An Introduction to
Russian History and Culture

by

IVAR SPECTOR

University of Washington

THIRD EDITION

D. VAN NOSTRAND COMPANY, INC.

PRINCETON, NEW JERSEY

TORONTO   LONDON

NEW YORK

D. VAN NOSTRAND COMPANY, INC.
120 Alexander St., Princeton, New Jersey (*Principal office*)
24 West 40 Street, New York 18, New York

D. VAN NOSTRAND COMPANY, LTD.
358, Kensington High Street, London, W.14, England

D. VAN NOSTRAND COMPANY (Canada) LTD.
25 Hollinger Road, Toronto 16, Canada

Library of Congress Catalogue Card No. 61-8545

———

First Published, August 1949
Two Reprintings

———

Second Edition, May 1954
Two Reprintings

———

Third Edition, January 1961
Reprinted February 1962

THE KREMLIN, SEAT OF RUSSIAN GOVERNMENT

To
My Father
VLADIMIR LVOVITCH

Preface

THIS work is a product of twenty-five years of teaching under-
graduates in the field of Russian history and civilization in the
Far Eastern Department of the University of Washington. In
its present form, it represents a revision and expansion of previous editions.

Since World War II, new emphasis has been placed not only on
formal history but on cultural backgrounds. The author therefore has
devoted considerable space to Russian and Soviet culture. This is particularly important because, as explained in this text, current events and
culture in Russia are so closely interwoven.

In the United States, where a constitutional system of government
has always prevailed, where Party platforms and Congressional debates
have reflected the thinking and needs of the people at large, and where
daily events have been chronicled by a free press, it is possible to teach
formal history and still provide a key to an understanding of the American people. In Russia, however, where there has never existed a strictly
civilian government, where policies both domestic and foreign reflected
not the will of the people so much as the will of the ruler, we must turn
to the novels, dramas, poems, music, and art—in other words, to Russian culture—for an understanding of the history of the Russian people
and their achievements. That is why no study of Russian history can
be complete without a parallel study of Russian culture.

This revision brings the history of the Soviet period up-to-date.
In recent years, even in the United States, foreign policy has taken
priority over domestic affairs. There have been substantial additions,
therefore, to the material on Soviet foreign policy. Soviet relations
with the countries of Asia, from the Near and Middle East to the Far
East, have received special consideration. The official Soviet version
of the Constitution of the USSR, as published in English in 1959, has
been used in this edition.

The writer wishes to express his thanks to all those professors and
instructors who have used this book and taken the trouble to offer suggestions for its improvement.

I.S.

March, 1960
University of Washington

Contents

PART ONE. RUSSIA FROM 862 TO 1917
THE RURIK DYNASTY

PART TWO. RUSSIA FROM 862 TO 1917
THE ROMANOV DYNASTY

List of Illustrations

(All photographs in the book unless otherwise credited are used with the permission of Sovfoto Agency, New York.)

Geography and Population

THE USSR embraces a territory of about 8,500,000 square miles, approximately one-sixth of the world's land surface, with a population of about 217,000,000. Including as it does the greater part of Europe and all of northern Asia, the USSR is as large as the United States, Alaska, Canada, and Mexico combined. In area it is nearly two and two-thirds times the size of the United States. Stretching from the Carpathian Mountains and the Baltic Sea on the west to the Pacific Ocean on the east, from the Arctic Ocean on the north to the Mongolian plains, the Pamirs, the Caucasus and the Black Sea on the south, the Soviet Union encompasses a vast and contiguous land mass with great diversity in topography, in climatic conditions, mineral resources, and vegetation. Thus in the north the USSR has to contend with the icy wastes of the Arctic, while in the south there are not only deserts and mountains, but also subtropical or irrigated areas where cotton and tea plantations, as well as citrus fruit orchards, flourish. The dominant feature of the topography of this vast land mass is the great plain, most of which is less than 1000 feet above sea level, that stretches from the western borders of the USSR east to the Yenisei River in Asiatic Russia, and is broken only by the Ural Mountains. The greater part of the country, most of which lies in the same latitudes as Canada, has a continental climate marked by extremes of heat and cold. In breadth the USSR spans 160 degrees of longitude, stretching almost halfway around the world. Travel from Leningrad to Vladivostok requires nine and one-half days via the Trans-Siberian Express.

The USSR, which is rich in strategic and industrial minerals and in raw materials, holds first place in the world for its resources of iron ore (with quartzites), oil, manganese, apatite, phosphorites, magnesium salts, niobium and peat, for its water power and timber reserves; it ranks second in coal, lead, zinc, and nickel.

In spite of its vast size and great natural wealth, however, large areas of the Soviet Union remain unproductive, either because they are too cold, too arid, too marshy, too mountainous, or too isolated from existing transportation facilities. The USSR has been handicapped in the past by its lack of ice-free ports, such as Murmansk, and by the fact that most of its long coastline fronts on the Arctic Ocean. Many of the greatest rivers of the Soviet Union, such as the Dvina, the Ob, the Yenisei, and the Lena flow into the Arctic, while the mighty Volga flows into the Caspian Sea, the largest landlocked body of water in the world. The USSR has partially overcome some of these obstacles by the development of the Northern Sea Route, by the use of ice-breakers to keep its harbors open, by air traffic to isolated regions, and by the construction of a highly important series of canals, still in process of completion, to link its major European rivers, the Dnieper, the Don, and the Volga with the Baltic and White Seas.

The Soviet Union is a multinational state, which comprises between 170 and 180 ethnic groups, with as many languages and dialects, although the basic element is Slavic and the Russian language predominates. Actually, three-quarters of the population are Slavs, while the rest are of Mongoloid, Iranian, or Turkic origin. The Russian people proper are the eastern branch of the Slavonic group. Being the largest member of the Slavic family, they are in turn subdivided into three distinct groups, namely, Great Russian, Little Russian (Ukrainian), and Byelorussian (White Russian). Among nearly 168,000,000 Slavs in the USSR, the Great Russians number more than 116,000,000, the Ukrainians about 40,000,000, and the Byelorussians 8,000,000. The Great Russians inhabit most of European Russia and Siberia, with scattered colonies in other parts of the Union. The Ukrainians live, for the most part, in the south and southwest regions of European Russia, bordering on Poland, Czechoslovakia, Hungary, Rumania, and the Black Sea. The White Russians are located in the west, adjacent to Latvia, Lithuania, Poland, and the Ukraine. The Mongoloid peoples of the Soviet Union are to be found mainly in the Baikal area and on the lower Volga. The Turkic peoples are in Central Asiatic Russia, the Volga valley, and Yakutia; those of Iranian extraction are mainly in the Caucasus and South Central Asia.

The USSR is a federation of fifteen republics, some of which include subsidiary autonomous republics. Although on paper these republics have certain powers delegated to them, including even the right to secede from the Union, in practice their association as members of the USSR is far from being voluntary. Their domestic and foreign policies are in reality controlled by Moscow. Attempts at independent action have resulted in drastic purges of key local officials and their replacement by Russian officials subservient to Moscow.

By far the largest of these republics is the Russian Soviet Federated Republic (RSFSR), which comprises 74 per cent of the area of the

USSR and over 50 per cent of its population, or 116,000,000 people, including more than 100 nationalities and ethnic groups. Non-Slavic elements in the population number about 45,000,000. The two principal cities of the RSFSR are Moscow, capital of both the USSR and of the Russian Republic, with a population of about 5,100,000, and Leningrad with a population of 2,814,000 (1956). The borders of the RSFSR extend from the Arctic Ocean, the Baltic states and the Ukraine, to the Mongolian plains and the Pacific Ocean. On the eve of World War II it produced about 70 per cent of the industrial and agricultural output of the USSR, about 20 per cent of the oil, more than 40 per cent of the coal, about 40 per cent of the pig iron, over 50 per cent of the steel, two-thirds of the electric power, and the greater part of the output of machinery, timber, textiles, grain, technical crops, and food products. The Ural Mountains, 1200 miles in length, ranging in height from approximately 1000 to 6200 feet, divide the European areas of the RSFSR from the Asiatic. Such large industrial centers as Sverdlovsk, Tchelyabinsk and Magnitogorsk are located here. World War II greatly hastened a process already emphasized in the prewar Five-Year Plans: the rapid development of the vast mineral wealth of the Ural region, as well as the industrial and agricultural development of Siberia, including the Soviet Far East. As of October 1945 the RSFSR was subdivided politically into 6 *Krais* (territories), 45 *Oblasts* (regions), 12 Autonomous Republics representing small nationalities, one Autonomous *Oblast* (Tuva), and the Koenigsberg *Okrug* (area) in what was formerly East Prussia, and which was acquired as a result of World War II.

The Ukrainian Soviet Socialist Republic, with an area of 223,000 square miles and a population of 40,000,000 (1956) ranks second in importance only to the RSFSR. The Ukraine, which is larger than France, is divided into 24 *Oblasts*. It includes many important cities, including Kiev, the capital (900,000), Kharkov (833,432), Odessa (604,223), and Dnepropetrovsk (576,000), the home of the famous Dnieper Dam. This republic has rich mineral resources and a fertile black soil. Before World War II, according to official figures, it produced 54 per cent of the coal, 60 per cent of the pig iron, 48 per cent of the steel, and 35 per cent of the manganese ore of the entire USSR. As a granary of major importance, it produced about half of the winter wheat and nearly three-quarters of the sugar-beet crop of the Union. In 1939, after the occupation of Southeastern Poland by the Red Army, the Ukraine acquired an additional 7,000,000 citizens. In 1940 it absorbed Northern Bukovina and part of Bessarabia, while in 1945, by agreement with Czechoslovakia, it took over the Carpatho-Ukraine (Ruthenia), with a population of some 725,000.

The Byelorussian Soviet Socialist Republic, which compares with Kansas in size, covers an area of 89,000 square miles and has a population of 8,000,000. Its main industrial centers include Minsk, the capital (239,000), Mogilev, Vitebsk, and Gomel. This republic is noted for its vast reserves of timber and peat, for its dairy farms and other agricultural processing industries. Like the Ukraine, it suffered major damage as a result of the Nazi invasion and occupation. The Byelorussian Republic almost doubled its size and population in 1939 when the White Russian areas of Northeastern Poland were taken over. White Russia includes most of the famous Pripet Marshes where extensive drainage projects have been undertaken to increase agricultural production. Postwar plans include the reclamation of 15,000 square miles of marsh land—an area larger than the Netherlands.

The region once known as the Transcaucasian SSR was in 1936 divided into three Union Republics: the Azerbaijan, Georgian, and Armenian Republics. Azerbaijan, with an area of 33,000 square miles and a population of 3,210,000, occupies the eastern part of Transcaucasia and lies on the border between the USSR and Iran. In size it is comparable to Maine. Its capital, Baku, on the Caspian Sea, which has a population above 600,000, is one of the greatest oil-producing centers in the world. The republic is also famous for its cotton production, its orchards, vineyards, tobacco plantations, silk and tea cultivation, and caviar output. The large industrial city of Kirovabad is known for its textile mills.

The Georgian SSR, situated in western Transcaucasia adjacent to Turkey, has an area of 27,000 square miles and a population of 4,000,000. Its capital is at Tbilisi, formerly known as Tiflis (635,000). Georgia is famous as a health resort, for its vineyards, and its subtropical crops of tea, lemons, and other citrus fruits. The extensive swamps of the Colchis lowland—the Soviet Riviera on the Black Sea— are being drained, and the reclaimed land transformed into citrus groves, tea plantations, and eucalyptus forests. The great manganese mines of Chiatura, once operated by an American syndicate headed by W. Averill Harriman, which the Germans tried to seize in World War II, are reputed to contain one-third of the world's deposits of this strategically important mineral. Today Georgia has important industries, including machine-building plants, textile mills, and boot and shoe works; a large new iron and steel mill, the first in the Transcaucasus, is now under construction. The famous Georgian Military Highway is a favorite route for Soviet tourists.

The Armenian SSR, with an area of 12,000 square miles, about the size of Belgium, and a population of 1,500,000, is located in the Caucasian highlands on the borders of Turkey and Iran. Its capital, Yerevan (200,000), lies in the shadow of the famous Mt. Ararat. In Armenia irrigation is extensively practiced for the growing of cotton, grapes, fruit, tobacco, and silk. A vast new power and irrigation project will harness the waters of Lake Sevan and the Zanga River. The republic has extensive reserves of copper and molybdenum and is also exploiting its resources of iron ore, chromite, and building materials. Its cotton and wine industries are expanding. To facilitate the further development of the country, the Soviet Union has encouraged the return of Armenians from abroad, especially from Turkey, Greece, Syria, and the United States.

In spite of the exploratory work undertaken by the Soviet Government in the Northern Caucasus, a leading Soviet engineer now a refugee in the United States, has stated that the republics in this area remain basically agrarian, with the present state of industry differing "very little from that which prevailed 32-33 years ago." [1]

An extensive area of the USSR east of the Caspian Sea and south of Siberia in Central Asia is now divided into five republics: the Turkmen, Uzbek, Tadjik, Kazakh, and Kirghiz Soviet Socialist Republics.

The Turkmen SSR, with an area of 187,000 square miles and a population of 1,500,000, is situated on the frontiers of Iran and Afghanistan. The Kara-Kum (Black Sands) Desert covers nearly 80 per cent of the territory of the republic, the capital of which is Ashkhabad (140,000). Although, under the tsarist regime, this region was inhabited mainly by nomadic tribes, extensive new irrigation projects have eliminated nomadism and led to large-scale production of cotton, silk, kok-sagyz—a rubber-bearing plant—fruits, etc., in addition to stock raising. The construction of the first unit of the Bolshoi Kara-Kum Canal, one of the largest irrigation projects not only in Turkmenistan but in the USSR, has already begun. It is expected to increase the total area of irrigated land in the southern and southeastern Kara-Kum by some 95,000 acres. Industry has now superseded agriculture in the Turkmenian economy, with new cotton and silk mills, shoe factories, and meat-packing plants taking precedence. Mineral deposits include sulphur, salt, and oil.

---

[1] *Construction Materials of the Northern Caucasus.* New York, Research Program on the U.S.S.R., Mimeographed Series, No. 20, 1952, p. 72.

The Uzbek SSR, which occupies a plateau in the heart of Central Asia, and extends to the Tien-Shan and Pamir Mountains on the frontier of Afghanistan, has an area of 160,000 square miles and a population of 8,500,000. Tashkent, the capital, was a city of nearly 778,000 in 1956. Irrigated agriculture is practiced on a large scale in Uzbekistan. The Great Stalin Ferghana Canal, 168 miles in length, provides irrigation for 1,250,000 acres of land. In 1947 the total length of the irrigation network reached over 120,000 miles. The canals alone extend over 600 miles. Among the new projects under construction is the Amu-Darya Canal (300 miles). Already the Uzbek Republic has more land under irrigation than the other Central Asiatic republics combined. As a result of the irrigation program, the Uzbek Republic has become the cotton belt of the Soviet Union, producing more than 60 per cent of all its cotton fiber. The republic is also noted for its stock breeding and for its caracul sheep. Today Uzbekistan has its own steel and rolled iron industries, its chemical, machine-building, textile, and food-processing industries. Its new industrial centers include Tchirtchik, with its chemical, power, and machine-building plants, Yangi-Yul, with its food production and light industry, Angren, the Uzbek "coal-pit" not far from Tashkent, and Kuvasai, a center for building materials. The ancient cities of Samarkand and Bokhara have well-developed silk and cotton industries respectively. Included among the minerals of the Republic are oil, copper, coal, and many rare metals. The new Tchardzhou-Kungrad Railroad, begun in 1947, will link the Kara-Kalpak ASSR, the Khorezm region of the Uzbek SSR, and the Tashauz region of the Turkmen SSR. The national economy of the Uzbek SSR is said to be developing faster, on the average, than that of the Union. This republic is often referred to in the Soviet press as the socialist beacon of the East.

The Tadjik SSR, with an area of 55,000 square miles and a population of 1,600,000, is situated in picturesque mountainous territory on the borders of Afghanistan and western China. It became a Union Republic in 1929. Its capital, the modern industrial city of Stalinabad, the youngest of the Soviet capital cities, has a population of 95,000. Regarded as one of the most ancient peoples of Central Asia, the Tadjiks are of Iranian origin. Soviet scientists have conducted many exploratory expeditions in the Pamirs, and an important program of road and railroad construction has been carried out. A new arterial highway runs from Stalinabad to the new town of Khorog in the Pamirs on the Afghan frontier. Stalinabad is linked with the Soviet Union by railroad. New air routes connect the capital with Khorog, with Leninabad, the center of the canning and silk-processing industries, and with the cotton area of the Vakhsh Valley. Extensive irrigation projects, such as the Vakhsh, Great Ferghana, and Gissar Canals have greatly increased the area under cultivation. In irrigated areas Egyptian cotton, fruits, and even sugar-cane are produced. By 1941 Tadjikistan was harvesting six times as much cotton as before the Revolution. The existence of more than 100 "millionaire" *kolkhozi* is indicative of the growing proseprity of agriculture in this republic. Important industries, including the textile, food, building materials, and mining industries, have been developed under the Soviet regime. More than 270 deposits of rare and nonferrous minerals have been discovered by Soviet geologists, seventy of which were already being exploited in 1947. Stalin Peak (25,600 feet), the highest mountain peak in the Soviet Union, is located in eastern Tadjikistan.

The Kazakh SSR, with its now famous capital of Alma-Ata, the Soviet Hollywood, covers an area of 1,560,000 square miles and has a population of 9,000,000. It stretches from the Caspian Sea to the Altai Mountains and the borders of Sinkiang. Kazakhstan, which became a Union Republic in 1936, ranks second in area among the republics of the USSR and is approximately one-third the size of the United States. More than 60 per cent of the republic consists of mountain and steppe pasture lands, with the result that Kazakhstan is one of the largest stock-raising regions in the USSR. Mechanized agriculture and irrigation projects have made it possible to reclaim extensive arid regions, including the virgin soil of sections of the Golodnaya (Hungry) Steppe. As a result cereals, sugar-beets, cotton, hemp, sunflower, tobacco, rubber plants, and other crops are now being cultivated. The Syr-Darya and Amu-Darya Rivers, which flow into the Aral Sea, fourth in size among the salt lakes in the world, are the center of important power projects for the republic. The completion in 1953 of the Ust-Kamenogorsk Hydroelectric Station, the largest in the republic, on the Irtysh River, will provide power for eastern Kazakhstan. Important industrial centers have sprung up in Kazakhstan, including Karaganda, Balkhash, Leninogorsk, Ust-Kamenogorsk, and others. During the Stalin Five-Year Plans great railroad trunk lines, such as the Turkestan-Siberian (Turksib), the Akmolinsk-Kartaly, and the Akmolinsk-Karaganda-Balkhash have been constructed. New airlines, radio, and telegraph communications have contributed to the progress of the republic. Kazakhstan ranks first in the USSR as a center for nonferrous metals and third in coal. In the Altai Mountains large deposits of lead, zinc, tin, silver, gold, copper and rare metals are being mined. Much of Kazakhstan's mineral wealth is still unexploited. The Karaganda coal basin north of Lake Balkhash and the important Emba oil fields northeast of the Caspian Sea are of great strategic importance for the Soviet Union.

Another Central Asiatic Republic, the Kirghiz SSR, has an area of 78,000 square miles and a population of about 1,900,000. Kirghizia, often termed the birthplace of the human race, is situated in the mountainous Tien-Shan range on the borders of Sinkiang. Its population, formerly nomadic, is now engaged in cattle-breeding, agriculture, and fruit production, or in such industries as the textile and meat-packing. Kirghiz industry is expanding rapidly. Such items as water-turbines, silk and woolen fabrics, agricultural machinery, sugar, canned goods, and cigarettes are now being produced. The city of Osh is the center of the republic's thriving silk industry. Rich mineral resources, including coal, oil, mercury, wolfram, lead, and antimony are being exploited. The construction of new irrigation canals in Kirghizia has increased the area under cultivation by 75 per cent. The Great Tchu Canal, now in process of construction, is expected to open up additional areas to agriculture and cattle-raising. The Great Kirghizian Highway leads from Frunze (100,000), the capital, into China.

Along the western frontiers of the USSR, as a result of Soviet seizure of former tsarist territory from 1939 to 1940, five additional Union Republics have been established: the Karelo-Finnish, Esthonian, Latvian, Lithuanian, and Moldavian. The Karelo-Finnish SSR,[1] which is situated between the Baltic and White Seas adjacent to the Finnish frontier in a region studded with lakes, has an area of some 92,000 square miles and a population of about 500,000. The capital is Petrozavodsk (70,000), the location of the Onega Metal Works, established in the time of Peter the Great. Because of the dense pine, fir, and birch forests characteristic of this region, timber is the basis of the republic's economy. The Stalin White Sea-Baltic Sea Canal, 140 miles in length, was completed in 1933 and constitutes one of the major achievements of the Five-Year Plans. Granite, marble, diabasis, and mica are mined.

The Esthonian SSR, with an area of 18,000 square miles and a population of 1,131,000, became a Union Republic in August, 1940. It is strategically located on the Baltic Coast between the Gulfs of Finland and Riga, with Tallin (147,000) as the capital. The production of food, shipbuilding, fishing, and the oil-shale refining industry constitute the principal occupations of Esthonians.

The Latvian SSR, the most industrialized of the Baltic Republics, has an area of 25,000 square miles and a population of 1,971,000. Riga

[1] Amalgamated into the RSFSR in July 1956.

565,000), the capital, is an important Baltic port. The republic has important textile and metal industries.

The Lithuanian SSR has an area of 24,000 square miles and a population of 2,880,000. The breeding of dairy cattle and pigs, as well as the cultivation of cereals, constitute the main branches of the country's economy. Vilnius (250,000), the capital, was the subject of a long dispute with Poland after World War I. Memel is the chief Lithuanian seaport of the Baltic.

In August 1940, after the recovery of the former Russian province of Bessarabia from Rumania, the Moldavian SSR was established, with its capital at Kishinev (110,000). The area of Moldavia is 13,000 square miles and the population numbers 2,700,000. Located southwest of the Ukraine on the borders of Rumania, this republic is a fertile black soil region, where cereal crops, sugar beets, and vineyards flourish.

As a result of World War II the distribution of Soviet industry and population underwent drastic changes. Not only was there enormous destruction of Soviet cities and villages, of Soviet industry and agriculture in European Russia as far east as Stalingrad and the suburbs of Moscow, but there was a great migration of industries and population eastward to Soviet Asia, beyond the reach of enemy attack. During the war years there was a veritable boom in Siberia, Soviet Central Asia, and even in the Soviet Arctic. Accurate statistics reflecting these changes are not yet available. It nevertheless appears that the redistribution of the population of the USSR, undertaken as an emergency measure in World War II, was continued as an integral part of the Stalin or Fourth Five-Year Plan (1946-1950). This redistribution was motivated by strategic as well as by economic factors. A careful examination of materials available to date suggests that a Slavic belt has been established along the borders of the USSR, especially on the Baltic coast and in Asiatic Russia. In the Baltic Republics, as a result of widespread deportation of the inhabitants during the postwar years, it is virtually impossible to estimate with any degree of accuracy how much of the native population remains. In some of the Central Asiatic Republics, the Slavs already outnumber the native inhabitants by as many as two or three to one. Whereas, in the prewar Five-Year Plans, emphasis was placed on the decentralization of industry as a security measure, the Fourth and Fifth Five-Year Plans, in addition to the above, seem to be accomplishing a permanent decentralization of population for economic and strategic reasons.

Geographical conditions in the Soviet Union are thus dynamic rather than static. Where a government has absolute power to determine which resources shall be developed and to distribute labor forces and specialists wherever necessary to accomplish this purpose, much can be done, albeit at great cost in terms of human values and efficiency, to change the face of nature. Since World War II, the Soviet Government has undertaken extensive, long-term afforestation and irrigation projects under what is known as the Stalin Plan for Remaking Nature, which it hoped would eventually banish drought and famine from large areas in the Volga-Don region and parts of Central Asia.

Americans who are impressed by the wealth and diversity of natural resources in the Soviet Union and by the nature of its dynamism should bear in mind that in spite of the herculean efforts of the Soviet Government the USSR is still far behind the United States in the exploitation of these resources, in the development of transportation and industry, and in the standard of living it is able to provide for the average citizen.

Note: The 1959 census report stated that the population of the USSR was 208,826,650. Early in 1960, Premier Nikita Khrushchev disclosed that the Soviet population had increased to about 212,000,000.

RUSSIA from 862 to 1917

The Rurik Dynasty
862 to 1598

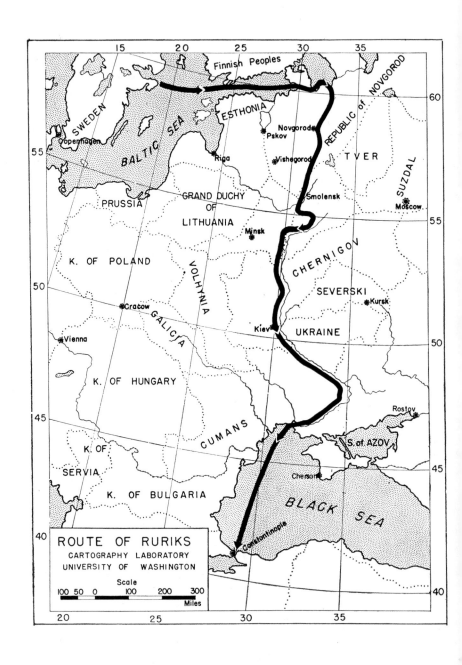

ROUTE OF RURIKS
CARTOGRAPHY LABORATORY
UNIVERSITY OF WASHINGTON

Scale
100 50 0   100   200   300
Miles

1

From Rurik to the Mongols
862-1243

LTHOUGH much has been written concerning the origin of the Russian people and the formation of their state, very little is known for a certainty about these vital facts of their history. Even the origin of the name "Russia" has been for many years a subject of speculation among native and foreign scholars, who have failed to reach any definite conclusions. We do know that the people who gave Russia its earliest rulers, and perhaps its name, were called *Rūs,* but who they really were has been a matter of conjecture. Some historians have maintained that they were Russian Slavs, whereas others have held that they were Norsemen or Varangians. Later authorities have stated that the Slavs used the term *Rūs* as a general designation for all Varangians. The Greeks used the name *Rūs* to identify Slavs and Norsemen living by the Black Sea, whereas they (the Greeks) called the Norsemen, who were in Greek service, Varangians. It is apparent that the name was loosely applied and that there has been no uniformity of opinion concerning the actual identity of the people. An examination of the works of distinguished historians concerning the earliest stage of Russian history reveals, at best, only theories based upon conjectures, hypotheses, and guesses.

Obviously the lack of authentic source material is responsible for the vagueness and obscurity which shroud early Russian history. The first account that purported to be historical was the *Original Chronicle,* traditionally ascribed to a certain monk, Nestor (1056-1114), of the Pechersky monastery at Kiev. Modern scholars, however, regard it as a compilation, the product of several generations of writers, which assumed its present form in the early part of the twelfth century

3

as the *Collection of Chronicles* or the *Chronicle of Ancient Years*.[1]
The *Chronicle* covers the period roughly from the middle of the ninth
century to the second decade of the twelfth century.

According to the *Chronicle,* the Russian state had its beginnings
about A.D. 862 when the Slavonic tribes of Russia had fallen into
disorder and confusion. Realizing their inability to promote peace
and establish justice among themselves, they sent messengers to the
tribe, *Rūs Varangians,* the implication of the *Chronicle* being that they
were a Scandinavian people living in the north, requesting that a prince
might be sent to govern their rich and vast dominion. The *Chronicle*
reports their message in these words: "Our land is great and rich, but
there is no order in it; come and rule and govern us." Three brothers
took advantage of this opportunity, and with their kinsmen and retain-
ers speedily established themselves in the land of the Slavs. Rurik,
the eldest, settled in Novgorod, Sineus, the second, on Lake Byelo-
ozero, and Truvor, the youngest, in Izborsk, near Pskov. The sovereignty, thus divided, became concentrated after their deaths in the
hands of Igor, the son of Rurik.

The foregoing account is distinguished chiefly for its inaccuracy
and obscurity. For instance, the date of the first arrival of the *Rūs,*
A.D. 862, conflicts with the fact that at least twenty years earlier they
were known to have been in the neighborhood of the Black Sea, engaged
in warfare with the Greeks, and that in June 860 they had laid siege
even to Constantinople. These facts alone suggest that they came
from the south rather than from the north. Furthermore the designation "Varangian" implies that they (the *Rūs*) were of Scandinavian
origin, which is at variance with the foregoing facts and also with the
distinction which the Greeks and Arabs of the period made between
the two peoples, namely, the *Rūs* and the Varangians.

---

[1] The principal Russian editions of the chronicle are St. Petersburg, 1767, and
1809-1819; Moscow, 1824. "In addition to numerous Russian editions, the *Chronicle of
Ancient Years* was translated and published abroad. Excerpts from it were quoted by
Herberstein; in 1771 a German translation was made in Göttingen (Schlözer, vol. I,
p. xxi); in 1860 it was published in Latin in Vienna by Fr. Miklošič. At the same time
Kotkowsky in Kiev published it with a translation in the Polish language. A German
translation was made by Josef Miller in Berlin in 1812, a French translation in Paris
in 1834 by Louis Paris, a Swedish translation in Helsingfors in 1849; it was translated
into the Czech language in 1864 by Jaromïr Erben in Prague, into the Danish language
in 1859 by Smith in Copenhagen. Louis Leger translated part of the annals in 1868
into French as an appendix to his doctor's dissertation, *The Nestor Annals.* He also
made a complete translation of these annals in 1884 and that same year they came out
in Lvov in Latin, the translation having been made by K. Luchakovsky. The *Chronicle*
was also translated into English in 1930 by S. H. Cross." (Academician B. D. Grekov,
The Culture of Kiev Rūs, pp. 118-119.)

THE LANDING OF RURIK

Many theories have prevailed as to the origin of the Slavs and the location of their ancient habitat. The famous Russian historians of the nineteenth century, S. M. Solovyev (1820-1879) and V. O. Klyutchevsky (1841-1911) were strongly influenced by the *Chronicle*. According to Klyutchevsky, the lands along the Danube were the original habitat of the Slavs, who later migrated to the northeastern foothills of the Carpathian Mountains, where their recorded history begins in the sixth century. The Russian historian and philologist, A. A. Shakhmatov (1864-1920) advanced a different theory. According to him, the original home of the Slavs was on the coast of the Baltic Sea, in the basin of the Western Dvina and the Lower Niemen Rivers, whence they migrated to the Lower Vistula, after the exodus of the Goths at the end of the second and the beginning of the third centuries. Finally, Shakhmatov believes that in the fourth century, following the expulsion of the Goths by the Huns from the steppes bordering on the Black Sea, the Slavs moved south to fill this gap. It should likewise be noted that the well-known Czech scholar, Lubor Niederle (1865-1944), placed the original habitat of the Slavs in parts of what is contemporary Poland, White Russia, and the lands on the right bank of the Dnieper. The consensus among outstanding German scholars, including Gustaf Kossinna (1858-1931), was that the proto-Europeans (Aryans) were originally located in northern Germany, Jutland, and southern Scandinavia, from which center they migrated and scattered throughout Europe and Asia as far as India, mixing with the native non-Aryan populations and thereby laying the foundation of the various Indo-European peoples (Aryans), including the Slavs.

⌊Soviet scholars, on the basis of extensive archeological investigation in European Russia, have established a new school of thought with regard to the early beginnings of the Slavs.⌉ They have refuted earlier accepted theories of the Scandinavian origin of the term *Rūs* and of a mass migration of Norsemen into what is now Russia. According to them the name *Rūs* was well established in South Russia as early as the fourth century and therefore antedates by some five centuries the use of the term by the Norsemen. The Slavs, according to Soviet interpretation, did not migrate to this region, but their ancestors were the autochthonic population of Central and Eastern Europe, dating back at least to 3000 B.C. It is their contention that neither the

---

[1] See Professor A. D. Udaltsov, "The Origin of the Slavs," *Voprosy Istorii*, No. 7, July 1947, pp. 95-100; *ibid.*, No. 9, September 1948, pp. 97-108; V. Mavrodin, "The Basic Stages of the Ethnical Development of the Russian People," *Voprosy Istorii*, No. 4, April 1950, pp. 55-70; see also, B. D. Grekov, *The Culture of Kiev Rūs*.

Goths nor the Scandinavians brought civilization to the *Rūs,* but rather they acquired a higher civilization from the *Rūs* and were absorbed by them.

Soviet archeological studies have indicated that there was an unbroken process of development of society in the Dnieper area, between the Carpathians and the Don, from the Scythians to the establishment of the Kiev state in the ninth century. Unfortunately, our knowledge of these ancient Scythians is not very extensive. The Greek historian, Herodotus, speaks of them at some length, but his account is superficial and unreliable. Archeological excavations in South Russia have revealed some details with regard to their civilization.[1] It has been established, for instance, that their territory lay between the Danube and the Don and thence extended inland to the edge of the forest region. The Scythians had numerous colonies, the chief of which were: Olbia, situated at the mouth of the Bug River; Tanais, at the mouth of the Don; Chersonesus, located approximately on the site of modern Sevastopol; Panticapea, now the city of Kertch; and Phanagoria, situated on the Taman peninsula. In these Scythian colonies, the inhabitants so thoroughly assimilated Greek culture that they became known as Greeks or Greek-Scythians. Although certain of the aforementioned sources of information would lead us to infer that the Scythians were regarded by their neighbors as the wildest of all barbarians, archeological discoveries tend to refute this and reveal them as a people of not inconsiderable cultural development. Their ill repute as barbarians may have arisen from an attempt on the part of their enemies to cast discredit upon their activities in war. Inasmuch as they early came in contact with at least three peoples of an advanced degree of culture, namely, the Arabs, the Hebrews, and the Greeks, it is unlikely that they remained in a state of extreme barbarism.

Arabic culture reached them through merchants of that race. Semitic influence was powerful not only upon the Scythians, but throughout the various Slavonic tribes, as is witnessed by the fact that the entire ruling class of the Khazars, together with some of their subjects, embraced Judaism in the eighth century. The Greek influence reached the Scythians chiefly through the Metics, or aliens residing in Athens, who included Thracians, Phrygians, Paphlagonians, Galatians, Lydians, Syrians, Egyptians, Hellenized Arabs, and He-

[1] See M. Rostovtzeff, *Iranians and Greeks in South Russia*; also by the same author, *A History of the Ancient World*, pp. 250 ff.; I. Tolstoy and N. Kondakov, *Russian Antiquities in the Monuments of Art*, Serials II, III, IV, 1889, 1890, 1891, St. Petersburg (in Russian); and George Vernadsky, *Ancient Russia*.

brews. These Greeks of foreign extraction brought with them elements of culture, distinctly Greek, which left an impress upon the Scythians, by whom they were shortly absorbed.

Although archeological research has not established a direct connection between the Scythian period and the history of the Eastern Slavs, scientists nevertheless believe that the Slavs are genetically related to the Scythians, and there is evidence of Scythian influence on the Slavs. Scythian ritual designs have been perpetuated in later Russian folk embroidery. On the banks of the Dnieper the burial mounds of the Scythian ploughmen, 1000 years older than the Slavonic barrows but similar to them, have been discovered, which afford additional evidence of the tenacity of Scythian influence.

Large numbers of Roman coins of the second and third centuries, discovered in the Dnieper region, indicate that active trade relations were established with the eastern provinces of the Roman Empire. But the barbarian invasions that brought about the fall of the West Roman Empire likewise led to mass migrations of peoples across the Danube into the Eastern Empire as Goths, Avars, and Huns occupied or swept across what is now the Soviet Ukraine.

Whether the Slavs as such were the descendants of these earlier peoples who occupied the southern plains of Russia, whether they were the basic stock of this region and had been subjugated by successive waves of invaders, or were newcomers who moved into a land already subjected to the depredations of barbarian tribes, are still matters of controversy. Irrespective of the various theories as to its origin, it is apparent that Slavonic civilization does not date, as was long assumed, from the ninth to the tenth centuries but actually had its beginnings much earlier. Modern archeological research has established the fact that an independent East Slavonic or *Rūs Ante* civilization had assumed form in the Dnieper region during the sixth to the eighth centuries. There is evidence to the effect that trade with Byzantium, and with the East via the Khazar Khanate on the Volga, flourished. Excavations at Sarskoye Gorodishche (the predecessor of Rostov) have disclosed a fortified city, where spinners, carpenters, tanners, jewelers, potters, smiths, and founders plied their trades in the seventh and eighth centuries. Many such city fortresses existed in South Russia and even as far north as Smolensk and Lake Ladoga at this time— cities which appear to have been at one and the same time centers of trade and places of refuge for the population of the surrounding countryside in the event of attack. It therefore seems clear that the highly developed civilization of Kiev *Rūs,* which long puzzled historians, was not a sudden development but was based on foundations laid many centuries earlier. This may well explain why the Norsemen, who came in the ninth century, and who, in other parts of Europe, rarely founded pioneer settlements, were attracted to the Dnieper region by the flourishing towns which already existed, as well as by the urge to push on to Byzantium. The Icelandic sagas lend support to the thesis that such wealthy, organized and fortified centers existed in Russia prior to the Viking settlements. Unfortunately there are no Russian written records prior to the coming of the Norsemen. As a result the *Chronicle,* highly traditional and far from complete as it is, of necessity has continued to serve as the main primary source for the beginnings of Russian history until almost the present day.

The history of the Russian state from its earliest beginnings to the Revolution of 1917 may be divided roughly into two dynasties, the Rurik and the Romanov. The first began with Rurik in A.D. 862 and ended with Tsar Fyodor, son of Ivan Grozny, in 1598. The Romanov dynasty began with Michael in 1613 and continued until the deposition of Nicholas II in 1917.

The founders of the Rurik dynasty were, as already indicated, of the *Rūs* tribe, later known as *Rūs*-Varangians. Under this dynasty the Russian state experienced both signal advances and bitter reverses, while two events of the most vital importance took place—the adoption of Christianity and the Mongol invasion. The greatest weakness of the Rurik government was the lack of centralization of power, resulting from a peculiar order of succession and feudal particularism. This led to bitter quarrels and endless dissension among claimants to the throne and caused the state to break up into a multiplicity of principalities. The lack of unity hastened and was, in a measure, responsible for the 240 years of Tartar domination, since the state was unable to meet attack with united strength.

The first ruler, Rurik (862-879), from whom the dynasty took its name, and whom succeeding princes, despite their mutual hostility, regarded as their common progenitor, appears to have been a man of foresight and considerable ability in statecraft. A good organizer, he left behind him a machinery of government which, considering the time and the difficulties which confronted him, was indeed excellent. At his death in 879 his son, Igor, had not attained his majority; hence a relative, Oleg, became regent and continued the policy of Rurik. This policy had been twofold: first, to establish order within his immediate jurisdiction and, second, to weld into an organized unit all the scattered and unorganized Slavonic tribes. Rurik succeeded in a measure in accomplishing the first, but it fell to the lot of his son, Igor, under the guidance of Oleg, to lay the foundation of the Russian state with Kiev, "Mother of Russian Cities," as the capital.)

For this reason the reign of Igor, as directed by Oleg, is of the utmost importance in early Russian history. Oleg was the first ruler to make a determined effort to check invasion by acquiring territory at the expense of the invaders. So successful was he in his conquests that in 907 he was able to organize a flotilla of some 2000 vessels and appear before Constantinople, forcing the Greeks to purchase immunity from further depredations. This expedition resulted in a commercial treaty, which granted Russian merchants special privileges at Constantinople. In 945 a more comprehensive treaty was negotiated by Igor which regulated all commercial and political relations between Kiev *Rūs* and Byzantium. Oleg's policy of eastern expansion was likewise followed by later rulers, who regarded Asia as the source of all the troubles and evils that beset *Rūs*. Because of Oleg's military success, Russian folklore abounds in tales of his prowess, while his deeds form the subject of many poems. In the nineteenth century, the famous Russian poet, Pushkin, wrote "The Lay of Oleg" (1822), a poem memorized and sung by generations of Russian children.[1] After his death Oleg came to be known by the name "Vieshchy," which means "the sage" or "the seer," and indicates that his contemporaries attributed to him unusual wisdom. Igor, deprived of the regent's ability and guidance, accomplished little.

Upon Igor's death, his widow, Olga, took control of the government on behalf of her infant son, Svyatoslav. Her assumption of power is an interesting revelation of the liberality of the Slavonic laws, which accorded to women a position considerably in advance of that enjoyed by them in other lands at this period. The *Chronicle* reveals that Olga was both astute and ruthless in her exercise of this power. Perhaps the most significant event of Olga's reign was her conversion to Christianity. In 957 she was baptized with the name of Helen, journeying for this purpose to Constantinople where the ceremony took place in the Byzantine court. The "Ceremonial Book" of Emperor Constantine Porphyrogenitus gives a detailed description of her reception. The account of the ceremony, which relates that certain honors were withheld because the convert was a woman, gives further evidence that Greek law was considerably less liberal than Slavonic law with respect to women, and that they enjoyed fewer privileges in the Byzantine

---

[1] For an English translation of this poem, see Yarmolinsky, A. (Editor), *The Works of Alexander Pushkin*, N. Y., 1936, pp. 55-58.

Empire than in Russia. Despite Olga's example, however, Christianity did not immediately became established in *Rūs*. Even her son,
Svyatoslav, refused to adopt the new religion, for fear the *druzhina* (re-
tainers) would laugh at him.

With the accession of Svyatoslav in 962, Russian expansion began
in earnest, and the state was so increased that it can be compared in
extent with the dominion of the Huns in the fourth and fifth centuries. It was at this time that considerable parts of the forest regions
were added to the steppes. Svyatoslav's conquests extended from the
stone Byzantine fortress of the Khazars at Sarkel on the Don to the
Bulgar base at Pereyaslavets on the Danube, where he established his
headquarters, and from which he was able to menace the cities of the
empire and to march against Byzantium. According to the *Chronicle,*
Svyatoslav preferred Pereyaslavets to Kiev as the center of his dominion, for it was an important crossroads where he could obtain silver,
cloth, fruit, and wine from Greece, silver and horses from Bohemia
and Hungary, furs, wax, honey, and slaves from *Rūs*. His imperialistic designs were retarded by the Pecheniegs, a Slavic-Turkish tribe,
who even laid siege to Kiev during his absence, and were definitely
checked by Emperor John Tsimiskes, a brilliant military leader of
Byzantium, who paid tribute to Svyatoslav but forced him to abandon
war against the empire in favor of an alliance. In 972 Svyatoslav
was killed in battle by the Pecheniegs. According to the *Chronicle,* a
prince of the Pechenieg tribe fashioned a drinking cup out of his skull.

After a prolonged struggle over the succession among the three
sons of Svyatoslav, one of them, Vladimir (980-1015), entered Kiev
in triumph and was recognized as "Grand Prince." His reign is of
especial importance from the religious and cultural standpoints, for
during this period Christianity became the official religion not merely
of the princely house but of the entire Kievan state.

Although there is evidence that the Greeks had tried to spread
Christianity among the Scythians in the first centuries of the Christian
era, and legend, as recorded in the *Chronicle,* claims that the Apostle
Andrew visited Kherson on the Black Sea and ascended the Dnieper
to the site of Kiev, *Rūs* paganism long resisted the pressure of the
Christian faith. The chief pagan gods of *Rūs* included Peroun, the
patron deity of the feudal-military class, Volos, the god of cattle, who
became the god of the merchants, Dazhbog, the sun god, Khors, the
sun god of the peoples of Central Asia, and Mokosh, a goddess of the
Finnish tribes to the north. There is evidence to the effect that Vladimir, before he accepted Christianity, had established a kind of pan-

theon in Kiev and Novgorod with his personal deity, Peroun, at
the head.)

How far Christianity had spread among the people of *Rūs* by the
time of Vladimir is not clear, but it seems evident that they were acquainted with the state religion of the Eastern Empire and that Olga
was by no means the only convert. That Christians were subject to
some persecution seems apparent from a record which reveals that in
983 two Christians were killed by a mob for failure to observe certain
pagan rites.)

As Christianity spread throughout Europe, there was considerable competition between Rome and Byzantium as to which should
win the Kievan state. By the reign of Vladimir the missionary efforts
of the Roman Church extended north to Scandinavia and the Poles
had accepted Roman Christianity from the Germans. The Eastern
Church, less aggressive than Rome in its efforts to propagate the faith,
was nevertheless reaching out into the Balkans to include Bulgaria
and the Black Sea coastal region.

The *Chronicle* relates that in 986 four faiths attempted to win the
prince Vladimir through their missionaries. The Bulgars of the Volga
presented the claims of Mohammedanism; Roman Catholicism was
represented by German emissaries, and Judaism by members of the
Khazar tribe. The Greek Orthodox Church sent one of its philosophers.
After listening to the arguments advanced, Vladimir sent envoys into
the various countries to investigate and verify what the missionaries
had said. These envoys returned, greatly impressed by the beauty and
solemnity of the Greek service at St. Sophia in Constantinople, and
submitted reports which in 987 led Vladimir to decide in favor of the
Greek Orthodox. Accompanied by his Varangian mercenaries, he
thereupon descended upon Kherson on the Black Sea and compelled
the Emperor Basilius to provide him with a Greek bride, part of the
bargain being that Vladimir himself should be baptized in the Christian faith. About 988-989 Vladimir enforced a general baptism on
the people of Kiev *Rūs,* and the Church was officially established. The
Roman Church apparently refused to recognize the decision as final,
however, for papal missions were sent to Vladimir in 991 and 1000.
Vladimir, in response, despatched his own envoys to Rome in 994
and 1001. The fact that Vladimir's wife, the Greek princess Anna, was
the aunt of Holy Roman Emperor Otto III may have led to increased
contacts, and the breach between the Eastern and Western Churches
was not yet recognized as final. Vladimir nevertheless pursued his
original course. There is a record of taxes collected by the Church in

996, and a statute with regard to Church courts appears in 1010. It may be assumed, therefore, that by the beginning of the eleventh century Orthodox Christianity was firmly established in Rūs.

It has been generally assumed that Christianity was responsible for the introduction of a written language among the Slavs. The Soviet scholar, B. D. Grekov, however, thinks that the Rūs may have had a written language in the eighth century, prior to the adoption of Christianity, using Latin and Greek characters, and that the Greek bishops, Kirill and Methodius, provided the Slavs with a Slavonic alphabet rather than a written language. Christianity, he claims, only increased the need for a written language and led to the improvement of the alphabet by the inclusion of Slavonic letters to represent sounds that could not be reproduced through the Latin and Greek alphabets.

Whether or not it was to the advantage of Rūs to cast its lot with Byzantium has long been a subject for debate. The decision, for one thing, led to religious division among the Slavs, some of whom, notably the Croatians, Czechs, Slovaks, and especially the Poles, accepted Roman Catholicism. There is every reason to believe that the antagonism of centuries between the Poles and the Russians was based to a very considerable degree on religious differences. On the favorable side, it has been suggested that the Byzantine Church, more tolerant than the Roman, permitted greater religious autonomy, which led to the rise of independent national churches among the Eastern Slavs. That the choice of Byzantium was the natural one for the Rūs there can be little doubt. Byzantium was still far in advance of the West as the foremost center of culture and wealth in the Christian world. Commercial contacts between Kievan Rūs and the capital of the Eastern Empire were already well established. The ancestors of the Rūs had many points of contact with the Greeks whereby they borrowed and shared elements of culture. The adoption of Orthodox Christianity, for a time at least, produced even closer ties with Byzantium. No doubt the Greek alliance enhanced the prestige and importance of Vladimir and the Kievan state among the countries of Europe, although historians have long speculated as to whether Vladimir, by his marriage with the Greek princess Anna and his baptism in the Orthodox faith, became a vassal or an ally of the emperor at Constantinople.[1]

After Vladimir's adoption of Orthodox Christianity, Byzantine influence was strong in Kiev Rūs. Greek priests and monks, sculptors,

---

[1] See Vasiliev, A. A., "Was Old Russia a Vassal State of Byzantium?" *Speculum,* Vol. VII, pp. 350 ff.

ikon painters, architects, and teachers flocked to Kiev. The metropolitan of Kiev, the head of the Church, was a Greek. The first of the great churches of Kiev, the Desyatinnaya (Church of the Tithe), was constructed of brick by Greek architects. Vladimir is said to have established a state school in Kiev to provide "book learning" for the children of the aristocracy. Church services, however, were held in Church Slavonic rather than in the Greek language—a factor of no inconsiderable importance in paving the way for a national church.

Following another bitter controversy over the succession—this time among the sons of Vladimir—Yaroslav, prince of Novgorod, later known as Yaroslav the Wise (1036-1054), finally gained possession of Kiev. Yaroslav was the first Russian ruler to establish an international position of some considerable importance in Europe. During his reign the princely house of Kiev was united with the royal lines of other Christian nations. His sister married Kazimir I of Poland. His wife was a Swedish princess. He married his daughters into the ruling families of France, Hungary, and Norway. Three of his sons married German princesses whereas a fourth married a relative of Constantine Monomachus, emperor of Byzantium.

It was Yaroslav's ambition to free himself from the dominance of Constantinople which, especially after the adoption of Christianity, was felt in all fields—religious, economic, and social. To this end he even launched an unsuccessful expedition against the Greeks in 1043. He sent traders to Germany, France, Hungary, and the Scandinavian countries. He invited and encouraged foreign artisans to settle in *Rūs*. He was instrumental in disseminating education, at least among members of the ruling class. He opened religious schools in connection with the churches and was probably the first Russian to establish a "Sunday School." The famous Pechersky monastery at Kiev, founded during Yaroslav's reign, came to have great political significance, since it supported his campaign for an independent Church and established a seminary for the training of Russian Church leaders. In 1051 Yaroslav even ventured to appoint the first Russian metropolitan, Hilarion, a highly educated man particularly well versed in homiletics, as is shown by one of his sermons yet extant. Despite the temporary appearance of a native metropolitan, however, Byzantium continued to send Greek metropolitans to Kiev until the thirteenth century.

Since it was his ambition that Kiev should vie with Constantinople in splendor, Yaroslav embellished it with many beautiful churches of stone, notable among which was the splendid cathedral of St. Sophia. That Kiev did more than just copy the patterns of Byzantium is evident from the fact that the Kiev Sophia had thirteen cupolas, and a fresco on the wall of this same cathedral depicted St. Nicholas not as a Greek but as a typical Russian. The tendency toward Russification was apparent in art as well as in politics. Other fine churches were built in Novgorod and in other cities of Kievan *Rūs.* Yaroslav also constructed the "Golden Gates of Kiev." It may be said that under him medieval Russian culture reached its zenith and that it was by no means inferior to that of the West.

Of great significance from the standpoint of internal policy was the promulgation by Yaroslav, first in Novgorod and later in Kiev, of the earliest Russian code of laws, the famous *Russkaya Pravda,*[1] which incorporated both Norse and Slavonic customs. This code restricted the hitherto prevalent exaction of blood vengeance for murder, substituting court procedure and payment of fines. It provided severe punishment for such crimes as theft, abduction, and concealment of slaves. As amended and expanded by Yaroslav's successors, this code became the most important written guide for the civil and Church courts of *Rūs.* The Yaroslav *Pravda,* as the historian George Vernadsky points out, affords many parallels with Frankish (Salic) law and with Anglo-Saxon law as depicted in the Wessex Code of Alfred the Great. Yaroslav's sons introduced provisions that afforded more protection to the princes and landholders.

At his death in 1054 much of the progress due to Yaroslav's efforts was lost when dissension of unusual bitterness broke out among the princes and continued with only occasional lulls until the reign of Ivan Grozny (1533-1584), who was strong enough to put a stop to it. During this long period of political confusion, the contending princes, with a total disregard for the interests of the country as a whole, often sought the alliance of foreign powers, such as Hungary and Poland, in their quarrels with one another. In consequence the principalities suffered severely from every standpoint, political, social and cultural, and the foundations were laid for the separation of the *Rūs* into three main branches, namely, Great Russians, White Russians, and Ukrainians (Little Russians). Had it not been for the dissension following the death of Yaroslav, it is doubtful if *Rūs* would ever have become so divided.

In 1113 the people became weary of continual confusion and, disregarding all rules of succession, elected a prince of their own choice,

---

[1] For an English translation, see Vernadsky, George, *Medieval Russian Laws,* N. Y., 1947, pp. 26-29. Revised and expanded versions of the same are also included, pp. 29-56.

Vladimir Monomakh (1113-1125), a grandson of Yaroslav. He was sixty years of age at the time of his election, wealthy and experienced and essentially a man of peace. Nevertheless he had displayed prowess in war against the Polovtsy (Cumani), a Turkish nomadic people from the steppe, which caused him to be feared and respected. He showed himself able to maintain order, and the people were loyal to him. During his reign education flourished; Vladimir himself was the author of several epistles which served as guides for conduct. In fact it is sometimes claimed that the *Chronicle* itself was a product of the intellectual activity characteristic of Vladimir's reign. The *Chronicle* places great emphasis upon the achievements of Vladimir, on his importance as the rallying point for all native elements against the foreign aggressor, on his role as a peacemaker, and as a popular hero. Additions to Yaroslav's *Pravda* in the Statute of Vladimir afforded protection to middle-class burghers and landowners of moderate means by limiting and regulating interest rates on short-term and long-term loans. In this connection it seems clear that in the commercial society of Eastern Europe the Orthodox Church failed to achieve the same results in regard to usury as did the Roman Catholic Church in the West.

After the death of Vladimir II, however, disorder broke out again. The city of Kiev began to decline, since it was frequently pillaged in civil wars among the princes. Kiev suffered a serious decline in 1169 when it was captured by Prince Bogolyubsky (1169-1174). Moreover, the raids of the warlike tribes of the Polovtsy against the lower Dnieper interrupted the trade via the "Varangian" route to the Black Sea and Constantinople. In 1204, when Constantinople was sacked by the Crusaders (the fourth Crusade), Kiev, being economically dependent upon the latter city, suffered even more severely. During the Mongol period (1240-1480), its glory definitely departed; and the political and cultural capital was transferred from the democratic "Cradle of Russia" in the south to autocratic Moscow in the north. Indeed, Moscow is said to have been founded by George Dolgoruky, the son of Vladimir Monomakh, as early as 1147.

For many years the throne of Kiev was regarded as the highest and most desirable position in the entire Russian state, and its occupant was recognized as the chief ruler, or grand prince. Consequently the eldest son in each successive ruling house did everything in his power to secure for himself the coveted honor. However, there were always other claimants who regarded themselves as at least eligible to the title and the power; hence there arose the jealousy and conflicts of the interested princes, which, as has already been noted, were especially bitter following the death of Yaroslav. As a result, by the middle of the twelfth century, instead of one strong national center at Kiev, there were a number of secondary centers or principalities, wherein disgruntled and disappointed aspirants to the title of "Grand Prince" sought solace in exercising local control. The most important of these were the Galician principality in the west, Novgorod in the north, and Vladimir-Suzdal in the northeast. In the south Kiev maintained its sway despite a constant decline in importance and population. Many of its inhabitants were attracted to other principalities and migrated there, not the least of the reasons being that the possession on the part of these principalities of forest lands offered a greater natural protection against invasions. Constantly the object of attacks which all too often ended in its defeat, and suffering from periods of economic depression, Kiev, nevertheless, remained the center of the Russian state in the real sense of the word. The history of the Russian people up to the time of the Mongol invasion is really the history of Kiev.

Before discussing the Mongol invasion and its disastrous effects, let us consider briefly the political, social, and religious structure of Russia preceding the cataclysm.

In all principalities the political structure was modeled upon that of Kiev, although there were minor variations due to local interests. In all cases, however, the government was semimonarchial, semiaristocratic, and semidemocratic. The monarchial element was represented by the ruling prince. His chief function was military, that is, it was his duty to protect the principality from outside foes. In addition judicial power was vested in him. For the exercise of this responsibility, he appointed special representatives to render judgment in litigations arising among his subjects.

The aristocratic element of the political structure was centered in the Council of the Prince, composed of the higher officers of his *druzhina*. This body discussed the most important matters of government and was instrumental in formulating the laws.

The democratic element found its expression in a popular gathering known as the *vieche,* almost the oldest of all socio-political Slavonic institutions and hence the one nearest to the hearts of the people. This gathering was not a representative assembly but was merely a meeting of all the adult males of any given town. The decision on any question had to be unanimous, the men indicating their wishes by shouts. In the event of any difference of opinion, the matter was settled by fisticuffs. This structure is reminiscent of the political organization of the

Homeric state wherein an uncrowned king represented the monarchial element, the Boule, the aristocratic, while the democratic element came into prominence in the assembly of the common citizens.

Although the three elements were always present, in the various regions one frequently took precedence over the others. Thus the monarchial element had ascendancy in northeastern Russia. The aristocratic element was predominant in southwestern Russia in the principalities of Galicia and Volyn. Here the *boyars,* or early nobility, influenced no doubt by ideas of Western feudalism reaching them through Poland and Hungary, compelled the ruling prince to make a choice between submitting to them or fighting them. The democratic element found its highest development in Novgorod[1] where there came to be a permanent assembly known as the *Vieche House,* through which means the principality attained complete and independent self-government with the *vieche* as the sole governing body.

During the tenth and eleventh centuries, Novgorod was governed from Kiev by the grand prince who appointed a viceroy, usually his son. After the death of Vladimir Monomakh in 1125, Novgorod took advantage of the fact that civil war had weakened the power of the princes and demanded and secured the privilege of electing its own prince. Through the *vieche* the principality was also rich and powerful enough to secure the right of appointing its own bishop from its own clergy. Up to the middle of the twelfth century this appointment had been made by the metropolitan of Kiev, but thereafter this authority was lost to him and he retained only the power of investiture.

The social structure of early Russia was composed of three groups, namely, freemen, semifreemen, and slaves. To the first group belonged the Churchmen, the *boyars,* that is, army officials and rich landowners, the townsmen who followed the crafts and trades, and the peasants. The semifree, or *zakupy,* were debtors who were obliged to work in order to repay debts contracted. There was a strong feeling among the *Rūs* that if a man could not pay in money, he must cancel his obligations by surrendering a portion of his personal liberty; hence there came into existence this semifree group. Originally the third group, the slaves, was composed mainly of prisoners taken in war, but, as time went on, slavery became a well-established institution and absorbed many of the native citizens as well; the usual reason advanced for its continuance was that it was necessary for the progress of civilization.

---

[1] For a translation of the Novgorod Charter of 1471, see Vernadsky, George, *op. cit.,* pp. 83-92.

As a rule, in a country which suffers from frequent invasion and devastation, agriculture does not occupy a very prominent place. Industry is likely to be more developed. Nevertheless in Kievan *Rūs* agriculture was a leading if not the most prominent occupation, and, in consequence, the peasants made up the bulk of the population. Agriculture did not, however, develop at the expense of industry, which, especially in the field of foreign trade, flourished remarkably.

To what extent the feudal system, which flourished in Western and Central Europe during this era, was characteristic of the Kievan state is still open to question. Soviet scholars, including B. D. Grekov, in recent years have devoted considerable attention to the study of this problem. The well-known historian, George Vernadsky, points out,[1] however, that serfdom was by no means universal in Kievan *Rūs,* whereas slave labor was used extensively; and that the Russian *boyars* and princes depended not only on agriculture but on trade, especially foreign trade, for their livelihood—all of which involved the growth of a money economy, as opposed to barter and services. He likewise contends that, although there was a marked development of political feudalism, as indicated by the relationship between suzerain and vassal in Suzdal (northeast) and Galicia (west) by the middle of the twelfth century, there was in reality a greater similarity between Kievan *Rūs* and the Byzantine Empire than between it and Western Europe.

Of highest importance, however, in pre-Mongol Russia was the Church, which had a vital and far-reaching influence upon the lives of the people. In common with other members of the Greek Orthodox faith, the Russians recognized as the head of the Church the patriarch of Constantinople. Directly subordinate to him was the metropolitan of Kiev who had jurisdiction over the bishops. They, in turn, had charge of the lower clergy. Thus there existed a closely knit ecclesiastical organization.

The Russian Church calls itself the Holy Catholic Apostolic and Orthodox Church. It has, with certain differences in administration, the same seven sacraments as the Roman Catholic Church, namely, baptism, confirmation, holy eucharist, penance, unction, holy orders, and matrimony. While the two Churches separated originally on minor questions of discipline, the gulf between them widened in the course of time with respect to questions of dogma. For example, the Orthodox Church denies the Dogma of Immaculate Conception in the sense that it is accepted by the Roman Church. According to the latter, all human

---

[1] See Vernadsky, George, *Kievan Russia,* Yale University Press, 1948, pp. 163-172, 209-212.

beings at birth bear the taint of original sin with the exception of the Holy Virgin. Further the Orthodox Church rejects the infallibility of the pope and refuses to recognize his authority over the Church as a whole. It affirms that the sole head of the Church is Jesus Christ, who has no vicar on earth. Thus the pope is the patriarch of the West but has no universal control. Considering the matter in the light of comparative religion, the Orthodox Church appears to approach Protestantism with respect to dogma, whereas in ritualism, it has more in common with the Roman Catholic faith.

In Orthodox worship the ikon plays an important role. Although the ikon portrays pictures of the holy family or saints or scenes from their lives, it is not regarded as a picture, but as a symbolic object of worship and veneration. Placed in a prominent position, with a lighted taper before it, it becomes the central point for the exercise of religious service. It is ever regarded as a symbol or reminder of the spiritual world, its purpose being to arouse noble spiritual aspirations.

It is impossible to overemphasize the importance of the spiritual life of Russia as it found expression in the Church of the period. The Church, like the spirit within a body, invisible yet all pervading, was the center from which all life both spiritual and secular radiated. Not only matters of a strictly religious nature but mundane affairs as well were discussed and decided within the Church. Yet the Church attempted no dominance. Such compulsion as was felt came from the efforts of overzealous princes. The Church itself was not the tool or instrument of any class or order but was the common possession of the people of all ranks and stations. In their devotion and mutual service to the institution, all met on a basis of equality. The pre-Mongol period may, therefore, be called the "honeymoon" of Orthodox Christianity in Russia.

Great credit is due the clergy of the period for the beneficial influence exerted by the Church. The Greeks sent their most capable and intelligent spiritual leaders, the very elite of the clergy. Yet the spiritual life remained in no sense an extraneous element in national life but immediately took on distinctly Russo-Slavonic characteristics. Thus the language of the Church service, which in the beginning was Greek, was gradually supplanted by Slavonic Bulgarian, which at that time was the dialect best adapted to translation from the Greek. As time passed, it assumed more and more Russian characteristics through the impress of Russo-Slavonic temperament. The service was often simplified, but at the same time a higher meaning was attributed to the symbolism, thereby sublimating it from the Slavonic standpoint.

A RUSSIAN IKON OF VIRGIN AND CHILD

In consideration of what has been said, it occasions no surprise that the first literature emanated from the Church and took the form of liturgies and prayers, mostly translations from the Greek. Secular literature, chiefly the epic, soon flourished side by side with it. Many literary critics have observed here a conscious effort on the part of secular literature to free itself from Church influence. This, however, was not the case. As has been stated previously, the Church made no effort to dominate secular life, hence there was no necessity for secular literature to free itself from a clerical control which never existed. It merely pictured a different phase of life and exhibited a variation from ecclesiastical literature. The best known of these secular epics, still in existence, is the *Tale of the Host of Igor*,[1] an account of a heroic but unsuccessful campaign which Igor made against the Polovtsy in 1185. Many other epics or "bylinas," proverbs and various forms of folklore originated in this period, but with the coming of the Mongols, material of incalculable value was lost.

Russian art, which was essentially religious, remained subordinate to the Orthodox Church until the time of Peter the Great. It was the Church which brought the ikon, and Russian monks, taught by the Greeks, developed the art of mural painting. Architecture was marked by greater diversity during the Kievan period. The cube-shaped churches of Novgorod and Pskov to the north, with their oval cupolas, high gabled roofs, and narrow windows were distinct Russian adaptations of Byzantine forms, and in decoration they even reflected the influence of Persia and India.[2] While Church influence prevailed, that is, until the close of the seventeenth century, there was no development of Russian sculpture. The iconoclastic struggle which rocked the Greek Orthodox Church in this respect left its imprint upon its Russian counterpart.

The pre-Mongol period in Russia was distinguished by great spiritual activity and not a little political and social progress. The stage was set for great cultural development, which might have had a far-reaching and beneficent influence not only upon Russia but upon the entire Western world. Outside foes, aided by internal discord, interrupted and retarded its development for many years to come.

---

[1] Now available in an English translation by Samuel H. Cross. See *Annuaire de l'Institut de Philologie et d'Histoire Orientales et Slaves,* Vol. VIII, pp. 151-179.
[2] For illustrations see Cross, S. H., *Mediaeval Russian Churches,* Cambridge, Mass., 1949.

2

The Mongol Period

1240-1480

T HE Mongol or Tartar invasion and domination of *Rūs,* which
began in the first half of the thirteenth century and lasted until
the latter part of the fifteenth, is of vital importance in the history of the country, the effects thereof being felt even to the
present day. During this long period of foreign control and influence,
the face of Russia was entirely changed. Not only were there territorial alterations, but the physical and mental characteristics of the
people were transformed to an almost unbelievable extent, so that the
break between Russian culture and Western culture became complete.
To be sure, this separation had begun automatically with the acceptance of the Greek Orthodox form of Christianity. This was especially
true after 1054, when the final division between Roman and Greek
Catholic Churches took place, marking the culmination of the original
division of 867. The Tartar period, however, brought about a change
which was much more vital and complete. It caused a division of the
Russian people proper into the Eastern group, subjugated by the Mongols, and the Western group, overcome by Lithuanians. Upon the
conquered peoples, the usurpers imposed their domination sometimes
subtly, sometimes by force; they succeeded not only in eradicating
many of the spiritual values which *Rūs* had attained through the adoption of Christianity, but it is sometimes claimed that they effected an
actual physical change in the people.

They accomplished these ends in several ways. In the first place,
the Mongol conquerors continuously practised polygamy and maintained many harems, which included Russian women. In addition
intermarriage between Tartars and Russians was of frequent occurrence. Then there was the shifting of population and consequent racial
transformation by the slave trade. Not only were slaves imported in

23

large numbers from other countries, but Russians were sold into slavery in the central market of Kaffa (Crimea) to be distributed thence to all parts of Asia Minor, Africa, and even Europe. This export trade in slaves arose from the Tartar practice of brutally crushing all opposition to their rule. Thus if a Russian prince had the temerity to indulge in disobedience, his territory was invaded and the inhabitants were sold into slavery.)

So extensive was this slave traffic that in al-Zahra the Umayyad Caliph of Cordova surrounded himself with a bodyguard of 3750 Slavs. Although the term *Slav* seems to have been applied at first to slaves and prisoners captured by the Germans and others from among the Slavonic tribes and later sold to the Arabs, it was later used to denote all purchased foreigners, whether Franks, Galicians, Lombards, or others.[1]

The Tartar influence upon the religious and spiritual life was more subtle but no less powerful. The Russian Church suffered comparatively little from interference or intolerance; nevertheless many customs, practices and ceremonies, distinctly Oriental, left their impress upon religion and daily life, and by reason of long duration they came to be regarded as of Christian origin.[2] For example, the free Russian woman of the pre-Mongol period was reduced to the status of the Mohammedan woman. She adopted the veil and began to lead a more and more secluded life. Thus when Peter the Great attempted by force to abolish this and other Asiatic practices, he encountered the most stubborn resistance, since they had become so completely ingrained in the daily life of his subjects that they were considered national customs of immemorial antiquity.

Although Tartar hordes brought misfortune and devastation to many other peoples and countries, the harm which they inflicted upon Russia was the greatest of all.

The prologue to the Mongol domination of Russia began in 1223 when wild hordes, headed by Chingis Khan (Jenghis Khan) and under the leadership of two brilliant generals, Djebe and Subutai, appeared in the southeast. Here they defeated the Polovtsy at the Khalka on the Dnieper and likewise put to rout a Russian army, which hastened to repel the invaders. During this battle the prince of Kiev was killed.

---

[1] See Hitti, Philip K., *History of the Arabs*, p. 525.
[2] See, however, Lobanov-Rostovsky, A., *Russia and Asia*, pp. 23-24, 305. See also Buslayev, F., *Sketches of the History of Russian Folklore and Art*, Vol. II, pp. 233-237. Compare Kunitz, Joshua, *Russian Liteature and the Jew*, Columbia University Press, 1929, pp. 2-3.

southern China as directed by Kublai Khan, emperor from 1257 to 1298 (Chinese records 1260-1294).

The Tartars, likewise, made no attempt to impose their own religion upon the subjugated Russians. Even after 1341, when Islam became the official religion of the Khans of the "Golden Horde," no effort was made to eradicate the Orthodox worship. The "Golden Horde" even permitted a Russian bishopric to be established in the city of Sarai, where the bishop not only enjoyed full freedom in holding services but was also allowed the privilege of proselytism.

Tartar rule was not entirely detrimental to Russia, especially during the first century of control. Comparative peace and order were maintained. Diplomatic and trade relations were established with many countries, and agreements concerning these relations were honorably kept. Trade routes were developed, which gave merchants assurance of safe transportation of their wares. In consequence a lively commerce grew up and flourished, and the country enjoyed a fair degree of tranquillity and prosperity. The stamp of Tartar rule, however, was upon everything and the country chafed because of the submergence of its nationalism.

Among the Russian princes, two attitudes prevailed toward the Tartar conquerors. The princes of one group gave apparent co-operation, biding their time until the foreign yoke could be thrown off. Meanwhile they availed themselves of Tartar assistance in repelling attacks from European neighbors, whose encroachments they feared even more than they did the Tartar dominance. Thus Prince Alexander Nevsky (died 1263) of Novgorod was aided by the Tartars in repulsing attacks of the Swedes, Finns, and Lithuanians against whom he won an outstanding victory on the River Neva (hence the name Nevsky) in 1240. He won a second triumph against the Germans (Teutonic Knights) in the famous "Battle of the Ice" at Lake Peipus in 1242 and drove the Lithuanians from Novgorod territory in 1245. The Russian Orthodox Church, which viewed Alexander Nevsky's victories as a decisive triumph over Roman Catholicism, later canonized its hero. His fame has been revived under the Soviet regime in the well-known film *Alexander Nevsky,* produced by the late Sergei Eisenstein. Even as Grand Prince of Vladimir, to which position he succeeded in 1246, Alexander Nevsky continued to recognize the dependence of the new Russia on the Tartars. When confronted simultaneously by danger from both the East and the West, he is reputed to have said: "The Mongol can wait." His example, in giving priority to European over

Asiatic affairs, has often characterized Russian and even Soviet foreign policy.

Another group of princes turned toward the West for assistance in freeing themselves from Tartar control. These princes, whose realms occupied most of northwestern Russia and Moscow, either made overtures to Western powers or adopted a policy of nonresistance toward Western invaders. One of their number, Daniel of Galicia, went so far as to offer to recognize the authority of the pope if the latter would start a crusade against the Tartars. When the help was not forthcoming, however, he relinquished his plans for securing Western aid and joined the Tartophile camp.

Of the Western powers, the one to make the most frequent raids upon Russian territory was Lithuania. The Lithuanians were aided in their invasions by the aforementioned policy of nonresistance on the part of those Russian princes who preferred them to the Tartars, and who believed they saw in the Lithuanian inroads an opportunity to rid themselves of their subjugators. They were aided, likewise, by the violent internal dissensions which by the middle of the thirteenth century had begun to disrupt the "Golden Horde," various pretenders quarreling for sovereignty very much as the native Russian princes had formerly contended for supremacy of Kiev. The Lithuanians were quick to take advantage of the weakening of the "Horde" and shortly brought under their control a considerable portion of Western Russia.

Originally the preference of the Russian princes for the Lithuanians as opposed to the Tartars or to other Western powers had been occasioned by the fact that the pagan Lithuanians had been very susceptible to Greek Orthodox influence, and the Orthodox Church had exerted considerable control over them. Toward the end of the fourteenth century, however, a change came about in religious policy. At that time the Lithuanian grand duke, Jagiello, was offered and accepted the Polish throne, which brought Lithuania under Polish influence. Moreover in 1386, the grand duke embraced Roman Catholicism, his example being rapidly followed by the pagan nobility of Lithuania. Even a part of the Russian nobility residing in Lithuanian territory became converted to the Roman faith.

The Russian princes, who had foreseen the political changes in Lithuania, now adopted a new policy whereby Tartophiles and their opponents joined forces to attain two objectives. In the first place, they resolved to take advantage of the quarrels among the Khans, attack them and drive them out from Russia as the Mongols were expelled from China in 1368.[1] This done, they planned to direct their energies toward winning back Russian territory from the Western invaders, the Lithuanians.

The first step was taken in 1380 when Dimitri, Grand Duke of Moscow (1350-1389), met and defeated the forces of Khan Mamai at Kulikovo Meadow on the Don River. Although the victory was not decisive and was followed by reprisals, including the ruthless sack of Moscow in 1382, the psychological effect upon the Russians was enormous. Heretofore the Tartars had been regarded as invincible, but now that this armor of invincibility had been pierced, the "Golden Horde" could never again inspire the same awe and terror as before. The year 1380, therefore, marks a turning point in the Mongol hegemony. The battle at Kulikovo Meadow had for the Russians the same significance that the battle of Marathon in 490 B.C. had for the Athenians, when their forces under Miltiades defeated the Persians, for "up to this time the very name of Medes was to the Hellenes a terror to hear." In recognition of this victory, Dimitri was given the surname Donskoi (of the Don). Among his other accomplishments, Dimitri is credited with the introduction of firearms into the army, and during his reign silver money came into general use. During the last years of his reign the Black Death, which had previously deprived him of his father, once again brought dire distress and want to the population of Russia. The Grand Duke Vasily (1389-1425), son of Dimitri, was forced to recognize once more the overlordship of the "Horde," but he cleverly availed himself of their aid against the Lithuanians. In a battle by the River Vorskla near Poltava in 1399, the Lithuanians were overwhelmingly defeated and their control of Russian territory ceased forthwith.

Dimitri's accomplishments, therefore, were twofold and of the greatest importance. In the first place, he proved that the Tartars could be defeated, and, secondly, his son and successor, Vasily, by playing one foe against another (also following the Chinese example), rid his land of Western invaders and was no longer a vassal of the "Golden Horde." Fully one hundred years were needed to rid the land entirely of Tartar dominance. This was accomplished in 1480 by Ivan III, known as Ivan the Great (1462-1505), who proved to be a statesman of outstanding ability.

---

[1] The Mongol period in China lasted from 1268 to 1368. Kublai Khan (1216-1294) was the first emperor of the Mongols in China. He made Buddhism the state religion.

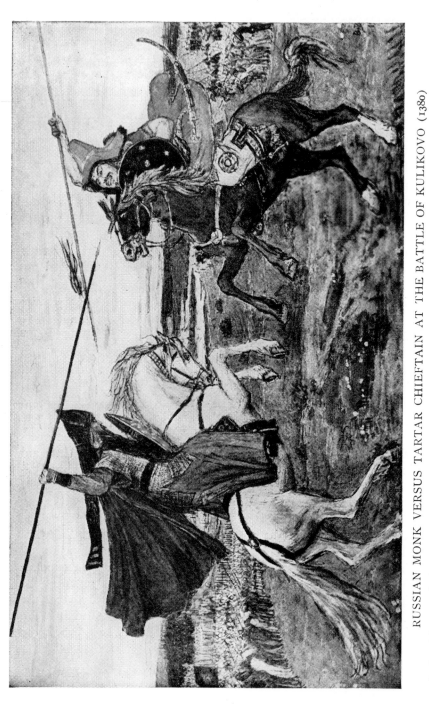

RUSSIAN MONK VERSUS TARTAR CHIEFTAIN AT THE BATTLE OF KULIKOVO (1380)

In Russia's struggle for survival against the Tartar hordes, the Church played a militant part. The painting, by Victor Vasnetsov, shows the monk Peresviet in single combat with the Mongol chief Tchelibey.

By the accession of Ivan III the principality of Moscow had emerged out of the confusion and disintegration to the extent that its grand prince was recognized as the leading suzerain of north Russia. His was not yet an extensive domain. Most of the south and southwest of Russia had been appropriated by Poland and Lithuania. On the south the principality of Moscow reached only as far as the River Oka on the edge of the steppes. To the east, Kazan was dominated by the Great Khan, who still claimed to be the overlord of Moscow, and to the north lay Novgorod, only nominally subject to the Grand Prince of Moscow.

Ivan III undertook to round out and consolidate his domain. From 1471-1479 he accomplished the complete subjugation of Novgorod, then a prosperous outpost of the Hanseatic League, which had entered into an alliance with Casimir of Poland and declared its independence of Moscow. This was followed, from 1484-1485, by the annexation of Tver and Ryazan. In 1480, Ivan having refused to pay tribute to the "Golden Horde," the Khan Akhmat invaded the principality of Moscow to enforce recognition of his suzerainty. The khan suddenly abandoned the field to his opponent, and the "Golden Horde" never reasserted its power over Moscow.

In 1472 Ivan III married Sophia Palaeologue, a niece and heiress of the last of the Byzantine emperors, who had taken refuge in Italy after the fall of Constantinople to the Turks in 1453. He then assumed the coat of arms of the former Byzantine Empire, namely the double-headed eagle, and began to regard himself as a "tsar" and successor to the Byzantine emperors. The expectations of the papacy and of some European sovereigns that, as a result of the marriage, he would join a Christian crusade against the Turks and effect a union of the Orthodox and Roman Catholic faiths, did not materialize.

Ivan did, however, enter into diplomatic relations with the West. He dispatched emissaries to Rome to secure armorers, engineers, artists, and artisans for Russia. In 1486 the Holy Roman Empire sent its first ambassador to Moscow. In 1493, following the subjugation of Novgorod, he entered into treaty relations with Denmark, another country which had contributed to the decline of the Hanseatic League and its trade monopoly in the Baltic. In reaching out to the West, and in particular toward the Baltic, he paved the way for his grandson, Ivan IV.

The dearth of public building during the Mongol period compelled Ivan III to devote considerable attention to the reconstruction of Moscow. Since Russian architects had become so ignorant, in the meantime, of the principles of good masonry that several churches collapsed before completion, Ivan brought Italian architects to Moscow, including Aristotle Fioravanti of Bologna and Pietro Antonio Solari of Milan. It was natural that the various churches and cathedrals restored by Italian artists should in many respects reflect the influence of the early Italian Renaissance. Since the Russians refused to abandon the old Russian-Byzantine forms, however, the chief contribution of the Italians seems to have been a better technique of construction. From them the Russians learned how to make better bricks and mortar and to reinforce their structures with iron instead of wood. Fioravanti reconstructed the Uspensky Cathedral (Cathedral of the Assumption), which became the Coronation Church of the tsars. Solari helped to build the first stone palace in the Kremlin and part of the Kremlin walls. The Cathedral of the Annunciation (Blagoveshchensky), which served as the Royal Chapel, and the Cathedral of the Archangel Michael, the burial place of the grand princes and tsars, were the work of Milanese architects, of whom the most notable was Aloisio da Carezano. In fact, the Kremlin was basically the work of the Italian colony of artists in Moscow.

In his reorganization of the administration, the army, and the system of land tenure, Ivan the Great contributed immensely to the centralization of authority and laid the foundations for Russian autocracy of the sixteenth century. The influence of Byzantine models and precedents in this respect is evident. Soviet scholars now regard the revival of Byzantine law and culture in Russia in the second half of the fifteenth century as something akin to a Renaissance. One phase of this revival was the renewed emphasis on jurisprudence, which resulted in the issuing in 1497 of a new code of laws, the *Sudebnik,* based upon the *Russkaya Pravda* of Kievan *Rūs.*

To handle the vastly increased amount of clerical work which his domestic and foreign program involved, Ivan drew heavily upon the ecclesiastical schools for trained secretaries and clerks. The Church, which became an important prop for the state, helped to lay the foundations of the tsarist bureaucracy. Like the Mongols, Ivan also maintained a highly efficient system of communications throughout his realm by the construction of post roads and the establishment of post stations to facilitate travel. Baron Herberstein, the emissary of the Holy Roman Emperor, Charles V, in Moscow from 1526 to 1533, who has left a first-hand account of his Russian sojourn, commented that his servant was able to travel from Novgorod to Moscow—a distance of some 600 *versts* (about 400 miles)—in seventy-two hours, with frequent changes of horses at the post stations.

Of special significance for the centralization of authority in the hands of the grand prince was the land policy instituted by Ivan III. Following the seizure of Novgorod and the wholesale slaughter and eviction of the *boyars* there, Ivan granted the land thus obtained to his subordinate officers on condition of constant service. This policy, which was pursued in the case of future annexations, built up a loyal and well-trained cavalry force, entirely subject to the grand prince. Although Russian scholars have termed this procedure a "manorial system" it might be more adequately defined as "royal feudalism" of the type instituted in England by William the Conqueror after 1066. No such military force had been available to the rulers of Kievan *Rūs*.

It should perhaps be noted here that at the very time when Ivan III was pursuing measures to centralize authority in his own hands, in the neighboring state of Poland the Polish aristocracy was successfully wresting authority from the hands of the monarch. Ivan III laid his foundations so well that they survived even the difficult period of the minority of his grandson, Ivan IV.

Russia emerged from her long Mongol subjugation (1240-1480) an entirely altered land. The capital had moved by stages from Kiev to Moscow, which had, likewise, become the ecclesiastical center, the metropolitan having taken up his residence here in preference to Kiev. The semidemocratic government of the Kievan period had been replaced by a rule of harsh autocracy. The Russian princes, following the example of the Tartars, whose government had been one of implacable despotism, had come to regard themselves as absolute monarchs.

Perhaps an even more disastrous result of the Mongol period was its influence upon the Church. Previous to the Tartar invasion, the Church, as already indicated, was a guiding and directing force toward the highest spiritual aims. Leading rather than compelling, it permeated all life to the extent that it became in reality the life of the people. It emerged from the Mongol period, however, as just one more autocratic institution, seeking supremacy. Like the Russian princes, the Church wished to make its authority felt; hence, having similar aims with the state, a close autocratic union developed between the two institutions.

Another result of Tartar rule was the development of monasticism, which in Russia was not so much a borrowed institution as an outgrowth of national distress. Although records show that there had

THE EASTERN FACADE OF THE CATHEDRAL OF OUR LADY OF
SMOLENSK AT THE NOVODYEVITCHI MONASTERY IN MOSCOW

been monasteries in Russia even before the Mongol invasion, they were few in number. Many individuals as well as groups, who chafed under the Tartar regime, often met outside the towns for the purpose of seeking solace in another environment. Here they frequently indulged in prayer and religious discussion, until by long continuance this led to the establishment of a religious organization, which developed later into the Russian monastery. While monasticism was responsible for many worthwhile accomplishments and even made valuable contributions to Russian culture, it began to decline in importance in proportion as Russia became independent of foreign influence. At no time did it enjoy particular favor from the government. Peter the Great began the practice of closing the monasteries, and those which remained down to modern times were closed by the Soviet government.

To sum up, the situation at the death of Ivan III in 1505 was as follows: Moscow, with a large mixed population of native Russians and assimilated Tartars, had transformed the Russian princes into despots, who punished with torture and death the least disobedience on the part of their subjects. Although the supremacy of the Tartars was forever broken, they still held control in several regions, especially in Kazan and Crimea where some time elapsed before they could be entirely shaken off. In the west, Poland, gradually controlling and absorbing Lithuania, was looming as a dangerous foe. What was now needed was a ruler who could put an end to the continual quarrels among the princes for supreme control so that outside foes might be met with united resistance. A strong leader was needed, who was more autocratic, more cruel, more merciless than any of the others, and such a person appeared in Ivan IV, or Ivan the Terrible, grandson of Ivan III.

3

Ivan Grozny[1] (Ivan IV)
the First Tsar
1530-1584

IVAN IV was but three years of age when his father, Vasily III, died in 1533, and his mother, Elena Glinskaya, assumed the regency. The country was in a state of great confusion. Not only were the princes constantly quarreling, but the *boyars* had taken a hand in the struggle for power. After the death of Vasily, the government fell into the hands of these *boyars* and passed from one prominent family to another, the exchange of authority being accompanied by atrocities and executions. Thus Ivan grew up in an atmosphere of dissension, cruelty, and murder, which in addition to his negative and unsystematic education predisposed him to his later abnormal brutality, especially toward the *boyars,* whom he hated with particular bitterness, deeming them responsible for the disrupted state of the country. In estimating his character and policies, it must be borne in mind also that he was a true child of his generation, a product of the Mongol period when self-interest, coupled with indifference to human suffering, had been the rule. Two hundred forty years of Tartar domination were necessary to produce a man like Ivan Grozny.[2] Yet strange as it may seem, he was the right man at the right time. He had sound judgment and vision and looked forward to a strong, united, mighty state under an autocratic monarchy, different from any that existed in Europe at that time.

---

[1] The customary English translation of *grozny* as "terrible" or "dreadful" is an incorrect rendition of the Russian term, which in reality means "awe-inspiring," "great," "wonderful," or "dreadful" in a reverential sense.

[2] Ivan IV was married seven times but left only two young sons at his death. In 1580 in a fit of fury he killed his eldest son, which action lent confirmation to the general belief that he suffered from insanity. His wives were as follows: Anastasia Romanov, Maria (Circassian), Martha, Anna, Anna Vasiltchikuf, and Maria Nagaya.

36

In 1547 the Metropolitan Macarius, a scholar steeped in Byzantine philosophy and predisposed toward a strong monarchy, declared Ivan of age but placed him under the guardianship of the Church until 1553. Ivan married Anastasia Romanov and assumed the title of "tsar," which was to be borne by all future emperors.[1] At first, Ivan attempted to deal diplomatically with the *boyars,* who sought to wrest his authority from him. He tried to win their support by concessions, now to one group, now to another, but these efforts on his part were interpreted as weakness by his opponents.

In his efforts to establish the supreme authority of the monarchy, Ivan was encouraged and advised by Ivan Peresvetov, a man of Lithuanian-Russian extraction, who had chosen to serve the tsar. Peresvetov, an avowed enemy of the *boyars,* exalted monarchial power and urged Ivan to consolidate his position by seeking support from the lesser aristocracy and by leaning upon the army. The military monarchy he advocated was modeled upon that of the Sultan of Turkey, Mohammed II, who had seized Constantinople in 1453.

The reign of Ivan IV was marked by almost continuous warfare. In his early military campaigns, for which he made elaborate preparations in regard to men and matériel, the tsar met with marked success. In 1552, with an army of 150,000 men and, according to one of his generals, 150 pieces of cannon, he seized the stronghold of Kazan from the Tartars, thereby securing a gateway to further Russian expansion in Asia. Thereafter he subdued the Volga region, captured Astrakhan in 1556, and, having reached the Caucasus, constructed several fortresses on the River Terek. Ivan distributed the lands of Kazan among his supporters, built numerous fortresses, and manned them by Russian troops. To commemorate the great victory of Kazan he began the construction of the famous, if somewhat grotesque, Church of St. Basil in Moscow—a work which was not completed until 1679. This remarkable building, which stands at one end of the Red Square in Moscow, and which is sometimes misrepresented as "typical" Russian architecture, is in reality a collection of some twenty-one chapels, all differing in shape and color, and with no two domes alike, the over-all structure of which bears some resemblance to the old wooden architecture of Russia.

While his military prestige was still high, the tsar in 1558 began

---

[1] It is extremely doubtful whether the title "tsar" (also Zarr, Czar, Czarr, Ksar, Tsar) is derived from the Latin "Caesar," as is usually contended. The Tartar princes of Kazan were also called "tsars." See Graham, S., *Ivan the Terrible,* pp. 39, 125-126; and Wipper, R., *Ivan Grozny,* p. 70.

THE SIEGE OF KAZAN BY IVAN GROZNY (1552)

A scene from the Soviet film Ivan the Terrible

his campaign for the seizure of Livonia on the Baltic coast, which was destined to last some twenty-four years and to end in failure. For this task he undertook an extensive mobilization of man power, bringing cavalry from the Volga, the Nogai Steppes, and even from the Terek to the Baltic. The capture of Narva and Dorpat gave him an outlet to the Baltic, which he would fain have extended by the inclusion of the larger and wealthier ports of Riga and Reval. Unfortunately his Baltic campaign constituted a threat to the Poles and Lithuanians, who held Riga, and to the Swedes, who held Reval. In 1563, with the capture of Polotsk on the Dvina from the Lithuanians, he added one more triumph to an already imposing succession of military victories.

By 1563 Ivan Grozny had reached the apex of his power and prestige. Even his limited successes on the Baltic, and the effectiveness of his artillery, aroused great fear in the West, especially in Sweden, Poland, and among the Germans. In 1560 Albrecht of Mecklenburg whose lands were in danger due to the advance of the "Moscow tyrant" called upon Western European nations to stop providing arms and provisions to the Russians. The German Reichstag, apprehensive about the possibility of a Russian fleet appearing in the Baltic, took measures to prevent trade with Russia via Narva.

An event of prime importance in the reign of Ivan Grozny was the establishment of trade relations with England, first by way of the Arctic and later via Narva and the Baltic. In 1553 Richard Chancellor, a survivor of the ill-fated English expedition of Sir Hugh Willoughby, which was searching for a passage to the Orient, arrived at the mouth of the Dvina on the ship *Bonaventure* (160 tons). Chancellor was welcomed and feted in true Russian style in Moscow. Having promised to furnish cloth and military supplies to the Russians via the Dvina, the English secured many concessions from the tsar in the years that followed. In 1555, following the conclusion of an Anglo-Russian trade agreement, Queen Mary of England granted the "Russia Company" a complete monopoly of English trade with Muscovy. Ivan likewise granted the English an exclusive monopoly of the Northern Route, to the great distress of the Swedes, and after 1558 permitted them free entry by way of Narva. The English not only secured the right to trade, duty free, throughout the Moscow state, but acquired exclusive rights to trade with Kazan and Astrakhan, together with the right of free transit by way of the Volga to Persia and Central Asia. By the Charter of 1569 an English company was given the right to prospect for iron and to erect a smelter near the River Vychegda. The English were permitted to mint English money at Russian mints, to use Russian post horses and to hire Russian labor—all at a time when the tsar was seeking the favor of Russian merchants in opposition to the troublesome *boyars*. It is not surprising that Ivan Grozny was upon occasion called the "English Tsar." Ivan later appears to have proposed marriage to Queen Elizabeth and, when that failed to materialize, to Lady Mary Hastings. Although he displayed keen interest in English trade, the tsar consistently rejected English efforts to secure a monopoly of all the commerce of his realm.

Of the English adventurers who traveled to Russia in the time of Ivan Grozny, Richard Chancellor and Anthony Jenkinson have left accounts of their experiences. One of Chancellor's statements was almost prophetic in nature: "If they (the Russians) knew their strength, no man were able to make match with them, nor they that dwell near them should have rest of them." [1] Both men were impressed by the wealth and luxury of the tsar's court, by his military might, and his autocratic authority.

It was toward the end of 1564 that Ivan adopted a course of action which was to bring him absolute authority and make it possible for him to crush the *boyars,* who were still conspiring against him. He suddenly and secretly left Moscow and took up his residence in the village of Alexandrovskaya Sloboda, near Trinity monastery, from whence he announced his abdication owing to the treachery of the *boyars*. This "abdication" immediately evoked terrified entreaties from the civil and ecclesiastical population to the effect that he should not forsake them. Thereupon Ivan laid down the conditions of his return and forthwith instituted a regime marked by great cruelty and atrocities.

Since his prime purpose was the complete destruction of the hated *boyar* class, Ivan demanded absolute and unquestioned authority to deal with the "traitors" as he saw fit. He further demanded that he be allowed to create a private guard for himself, which came to be known as the *Oprichnina*. The term, which was coined in the time of Ivan IV, means a "separate" or "private" household or court. The members of the *Oprichnina* were men who, regardless of rank and station, abandoned everything in order to devote themselves exclusively to the service of the tsar. They numbered about 6000, held the rank of monks, and wore a special uniform consisting of "black cassocks over sable necklets and cloth of gold." They became Ivan's most powerful agent in his purge of treason from within. He gave the *Oprich-*

---

[1] See Hakluyt's *Voyages*, N. Y., 1903, Vol. II, p. 232.

nina license to slay and drive out the *boyars,* whose lands they secured eventually for themselves. There followed an "open season" for *boyars,* who had lost all protection of life and property.

One method of execution, much in favor with Ivan, consisted in inviting to dinner a group of *boyars* who were hostile to him. When they had been reduced to a semi-comatose state by gluttony and drunkenness, the waiting *Oprichnina* would fall upon them and indulge in wholesale decapitation. The country at large, although not exactly approving of Ivan's course of procedure, regarded it with more or less indifference, since the policies of the *boyars* had brought extreme hardships to the people. Ivan, himself, who was firmly convinced that Russia's future demanded the destruction of this class, continued his ruthlessness until he had attained his objective. The *boyars* who managed to remain alive either fled from the country or were rendered impotent by being stripped of all wealth and position. In this fashion Ivan strengthened the monarchy by a policy of terrorism. Like Ivan III before him, he broke up the strongholds of untrustworthy *boyars,* disbanded their private armies, confiscated their property, and substituted a service class, composed of new men of obscure lineage who were dependent on him alone. These he settled on lands beyond Moscow, and they proved to be an important factor in the maintenance of the tsar's authority in the long years of warfare and defeat that followed. Ivan's new group of courtiers later became known as the *dvorianie.* From the *Oprichnina* there gradually developed a new landowning, politically powerful class, known as the *pomiestchiki,* who earned their wealth and preferment by service for the tsar. This group continued to be a factor to be reckoned with as late as the middle of the nineteenth century.

Shortly after the establishment of the *Oprichnina,* Ivan, in order to win public backing for a renewal of the war for the possession of Livonia, summoned in 1566 what is ordinarily termed the first genuine *Zemsky Sobor*—an assembly of representatives of the clergy, the princes, the government bureaucracy, as well as the merchants and traders. The merchants and traders were invited for the first time, and this step affords one more indication of Ivan's efforts to win the support of other classes against the hated *boyars.* Ivan's calling of the *Zemsky Sobor* recalls the comparable action in England of Simon de Montfort in 1265 and Edward I in 1295.

The second half of Ivan's reign, especially the years from 1571 to 1583, was marked by constant warfare, in which Russia was under attack from the Crimean Tartars in the south and from the Poles and

Swedes in the west. Although Russia had virtually thrown off Tartar control, the khans were still powerful enough to threaten seriously the peace and security of the country. In 1571 Devlet Girei, Khan of Crimea, conducted a raid into the interior of Russia, sacking and burning Moscow. The following year he made another raid, and only the united forces of all Russia were able to drive him off. In the west, where Ivan failed to secure election to the vacant Polish throne in 1573 and 1575, he was soon involved by his successful rival, Stephen Bathory (1576-1586), a Magyar nobleman of great military ability, in a renewal of the struggle for Livonia. Bathory, who had been in the service of the Sultan of Turkey before he acquired the Polish throne, did not hesitate to ally himself with the Crimean Tartars against his Russian adversary. Poland and Lithuania having been united since 1569, Bathory conceived the idea of an even greater union by the ultimate inclusion of Russia and its conversion to Roman Catholicism. He captured Polotsk and the important Russian fortress of Velikie Luki, but the heroic defense of the city of Pskov stopped his advance. By the peace that followed in 1582 Ivan Grozny renounced his claims to Livonia and abandoned his previous Lithuanian conquests, in return for which Poland recognized his title as "Tsar." In the following year Ivan was forced to surrender Esthonia to the Swedes. Thus ended, for the time being, Ivan's persistent effort to secure access to the Baltic and thereby to the West. The long war, which had begun in 1558, had strained the resources of the country to the limit.

It was in Ivan's reign that the foundation was laid for the institution of serfdom. No matter who the various landowners in Russia had been, the peasants were the people who lived on the land and cultivated the soil. They had been free to move from one estate to another in accordance with their economic needs and desires. In 1497, however, Ivan III had restricted their freedom of movement to St. George's Day, in the late autumn. The *pomiestchiki* found even this migration distinctly disadvantageous to them and, as the long period of warfare drew to a close, they secured further legislation for its limitation. Beginning in 1581, certain years were designated as "prohibited," and the peasant had to remain on a given estate during such a year. It was but a step, then, to make all years "prohibited," and the peasant became "attached" to the soil without freedom to leave. Thus the formerly free peasants were reduced to the status of serfs.

A census begun by Ivan in 1581 and completed after his death in 1592 afforded further evidence that by this time serfdom had become

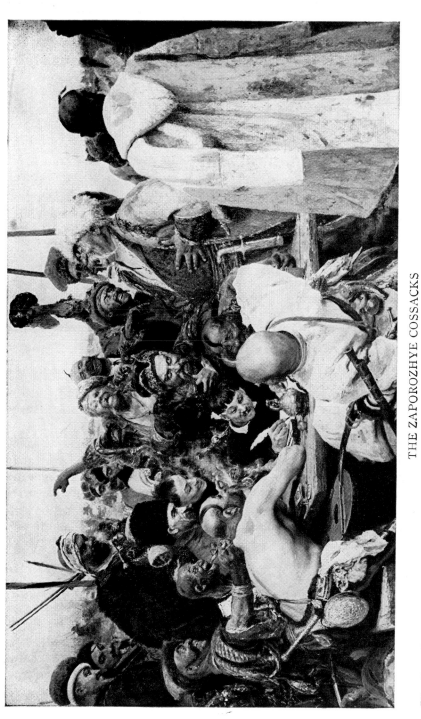

THE ZAPOROZHYE COSSACKS

The Cossacks are composing a provocative letter to Sultan Mahomet IV of Turkey. The painting is by the Russian artist Ilya Repin.

well established. In addition to the legislation against migration, the peasants had fallen into debt to the landowners and were prevented from leaving the land. The peasants, therefore, were registered as belonging to the land. They were not slaves in the sense that they were personal property of the landowner, for when the land was sold they were transferred with it. In addition to the serfs there were, however, house servants, or *kholopy,* who belonged to the owner and hence were true slaves.

Ivan's policy of ferocity did much to hasten the formation of the Cossack states, if it did not actually create them. These states first came into existence in this wise. In the fourteenth century, the Ukraine was conquered by the Lithuanian forces under Prince Gedimin and became entirely separated from the North and from Tartar jurisdiction. By the middle of the fifteenth century Russians and even Tartars, who found Tartar or Lithuanian control entirely unbearable, would seek homes in border territories by the southern steppes where they enjoyed a high degree of independence. One of their most profitable occupations consisted in robbing caravans. These freebooters were called *Cossacks* by Turks and Tartars alike. The Turkish word for robber is *Kazak.* The same word is found in the Tartar language, but means a "light-armed warrior."

When the oppression of Ivan Grozny became excessive, many persons, especially of the lower classes, fled to this Cossack "land of the free and the home of the brave." In time this heterogeneous population established two states: the Host of the Don in southeastern Russia and the Zaporog Host in southwestern Russia.[1] The government of these states was quite democratic. All citizens were regarded as equal, and all property was held in common. At the head of the state was the Ataman or Hetman, elected by universal suffrage and in pos-

---

[1] The literal meaning of "Zaporog" is "beyond the Cataracts" and refers to those of the Dnieper River. It is interesting to note that the Soviet Government, as part of the Five-Year Plan, constructed in the neighborhood of these cataracts the modern Dnieprostroy, the largest hydroelectric plant in Europe. The following book gives a vivid portrayal of the Zaporog Cossacks: *Taras Bulba,* a short historical novel by Gogol. *The Cossacks* and *Hadji Murad* by Leo Tolstoy are interesting, fictional accounts of Cossack life in general. For a description of Cossack life before and during the Great War and the Civil War in Russia, see *The Silent Don,* by Sholokhov. See also, *The Cossacks* by Maurice Hindus (N. Y., 1945).

IVAN GROZNY RECEIVES THE ENVOYS OF YERMAK

The envoys have come to offer Siberia to Ivan in return for a pardon for Yermak and his followers.

session of strictly limited authority. Judicial power resided in the popular council or the "Circle." Serious offenses were punished by drowning. A peculiar feature of the government was the imposition of celibacy upon members of the ruling class. The states were completely indifferent in their allegiance to their "Mother" land, fighting either for or against Russia as it suited their humor and interests. Their service to Christian civilization was rendered unconsciously but was none the less effective. It consisted in their acting as buffer states to check further Mohammedan encroachment. These rude Cossacks of mixed antecedents were fully as fierce as the Asiatic invaders and kept the latter from completely overrunning Europe.

Since fighting and depredation occupied most of their time, as a matter of course the Cossacks developed a system of military training and became adept in a kind of brutal warfare. Compulsory military service began when a youth reached the age of eighteen and entered the *stanitsa*. It continued for seventeen years, twelve of which were spent in active service. In addition to active service, there were two other types or classes of service, that is, on furlough with arms and horses and on furlough with arms but not with horses. The soldiers were equipped and clothed by the army or "host" from revenue granted by the government. At the beginning of World War I their forces numbered about 3,000,000 with 300,000 ready for immediate active service. They were divided into eleven hosts or corps, namely, Don, Kuban, Terek, Astrakhan, Orenburg, Ural, Siberian, Semiryetchensk, Transbaikal, Amur, and Ussuri.

The Cossacks were instrumental in adding the realm of Siberia, then dominated by Kuchum Khan, to the expanding empire of Ivan Grozny. As early as 1555 Ivan had secured Siberian recognition of the supremacy of Moscow and exacted an annual tribute of furs. When this was ignored by Kuchum Khan, Ivan IV in 1571 bestowed upon the powerful feudal family of the Stroganovs, located west of the Urals, a huge tract of territory east of that range in the control of the khan. The Stroganovs made use of a strong and troublesome band of Cossacks under the leadership of Yermak to enforce the tsar's edict east of the Urals. In 1580 Yermak and some 1600 of his warriors crossed the Urals to Siberia. Few in numbers though they were, their firearms and cannon proved too much for the khan's troops, who were armed only with bows and arrows, and Yermak captured Iskar on the Irtysh, the capital of Siberia. Siberia was annexed in 1584. Ivan

Grozny had greatly expanded Russia's possessions and, in spite of his defeats on the Baltic, had built up one of the largest kingdoms in the world.

Perhaps the greatest achievement of Ivan IV was his victory over the Mohammedan world which, at the time of his accession, extended as far west as the gates of Vienna. By his conquest of Kazan and Astrakhan he not only stemmed the tide of Mohammedan conquest but reversed the trend. Not only did Russian expansion in Asia date from his reign, but Russia broke the ground for other European nations in this respect. A recent Soviet biography has depicted Ivan Grozny as "one of the great political and military leaders of Europe of the sixteenth century."[1]

---

[1] Wipper, R., *Ivan Grozny*, Moscow, 1947, p. 231.

4

The End of the Rurik Dynasty
1598

AT HIS death in 1584 (March, Kyril's Day), Ivan Grozny left two sons, Fyodor (1584-1598), who became the second tsar of Russia, and Tsarevitch Dimitri, who was mysteriously murdered in 1591.[1] Indeed the entire reign of Tsar Fyodor is shrouded in deep mystery, and no one knows for certain what dark deeds marked the closing years of the Rurik dynasty. Tsar Fyodor Ivanovitch was weak of will, fearful and lacking in initiative, the complete opposite of his father. Consequently it was easy for his brother-in-law, Boris Godunov, to direct the policy of the government.

Concerning the personality and character of this man, Boris Godunov, historians have come to no agreement. Some declare that he was a true patriot, who endeavored to render his country real service. Others maintain that he was influenced solely by motives of self-interest, his main purpose being to usurp the throne. It must be said that there is evidence to justify either opinion. There can be no doubt that as the person who virtually ruled Russia during the last years of the reign of Ivan Grozny and throughout the reign of Fyodor, he was responsible for many a cruel edict, including the *ukaz* of 1581 by which serfdom was instituted. On the other hand, he exhibited ability as a statesman and not a few of his acts bear the stamp of true patriotism as it was understood in his time. In any event when Tsar Fyodor died childless on the eighth of January, 1598, thus bringing to an end the Rurik dynasty, Boris Godunov was elected tsar by the *Zemsky Sobor*, a popular assembly organized by Ivan IV in 1566. Since he was re-

---

[1] Early historians accused Boris Godunov of instigating this murder in order to remove a troublesome obstacle to his usurpation of the throne. For a different point of view consult *Boris Godunov* by S. F. Platonov, Petrograd, 1921; *Pushkin* by Prince D. S. Mirsky, 1926, pp. 156-157; and *Boris Godunof* by Stephen Graham, Yale, 1933. For literature dealing with this event see: Pushkin, *Boris Godunov*; also Count A. K. Tolstoy's trilogy: *Ivan the Terrible, Tsar Fyodor Ivanovitch*, and *Boris Godunov*.

sponsible for raising the metropolitan of Moscow to the rank of patriarch (1588-1589), it is not surprising that his election received the
backing of the Church. Like Ivan IV, Boris Godunov (1598-1605)
recognized the importance of a strong middle class and tried to advance
its interests. This policy, however, merely served to alienate the
boyars and rich, untitled nobility, whereas the middle class had not
yet sufficient strength to take advantage of its opportunities and counteract the dissatisfaction not only of the upper classes but also that of
the other extreme of society, namely, the lower classes. Boris Godunov's policy in this respect and its results call to mind similar efforts
and similar results on the part of Stolypin in the reign of Nicholas II,
1906-1911. While the upper classes were enraged because of curtailment of their political power, the lower classes were suffering dire
want, especially during the years of famine in 1601, 1602, and 1603.
Hence the ruler had two problems to handle, one political, and the
other, economic. Boris Godunov did his best to solve both and made
concessions and advances to all classes of society, without, however,
gaining any support. This was not due solely to the fact that in endeavoring to satisfy one group, he estranged the others, but chiefly
because he did not belong to the Rurik royal line. The people would
tolerate a weak or cruel legitimate ruler, but when it came to enduring
oppression and suffering from an elected tsar of Tartar extraction,
that was an entirely different matter.

The dissatisfied *boyars* finally declared void the election of the
Zemsky Sobor by which Boris Godunov had become tsar. They announced that the real ruler was in Poland, thus again bringing foreign
influence to bear upon Russian affairs. In the Pretender, they claimed
to have discovered the Prince Dimitri who, they said, had not been
murdered in 1591 after all but had found refuge in Poland.

Under Sigismund III (1587-1632), a Swedish prince who was
elected to the throne of Poland following the death of Stephen Bathory,
the Polish Empire was one of the largest in Europe. The successful
Polonization of the Lithuanian upper classes after the dynastic union
of 1569 encouraged the Poles and the Jesuits, who were active in
Poland after 1565, to believe that a larger union and the conversion of
the Russians to the Roman Catholic faith were both possible and desirable. The religious controversy between the Poles and the Russians,
especially during the era of the Counter-Reformation, assumed a bitterness not unlike that engendered by the ideological struggle between
the USSR and the West in later years. Sigismund of Poland and the
Jesuits therefore viewed the appearance of the "False Dimitri" with

delight, for they saw an opportunity to widen the sphere of both Polish and Catholic influence.

Encouraged by the promise of support both within and outside Russia, the Pretender appeared in Moscow in 1605. Immediately insurrection broke out, and still another "Tsarevitch Dimitri" appeared, this time the candidate of the lower classes, who had risen under the leadership of an escaped serf, Ivan Bolotnikov. Hardly had this revolt been put down when the Cossacks led another uprising. In a short time Russia was embroiled in the most bitter civil war and anarchy, and hence an easy prey to external foes, especially the Poles and Swedes, who made haste to occupy Russian territory. The Swedes occupied Novgorod, while the Poles seized Smolensk and entered Moscow in 1610. Vladislav, the son of Sigismund III, was installed as tsar in Moscow from 1610 to 1612.

The invaders, however, pressed their advantage too far and brought about a reaction which led to their expulsion. During the Polish occupation of Moscow, the patriarch of that city, Hermogen, refused to recognize foreign domination, and in punishment he was starved to death by the enraged Poles. This, together with other atrocities, aroused a religious and nationalistic feeling among the Russians. A middle-class meat merchant of Nizhni-Novgorod, K. Minin by name, took the initiative[1] in arousing his own class and bringing about a union with the nobility, led by Prince Dimitri Pozharsky, against the foreign encroachments. Aided by the more moderate of the Cossacks, they succeeded in driving out the Poles and in taking possession of Moscow in 1612. The Poles nevertheless retained Smolensk and it was five years before the Russians recovered Novgorod from the Swedes. A few sporadic and minor uprisings still called for suppression, but in the course of another year these were checked and the country gradually returned to more normal conditions. In 1613 the *Zemsky Sobor* elected as tsar of Russia a young *boyar*, Michael Romanov, with whom the Romanov dynasty began. The "Time of Trouble," as the years 1605 to 1613 were called, had come to an end. Although the Poles thereafter abandoned their efforts to win Russia for Roman Catholicism, the Russians did not soon forget the part played by the Poles in Moscow during the "Time of Trouble" and it served to accentuate the bitterness between the two peoples.

---

1 This indicates that in recognizing the important potentialities of the middle class both Ivan IV and Boris Godunov exhibited sound judgment.

II

RUSSIA from 862 to 1917

The Romanov Dynasty
1613-1917

5

From Tsar to Emperor
(Michael to Peter I)
1613-1682

REIGN OF TSAR MICHAEL FYODOROVITCH (1613-1645)

HE *Zemsky Sobor* elected the new tsar without a dissenting vote, despite the fact that he was very young and not in particularly robust health. The problem which confronted him was difficult indeed and would have tested the powers of a mature man; nevertheless, Tsar Michael approached his task with praiseworthy energy and good judgment. The insurrectionists of the "Time of Trouble"—Cossacks, peasants, and others—had produced a condition of chaotic confusion in the state and had been guilty of atrocities which caused the deeds of Ivan Grozny to pale into insignificance. The tsar's first efforts, therefore, were directed toward the suppression of the activities of various brigands and outlaws. Scarcely had he succeeded in producing a degree of order in his distracted country when he had to cope with a yet more difficult problem; the *boyars* resumed their old tactics of exploitation of the country for their private ends. Stooping to any despicable means of attaining their purpose, they were able to secure the most desirable "pork barrel" appointments, and the treasury became a prey to their systematic plundering. One of their most dastardly practices was their custom of demanding of the tsarina that she use her influence to further their nefarious schemes. Failure on her part to comply endangered her career and even her life. Thus they secured by false charges the expulsion from the palace of Michael's first bride, whereas her successor was poisoned. It was the general knowledge of this atrocious procedure which caused the King of Denmark to refuse to permit his niece to become Michael's wife.

Fortunately an able adviser came to Michael's assistance in this crisis. In 1619 his father, Philaret Romanov, was returned as an exchange prisoner after nine years of captivity in Poland. He was immediately consecrated patriarch as successor to the martyred Hermogen, the office having remained vacant up to this time in anticipation of his return. His ecclesiastical duties, which he performed with great efficiency, did not prevent him from aiding his son in the most effectual manner. In fact, although Michael retained the title of tsar, it was his father who, to all intents and purposes, was the real ruler. The country benefited enormously under the direction of this able statesman, who was well versed in all worldly, as well as clerical matters, and whose impelling and brilliant oratory swayed the people to his will. Under his guidance, Michael checked the depredations of the *boyars*, established internal order, and set about adjusting Russian foreign relations.

The Swedes and the Poles constituted the most serious menace to the national integrity of the country, the latter even laying claim to the throne of Moscow. Russia was not yet strong enough to force her assailants to make a satisfactory peace. Thus the Treaty of Stolbovo which Michael was able to secure from the Swedes in 1617 was far from favorable to his country. Although the Russians recovered Novgorod and Pskov, they were still cut off entirely from the Baltic Sea, with Archangel as the sole port for direct water communication with the rest of Europe.

Although Poland, like other states adjacent to Russia, had become distinctly uneasy about the spread of anarchy during the "Time of Trouble," no agreement between the Poles and the Russians was immediately forthcoming. After a new Polish invasion led by Prince Vladislav was repulsed at Moscow, the tide began to turn in favor of the Russians. Other European governments, including that of Sultan Osman of Turkey, which were more than a little relieved by the restoration of order in Russia, offered their assistance in checking Polish pretensions. In the war against Poland (1632-1634), the Russians tried unsuccessfully to recover Smolensk. The "perpetual" peace of Polyanovka in 1634 proved indecisive, although the Poles finally recognized Michael as tsar.

One of the most beneficial results of Russia's relations with the Western powers was the importation of foreign goods and the influx of a large number of foreigners. Although James I of England loaned Russia 20,000 rubles—a loan which was promptly repaid—Moscow refused to grant England the exclusive use of two trade routes, one by way of the Volga to Persia and the other through Siberia to Hindustan. The tsar did afford, nevertheless, wide facilities to English and Dutch merchants for trade inside Russia. He encouraged foreign merchants and craftsmen, military officers, scientists, and physicians of various nationalities to take up residence in the country and did his best to stimulate foreign trade. Thus Western influence was considerably extended during his reign, and his subjects began to adopt some of the customs of their European neighbors and hence had more in common with them. Not all European customs, however, met with equal favor. Thus the people were commanded to abstain from the use of tobacco, while snuff addicts were discouraged to the extent of having their noses cut off.

It will be remembered that during the reign of Ivan Grozny the peasants lost their freedom and became "attached" to the soil, the length of time which they were obliged to spend upon a given estate being gradually lengthened. Nevertheless, the landowners were not satisfied but were continually clamoring for legislation to deprive the wretched peasants of the modicum of liberty left to them and to "attach" them permanently to the estates. The peasants, for their part, were immeasurably discontented with their hard lot and were constantly seeking some alleviation of their misery. In consequence, there was much ill-will and strife between them and the landowners, and fugitives from the estates increased in number. In order to relieve the situation, laws were passed during Michael's reign which, however, were entirely in favor of the owners of the estates, and which established serfdom even more firmly than before. The term of "fixation" to the soil was extended from the five-year period instituted by Boris Godunov to ten and even fifteen years and landowners were given the right to reclaim fugitive peasants.

To sum up, Michael, during his reign, restored internal peace and established important foreign relations. He maintained an "open door" policy toward foreign trade and foreign tradesmen. He rescued Russia from a state of anarchy and secured for her the recognition of Europe as a power which must be respected. He developed a national feeling so that the people no longer regarded themselves as members of various principalities but as Russians, natives of a united state with a central authority emanating from Moscow. It was Ivan Grozny who from the principalities forged the state of Moscow and placed the tsar above all princes, who had a claim to the throne or any connection with the royal line. Michael, for his part, made the Moscow tsardom the entity which later developed into the Russian Empire. His most negative policy was the strengthening of serfdom which rendered the peasant problem still more acute, and which was to become an increasing source of difficulty to the country. Some historians are wont to compare Michael's reign with the reign of Henry IV of France. There were many similarities in the problems and difficulties, both domestic and foreign, which confronted the two monarchs.

REIGN OF TSAR ALEXEI MIKHAILOVITCH (1645-1676)

Michael was succeeded by his sixteen-year-old son, Alexei. The most important event of the latter's reign was the *Raskol,* or Schism, which resulted from the development of two opposing groups in the Church. Of these, the Old Believers, or fundamentalists, vigorously opposed any changes in the existing creed and liturgy, whereas the Reformers, or modernists, advocated certain ritualistic modifications. Heretofore Russians had been little concerned with religious controversy. Isolated even from Byzantine religious influences from the twelfth to the fifteenth centuries, the Russian Church had tenaciously clung to the ritual and customs established in the Kievan era. To be sure, some faint echoes of the Protestant Reformation reached the country. Even Ivan Grozny had been sufficiently interested to make investigations concerning the new faith. The terrific altercations, however, which were rocking all other European nations, did not affect Russia to any marked extent. The problems which arose as an aftermath of the Mongol period, together with the serious disorders of the "Time of Trouble," had so occupied all classes of society that they had little time or inclination to engage in doctrinal disputes. In the seventeenth century, however, increased contacts via Kiev with the Orthodox centers of Constantinople, Antioch, and Jerusalem, and the trek of Greek, Arab, and Slavonic pilgrims to Moscow to enlist Russian aid against the Turks, produced an awareness on the part of certain Church leaders of the discrepancies between Greek and Russian ritualistic observances. Stephen Vonifatiev, chaplain to Alexei, inaugurated a movement to raise the standards of the Russian clergy, to improve their education, and to encourage a return to the purer traditions of the Church.

On July 23, 1652, Nikon, an able and ambitious Churchman of distinctly modernist tendencies, became patriarch in Moscow. He at once set to work to introduce the ritualistic changes and reforms he regarded as essential. In a Pastoral Letter of 1653 he directed the

Russians to follow the Greek practice of joining three fingers in making the sign of the cross, thus symbolizing the Trinity. The Russians had been accustomed to join two fingers to denote the dual nature of Jesus Christ. Nikon met with no little opposition on the part of both clergy and laity, who bitterly resented any innovations, particularly if these seemed to indicate an imitation of Western practices. In their opinion, Moscow was the "Third Rome" and the Russian Church alone had retained Christianity in its original purity, even the Greek Church having deteriorated to a lamentable extent. Any changes, therefore, assumed in their eyes the aspect of a disastrous retrogression. To understand why such an issue was made of Nikon's program, it is necessary to realize the vital importance the Russians attached to ritualistic observances and their deep-seated distrust of the Greeks, whom they suspected of subservience to Roman Catholicism.

Nikon pursued his headstrong course, brought scholars from Kiev to Moscow to support his cause, and appealed to Greek spiritual leaders for a decision. He was so successful that in 1654, 1655, and 1656 his reforms were approved by Church Councils and incorporated in canons and rituals. In the beginning the nonconformists were given an opportunity to present their case, which, under the leadership of the Archpriest Avvakum,[1] they did effectively and produced a valuable literature on the subject. Nevertheless, under pressure from the Eastern patriarchs, the Old Believers were excommunicated by a Church Council in 1667. Moreover, the state, with a view to assuming the role of protector of all Orthodox Christians persecuted abroad, and incited by Nikon, took a hand in the matter and began to persecute dissenters by torture, imprisonment, and death at the stake.

Even these measures failed to bring conformity. For the Old Believers, the changes in the Church bore all the marks of a world catastrophe, and they subbornly refused to relinquish their principles. Persecution made fanatics of the dissenters, whose ranks originally included many progressive priests and reformers. It is recorded that more than 20,000 of them voluntarily sought death at the stake rather than accept the new forms of worship. Others buried themselves alive. Being unwilling to participate in services following the new order, they either dispensed with priests entirely or chose from among themselves men to act as their leaders, who unfortunately were often ignorant and untrained. Sometimes they availed themselves of

---

[1] *The Life of the Archpriest Avvakum Written by Himself* has been translated by Jane Harrison and Hope Mirlees (London, 1924).

the services of priests, who came from southwestern Russia. These priests, by reason of their frequent contact with Roman Catholic Poles, had become very argumentative. They, as well as their untrained brethren, brought distinctly undesirable elements into the Russian priesthood. A detailed description of the life of the Old Believers can be found in the two novels of Andrei Petchersky (P. I. Melnikov), *In the Forests* and *On the Mountains.*

The persecution of the Old Believers proved to be an important factor in Russian colonization and expansion. Many were exiled or fled to the vast open spaces of the north and Siberia, to the Volga, the Don, the Urals, the Kuban, and the Caucasus, where they established new settlements. Avvakum and his wife were exiled first to Tobolsk and Yeniseisk in Siberia, later to the White Sea, and finally to Pustozersk on the Petchora in the Arctic, where he spent fourteen years and was burned at the stake in 1681. Dispersed in this fashion the Old Believers were unable to offer effective opposition to the government, although in their new localities they sometimes supplied a nucleus for dissident elements of the population. Others fled abroad as refugees to Poland, Prussia, Rumania, Turkey, and even to China. There are no reliable statistics as to the numbers of the Old Believers. Nevertheless their views persisted, and it is estimated that at the time of the Revolution their ranks included from twenty to twenty-five million persons in Russia.

Having secured official adoption and governmental support of his reforms, Nikon could afford to disregard the ineffective resistance of the dissenters, and he turned his energies in another direction. Following the precedent set by Philaret Romanov, he reached out for temporal power, dreaming of a future in which the head of the Church should stand above the tsar, in spiritual matters at least. His efforts to bring this about led to the first serious clash between Church and state in Russia and caused his own downfall. In 1666 he was deposed from his patriarchate and exiled. He died in 1681. Within forty years of his death the Russian patriarchate itself was abolished by Peter the Great.

The religious controversy gave rise to discussions, which embraced social issues, as well as purely religious interests. In a sense they constituted a manifestation of social opposition to the growing centralization of power in both Church and state. Eventually two rather sharply opposed groups made their appearance. One was intensely national in outlook. Its supporters had much in common with the Old Believers, inasmuch as they also maintained that pure Christianity was to be found in Russia alone and that Moscow was the "Third Rome." Further they maintained that the Russian people constituted a "New Israel," over which the tsar reigned as the sovereign of all Orthodoxy. As a matter of course, they did not favor innovations or foreign "isms" but sought rather to develop and intensify that which was national and innate, either in spiritual or material concerns.

Those who favored a Western orientation, on the other hand, welcomed foreign ideas much as their predecessors of the Mongol period had welcomed foreign armies. They believed that Russia was behind other European countries, both in the field of thought and in material progress, and that, in consequence, the West had much to give her that was beneficial. Hence they favored the adoption and incorporation into the national life of any elements which would contribute to the national welfare and progress. They sedulously cultivated, therefore, all foreign contacts and endeavored to govern their lives in accordance with Western ideals.

One potent source of Western influence much utilized by them was to be found in the colonies of foreigners established within the country. While, during the reign of Alexei, tradesmen of foreign extraction were compelled to confine their activities to the neighborhood of Archangel, the same restrictions were not imposed upon foreign intelligentsia. Many of the latter of German or Anglo-Saxon antecedents settled more or less permanently in Russia, particularly in the neighborhood of Moscow, from whence they contributed to the dissemination of reforms in line with Western concepts.

These exponents of the two opposing ideals for national betterment continued to advocate their principles with the utmost energy. The respective movements gained such momentum that by the nineteenth century, when they came to be known as Westernizers and Slavophiles, they occupied a disproportionate amount of public thought and discussion, as is so ably revealed in the writings of Turgenev and Dostoyevsky.

In Alexei's reign a committee headed by Odoyevsky achieved further progress in the codification of Muscovite law. The *Ulozhenie* of 1649, some 2000 copies of which were printed in 1650 and distributed throughout the country, continued to serve as a landmark in Russian jurisprudence until the reforms of Speransky in 1833. The new code included provisions which forbade the clergy to acquire more land, restricted foreigners to Archangel for trade, and bound the peasants more closely to the soil.

While the various religionists and national idealists were consuming their energies in what were often mere hairsplitting controversies, the mass of the population was in dire need of a practical handling of serious economic and social problems. Unemployment had increased alarmingly, and the discontent engendered thereby constituted a serious menace to national peace and welfare. The bondage of the serfs had become so increasingly oppressive that they were raging in impotent misery. Among all orders of society, intense and dangerous class hatred prevailed. A contributory cause of this class feeling was the legislation which Alexei, in imitation of his predecessors of the Rurik dynasty, had enacted with the intent of advancing the interests of the slowly developing middle class, or minor nobility. As a result both the upper nobility and the lower were equally enraged by discriminating laws, while the middle class was neither of sufficient size nor strength to take advantage of its privileges and assume a position of leadership.

The general and widespread dissatisfaction found an outlet among the lower classes in the years 1667 to 1671 in an uprising headed by Stepan (Stenka) Razin, the Russian Robin Hood. This man, who proclaimed himself an enemy of the rich *boyars* and merchants and a brother of the poor, had none of the qualities of an able leader, who could inaugurate beneficial social reforms. He was merely a bandit at the head of a motley crew of robbers and murderers. He drew his first followers from the most indigent Cossacks, the "Naked," as they were called. With a force augmented by recruits from the dissatisfied villagers, he quickly overran a great expanse of territory, plundering wherever the opportunity offered and murdering *boyars,* public officials, and even members of the clergy. Alternately appeased and threatened by Moscow, he not only subdued the Lower Volga and invaded Persian territory along the Caspian, but he seized the Volga river posts of Tsaritsyn (Stalingrad), Samara (Kuibyshev), and Saratov, and established himself at Astrakhan. Finally his own Cossacks turned against him and betrayed him to the authorities. After being put to torture, he was executed in Moscow in 1671, and the uprising came to an end.

The following song is attributed to Razin, who is said to have left it as a "bequest" to his followers:

> Bury me, brothers, between three roads,
> The Kiev, and the Moscow, and the Murom, famed in story.
> At my feet fasten my horse;
> At my head set a life-bestowing cross;

In my right arm place my keen sabre.
Whoever passes by will stop;
Before my life-bestowing cross will he utter a prayer;
At the sight of my black steed will he be startled;
At the sight of my keen sword will he be terrified.
"Surely, this is a brigand who is buried here!
A son of a brigand, the bold Stenka Razin." [1]

The internal disorders of Alexei's reign were paralleled by external troubles. Extended and bitter wars with Poland and Lithuania over the possession of Little Russia, or the Ukraine, occupied many years. Heretofore the Western powers had always been the aggressors, and Russia had not been strong enough to check their encroachment effectively. This time, however, she took the offensive and succeeded in acquiring control of much territory, which had been wrested from her in former years. Faced with rebellion at home, trouble with the Cossacks on the Dnieper (1648-1657), under the leadership of the Ukrainian Cossack, Bogdan Khmelnitsky, and foreign intervention, the Poles were engulfed in their own "Time of Trouble," ordinarily referred to as "the deluge" (1654-1667). By the Treaty of Andrusovo in 1667 they were forced to cede to the Russians Smolensk, Sieversk, Kiev, and that part of the Ukraine located on the left bank of the Dnieper. Although the cession was for two years, Moscow retained these territories, which never again reverted to the Poles. Kiev was ceded permanently to the Russians in 1686. Out of the conflict with Poland there developed struggles with Sweden and Turkey, which were, however, of little significance. The combatants withdrew from the Swedish War (1656-1659) without gain or loss of territory on either side. A few skirmishes on the banks of the Dnieper constituted the whole of the war with the Turks. In Siberia, the Russians continued their expansion toward the Pacific, and entered into diplomatic negotiations with the Manchus at Peking.

REIGN OF TSAR FYODOR ALEXEYEVITCH (1676-1682)

Tsar Alexei left three sons and a daughter, Fyodor, Ivan, and Sophia, children of his first wife, Maria Miloslavskaya, and Peter, son of his second wife, Natalia Narishkina. Fyodor succeeded his father to the throne. He was a man lacking in ability and ambition, and of so feeble a constitution that he survived Alexei by only six years, dying in 1682. After his death a bitter feud broke out between two

---

[1] Ralston, Sh., *Songs of the Russian People*, p. 46.

opposing court parties. One of these supported Ivan's claim to the throne, calling themselves Miloslavskys in honor of his mother. The other party, known as the Narishkins, demanded the accession of Peter on the ground that Ivan was incapacitated. Supported by the patriarch, the *boyars* and a considerable number of the citizens, the Narishkins succeeded in gaining their point temporarily. The Miloslavskys, however, stirred up the *Streltsy,*[1] who demanded that Ivan be given his rightful place in the succession and instituted a period of such confusion and bloodshed that a compromise became necessary. It was decided that the throne should be held jointly by Ivan and Peter, with their elder sister, Sophia, as regent. Thus governmental control was in reality in the hands of the Miloslavskys.

Although Tsarevna Sophia (1682-1689) was a woman of much intelligence and ability, she was not a successful ruler; especially was her foreign policy disapproved by her subjects, despite the fact that in 1686 she succeeded in making a treaty of "perpetual" peace with Poland, thereby securing an alliance with the Poles against the Turks. It was by this treaty that the Polish ruler, Jan Sobieski, recognized as permanent the cession of Kiev to Russia.

The last official act of the regency of Sophia—the signing of the Treaty of Nertchinsk on August 26, 1689—was of considerable consequence for Russian expansion in the Far East. In the middle of the seventeenth century Russian traders and adventurers had reached the Amur River, where they soon clashed with the Manchu-led Chinese army and with the Buryat Mongols. In a manner reminiscent of French and English expansion in North America, the Russians constructed a line of forts (*ostrogs*) from Lake Baikal to the left bank of the Amur. In their efforts to oust the Russians from the Amur basin, the Chinese conducted a successful offensive against the Russian fortress of Albazin, following which peace negotiations were held at Nertchinsk, with Count F. A. Golovin representing the Russians and a Jesuit missionary serving as intermediary for the Chinese.

The Treaty of Nertchinsk, which delimited the frontiers between China and Russia and made provision for a Russian mission at Peking, was the first that China signed with any Western power. By excluding Russia from the Amur, this treaty served to stem the tide of Rus-

---

[1] As a protection for Moscow, Ivan Grozny had organized several regiments of infantry, known as the *Streltsy*. This body became very powerful by reason of its good military organization and the special privileges granted to it. It eventually became so independent and arrogant that it was able to enforce its will upon the government, which did not dare to check its activities.

sian expansion to the Pacific until the nineteenth century. Since Peter the Great was primarily concerned about an outlet on the Baltic, the Treaty of Nertchinsk proved to be of mutual advantage to the Chinese and the Russians. The discrepancies in the Manchu, Chinese, Mongol, Russian, and official Latin versions provided the Russians, some 150 years later, with a pretext for further claims against the Chinese.

Meanwhile Sophia, who hated and feared her half-brother, Peter, recognized in him a dangerous menace to the continuation of her authority and considered ways and means for his removal. He was not unaware of her animosity, and discovering that she was plotting against his life, he took measures to secure her overthrow. With the support of one faction of the *Streltsy,* he brought about a *coup d'état* in 1689, which wrested the government from Sophia's hands. She was sent to a convent, where she was virtually a prisoner, and Peter assumed absolute control, although his brother, Ivan, lived until 1696.

6

From Reformer to Reformer (Peter I to Alexander II)
1682-1855

REIGN OF PETER I, THE GREAT, THE FIRST EMPEROR
(1682-1725)

PETER was only seventeen years of age when he made himself master of Russia, but he had already attained mental and physical maturity. His superior intelligence had been manifest at an early age when he had rapidly mastered the subjects which constituted a liberal education of his day. His interests and abilities were not exclusively academic, however, for ships and shipbuilding had a great fascination for him. He also had a strong militaristic bent, which led him as a very young boy to begin the organization of regiments among his youthful companions, which regiments later served him well.

Peter's formal instruction was interrupted by the hostilities following the death of his brother, Fyodor. When Sophia became regent, she selected tutors for him, but his mother so strongly disapproved of them that she withdrew with him to the village of Preobrazhenskoye. This village was near the German Suburb, the rendezvous of all sorts and conditions of foreigners. The German Suburb was originally founded by some adventurous Englishmen and a group of soldiers from the army of the Austrian general, Albrecht von Wallenstein, famous for his defeat of Gustavus Adolphus and the Swedish forces in the Thirty Years' War. Later some 3000 Scottish refugees, who fled from their homeland following the imprisonment of Charles I of England, joined the community. As time went on the population became exceedingly cosmopolitan. Since very few of the inhabitants could speak Russian,

RULERS OF RUSSIA
(A.D. 862-1917)

I. RURIK DYNASTY (862-1598)

Princes

Rurik	862- 879
Oleg	879- 912
Igor	913- 945
Olga, his widow	945- 969
Svyatoslav	962- 972
Yaropolk	973- 980
Vladimir, the Saint	980-1015
Sviatopolk	1015-1019
Yaroslav, The Wise	1036-1054
Vladimir Monomakh	1113-1125

Grand Princes of Moscow

Ivan I, Kalita	1328-1341
Simeon, the Proud	1341-1359
Ivan II, the Red	1353-1359
Dimitry II	1359-1362
Dimitry III, Donskoi	1362-1389
Vasili Dimitrievitch I	1389-1425
Vasili Vasilievitch II	1425-1462
Ivan III, the Great	1462-1505
Vasili, Ivanovitch III	1505-1533

Tsars

Ivan IV, Grozny	1533-1584
Fyodor Ivanovitch	1584-1598

II. ROMANOV DYNASTY (1613-1917)

Tsars

Michael Fyodorovitch	1613-1645
Alexei Mikhailovitch	1645-1676
Fyodor Alexeyevitch	1676-1682
Ivan V, and Peter I	1682-1689

Emperors and Empresses

Peter I, the Great	1682-1725
Catherine I	1725-1727
Peter II	1727-1730
Anna	1730-1740
Ivan VI	1740-1741
Elizabeth	1741-1762
Peter III	1762
Catherine II, the Great	1762-1796
Paul	1796-1801
Alexander I	1801-1825
Nicholas I	1825-1855
Alexander II	1855-1881
Alexander III	1881-1894
Nicholas II	1894-1917

Note: The period from 1598 to 1613 is called the "Time of Trouble." None of the rulers, including Boris Godunov (1598-1605) who reigned during this time of unrest and anarchy, was fully acknowledged.

the Russians applied to all of them the name, *Nemetz* (German), from *Nemoi,* meaning speechless. The Church regarded the colony as a resort of heretics and an abode of evil and reluctantly tolerated its existence. Patriarch Joachim, who died in 1690, left as a bequest to Peter the injunction not to associate with Lutherans, Calvinists, Catholics, and like heretics, but rather to banish them from the country and raze their places of worship to the ground. The German Suburb was, nevertheless, much frequented by Russians who found stimulus in the varied intellectual contacts which it offered, or who sought relaxation from the restraints imposed by Russian conventions. An English historian, B. H. Sumner, has rather appropriately termed the colony "a little fragment of industrious, ingenius, Protestant Europe." [1]

Peter visited the German Suburb often and made numerous friends and acquaintances among its inhabitants. Through his association with philosophers, scholars, and technicians of various nationalities, and with Protestant missionaries of German and Dutch extraction, he became imbued with Western ideas and turned a critical eye upon conditions in his own country. From the Scottish members of the German Suburb—among them the Gordons, the Ogilvies, and the Carmichaels—he learned much of English naval and military techniques, and he planned to reorganize the armed forces of Russia in conformity with those of Western Europe. He began to study Russian history and became convinced that in pre-Mongol days Russia had possessed a degree of culture and had reached a stage of development which would have enabled her easily to keep abreast of, or even to outstrip, other European nations. He also saw that the Mongol invasion and the long period of foreign bondage, which completely severed Russia from cultural contacts with the West, had resulted in a fearful retardation of her civilization, so that she was centuries behind her neighbors. In order to bridge the gulf which separated Russia from Western culture, he determined to effect by force a complete change in the customs, ideas, and character of his people by the eradication of all relics of Mongolism and the substitution of European civilization. Whereas the Tartars had *trans*formed Russia, it was his purpose to *re*form her in accordance with Western ideals, toward which end he proceeded with relentless determination.

INTERNAL POLICY

In order to understand Peter's internal policy, we must bear in mind that his prime purpose was to make of Russia a European nation.

---

[1] Sumner, B. H., *A Short History of Russia* (New York, 1943), p. 319.

His program of Europeanization was modeled largely after the Protestant countries of northern Europe, and many of his reforms were accomplished at the expense of the Orthodox Church. As has been noted previously, during the Mongol period the Church incorporated within itself many Oriental features, the origin of which came to be forgotten in the course of centuries. Peter was keenly alive to this source of Oriental and, in his opinion, pernicious influence, and knew that it must be destroyed if his program of Europeanization was to succeed. Moreover, he resented the efforts of the Church to secure temporal power and resolved to crush such pretensions without delay. Thus, although he joined with the Church in its persecution of the Old Believers, whom he likewise regarded as a troublesome obstacle to progress, he omitted nothing which would serve to injure ecclesiastical power and prestige and render its influence ineffective. In consequence his procedure was bitterly resented by many Churchmen, who voiced their indignation so emphatically that for many years he was referred to as an infidel, the "Anti-Christ," whose rule had wrought incomparable harm to his country.

One of Peter's most effective blows against the Church was the abolition of the patriarchate upon the death of the Patriarch Adrian in 1700. There was no supreme ecclesiastical authority until 1721 when Peter instituted a Synod, or Committee of Bishops, in accordance with German Protestant practice; but as this body could act only at his direction, he himself became thereby the actual head of the Church. He also turned against Moscow—the "Third Rome," the "Second Jerusalem"—and robbed it of its glory by removing his capital to the new city of St. Petersburg, founded in 1703 at the marshy estuary of the Neva. To be sure, he had selected this site because he considered that the capital needed a more strategic location than Moscow afforded, but he also had in mind the entire separation of the government from any possibility of Church control or influence. So determined was he to stamp out this influence that when he learned that his son, Alexei, had promised the clergy to restore the capital and to reassert the authority of the Church upon his accession, he had the young man murdered (1718).

By this time monasticism had become a well-established institution in the Church and exerted no little influence along educational lines. Peter, however, made it the object of ridicule upon all occasions, passed laws to eradicate it, and deprived its members of any public offices that they had secured. For example, the Department of Education had been in charge of an Orthodox monk; Peter dismissed him and gave the office to a Protestant pastor.

As a further "Church reform," in 1721 he discarded the title of "Tsar" because of its Oriental and ecclesiastical implications and substituted for it the Western title of "Emperor." The people in general, however, continued to call their ruler the "Tsar." In order to give this change special significance, Peter selected as the day for announcing it, November 4, the anniversary of the freeing of Moscow from the Poles in 1612. As a matter of course, he also changed the name "Grand States of the Russian Tsardom," to the "Empire of all the Russias" to conform with European usage. Already, as early as 1708, he had reorganized the country into provinces in accordance with European principles of government.

Second only to the Church, Peter regarded the *boyars* as a reactionary and detrimental force. Although he did not seek to annihilate them as did Ivan Grozny, he effectively deprived them of all political and social power. Thus in 1711 he established the Administrative Senate, a body of officials who enjoyed Peter's confidence, and who soon began to exercise supervision over state finances, the judiciary, and the provincial governors, in practice superseding the Boyar's Duma. Peter further transformed the haphazard Muscovite bureaucracy in 1718 by reducing the number of government departments to eight "Colleges," each headed by a board, and by adding two new ones to handle commerce, and mines and manufactures. In January 1722 he published the well-known "Table of Ranks" which, in place of the old aristocracy by right of birth established a new aristocracy, the *dvorianstvo*, whose titles were bestowed because of service to the government. Military, civil, and court services were organized in an ascending series of ranks (*tchins*), fourteen for military and naval service, and parallel to them, another fourteen for civilian service. In practice the upper eight came to be identified with the nobility. Peter thus made possible a career open to talent, irrespective of birth and social origin. Several of his top administrators, including Alexander D. Menshikov (1670-1729), were of lowly origin. The "Table of Ranks" was abolished on December 10, 1917.

In accordance with the prevailing mercantile theories of his day, it was Peter's objective to develop Russian industry and make Russia economically independent of foreign lands. Peter's hostility to the Church and to the *boyars* rested, in part, on their uncompromising opposition to his program of Westernization and industrialization. Nevertheless he soon found himself handicapped by the lack of a middle class capable of building up the Russian mining and manufacturing industries necessary to provide the nation with iron, steel, munitions, and textiles. Although state economic control was greatly extended during his reign, Peter was forced to grant monopolies of certain industries to members of the nobility and to attach villages of serfs to their factories to provide the necessary labor, thereby initiating factory-serfdom. During Peter's reign more than two hundred factories and mills were established in Russia, including important new iron works and textile mills in the Urals. The abiding interest of the state in the new enterprises was evinced by the establishment of a Ministry (College) of Mines and Manufactures in the government, and by a policy of generous state subsidies for industry.

In the field of education and science, Peter adopted a distinctly constructive policy and was responsible for much valuable progress. Among other things, his adoption of the Julian calendar on January 1, 1700, brought Russia into line with the majority of the countries of Western Europe. The Academy of Science, organized in imitation of a similar institution in Paris and the Royal Society in London, was founded at the close of his reign. It speedily attracted scientists and mathematicians in great numbers and contributed much to progress along scientific and technical lines. Its most valuable accomplishments were the geographical survey of Siberia and the great Siberian expedition of 1733 to 1743. To assist the work of the Academy, Peter also had books on technical subjects translated from various European languages. His instructions to the translators show that he had a true comprehension of what constitutes the art of translation. He admonished them to acquire a thorough understanding of the content and to translate the thought rather than mere words. In regard to language, Peter was likewise responsible for the simplification of the old Church Slavonic script in order to facilitate the production of secular literature, including technical and historical works.

With the capture of an outlet on the Baltic it became Peter's ambition to create a great occidental capital at Petersburg (now Leningrad), one that differed in every respect from Moscow. For this purpose he secured the services of European architects, engineers and artists, the most outstanding of whom were the Frenchman, A. Leblond, and the Italian, Domenico Trezzini. The best-known work of the latter was the Church of Saint Peter and Saint Paul, which was far removed in design from the traditional Russian-Byzantine churches. Leblond built the summer residence of the tsar, the palace of Peterhof, in the Regency style, later altered by Rastrelli.

THE VICTORY AT POLTAVA (1709)

The Russian artist A. Kotsebu depicts Peter the Great on horseback.

Of the numerous Dutch, German, French and Italian architects and craftsmen employed by Peter, the majority were, unfortunately, second or third rate. Not infrequently a structure designed by an Italian, started by a German, was continued by a Frenchman or Dutchman, with the inevitable result that the new capital on the Neva lacked architectural unity. St. Petersburg became a hodgepodge of French, Dutch, German and Italian Baroque, and little or no attempt was made to assimilate the foreign styles with the Russian.[1] With the advent of Peter, Russian art, which had been essentially religious, became secular and was divorced from the art of the people. The new Western forms appealed only to the aristocracy. It remained for a later generation of Russian artists, trained abroad, to improve the architecture of St. Petersburg.

With his customary energy, the tsar took the initial steps to provide a modicum of secular education for children of the nobility and gentry. With very limited success, his schools attempted to promote the study of the three R's, mathematics, and science, as a minimum, in order to enable young Russians to qualify for service under the requirements of the new "Table of Ranks." With a view to furthering education of a more popular character, Peter established the first public newspaper, *Vedomosty,* in 1703, and in the same year authorized the erection of the first public theater, the Comedy House, at Red Square.[2] Thus the initiative in education, as in so many other fields, came from the state, and education was thereafter carefully controlled by the state.

In his zeal to reform his subjects, Peter did not forbear to interfere with the minor details of their daily lives. He commanded all of them to adopt European dress. He forced the men to shave their abundant beards and made the women abandon their Oriental seclusion. Although such regulations could not be enforced throughout the length and breadth of Peter's domains, his officials and those Russians within the reach of the long arm of the Government had to conform. Taxes were imposed on those who failed to do so. Despite Peter's harsh rule, he won popular respect by his unaffected, oft-times coarse behavior, and because he often conducted himself as if he were one of the "common people." His great height of six feet seven and his huge frame were also not without effect in arousing respect and inspiring fear.

---

[1] See Voyce, A., *Russian Architecture,* pp. 11-13.

[2] In 1672 the Comedy *Khoromina* was constructed near Moscow at the summer residence of Tsar Alexei Mikhailovitch. Nine plays were presented there, the majority on biblical themes. This was not, however, a public theater.

The clergy, the *boyars,* and those who opposed Western ideas in general, censured his methods, citing his private life, which was indeed far from immaculate, as an evidence of his depravity and characterizing him as the "Deformer" of Russia. He was, however, above all things, heart and soul a Russian, and the practices and customs which he opposed were for the most part outmoded or were relics of the Mongol period. The reforms which he forced upon his people contributed in general to their welfare and progress. His vision extended far beyond that of his Russian contemporaries. He had a great intellect and a great mission, and from this standpoint he was indeed the Reformer of Russia.

Unfortunately the institution of serfdom became more firmly established during his reign. His great building projects, for instance the construction of St. Petersburg and his initiation of a canal project to link the capital with the upper Volga, required much forced labor by the serfs, which caused control of them to become stricter and more harsh. To meet the increased burdens of government, Peter resorted to innumerable taxes on land, wearing apparel, implements, food, birth, and marriage, most of which weighed upon the peasants. His poll tax and his passport system, which made it illegal for peasants to move from a locality without the proper credentials, contributed still further to bind them to the soil. The only mitigation in the lot of the serf was the introduction of a law forbidding the sale of individuals among them; henceforward "the family must be disposed of as a unit."

Years later the opposition to Peter's reforms was still reflected in the works of the renowned Russian historian, N. M. Karamzin (1766-1826), who voiced the sentiment of the nineteenth century Slavophiles as follows: "We became citizens of the world, but ceased in some respects to be citizens of Russia." Under the Soviet regime, especially since the inauguration of the Five-Year Plans, new emphasis has been placed by Soviet writers on the constructive aspects of the policies of Peter the Great. They have found much to approve in Peter's program of industrialization, his attitude toward the *boyars* and the Church, his emphasis on the obligation of all individuals to serve the state, his tolerance of minorities, and his establishment of Russia's "window" on the Baltic. They have been inclined to see in Peter's program the beginnings of a planned society which is now a major aspect of Soviet policy. The historical novel, *Peter I,* by Alexei N. Tolstoy, and Sergei Eisenstein's film based upon it, have done much to rehabilitate and popularize Peter in the USSR.

EXTERNAL POLICY

At Peter's accession in 1682 Russia had already wrung from Poland at least nominal sovereignty over the Ukraine, although the Turks still barred the way to the Black Sea and the Swedes prevented access to the Baltic. Peter energetically addressed himself to the task of further Russian expansion at the expense of Turkey and especially of Sweden. During his long reign there were scarcely two years of peace. Nevertheless Peter established Russia as a first-rate military and naval power, with an ice-free port on the Baltic.

As the first step in his plan of expansion, he resolved to advance against the impregnable Turkish stronghold of Azov. A campaign of this nature necessitated an army drilled to the last degree of perfection in military tactics, and Peter had long been preparing such a force. The regiments which he had drilled as a boy in the village of Preobrazhenskoye were now seasoned, disciplined troops. Their long training produced valuable results, for in spite of initial setbacks the unconquerable Azov was surrendered to the Russians in 1696. During Michael's reign it had once been taken by the Cossacks, but they had been unable to hold it without assistance from Moscow. Turkey was to regain the fortress by the Treaty of Pruth in 1711, but the Russians recovered it in 1736. The effect of Peter's victory upon Russia and all Europe can hardly be overestimated. At one stroke, he made of Russia a power which could no longer be ignored in European politics. It became clear that Russian armies, organized and armed in accordance with Western techniques, were once again, as in the days of Ivan Grozny, assuming the offensive. Peter promptly fortified the Azov area and established a fleet of some eighty vessels there in 1699. In the same year the appearance of his fleet at Kertch constituted a demonstration of Russian naval power in the Black Sea, and a challenge to exclusive Turkish domination of that area, which prompted the Sultan to conclude a thirty-year truce with Russia. At home Peter took care to ascribe his success to his European reforms and gained thereby much support for his policy of Europeanization.

After the success at Azov, Peter resolved to attempt a peaceful penetration of the West before following up his plans against Sweden. He hoped to bring about an alliance of all Christian European nations, with Russia as the leader, against the Turks and Mohammedans in general. If this plan succeeded, he believed that he would be able to deal with Sweden and to acquire the territory he sought without war. He therefore began to organize a suite which should accompany him on a tour of the principal countries of Europe, for the purpose of observing and studying all phases of the life of the people. This suite was known as "The Great Ambassadors of the Tsar" and consisted of some 270 persons selected with the greatest care by Peter himself. Although their mission was unofficial and Peter traveled incognito as Peter Mikhailovitch, its prime purpose and his great ambition was to secure for Russia a place of dominance among the nations.

The "ambassadors" left Russia in March 1697 and visited many of the chief cities of Europe, such as Riga, Königsberg, Amsterdam, London, Leipzig, Dresden, Prague, and Vienna, gaining much valuable information thereby, but Peter's plan for a great European alliance did not materialize. The time was not propitious. Europe was torn by the conflicts of the Hapsburgs and the Bourbons, and although there had been general satisfaction over the fall of Azov, the great powers had no intention of looking to Russia for future leadership. Realizing that he could not secure the alliance, Peter abandoned his efforts and returned to Moscow in August 1698.

In this connection it is important to note that the group of carefully selected young men who accompanied Peter abroad and who were expected thereafter to play a leading role in the Europeanization of Russia, also imbibed the advanced political theories current in Britain and other parts of Western Europe. No sooner was Peter dead than they demanded a constitutional government for Russia. They may, in fact, be regarded as the progenitors of the Decembrists of 1825 and of subsequent agitators for political reform.

Immediately after his first European tour Peter began preparations for a campaign against the Swedes, whose military prestige, under the brilliant leadership of Charles XII (1682-1718), was soon to startle the world. In order that he might not be harassed by attacks from other sources, he sought and secured treaties with King Augustus II of Poland and King Christian of Denmark. By the summer of 1700 he had also negotiated a treaty of peace with Turkey. Thus assured, he began the campaign against Sweden, which developed into the Great Northern War (1700-1721). In his initial efforts Peter met with constant reverses. The battle of Narva ended in a disastrous defeat for the Russian forces, and it required four years of dogged persistence and stubborn fighting on his part before he was able to conquer the desired Swedish territory of Ingria. Finally he became master of the site which he had long had in mind as a desirable "window to Europe," and in May 1703, he was at last able to found his new capital of St. Petersburg and make arrangements for the creation of a

PETER THE GREAT

Baltic fleet. The campaign and the building of the city caused so much suffering and cost so many lives that discontent and rebellion became general. Peter was nevertheless able to put down all revolts effectively. Then came the overwhelming defeat of the Swedes in the great battle of Poltava in 1709 in the Ukraine. Peter was once more the national idol, and popular discontent was stilled.

Peter's initial reverses in his conflict with the Swedes led to the introduction of important military reforms in Russia. To secure a larger professional army he instituted a kind of compulsory universal service, by which all single men from fifteen to twenty, and all married men from twenty to thirty, were liable for service and received a modicum of training to prepare them for the regular army, into which they were drafted as needed. From 1705 to 1709 Peter resorted to annual conscription to raise an army of around 300,000 men, with which he was able to rout the Swedish forces at Poltava.

Although Sweden's power was broken and she was henceforth forced to assume the defensive, Charles XII escaped to Turkey. There he had little difficulty in inciting the Turks, never very friendly to Russia, to declare war late in 1710. The struggle which followed was nothing but a series of defeats for the Russian forces. The situation seemed so hopeless that Peter was ready to sue for peace when overtures for a cessation of hostilities came from Turkey. By the Treaty of Pruth in 1711, Russia lost Azov, but was not compelled to pay any more severely for her sorry showing throughout the war. This fortunate turn of affairs for Russia has been credited to efforts put forth by Peter's second wife, Catherine.

In 1716, five years after the Russo-Turkish War (1710-1711), Peter the Great made a second European tour. His first visit, nineteen years earlier in 1697, had been chiefly for the purpose of collecting information and establishing diplomatic relations. Upon this occasion, however, he was concerned mainly with scientific matters. At a very early age he had evinced a deep interest in science, and during his reign he had lent encouragement and assistance to scientific enterprise. Thus, immediately upon his accession to the throne, he had taken cognizance of the efforts of his energetic Cossacks, who were blazing new trails in Siberia, and had sent to their aid certain Swedish prisoners of war, who gave them intelligent guidance and taught them "to build sea-going vessels, to use nautical instruments and to construct modern maps." Peter was likewise instrumental in bringing about the discovery and exploration of Kamtchatka and the Kurile Islands, which took place between 1700 and 1715. When reports of these accomplishments reached the scientific world, the scholars of Western Europe began to pay homage to Peter and to the achievements of Russian men of science. Oxford University conferred upon him an honorary doctor's degree, and the Paris Academy made him one of its members. Therefore when he came among European scientists in 1716-1717, he was cordially received and urged to make explorations for the purpose of determining once and for all whether Asia and America were united.

Upon his return to Russia in 1718, Peter therefore ordered two of his officers, Fyodor Luzhin and Ivan Yevreinov, "to go to Kamtchatka and farther . . . , and determine whether Asia and America are united; and go not only north and south but east and west, and put on a chart all that you see." Although this expedition (1719-1722) failed to establish the fact in question, it was not entirely without results.[1] Peter's interest did not flag and on December 23, 1724, shortly before his death, he drew up orders for further explorations, thereby paving the way for the famous Bering[2] expeditions (1725-1730; 1733-1742), the Gvozdev[3] expedition (1731-1733), and the Baranov[4] explorations (1790-1818).

---

[1] The question whether Asia and America were united was not answered until the coming of another Russian, Baron Ferdinand Wrangel, who, during the winters of 1821 and 1823, walked along the Arctic coast from the Kolyma to Kolyutchin Island.

[2] Vitus Bering, born in 1681 at Horsens, Denmark; died in 1741 on Bering Island. In 1704 he joined the Russian navy with the rank of sublieutenant. By 1724 he was promoted to captain of the first rank and was put in charge of the expedition. See Lauridsen, Peter, *Vitus Bering*, translated by Olson, Chicago, 1889; Golder, F. A., *Bering's Voyages*, Vol. I, 1922, p. 8. See also Berg, L. S., "The Three-Hundredth Anniversary of the Discovery of Bering Strait by Semyon Dezhnev (1648-1948)," *Soviet Press Translations*, Vol. IV, March 15, 1949, pp. 178-184.

[3] Michael Spiridonovitch Gvozdev, a Russian officer, is believed to be the first of his nationality to sight America, although he was not aware of the fact. He saw the American coast on September 1, 1732, but thought, however, that he had discovered an "island."

[4] Alexander Andreyevitch Baranov (1746-1819), head of the Russian American Company for nearly twenty-eight years and first governor of Russian America, rendered valuable service in the North Pacific. Under his direction the Russian possessions in the New World attained their widest extent. In 1796 he established a colony on Bering Strait. In 1799 he took possession of the largest of the Sitka Islands (now Baranov Islands), began trade with the natives, and subsequently extended his operations to Canton, the Hawaiian Islands, Boston, New York and other distant regions. He also founded a small colony in California, near the present site of San Francisco. See Andrews, C. L., "Baranof the Builder," *The Washington Historical Quarterly*, Vol. VII, No. 3, pp. 215-216; and Kiril Khlebnikov's *Zhizneopisanie Alexandra Andreyevitcha Baranova* (*The Life of A. A. Baranov*), St. Petersburg (Russia), 1835. Consult also Golder, F. A., *Guide to Materials for American History in Russian Archives*, Washington, D. C., 1917; Golder, F. A., *Russian Expansion on the Pacific, 1641-1850*. Cleveland, 1914.

"When Bering's second expedition came to an end in 1749," says F. A. Golder,[1] "Bering Strait had been discovered, the Arctic coast of Asia from the White Sea to the Kolyma River had been charted, and the North Pacific coast of America from Cape Addington to Bering Island had been placed on the map. This was Russia's share in the work of discovery and exploration, and a very important contribution to geographical knowledge it was."

Thus it was that, stimulated by Peter's energy and encouragement, explorations were made which opened a window to America and eventually solved the problem as to "whether Asia and America are united." Although Russia's territorial expansion elsewhere was distinctly imperialistic, the explorations in America were motivated chiefly by scientific interest, albeit "for the benefit and glory of Russia" (Russian Senate).

Despite the loss of prestige which the clash with Turkey had cost him, Peter did not relinquish his efforts to force from the Swedes the Baltic territory he desired. In 1721 his persistence finally triumphed, when Sweden by the terms of the Treaty of Nystadt ceded to Russia the entire Baltic coast from the strategic port of Viborg (Viipuri) to Riga, thus bringing to an end several centuries of conflict. Finland proper was to remain in Swedish possession until 1809. Russia, having eclipsed Sweden, now loomed as one of the major powers, a fitting rival of France, Prussia, and England. Peter's window on the Baltic was to have important economic and cultural effects upon Russia. In recognition of his conquests the grateful Senate bestowed upon him the titles, "Father of his Country," "Emperor," and "The Great" (Pater Patriae, Imperator Maximum). In order to strengthen his hold upon the Baltic region, Peter sought to win foreign support by means of diplomatic marriages. His daughter, Anna, was married to the Duke of Holstein; his niece, Catherine, to the Duke of Mecklenburg, whereas another niece became the wife of the Duke of Courland. These marriages for the sake of diplomacy were productive later of much misfortune to Russia. With his window on the Baltic secure, Peter in 1722 turned to the southeast to the Caspian Sea, where in the course of the following year he was able to win an important cession of territory, including Baku, from the Shah of Persia.

Peter's success in the Baltic may be said to have marked the culmination and well nigh the end of his career. Despite his robust constitution, he was not destined to reach extreme old age. Early in No-

---

[1] *Bering's Voyages*, p. 5.

vember 1724, he happened to see a boat in distress. Always courageous, he plunged into the icy water to go to its assistance. He was seized with an illness as a result of this exposure from which he never recovered. He died on February 5, 1725, at the age of fifty-three.

THE SUCCESSORS OF PETER THE GREAT, 1725-1762

Peter's heir apparent, his son Alexei by his first wife, Eudokia Lopukhina, whom he put away in 1698, had been murdered by Peter's own orders in 1718. Another son, Alexander, died at an early age. Although Peter in 1722 had issued a law enabling the tsar to select his own successor, he died without expressing a decision in this respect. Because of the influence of Menshikov and his lieutenants, Peter's second wife succeeded to the throne as Empress Catherine I (1725-1727), the first of a series of women to become autocrat of all the Russias. Her accession, which was an unheard-of innovation, far greater than the regency of Sophia, aroused the bitterest opposition, and many adherents of the Orthodox Church submitted to torture rather than take an oath of allegiance to her. They objected to her not only because she was a woman and not of royal descent, but also because she had been a captive and, although legally the second wife of Peter, her repute was scarcely more than that of his mistress.[1] Nevertheless, despite all opposition she was crowned Empress in May 1724 and succeeded him to the throne on February 19, 1725. Her short reign was marked by no significant event and was in reality merely a sequel to the reign of Peter. Shortly before her death (May 17), she named as her successor Peter's grandson, Peter, son of the murdered Alexei by his first wife, Sophia Charlotte of Wolfenbüttel. Next in the line of succession she named her daughters, Anna of Holstein and Elizabeth.

Peter II was twelve years old at the time of his accession and lived only three years longer, dying of smallpox on the eve of his marriage. Considering his extreme youth and short reign, we would not look for any startling changes or spectacular events during this period. As

---

[1] She was of obscure origin, possibly Lithuanian, and a Lutheran. Her parents died when she was very young and a preacher's family, Glück by name, took her into their home as a servant. In 1701 she married a soldier in the Swedish army, but, only two days after the marriage, she was taken prisoner by Russian soldiers and separated forever from her husband. Because of her beauty, Field Marshall Boris Petrovitch Sheremetiev made her his mistress. Later General Menshikov took her into his house. Here Peter I saw her and fell in love with her, made her his mistress, and three years later, his wife. She was only twenty years old at the time of her marriage to Peter.

a matter of fact, however, his reign was marked by certain significant occurrences, which seemed to give confirmation to the fears of Peter I that his reactionary offspring would utterly destroy everything that he (Peter) had accomplished with so much difficulty. In any event, the Church and the *boyars* again became active participants in public affairs and the Imperial Court was transferred from St. Petersburg to Moscow, although the former city still remained the capital.

When Peter II died the Supreme Secret Council took up the matter of succession, and passing over the daughters of Peter the Great, offered the throne to Anna of Courland (1730-1740), allegedly the daughter of Ivan, who had shared the throne with Peter I until 1696. Before her coronation, a movement was set on foot to transform the government from an absolute to a limited monarchy, in accordance with the English example of 1688. The sponsors of this change were not able to rally enough adherents to their support and the attempt failed.

Anna's reign was a period of debauchery and foreign influence. Governmental and court positions were in the hands of Germans from the Baltic area. These officials, who knew nothing and cared less about Russian ideals and temperament, and who could not even speak the language, rode roughshod over the people's rights and outraged every national feeling. Chief among them was Anna's favorite, Count Johann Ernst Biron, Duke of Courland (1690-1772), who enjoys the unenviable reputation of being the most unpopular German in Russian history, and who, to all intents and purposes, became the real ruler of Russia. Under his direction the foreign policy of the country was characterized by disgraceful retrogression. Russia's meddling in Polish affairs brought her little credit. In a war with Turkey (1733-1739), General Münnich won brilliant victories, but since no advantage was taken of them, Russia failed to secure access to the Black Sea. Even the Persian conquests of Peter the Great were lost, when in 1732 Russia voluntarily relinquished to Persia certain cities on the Caspian Sea. Although Russia participated in an alliance with Austria and England against France and Prussia in the War of the Austrian Succession (1740-1748), she was snubbed by both sides and peace was made at Aix-la-Chapelle without her.

Anna led so corrupt a life that it shattered her health and caused her death. She had named as her successor her young grandnephew, Ivan VI, but had appointed Biron as regent. The country, however, had had more than enough of Biron. As has been indicated elsewhere, the Russian people would tolerate debauchery and misrule in the case of a legitimate ruler but absolutely refused to endure the same things

a foreigner. Biron was speedily removed from power and sent to
ia, where he remained for twenty years. Anna's choice of a successor was disregarded, and the crown was offered to Elizabeth,
daughter of Peter the Great. She became Empress on November 25,
1741, and early the following year the boy, Ivan, was put under arrest
in order to avoid complications and plots.

During the years 1725 to 1741, Russia was almost constantly
subject to foreign influence. One foreign party or another at court
was usually able to control the governmental policy and the distribution of official positions. By reason of their family connection with
the royal line, the Germans were the most numerous and powerful
among the foreign favorites. The period came to be known as the
"period of favorites."

The Empress Elizabeth (1741-1762) began her reign auspiciously
by removing Germans from office and appointing Russians in their
places. This produced universal satisfaction among all classes, which
welcomed the end of the "German yoke." The rejoicing was somewhat premature, for although the period of favorites had come to an
end, foreign influence was by no means eliminated. In Elizabeth's
reign French influence came into prominence, especially along cultural
lines, where it contended for supremacy with German and English
influence until the middle of the nineteenth century. Russia stood on
the threshold of the Age of Enlightenment which reached its zenith
under Catherine II.

In establishing intellectual contacts with France, Elizabeth was
inspired by a sincere desire to contribute to the cultural advance of
her country. Her ideas of progress were in accord with those of her
father and she directed her efforts toward the education and improvement of her subjects. With this in mind and realizing that the theater
was an educational force of tremendous power, she established the
Russian Theatre by the *ukaz* of August 30, 1756, and provided for a
theatrical staff. Elizabeth was determined that her subjects should
have the benefits of the theater whether they wished it or not. Therefore, when performances were scheduled, she sent her servants into
the streets with directions to secure an audience by force if necessary.
Likewise when she discovered that the clergy had become deplorably
lax, both morally and intellectually, she made a determined effort to
raise ecclesiastical standards.

Stimulated by her encouragement, the progress made in arts and
letters was noteworthy. The year 1755 (January 25) marked the
founding of the University of Moscow, which soon attained academic

prestige and contributed greatly to the.development of Russian scholarship. Among the leading scholars of the time we find the famous physicist, poet, and artist, Mikhail V. Lomonosov (1711-1765), son of a lowly fisherman from the White Sea region, and the historian, V. N. Tatishtchev (1686-1750), who began writing his *History of Russia from the Most Ancient Times,* which appeared during the reign of Catherine II. Several other writers, who were to become prominent during the latter's reign, began their work under Elizabeth. Among them was the great artist and playwright, A. P. Sumarokov (1718-1777), director of the first St. Petersburg theater, who has been called the "Russian Racine."

Elizabeth shared Peter's zeal for new construction. The chief architect of her reign, Rastrelli the Younger, trained in France, built the Winter Palace, an outstanding example of Russian Baroque, and also Tsarskoe Selo, the Russian "Windsor Castle," the interior of which was noted for its lavish rococo decoration. In 1758 Elizabeth founded the Academy of Fine Arts, which she staffed with French artists from the Académie Française, and which in the course of time produced a new generation of Russian architects, such as Starov, Bazhenov, Kazakov, Veronikhin, and Zakharov.

Elizabeth's government also took steps to stimulate agriculture and industry. Banks were established, from which landowners could borrow money for the improvement of their estates. Promising sons of merchants were sent to Holland at government expense in order to become acquainted with the latest methods of business procedure. The mining industry was encouraged, and commerce with the East increased enormously in volume.

Despite her subservience to French intellectual influence, Elizabeth was intensely patriotic and won the good will of her subjects thereby. She intended to treat them kindly but often failed, either through the influence of bad advisers or through a mistaken conception of justice. For example, she was of a very liberal turn of mind and left to herself would have been very tolerant, no doubt, in her dealings with the various religious minorities in her realm. Members of the clergy, however, brought pressure upon her, and at their instigation she closed Roman Catholic churches and Mohammedan mosques and forced many Jews to leave the country. When there was a rebellion to be put down or a vice to be checked, she shrank from exacting a death penalty, resorting instead to banishment and flogging as punishment for crimes. However, the floggings were so severe that they usually caused the victim's death!

Elizabeth's reign was marked by several events of importance in foreign relations. In 1743, Sweden ceded to Russia the territory of the Finns east of the Kuno River. In the Seven Years' War (1756-1763), Russia joined with Austria and France against Frederick the Great of Prussia. In conjunction with the Austrians, Russian forces under General Saltykov defeated Frederick in battle at Kunersdorf in 1759. In 1760 Russian troops temporarily took possession of the city of Berlin but reaped no benefits therefrom, for Elizabeth died and her successor, a fanatical admirer of Frederick the Great, brought the campaign to an abrupt termination.

Immediately after her ascent to the throne, Elizabeth had named as her successor, her nephew, Karl Peter Ulrich, Duke of Holstein, son of her sister Anna. In 1742 he came to St. Petersburg, where he adopted the Greek Orthodox faith and was baptized as Grand Duke Peter Fyodorovitch. He was then proclaimed the heir apparent. Elizabeth selected as his wife Sophia Augusta, daughter of the Prince of Anhalt-Zerbst. She likewise accepted the Greek Orthodox faith, being baptized as Catherine. This princess later became Catherine II, known as Catherine the Great.

Peter's sympathies had always been intensely pro-German, and upon Elizabeth's death he speedily restored the German influence which she had been at such pains to eradicate. "Bironism" returned once more to plague the country. The new emperor's first step was to make a peace with Prussia on April 22, 1762, by the terms of which Russia lost every shred of the advantage which her victories should have brought her. Nevertheless the presence of large numbers of Russian troops in Prussia made a lasting impression upon Western Europe and may well have served to prevent the further expansion of Prussia at the expense of Russia. Peter would have been glad to ally himself with Frederick the Great of Prussia against Austria and France, but popular feeling ran too high to make it expedient for him to go so far. As it was, his complete about-face in foreign policy estranged Russia's former allies in Western Europe.

In order to detract attention from his unpopular foreign policy, Peter followed the suggestion of certain of his German advisers and on March 2, 1762, issued a manifesto with the intent of disarming the hostility of the nobles. This manifesto freed them from compulsory service to the state, and while it did, in a measure, do away with their opposition, it stirred up discontent in another quarter, which was productive of nearly a century of seething ill-will. The peasants, whose lot was still immeasurably wretched, had their hopes raised by the manifesto and eagerly awaited a second manifesto which would alleviate their predicament. With perfect logic they reasoned as follows. The nobility had held their lands contingent upon service to the state, that is, they were required to furnish revenue and, in time of war, men. The peasants, who were attached to the land, served the nobles and hence indirectly the state. Since the nobles were now freed from compulsory state service, they could no longer demand service from the peasants. However justified their expectations were, the unfortunate peasants were doomed to disappointment, for the manifesto freeing them did not appear until March 3, 1861.

Peter alienated and disgusted his subjects by his vulgar and ridiculous behavior, not less than by his unpatriotic foreign policies and sympathies. When under the influence of drink, he would rail against everything Russian and heap abuse upon the clergy and the Orthodox Church. Toward his wife, he was brutal, not forbearing to insult her publicly. With great astuteness, she never permitted him to shake her self-control. She was ever on the alert, however, to seize any opportunity of ridding herself and the country of a creature who had none of the qualities of a sovereign. When Peter had finally tried the patience of Russia beyond endurance, she took an active part in stirring up the revolt which deprived him of his throne. She was aided and abetted in this by certain officers of the Guard, some of whom later became her favorites.

On July 12, 1762, less than a year after his accession, Peter was forced to abdicate. His death followed shortly afterwards. It was officially announced that he died of colic, but a current rumor attributed his demise to a wound given him in the course of a drunken brawl by one of Catherine's favorites. Catherine had already been proclaimed Empress and absolute monarch. Her son, Grand Duke Paul, was named as her successor.

REIGN OF EMPRESS CATHERINE II, THE GREAT (1762-1796)

INTERNAL POLICY

The internal reforms and foreign policies of Catherine the Great, the outstanding representative of enlightened despotism in Russia, were in many respects an extension of those instituted by Peter I, while in Russian annals her reign stands second in importance to his alone. An indefatigable worker and the possessor of a fine intellect, she spared no pains to increase her own intellectual equipment or to promote the interests of her country as she saw them. Perhaps her most short-sighted policy was her intensification of the bondage of the serfs and her continual support of the upper classes at their expense. Although she was keen enough to realize, as later events have borne out, that an autocracy which has the support of the powerful upper classes need not trouble itself about the discontent of the impotent submerged groups, she failed to comprehend that the peasant problem was a kind of social volcano, upon which the superstructure of society rested precariously. One of the most significant occurrences of her reign, although not the first in chronological order, was the peasant revolt, which arose from her failure to ameliorate the lot of these people.

It will be remembered that the peasant population eagerly hoped for a manifesto in their favor, following the nobles' manifesto of 1762. Time went on, however, and nothing was done to improve their condition, which, on the contrary, rapidly became more wretched. To be sure, Catherine passed a law to prevent free men and freed peasants from being reduced to the status of serfs and likewise forbade the selling of peasants during times of military conscription. The serfs on Church lands also benefited by her legislation, but in general she showed an absolute lack of comprehension of the plight of the peasants and the serious problem created thereby. By her legislation, they lost the small remnant of liberty still left them and became actual slaves, the personal property of their respective owners. She even instituted laws which forbade them to complain of the treatment they received from their masters!

The nobles, on the other hand, were granted an increasing number of privileges, among which were exemption from taxation and military service. They even gained the right in 1765 to banish rebellious serfs to Siberia and, in general, disregarded all claims of humanity in dealing with them. In addition Catherine constantly favored the upper classes with a view to strengthening her numerous favorites, who enjoyed unusual benefits.[1] Consequently revolts of the lower classes, espe-

---

[1] Catherine's favorites, while numerous, were often men of ability, who gave her efficient service in furthering her policies of internal reform and foreign expansion. Among these favorites were the Orlov brothers, Gregory and Alexei. Above all others, however, stood Gregory Potemkin (1739-1791) who enjoyed Catherine's favor to an extent without precedent. She esteemed him for his loyalty and intelligence, showered great wealth upon him and made him governor of "New Russia," as the southern territory was called. Much of this was conquered by him. See Kyzevetter, A., *Istoritcheskie Siluety,* Berlin, 1931, pp. 7-123.

cially the Cossacks, became frequent, and in 1773 the matter came to a head.

In that year there appeared in the Urals a Cossack by the name of Emelian Pugatchev (1726-1775), who proclaimed that he was the Emperor Peter III. The death of the latter had been so sudden, and the circumstances surrounding it so clothed in secrecy, that several persons had already claimed to be the deposed ruler. Although Peter had had neither the respect nor the liking of his subjects, the oppressed classes merely sought an excuse for an uprising, and his reinstatement furnished as good a pretext as any. In addition to announcing a program for the extermination of the hated nobility, Pugatchev also injected into his revolt a religious element. He was one of the Old Believers, who had suffered more than a little through the Church reforms. Indeed the peasants had become convinced that they owed their wretchedness in great part to these reforms which had seemed to advance merely the interests of the upper classes while their lot became continually worse. Moreover the country had just been ravaged by an epidemic of cholera which appeared to indicate the aroused wrath of an outraged deity. Hence Pugatchev had little difficulty in giving his revolt religious significance. In addition Russia's war with Turkey and Poland made the moment for revolt most propitious. He announced his purpose as follows: "We shall behead every noble in the land. We shall make the true faith prevail and take over the land for ourselves." In a brief space of time, he collected a large number of followers with whom he instituted one of the most ghastly periods of bloodshed in the history of Russia. As in the case of Razin, he was betrayed by his own followers and was executed in 1775. His uprising, however, was not without results. Since it coincided with the American Revolution, it aroused serious concern in Russia. The more thoughtful among the upper classes began to feel that something must be done to improve the condition of the serfs and keep the system from spreading. This popular demand for a more even-handed justice to all classes of society did, after many years, produce some readjustments.[1] For the time being, however, the government was content to take measures to strengthen the landowners against any possible repetition of the revolt.

Fifteen years later the plight of the serfs was boldly described in the guise of a dream by a nobleman, Alexander N. Radishchev (1749-1802), in *A Journey from St. Petersburg to Moscow*

---

[1] See *The Evil Empress* by Grand Duke Alexander of Russia. Philadelphia, 1934.

(1790). Radishchev, who had been sent abroad to study at the University of Leipzig, was imbued with the ideas of the French philosophers of the Age of Enlightenment, including those of Voltaire, Montesquieu, Mably, and Rousseau. Upon his return he served in the Senate and in the "College" of Commerce, where he became head of the St. Petersburg Customs House. His *Journey*, printed by his own private press, was the first Russian book to attack the institutions of serfdom and autocracy, thereby antedating Turgenev's famous *Memoirs of a Sportsman* (1847-1852) by half a century. "Tremble, hard-hearted landlord," said Radishchev, "for on the brow of each of your peasants I read your condemnation." The Pugatchev revolt and the French Revolution having cooled Catherine's ardor for reform, she denounced Radishchev as a worse rebel than Pugatchev. He was condemned to death, but the sentence was commuted to exile in Siberia, where Radishchev remained until after Catherine's death.

Whereas Catherine's policy in regard to the serfs was narrow and short-sighted,[1] in other respects she was very liberal. In imitation of Peter the Great, she was careful to limit the powers of the Church and kept it strictly subordinate to the state; however, she engaged in no religious persecutions. On the contrary, she offered a refuge to all who suffered such persecution in other lands. In 1771 as many as 26,000 refugees came to Russia. In 1785 she followed the example of Emperor Joseph II (1741-1790) of Austria and issued an "Edict of Toleration," which permitted freedom of worship to all creeds. She even gave official support to Mohammedanism, which flourished especially in the middle eastern part of Russia. Pursuant to her policy of toleration, she at first befriended and protected the organization of Free Masons, which began to spread throughout Russia at this time. Later, however, the mystery with which they surrounded their rites aroused her suspicions, and, fearing that they were engaging in political intrigues, she enacted laws against the organization and imprisoned its leaders.

---

[1] Recognizing that nothing was to be hoped for from Catherine in this matter, those who wished to bring about an amelioration of the lot of the serfs and at the same time a limitation of the powers of the nobles, sought the support of Catherine's son, Paul. He feared for himself the fate of Tsarevitch Alexei, son of Peter I. Indeed at the time of her death in 1796, Catherine actually had in preparation a manifesto which was to deprive Paul of his right of succession and give the throne to her grandson, Alexander. See Maroger, Dominique, *The Memoirs of Catherine the Great,* London, 1955; and Fitzlyon, K. (ed. and trans.) *The Memoirs of Princess Dashkov,* London, 1958.

In matters of education Catherine was unusually progressive, so that her reign was a period of unparalleled intellectual activity, although French influence was measurably increased. During the first part of her reign she took great delight in French ideas and did much to disseminate them throughout the country. She admired Voltaire greatly and corresponded with him from 1763 until his death in 1778. She likewise carried on a correspondence with Diderot, D'Alembert, Grimm, and other leading representatives of the Age of Enlightenment. Under her influence, French, the international language of Europe in the eighteenth century, became the language of the Russian court; and Russian writers began to translate the works of Molière, Racine, Corneille, LaFontaine, Montesquieu, and, above all, Voltaire, and to compose works of their own in imitation. Indeed French became the chief medium through which the ancient classics of Greece and Rome, as well as those of English and German origin, reached Russia. The Russian aristocracy was thus subjected to an infusion of Western culture, and its members hired French tutors for their children.

Like the enlightened despots of her time, and like her immediate predecessors in Russia, Catherine had a passion for building. Already throughout Europe the ornate baroque style was giving way to Roman classicism. Catherine II, who shared the revived European interest in the classical monuments of ancient Rome, with characteristic energy devoted her attention to the construction of palaces, public buildings, villas, and private residences. The Russian architect, Starov (1743-1808), the first of the Classic School to graduate from Elizabeth's Academy of Fine Arts, built the Tauride Palace of Prince Potemkin, which in later years housed the Russian Duma. Catherine showered her favorites with villas and residences. Other structures of note in the classic style include Quarenghi's Theater of the Hermitage, Cameron's addition to Tsarskoe Selo, and his restoration of the fifteenth century Palace of the Khans in the Crimea. Such classical models were copied throughout Russia by members of the Russian aristocracy. Catherine's grandson, Alexander I, carried on the classical tradition, although his predilection was for Greek rather than Roman models.

Catherine was much in advance of her contemporaries in realizing the value of popular education and its importance with regard to character and training for citizenship. In order, therefore, to make education more general, she appointed in 1782 a "Committee for the Establishment of Public Schools." Although she did not believe universal education to be feasible for a country the size of Russia, she did give

CATHERINE THE GREAT

additional stimulus to the schools for children of the nobility, which she had founded as early as 1764.

Following in the footsteps of Peter the Great, Catherine established a Russian Academy in 1783. She encouraged the study of medicine, sending for foreign physicians, who could bring new knowledge and practices to her countrymen. At that time smallpox was widespread and usually fatal. Louis XV of France and the children of the King of Spain were among the royal victims of the dread disease. Inoculation was just coming into use and to introduce it into her country, Catherine took the decisive step of being the first to submit to the process. This took no little courage, considering the superstition of the day and her own age of 40 years. The people soon followed her example and inoculation became general. The Senate bestowed upon her twelve gold medals and put up the following inscription in the Senate House: "She saved others to the danger of herself." It was due to her efforts that a Department of the College of Pharmacy was founded at Moscow. Always a patron of arts and artists of whatever nationality, she set aside in one year 1,000,000 rubles for the purchase of valuable works of art. She also gave to the new Russian theater the benefit of her patronage.

Catherine's personal accomplishments along intellectual lines are little short of amazing. She read widely, studied constantly, and became exceedingly well versed in European literature and philosophy. She neither inaugurated any new policy nor instituted any reform without having made it the subject of painstaking study and investigation. Her intellectual accomplishments were not merely the passive results of scholarship, for she wrote extensively on subjects which ranged from fairy tales and satires on manners to erudite treatises on pedagogy and the science of government. Thus for her grandsons, Alexander and Constantine, she compiled the first children's textbook in Russia. It was known as the "Grandmother's A B C Book" and consisted of tales of history. One of her most scholarly accomplishments was the compilation of "Complementary Notes" for the first volume of the first dictionary of the Russian language, which was issued in six volumes, during the years 1789 to 1799 and contained 43,257 words. The work was re-edited from 1840 to 1850.

Under the influence of her example and the encouragement of her patronage, it is not surprising that able men of letters made their appearance and that there was an unprecedented increase in literary productivity. The period boasts such great men as G. R. Derzhavin (1743-1816) and Denis Ivanovitch Fonvisin (1745-1792), together with a host of lesser literary lights. In addition, following Catherine's example, approximately seventy other women took to writing during her reign and made valuable contributions to Russian letters. As a result of their beginning the nineteenth century produced some 1200 emulators among Russian women in the field of Russian literature. Outstanding among them were U. V. Zhadovskaya, Marko Vovtchok, and Gan. Activity was likewise manifested in journalism, and several periodicals made their appearance. In short, Catherine's broad culture and intelligent patronage of the arts, sciences, and letters gave Russia much intellectual prestige throughout Europe.

It was while Catherine was still under the influence of Montesquieu and Beccaria that in 1767 she summoned a Legislative Commission of 564 delegates, representative of all parts of the country and of all classes, except the serfs and the clergy. Her immediate objective was the formulation of a new code of laws. Catherine's *Instructions* (*Nakaz*)[1] to the deputies, according to the Russian historian, V. O. Kliutchevsky, constitute her "political confession," and Voltaire lauded them as the finest monument of the eighteenth century. The *Instructions* were, within a few years, translated into practically every language in Europe, with the result that Catherine became, for a time, the cynosure of all reformers.

In the *Instructions* Catherine expressed herself unqualifiedly in favor of religious toleration and in opposition to the use of torture and capital punishment. She called for a Code of Laws, written in the vernacular and available to all at no greater cost than the Catechism. On the subject of slavery, Catherine's conclusions were even at this time largely negative. She urged the deputies to shun all occasions for the further reduction of people to slavery, except in cases of dire necessity, but opposed any general measure of emancipation. Other sections of the *Instructions* bearing upon economic conditions called for a more judicious method of taxing the peasants, encouragement of agriculture, greater freedom of commerce with all peoples, and other progressive ideas. In view of the fact that England was at this time on the eve of the Industrial Revolution, it is of interest to note Catherine's skepticism about the use of machines in manufacturing, except in the case of goods for export. As regards education, her advice was chiefly directed toward parents, who were enjoined to imbue their children with fear of God and love of country.

---

[1] See Reddaway, W. A. (ed.), *Documents of Catherine the Great* (Cambridge, England, 1931), pp. 215-309.

These and other recommendations indicate that Catherine covered a wide range of subjects, and that, although she took pains to justify her own absolute authority, she was sincerely convinced that even an absolute ruler should govern in the interests of the people. The members of the Legislative Commission, who were required to re-read her *Instructions* monthly, worked diligently for seventeen months, but with the outbreak of the Turkish War in 1768 their sessions were suspended. There seems little doubt, however, that Catherine had implanted in the minds of many people the idea that the best government was the one that shackled freedom the least. The precepts to which she committed herself in writing, although soon violated and never incorporated in the projected code, could scarcely be eradicated.

It is not without interest that the Russian dramatist, Fonvisin, in his play, *The Minor,* was able even as late as 1782 to make guarded references as to how a monarch should conduct himself. In the words of Fonvisin:

The most stupid peasant in the village is usually chosen to pasture the herd, because it does not require much wit to tend cattle. A Tsar who is worthy of his crown endeavors to elevate the souls of his subjects. This we see with our own eyes. . . . [1]

The final statement is, of course, a direct reference to Catherine.

As indicated by the *Instructions,* Catherine gave serious thought to the economic problems of the country. To improve the credit system, she abolished the banks that Elizabeth had established for the benefit of the landowners and opened in their place a "State Loan Bank" with a capital of 1,000,000 rubles, which lent money to all classes at an established interest rate of 5 percent. It was also empowered to issue bank notes. Soon paper currency likewise came into general use. With the improvement of credit, factories began to spring up. More than 2000 were built, which employed a steadily increasing number of workmen. Under Catherine's encouragement and protection, foreign colonists began to enter the country. The population increased from 13,000,000 at the end of the reign of Peter I to 40,000,000, which led to the founding of nearly 200 towns. This, together with the new territory acquired by expansion, led to a re-division of the empire in 1775 on the basis of the census, whereby the twenty provinces of Peter I were increased to fifty.

[1] See Noyes, G. R., *Masterpieces of the Russian Drama* (1933), pp. 76 ff.

FOREIGN AFFAIRS

The period under consideration was marked by the acquisition of much territory by Russia. The possibility of expansion in the Far East began to arouse considerable interest, but the central government was too much occupied with foreign affairs nearer at hand to give the matter much attention. Therefore such progress as was made in that direction was the work for the most part of adventurous traders, who penetrated into the most remote regions. It must not be overlooked, however, that Catherine's policy of religious toleration to all creeds contributed not a little to this program of expansion, inasmuch as the population of the eastern territories was largely Mohammedan. In the course of time, settlements were planted as far east as Alaska and the neighboring islands. This advance, however, was not adequately followed up until a later day.

In the West the problem of foreign expansion was much more immediate. Catherine was determined to regain the considerable Russian territory which had come under Polish control and to wrest from the Turks that region extending to the natural frontier of Russia on the shores of the Black Sea. The Turks, alarmed at the prospects of further Russian expansion at their expense, precipitated a conflict in 1768 by invading the Crimea. In the course of the first Turkish War General Peter Rumyantsev (1725-1796) was able to defeat the Turks and cross the Danube. This war was likewise notable, in that it marked the first appearance of the Russian Baltic fleet in the Mediterranean, with the subsequent annihilation of the Turkish Navy in the Aegean (1770).

The Treaty of Küchük Kainarji in 1774, concluded largely as a result of the Pugatchev revolt, is a landmark in Russian diplomacy. By this treaty Russia became a Black Sea power, her right to free navigation of its waters being duly recognized, as was her control of its northern shores from the Bug to the Dnieper. With a Turkish pledge to permit freedom of religion in the provinces of Moldavia and Wallachia, Russia emerged as the champion of Orthodoxy in the Balkans. Although the treaty merely stipulated the "independence" of the Crimea, this region was annexed by Catherine within a decade (1783). The treaty of 1774 was of great significance in all future international settlements with reference to the Black Sea and the question of the Dardanelles, as well as in regard to the protection of Orthodox Christians under the Ottoman Empire. The stage was set for the role of Turkey as the "sick man of Europe" in the nineteenth century. One of Catherine's favorites, Gregory Potemkin, was placed in charge of the newly acquired territory and he lost no time in promoting its development.

It is sometimes customary to divide Catherine's foreign policy in the West into two periods, with the year 1780 as the line of demarcation. The so-called first period, prior to 1780, witnessed the establishment of the "Northern Accord," an alliance of Russia, Prussia, Poland, Sweden, Denmark, and England against Austria and France. The fact that Poland was a member of the "Accord" did not prevent Catherine from taking steps to secure the coveted Polish territory, with the result that Poland was arbitrarily partitioned three times in the course of her reign in 1773, 1793, and 1795.

With regard to Poland, Catherine as early as 1763 had intrigued to place her own candidate, Stanislas Poniatovski, on the Polish throne. Using the religious issue—a cardinal feature of her policy toward both Turkey and Poland—Catherine joined forces with Frederick the Great of Prussia and Maria Theresa of Austria to effect the first partition in 1773. Poland helped to precipitate her own downfall by her internal dissensions, her failure to respect treaties, and her persecution of various religious sects, particularly Orthodox worshippers.[1] Nor was the entire population of Poland hostile to the advent of Russian control. Many of the nobility and the Catholic priests, as well as the Jewish population [2] of the Polish Ukraine, had suffered horribly at the hands of the Ukrainian Cossacks, the "Haidamaki." From time to time these "Haidamaki" would rise in retaliation for the persecution of Orthodox believers and leave a trail of massacre and devastation in the regions inhabited by the aforementioned classes of citizens. Those who believed that Russia would put an end to this reign of terror were not averse to partiton, and there was always a small faction—in contem-

[1] As early as 1591, certain Orthodox bishops, residing in territory taken by Poland from Russia, were advised to approach King Sigismund III with suggestions of the desirability of a union between the Orthodox and Catholic Churches. As a result, in 1595, a petition was presented to the Pope, asking him to take over the control of the West Russian Church and a council was called for the following year to consummate the union. The deliberation of the council resulted in a disagreement between the Uniates and their opponents. Naturally the king supported the Uniates and maintained that a union of the Churches had been effected. Orthodox believers who refused to conform were deprived of the right to hold public office of any kind and were heavily taxed for the benefit of the Catholics. Their religious books were subject to Catholic censorship, and they were not permitted to repair, much less build, churches.

[2] The Jews, because of their business ability and knowledge of languages, were extensively employed by the Polish government to collect taxes and enforce certain unpopular measures. Acting under instructions, they were often compelled to resort to drastic methods, which aroused great hostility against them.

porary terminology, a fifth column—that actively supported it. Of course the masses of the people bitterly resented foreign dominance, as their frequent revolts have testified.

Russian acquisitions by the first partition were confined to territory in northeastern Poland, occupied mainly by White Russians. In the years that followed the Poles proved unsuccessful in reorganizing their government to resist outside pressures, although the interlude between the first and second partitions was one of marked progress in the intellectual and financial spheres. Even the new Polish Constitution of 1791 —which provided for a hereditary instead of an elective monarchy, abolished the notorious *liberum veto,* and introduced a bicameral legislature—promoted internal dissension. The French Revolution and the preoccupation of Austria with French affairs made it possible for Prussia and Russia to carry off a second and more drastic partition in 1793. Indeed Catherine discreetly let it be known abroad that she was curbing Jacobinism in Warsaw while her allies sought to do the same in Paris. The heroic efforts of the renowned Polish patriot, Thaddeus Kosciuszko, failed to offset the losses Poland had suffered or to prevent the final partition of that unhappy land among the Russians, Austrians, and Prussians in 1795.

By the three partitions Russia secured Eastern Poland, including the old Grand Duchy of Lithuania and large areas occupied mainly by White Russians and Ukrainians (Little Russians). It was only in the final partition that the Russians acquired large numbers of Polish subjects. The new Russian frontier, except for eastern Galicia, was not unlike that re-established by the Soviet Government in the fall of 1939, after the outbreak of World War II.

The transition to the second period of Catherine's foreign policy was marked by the proclamation of the "Act of Armed Neutrality" (1780). This measure affirmed the right of neutral ships to trade with belligerent nations in all commodities save war supplies. It was a product of the American War of Independence and was designed to obstruct the English in their efforts to subdue the rebellious colonies. It should not be assumed, however, that Catherine, already embittered by the Pugatchev revolt, looked with favor on American revolutionaries. Although the United States, as early as 1781, sent Francis Dana to St. Petersburg to obtain recognition of the young republic, he accomplished nothing. Indeed, Catherine viewed the American "rebels" in much the same light as many Americans have regarded Russian Communists in our own day. Thirty-three years elapsed before Russia finally recognized the American Government in 1809.

Catherine was more concerned, during these years, with the implementation of her famous "Greek Project" (1782), which was announced during the celebration of the birth of her grandson, who was appropriately enough named Constantine. Voltaire was responsible for giving Catherine the idea of the "Greek Project," which he discussed in detail with her. This project had as its objective the banishment of Turkey from Europe, the establishment of a Greek Empire under an Orthodox monarch at Constantinople, and the division of the remaining Turkish possessions among European nations. As a first step in this direction Catherine established an alliance with Austria. Of course the immediate result was a conflict with Turkey, which was further complicated by a struggle with Sweden, not to mention the usual Polish problem. Although the "Greek Project" failed to materialize, Russia consolidated her territorial gains and put an end to the Tartar menace. Turkey continued to resent Catherine's imperialistic designs, and in 1787, partly as a result of English pressure, hostilities began on a large scale. Under the leadership of the brilliant Russian general, Alexander Suvorov (1730-1800), who stormed the great fortress of Ismail, Russia again emerged triumphant, and by the Treaty of Yassy in 1791 acquired additional territory on the Black Sea between the Bug and the Dniester and on the Sea of Azov, including the fortress of Otchakov. The entire north shore of the Black Sea fell into Russian hands.

Sweden had taken advantage of the Turkish war to attack Russia in 1788. Two years later, however, the Peace of Verela left the boundaries of the two countries as they were before hostilities began. Thus, under Catherine, Russia regained all the "Western Lands" lost in previous centuries, with the exception of Galicia, and extended her boundaries to the Black and Azov Seas. By way of analogy it may be said that both Peter and Catherine strove to increase Russia's prestige among the powers. But whereas Peter's methods were autocratic and based on the use of force, Catherine, as in the case of the Polish partitions, made effective use of diplomacy.

As elsewhere in Europe, the outbreak of the French Revolution in 1789 at first evoked great enthusiasm in Russia among the nobility and intellectuals—even those as high in station as the grandsons of the empress, Alexander and Constantine.[1] In Paris a prominent representative of the Russian colony, Count Paul Stroganov, even joined the Jacobin Club and expressed a desire to witness a similar cataclysm in

---

[1] See Lobanov-Rostovsky, Andrei, *Russia and Europe, 1789-1825*, Chap. I, pp. 3-30.

Russia. The excesses of the revolutionaries soon dampened the enthusiasm of the proponents of the revolution in Russia, and Catherine, who had never shared it, severed diplomatic relations with France in October 1789. Although she confined herself to promises of aid for her Austrian ally, granted subsidies to needy French *émigrés,* and signed a treaty of "friendship" with England in 1793, by which, among other things, she agreed to close Russian ports to French ships, Catherine bluntly rejected a British request that she send an expeditionary force to the Rhine. In spite of her opposition to the French Revolution, Catherine continued to pursue measures short of war until her death in 1796.

That Catherine was able to reign over Russia for thirty-four years, without an altogether legitimate claim to the throne, is a real tribute to her political genius. There can be no doubt but that her initial role as the patron of liberal and progressive ideas, regardless of the fact that she failed in large measure to put them into practice, contributed to her popularity, not only in Europe, but in Russia, especially among the upper classes. Thus her reputation was that of an "enlightened" despot. Moreover, her consistent support of the upper classes, often at the expense of the masses, helped to establish the security of her position. Revolt, as in the case of the Pugatchev uprising, came mainly from the lower classes, and, without leadership and organization from above, it was suppressed. Chiefly, however, Russian military victories and territorial acquisitions from Turkey and Poland contributed greatly to Catherine's prestige and served, as such expansion has always served under a despotic regime, to quell discontent at home.

REIGN OF EMPEROR PAUL (1796-1801)

INTERNAL POLICY

Paul was in many respects the direct opposite of his mother, Catherine II. At an early age he had been taken by the Empress Elizabeth and reared under her supervision. As a result he was scarcely acquainted with his parents and early developed a great antagonism toward his mother, which increased with the years. He held her responsible for the death of his father and disapproved of her private life and governmental policies, including the partition of Poland. Upon his ascent to the throne he was forty-two years of age, but so physically and mentally broken that many of his contemporaries, as well as later historians, believed him to be insane. Despite this, and his short reign of five years, he was responsible for some very important innovations in the laws and customs of the land, not all of which were detrimental. Intent upon reversing, or at least mitigating, the results of some of Catherine's policies, Paul hastened to release all Polish prisoners in St. Petersburg, including Kosciuszko, who received a grant of 60,000 rubles and permission to set out for the United States.

Paul had long been of the opinion that, with the exception of the peasants, all classes of society had been granted too many concessions by his predecessors, with the result that the monarch had lost much of his autocratic power. He began his reign, therefore, with a reassertion of the principle of absolute autocracy, plus a strengthening in every possible way of his own personal authority. That all classes of society might feel the weight of his authority, he issued statements and promulgated legislation which established him as the supreme head of all institions, both civil and ecclesiastical.

It will be recalled that by the reforms of Peter I the Church became distinctly subordinate to the state, and was placed under the control of a specialized department of the government, the Synod. At this time, as far as the government and the upper classes were concerned, it lost its worth as a source of spiritual influence. It was tolerated solely as an institution, which dispensed a necessary moral "opiate" to the lower classes and thus reconciled them to their miserable condition. Paul revived the power of the Church as a moral influence but, at the same time, made it completely subject to his authority. He was the first to give precise expression to the doctrine, "The Tsar is the head of the Church." This doctrine was definitely incorporated into the laws of the empire under Nicholas I (1825-1855). In this way he made Church control synonymous with autocratic control and despotism, for which reason the Church never gained the support of the upper classes of society and the intelligentsia. From the reign of Paul almost up to 1917, the more thoughtful classes of society recognized that the revival of Church authority meant the institution of reactionary policies and despotic rule.

In order to compel general recognition of his supreme authority, Paul demanded that his subjects pay him the most servile homage upon all occasions. When he appeared in public all persons were required to fall upon their knees in token of their submission, irrespective of the condition of the streets at the time. Anything which savored of democracy and equality was anathema to him; hence he was extremely hostile to such tendencies as were manifested in France. He even forbade the wearing of certain articles of apparel which were in vogue among the

French Jacobins, while he eliminated from court language some of their favorite words, such as "citizen." Moreover no Frenchman was allowed to enter Russia unless he had a passport bearing the signature of the Bourbon princes, thus proving that he would not be a source of revolutionary propaganda.

In order to isolate his subjects from the slightest taint of foreign revolutionary influence, Paul no longer permitted foreign books, or even music, to be imported. Permission was also refused to any who sought to leave the country for travel or study and those who had already done so received peremptory orders to return. As a matter of course, the theater and press were subjected to the most rigid censorship.

In contrast to his dislike and suspicion of everything which ema·nated from democratic France, Paul had a considerable predilection for anything of Prussian origin. For instance he abolished the army uniform so admirably adapted to Russian needs and substituted in its place Prussian military dress, which was characterized by powdered wigs, buckled shoes, and similar unsuitable articles of attire. General Suvorov regarded the new uniforms as objectionable in the extreme and is reported to have said: "Wig powder is not gun powder; curls are not cannons; a pigtail is not a sabre; I am not a Prussian, but a Russian." He paid for this expression of opinion by being exiled to his village.

As the culmination of his efforts to re-establish an absolute autocracy, Paul issued on April 5, 1797, the "Law of Succession to the Throne." This law established the principle of primogeniture in Russia.

In the measures considered thus far, the policy of the emperor was reactionary. On the other hand, his attitude toward the serfs revealed him to be far more progressive than any of his immediate predecessors; the *ukaz* which he promulgated in their behalf was of the greatest importance and subsequent influence. As will be remembered, serfdom had its beginnings in 1581 during the reign of Ivan Grozny, when the peasants became "fixed' to the soil for a limited term of years. From that time forth, the period of fixation was continuously lengthened, and the liberties of the peasants were increasingly curtailed until they virtually became slaves through the legislation of Catherine II. Not the least of Paul's objections to what he deemed the injudicious concessions of his mother to the upper classes originated from his conviction that these concessions were made at the expense of the peasants, who were existing under oppression well-nigh unendurable. It had also been pointed out to him that in time of war the serfs constituted a most serious problem. He was therefore the first ruler for many generations to enact legislation in their favor. While he was not able to institute so revolutionary a measure as a complete emancipation of the serfs, he issued an *ukaz* limiting their compulsory service to three days a week. Although this law was not strictly enforced, it became a guiding principle for succeeding monarchs. Whereas all rulers before Paul aided in intensifying the bondage of the serfs, each one thereafter made serious efforts to improve their condition until they finally attained their freedom under Alexander II.

FOREIGN POLICY

Despite the stigma of insanity attached to him, Paul did manifest some good judgment in his foreign policies. As a gesture of peace, he recalled Russian forces stationed in Persia and relinquished suzerainty over the state of Georgia. He also sought and secured a friendly understanding with Turkey, hoping by this means, rather than by force of arms, to extend the scope of Russian influence to include the regions bordering on the Mediterranean and Adriatic Seas.

Affairs in Europe were destined to assist him in his ambitions in this direction. The chief European powers had become exceedingly alarmed by the aggression of France and her steady expansion. Already she had brought under her control all of Switzerland, northern Italy, and the Ionian Islands, where Orthodox Greeks made up the bulk of the population. Although under Catherine Russia had played no more than a nominal role in the First Coalition against France, and Paul at first abandoned all idea of sending an expeditionary force to the Rhine, he was gradually converted to the need for concerted European action to forestall further pretensions on the part of the French. Paradoxically enough, Paul, who entered into negotiations with the Knights of St. John over their property rights in Poland, was persuaded to assume the position of Grand Master of this Catholic Order, when in 1798 Napoleon occupied their headquarters at Malta. Paul seems to have dreamed of the possibility of a crusade against France. Concerned about the French threat in the eastern Mediterranean following Napoleon's occupation of Egypt, Paul was persuaded in December 1798 by William Pitt the Younger to join the Second Coalition, which ultimately included Austria, England, the Kingdom of Naples, Russia, and her ally, Turkey.

Meanwhile, in collaboration with Turkey, he undertook to liberate the Ionian Islands from French "tyranny." A Black Sea squadron under the command of Admiral Ushakov was ordered to proceed to the

Adriatic where, with the backing of a few Turkish warships, the public support of the Greek patriarch at Constantinople, and the favorable disposition of the local population, the French were expelled from the Islands. A republic was established in the Ionian Islands, nominally under Turkish control, but in reality a dependency of Russia. Thus Paul's ambition approached realization, since a Russian base had been secured in the Adriatic, from which he could exercise control over the Orthodox and Slavonic population of the Balkan regions. In 1799 the Prince-Bishop of Montenegro, a country which had maintained relations with Russia since the reign of Peter the Great, voluntarily sought an alliance with the Russian emperor, thereby promoting still further his designs in the Adriatic.

In accordance with the terms of his alliance with Austria, Paul dispatched a Russian expeditionary force to Italy under the leadership of the brilliant General Suvorov, who had been designated commander-in-chief of the Austro-Russian armies in that part of Europe, which included some 52,000 men. Suvorov's spectacular offensive drove the French from Italy, and the elderly Russian general became a popular idol in Western Europe. Suvorov medals, hats, feathers, portraits, etc., became the fashion of the day. Suvorov, himself, when directed to evict the French from Switzerland, performed the well-nigh impossible task of crossing the Alps late in the season via the St. Gothard Pass. Unfortunately friction had developed between Suvorov and the Austrians, who were none too enthusiastic about the whirlwind Russian campaign which they were unable to control, and they withdrew from Switzerland, leaving Suvorov to face French armies that were greatly superior in numbers. As a result the Russian losses were heavy.

Another expeditionary force of 12,000 men, which Paul had dispatched by sea to effect a joint landing with the English in Holland, met with disaster, allegedly because of the military inefficiency of the Duke of York. Convinced that both his Austrian and English allies had failed to co-operate, and incensed by the English occupation of Malta in 1800, Paul abruptly recalled his armies and withdrew from the Second Coalition. Making a complete about-face in policy he revived Catherine's League of Armed Neutrality against England and entered into peace negotiations with Napoleon. The two erstwhile enemies planned a joint expedition against the English possessions in India. On January 12, 1801, Paul actually ordered the dispatch of 22,000 Cossacks by the overland route to India. He pictured in the most glowing terms the glory, wealth, and imperial favor these Cossacks would gain and the service they would render their country.

No adequate preparations had been made, however, for the long and arduous march they were to undertake. In consequence, although eleven regiments actually set out, half of their horses were lost in the desert, the forces became utterly demoralized, and the campaign dwindled to a miserable conclusion.

The break with England had disastrous consequences for Paul. His autocratic and violent rule had aroused much hostility against him in Russia, especially in military circles, where his wrath found vent in wholesale banishments. The English, who were aware of this, proceeded to make use of it to their own advantage. An English fleet under Nelson was dispatched to the Baltic, where it completely destroyed the Danish fleet at Copenhagen. English agents began to foment opposition against Paul, who was assassinated on March 24, 1801. He was succeeded by his son, Alexander I.

REIGN OF EMPEROR ALEXANDER I (1801-1825)

Like his father, Alexander was brought up apart from his parents, for the Empress Catherine II had taken him at an early age and had trained him as her own son. The tutors she selected were instructed to educate him "in accordance with the laws of reason and the principles of virtue." One of these men was Frederick Caesar Laharpe (1754-1838), a native of Switzerland and a devotee of liberalism and republicanism. A great friendship grew up between teacher and pupil, and Alexander became so imbued with the principles he was taught that he believed to the end of his life that he was a republican. Shortly before his death, Alexander said: "They may say of me what they will; but I have lived and shall die a republican." Although the republicanism which he championed bore little resemblance to present-day conceptions, nevertheless his policies and government were regarded by his subjects as such an improvement over those of his father that they referred to him as the "angel." Many of them, however, especially those closely associated with him, were not unaware of his subtle and devious diplomacy. Possessed of a pleasing personality and a persuasive tongue, he was able to win people to his way of thinking and then, by skillful flattery, he led them to believe that the ideas in question had originated with them. In this way he gained support and avoided opposition. He also accomplished much by winning the favor of women, with whom he was very popular because of his personal charm. These practices caused certain of his contemporaries to characterize him as being "as sharp as a pin, as fine as a razor, and as false as seafoam."

In conformity with his republican leanings, Alexander began his reign with very liberal ideas. The censorship was relaxed, foreign books were once again imported, and the ban on foreign travel was withdrawn. Alexander commissioned a group of his progressive friends, including Count Paul Stroganov, Prince Adam Czartoryski, Nicholas Novosiltsev, and Count Victor Kochubey, to serve as a Committee of Public Welfare with the object of drafting a program of reform for Russia. Laharpe was called back to St. Petersburg to advise them. However, the opposition of the conservative nobility and the course of European events outside Russia were destined to cool Alexander's ardor for reform. His "splendid beginnings" gave way to a regime of reaction and autocracy. Inasmuch as outside influences were so potent in altering internal policies, it seems appropriate to turn first to the foreign policy of Alexander I.

FOREIGN AFFAIRS

With respect to foreign affairs, the reign of Alexander tends to divide itself naturally into two periods. The first period extended from 1801 to 1815 and was occupied chiefly by the struggle with Napoleon. The second period embraced the years 1815 to 1825 and witnessed the concerted efforts of the powers, under the aegis of the Holy Alliance, to maintain the *status quo* in Europe against the resurgent forces of revolution.

Although Alexander's initial move, upon his accession to the throne, was to recall Paul's India expediton, thereby preventing a possible war with England, his relations with France remained for the time being outwardly friendly. The murder of the Duke d'Enghien at the instigation of the French Government in 1804 led to a breach of relations with France and to Russian participation in the Third Coalition (1804-1807) of Russia, Austria, England, and Sweden against Napoleon. There followed a series of setbacks for the Russian forces at Austerlitz (1805), Eylau (1807), and Friedland (1807) which, after the brilliant victories of Rumyantsev and Suvorov in the preceding reigns of Catherine and Paul, Alexander found particularly humiliating, especially since he had disregarded the advice of his commanding general, Mikhail Kutuzov (1745-1813), a former pupil of Surorov. The Russian emperor was equally bitter over lack of support from his Austrian and Prussian allies, the latter having met with complete disaster at Jena (1806), and at the failure of England to furnish a promised detachment of 10,000 to 15,000 troops. He thereupon performed an about-face in foreign policy, as startling as that executed by the Emperor Paul before him, when, on June 25, 1807, he came to terms with Napoleon at Tilsit on the Niemen River in East Prussia, and the two leaders prepared to divide the world between them.

By the terms of the Treaty of Tilsit Alexander was given a free hand against Sweden, including the right to annex Finland and thereby remove a threat to the near-by capital of St. Petersburg. In return he agreed to adhere to Napoleon's Continental System, which prohibited all trade with England, and, should the English refuse to make peace, even to enter the conflict against her as an ally of the French. The alliance envisaged the eventual partition of the Ottoman Empire, provided that the Turks failed to come to terms with Russia. Thus Alexander, the former leader of the anti-French bloc on the continent, became the ally of Napoleon and his partner in the struggle for world domination. This reversal in foreign policy was extremely unpopular among the Russian nobility in general, but it did provide the Russian armies with a breathing spell, which was used by Alexander to secure possession of Finland (1809) in a war against Sweden, to bring about the termination of hostilities with Turkey, which had dragged on from 1806 to 1812, as a result of which the Russians acquired Bessarabia, and to reorganize the Russian forces for a renewal of the struggle with Napoleon.[1]

The Franco-Russian alliance did not put an end to the mutual distrust of Napoleon and Alexander. The involvement of Napoleon in the uprising in Spain after 1809 led the Russians to encourage Austrian and Prussian opposition to Napoleonic domination, and Alexander became more evasive in his dealings with the French emperor. In 1810 a revised Russian tariff, designed to offset some of the detrimental effects of the Continental System in Russia, placed heavy duties on wines and luxuries, most of which were imported from France. Both sides violated the terms of the Treaty of Tilsit, the French by annexing the Grand Duchy of Oldenberg, whose ruler was an uncle of the tsar, and the Russians by failing to live up to the letter of the Continental System. By 1811 it became apparent that the renewal of hostilities between France and Russia was just a matter of time.

---

[1] For an opinion to the effect that Alexander never considered the agreement at Tilsit as other than a truce in his struggle against Napoleon, see Strakhovsky, Leonid I., *Alexander I of Russia*, N. Y., Norton, 1947, pp. 71-108.

Both Napoleon and Alexander began to prepare feverishly for the approaching struggle. Napoleon assembled some 600,000 men (the Grand Army), and was in a position to array all of Europe, with the possible exception of Sweden and Turkey, against Russia. In spite of the timely warning of General Armand de Caulaincourt (1772-1827), French Ambassador in St. Petersburg, to the effect that Napoleon would encounter stiff resistance from a united Russian nation, the Grand Army crossed the Russian frontier at the Niemen River near Kovno in June 1812.

It is inevitable, as a result of World War II, that the invasion of Russia in June 1812 by Napoleon should recall the invasion in June 1941 by Nazi Germany. Like Hitler, Napoleon seems to have expected that *Blitzkrieg* tactics and one resounding victory like Austerlitz or Friedland would bring Alexander quickly to terms. After all, he had an army of 600,000 at his disposal as compared with fewer than 200,000 for the Russians. But the Russian armies retreated before him, avoiding battle wherever possible, and carrying out a scorched earth policy. After the French capture of Smolensk, popular outcry resulted in the recall of Kutuzov to command the Russian forces. Kutuzov faced the French army at Borodino, about seventy-five miles west of Moscow. In one of the bloodiest battles of the war, the French lost 30,000 men, together with 49 generals, and the Russians, 18 generals, 1732 other officers, and 35,000 men. The Russian retreat nevertheless continued, even Moscow being evacuated and abandoned to the enemy.

The burning of Moscow has been termed the turning point of the war.[1] Napoleon was confronted with the prospect of spending the winter in a devastated and looted city, without adequate supplies of food and clothing, in the midst of a hostile population. Any expectations he may have had of arousing the peasants against the tsar had failed to materialize. Any hopes that he may have entertained of dictating peace in Moscow were likewise doomed to disappointment. For the Russians this had become a war for national survival.

When, on October 20, Napoleon undertook his now famous retreat from Moscow, over the same route by which he invaded Russia, Cossack cavalry harried his rear, Russian partisans prevented his army from acquiring the necessary supplies, and Kutuzov's armies virtually destroyed his forces. When the French crossed the Russian frontier into Prussia early in December, the Grand Army had been reduced to a

---

1 See Lobanov-Rostovsky, *op. cit.,* p. 228.

NAPOLEON'S RETREAT FROM MOSCOW

bare 30,000 of the 600,000 troops that had entered Russia just six months before.

Many reasons have been assigned for the defeat of the Napoleonic forces in the campaign of 1812. It has been ascribed to the weather, to the vast open spaces of Russia, to the polyglot composition of Napoleon's armies, to the Russian tactics of retreat, to the fact that Napoleon extended his lines too far, to the resistance of the Russian people, and to other reasons. In this connection, the well-known historian, Lobanov-Rostovsky, gives the following estimate:

> No war has been more generally misinterpreted in history than Napoleon's campaign in Russia. Too readily it has been dismissed with the statement that Napoleon was driven out by the cold. In saying this, historians forget that they thereby merely endorse Napoleon's "war propaganda"— the official explanation which Napoleon gave Europe to account for his defeat and make it appear an "act of God" for which he could not be responsible. Thus accepted, the legend of the defeat of the Grand Army by the cold in Russia has crept into history, and this superficial view has been repeated glibly ever since.[1]

He goes on to point out that the French defeat was due to a combination of military, national, and geographical factors. The contemporary Soviet historian, Eugene Tarle, interprets the campaign of 1812 as a people's war and suggests an interesting parallel between the Russian and Spanish campaigns:

> Not the cold and not Russia's vast expanses conquered Napoleon, but the resistance of the Russian people.
>
> The Russian people asserted their right to an independent national existence; they asserted it with an indomitable will to victory, with the true heroism that despises all phrases, with a surge of spirit unequalled by any other nation save the Spanish.
>
> The Russians revealed greater physical strength and material potentialities than Spain. Within six months Napoleon's hordes were dispersed and destroyed in Russia, while the Spaniards, despite their equally indisputable heroism, took five years, even with the immense help given them by England, to get rid of Napoleon—and ultimately succeeded in 1813 in direct consequence of Napoleon's defeat in Russia.[2]

With the liberation of Russian territory from the invader, Alexander was at once faced with the decision as to whether to carry the conflict

---

[1] Lobanov-Rostovsky, *op. cit.,* p. 212.
[2] Tarle, Eugene, *Napoleon's Invasion of Russia—1812,* N. Y., Oxford, 1942, pp. 408-409.

to foreign soil or to make peace with Napoleon. Contrary to the advice of the ailing Kutuzov, the tsar decided to continue the conflict until Napoleon's downfall was assured. The war lasted another two years, during which time Russian losses in man power were greater than those of any other nation which joined the Fourth and Fifth Coalitions. Napoleon's retreat was marked by the great Battle of Leipzig, September 16-19, 1813, commemorated as the Battle of the Nations. In January-February 1814 the allied armies crossed the Rhine into France. Although England and Austria were at first disposed to make peace with France without further delay—a development which evoked profound discord among the allies—Alexander, with the support of Prussia, insisted on the continuation of the conflict until Napoleon was overthrown. At Chaumont the four great powers, upon British initiative, signed a twenty-year alliance by which they agreed to continue the war and to make no separate peace. On March 31, 1814, the allied troops entered Paris. Shortly thereafter Napoleon abdicated, and on May 30, 1814, the First Treaty of Paris was signed, leaving France with the boundaries of 1792.

No sooner was victory in sight than the deep-rooted divergences of opinion among the great powers came to the fore. Alexander had entered Paris in triumph as the liberator and "savior" of Europe. The unprecedented display of power by the Russian army, and Russian pressure in favor of moderate terms for defeated France, aroused the fear and jealousy of England and Austria, whose representatives, Metternich and Castlereagh, began to suspect that they had destroyed one colossus only to be confronted with another, and that Alexander's expansionist program constituted a threat second only to that of Napoleon.

This rift among the allies reached its climax at the Congress of Vienna, which began in October 1814. Here Alexander's program for a united Poland, with himself as monarch, and with compensation elsewhere in Europe for Prussia and Austria, almost broke up the Conference. The efforts of Castlereagh and Metternich to line up all the powers, including France, in opposition to Russia failed when Prussia, in the expectation of compensation in Saxony, continued to support Alexander. The deadlock over the Polish-Saxon issue was broken by the sudden return of Napoleon from Elba, which rendered compromise imperative and Russian military participation indispensable. In the compromise that ensued it was agreed that the greater part of Poland should be established as a constitutional monarchy under Alexander, with Prussia receiving two-fifths of Saxony. Russian expansion on the continent proved to be moderate, as compared with the acquisitions of Prussia and Austria, as well as the colonial acquisitions of Britain.[1] Following the defeat of Napoleon at Waterloo and the conclusion of the Second Treaty of Paris on November 20, 1815, the Russians for several years maintained an army of occupation of 27,000 men in France.

It was at Paris, in September 1815 that Alexander proclaimed his celebrated Holy Alliance of European powers pledged to conduct their relations in accordance with the "precepts of justice, Christianity, charity, and peace." During the closing stages of the Napoleonic conflict Alexander had come under the influence of the Baroness Julia von Krüdener, an exponent of the mysticism and pietism then spreading rapidly throughout Europe in the wake of the war. He became convinced that the principles of Christianity, if applied to international policies, would lead to an exalted conception of international relations and thus prevent wars in the future.

The Holy Alliance was signed by all European nations with the exception of England, the Papal State, and Turkey. Its "Covenant" stated that the "supreme truths dictated by the eternal law of God the Saviour" should be the basis of the government of the league and that international questions should be decided "by no other rules but the commandments of this sacred faith, the commandments of love, truth, and peace." However, there was a further stipulation in the pact which was extremely significant. The members of the Alliance were to govern their various subjects "as fathers of their families," and each was pledged to go to the assistance of any other if need arose. Although the Holy Alliance was generally regarded as too vague and mystical to be practical, the renewal by the Second Treaty of Paris of the twenty-year alliance of the four great powers (Quadruple Alliance) provided the machinery for the implementation of these precepts.

After the European settlement of 1815 the power and prestige of Russia remained undeniably great in Western Europe. Through the French foreign minister, the Duke de Richelieu, who had spent many years in the service of Russia, Alexander for some time exercised a preponderant influence over the affairs of France. That influence was exerted in 1818 at the Congress of Aix-la-Chapelle, to secure the withdrawal of the allied occupation forces from France and the admission

---

[1] Russia obtained 2100 square miles of territory with a population of more than 3,000,000; Austria received 2300 square miles and a population of 10,000,000; and Prussia got 2217 square miles, with a population of 5,360,000. (See Lobanov-Rostovsky, *op. cit.,* p. 352.) England obtained from France the islands of Malta, St. Lucia, Tobago, Mauritius, and the Ionian Islands; from the Netherlands, Ceylon, part of Dutch Guiana, and South Africa; and from Denmark she took Heligoland.

of that country to the Concert of Europe. Although Alexander at first supported the establishment of liberal constitutions in the German states of Saxe-Weimar, Württemberg, and Baden, with the resurgence of revolution and violence in Europe, he became increasingly alarmed. Beginning with the Conferences of Troppau (1820) and Verona (1822), which were concerned respectively with revolution in Naples and Spain, Russia lined up with Metternich on the side of legitimacy and the *status quo*. Henceforth the Holy Alliance began to serve in practice to make the world safe for autocracy. Thus in 1821, when the Greek Christians rebelled against Turkish despotism, they met with no sympathy at first on account of their disobedience to a lawful ruler.

The United States was invited to become a member of the Holy Alliance, a league which at first Americans regarded sympathetically. When it became apparent that the Alliance served as a tool of despotism and reaction in Europe, however, American sympathy was alienated. While the Alliance curbed the expansionist ambitions of its members in Europe, including those of Russia, it may have served to direct Alexander's attention to the Pacific Northwest. In 1821, in what amounted to unilateral action, he issued an official *ukaz* which closed the entire North Pacific from the Bering Straits to the fifty-first parallel to the trade and navigation of any foreign power. Only Russian ships were to be permitted to approach within 100 Italian miles (115 English miles) of the territory of the tsar in this region. Needless to say, this *ukaz* aroused the antagonism of all Americans, especially the commercial and fur-trading interests of New England, who were concerned about the future of the Pacific Coast. In 1822, when Russia and France, as members of the Holy Alliance, expressed their readiness to lend military support to Spain in her efforts to recover Spanish America, the United States was still more alarmed by the extent of European encroachments, which by now amounted to a pincer movement. The immediate result was the proclamation of the Monroe Doctrine on December 2, 1823, which warned Russia and all other powers against intervention in the American hemisphere. On April 17, 1824, the United States and Russia reached an accord with regard to the Northwest which removed the danger of a future clash between these two countries in the Pacific.

As a result of World War II and the obvious parallels afforded by the Nazi and Napoleonic invasions of Russia, there has been in the Soviet Union a great revival of interest in, and a general reinterpretation of, the age of Alexander I.

INTERNAL POLICY

As previously stated, Alexander began his rule with liberal ideas. Two serious problems confronted him, both of which he endeavored to solve in accordance with humanitarian and progressive ideals. The first had to do with the institution of serfdom. Alexander would have been glad to free the serfs outright but was unable to take so decisive a step for fear of antagonizing the landowners. He did set aside 1,000,000 rubles per year with which to redeem for the state land held in private ownership. Since the peasants were attached to the land, they, of course, went with it. Thus they came directly under state control, and fully 50,000 were redeemed in this way during his reign. Although they were still serfs, their lot was immeasurably improved. There were other measures designed to alleviate the condition of the serfs. As early as 1802 landlords were forbidden to exile their serfs to hard labor. A few years later, in 1808, the public sale of serfs in the market place was banned. The liberation of Polish serfs in the Duchy of Warsaw in 1807 (by the French), and their emancipation in the Baltic Province, 1816-1819, served as a clear indication of the trend of the times. Nevertheless these steps involved only a fraction of the serfs in the Russian Empire, and as Alexander succumbed more and more to conservative pressures the prospects for any general settlement of the problem receded.

The other major problem that confronted Alexander was the reorganization of the government along republican ideas of popular representation as they had found expression in France or in regions under Anglo-American control. Upon his accession, as previously noted, he had established a commission to handle this problem. As the first step toward governmental reform he limited the functions of the Senate chiefly to judicial questions. This was followed in 1802 by a continuation of a policy already begun by Paul, namely, the creation of eight administrative departments of government, or ministries. These were the departments of foreign affairs, war, navy, justice, interior, finance, commerce, and education.

In his investigation of Anglo-American and French republicanism, Alexander enlisted the services of able statesmen, two of whom brought considerable distinction to themselves. One of these, Michael Speransky (1772-1839),[1] favored a centralized state in accordance with the French form of government. The other, Nicholas Novosiltsev (1761-1836), inclined to the United States conception and urged a federal state within the boundaries of the Russian Empire.

---

[1] See Raeff, Marc, "The Political Philosophy of Speransky," *The American Slavic and East European Review,* February 1953, pp. 1-21.

In 1806 Alexander began a correspondence with President Jefferson relative to the governmental organization of the United States. This correspondence, however, was productive of no results in Russia. Although the time was ripe for the development of a republican, or at least of some form of constitutional government in Russia, the war and the conservative nobility, who fiercely opposed such a change, prevented further political reform in Russia proper. The projects of Speransky and Novosiltsev were rejected. The temper of the reactionaries perhaps was best illustrated by the memorandum of the renowned historian, Nicholas Karamzin, to Alexander I in 1812, entitled *Old and New Russia*. Karamzin scoffed at the reforms proposed by Speransky and called in no uncertain terms for the maintenance of the *status quo,* with a strong monarchial government, free from such trimmings as a Senate, a State Council, or any representative institutions. Paradoxically enough, Alexander had granted a constitution to Finland, following its conquest from Sweden in 1809. With the reconstitution of the Kingdom of Poland under Alexander in 1815, that country secured, for a time, one of the most liberal constitutions in Europe. Thus Alexander, still an autocrat in St. Petersburg, was a constitutional monarch in Warsaw and Helsinki, an anomaly which many of his subjects found it increasingly difficult to understand.

In the period of political reaction which followed the Napoleonic Wars, Alexander employed ultra-conservative ministers like Count Alexander Araktcheyev (1769-1834) and Prince A. Golitsyn, head of the Holy Synod and subsequently of the Ministry of Education, to conduct a campaign against subversive, un-Russian ideas, which savored of Jacobinism, "false reasoning," "free thinking," and "atheism." The five Russian universities were among the first to suffer from the repression of free thought, and many professors were expelled because of their predilections for a constitutional form of government. In 1823 Russian students were forbidden to attend German universities. Drastic censorship was likewise imposed upon the press, which was forbidden to discuss the problem of serfdom or constitutional questions. Schiller's *Jeanne D'Arc* and Zhukovsky's translation of Sir Walter Scott's ballad *The Eve of St. John* were banned as immoral by the literary censor. One of the most unpopular measures of this era of reaction was the revival of an earlier project for the establishment of military colonies in such places as St. Petersburg, Novgorod, Mogilev, Ekaterinoslav (Dnepropetrovsk), and Kherson, under the direction of the iron disciplinarian, Araktcheyev.

Such persecution led to the organization of secret societies and subsequently to the Decembrist uprising of 1825, which has been called the
First Russian Revolution.[1] Many Russians representative of the liberal nobility, the Guards, and younger officers who were veterans of
the Napoleonic campaigns, were bitterly disillusioned with the failure of
the government to achieve basic political and social reforms over a
period of many years—in fact, since the days of Catherine the Great.
Some had been exhorted to fight Napoleonic despotism abroad and had
returned to find even worse political and economic conditions. Nearly
all of these discontented and conscience-stricken noblemen later acknowledged that they had derived their liberal convictions from foreign literature and from exposure to the revolutionary movements abroad. They
were unanimous in their opposition to the institution of serfdom and in
their demand for some form of constitutional government.

Two secret organizations were established. The Northern Society,
with its headquarters at St. Petersburg, had for its leaders the Muraviev brothers, Nikita and Alexander, the poet Ryleyev (1795-1826),
and Prince Sergei Trubetskoy. The leader of the Southern Society was
Colonel Paul Pestel, a veteran of the Battle of Borodino. Although the
Northern Society aimed at the establishment of a limited monarchy,
and its southern counterpart favored a republic after the model of the
United States, both came eventually to have one chief purpose, namely,
the precipitation of a revolution. Colonel Pestel, one of the most radical
leaders, has been called a Russian Jacobin. The two societies kept in
constant communication and only awaited a favorable opportunity to
test their strength. This opportunity did not arise in Alexander's lifetime, but at his death in 1825 a misunderstanding in regard to the succession provided an opportunity for the revolutionaries.

According to the "Law of Succession" promulgated by Paul in
1797, Alexander should have been succeeded by his brother Constantine.
But Constantine, who was stationed in Warsaw as commander-in-chief,
had never been enthusiastic about the succession, being well aware of
the revolutionary trend of the times. In 1823 Alexander therefore
appointed his third brother, Nicholas, as his successor, but failed to
make this momentous decision public. When Alexander died Constantine promptly swore allegiance to Nicholas, who, either in real or feigned
ignorance, swore allegiance to Constantine. By reason of the poor
means of communication, much time elapsed before it became known
that Nicholas was the rightful ruler.

[1] See Mazour, Anatole, *The First Russian Revolution, 1825,* Berkeley, 1937, for
an interesting study of this revolt, its background, leaders, and results.

Nicholas was known to be a reactionary with a predilection for Prussianism, hence the revolutionaries and others of liberal leanings were very much disturbed. The former decided not to delay action any longer and chose as the day for instituting their revolt December 26 (hence the term, Decembrists), on which day the oath of loyalty to the new emperor was to be taken. The uprising was poorly organized and consisted of little more than demonstrations of disapproval. Certain revolutionaries among the army officers induced two regiments of soldiers to refuse to take the oath, telling them that Nicholas was a usurper. They instructed the soldiers to proceed to a given point and cheer for Constantine and the Constitution. The soldiers were so densely ignorant that they thought that "Constitution" was Constantine's wife. Nicholas had no trouble in putting down the uprising. He executed five of the ringleaders, sent more than one hundred to Siberia, and granted a conditional pardon to the less active.

Although the Decembrist revolt was of short duration and without immediate results, it was, nevertheless, of profound significance, partly because the center of the revolt was the capital, St. Petersburg, and its leaders, far from being counterparts of Pugatchev and Razin, represented in many instances the flower of the Russian nobility and some of the most powerful families in Russia. They came to be regarded as martyrs to the constitutional cause, and were celebrated as such by the writer, Alexander Herzen, from his refuge in London. Although the suppression of the uprising amounted to a serious setback for the Russian constitutional movement, it did serve, as we shall see, to focus the government's attention on domestic conditions, with a view to preventing a repetition of the revolt. Those Decembrists who were exiled to Siberia formed the nucleus of an intelligentsia there, and in spite of the restrictions imposed upon them, they contributed greatly to the development of education, better agricultural methods, medical knowledge, improved administrative methods, and to the scientific study of the region in general. The Decembrist uprising has been called "the logical prologue to the drama which found its apotheosis in 1917." [1]

The reign of Alexander witnessed the increase and spread of sectarianism. The Old Believers, who opposed Nikon, had been the object of governmental persecution almost constantly since 1653. In the course of time, these original dissenters became divided into various denominations or sects. Toward the close of the seventeenth century, there appeared a mystic sect, the *Khlysty* (flagellants), which was second only to the Old Believers in numbers and importance. The *Khlysty* held that

---

[1] Mazour, *op. cit.*, p. xvii.

God could become incarnate in a human being and sought to produce this incarnation by means of ecstatic dancing. Their gyrations often terminated in sexual orgies, which brought them ill repute.[1]

Some members of the sect, to whom certain of its practices became repugnant, withdrew about the middle of the eighteenth century and formed another group which rapidly gained followers. The sect took the name *Dukhobors* and was made up largely of peasants, who had communistic leanings and objected to war. Because of the latter principle, they suffered much persecution from the government. In southern Russia a number of their leaders were condemned to death at the stake in 1792, but Catherine II commuted the sentence to exile. Under Nicholas II, members of the Society of Friends in England and America, hearing of their sufferings, raised funds to assist the Dukhobors. The Emperor's consent to their departure from Russia was obtained. In 1898, 1150 refugees came to Cyprus. In the following year an asylum was offered them in Canada, and 4000 availed themselves of the offer. Their numbers were soon increased by the arrival of those who had originally gone to Cyprus, together with 2000 additional refugees. Leo Tolstoy gave to them all the money which he realized from his novel, *Resurrection.*

The late eighteenth century witnessed the development of yet another sect, an offshoot of the Dukhobors, the Molokane, who rejected many rituals of the Orthodox Church. Although all of the sects drew their numbers at first almost exclusively from the peasant and small trader classes, in the reign of Alexander I they began to win many adherents in the upper orders of society. This was especially true in St. Petersburg.

While the present reign was not so distinguished along intellectual lines as certain other periods in Russian history, it was not without its great names. Alexander Pushkin, the poet, who became famous during the succeeding reign, began to attract attention at this time. The ripest accomplishment within the compass of the reign was the work of the historian Nicholas Karamzin (1766-1826), whose eleven-volume *History of the Russian State* (1818) represents the first attempt to treat the history of Russia from a scientific standpoint.

REIGN OF EMPEROR NICHOLAS I (1825-1855)

INTERNAL AFFAIRS

Nicholas I was born in 1796 and hence was almost twenty years Alexander's junior. He was the exponent of absolutism and reactionary

---
[1] Gregory Rasputin was a member of the *Khlysty.*

aristocracy. As Nicholas informed the Marquis de Custine, during his sojourn in St. Petersburg in 1839: "I can understand the republic—it is an open and sincere government, or at least it can be; I can under-

Courtesy Sovfoto

DECEMBRIST REVOLT, December 14, 1825

stand the absolute monarchy, since I am the head of such a government; but I cannot comprehend the representative monarchy—it is a government of lies, of fraud and corruption, and I would withdraw as far as China rather than ever adopt it." [1]

---

[1] Kohler, P. P. (ed. and trans.), *Journey for Our Time: The Journals of the Marquis de Custine,* New York, 1951, pp. 124-125. See also de Grunwald, Constantin, *Tsar Nicholas I,* New York, 1955.

Since Nicholas was not expected to succeed to the throne, he had not been educated in politics and diplomacy. Strongly militaristic, he was a great admirer of Prussianism in all its phases and his contacts therewith were greatly increased by his marriage with Alexandra, daughter of King Frederick William III of Prussia. The main objective of his reign was the development of a strong, well-disciplined army, modeled after Prussian standards. With such an army he thought to police all Europe and thereby bring about an immense expansion of Russian territory and influence. At the same time, through the process of building up his army, he planned to weld the heterogeneous elements of his nation into a homogeneous whole.

Despite his determination to militarize Russia, and the fact that he had put down the Decembrist movement with a firm hand, he, nevertheless, gave consideration to the causes and grievances responsible for the movement before devoting himself exclusively to his main purpose. The chief complaints of the Decembrists were as follows: (1) The legal machinery of the country was antiquated, unsystematic, and inefficient; (2) finances were in a lamentable tangle due to over-issuance of currency and consequent depreciation; (3) opportunities for education were so limited that the majority of the populace was condemned to dense ignorance; and (4) the institution of serfdom was a constantly increasing source of danger to national peace and security. This last point was the one which caused the Decembrists the most concern and the one upon which they were the most insistent.

While Nicholas I disapproved of an extension of educational opportunities, in other respects he recognized the justice of the criticism of the Decembrists and proceeded to institute certain reforms. In 1826 he appointed the statesman, Speransky, to examine the Russian legal code with the intent of bringing order and system out of the existing confusion. Speransky fulfilled his commission in a most able manner. His "Complete Collection of Russian Laws" consisted of forty-five volumes, in which the laws of the empire were arranged in chronological order from 1649 to 1825. The value and importance of this codification to the Russian courts cannot be overestimated. This code became the basis for a "Systematic Code of Laws of the Russian Empire," compiled in 1832.

Nicholas, with the help of Count P. D. Kiselev (1788-1872), an early exponent of emancipation, gave some attention to ameliorating the lot of the serfs. In 1826 slavery was officially prohibited in Siberia. He passed a law in 1827 which forbade the purchase of peasants unless they could be supplied with sufficient land to eke out an existence. This was followed by a law in 1833 which made it illegal to separate families by sale. In 1842, shortly after the publication of Nikolai Gogol's *Dead Souls,* provision was made whereby serfs could be emancipated by their landlords but remained "bound" by the terms imposed. So far as Russian landlords were concerned, this law remained a dead letter. Kiselev devoted his efforts mainly to the Crown peasants, seeking to introduce better agricultural methods, to supply grain in the event of crop failure, and to lay the foundations for self-government among them. However, the condition of the peasants at large was not greatly improved. The landowners, the *pomiestchiki,* were firmly entrenched in their prerogatives and did not permit themselves to be hampered too much by legislation in favor of the peasants. They had become increasingly arrogant and independent in proportion to their privileges and exemptions. Up to the time of Catherine II, land had been granted only in return for service—no service, no land! Catherine desired to advance the interests of certain of her favorites, and in her *nakaz* of 1776 did away with the requirements for land grants. In consequence the owners began to regard their estates strictly in the light of private property and governed themselves accordingly. It is interesting to note that before the time of Catherine II.Russian law did not contain a term which meant "property" in the English sense of the word. During her reign however the word *sobstvennost,* or private property, as we understand it, came into use. Like Catherine, Nicholas was inclined to regard the landlords as the bulwark of the Crown and the "watch-dog" of the state. He believed that emancipation was premature.

As indicated earlier, Nicholas I had no sympathy with the idea of education for the masses. He foresaw that an educated citizenry might put obstacles in the way of his complete militarization of the country and in other ways become difficult to handle. When he turned his attention, therefore, toward public education, he made at first some concessions, by establishing technical schools, teachers' colleges and even several women's institutes, but soon reversed his procedure and tried to limit it even more than heretofore. The dictum went forth from the office of the Minister of Public Instruction, Count S. S. Uvarov (1786-1855), that the gymnasiums were in general to be closed to all save the children of nobles and state officials. Count Uvarov's predecessor had stated that knowledge to be useful should be used sparingly like salt in proportion to the people's circumstances and needs. He maintained further that it would be actually harmful to teach the masses to read. The children of merchants and mechanics were given limited instruction in special secondary schools, but were discouraged from seeking a higher education.

The emperor also regarded the universities with a certain suspicion as institutions for fomenting radicalism. Once he remarked while passing the University of Moscow, "There is the wolf's den." The universities, together with the gymnasiums, were reorganized upon strict military lines and placed under the supervision of pronounced reactionaries. The maximum number of students at a given university was not permitted to exceed 300, and the curriculum was curtailed, philosophy being one of the subjects eliminated. Although foreign languages and literatures were likewise curtailed, greater emphasis was placed upon the study of the Russian language, literature, and history. Study abroad by professors or students was emphatically discouraged. This type of "higher" education was designed to turn out a number of standardized individuals of safe mediocrity who could be relied upon not to engage in too much thinking. Very often it attained its purpose, but not infrequently it also produced a rebel who dared to think for himself, and whose thoughts were often radical and anarchistic.

Before 1825 the intelligentsia,[1] or intellectual class, was made up entirely of nobles. By reason of their position and training, these intellectuals tended to be conservatives, who accepted the established order without much desire for change. This is the reason that the Decembrist movement was such an innovation and made so great an impression upon all classes, since heretofore, with the exception of a feeble effort in 1730, no such revolutionary tendencies had been observable among the nobles. The early concessions of Nicholas I in the matter of popular education, inaugurated with a view to satisfying these Decembrists, put education within the reach of an entirely new class, the *raznotchintsy* (plebeian, commoner), who eagerly and enthusiastically embraced the opportunities offered. When the emperor, alarmed by this zeal for education, repented of his liberality and imposed restrictions, it was too late. The young people of the *raznotchintsy* had had a taste of knowledge and were not to be restrained. If they were forbidden to attend the higher institutions of learning, they studied either privately or with the aid of tutors. This encouraged the practice of studying privately for an examination covering several grades of a government gymnasium. Passing such an examination entitled the student to a certificate or diploma, the latter of which admitted him to the university. The student was said to *externitchat;* he himself was called an *extern.* The new intellectual class had had experiences very different from those of the nobles. Its mem-

---

[1] See pp. 260-261.

bers had been hampered by discriminatory laws and had even suffered oppression. In consequence they were much more susceptible to radical and advanced ideas than the earlier intelligentsia. The influence of these newcomers was such as to change entirely the face of the Russian intelligentsia, so that through succeeding generations this order of society manifested more and more revolutionary tendencies.

For the purpose of preventing a recurrence of the Decembrist uprising, Nicholas I organized in 1826 a police division, which was designated as the Third Division, or *Gendarmerie*. This body had instructions to crush without mercy any demonstrations of dissatisfaction or revolt. In order that its members might not be troubled by any conscientious scruples, they were selected for their brutality and lack of education. As a result, police standards, which had risen considerably under Catherine II, sank to a very low level. Under its control, freedom of speech and freedom of the press almost vanished from the land. No group or individual was safe from its high-handed repression and abuse. Even conservatives, such as Yuri Samarin (1819-1876) and Fyodor Dostoyevsky (1822-1881), fell victims to its suspicions. The establishment of the "police state" drove radicals underground, and Russian writers resorted to fiction as the only available medium for the expression of social and political thought. The *Gendarmerie* retained its power until 1917 and was responsible for much suffering and loss of life.

The Jewish population in Russia had grown considerably despite manifestations of ill will and governmental restrictions. The restrictions imposed upon them were of two kinds, namely, religious and economic. The Orthodox clergy, who acted as tutors for the future rulers of Russia and the nobility, had been in the habit of instilling in them the most bitter hatred against Protestants, Roman Catholics, and most of all against the Jews.[1] This method of instruction, from a modern standpoint, vicious in the extreme, had the result of breeding great intolerance, which found vent in discriminatory religious laws from which the Jews as a minority group suffered especially.

As has been mentioned before, Catherine II did not indulge in religious persecutions and even offered an asylum to the persecuted of other lands; nevertheless, she placed restrictions upon the Jews. She was constrained to do this both by the clergy and by certain business people, who were finding it increasingly difficult to compete successfully with the Jews. Catherine, therefore, in 1791 established a Pale of Settlement, or

---

[1] This practice continued to 1917. See Alexander, Grand Duke of Russia, *Once a Grand Duke*, pp. 91-93; Graham, Stephen, *Tsar of Freedom: Alexander II* (1935), pp. 72, 237.

segregated district, in which the Jews were compelled to live. In these districts, or Ghettos, they came in contact with few Russians other than uneducated peasants, together with a few unfriendly and prejudiced members of the clergy and public officials. These latter oppressed and bled the Jews whenever the occasion offered. Educational opportunities being as limited as they were, Jews had not the least chance of entering Russian schools. Consequently they remained entirely ignorant of the Russian language and Russian life. They lived to themselves and used the Talmud as their sole spiritual and cultural guide. It is not surprising, therefore, that by reason of association with the most ignorant and oppressive among the Gentiles, they began to regard all of them with detestation and distrust. On the other hand, any members of the upper classes, who occasionally came in contact with the Jews, considered them uncultured and often lacking in cleanliness. Thus there existed mutual misunderstanding and hostility. Despite this, however, the Jews were very loyal to the emperors and built up industry greatly in their districts.

This, then, was the situation at the accession of Nicholas I, who had his own ideas concerning the handling of the Jewish problem in his territories. Under his personal supervision, almost 600 laws were promulgated concerning the Jews, most of which were in line with his general policy of militarizing and amalgamating the diverse elements of his empire. In 1827, for the first time, Jews were required to render active service in the army. Heretofore it was generally accepted that, if conscripted, they could pay a specified sum for exemption. Nicholas, however, looked upon this service as an effective method of solving the Jewish problem. Recruits were taken from the ages of twelve to twenty-five for a compulsory military service of twenty-five years. The emperor foresaw that during this long period, far from their homes, they would not only become superlatively well-trained soldiers, but they would also forget their early religious teaching and accept the Orthodox faith. This amounted to compulsory conversion.

In order to encourage still further the acceptance of the Orthodox faith, the government resorted to various expedients, not the least of which was the offer of all the rights and privileges of Christians to baptized Jews. Two measures in their favor also met with response and approbation from some of the more far-sighted among them. One opened Russian schools to the Jews, the other made it possible for them to enter into agricultural pursuits. However, because in the past they had frequently been the victims of tricks and deception, the majority of them looked with suspicion upon any overtures of good will on the part of the government, sensing therein a subtle attack which would rob them of their Judaism. It is unfortunate in the extreme that there was not a more general response among them to the agricultural program. Had they left the congested cities and settled upon the land they would have escaped much persecution, and the country would not have been disgraced by pogroms. There were, to be sure, many Jewish colonies established in the provinces of Ekaterinoslav (now Dnepropetrovsk) and Kherson, while by the time of the Revolution of 1917, some 100,000 Jews were engaged in tilling the soil. These Jewish farmers had not suffered nearly so much persecution during the years as had their coreligionists in the cities.

It will be recalled that during the reign of Alexei there were two movements representing opposing theories as to how Russia could best fulfill her destiny. Under the impetus of the Decembrist uprising, these movements became well-organized groups, possessed of well-defined ideology. At this time they came to be known as Slavophiles and Westernizers.[1] The leaders of the former, in theory at least, were A. S. Khomyakov, the Kireyevsky brothers, Yuri Samarin, and the Aksakov brothers. They held that if Russia would assert herself and follow her own natural lines of development, she would attain results beneficial to herself and to all humanity. Never would she realize her true destiny by imitation or adaptation of Western ideas, for every nation as well as every individual was possessed of a unique personality, and only by full development of this true personality could success be attained. Furthermore they believed that in the Orthodox faith Russia had preserved the purest form of Christianity, far superior to anything which the West had to offer. Thus when Peter the Great had weakened the influence of the Orthodox faith and had forcibly introduced Western innovations, he had torn the land asunder, wresting from it its true tradition, and doing incomparable harm thereby. The only salvation lay in a return to former beliefs, ideals, and modes of life. It occasions no surprise that Nicholas I was in reality a Slavophile in outlook, since for him Orthodoxy and autocracy were the inviolable principles of government.

In contrast to all of this, the Westernizers, whose leaders were V. G. Belinsky, T. N. Granovsky, A. I. Herzen, I. S. Turgenev, and others, advocated following the course of European progress. They opposed the reactionary clergy and favored liberalism or socialism in politics. For them a return to the old order of the days preceding Peter I was equivalent to a return to the dark ages. They approved of Peter's reforms and held that he had rendered an inestimable service by his program of Europeanization. Both Slavophiles and Westernizers

---

See pp. 200-202.

consulted German philosophy, as expressed by Schelling and Hegel, in an effort to find support for their theories.

The most important internal improvements of the reign of Nicholas I were in the field of transportation and communications. In 1838 a private company undertook the construction of Russia's first railroad, which was completed between St. Petersburg and Tsarskoye Selo, a distance of sixteen miles. By 1842 another railroad was begun between St. Petersburg and Moscow, this time at state expense. The completion of this road took eight years and cost 100,000,000 rubles, even with the employment of slave labor. By 1875 there had been constructed in Russia 17,000 *versts* [1] of railroad, or nearly 13,000 miles. In 1851 St. Petersburg and Moscow were also connected by telegraph. The general backwardness of transportation and communications facilities was to prove a serious handicap during the Crimean War.

FOREIGN AFFAIRS

Nicholas I did not favor revolution abroad any more than at home and was ever ready to throw the weight of his influence against it. He never permitted himself to forget that the Decembrists had acquired their revolutionary ideas from the West. The chief object of his foreign policy, as far as Western Europe was concerned, was the maintenance of the settlement reached at the Congress of Vienna. For example, when the Bourbons in France were overthrown by the July Revolution of 1830, Nicholas prepared to intervene in their favor and was only prevented from so doing by the outbreak of a revolution in Poland.[2] At Munchengratz in 1833 Nicholas and Metternich reached an understanding which virtually amounted to a revival of the principles and policies of the Holy Alliance. For the next fifteen years Nicholas remained in fact the foremost leader of reaction in Europe, in opposition to the dangerous doctrines of liberalism, socialism, and nationalism. In 1848-1849, when most of Europe, including Belgium, France, Italy, Germany and Austria, was swept by revolt, Nicholas made one last attempt to save the European system established at Vienna. In response to the request of Emperor Francis Joseph of Austria in 1849 he dispatched

---

[1] A *verst* is equal to 0.6629 miles.

[2] Toward the close of the year 1830, the Poles, encouraged by the French and Belgian revolutions, raised an army of 80,000 men and staged a revolt of their own. They took possession of Warsaw, forcing the troops of Grand Duke Constantine to evacuate the city. They then demanded their independence, together with the surrender of Lithuania and Western Russia. The emperor's answer was to send a strong force against Poland under General Diebitsch. The revolt was crushed, and Poland was made part of the empire and divided into provinces like the rest of Russia.

General Ivan Paskevitch (1782-1856) and 100,000 troops to put down the Hungarian revolt led by the man who had become Europe's number one revolutionary, Louis Kossuth. The fact that Kossuth's forces included more than a thousand Polish refugees may well have contributed to the emperor's zeal, but his action served immeasurably to foster the development of anti-Russian sentiment in Hungary. His service to Austria at this time earned him the title of "the policeman of Europe."

Wars in the Near and Middle East broke out shortly after the accession of Nicholas I. The first of these was with Persia, where English officers had entered the service of the shah, and the mullahs preached a holy war against Russia. The Persian forces, which initiated the conflict, retreated before the army of General Paskevitch, who crossed the Araxes, seized the important stronghold of Yerevan, and proceeded to march on Teheran. In alarm the shah, who failed to receive the expected aid from England, hastened to conclude the Treaty of Turkmantchay in 1828, by which the Russians acquired the left bank of the Araxes, and a large part of Armenia, including Yerevan. In addition Persia paid a huge indemnity of 36,000,000 rubles and abandoned her claim to the Caucasus. Almost immediately, however, the Muridist revolution, a religious movement, broke out among the Moslem mountaineers in the Caucasus. Under the leadership of able *imams* and sheikhs, the best known of whom were Kazi-Mullah, who was killed in 1831, and Shamyl (1797-1871), who was captured by the Russians in 1859, the revolutionaries maintained a long and stubborn resistance and were not fully subdued until the reign of Alexander II. The conquest of the Caucasus took in all 137 years, from 1722 to 1859.

Scarcely had peace been concluded with Persia, when Russia was again involved in war, this time with Turkey. This conflict grew out of the Greek struggle for independence (1821-1829). For some time, in conformity with the sentiment of the Holy Alliance, Europe rendered no formal military assistance to the Greek rebels. In Russia, Alexander's opposition to revolution was somewhat compromised by the fact that the *Hetairia Philike,* a leading Greek revolutionary society, had been founded in Odessa in 1814 and many wealthy Greek merchants of that city extended very considerable financial aid to their rebel kinsmen. Although the possibility of supporting Orthodox Christians against the Turks was an idea that traditionally appealed to Russians, Alexander nevertheless promptly disavowed Prince Ypsilanti, pro-Russian leader of the Greek revolt and, until his death in 1825, refused to intervene actively on the side of the Greeks. However, his more militaristic brother, Nicholas I, who stood for the *status quo* in Western Europe, by no means applied the same principle to Turkey and the Balkans. The ruthless campaign of the sultan's vassal, Ibrahim Pasha of Egypt, against the Greeks had aroused popular opinion throughout Europe. This led to joint intervention on the part of England, France, and Russia to enforce a diplomatic settlement, and when that failed their combined fleets destroyed a Turko-Egyptian squadron in the Battle of Navarino in 1827. In the following year Nicholas, acting unilaterally, declared war on Turkey, and the Russian army, supported by the Serbs, almost reached Constantinople. The Treaty of Adrianople, which brought the war to a close in September 1829, was highly favorable to Russia and marked an important stage in the dismemberment of the Ottoman Empire. By its terms Russia gained possession of the mouth of the Danube and the coast of the Black Sea to Poti. Turkey also acceded to Russia's demand for a protectorate over Orthodox peoples living in Turkish territories and granted commercial privileges to Russian subjects in the same regions. In addition to her concessions to Russia, Turkey agreed to recognize the independence of the Greeks (1830) and to open the Bosporus and Dardanelles to friendly nations. Moreover certain dependencies of Turkey, namely, Moldavia, Wallachia, Serbia, and the principalities of the Danube, were granted autonomy under Turkish suzerainty.

Nicholas might have exacted far more by the Treaty of Adrianople, but he preferred to moderate his demands and pursue a policy of expansion by peaceful penetration, in conformity with the tactics of Catherine II in the Middle and Far East and those of Paul in the Near East. Therefore, when Mehemet Ali, the Pasha of Egypt, began hostilities against the sultan in 1833, Nicholas sent a force to Asia Minor to protect the Bosporus. This resulted in the Treaty of Unkiar-Skelessi in August 1833, by which the emperor's diplomacy scored a great victory, since Turkey agreed to close the Bosporus and the Dardanelles to the warships of all foreign powers, with the exception of Russia. With this treaty Russian influence at Constantinople reached its zenith. The implementation of its terms would have made a Russian satellite of the Ottoman Empire.

The unilateral policy of Nicholas in regard to Turkey in 1828 and 1833 aroused the fear of Austria and the antagonism of England and France. In spite of the Holy Alliance, Austria found herself increasingly at odds with Russia over the Christian principalities in the Balkans as a result of the Treaty of Adrianople. Since the reign of Catherine II England had watched, with increasing concern, the expansion of Russia at the expense of Turkey, Persia, and Afghanistan. With the appointment of Viscount Palmerston as foreign secretary in 1830, Anglo-Russian relations began to deteriorate rapidly. France, as the ally of Mehemet Ali, had her own reasons for discomfiture with regard to Russian policy toward Turkey. The groundwork was being laid for the formation of an anti-Russian bloc, which was before long to challenge Russia in the Crimean War.

In 1839 Nicholas, envisaging an opportunity to collaborate with England in the solution of the Turkish problem, agreed to let the Treaty of Unkiar-Skelessi lapse. In 1840, in a move to isolate France, the four great powers—Russia, Prussia, England, and Austria—signed the London Convention, which defined the position of Mehemet Ali in the Ottoman Empire and closed the Straits of the Bosporus and Dardanelles to the warships of all foreign powers in time of peace. These terms were confirmed by the Treaty of London in 1841, which included France. Still seeking English collaboration, Nicholas visited London in 1844, in order to obtain some assurance of English neutrality in the event of another Russian war against Turkey, or English participation in the dismemberment of Turkey, which he labeled "the Sick Man of Europe." His visit did little to allay English suspicions of Russian designs on the Ottoman Empire.

The foreign policy of Nicholas I during the breathing spell of the 1840's was characterized by two fixed ideas: (1) a firm determination to stop the spread of democracy and liberalism in Europe; and (2) the acquisition of the Dardanelles and Constantinople. In reality Nicholas achieved neither of his objectives. Not only did he fail to call a halt to democratic and liberal trends in Europe, but that continent became a hotbed of revolution in 1848, the year which marked the appearance of Karl Marx's *Communist Manifesto*. By using Russian troops for the suppression of revolt abroad, Nicholas brought Russia into still further disrepute among Western liberals as a reactionary and autocratic country. In the second place Nicholas's bid for Constantinople and the Dardanelles led directly to the Crimean War (1853-1856).

The immediate cause of the Crimean War, however, grew out of the efforts of Napoleon III of France to strengthen French influence and prestige in the Near East, particularly in the Holy Land. He demanded and obtained from Turkey concessions for Roman Catholics living in the Holy Land. He obtained for them also possession of the keys of the Church of Bethlehem, which by the Treaty of Küchük Kainarji (1774) had been assigned to the keeping of the Orthodox Church. Nicholas promptly demanded of the Turks that the treaty be respected and Orthodox rights restored. When Turkey temporized, Nicholas countered with a demand for the recognition of Russian claims for protection over Orthodox Christians throughout the Ottoman Empire, and Russian troops invaded the Turkish provinces of Moldavia and Wallachia to enforce these demands. The sultan, encouraged by Lord Stratford (Stratford Canning), the English ambassador in Constantinople, to believe that English and French aid would be forthcoming, declared war on Russia on October 1, 1853.

Russia's first move was to dispatch Russian warships to Sinope, where a Turkish squadron was destroyed. Anglo-French naval forces entered the Black Sea, and, after a futile effort to achieve a diplomatic settlement at Vienna, England and France declared war on Russia on March 27, 1854. They were later joined by the ambitious King of Sardinia. Austria and Prussia, from whom Nicholas expected a display of friendship, preserved a hostile neutrality. Russia was thus left alone to face an enemy alignment of the chief powers of Western Europe. In September 1854 the allied forces landed in Crimea near Eupatoria and laid siege to Sevastopol. The city surrendered after a siege which lacked only fifteen days of lasting a year. Nicholas did not live to see its downfall, for he died on March 2, 1855. It was rumored that he committed suicide by taking poison because he was unable to outlive the defeat of all his plans and the collapse of Russian military power. Peace was concluded in 1856 by his son, Alexander II, under the terms of the Treaty of Paris.

The Crimean War revealed the backwardness of tsarist military and naval equipment and Russia's lack of adequate transportation and communications facilities. Russian generals even lacked good maps of the Crimean peninsula. Whereas the Russian fleet was still predominately a sailing fleet, the ironclad British and French warships were run by steam, and their guns had a range double that of the Russian shore batteries. It must not be forgotten, however, that the Russians not only fought in the Crimea, but had to maintain fronts in the Caucasus and the Baltic, while large forces were immobilized throughout the war on the Austrian frontier. Even in the Pacific, units of the Anglo-French fleets attacked the port of Petropavlovsk on the Kamchatka Peninsula in 1854. In spite of this "encirclement," Russian troops after the fall of Sevastopol won a signal victory against the Turks at Kars in Asia. In the final analysis, the Crimean War demonstrated rather clearly how ineffective was naval power without the backing of huge armies, when pitted against a great land power. At no time did Anglo-French military forces penetrate more than a few miles beyond the Crimean coast. For classic literature on this war, the reader will do well to consult *Sevasto-*

pol, three sketches by Leo Tolstoy, who himself took part in the Crimean campaign.

All the belligerent nations suffered heavily in the war, although Russia's loss of a quarter of a million men was the greatest. The French lost 80,000 men and the English 22,000. In view of the fame of Florence Nightingale, whose name is ordinarily associated with the care of the wounded in this war, it is perhaps worth while to note that the famous Russian surgeon, Nicholas Pirogov (1810-1881), did much to promote the development of antiseptic surgery in the field, established first-aid stations behind the Russian lines, and organized an order of nursing sisters to tend the Russian wounded. One of these nurses, Darya Sevastopolskaya, became as celebrated in Russian annals as Florence Nightingale in England. The Treaty of Paris destroyed at one stroke the results of two centuries of effort on the part of Russian rulers. While Sevastopol remained in her possession, Russia temporarily lost control of the Black Sea. She was also compelled to relinquish her exclusive protectorate over Orthodox Christians in the Near East, all the great powers sharing the responsibility for Christian residents in Turkish lands. By the cession of southern Bessarabia Russia was likewise excluded from the mouth of the Danube. In addition the Bosporus and the Dardanelles were closed to the armed fleets of all nations. Thus the military prestige which Russia had built up under Suvorov and Kutuzov, and the stabilizing influence she had been able to exert throughout Europe since 1815, were swept away. The Treaty of Paris sounded the beginning of the end of tsarist expansion in Europe. More important still, Russia remained isolated from the Concert of Europe, while, in the years that followed the Treaty of Paris, the balance of power in the West was completely upset by the rise of Germany and Italy as national states.

7

From Liberator to the Last Emperor (Alexander II to Nicholas II)

1855-1894

REIGN OF EMPEROR ALEXANDER II (1855-1881)

LTHOUGH Alexander became emperor by the death of his father on March 2, 1855, the continuation of the Crimean War and the events following its conclusion delayed his coronation until the next year. Because of the noteworthy and beneficial reforms which he introduced into his distracted country, he was very much praised by subsequent generations, who bestowed upon him such titles as the White Tsar, the Liberator, the Great Reformer, the Abraham Lincoln of Russia. At the beginning of his reforms the Westernizers rejoiced greatly in his liberalism.

Born in St. Petersburg on April 29, 1818, Alexander became emperor at the age of thirty-six. Whereas his father, Nicholas I, had received no special training for the responsibilities of an emperor, inasmuch as his accession had seemed remote, all of Alexander's training was directed with a view to preparing him adequately for his high office. His education had been most liberal and his experience in statecraft most adequate by the time he was called upon to assume the reins of government. One of his tutors was the poet Zhukovsky, who translated the *Iliad* and the *Odyssey* into Russian and whose nobility of character was generally recognized. At the age of twenty-three, he married Maria Alexandrovna, Princess of Hesse-Darmstadt. They had eight children, six sons and two daughters.

ALEXANDER II ANNOUNCING TO HIS COURT
THE EMANCIPATION OF THE SERFS

INTERNAL REFORMS

It is no secret that shortly before his death, Nicholas I, with unusual honesty and recognition of fact, admitted to his son that he had erred in his Slavophile and autocratic policies. The crumbling of the Russian defense before a Western European attack had made it clear that a government of such extreme autocracy as that which Nicholas I had instituted was suited, if at all, only to Asiatic peoples. This was generally admitted even by enthusiastic Slavophiles. Thus Aksakov affirmed that "Sevastopol fell that God might reveal all the rottenness of the system of government." Yet another ardent Slavophile, Samarin, said: "We have fallen, not before the forces of the Western Alliance, but as a result of our own internal weakness."

Nicholas advised Alexander, therefore, to follow more liberal methods upon his accession. Although publicly Alexander expressed diplomatic vindication of his father's policy and attempted to smooth over the humiliating terms of the Treaty of Paris, he lost no time in instituting a different policy of his own, devised to repair the ravages of past mistakes. The day of his coronation was marked by the issuance of a manifesto of thirty-eight articles. Among its provisions was an amnesty for surviving Decembrists of the 1825 uprising and for Polish conspirators of the 1831 revolution. Moreover, children who had been forcibly inducted into the army and navy were to be returned to their families and permitted to make their own choice of a profession.

With these beginnings, Alexander II undertook at once the major problems which confronted him and, in the course of time, instituted reforms in respect to the following: serfdom, zemstvos, court procedure, and universal military service. We shall now proceed to consider his reforms in order, beginning with the one which he considered of major importance.

At the time of Alexander's accession, the population of Russia was about 70,000,000. Of this number 47,000,000 were living in a more or less arduous condition of serfdom. Some of them, to be sure, were free in everything but name. These were the 20,000,000 Crown peasants, who had become dependents of the state by the process of redemption previously mentioned. In addition to these, there were 4,700,000 on appanages, or *Udyely*. These peasants had their own communities, wherein they exercised a degree of self-government and managed their private affairs in accordance with their own traditions. The problem which they presented to the state was comparatively easy to handle, consisting as it did of little more than official confirmation of the freedom which they already enjoyed. By the middle of 1858, an edict of the government made them free in law as well as in fact.

The cancerous spot in the system of serfdom, which required the most diplomatic treatment to effect its cure, was to be found in private ownership of serfs; actually some 22,400,000 peasants were virtually slaves of individual landowners. The bondage of the 1,400,000 of these who served as domestic servants (*Dvorovie* or *Kholopy*) was especially strict; Alexander II directed his efforts, therefore, toward the abolition of this type of servitude.

He was obliged to move with caution and circumspection, for, although a large majority of the people was in favor of freeing the serfs, there was an opposing faction, composed of rich landowners and reactionary public officials, who were both influential and powerful. It was necessary to secure their support before a drastic reform could be instituted with any hope of success. The emperor, therefore, sought to win the co-operation of these classes by an appeal to practical reasoning. In an address delivered before their leaders in Moscow, he pointed out succinctly that it was much better for them to handle the problem while it was still under their control, than to wait until their hands were forced by uprisings, which would result in destruction of property and loss of life. "Better that the reform should come from above than wait until serfdom is abolished from below." This made a great impression, for the owners of the serfs could not fail to recognize the soundness of his reasoning. Every effort was made to convince the landlords that the existing system of land tenure was becoming economically more unprofitable and prevented the adoption of more up-to-date agricultural methods. Whereas this situation had long been apparent to many impoverished landlords, those who had serfs out on the *obrok* system, working in factories or at some trade, and who derived a handsome income thereby, were particularly hard to convince. Even those landlords converted to emancipation were likely to hold out for compensation in order that they might use the capital so acquired to modernize their farm equipment and agricultural methods.

The minister of the interior, Count Sergei Lanskoy (1787-1862) and the adjutant-general, Y. I. Rostovtsev (1803-1860), took an active part in the preparations for emancipation. Committees established in each province submitted recommendations, which were in turn examined by the Tsar's General Committee. Alexander himself toured the provinces to get a first-hand picture of conditions and spent hours in session with his General Committee. The main issue to be decided was whether to grant the peasant his personal freedom, without land, as in the case of the Baltic Provinces (1816-1819), and thus create a huge landless proletariat in Russia, or to grant the peasant both freedom and land, a procedure which, unless accompanied by compensation for the landlord, might well lead to the ruin of the latter. The state treasury, following the Crimean War, was scarcely in a position to shoulder the financial burden. It was therefore concluded that if the peasant was to receive the land, he himself must pay for it. Practical considerations for the handling of the matter necessitated long discussions, deliberations, and adjustments, but finally on March 3, 1861, the sixth anniversary of his accession, the emperor issued the manifesto abolishing serfdom from Russia. If the reign of Alexander had been distinguished solely by the issuance of this manifesto it would merit a place of importance in Russian annals, and he himself would be entitled to the gratitude accorded him by his subjects.

Despite the emancipation, however, the peasant problem was far from solved. The solution adopted was essentially a compromise, by which the landlords received no formal compensation for services lost but retained the ownership of the land. The peasants continued to live on the land and till the soil, but as freemen they were obliged to pay for these privileges either in money, produce, or services. Provision was made whereby the liberated peasant could purchase land and pay for it over a period of years. The system of redemption was, however, highly complicated. Where the peasants agreed to take one-quarter of their allotment, the issue could be settled with the landlords direct. If they had 20 percent of the purchase price available, the state would advance the balance to the landlord in the expectation of collecting from the peasants later. In accordance with these arrangements, the Crown peasant received an *average* allotment of twenty-three acres, the appanage peasant one of fifteen acres, and the privately owned serf nine acres. Although circumstances varied considerably in different parts of the country, except in the north and west the liberated serfs obtained less land than they had tilled prior to emancipation, and they were often handicapped by lack of pasturage, hayfields, wood, and even water. In the majority of cases the transfer of the land was not accompanied by any move to consolidate the strip holdings of the peasant, and an already antiquated system of cultivation was therefore perpetuated. By the death of Alexander in 1881, however, more than 80 percent of the landowners had sold out to the peasants.

One further aspect of the process of emancipation deserves some consideration, since it helps to explain much of Russia's later economic and social difficulties. The land thus acquired by the peasants did not belong to them individually but was held in communal ownership by the *mir*, or village commune, an institution of peculiarly Slavonic origin. It was the *mir* that assumed responsibility for the payment of the peasant's redemption dues, his taxes, and his forced labor. The peasant soon found that his hard-won liberty was qualified by the fact that the authority of his local *mir* had superseded the authority of his former landlord.[1] Although theoretically the principle of equality prevailed among the village peasants who comprised the *mir,* in practice the institution came to be dominated by its more aggressive and well-to-do representatives. The resentment of the peasant, who was often compelled to pay more than the market value for land he regarded as his own in the first place, and who was in the process subjected to restrictions imposed upon his household by the *mir,* was amply demonstrated by the more than 2000 peasant uprisings which occurred in the country from 1861 to 1863. In view of later developments in Russia, it is important to emphasize here that, although each peasant member of the *mir* shared in the responsibility of paying off the purchase price of the land, none of it became his private possession. It is apparent that such an arrangement closely resembled a Soviet *kolkhoz,* or collective farm, of the 1920's and in fact served as the best possible training for subsequent economic developments.

It should be recognized that the problem of land-ownership was not efficiently handled and that the failure to do so without doubt precipitated the Revolutions of 1905 and 1917. What could have been done to produce more general satisfaction and thereby avoid the aforementioned social catastrophies? It has been most ably demonstrated that there were two possible solutions, either of which would in all probability have prevented later misfortunes.[2] The government might have elected to give the peasants merely their personal freedom and to assist individuals, rather than groups or communes, to purchase the land from the original owners. As a second mode of procedure, the government might have taken over the land with suitable compensation to its former owners and then parceled it out among the peasants, again on an individual basis. In either case, by the year 1917, there would have been in Russia millions of *farmers* instead of millions of *peasants,* who would

---

[1] See Maynard, Sir John, *Russia in Flux,* N. Y., 1948, Chapter II, "The Peasant in the Nineteenth Century," pp. 22-38. On the whole subject of peasant conditions from the emancipation to 1917, see Robinson, G. T., *Rural Russia Under the Old Regime,* N. Y., 1932, pp. 64 ff.

[2] In this matter the author concurs entirely with George Vernadsky. See *A History of Russia,* New Haven, Yale University Press, 1930, pp. 154-155. See also Maxwell, B. W., *The Soviet State,* 1934, pp. 258-259.

have constituted a conservative, agricultural middle class. It was for the purpose of developing such a class that Premier Stolypin instituted his reforms of 1906-1911, but it was then too late. There is no doubt that the success of Russia's social revolution was due to the lack of a middle class.

The stability of any country is in a large measure dependent upon the middle class, and in proportion as this class is strong and well established, the danger of a social revolution along communist or fascist lines is lessened. The capitalist, with extensive schemes and high ambitions, may risk his entire capital in a speculative venture. He may lose everything, but on the other hand, his gains may exceed all dreams of avarice. He enjoys playing for a great stake. The laborer, especially in Europe, has very little to lose while he may gain much by a change in the social order. Hence a revolution becomes his speculative venture. A member of the middle class, however, is in an entirely different position from either of these representatives of two social extremes. He possesses a little property or a small capital, which has cost him years of toil and self-denial to accumulate. He has become accustomed to some modest comforts. A revolution would rob him of all of this and plunge him into an abyss of destitution and privation. He has nothing to gain and everything to lose, hence he is conservative in the extreme. Any government which takes cognizance of its middle class and furthers its interests has little to fear in respect to revolution and communism. This is the case in the United States where the middle class is very large and has a somewhat high standard of living. The chief reason why other European countries did not go communistic after World War I, as did Russia, is to be found in their possession of a relatively large middle class. This explains also why the Soviet government in pursuance of its communistic ends was so ruthless in its treatment of the *kulak* farmers, a product of the Stolypin reforms, 1906-1911. In passing, "If Russia had had a middle class of any size," says Maurice Hindus,[1] "the Bolshevik Revolution might never have become an active fact, or, if it had, it surely would have failed."

The emancipation of the serfs in Russia in 1861 inevitably calls to mind the parallel emancipation of the slaves in the United States in 1863 and invites comparisons. Whereas in the United States the Negroes achieved their freedom only as a result of the prolonged and bloody Civil War (1861-1865), in autocratic Russia the change was inaugurated peaceably after years of investigation and preparation. It is im-

---

[1] *The Great Offensive*, N. Y., 1933, p. 357. See also pp. 357-368. See Chamberlin, W. N., *Russia's Iron Age*, 1934, pp. 228-229.

portant to note that, while in the United States the liberated population constituted a racial minority of Negroes, in Russia the liberated serfs were Russians and no racial antagonism complicated the search for a solution.[1] Aside from this fact, emancipation in Russia was productive of more profound and far-reaching consequences, since the 22,400,000 Russian serfs constituted approximately one-third of the population and were scattered throughout Russia proper, whereas the 3,500,000 Negroes amounted to somewhat less than one-ninth of the population of the United States and were located in one region, the South. Although in both countries the aftermath of liberation involved untold hardship and suffering, in Russia, which remained basically an agricultural country, the effects were perhaps more profound than in America where the rapid industrialization of the North offset in part, for the country as a whole, some of the dislocation that accompanied emancipation. In Russia a considerable number of liberated serfs had been engaged, under the *obrok* system, in manufacturing and trade, and a few had accumulated wealth even prior to their liberation.

With the abolition of serfdom, a change in rural government soon became necessary. Previously the nobility of a province had governed in behalf of all freemen residing therein. In 1864 a form of representative government, known as the zemstvo (from *zemlya,* land), was introduced into thirty-four provinces. Under this order, all property owners were allowed to participate in local affairs, although the nobility had precedence in all respects. By representative vote an "Executive Committee" or "Zemstvo Committee" was elected for a term of three years. This body took charge of the local affairs of a province. By 1870 town government was managed by a similar system. The zemstvos could levy taxes and had the supervision of roads, public charity, public health, and schools. The central government, which had a veto in all matters, was careful to restrict the zemstvo to local affairs and often interfered even in this field. This was especially true in regard to the schools, which, as directed by the zemstvos, were usually more liberal than the government desired. Hence there was considerable governmental supervision of the teaching body. Yet often, in spite of the interference of the government, the zemstvo schools produced noteworthy results in their efforts to banish ignorance from the rural districts. Both the provincial zemstvo and the town government were responsible for much material and cultural progress previous to the Revolution of 1917. If this had not been the case, the Revolution would have been

---

[1] See pp. 202-203.

marked by even more horrors and bloodshed. In 1914 the expenditure of the zemstvos of forty-three provinces was in the neighborhood of 400,000,000 rubles. Of this, the sum of 106,000,000 rubles was devoted to public education. There were 50,000 zemstvo schools employing 80,000 teachers and furnishing instruction to 3,000,000 children. All of this came to an end in 1917.

Of equal importance to the reforms in local government were the reforms in the judiciary in 1864. The most outstanding of these were an alteration and improvement in court procedure, the introduction of trial by jury, and the organization of lawyers into a formal bar. Thus strengthened, the courts operated with a considerable degree of efficiency. Their prestige was enhanced by the recognition of their independence from administrative interference, by provision for better pay and improved training for judges, whose appointment was permanent, and by regulations requiring public hearings in cases that came before these courts. The principle of equality before the law was recognized.

Another important reform of the reign of Alexander was the introduction in 1874 of compulsory universal military service. However, it was by no means so rigid and autocratic as it had been under Nicholas I. Thus the long term of service was shortened to six years, and family ties and responsibilities were respected. An only son, an only grandson, or a son who was the sole support of a family, registered in what was known as the reserve of the Second Category (*Vtoroye Opolt-chenie*). This reserve, previous to World War I, was never called into active service. Likewise recruits possessing a secondary education received consideration in respect to term of service, promotion, and certain privileges. Although the officers of the Guard were drawn exclusively from the aristocracy, the rest of the army was the most democratic institution in all Russia. Here the diverse races and creeds of the great expanse of the empire met on a footing of equality and began to develop a better understanding of each other.

Much of the harsh, restrictive legislation of Nicholas I was repealed, and a more liberal, humanitarian policy adopted. In the army and the imperial tribunals, corporal punishment was legally abolished, although sometimes resorted to, nevertheless. In the peasant tribunals it still remained in force. Censorship of the press was relaxed in its vigilance, and soon there sprang up in St. Petersburg and Moscow periodicals which had a brisk circulation. By 1860 full civil rights were granted to foreign residents, in conformity with the practice followed by other European countries. This did much to break down the barriers which the policy of Nicholas I had created between Russia and her neighbors.

Restrictions were removed from the universities. The number of students was no longer limited to 300; the cost of tuition was lowered, and scholarships were offered for the encouragement of talent and ability.

Alexander II likewise extended many privileges to the Jews. On March 16, 1857, and November 27, 1861, he enacted laws which permitted Jewish scholars, university graduates, wholesale merchants, and manufacturers to reside outside the Pale of Settlement. In 1865 this privilege, with certain restrictions, was also granted to artisans. The emperor would have been glad to abolish the Pales entirely, but he dared not oppose the bureaucracy. The Jews were fully cognizant of his good will, and his policy did more to Russianize them than all previous resorts to force and compulsion. Indeed if the Jews had continued to enjoy these privileges and had been allowed to associate with other citizens on a basis of freedom and equality, by 1917 many of them would have been completely absorbed by the Russian people. The pogroms, following the reign of Alexander II, once more set them apart and made them keenly aware of their Judaism.

In pursuance of his policy of liberalism, Alexander II tried to calm the seething unrest in Poland by granting the country self-government. He appointed Grank Duke Constantine Nikolayevitch as viceroy, because of the latter's Polish sympathies and liberalism, and established complete local autonomy under him. Poland, however, responded to the overtures of the emperor by an outbreak of rebellion in January 1863. Russian garrisons in Poland and Lithuania were attacked, and the revolt began to assume formidable proportions. The seriousness of the situation was further intensified by the possibility of interference by Austria, France, and England on the basis of the international settlement at Vienna. The reactionaries now took the opportunity to charge that the reforms had been carried to extremes and were the cause of all sorts of confusion and disaster. The emperor yielded to their insistence, suppressed the revolt without mercy, and then deprived the Poles of local autonomy. In order to gain some support in the rebellious territory, he granted privileges to the peasants at the expense of the nobles.

Among his other problems Alexander confronted serious financial difficulties, some of which emanated from the huge expenditures and wholesale graft that occurred during the Crimean War, some from the excess of imports over exports subsequent to the war, as a result of which there was an alarming depreciation of the ruble. The emperor secured an able financial administrator in M. Kh. Reutern (1820-1890), who directed his efforts toward economy at home and the increase of exports abroad, especially the export of wheat. With this last object in

view, he encouraged the construction of railways to Russia's leading
ports on the Baltic and Black Seas. Incidentally, the export of Russian
grain to western Europe adversely affected American farm prices and
contributed to an agricultural depression in the United States. The
Russian economy was continually handicapped, however, by the difficulty of attracting foreign capital, and Russia was forced in the main to
fall back on her own resources. As previously indicated, there were only
13,000 miles of railroad in Russia by 1875, as compared with the 35,000
miles in operation in the United States at the close of the Civil War. It
is significant that even the $7,200,000 secured from the sale of Alaska
to America in 1867 were earmarked by Reutern for railroad construction. Although by dint of great effort Reutern succeeded temporarily
in stabilizing the financial situation in Russia by 1875, the renewal of
war with Turkey in 1877 threatened to undo much of the good he
accomplished.

FOREIGN POLICY

The defeat of Russia in the Crimean War by no means put an end to
Russian efforts in the direction of territorial expansion. It was scarcely
to be expected that Russia, which held more than 1000 miles of coastline on the Black Sea, would accept indefinitely the unrealistic provision
in the Treaty of Paris that excluded her fleet from that sea and forbade
the construction of fortifications along its shores. Russians likewise
regarded their exclusion from the mouth of the Danube as intolerable.
Alexander II merely awaited a favorable opportunity to dispose of
"these two nightmares." Moreover, Anglo-French success in "block-
ing" Russian expansion in the direction of the Mediterranean in 1856
merely deflected the tsarist program of expansion to the Middle and
Far East, with the result that England, in particular, soon had further
occasion for anxiety.

The favorable opportunity Alexander sought was afforded by the
Franco-Prussian War (1870-1871). Under the circumstances it was
greatly to Bismarck's advantage to promote discord between England
and Russia, while Germany settled her score with France. In October
1870, therefore, with the prior consent and perhaps even at the instigation of Bismarck, Prince Alexander Gortchakov, the Russian foreign
minister, announced Russia's unilateral denunciation of the Black Sea
clauses of the Treaty of Paris. In return for the "benevolent neutrality"
of Russia during the Austro-Prussian War (1866) and the Franco-
Prussian War, Prussia at once refused to join England in any protest
against Russian action. As a result, the offensive clauses were formally

repealed by the signatories of the Treaty of Paris at a conference held in London in 1871. At the same time, in a face-saving gesture, the powers reaffirmed those clauses which provided for the closing of the Straits to the warships of all nations, except at the invitation of the Sultan of Turkey.

Meanwhile, news of Russian expansion in Central Asia began to arouse concern among the European powers, especially England. After the successful completion of the conquest of the Caucasus in 1859, the Russian army continued its efforts to revive the military prestige of the Tsarist Empire by new victories in Asia and to establish a defensible frontier there. In a rapid succession of victories during the next twenty years the Russians captured the Uzbek city of Tashkent (1865) and made it the capital of the new province of Turkestan, occupied Samarkand (1868), the famous capital of the Empire of Tamerlane, and converted the Khanate of Bokhara into a Russian protectorate. England, greatly alarmed at the strides the tsarist forces were taking in the direction of India, proposed the recognition of a series of "buffer states," including Afghanistan. Although Russia somewhat tentatively accepted this proposition, the instability of conditions in Central Asia and the absence of a natural frontier led to the occupation of Khiva (1873) and of the Khanate of Kokand (1876), thereby extending Russian frontiers to the mountainous northwest borders of China. Russian forces then proceeded to subjugate the warlike Turkoman tribes in the Trans-Caspian region. Thus Russia carved out for herself a new and rich Asiatic empire. In the wake of Russian armies came merchants and traders. It was not long until American cotton was being cultivated in Central Asia. About the same time Russian relations with Persia assumed a new aspect, when in 1878 the shah requested the Russian government to undertake the training of the Persian armed forces.

Before the Crimean War, official Russian opinion was divided as to the wisdom of expansion in the Far East. Such expansion as took place was mainly the product of individual initiative. As a result of the Russian defeat in Europe, however, the monarchy lent official sanction and support to prominent and colorful Russian expansionists like Count Nikolai N. Muraviev (1809-1881). Indeed Muraviev may be said to have established the pattern for a Russian foreign policy in the Pacific, based upon two premises: cultivation of friendship toward the United States and expansion at the expense of China. Judging by materials extant he was the first to suggest, as early as January 1853, the cession of Russian America, including Alaska, to the United States as a guarantee against any future clash between the two countries. As a result of his energy and activity Russia's territorial gains in the Far East were considerable. By the Treaty of Aigun in 1858 the Amur region, which had been abandoned to China in 1689 by the Treaty of Nertchinsk, was regained. In the same year the Treaty of Tientsin conferred upon Russia the extraterritorial privileges already acquired by other Western powers. Two years later, in 1860, Russia acquired the Maritime Province as a result of the Treaty of Peking. The Chinese government recognized the right of Russia to engage in free trade in Mongolia in 1862. Within another ten years there was a flourishing seaport and naval station at Vladivostok on the Sea of Japan. Nor was Russian expansion confined to the mainland in the years that followed. In 1875 Russia entered into an agreement with Japan, whereby she exchanged the Kurile Islands for the southern half of the Island of Sakhalin.

Realizing the hostility of the European powers, Russia from time to time had sought a *rapprochement* with the United States. The suspicion and dislike which both countries felt for England and a certain similarity in their social problems of serfdom and slavery made a mutual understanding not improbable. Nevertheless the *rapprochement* did not progress beyond the lending of moral support upon a few occasions. For instance, the United States demonstrated its good will to Russia at the time of the Crimean War. In return for this the Russian government came out openly in favor of the Union forces during the critical stage of the Civil War. The dispatch of units of the Russian fleet to New York and San Francisco in the fall of 1863 may have been motivated by self-interest, in view of Anglo-French hostility toward Russia during the Polish insurrection, but it led Gideon Welles, Secretary of the United States Navy, to exclaim in all sincerity: "God bless the Russians!" Admiral Popov's sojourn in San Francisco during the winter of 1863-1864 served to discourage any hostile action on the part of Confederate cruisers against that port. The pro-Russian sentiment which swept the Union at this time played an important role in connection with William H. Seward's purchase of Alaska for $7,200,000 in 1867.[1] However, Alexander's policy of imperialism won no approval in the United States, and American diplomacy was, as yet, definitely committed to the policy of avoiding "foreign entanglements." Therefore Alexander abandoned any effort to bring about a closer understanding with the United States and in 1872 joined with William I of Germany and Francis Joseph of Austria in the Three Emperors' League.

In 1875 the Near Eastern question came once again to the fore, with

---

[1] See Farrar, Victor J., *The Annexation of Russian America to the United States*, Washington, 1937, p. 61.

the outbreak of disturbances, first in the Turkish provinces of Bosnia and Herzogovina, and later in Bulgaria, in protest against Turkish oppression. The Bulgarian massacres that marked the suppression of the revolt aroused public opinion throughout Europe, and among the Slavic peoples in particular. Although the signatories of the Treaty of Paris had assumed the role of protectors of the Christian peoples under Turkish domination, they failed to take any decisive action in the face of Turkish atrocities. England had acquired a vested interest in Turkey, having extended loans to that country amounting by 1875 to some £200,000,000, and although Gladstone made political capital out of the Bulgarian atrocities, Disraeli, the prime minister, refused to act in concert with the powers. Bismarck, estranged by Alexander's intervention to forestall a preventive war on the part of Germany against France in 1875, rejected Gortchakov's proposal to call a conference and pursued a policy calculated to embroil England with Russia, thereby fanning the flames of war in the Near East.[1] In 1876 the small Balkan states of Serbia and Montenegro made war on Turkey, and the former placed its army under the command of an able Russian general. The Serbs were, nevertheless, confronted with the certainty of overwhelming defeat, when, on April 24, 1877, Russia took unilateral action and declared war on Turkey.

Although the Turkish forces were supplied with up-to-date English equipment, the outcome of the war soon became apparent, as the Russian army continued its relentless march on Constantinople. Although war hysteria ran high in England, Disraeli did not wish to fight alone, and his efforts to secure active Austrian intervention proved futile. France was more concerned with the German menace than with Turkey. As Russian troops approached Constantinople, England dispatched a fleet to the Sea of Marmora, and the hostile Anglo-Russian forces faced one another for a time at San Stefano. Since Austria joined England in threatening to break off diplomatic relations with Russia in the event that Russian troops occupied Constantinople, the tsar, anxious to avoid a general conflict, halted his army just outside the city. On March 3, 1878, the Turks made peace with Russia by the Treaty of San Stefano.

The terms of this treaty bore witness to the overwhelming defeat of the Turks. They provided for the creation of a new and greatly enlarged principality of Bulgaria, the independence of Montenegro, Rumania, and Serbia, and administrative reforms in Bosnia and Herzogovina. For her share, Russia regained the mouth of the Danube,

---

[1] See Potemkin, Academician V. P., Editor, *History of Diplomacy* (in Russian), Moscow, 1945, Vol. II, pp. 30-39.

which she had lost in 1856, together with Batum, Kars, and Ardahan in Transcaucasia, and a financial indemnity. In demanding so much from Turkey Alexander committed a diplomatic error. He aroused the envy and fear of other powers having interests in the Balkans, namely England and Austria. Since, in 1875, in response to the urgent appeal of Queen Victoria, Alexander had exerted pressure upon Germany to prevent the renewal of war against France, he had assumed that both England and France would allow him a free hand in the Balkans. This did not prove to be the case. Austria, seeking compensation in the south for what she had lost to Germany, joined England in demanding a European conference to settle the whole problem of peace in the Balkans. For a time a general European war seemed imminent. However, Germany took the initiative through her chancellor, Bismarck, who assumed the role of an "honest broker" and called a conference at Berlin in 1878 to revise the Treaty of San Stefano.

At Berlin, Gortchakov confronted an anti-Russian bloc, with the result that Russia lost by diplomacy a large part of what she had gained by force of arms. The provisions of the Treaty of San Stefano regarding Bessarabia, the Dobruja, and the independence of Montenegro, Serbia, and Rumania were allowed to stand. The territory of Bulgaria was, however, drastically reduced. Macedonia was restored to Turkey, and the remaining region was divided into two parts, namely, Bulgaria and Eastern Rumelia, both of which were reduced to dependencies of Turkey. Austria was permitted to occupy Bosnia and Herzogovina "temporarily," as well as to station troops in the Sanjak of Novibazar. Since the Russians insisted on retaining Kars, Batum, and Ardahan in Transcaucasia, England took Cyprus as "compensation."

Thus although Russia, in spite of her complete isolation by the great powers at Berlin, retained her own territorial gains, she once again lost her sphere of influence in the Balkans, and with it her prestige among the Slavic peoples of that area, who felt that their interests had been sacrificed. Alexander II, like Nicholas I before him, had failed to settle the Turkish question by unilateral action. As for the "defenders" of Turkey, Austria and England, without having fired a shot in the war they participated in what actually amounted to another partial partition of the Ottoman Empire. Bismarck's support of Austria's interests over and above those of Russia at the Congress of Berlin effected a breach in the Three Emperors' League. Moreover Russia's isolation in Europe was still further emphasized by the establishment of the Triple Alliance of Germany, Austria, and Italy (1879-1881). As in the case of the Crimean War, Russia turned her back upon Europe and proceeded to concentrate upon further expansion in Asia, especially in the Far East.

The diplomatic defeat at Berlin led to increased criticism of Alexander II at home. Had he succeeded in winning Constantinople, or even in preserving intact the terms of the Treaty of San Stefano, public criticism would have been in large measure silenced, especially among the conservative Slavophiles. The reactionaries had long raised the cry that his domestic reforms were undermining the very foundations of the government. They now claimed that his foreign policy had humiliated Russia in the eyes of the world. The liberals, too, had long accused Alexander of procrastination in instituting reforms, which, when they came, proved to be halfway measures. Many of the more radical intellectuals had already preached Nihilism,[1] as did Michael Bakunin (1814-1876) from his refuge in Switzerland, or anarchism, like the scholarly Prince Peter Kropotkin (1842-1921), and regarded revolution as the only solution. Young intellectuals were distributing revolutionary and seditious literature among the people. In 1877, during the Turkish War, some 183 Nihilists had been arraigned in St. Petersburg for sedition, and were regarded by many as martyrs to the cause of liberalism. In 1879, however, an abortive attempt was made on the life of the emperor. When it was learned that the tsar had been condemned to death by a secret society with widespread affiliations, the government struck back with blind fury and conducted a campaign of repression throughout the country. Several other attempts were made upon Alexander's life before he was finally assassinated on March 13, 1881, by a member of a terrorist organization known as "The Will of the People."[2] Ironically enough, Alexander was assassinated immediately following his acceptance of a constitution for Russia—a constitution on which a Preparatory Committee, headed by Count Loris-Melikov (1825-1888) had been working since 1880. His son and heir, Alexander III, rescinded the constitution and the *ukaz* of Alexander II, which had been signed, was never proclaimed.

REIGN OF EMPEROR ALEXANDER III (1881-1894)

The entire country was shocked by the assassination of Alexander II, with the result that the stage was set for a general reaction against liberalism. The accession of Alexander III coincided with a period of

[1] See pp. 206-207.
[2] A graphic account of the conspiracy against the life of Alexander II is to be found in fictionalized form in Mark Aldanov's novel, *Before the Deluge*, N. Y., 1947.

economic depression (1880-1885)—an aftermath of the European slump of 1876—which affected prices and led to industrial strikes of weavers, railwaymen, and dock laborers. This depression likewise contributed to the impoverishment of the landowning nobility, many of whom had to sell their estates and move to the towns. Here they agitated incessantly for a return to a more autocratic policy in government under a strong, reactionary ruler. Such a ruler Alexander III proved to be.

All Alexander's governmental measures were directed toward the restoration of absolute autocracy and the suppression of everything which savored of liberalism and revolution. Privileges were curtailed, and former restrictions revived and intensified. In this favorable atmosphere religious persecution began once again to make itself manifest, as if it had been merely biding its time in anticipation of such an opportunity. Since in Russia, autocratic government has always been closely associated with the Church, it occasions no surprise that the emperor's former tutor, Constantine Pobyedonostsev (1827-1907), Procurator of the Holy Synod from 1880 to 1905, was the directing spirit behind much of the reign of terror which broke out shortly after the accession of Alexander III. Pobyedonostsev was a former Professor of Civil Law at the University of Moscow and a jurist of some repute, the author of a *Course of Civil Law* (1868-1875). In his political philosophy, however, he was the advocate of autocracy and an uncompromising opponent of constitutional reform. In Russia his name became synonymous with black reaction and religious persecution under the guise of Russification.

Whereas all non-Orthodox peoples and dissenters in general suffered from this campaign, it was the Jews who were especially singled out for bitter and relentless persecution. Within a few weeks of the accession of Alexander III a series of atrocities were committed against the Jews in some 170 places in the southern parts of European Russia. These pogroms, as they were called, had the official sanction of the government and elicited no protest from the Orthodox Church. They were devised to distract attention from certain revolutionary movements that were threatening tsardom, and since some Jewish youths had joined their Gentile compatriots in a movement against autocracy, the government pointed to the pogroms as an indication that the Russian people "had given vent" to their fury against revolutionaries and like enemies of the emperor.

As already indicated, religious persecution was not confined to the Jews alone, Roman Catholics and Protestants also being subject to it.

In their case, however, the persecution consisted more in a curtailment of liberties, with the purpose of forcing religious conformity and achieving Russification. Thus throughout Poland further restrictions were placed on the acquisition of land by Poles, and the Bank of Poland was replaced by the Bank of Russia. Even in Finland a campaign of Russification was begun. In the Baltic Province an attempt was made to eradicate German cultural influence, the German language being replaced by Russian in the courts and schools. In the Caucasus Tartars and Georgians were subject to corresponding restrictions.

Against political offenders the law became so severe that all radicalism and terrorist organizations like "The Will of the People" were driven underground. The following excerpt from the law on political offenses signed by Alexander III in 1881 affords eloquent testimony of the conditions which existed in Russia at this time:

Section 249. All persons who shall engage in rebellion against the Supreme Authority—that is, who shall take part in collective and conspirative insurrection against the Gossudar (the Emperor) and the Empire; and also all persons who shall plan the overthrow of the Government in the Empire as a whole, or in any part thereof; or who shall intend to change the existing form of government, or the order of succession to the throne established by law; all persons who, for the attainment of these ends, shall organize or take part in a conspiracy, either actively and with knowledge of its object, or by participation in a conspirative meeting, or by storing or distributing weapons, or by other preparations for insurrection—all such persons, including not only those most guilty, but their associates, instigators, prompters, helpers, and concealers, shall be deprived of all civil rights and be put to death. Those who have knowledge of such evil intentions, and of preparations to carry them into execution, and who, having power to inform the Government thereof, do not fulfill that duty, shall be subjected to the same punishment.

Section 250. If the guilty persons have not manifested an intention to resort to violence, but have organized a society or association intended to attain, at a more or less remote time in the future, the objects set forth in Section 249, or have joined such an association, they shall be sentenced, according to the degree of their criminality, either to from four to six years of penal servitude, with deprivation of all civil rights (including exile to Siberia for life) . . . or to colonization in Siberia (without penal servitude), or to imprisonment in a fortress from one year and four months to four years.[1]

Under such a system parents were exiled because their children were engaged in revolutionary activity. Even the well-known Russian novel-

---

[1] See Kennan, George, *Siberia and the Exile System,* Vol. II, p. 509.

ist, Vladimir Korolenko (1853-1921), after having been reprieved from exile in Siberia due to an official error, was banished again when he refused to betray friends and acquaintances who opposed the government. In 1885 an American by the name of George Kennan, who had been in Russia on previous occasions, undertook for *The Century Magazine* to make a study of the exile system. His classic two-volume report (*Siberia and the Exile System,* New York, 1891) so aroused public sentiment in the West that it even led to the adoption of some reforms in Siberia.

It naturally follows that government censorship permeated every phase of life. The press and the universities, which were reorganized in 1884, were stripped of every semblance of liberty. There was outright interference with the courts, especially as regards the independence of judges and the jury system. The police exercised a supervision and operated with a license unheard of even in the days of Nicholas I. Political prisoners were regarded as having lost all rights and were subjected to shocking brutality. A greater contrast to the liberalism of Alexander II could not well be imagined than that presented by the absolutism of Alexander III. In 1887 a plot to assassinate Alexander III was uncovered by the police. The leaders of the conspiracy were executed. Among them was Alexander Ulyanov, Lenin's eldest brother.

While the baleful influence of political reaction hung over the country like a pall, important advances were made in the economic development and industrialization of Russia. In order to free the country from economic dependence on Germany, Professor Ivan Vyshnegradsky, minister of finance, in 1891 inaugurated a policy of tariff protectionism, which served as a spur to domestic industrial enterprise, especially the production of such items as iron, coal and cotton. Banks were established to aid in the rehabilitation of the destitute nobility and to care for the needs of the peasants. Certain labor legislation was also enacted by which exploitation of employees by employers was somewhat limited. The state derived huge profits from the establishment in 1893 of a government monopoly of the sale of intoxicating liquors. Of particular importance were the steps taken in the direction of the stabilization of the ruble, which led in 1897 to the adoption of the gold standard, thereby facilitating business at home and abroad.

The outstanding material accomplishment of the period was the construction of the Trans-Siberian Railway, decided upon in 1885 and actually begun from both Vladivostok and Tchelyabinsk in 1891. Whereas in the United States railway construction ordinarily preceded the population of a region, in Russia it had served heretofore to open up to trade and industry many areas that were thickly populated. Already by 1880 the railroad had crossed the Volga and reached the Urals. Although it was well known that a railway across Siberia would promote the economic development and settlement of the country, the project was delayed by failure to agree on a suitable route across the Urals. Rumors of a Chinese railway project under English auspices finally galvanized the government into action.[1] The Trans-Siberian Railway was constructed by the state between 1891 and 1904 at a cost of 400,000,000 rubles. Although in its inception the project was primarily economic rather than strategic in design, after 1891 its strategic importance became ever more apparent. In reality this railroad made Siberia an integral part of the Russian Empire. Moreover, as events were soon to prove, it outflanked the British fleet in the Pacific.

Much of the success of the new national economic policies referred to above must go to Count Sergei Witte (1849-1915), who succeeded Vyshnegradsky as minister of finance from 1892 to 1903. Adopting as his own the policy of tariff protectionism inaugurated by his predecessor, Witte secured a favorable commercial treaty from Germany in 1894, thereby ending a tariff war between the two countries. Witte's primary objective was the economic development of Russia by means of industrialization and railroad construction, which he placed ahead of agrarian reform. Perhaps the secret of his success was that he left the delicate agrarian problem strictly to the emperor to handle, while he devoted himself to business and avoided arousing the antagonism of the landlords. In Russia, where agriculture was still the backbone of the nation, the interference of the government in the affairs of the landlords was likely to be as productive of trouble as government interference in business in the United States.

Witte was perhaps the first trained economist to be able to make his policy felt in the Emperor's Council to the extent that it superseded for a time that of the militarists and strategists. The impression is that he was tolerated rather than fully appreciated. Since he spoke the language of the industrial European nations, he was able to obtain much-needed foreign loans for the development of domestic industry. With his good neighbor policy he accomplished more, especially in the Far East, than his successors who pursued a policy of imperialistic expansion. The only man who has rivaled Witte in internal affairs, although his emphasis was on agrarian rather than industrial development, was Peter Stolypin (1862-1911), who was prime minister under Nicholas II,

[1] See Mayor, James, *An Economic History of Russia*, N. Y., 1914, Vol. II, pp 226-228.

1906-1911. Both men subordinated foreign affairs to domestic well-being, and, although their methods differed, under both the country enjoyed a modicum of prosperity. In both cases their successors proved unable to check the imperialistic struggle for aggrandizement, and Russia was plunged into war in 1904 and 1914 respectively.

Under Alexander III, Russia, for the most part, stood aloof from European affairs and ceased to interfere in the concerns of other nations. This policy of "hands off" had come increasingly into favor following the Congress of Berlin in 1878. The emperor trusted no foreign power, had an especial hatred for England, and tolerated no outside meddling as a return for his own noninterference. During his reign, Russia but once had resort to arms. This was the conflict on the Kushk River with the Afghans in 1885. At its conclusion Russia came into possession of the Merv and Pendeh Oases.

Alexander III was nevertheless responsible for what turned out to be a momentous reorientation of Russia's foreign policy in the West. The formation of the Triple Alliance in Central Europe following the Congress of Berlin had aroused serious misgivings in Russia due to the clash of Austrian and Russian interests in the Balkans. In 1886 the prominent Russian publicist, Katkov, inaugurated a violent anti-German campaign in the Russian press, comparing Russian pilgrimages to Berlin with those of the Golden Horde, and called for a French alliance. Although the Three Emperors' League was renewed, with some recognition of Russia's primary interest in the Balkans, by the Reinsurance Treaty of 1887, this dynastic link was permitted to lapse after the fall of Bismarck in 1890. The new course of German policy under Kaiser William II, together with Bismarck's blunder in excluding Russian loans from the German market, which led to economic strife between the two countries, led Alexander III with reluctance to seek both security and economic aid elsewhere.

In 1888 the first of a series of French loans, which by 1891 amounted to three and one-quarter billion francs, paved the way for a realignment of Russian foreign policy. The French government promoted better feeling by arresting, at the request of the Russian ambassador, a group of Russian Nihilists in Paris. In 1891 a French squadron entered Russian naval waters for the first time since the Crimean War and was enthusiastically received at the Russian naval base at Kronstadt, where the tsar climaxed the official welcome by ordering the Russian band to play the hitherto forbidden French national anthem, the *Marseillaise*. It was during this visit that a Franco-Russian *rapprochement* was effected.

The Dual Alliance between Russia and France in 1891, by which both powers agreed to confer and to take concerted measures in the event of a threat of aggression, brought an end to Russian isolation in Europe. It remained only to implement the alliance by a military convention defining the terms of aid, which was accomplished in 1893. Although the existence of the alliance was not proclaimed until 1895, following the accession of Nicholas II, it remained an open secret in Europe. The Franco-Russian alliance was a significant event both for Russia and for Europe. From France Russia was able to secure the capital necessary for the construction of the Trans-Siberian Railway which changed the balance of power in Asia. In Europe it eventually paved the way for the division of the continent into the two armed camps which clashed in 1914 in World War I.

8

The Last of the Romanovs
(Nicholas II)

REIGN OF EMPEROR NICHOLAS II (1894-1917)

NICHOLAS II came to the throne on November 1, 1894, and was crowned in Moscow on May 14, 1896. He lacked both the temperament and the training necessary for an able ruler. His unyielding obstinacy alternated with a weak vacillation. At times he was very susceptible to influence, but almost invariably seemed to yield to that which was most pernicious. While fairly well versed in the field of general literature, he had only the most inadequate and incorrect knowledge of the science of government. Like the majority of Russian princes and grand dukes, he had received an early education which had served to implant in him unreasoning and stubborn prejudices toward certain races and individuals.

In November 1894, he married a German princess of the House of Hesse, who accepted the Orthodox faith, and assumed the name of Alexandra Fyodorovna. From the first the new empress was very unpopular. Since her first appearance among the Russians coincided with the elaborate funeral ceremonies of Alexander III, she came to be known as the "funeral bride." [1] Because of her lack of Russian sympathies and her inability to adapt herself to Russian life, she was constantly the object of suspicion and distrust. Many people resented the fact that she refused to speak Russian unless obliged to do so, and made English and French the preferred languages at court. Her influence over Nicholas II was believed to be great, hence she received the blame

---

[1] At the height of the coronation festivities a horrible tragedy occurred. Thousands of spectators, who were waiting for the royal cortège, suddenly broke through the police lines. A panic ensued, in which some 2000 persons were crushed and trampled to death. In spite of this disaster which plunged the city into mourning, the usual state ball was held in the evening at the French Consulate. This was a great blunder on the part of the sovereigns and contributed much to their unpopularity.

for many reactionary measures. It is true that she was even more prejudiced and narrow-minded than he and, upon occasion, prevented him from making much-needed concessions. However, on his own responsibility Nicholas made it extremely plain shortly after his accession that he intended to follow the policy of his father. This he did by tightening government control and censorship in all fields where independent thought or action might be suspected of making an appearance.

As previously indicated, Alexander III had succeeded in re-establishing autocratic rule, which had been somewhat weakened by the reforms of Alexander II. He was able to do this because he very carefully kept out of foreign entanglements which were likely to weaken his prestige and authority at home. On the other hand, Nicholas II permitted himself to become involved in foreign affairs to his and to the country's exceeding disadvantage. The failure of his foreign policy was largely responsible for the social disorders which marred his reign.

Despite the recent financial and political ties with France, Nicholas II realized that Russia's position was by no means secure. In addition to being constantly pressed for money, he had an army, which was but poorly equipped as compared with the military forces of his European neighbors. In consideration of these facts, he took the initiative in calling for a conference of the Great Powers in the interests of international peace. The first Peace Conference convened at The Hague in 1899. In 1907, when Russia was much weakened by the Japanese War and the Revolution of 1905, the second Hague Peace Conference was called. Although the second Conference assembled at the invitation of Nicholas II, the suggestion for it came from President Theodore Roosevelt. Neither conference succeeded in bringing about any practical and lasting adjustments. The Great Powers were much too distrustful and jealous of one another to render any understanding possible. England resented the Franco-Russian alliance, Germany was wary of England, and Russia was suspicious of all of them.

Although international peace was of supreme importance to all Europe, no country stood in greater need of it than Russia. Even before the first Hague Conference in 1899, a group of farsighted statesmen, under the leadership of Witte, had seriously urged the abandonment, at least temporarily, of the policy of territorial expansion in favor of an economic expansion in the markets of the Middle and Far East. This, they believed, would contribute materially toward the establishment of internal stability; for the attainment of this end, however, there must be guarantees of external peace. A step in this direction was the under--

standing with France, which was much to the interest of both countries in view of Germany's growing militarism.

Germany, for her part, maintained peace with Russia and rendered her rather valuable assistance in European politics, because it was to her own interests to do so. She particularly favored Russia's activities in the Middle and Far East for two reasons. Her own immediate objectives in the *Drang nach Osten* were in the Near East, in Turkey. If Russia were occupied further afield, she would not meddle with Turkey, and at the same time would draw away the attention of England from the region in question. Russia's pretensions in the Far East were, at that time, of no particular interest to any nation but Japan, and hence were not as yet a factor to be considered in European politics. The mutual rivalry of Russia and Austria in the Balkans alone threatened to lead to immediate hostilities in the course of adjustment. To be sure, Alexander III had been strongly in favor of leaving the Slavonic peoples of the Balkans to their fate after Bulgaria and Serbia had demonstrated their "ingratitude" following the Congress of Berlin. After his death, however, there was a revival of interest in the "tradition" of the Near East. Germany again came to the fore and prevented a clash between Russia and Austria by engineering a *modus vivendi* between them with with respect to the Balkans.

Nicholas II, whose accession to the throne in 1894 coincided with the Sino-Japanese War, had a particular interest in the Far East. As heir apparent he had traveled widely in Asia, including Japan. On his return trip he laid the foundation stone for the eastern terminus of the Trans-Siberian Railway and subsequently became chairman of the committee on the construction of this road. Thus he was the first Russian monarch to have acquired first-hand information of Siberia and the Far East,[1] and the experience kindled his imagination. When, after a brief but decisive war, Japan defeated China and seized part of Manchuria and the Liaotung Peninsula, Nicholas, supported by Witte, secured the collaboration of Germany and France to force Japan to revise the Treaty of Shimonoseki (1895) and relinquish the conquered territory. On July 6, 1895, Russia, together with France, loaned China 400,000,000 francs to pay the Japanese indemnity. England and Germany also made loans to China, amounting to £16,000,000 each. In gratitude for this assistance, China was persuaded by Witte to make a treaty with Russia (June 3, 1896), whereby the latter secured permission to build railroads in Manchuria across the Provinces of Heilung-

---

[1] Gurko, V. I., *Features and Figures of the Past,* Stanford University, 1939, p. 256.

kiang and Kirin in the direction of Vladivostok. The Chinese Eastern Railway Company was organized and financed with the aid of France and Germany. According to the original plans, this railroad was to connect Tchita and Vladivostok and to operate only in northern Manchuria. In return for this concession, Russia guaranteed to come to the aid of China in case the latter was attacked by a third party. It was understood that this clause was aimed at Japan.

Russia had now laid a firm foundation for a policy of peaceful, economic penetration of China, which policy, if continued, would have redounded very considerably to her material advantage and averted the disastrous conflict with Japan in 1904-1905. Unfortunately Nicholas II and his advisers had more imperialistic aims. When Germany, after openly advocating the occupation of Chinese ports by European nations as a guarantee of their financial interests, took the lead and seized Kiaochow, Nicholas was persuaded, against the advice of Witte, to take parallel action. Russian warships appeared at Port Arthur a week later, and on March 27, 1898, Russia by resort to bribery forced China to surrender to her on a twenty-five year lease the Liaotung Peninsula, the very territory that Japan had been forced to evacuate after the peace of Shimonoseki, while France occupied Kwangchowan and Great Britain took Weihaiwei "for so long a period as Port Arthur shall remain in possession of Russia." It is worthy of note that like the Liaotung Peninsula, Weihaiwei had also been occupied by Japan during the Sino-Japanese War but had been voluntarily relinquished. Thus the good results of the Russo-Chinese Treaty of 1896 were entirely destroyed. China was bitterly resentful toward all the European powers, but most of all toward Russia for her breach of friendship. The situation was not improved when in 1900 Russia and other European countries intervened for the purpose of suppressing the Boxer Rebellion. Russian troops occupied Manchuria and committed many acts of violence against the Chinese civilian population in this region.

Many causes contributed to the deterioration of relations between Russia and Japan. As a matter of course, Japan had deeply resented Russia's interference in 1894-1895. Then the latter's occupation of the Liaotung Peninsula in 1898, and of Manchuria in 1900, had aroused throughout Japan the most serious fears of a further extension of Russian imperialism. From 1900 on Nicholas II fell more and more under the influence of an irresponsible group of adventurers, whose reckless policy led Russia to drift into war with Japan. The so-called Bezobrazov Circle, which in addition to the ambitious schemer, A. M. Bezobrazov, included Admiral Alexeyev, whom Nicholas in 1903 appointed his Viceroy in the Far East, and Admiral Abaza, a representative of the Yalu Company for the development of the forest resources of Northern Korea, favored a policy of outright expansion and intervention in Manchuria and Korea. They vigorously opposed Witte's policy of caution and peaceful penetration. Hence Japan not only feared severe economic competition with Russia, especially in Korea, but she was likewise apprehensive lest this region fall a prey to Russian expansion. The Japanese felt that their very existence was at stake. Moreover Admiral Alexeyev pursued a policy in regard to Japan which, by reason of its domineering tactlessness, tended to render the situation more and more acute. By 1902, the construction of the Trans-Siberian Railroad, by means of which Russia outflanked the British fleet in the Far East, led to the conclusion of an Anglo-Japanese Alliance directed against Russia. Before the construction of this railroad, Eastern Siberia was little more than a distant Russian hinterland. The advent of the Trans-Siberian route, however, indicated clearly enough to both Britain and Japan that Russia intended to become a leading Pacific power—a situation they were anxious to prevent. It is significant to note, however, that prior to signing an alliance with Great Britain the Japanese statesman, Prince Ito, tried ineffectually to reach an understanding with Russia regarding Korea.

Meanwhile the Russian government, dominated as it was by the expansionists after the removal of Witte in 1903, felt the necessity of "a small victorious war," which would unite the people and divert their attention from unsatisfactory internal conditions. For some time, as an outgrowth of the repressive policies of V. K. Plehve (1846-1904), minister of the interior, and an inveterate opponent of Witte, there had been mutterings of a revolutionary nature, and nothing could be better calculated to check these than a brilliant victory in some foreign field. The country was in no condition to engage in a test of strength with any European power, but Russia had never yet lost a war with a non-European nation. Hence the situation in regard to Japan seemed to be made to order.

England also was much interested in the possibility of a struggle between Russia and Japan. In such an event, Russia would be drawn away from the Middle East, where she had long been a thorn in the flesh to Great Britain. Moreover, the latter, in common with other European powers, had become more and more interested in the Far East, and Russia's expansion in that direction, which a few years earlier had been of no especial importance to her, was now regarded by England with the most lively concern.

England and Japan, it should be said, were not the only countries alarmed by Russian expansion in the Far East. The United States, which, following the Spanish-American War (1898), watched with growing concern the tightening of the Russian grip on Manchuria, was vitally interested in the opening up of this region to American investment. While John Hay's call for the preservation of the Open Door in China (1899-1900) was not aimed solely at Russia, the American secretary of state was motivated largely by his fear that Russia would obtain exclusive rights in Manchuria to the detriment of American interests. For similar reasons the United States government regarded with satisfaction the Anglo-Japanese Alliance of 1902, which recognized Japan's special interests in Korea. In fact, less than a month before the outbreak of hostilities between Russia and Japan the United States assured the Japanese government of its "benevolence" in the event of war. Thus by 1904 Russian policy in the Far East had not only alienated China and brought about an alliance between England and Japan, but it had led the United States to lend moral support to Japanese expansionism in order to counteract that of Russia.

Under such circumstances, all that was needed to precipitate a crisis was some excuse or overt act. This Japan furnished on February 8, 1904, when without warning her fleet attacked Russian warships moored in the outer harbor of Port Arthur. A declaration of war by Russia followed, and the struggle was on. In its initial stages, the Korean Peninsula was the locale of land fighting between the Russians and the Japanese. In fact, Russo-Japanese rivalry for the control of Korea was a leading casus belli in this conflict.

The war did not go well for the Russians. Although the incompetent Alexeyev was superseded as commander-in-chief by the minister of war, General Kuropatkin, the former remained viceroy in the Far East, with the result that there was no real co-ordination of effort, such as was displayed by the Japanese. In September 1904 the Russians were defeated in the important Battle of Liaoyang. On January 1, 1905, General Stoessel, in what practically amounted to treason, surrendered Port Arthur without calling a Council of War, although the garrison still had a three months' supply of food and more than 2,000,000 rounds of ammunition. The defense of this important port cost the Russians more than 28,000 men and the Japanese more than twice that number. With reinforcements from Port Arthur, the Japanese were able to win the Battle of Mukden in March 1905, although in the course of two weeks' fighting both sides lost 70,000 men. Whereas the main forces of the Russian army were never sent to the Far East, Admiral Rozhdestvensky sailed the Baltic fleet halfway around the world, only to meet with overwhelming defeat at the hands of Admiral Togo in the Battle of the Tsushima Straits in May 1905. The Russians lost thirty out of forty-seven ships, and only three managed to reach Vladivostok.

This disastrous turn of affairs naturally produced internal results far different from those which the Russian government had anticipated. The Russian people had never been particularly interested in the war, seeing no good reason why they should fight Japan for Chinese territory when China herself remained consistently neutral. The series of defeats produced financial disturbances, which in turn provoked internal disorders. Far from diverting popular attention from revolutionary activities, the war provoked an uprising. The Russian government was ready to secure peace on almost any terms, so that the army might be used to crush internal revolt. The Japanese were not unaware of the collapse of their foe, but they themselves were well-nigh exhausted and were too eager for peace to press very far the advantage which their victories gave them. At this critical juncture, President Theodore Roosevelt tendered his good offices, with the result that a treaty of peace was signed on September 5, 1905, at Portsmouth, New Hampshire.

Throughout the war American public opinion had remained overwhelmingly favorable to Japan. Roosevelt's own pro-Japanese stand is clearly indicated in a letter which he sent to his friend Cecil Spring-Rice, the British ambassador in St. Petersburg:

As soon as this war broke out, I notified Germany and France in the most polite and discreet fashion that in the event of a combination against Japan to try to do what Russia, Germany, and France did to her in 1894 (*sic*) I would promptly side with Japan and proceed to whatever length was necessary on her behalf.[1]

The American press represented the Japanese war effort as a struggle for self-preservation against "a vicious despotism," as well as for the maintenance of the Open Door and the integrity of China. It was even claimed that Japan was fighting America's battle in the Far East and stood for the preservation of Anglo-Saxon civilization![2] Anglo-American loans practically financed the Japanese war. As the conflict pro-

---

[1] Quoted in Zabriskie, *op. cit.*, p. 104.

[2] For an interesting analysis of American public opinion during the war and the peace conference, see Thorson, Winston B., "American Public Opinion and the Portsmouth Peace Conference," *American Historical Review*, Vol. LIII, No. 3, April 1948, pp. 439-464; and by the same author, "Pacific Northwest Opinion on the Russo-Japanese War of 1904-1905," *Pacific Northwest Quarterly*, XXXV (October 1944), pp. 305-322.

gressed, Roosevelt became somewhat concerned lest Japanese victories should lead to Japanese predominance in the Far East and constitute a threat to American interests. He visualized a long war, with the ultimate exhaustion of both belligerents, as most likely to redound to the interests of the United States. The official Russian press, for its part, openly blamed the United States for instigating the war and speculated about American designs on Eastern Siberia. It was largely in the expectation that Roosevelt might use his influence with Japan to secure reasonable peace terms that the Russians agreed to his mediation and the holding of the peace conference in the United States.

Nicholas II, anxious to secure the best possible terms, wisely appointed the previously discredited Witte as the head of the Russian delegation, with instructions not to pay "a kopeck of indemnity or yield an inch of land." At Portsmouth the Japanese demanded (1) an indemnity of $750,000,000, (2) the cession of the entire island of Sakhalin, (3) the lease of the Liaotung Peninsula, and (4) the limitation of Russian naval power in the Far East. A deadlock ensued, but since both powers stood in dire need of peace and could float no more loans in the foreign market to carry on the conflict, pressure was brought to effect a compromise. By the terms of the Treaty of Portsmouth Japan secured only the southern half of the island of Sakhalin and Russia's lease of the Liaotung Peninsula, including Port Arthur. Since the Russians to the bitter end remained obdurate on the subject of paying "tribute" to an Asian power, the Japanese finally abandoned their demand for a cash indemnity. Since Japan acquired important political, military, and economic concessions with regard to Korea, thereby replacing Russia, and the two belligerents agreed to evacuate Manchuria and return it to China, the United States government felt reasonably satisfied that the balance of power had been restored in Asia. Whether or not President Roosevelt was influenced by considerations unfavorable to Japan, the fact remains that he tendered a service of inestimable value to both combatants. In Russia, however, the "favorable" terms of the treaty were attributed, not to him, but to the leader of the Russian delegation, Sergei Witte, who received the title of "Count" as a reward for his services.[1] The Japanese, in spite of their very considerable gains, resented the fact that they had been deprived of the just "fruits of victory" and regarded the treaty as "a national disgrace." There was little or no indication at the time, however, that Japan and Russia would soon join forces to curb American expansion in the Pacific.

---

[1] See, however, Lobanov-Rostovsky, Andrei, *Russia and Asia*, 1933, p. 234.

POLITICAL PARTIES AND THE REVOLUTION OF 1905

In Russia the emergence of political parties was obstructed by the reaction that marked the period from the closing years of the reign of Alexander II until 1905, during which all political as well as terrorist organizations were driven underground or of necessity found asylum abroad. George Plekhanov (1857-1918), for example, a one-time exponent of "The Will of the People," fled to Switzerland, where he adopted Marxism and in 1883 founded the first Russian group of avowed Marxists under the name, "Liberation of Labor." Its members translated into Russian the works of Marx and Engels and distributed them secretly in Russia. By 1893 the term "Social Democrats," borrowed from Germany, was being applied to Russian Marxists. One of their number, Nikolai Lenin (Vladimir Ilyitch Ulyanov, 1870-1924), who had joined a Marxist group in Kazan, where he was expelled from the University for engaging in subversive student activities, in 1895 organized among the workers' circle of St. Petersburg a League of Struggle for the Emancipation of the Working Class. Similar leagues were formed in other cities, and the most immediate result of their activities was an increase in strikes.

Against the background of a severe economic crisis, a secret convention of nine delegates was held in Minsk in 1898 to unite these leagues into a Russian Social Democratic Workers' Party, an avowedly Marxist group, such as Plekhanov had advocated. Lenin, first in Munich and later in London, edited its first newspaper, *Iskra* (*The Spark*), which was smuggled into Russia, where as the foremost revolutionary sheet of its time it exercised an important influence on the Revolution of 1905. Another revolutionary, Leon Trotsky (Lev Davidovitch Bronstein, 1879-1940), joined the editorial staff of *Iskra* in London. In 1903, when these Social Democrats held a second congress in Brussels and London, their deliberations resulted in a Party split. The minority, or Mensheviks, lost in the balloting by only two votes (25:23). It was their contention that the social revolution must be achieved only after a careful and intensive preparatory campaign of education had trained the masses for a democratic regime. The majority, or Bolsheviks, had no patience with such deliberate methods, but favored an abrupt overthrow of the existing social and political order by a resort to force. Lenin was the leader of the Bolsheviks, while Plekhanov, and for a time, Trotsky, supported the Mensheviks. Both groups aimed at the overthrow of tsarist autocracy and the organization of socialist revolution. The difference between them was one of methods rather than of aims. Not until 1912, at a conference in Prague, were the Mensheviks expelled from the Party. In the same year the now well-known newspaper, *Pravda* (*Truth*), was founded as the organ of the Party.

The Social Revolutionary Party was organized about the same time (1901-1902) as that of the Social Democrats, the latter's activities perhaps serving as an impetus to their own. The S.R.s, as they were called, were, however, primarily concerned with the interests of the peasants, in contrast to the S.D.s who championed the cause of the workers in the city. They drew inspiration from the *Narodniki* (Populists) of the 1870's and sought to develop political consciousness among the peasants, contending that the land should belong to those who tilled it. Like the S.D.s they stood for the socialization of the land rather than for private ownership. Aroused by the appalling famine on the Volga, 1891-1892, and the unsatisfactory agricultural conditions in general, they encouraged agrarian disturbances. Moreover, a minority among them sought to arouse popular feeling against the government by a series of terroristic acts, whereas the S.D.s sought the same end by somewhat less violent means, such as strikes and popular demonstrations. One of their number was responsible for the assassination of Dmitry Sipyagin, minister of the interior, in 1902, while another killed the highly unpopular Plehve in 1904, and still another disposed of the Grand Duke Serge, uncle of the emperor and governor-general of Moscow, in the spring of 1905. The S.R.s did not accept Marxism in its entirety, being influenced in part by the "Utopian" School of Socialism in France, and by the thinking of some Russian novelists and literary critics. As in the case of the S.D.s, a wide divergence of opinion among the membership caused them to separate into "Right" and "Left" wings. The S.R.s soon became the largest political party in Russia. Both the S.D.s and the S.R.s had a following among university students and included in their membership representatives from the professions of law, medicine, and education. The leaders of both parties of necessity had to live abroad.

The Constitutional Democratic Party was composed of both conservative and liberal members of the intelligentsia, who disapproved of the radical theories and practices of the earlier groups. Its members advocated a policy of liberalism, which gradually and by peaceful means would displace absolute autocracy by a constitutional government, modeled upon the parliamentary system of England or France. The most learned men of the nation and many liberal landowners either belonged to this party or sympathized with its aims. The party, although organized in 1903, did not begin to make its influence felt until 1905. Prior to that time it was, like all other political parties, banned by the government and was obliged to work in secret. No group was more influential throughout the country during the years from 1905 to 1917. The party came to be known as the Kadets, or the K.D.s, from the first letters of the Russian words for Constitutional Democrats.

Inasmuch as all parties thus far considered had as their common aim the abolition of autocracy in favor of a representative government chosen by the people, the tsarist regime was absolutely without popular support. To repair this lack and offset the activities of the various social reform groups, a counter-revolutionary organization known as the Black Hundred was built up at the initiative of the government and secretly under the direct patronage and protection of Nicholas II himself. Its members were drawn from the ranks of the Orthodox clergy and from the most reactionary elements of the country. While there were sincere and upright monarchists among them, there was also present a most vicious and undesirable element. This was made up of ordinary hoodlums, who delighted in pogroms and similar atrocities and who took advantage of the government immunity to indulge in all forms of lawlessness and violence against the "enemies of the emperor." Their propaganda often incited the rabble to take violent action against non-Russian elements in the population, such as the Poles, Armenians, and Jews. Their connection with the notorious Kishinev pogroms of 1903 brought discredit to the government both at home and abroad. However when the more decent monarchists ventured to call the attention of the emperor to these abuses, both he and the empress refused to listen to their protests.

By the outbreak of the Russo-Japanese War in 1904, in spite of all the efforts of the government to wipe out subversive activities, there existed a rather widespread revolutionary movement. Under the police department's direction, government agents, or spies, were instructed to join the various revolutionary groups to obtain evidence against their leaders. Although many such leaders fell victims to the machinations of these agents, some of the latter became so active in revolutionary circles that the government was in doubt as to their real affiliations and sympathies. The government made various and fruitless efforts to divert the attention of the revolutionaries. The failure of the war with Japan in this connection has already been mentioned. With every defeat abroad the revolutionary movement at home gained momentum and became more threatening. At the instigation of both wings of the Social Democrats, strikes broke out on a large scale and spread with an unprecedented rapidity. At one time in 1905 there were 1,834,000 workmen engaged in major strikes, the largest number ever participating at one time in such demonstrations. The years 1903 to 1917 witnessed fifteen major strikes in Russia.

The peasants, likewise, had become disaffected under the influence of propaganda spread by the Social Revolutionaries. They demanded land on a large scale and on the basis of strictly private ownership. In the old days of serfdom, they had been accustomed to say to the landowners, "We are yours, but the land is ours." Now their terroristic cry had become: "Kill the landowners and seize the land." Thereupon they fell upon many of the rich landowners, murdered them, and looted and burned their property.

Although the majority of the leaders among the clergy gave their support to the reactionary forces, which were endeavoring to suppress popular dissatisfaction either by violent or subtle means, there were others among them who felt that the Church had a duty to perform toward the people. It was their belief that the clergy should assume the leadership of the hundreds of thousands of illiterate and misguided workers in the towns and on the farms and direct them toward constructive efforts, by which they and the country at large would be benefited. Most prominent among these ecclesiastical leaders was Father George Gapon. Many conflicting opinions have been expressed in regard to this man's character and deeds, but we may assume that he was absolutely sincere in his efforts to procure by religious means that adjustment of social conditions, which government oppression and revolutionary activities had alike failed to accomplish. He began to hold meetings for the workingman, opening and closing each gathering with prayers for divine guidance. He begged the workers to refrain from violence and seek redress of their wrongs through peaceful measures. He told them that the emperor did not know what conditions were really like since he was misinformed by deceitful advisers, who were responsible for all the sufferings of the people. Great crowds flocked to hear him preach his simple logic which was comprehensible to a simple people.

By tireless efforts and ceaseless persuasion he convinced large numbers of workers that they should abandon the revolutionary and socialistic organizations and cast their lot with him. Then he decided that the time was ripe for a personal appeal to the "Little Father." Sunday, January 22, 1905, was selected as the day for this appeal. Thousands of workingmen with their wives and children assembled for a religious service, after which the entire multitude marched to the Winter Palace with Father Gapon at their head. Reverently bearing aloft portraits of the emperor and members of the royal family and singing hymns, they presented the aspect of a devout religious procession. Anything less like a revolutionary demonstration cannot well be imagined. Father Gapon had told them that the emperor would no doubt receive them himself and instructed them to fall upon their knees when he appeared in token of their loyalty and submission.

It is difficult to believe that Nicholas II was not well informed by his various spies of the spirit and purpose of this march.[1] Had he or one of his representatives afforded the marchers a brief hearing, they would in all probability have dispersed quietly with that gratitude and respect in their hearts which might have served later to save the life of Nicholas II, if not his throne. With a blind obtuseness of judgment, which finds few parallels in history, soldiers and Cossacks were ordered to open fire without warning upon the assembled crowd. Estimates of the number of victims range from 70 to 500 or more killed, and 250 to 3500 wounded. Whatever the numbers, the government had committed an unpardonable blunder, the repercussions of which were felt throughout the country. No words can depict the terror and the wrath of the people over the horrors of Bloody Sunday. Those who had lost friends or relatives vowed an undying vengeance, the intensity and fervency of which only increased with the passing years. Wrath also fell upon the Church, because the people were fully convinced that they had been betrayed and entrapped by its emissaries. From this time forth the workers aligned themselves wholeheartedly with revolutionary and socialist forces. "Bloody Sunday" marked a crisis in the revolutionary movement.

On the evening of Bloody Sunday, Maxim Gorky led Father Gapon to the rostrum of a protest meeting, where the priest spoke as follows:

Dear blood brethren, the bullets of the Imperial soldiers have killed our faith in the Tsar. Let's take vengeance on him and his entire family. Vengeance on all his ministers and all the exploiters of Russian soil. Go, pillage the imperial palaces! All the soldiers and officers who killed our innocent wives and children, all the tyrants, all the oppressors of the Russian people, I herewith smite with my priestly curse.

---

[1] For a different account of Bloody Sunday, see Alexander Grand Duke of Russia, *Once a Grand Duke,* New York. See also Walsh, E. A., *The Fall of the Russian Empire,* N. Y., 1931, pp. 74-76, and General P. G. Kurlov, *Fall of the Russian Empire* (in Russian), Berlin, 1923, pp. 16, 36.

BLOODY SUNDAY, JANUARY 22, 1905

Father Gapon was forced to flee to Switzerland, from whence for a time he directed bitter philippics against the Russian government. His later movements are something of a mystery. He met his death in a small village in Finland, where he was murdered by workingmen who denounced him as a "provocateur."

Throughout the country there was prompt reaction to Bloody Sunday. In Poland a general strike was proclaimed. In western Georgia Russian officials were ousted, and the inhabitants organized and maintained their own government for a period of several months. Widespread peasant uprisings took place throughout European Russia. Disorders and strikes occurred in cities from St. Petersburg to the Caucasus, with workers and members of the intelligentsia demanding a Constituent Assembly and an eight-hour day. When news arrived of the destruction of the Russian Baltic Fleet in the Battle of Tsushima, workers called for the end of the war, and the crew of the battleship *Potemkin,* anchored off Odessa, mutinied and escaped to a Rumanian port. In brief, over a wide area of the country, government authority ceased to function.

Under the pressure of military reverses and internal revolt, the government decided to make a gesture in the way of political reforms. This indicated a belated and withal limited recognition of a principle confirmed by historical facts that a government which would continue must never yield to a mob but should take due cognizance of any demands made by a considerable number of reliable citizens. On August 19, 1905, the Government's own plan for a Duma was announced. Since this plan envisaged only a consultative body, to be chosen by indirect election on the basis of a narrowly restricted franchise conferred chiefly upon landowners, it completely failed to quell the dissatisfaction of all those who demanded a constituent assembly with broad legislative powers. Here again the Imperial government of Russia missed an opportunity of taking measures to avert its downfall.

The internal situation grew more and more critical. The agitation of the Social Democrats resulted in bringing about a general strike among public utility workers. Railroads ceased to operate, and cities were without electric lights and without water. At this juncture a new organization came into being in St. Petersburg, the Soviet of Workers' Deputies. *Soviet* is the Russian word for "council." Originally its members were drawn from all Socialist groups, but the Bolsheviks comprised only an insignificant minority. This organization was in the nature of a representative council of socialist groups and workers.

Its first chairman or president was Khrustalev-Nosar, a lawyer by profession. His importance, however, was soon overshadowed by that of the vice-president, who then went by the name of Bronstein, but who is better known as Leon Trotsky. Trotsky was at that time a leader of influence among the Mensheviks (Moderate Socialists), who controlled a majority in the Soviet. This council was regarded with much disfavor by the Bolsheviks, who repeatedly warned the Mensheviks that there was no safety in the latter's policy of deliberate methods and co-operation with the government. The Bolsheviks demanded rapid action and complete severance from a government which would only "double cross" them in the end.

It is uncertain what the Soviets might have instituted or accomplished at this time, for they were forestalled by the government before they had a chance to become very numerous or very powerful. According to Witte, the peasant disorders, which wrecked some 2000 estates in 1905, caused more concern in government circles than the Soviet of Workers' Deputies and its general strike. Nicholas II and his advisers had finally become thoroughly alarmed, in view of the relentless advance of the revolutionary forces and the threatened collapse of the government. Count Witte, who was noted for his liberal ideas, and Grand Duke Nicholas Nicholayevitch, Jr., succeeded in exerting sufficient influence and pressure to produce a Manifesto for the instituting of political reform. This Manifesto, which was issued on October 30, 1905, startled even the most radical of the socialists by its liberal provisions. It granted practically everything for which the Liberals and moderate Socialists had been asking, that is, freedom of speech, freedom of assembly, universal suffrage, and a representative and legislative Duma. It clearly aimed at winning over the liberal groups among the revolutionaries, who would be rendered powerless by the loss of their most able members. Count Witte was made prime minister and given the power to select his own cabinet. Promptly he invited the co-operation of the Liberals. This was a remarkable opportunity for them, which, if it had been accepted, would have given them almost absolute control of the government and redounded much to their prestige. However in this year, 1905, they failed, as they did later in 1917, by exhibiting a deplorably weak hesitation and vacillation when the time came to act. Despite the excellence and thoroughness of their campaign for just such reforms as the October Manifesto offered, they did not respond to any extent to the invitation of the prime minister, and the psychological moment passed.

The radical Socialists, after recovering from the first surprise occasioned by the Manifesto, expressed their disapproval of it as a halfway measure, for now nothing short of a social upheaval would satisfy them. The Bolsheviks came out strongly against it under the leadership of Lenin, who had just returned to Russia. Despite its failure to win the support of the various parties, the Manifesto gave a moral victory to the government and saved it from an immediate collapse. The general public was pleased with the liberalism of the document and lost for the time being the desire for revolt. The Manifesto of 1905 came to be regarded as even more important than the Manifesto of 1861, abolishing serfdom.

Disappointed at the lukewarm reception accorded the Manifesto by the Liberals, the government turned to other means of suppressing revolutionary activities. Using as an excuse the well-known fact that certain Jews had become affiliated with the various organizations sponsoring revolt, another series of pogroms was instituted. The atrocities which followed were the most ghastly in the history of pogroms, largely because the worst element of the Black Hundred participated and was chiefly responsible for all that occurred. In Odessa, for example, where seven hundred were killed, the Cossacks of the Black Hundred bayoneted women and children and threw some of the latter from fifth and sixth story windows. The victims were almost entirely innocent persons, who had no idea of engaging in any activities against the government. The real Jewish revolutionaries for the most part managed to escape.

Armed insurrection broke out in Moscow toward the end of December 1905. The government knew that such a demonstration was threatening and for that reason, as has been previously mentioned, was very anxious to end the war with Japan and get the troops home. They began to return immediately following the Peace of Portsmouth in September, so that by December the majority was available. In comparison with their losing fight with the Japanese, the suppression of an internal revolt seemed very simple and easy. Moreover, inasmuch as the Manifesto had satisfied many influential persons, the revolt did not become as widespread as in 1917. Nevertheless, the second Russian Revolution of 1905 caused the death of thousands, the wounding of tens of thousands, and the exiling of many more. Between 1905 and 1909 the number of political prisoners rose from 85,000 to 200,000 annually.

The Revolution of 1905 shook the autocracy to its very foundations. The concessions made in time of dire emergency in the direction of a constitutional regime, although whittled down in the process of the counter-revolution, could never be scrapped entirely. The government, jarred into action, attempted in the years that followed to tackle some of the basic problems that confronted Russia, such as the agrarian issue, mass illiteracy, and military reorganization. The time available for what amounted in some respects to a revolutionary transformation of the country was, as events were to prove, all too short. At least a generation of peace was needed. World War I overtook Russia before the fundamental changes under way could be expected to produce the desired results, and the monarchy, which unknowingly faced its last great test following the Revolution of 1905, went down to defeat amid the chaos of 1917.

THE DUMAS; STOLYPIN

When the Revolution of 1905 had been crushed, a general assembly was called in accordance with the provision of the Manifesto of October 30, 1905. This was the first of a series of four Dumas which were called before 1917. The term, "Duma," which is derived from the verb *dumat,* meaning "to think," was linked in Russia with the traditions of the past. The *Boyarskaya Duma,* a consultative council which had made recommendations to the tsar, and which was replaced by the Administrative Senate under Peter the Great in 1711, was never in any true sense of the word a legislative body. Although Nicholas II would have preferred that the new Duma should perform a similarly restricted function, the emergency had forced him to make greater concessions. Although hedged about by many restrictions, the Imperial Duma was nevertheless a legislative body, chosen by indirect, but very nearly universal male suffrage for a period of five years.

Although the October Manifesto had provided the forms of Western democracy, including the five freedoms of person, conscience, speech, meeting, and association, it remained to be seen how they would take root in the alien Russian soil. Witte's additions to the fundamental laws, enacted on the very eve of the inauguration of this experiment in constitutional government, arbitrarily placed the army, navy, and foreign loans outside the competence of the Duma, thereby violating the spirit, if not the letter, of the October Manifesto, which provided that "no law can obtain force without the consent of the State Duma." Witte likewise made good use of his reputation abroad to secure a large loan from France, which served at a most critical time to make the administration independent of the new Duma. It was not an auspicious beginning.

The First Duma, convened on May 10, 1906, which was boycotted by the radical Socialists, included, in the words of Sir Bernard Pares, "the cream of the Russian intelligentsia." [1] Of its 478 members, 187 were Constitutional Democrats (Kadets), and 85 represented the moderate Labor Party. Among the 204 peasants elected, only two were recorded as illiterate. The session was opened by the emperor in person, and S. M. Muromtsev, a lawyer and author, as well as a member of the Kadets, was elected President. The members promptly turned to the discussion of such controversial issues as the activities of the Black Hundred in connection with the pogroms, the desirability of an amnesty for revolutionary offenders, the abolition of capital punishment even for political offenses, the end of the extraordinary courts and the passport system, and compulsory expropriation of the land. They even passed a vote of censure on the emperor's ministers, although the principle of executive responsibility to the legislature had not been conceded by the Manifesto. Although Article 14 of the Statute of the Duma and Article 26 of the Statute of the State Council guaranteed freedom of speech, Nicholas II could not endure the criticism of governmental policies resorted to by the delegates, and with the approval of reactionary bureaucrats he arbitrarily dissolved it on July 21, after a session of seventy-two days, and with a total disregard for its five-year term. From Finland, where some 200 of the disillusioned Kadets and Labor members sought refuge, was issued the Viborg Manifesto, which protested the dissolution of the Duma, called for civil disobedience to the government, and nonrecognition of foreign loans negotiated without the consent of the Duma. The country, weary of revolution and violence, failed to rise to the support of the Duma.

The Second Duma, which convened on March 5, 1907, and which was selected in accordance with the same franchise, fared no better than the first. All those who had participated in the Viborg Manifesto were barred from re-election. Lenin had reversed his earlier position in regard to the boycott of the Duma, and the new assembly included 180 Socialists, who proved to be far more hostile to the government than their predecessors. Unfortunately they dissipated their energies by making denunciatory speeches, instead of undertaking worth-while reforms. When the police uncovered two plots in which both revolutionary parties, the S.D.s and the S.R.s, were implicated, the Second

[1] See Pares, Bernard, *The Fall of the Russian Monarchy*, p. 94.

Duma was dissolved unceremoniously on June 16 for plotting against the emperor.

Peter Stolypin, who had been appointed prime minister by Nicholas II on the eve of the dissolution of the First Duma, had already made arrangements for a drastic revision of the electoral law, as a result of which the Third Duma, which met in the fall of 1907, could no longer be said to represent the people as a whole but mainly the conservative propertied classes among the Great Russians. Even the peasant members of the Third Duma, it was claimed, were elected by the gentry. An illustration of how drastic was the restriction of the franchise is provided by Sir Bernard Pares, who was informed by one member of this Duma that all his constituents could be assembled in one room.[1] The Third Duma, nevertheless, included some able men, and since the monarchy had no occasion to question their loyalty, they were able, through the organization of special commissions, to effect important agrarian and military reforms and to remain in session for the full term of five years.

Sir Bernard Pares, already mentioned above, who spent some time each year in Russia from 1904 to 1919, and observed the operation of the Dumas at first hand, has commented on them as follows:

> . . . The Duma had the freshness of a school, with something of surprise at the simplicity with which differences that had seemed formidable could be removed. One could feel the pleasure with which the Members were finding their way into common work for the good of the whole country. In the First Duma peasants had picked out as their chief impression the realization that Russia was a great family, that there were so many others with thoughts and hopes like their own. "It went past like a dream," one of them said to me. The Second Duma was fast growing more and more into a family when it was prematurely dissolved. The Third Duma, though its horizon was much more limited, did come to stay, and its membership was better qualified to take practical advantage of the education which it offered. Some seventy persons at least, forming the nucleus of the more important commissions, were learning in detail to understand the problems and difficulties of administration and therefore to understand both each other and the Government. One could see political competence growing day by day. And to a constant observer it was becoming more and more an open secret that the distinctions of party meant little, and that in the social warmth of their public work for Russia all these men were becoming friends.[2]

---

[1] Pares, *op. cit.*, p. 103.
[2] *Ibid.*, pp. 117-118.

Much of the credit for the handling of the agrarian situation must go, however, not to the Duma, but to Peter Stolypin, who served as Nicholas II's prime minister from 1906 to 1911. Stolypin had had much practical experience in politics, having served as Governor of Saratov Province, as well as minister of the interior. Although less brilliant than Witte, he was straightforward, honest, courageous, and energetic in his efforts to improve domestic conditions in Russia. Having achieved the restriction of the franchise and suppressed the revolutionaries by establishing a series of military courts, he turned to more constructive measures, especially to the agrarian situation. During the First Duma the Constitutional Democrats had introduced a bill advocating that the government take over the large estates upon the payment of suitable compensation to the owners and then allot the land to the peasants. Stolypin opposed such abrupt measures, which were sure to antagonize the large landowners, and substituted his own solution for the agrarian problem. By a truly revolutionary decree of November 22, 1906, he provided for the abolition of the peasant commune, or *mir*, in favor of individual ownership and the consolidation of peasant holdings. Stolypin's objective was to transform Russia from a nation of peasants into a nation of farmers. Each peasant, he insisted, was entitled to a farm of his own, as well as to government aid in financing it. Hence reforms were effected in the Peasants' Land Bank to facilitate the financing of this program. Peasants in the overcrowded Black Soil areas were encouraged to migrate to Siberia. Better agricultural methods, including the use of machines and fertilizers, were fostered. Stolypin's program was first introduced by imperial *ukaz*, over the protests of the Duma, and did not actually become law until it was ratified by the Third Duma on June 14, 1910. In the meantime, however, Stolypin continued to carry on his reforms. No doubt the success of the program was due in part to the fact that for a decade following 1907 Russian agriculture produced bumper crops, and the country enjoyed almost unprecedented prosperity.

By 1911, Stolypin's reforms had brought into existence from one to two million such peasant farms, the owners of which were later known in Soviet Russia as "kulaks." If Stolypin had been permitted to continue this work, the number of these farms would have doubled and trebled, with the result that the Revolution of 1917 might have taken an entirely different course. Unfortunately for the peasants, Stolypin was assassinated on September 14, 1911. The assassination was the work of a young lawyer, Bogrov by name, a Social Revolutionary. It occurred in the Kiev Opera House in the course of a performance given in honor of a visit of the emperor. Stolypin's harsh methods in dealing with political opposition were given as a cause. Nearly 3000 persons are said to have been executed during the five years that he was in power. Although the more radical peasants may not have appreciated his efforts on their behalf, he nevertheless contributed much to their welfare, and his death operated as a distinct check to reforms in their favor.

The election of the Fourth Duma in 1912 was accomplished with an even greater disregard for the right of popular suffrage. The Procurator of the Holy Synod, Sabler, a strong reactionary, desired that certain members of the clergy should serve as deputies in the Duma. In order to make their election certain, the minister of the interior arbitrarily rearranged electoral districts. While the First Duma had 6 clergymen, and the Second Duma 13, including two bishops, the Third included 45 and the Fourth 46. Thus once more the clergy evinced its willingness to co-operate with the government in restricting the liberties of the people. The Fourth Duma startled the people by the course of its procedure. It was this Duma which brought about the overthrow of the Romanov dynasty.

Very powerful in directing the election of the Duma was the so-called "Mad Monk," Rasputin (1871-1916). Beginning with 1905, when his influence first began to be felt, he exercised almost unlimited authority in the appointment of public officials and the shaping of foreign policy. There are few stranger tales in history than that dealing with the career of this man. He was neither a priest nor a member of any religious order but was a mere wanderer, who combined the characteristics of a picaresque rover with those of a pilgrim. He did not even go by his right name, which was Novikh, but adopted the epithet, which his fellow peasants in his native Siberian village had bestowed upon him because of his well-known course of immorality and crime. His chief claim to superiority apparently consisted in the possession of a personal magnetism of such force that he was able to bend many persons to his will and even bring healing to the sick. It is said that in his capacity as a "healer" he attracted the attention of a wealthy lady, who was responsible for his coming to St. Petersburg and for his subsequent introduction to the empress. Since he appeared to benefit the sickly Prince Alexis [1] as no doctor had been

---

[1] Alexis, the long-awaited heir to the throne, was born August 12, 1904. When he was three years old, he fell while playing and received an injury which began to bleed. When the court physician was unable to check this bleeding, the empress sank in a swoon. She realized that she had transmitted to her only son the disease known as hemophilia, which had afflicted males of her father's family for 300 years.

able to do, the empress believed that he was possessed of divine power and surrendered entirely to his direction. The emperor, likewise, came under his influence, so that the licentious adventurer was for a time the real ruler. Bitter protests came from all sources, but neither Nicholas nor the empress would listen to them. At last members of the nobility took matters into their own hands, and Rasputin was assassinated in December 1916, by the wealthy Prince Felix Yusupov, whose wife was a niece of Nicholas II, and his fellow conspirators, the Grand Duke Dmitry Pavlovitch, a cousin of the emperor, and the ultra-reactionary, Vladimir Purishkevitch.

POLITICAL, SOCIAL AND ECONOMIC CONDITIONS
ON THE EVE OF WORLD WAR I

Disturbed by the Anglo-French *Entente Cordiale* of 1904, which was an outgrowth of Russia's involvement in the Far East, Nicholas II promptly sought to re-establish better relations with Germany. In July 1905, while the Russo-Japanese War was still in progress, the German emperor and the tsar reached a secret agreement at Bjorko, which virtually amounted to a Russo-German alliance. Since this private "deal" constituted, for all practical purposes, an abrogation of the Franco-Russian alliance of 1894, the ministers of Nicholas II forced him to annul it. Not the least of the reasons for avoiding a break with France was Russia's constant need of money, in view of her struggle against internal disorder and her reverses in the war. When on April 16, 1906, France, in return for Russia's support against Germany at Algeciras (1906), extended to her a huge loan, this aid came at a most critical and opportune moment and did much to bind Russia more firmly to France.

The *rapprochement* with France, together with the outcome of the Japanese War, led the Russian foreign minister, A. P. Izvolsky, to seek improved relations with Great Britain. In an agreement with the latter country in August, 1907, known as the Anglo-Russian Entente, Russia materially modified her claims upon territory in Central Asia, thereby relieving the uneasiness of England in respect to India. By this agreement, Russia recognized Afghanistan as a British sphere, both powers consented to maintain a "hands off" policy in Tibet, and each retained a sphere of influence in Persia— the Russians in the north and the British in the south. A famous cartoon in the English magazine *Punch* portrayed the British lion and the Russian bear mauling the Persian cat! Inasmuch as the Japanese War had all but ruined Russia's pretensions in the Far East, Great Britain had gained all her ends. Her hostility, therefore, was considerably abated, and the way was paved for a better understanding between the two powers.

The second Hague Peace Conference of 1907 and its failure to accomplish disarmament have already been mentioned. Russia would have been glad to devote the French loan ($400,000,000) of 1906 to internal improvements rather than to armament. However her recent defeat by Japan and the fact that other European countries, especially Germany, were armed to the teeth, made her position extremely precarious and her need of armament imperative. It was these considerations which led her to take the initiative in calling a Peace Conference in the hope of averting future wars. The failure of this earnest attempt on the part of Russia was a great disaster to her. It had, however, a very significant result, that is, the alignment of Germany and Austria against the Triple Entente made up of Russia, Great Britain, and France. The course of European politics was such that Great Britain soon began to fear Germany far more than she ever had feared Russia. The events growing out of the Turkish revolution, 1908, intensified this fear and also served to cement more firmly the alliance of the Triple Entente against Germany. The aforementioned revolution brought a pro-German government into power in Turkey. In October of the same year, to the consternation of the Triple Entente, Austria suddenly annexed Bosnia and Herzegovina, which she had occupied temporarily in 1878. Although Germany's part in the annexation was clearly discernible, the Russian government was in no position to do anything about the matter, and the Triple Entente accepted perforce the *fait accompli*. The fact was that Izvolsky, in trying to make a deal with Austria whereby he might secure Austrian support of Russian interests in the Straits, had been completely outwitted by the Austrian foreign minister, Aehrenthal. Worse still, the Bulgars, obviously acting by preconcerted arrangement with Austria, seized this opportunity to proclaim their final independence from Turkey. The upshot of the Balkan crisis of 1908, which has sometimes been termed a dress rehearsal for 1914, was that Pan-Slav sentiment in Russia was thoroughly aroused, Serbia looked to Russia for aid against Austria, and the Triple Entente was further consolidated by its opposition to the new *Drang nach Osten* on the part of the Central Powers.

Germany's next move came in the summer of 1911, when the German gunboat *Panther* was sent to Agadir, ostensibly to protect German interests in Morocco but really for the purpose of attempting once more to secure a foothold in that territory. Powerful Arab leaders of South Morocco were entertained by the officers of the *Panther,* who promised German assistance if they made an attempt to throw off French control. As in 1905-1906, at Algeciras, French diplomacy won the victory. France's right to a protectorate in Morocco was recognized, November 4, 1911, but in return she ceded to Germany some 250,000 square kilometers of her possessions in the northern Congo.

There was no reason to believe that the Central Powers would be satisfied with the outcome of the Agadir affair, and European relations became tense. Inside Russia, German-Austrian diplomacy had long been active in increasing the tension existing between the Russian people and their government. For example, Austria sedulously fostered Ukrainian "culture" in her territory of Galicia, from whence it spread to Russian territory and exerted a subversive influence. The purpose of this was to create among Ukrainians a sentiment of good will toward the Central Powers and a desire to separate themselves from Russia. In retaliation for this propaganda, Russia brought about the union of Serbia, Bulgaria, and Greece against Turkey in the First Balkan War, 1912-1913. This was intended as an indirect blow against Austria. The Central Powers, however, succeeded in stirring up dissension among these minor powers, which, after defeating Turkey and stripping her of most of her European possessions, divided their allegiance, Serbia turning to the *Entente,* and Bulgaria seeking the patronage of the Central Powers. In the Second Balkan War (1913), Bulgaria was defeated by the combined action of Serbia, Greece, and Rumania. But the Germans, at the request of Turkey, dispatched a military mission under General Liman von Sanders to Constantinople to reorganize the Turkish army. While Germans dreamed of a Berlin-to-Bagdad railway, Russians regarded the German interest in the Near East as a direct threat to Russian interests at the Dardanelles. The Balkans remained a veritable powder keg. It required only a slight pretext to cause the mutual hostility to explode, and this was afforded by the events of the summer of 1914.

In Russia internal conditions on the eve of World War I could hardly have been worse. Not only was there an alarming lack of political stability, but economic conditions were in a precarious state. The strikes alone were almost as universal and involved almost as

TSAR NICHOLAS II REVIEWING HIS BODYGUARD AT KRASNOY SELO IN AUGUST 1911

many persons as in 1905. There were 1,059,000 workmen engaged in strikes as compared with 1,843,000 in 1905. The government sought desperately to divert public attention from the rotten politics and wretched economic conditions and eagerly seized upon a means offered it by the Black Hundred in the city of Kiev. This organization had brought charges against Mendel Beilis, a Jew, of the ritual murder of a Gentile boy named Andrey Yushtchinsky. A conviction would have resulted in a series of pogroms against the Jews, whereby the authorities hoped to exhaust the people in an orgy of blood. Instead of diverting popular attention, this farcical trial merely brought into glaring prominence the entire rottenness of the system of government. The people were much aroused over the manifest injustice of the accusation against Beilis. Protests poured in not only from organizations in Russia but also from foreign countries, including the United States. Despite this, the case dragged on for two years, from July 1911 to November 1913. However public opinion and especially world opinion were too strong to be disregarded and in the end Beilis was acquitted. Russian officials were of the opinion that German-Austrian diplomacy utilized this famous case to further several ends: first, to stir up unrest among Russian Jews; second, to injure Russia's world prestige; and finally, to divert Russia's attention from German militarism.

There were, however, lights as well as shadows in the picture presented by Russia prior to World War I. Heroic efforts of Liberals in the Duma had resulted in significant achievements, one of the most important being in the field of education. On May 16, 1908, a law was passed which provided for four years of elementary instruction for all children between the ages of eight and eleven. By 1914 there were 149,000 elementary schools, in which about half the children of school age were enrolled. Educational authorities estimated that by 1922 more than twice that number of schools would be needed to accommodate the increasing school population. Despite the obstructive measures of a reactionary government and the opposition of the Orthodox Church, there is little doubt that the hopes of the Liberals for universal education would have become a reality by 1922. The war and the revolution of 1917, however, interrupted the educational campaign.

As a result of the reforms of Stolypin, the bulk of the peasants was in possession of full civil rights and enjoyed a fair degree of prosperity. Whereas agriculture was, as always, the basic industry in Russia, it was not especially well developed because of antiquated tools and methods. Thus, although large areas were under cultivation,

Russia ranked fourth in the world production of grain. Hours of work in the various trades and occupations had been shortened, a working day now averaging from ten to twelve hours. For this the worker received on an average about $150 a year, which according to Russian standards, was a very fair wage. The country's chief source of income came from the alcohol monopoly introduced by Witte, which in 1913 yielded a revenue of $335,000,000. Since the building of the great Trans-Siberian Railway, previously mentioned, the number of railroads had steadily increased, supplying work for many and making some progress toward uniting the scattered settlements of Russia's vast expanse of territory. The area of Russia at this time was 8,764,586 square miles, almost three times that of the United States. This supported a population that approached 180,000,000, which represented 169 ethnic groups with as many dialects.

The support of the royal family cost the country 11,000,000 rubles (about $5,450,000) annually. In addition the emperor derived an income equal in amount from estates known as *Udyely* belonging to the royal family, and from deposits which he kept in banks in England and Germany. In London banks he had £20,000,000, which, according to the Grand Duke Alexander, he is said to have devoted in its entirety to charity during the years 1915-1917. The imperial family also possessed rare jewels valued at $80,000,000. These jewels had been collected during the three centuries of Romanov rule.

In view of all that has been said of strained European relations, it may seem strange that there was not an earlier outbreak of hostilities. As a matter of fact a general war was delayed solely by the race for armament, each country seeking to oustrip the other. Of course this in itself increased international tension, but each nation hoped to gain military superiority before the advent of the inevitable combat. As has been indicated elsewhere, Russia was behind other European countries in the matter of armament but had, nevertheless, made considerable progress. The improvements had given the Russian junkers a most exaggerated idea of their ability. They thought they could fight anyone and burned with a desire to recover the prestige lost in the war with Japan.

Despite the machinations of Germany, which have been discussed earlier, it would be unreasonable and unfair from a historical standpoint to attribute to her the entire responsibility and blame for World War I. A careful study of all phases of the situation leads to the conclusion that the war was a divided responsibility, and that all the major powers of Europe had a hand in precipitating the catastrophe. To be sure,

THE NEVSKY PROSPECT, ST. PETERSBURG, ABOUT 1910

Germany was eager to carry out the Moltke Plan,[1] and Austria dreamt of domination in the Balkans. On the other hand, however, French resentment over the outcome of the Franco-Prussian War and the loss of Alsace-Lorraine was as alive as ever, and France never relinquished her hope of retaking this territory. Moreover she wished to put an end to German interference in her African colonies and protectorates, especially in Morocco. It is a well-established fact that French emissaries in various parts of the world had disseminated propaganda against Germany in the early 1890's. England, indeed, did not want war in 1914 and tried very hard to prevent it. The efforts of Sir Edward Grey to avert hostilities are well known. Nevertheless, England regarded Germany as a dangerous competitor, whose power she wished to see curbed. This Grey hoped to do without actual participation in the war but by acting in the capacity of a powerful neutral country, which would be in a position to dictate terms.

As for Russia, we may say by way of recapitulation, that the governmental authorities were exceedingly anxious for war, inasmuch as the Beilis case and the failure of Russian diplomacy in the Balkans in 1912 had brought them into exceedingly bad repute with the people. Foreign propaganda, such as that disseminated by Austria and the fomenting of strikes by various and sundry agitators and agencies contributed to the unrest among the masses. The upper classes, for their part, were disgusted and alienated by the power given to Rasputin. The government was tottering, and a brilliant military campaign was urgently needed to restore its prestige and stability. Thus when war loomed, the country was plunged into the conflict with the speed of lightning by officials who were making one last desperate effort to maintain their sway over the Russian people. General Lukomsky, who had charge of Russian mobilization, proceeded with incredible rapidity. Whether he did so with the encouragement of France or under the influence of Russian jingoists is uncertain. In any event, the speed with which the Russian army was mobilized had much to do with hastening the outbreak of the war.

The immediate cause, or rather pretext, for the war was the assassination of the Austrian archduke, Franz Ferdinand, on June 28, 1914, in the heretofore unimportant town of Sarajevo in Bosnia. Austria, alleging that the assassination had been perpetrated with the

---

[1] The Moltke Plan originated with General Helmuth von Moltke, Chief of the German General Staff, 1906-1914. He had detailed topographical surveys made of all neighboring countries, especially of Russia, France, and Belgium. These surveys were studied by officers in preparation for possible wars.

sanction of the government of Serbia, issued an ultimatum to the
latter country on July 23, 1914. One clause of the ultimatum demanded
the participation of Austrian officials in the investigation of the murder
and the apprehension of the conspirators. No doubt Serbia was correct
in believing that, if permitted, this Austrian "participation" would lead
to an occupation of a part of Serbian territory by Austrian troops on
the pretense that the investigating officials must be protected. The
occupation of Serbian territory would in turn lead to absorption by
Austria. Even so, Serbia might have yielded to the demands of a
stronger country, especially since she was on bad terms with Bulgaria,
who had been plotting for revenge ever since the Balkan War in 1912.
However Serbia, certain of Russia's support, gave only a qualified
acceptance to the Austrian ultimatum. In consequence, Austria, in
spite of German pressure to the contrary, declared war upon Serbia
on July 28, 1914, and immediately invaded Serbian territory.

   In view of the two opposing systems of alliance that had been
established German hopes for the "localization" of the Austro-Serbian
conflict proved untenable. Russia and France refused to permit Austria
to have a free hand in Serbia. Because of the Parliamentary situation
in England, Sir Edward Grey found it inadvisable or impossible to
align his country unqualifiedly with either side or to exert sufficient
pressure on Germany to prevent the latter from granting Austria a
carte blanche against Serbia. Russian bureaucrats, including Minister
of Foreign Affairs S. D. Sazonov, fearful that a delay in Russian
mobilization would result in an undue advantage for the highly mobile
German armies, induced the tsar to resort to general mobilization,
which, in view of the terms of the Franco-Russian alliance, was practically equivalent to war. It culminated in a German declaration of
war against Russia on August 1, followed by similar action against
France two days later. German violation of the neutrality of Belgium
brought England into the war on August 4, followed by her ally, Japan,
on August 22. Turkey entered the conflict on the side of the Central
Powers in October, thereby closing what might have been an important
allied supply route to Russia. Thus the great powers blundered into
World War I.

RUSSIA AT WAR, 1914-1917

   Once Germany had declared war, Nicholas II called upon all
Russians to rally to the defense of their country. His appeal met
with an immediate and enthusiastic response from all classes of the

people, especially as the governmental policy was approved by the Fourth Duma and the zemstvos. The participation of England and France did much to win popular support of the war in Russia and avert those disorders which Germany had hoped, not without reason, would follow the mobilization of the Russian army. Even the radicals saw hope for the future of Russia if she took part in a war in which France, a republic, and England, a true democracy, were opposed to monarchial Germany. They felt that if Russia associated herself with these countries as an ally, she too might be able in the end to secure a democratic form of government. For this reason many volunteered without waiting for their turn to be called to arms. However, in those early days few in Russia or elsewhere believed that the war would be of long duration. It was thought that the regular army alone would be engaged in the actual conflict. Therefore the readiness to take up arms meant nothing more than an expression of loyalty to Russia. There was another reason for popular support of the war. In his appeals for the co-operation of the people, Nicholas II emphasized the element of Slavonic emancipation. An address by the emperor to the Duma on August 8, 1914, contained the following statement: "We are not only defending the dignity and honor of our country, but we are also fighting for our Slavic brothers, the Serbs, our coreligionists and kinsmen, and at this moment I behold with joy how the Union of all the Slavs with Russia is being strongly and unremittingly carried to consummation." Poland was also guaranteed the restoration of her ethnic boundaries under Russian suzerainty.

The war enthusiasm was, however, of short duration in Russia. Within a few weeks it had been greatly lessened by fear. On August 17, 1914, upon the insistence of her allies, Russian forces under General Rennenkampf entered East Prussia. They were thus the first allied forces to set foot on enemy soil, a factor of great psychological importance. Troops under General Samsonov followed up this offensive. This army numbered about 200,000 men and represented the very flower of the Russian military system. It was, nevertheless, destined for defeat, because German strategy had carefully laid a trap in the invaded region. General Hindenburg, with Ludendorff as chief of staff, attacked the Russian forces on August 31, 1914, at Tannenberg. The battle resulted in an overwhelming defeat for Russia. The Germans drove their foes into the Mazurian Swamps of East Prussia. Here 30,000 were either drowned or bayoneted, and 90,000 were taken prisoners. This disastrous defeat struck terror to the heart of the Russian masses. The German front was regarded as impregnable, and an order to report to this front was looked upon by many as a sentence of death. Whereas the blow to Russia was irreparable, France profited exceedingly by the Battle of Tannenberg, inasmuch as it withdrew six divisions of German troops and one cavalry division from the Western Front. This reduction of the invading forces made it possible for the French and English to check the German advance at the first Battle of the Marne and thereby change the entire course of the war.

The military plans worked out in advance of the war by Russian strategists had called, first of all, for the invasion of the Austro-Hungarian Empire and the destruction of its not so formidable military might. Only when that was accomplished did the Russian General Staff plan to undertake an offensive against Germany. Furthermore, the Schlieffen-Moltke plan of operations likewise envisaged a German offensive against France before the German armies would be called upon to face the slow-moving Russians. Thus the allied appeal to Russia for an offensive against Germany in August 1914 not only disrupted Russian strategy but likewise that of Germany.

In the light of what happened in World War II, it is now clear that it was Russia that provided the "second front" for the allied armies in the first world war. Whenever the situation on the Western front became threatening, the Allies invariably demanded that Russia come to their aid by launching a counter-offensive against Germany. On the other hand, in 1915 when Russia was sorely pressed, and in dire need of support because of the retreat of her army and the collapse of Serbia, the Allies did not stage any large drives on the Western front, which would have drawn off the armies of the Central Powers. To be sure, the Allies tried to render assistance at the Dardanelles and thereby put an end to the isolation of Russia, but with no results. In the spring of 1915, however, "the immemorial and sacred dream of the Russian people" appeared to be near fruition, when Russian Foreign Minister Sazonov reached a secret agreement with England and France whereby, in the event of an Allied victory, Constantinople and the Straits zone would be annexed to Russia. The entrance of Italy into the war in May, 1915, was productive of no benefits to Russia. For the most part she was left to her fate. Yet despite her defeat by the Germans, Russian man power rendered valuable service to the Allies, aside from serving as a means of diverting attention from the Western Front.

While the armies of the Western Allies bogged down in France and Belgium and failed to reach enemy soil until 1918, Russia launched four armies against Austria-Hungary in 1914 and occupied Austrian

Galicia. The Russian army likewise carried on offensive operations against Turkey on Turkish soil, seizing large slices of Armenia and Eastern Anatolia in 1915. In fact British success against Turkey under General Allenby later in the war was greatly facilitated by Russian action against the Turks in the Caucasus. Russian man power not only played an important role against Austria and Turkey, but in accordance with a Franco-Russian deal of December 19, 1915, five Russian brigades were dispatched via the Chinese Eastern Railway and the port of Dairen to the Western Front and Salonika.[1] In return France promised Nicholas II badly needed supplies of munitions.

The losses and failures, which marked the year 1915, greatly weakened the morale of the army and the people at large, which in turn led to serious political problems. The army had been found most inadequately prepared to meet the Central Powers, whose men were equipped with the most modern and deadly machinery of warfare. This was not due solely to the fact that prior to the war Russia had not been able to keep pace with her neighbors in armament. Graft and treason among high officials had criminally reduced army equipment. Upon the occasion of the Russian retreat from the Carpathian Mountain region, when a hail of sharpnel was descending upon the troops, the following order was issued: "Do not fire unnecessarily and take the ammunition from the killed and wounded." One of the officials, who was found to be chiefly responsible for the inadequate equipment of the Russian Army was General Sukhomlinov. He was dismissed in August 1915.

As the year 1915 advanced, the Duma and the emperor were increasingly unable to agree. Finally the Duma demanded a new cabinet composed of responsible leaders who would restore public confidence. The emperor did not want to yield to this demand and in order to avoid doing so assumed the command of the Russian army. The former commander-in-chief, Grand Duke Nicholas, was transferred to the Caucasian front. All this was done at the suggestion of Rasputin, whose influence was also responsible for the unreasonable supplanting of one ministry after another. The Duma wished to continue the war and hence had the support of the Allies in all its disagreements with the emperor. Certain influential government officials, however, were in favor of making a separate peace with Germany. Their first step was to win over Rasputin, who brought about the dismissal of Minister of Foreign Affairs Sazonov who was pro-Ally.

---

[1] See *Red Archives*, No. 2 (99), 1940, and *Ibid.*, 4 (101), 1940, pp. 228-235.

His place was taken by B. V. Sturmer, whose pro-German sympathies were well known. Naturally this aroused the suspicions of the Allies.

As for Nicholas II, he found himself in a most unusual and precarious position. Almost within his very palace, there was a strong combine using every means in its power to bring about a separate peace with Germany. The Duma was pro-Ally and hence opposed to a separate peace, but its policies were so at variance with his own that they were constantly at loggerheads. Moreover the military situation was becoming progressively worse. Russian armies had won successes against the Austrians and Turks only to meet defeat at the hands of the Germans under General Mackensen. In 1915 Germany had conquered Poland, Lithuania, and part of Latvia, thereby constituting a potential threat to the Russian capital. As compared with eighty-four divisions on the Western Front, where the Allies remained on the defensive, the Germans had massed one hundred sixty-one divisions against the Russians by the fall of 1915.

By the winter of 1916-1917, the Duma's dissatisfaction with the emperor had reached a high pitch. The empress also became the object of its displeasure, and at the November session several speeches were made, openly charging her with exerting a pernicious influence. Nor were the charges groundless. She was constantly urging her husband with all the eloquence at her command to defy the Duma and crush those who opposed him. In a letter written to him while he was at the front in 1916, she advised that the premier be hanged and that several high officials be exiled to Siberia. In all the words and deeds of the sovereigns the influence of Rasputin was evident, but even after his assassination on December 29, 1916, their stubborn temper did not change and they made no concessions to the demands of the representatives of the people. It was then that a plot began to develop in court circles, approved and supported by members of the Allied corps, which had as its aim the deposition of the emperor in favor of some other member of the royal family.

The situation in Russia on the eve of the Revolution was briefly as follows. There was an army of about 15,000,000 men, counting the reserve troops in the rear and the wounded, as well as those in active service at the front. All of them were discouraged and heartily sick of the war which seemed to drag on indefinitely. Among them were some 600,000 Jewish soldiers, whose loyalty and sacrifices had won the praise of even the greatest reactionaries at the beginning of the war. Nevertheless, they were in constant terror for the safety of their families

who might be made the object of pogroms. There were the two opposing movements, the separatist and pro-Ally. There was an emperor,
who was not supported by the Duma, but who stubbornly refused to
make any concessions. There were liberals and radicals who feared
that their opposition to imperial policies would mean a sentence of exile
or death as soon as the emperor had time to give the matter his attention after the war. Worst of all, there was a serious food shortage,
which was rendered more desperate by the presence of some 2,500,000
refugees from the front. Clearly the only possible remedy lay in a complete change of government and a new ruler, since Nicholas II had
neither respected the wishes of the people nor kept his promises to them.

By March 10, 1917, the food shortage had become very great, and
distress was widespread and acute. Especially alarming was the situation in Petrograd,[1] where crowds marched through the streets bearing
red flags and shouted "Down with the German woman" (the empress),
and where revolt threatened to break out at any moment. Thereupon,
M. V. Rodzyanko, president of the Duma, once more implored the
emperor to form a new cabinet and restore public confidence. This
measure was approved and supported also by Grand Duke Michael
Alexandrovitch, brother of the emperor, as well as the prime minister,
Prince N. D. Golitsyn. The emperor's answer to their pleas was the *ukaz*
of March 11, which dissolved the Duma. He then sent one battalion
under General Ivanov to Petrograd with orders to put down the threatening revolt.

In defiance of the imperial *ukaz,* the Duma met on March 12, in
which move it was supported by the soldiers of the local garrison. After
much deliberation and bickering, the Duma decided to launch a revolution, and a temporary committee of twelve was appointed to lead the
movement and to organize a provisional government. The members of
the committee were liberals and moderate conservatives, with the exception of two, Alexander Kerensky, then in his early thirties, and Nicholas
Tchkheidze, both of whom were socialists. Tchkheidze resigned from
the committee immediately.

While the Duma was deliberating, a mob spirit reigned in the streets
of Moscow and Petrograd. Police control had virtually disappeared,
for many members of the force had joined the mob. Some of the mob on
their own responsibility proceeded to "arrest" officials and ministers of
reactionary tendencies and bring them by force to the building in which

---

[1] At the beginning of the war in 1914, the name *Petrograd* was substituted for
St. Petersburg because of the German origin of the latter.

the Duma was in session. In the meantime a most significant develop-ment was taking place in Petrograd. A Soviet of Workers' and Soldiers' Deputies on the 1905 model had been organized and Tchkheidze, the aforementioned Social Democratic deputy of the Duma, had been elected chairman, with Kerensky serving as a vice-president. The Soviet estab-lished its headquarters at the Duma, where, with its military backing, it soon threatened to become the real master of the capital. The Bol-sheviks, in the beginning, were very much in the minority in the Soviet.

On March 14, the committee of the Duma succeeded in forming a provisional government, which was to act pending the election of a per-manent government by a representative assembly. The chairman of the new government was Prince George E. Lvov, head of the Zemstvo Red Cross, who was assisted by the following ministers: Alexander Gutch-kov, minister of war, Professor Paul Milyukov, minister of foreign affairs, and Alexander Kerensky, minister of justice. These men and all who were given responsible positions by the new government were liberals or socialists. The revolution was moving too fast and the gen-eral temper was becoming too radical to permit conservatives to find any favor as candidates for public office. Rodzyanko, former president of the Duma, a conservative liberal, had been elected chairman of the Temporary Committee, but, with the formation of the Provisional Gov-ernment, he was no longer considered. The first act of the Provisional Government was to demand the abdication of the emperor. On March 15, Nicholas II abdicated in favor of his brother, the Grand Duke Michael, but the latter renounced his claims, and the Romanov dynasty ceased to rule. Shortly after the abdication, the emperor and empress and their children were arrested and exiled to Siberia. Early in 1918 the Soviet Government sent them to Ekaterinburg (now Sverdlovsk). Here they were murdered on July 16, 1918.

It was in June 1915 that a Russian industrialist, in conversation with Maurice Paléologue, French ambassador to Russia, made the following remarkable prophecy as to the coming and ultimate course of the Rus-sian Revolution:

The days of Tsarism are numbered. It is beyond hope. But Tsarism is the very framework of Russia and the sole bond of unity for the nation. Revolution is now inevitable, it is only waiting for a favourable opportunity. Such an opportunity will come with military defeat, a famine in the prov-inces, a strike in Petrograd, a riot in Moscow, some scandal or tragedy at the Palace. . . . With us (in Russia) revolution can only be destructive because the educated class is only a tiny minority, without organization, political experience or contact with the masses. To my mind that is the greatest crime of Tsarism. . . . No doubt it will be the *bourgeois,* intellectuals, "Cadets," who will give the signal for the Revolution, thinking they are saving Russia. But from the *bourgeois* revolution we shall at once descend to the working-class revolution, and soon after to the peasant revolution. And then will begin anarchy, interminable anarchy! . . . We shall see the days of Pugachev again and perhaps worse![1]

---

[1] Paléologue, Maurice, *An Ambassador's Memoirs,* London, 1923, Vol. I, pp. 349-350.

9

A Century of Russian Culture[1]
1815-1917

LITERATURE

WHEN we speak of Russian culture, we mean primarily that of the nineteenth and early twentieth centuries, and especially the literature. Although much was accomplished in music, ballet, painting, and so forth, the main contribution was in the field of literature.

The Russian literary renaissance of the nineteenth century was a product of many factors and literary influences. It received its immediate impetus, however, from two major forces: one cultural, the other political. The first was the appearance in the year 1800 of the manuscript of the *Tale of the Host of Igor,* which created a stir in Russian literary circles, and which inspired Russian authors to cast aside their foreign models in order to emulate the quality of work produced by their ancestors. In the second place Russian literature owed a great deal to the upsurge of nationalism which resulted from the Napoleonic invasion of Russia. During the French invasion there came a strong reaction against foreign influence in general—against French influence in particular. In spite of the fact that the Russian officers who fought Napoleon spoke French among themselves, the bulk of the Russian people despised it. Following the trend of popular opinion, and stimulated by the discovery of ancient manuscripts, Russian authors chose Russian themes as their literary medium during the golden age.

Unlike other literatures, where poetry occupies the most prominent place, prose, especially the novel, is foremost in Russian literature. For various reasons, the Russian genius expressed itself much better in prose. The majority of Russian writers considered poetry as entertaining literature—but Russian literature, regarded in its entirety, is not entertaining. It is closely interwoven with current events and deals with problems of utmost importance to the individual, to the nation, or

---

[1] In this chapter the writer has drawn extensively upon his book, *The Golden Age of Russian Literature* (1952).

to society as a whole. The most significant reason for this phenomenon was the censorship that existed in Russia during the period in question. In Russia writers were not permitted to express themselves directly on any controversial subject. Much material, which in other countries would have found its way into scientific or theological journals, in Russia, found an outlet in fiction. For example, it was impossible to have the same debates and discussions over the condition of the serfs in Russia as occurred in the United States over the abolition of slavery. Russian champions of emancipation had to resort to fiction—to novels and short stories in which they discussed the pros and cons of the problem. It will suffice to mention Gogol's *Dead Souls,* Turgenev's *Memoirs of a Sportsman,* or Pisemsky's works. In the light of this situation there is perhaps no such thing as Russian fiction (as the term is usually understood), for each novel dealt with the burning issues of the day. In other words, if one were to substitute the real names for the fictitious names, one could easily reproduce an important part of Russian history in the nineteenth century. In this connection it is well to remember that the reading public in Russia during the period, although small in proportion to the total population, was, generally speaking, a highly intelligent group, capable of grasping the underlying facts behind the so-called fiction.

Although the novel occupies the most prominent place in Russian literature, we can hardly afford to overlook the role of the drama. Briefly, classical Russian drama is a purely secular institution. Unlike the drama of Western Europe, whose beginnings are traceable to the Church, the Russian classical drama was founded and developed outside the Church; in fact, it was established and flourished in spite of the Church.

Although the novel afforded a medium for the highest expression of Russian tragedy, the genius of Russian drama lay in the comedy. For this reason, in Russian literature the novel and the play are closely interwoven and inseparable—the one complementing the other. Closer examination reveals, moreover, that the technical structure of the best Russian fiction was based upon the play. In view of these facts it is not surprising to find that practically every Russian novelist of renown was also a playwright and *vice versa.*

The novel reflected life as it was too often in Russia at this time—a tale of frustrations and defeat. Strictly speaking, the comedy interpreted the novel. That is, by exposing the corruption prevalent among public officials and by holding up to ridicule their mismanagement of public affairs, the comedy often revealed the source of the tragedy in Russian life. In a country where universal education did not yet exist, and where the majority of the ruling class could scarcely be called literary-minded, the stage had, potentially at least, a wider audience than the novel. This may partially explain why the censor was more lenient with the novel than with the play and why the novel became the main channel of expression in Russian literature.

The founder and the most outstanding leader of this Russian national literary renaissance was Alexander Sergeyevitch Pushkin (1799-1837). Pushkin has done more for the Russian language than Shakespeare for the English. As Peter the Great, in the time of one short life, sought to bridge the gap created by the Mongolian invasions, Pushkin cherished the same dream for Russian literature and the Russian language. He found it a rough, uncut diamond with great potentialities, and he left it a polished medium of expression unsurpassed by other modern languages. Even into the foreign words he borrowed, he breathed a new spirit. In the Russian language he was able to give expression to the pent-up thoughts and emotions of a previous generation as well as of his own contemporaries. He gave wings to the Russian language in poetry.

Pushkin's liberal leanings, radical associates, and revolutionary poems and epigrams, directed even against the highest functionaries of the government, including the Tsar, soon rendered him suspect. His *Ode to Liberty* (1817), which constituted a summons to revolt against an unregenerate autocracy, *The Village,* which depicted the evils of serfdom, and other Pushkin poems were widely circulated in manuscript form among his friends. Alexander I, antagonized by the rash young poet's boldness in deluging the country with shocking verses, banished him to South Russia in 1820. Although ostensibly he made his peace with autocracy under Nicholas I, his *Message to Siberia* (1827) revealed the poet's strong sympathy for the exiled Decembrists.

Until Pushkin, Russian writers were for the most part of the dilettante type—for it was an unwritten tradition that each outstanding noble family should produce at least one manscript of merit in each generation. Pushkin, however, in addition to his other contributions, made a profession of writing.

Pushkin transmitted to others the inspiration and ambition to continue that which he himself was not able to complete in the brief span of his own life. His influence is clearly discernible throughout the entire period, many ideas being directly traceable to him. For instance, his *Eugene Onegin,* a novel in verse, provided the pattern for all subsequent novelists in Russia. His *Dubrovsky* forms an excellent background for Turgenev's *Memoirs of a Sportsman.* Tolstoy's *War and Peace* was

FYODOR DOSTOYEVSKY

patterned after Pushkin's *The Captain's Daughter,* while *The Queen of Spades* by Pushkin may have inspired Dostoyevsky's *Crime and Punishment.* To be sure, Dostoyevsky always acknowledged his indebtedness to Pushkin. For it was he who made Pushkin famous by evincing his admiration for *The Prophet.* If Belinsky (1810-1848), the Russian Lessing, was chiefly responsible for discovering Pushkin's talent, it fell to the lot of Dostoyevsky to proclaim him the greatest poet of the world and the national poet laureate of Russia.

As the first writer of Russian tragedies, foreign in form but Russian in content, Pushkin also made his contribution to the field of drama. Of these the best example is *Boris Godunov,* upon which Mussorgsky later based his opera of the same name. But Pushkin's real genius lay in poetry. It was through his verse that the young poet voiced the true sentiment of literary Russia. His greatest achievement, and one which alone would have ensured for him the literary immortality he sought, was the incomparable *Eugene Onegin.*

Few poets can claim to have exerted such an influence on their country's music as did Pushkin. His dramatic poems and fairy tales provided themes for most of the oustanding Russian composers of the nineteenth and twentieth centuries. The impressive list includes the best-known Russian operas, such as Glinka's *Ruslan and Lyudmila,* Dargomyzhsky's *The Stone Guest,* Mussorgsky's *Boris Godunov* (as revised by Rimsky-Korsakov), Tchaikovsky's *Eugene Onegin, Mazeppa* (*Poltava*), and *The Queen of Spades,* Rimsky-Korsakov's *Tale of the Tsar Saltan, The Golden Cockerel,* and *Mozart and Salieri,* Rachmaninov's *Aleko* (*The Gypsies*) and *The Avaricious Knight,* and the ballets of the Soviet composer Asafyev, based on *The Fountain of Bakhchisarai* and *The Prisoner of the Caucasus.*

Next in importance to Pushkin was Mikhail Yurevitch Lermontov (1814-1841), whose fame rests primarily on his poems *The Demon, The Angel, On the Death of a Poet,* and on his prose novel, *The Hero of Our Times.* Unlike Pushkin, whose writings reflect the past and present of Russia and afford a glimpse into her future, Lermontov is primarily the poet of the Caucasus. He first visited this region as a lad, and was twice banished there—a punishment which proved to be a blessing in disguise. The prerequisite for a full appreciation of Lermontov's poetry is a knowledge of the Caucasus region as it was in the early nineteenth century. The Caucasus made of Lermontov more than a mere successor to Pushkin. It was due to the scenic grandeur of that environment that he inaugurated the age of romanticism in Russian literature.

His main contribution to Russian literature was that he revealed a new world in the Caucasus, a hitherto comparatively unknown region then in the process of conquest by the Russians. The Caucasus, in those days, stood in much the same relation to Russia as the Wild West to the Eastern states in America. The Cossacks were the Russian cowboys and the native tribesmen their Indians, who carried on an unrelenting guerrilla warfare against Russia for 137 years.

Lermontov was the first Russian poet to depict not only the magnificent grandeur of Caucasian scenery, but also to describe Caucasian culture, itself an elongation of the Near East, and to record the hitherto unwritten folk tales and ballads of the native peoples. In this light, his contribution was not only to Russian literature but to Oriental studies in general; for, although the Caucasus has long belonged to Russia, it has remained linguistically and culturally Near Eastern. During recent years when the Soviet Government has encouraged a real renaissance of Caucasian culture, the inspiration and value of Lermontov's work have become even more apparent.

It is in part due to Lermontov that Russian literature—a literature in which the East and West meet—has such a fascination. Pushkin primarily interpreted western Russia to the Eastern world, whereas Lermontov, through the Caucasus, interpreted the East to western Russia and the world.

One of the outstanding dramatists of this period, a contemporary of Pushkin and Lermontov, was Alexander Sergeyevitch Griboyedov (1795-1829). His masterpiece, and the most widely discussed comedy in the Russia of his time, was *The Misfortune of Being Clever*. The chief character was Tchatsky, who voiced the sentiment of a considerable part of the intelligentsia against the foreign influences which permeated the Russian ruling classes, and who advocated reform in preference to violent revolution. However, Tchatsky's "tirades," after a period of crystallization, reached their climax in the abortive Decembrist revolt of 1825—the first Russian revolution.

The influence of this play did not end with the Decembrist revolt. Subsequent Russian writers and leaders studied its verses by heart. Its influence is clearly discernible in Dostoyevsky's work. Tchatsky was undoubtedly a model for Dostoyevsky's Prince Myshkin in *The Idiot*.

In brief, *The Misfortune of Being Clever* was written for the elite. It was both a confession of and a protest against the corruption of the official world and the excesses of the younger generation. The shadow of Tchatsky hovered over Russian literature almost to the outbreak of the Russian Revolution of 1917. Its great, although indirect, influence on the latter event can hardly be overestimated.

In the history of Russian literature, 1842 should be hailed as a red-letter year. For the appearance of *Dead Souls* by Nikolai Vasilyevitch Gogol (1809-1852) in that year marked the birth of the genuinely realistic Russian novel, thereby inaugurating the age of prose in Russian literature. Gogol was the father of the Russian novel, and, as previously stated, it was the novel which occupied the most prominent place in the field of Russian letters.

Although Gogol's work reflected Russian life as a whole, we immediately associate it with South Russia. Just as when we speak of Lermontov we visualize the Caucasus, when we turn to Gogol we think chiefly in terms of the Ukraine. Gogol first attained popularity by his sketches of Ukrainian life. These sketches were widely read, not because of their rich content, but chiefly because they revealed a new world to the people of Great Russia. The North Russians of the period in question looked upon Southern Russia as the Americans for many years regarded the West. Just as the stories of the Wild West, real or fictitious, made a tremendous appeal to men in the more settled parts of the United States, so Gogol's early sketches of Ukrainian life, present or past, stirred the imagination of Russians elsewhere. His historical novel, *Taras Bulba,* became the first and foremost classic on the Russian Cossacks. The sixteenth-century Cossacks depicted in this novel held the same appeal for the Russian reader as the exploits of the Western cowboys for Americans. These tales hold the key to Gogol's widespread popularity.

Gogol's famous story *The Cloak* also broke new ground in Russian letters. *The Cloak* is not the best story in Russian literature, as some critics claim, but it was the most epoch-making literary production. Here, for the first time, the sad plight of the low-salaried chancery clerk attracted the attention of Russian society. Prior to this, the Akaky Akakiyevitches, if they were ever mentioned, received only incidental recognition and never captured a leading role. There were thousands of them in Russia, toiling for a mere pittance, yet striving to maintain the standard of living demanded of them. In *The Cloak* they received for the first time a new recognition when Gogol relegated the titled bureaucracy to the background in a story which was essentially economic and social. He therefore gave a new tone to Russian literature. That note of sympathy for the oppressed, so characteristic of later Russian writers, who selected now one group, now another, as the object of their concern, reached its zenith under Dostoyevsky. Gogol, in addition to arousing the public conscience, laid the foundations for a new literary school in which many of his successors were trained. It is hardly an exaggeration to say in the words of one great Russian author, Dostoyevsky, that all Russian literature emanated from that cloak! So great was its influence that Russian literary critics have enumerated about two hundred stories written in the same vein.

Gogol wrote many plays, but the best of all was *The Revizor* (*The Inspector-General*). *The Revizor* is the national comedy of Russia, and ever since its initial performance it has retained its crown of popularity. Because it holds up corruption and inefficient bureaucracy to ridicule, it is a play that will endure under any regime. Although some Western critics who approach the analysis of Russian plays with Western tools have maintained that there is no such thing as Russian drama, they have failed to realize that the Russian playwright, consciously or unconsciously, stresses character portrayal at the expense of action and other technicalities that loom so large to the Western mind. In the typical Russian play the plot evolves from and is an outgrowth of character portrayal. The same is true, not only of Russian drama, but of Russian literature in general. Russians emphasize the *who,* not the *what.* With reference to *The Revizor,* however, it is universally conceded that even technically speaking the play measures up to the standards of a Western drama.

The Revizor has done more to effect a bureaucratic housecleaning than any number of serious articles directed against a corrupt officialdom. The fact that Emperor Nicholas I himself overruled the censor and granted permission to stage the play was sufficient to stir up some activity in the various chancelleries of autocratic Russia. The emperor's position in this matter was obvious. He wanted to show a corrupt officialdom that he was aware of what was going on in Russia.

A closer analysis of *The Revizor* reveals that Gogol, in spite of his merciless exposure of the bureaucracy, did not attack the institution of autocracy. He merely pointed out the incongruity between the office and the behavior of its incumbent, between duty and abuse of power or privilege. Gogol's criticism was constructive rather than destructive. Constructive criticism is indispensable in every field of human endeavor, particularly in the state. For this reason Nicholas I, the most auto- cratic tsar of the nineteenth century, permitted the staging of *The Revizor.*

Whereas the scene of *The Revizor* was laid in a small locality, its message was national. Encouraged by the emperor's support and by the elite of Russian society—in spite of the bitter criticism of officials at whom the play was aimed—Gogol conceived a new work, almost a sequel to *The Revizor,* which was destined to play a greater role in the history of Russia, and which dealt a severe blow to the institution of serfdom. The work in question, which has come to be of the utmost his- torical importance, was later called *Dead Souls.*

Whereas the action of *The Revizor* took place in a single town and was confined to one restricted group of people among whom there was not a single redeeming feature—worse than Sodom and Gomorrah— the setting for *Dead Souls* was Russia in miniature. It embraced vari- ous classes and social strata, officials and civilians, landowners and serfs, who pass before the reader as on a literary screen. These characters had their prototypes in real life. *Dead Souls* may therefore be termed the first genuinely realistic Russian novel, because it dealt with Russian life *per se,* with a burning issue which occupied the best minds of Russia throughout the nineteenth century—the problem of serfdom—a parallel to which, against a different background, may be found in the United States. The chief difference is that the Russian serfs, unlike the Ameri- can Negroes, were of the same stock and the same religion as their masters.

To understand Gogol, one must remember that his criticism was constructive. He aimed at individuals—not at the body politic. He held up corruption to ridicule but did not question the divine authority of autocracy. He rather aimed at those who by their very abuse of power undermined it, as subsequent events were to show. In the light of his constructive criticism and profound knowledge of Russian institutions *Dead Souls* represented the accurate diagnosis of a competent physician; the appellation *Dead Souls* can be attributed not only to the deceased serfs in the novel, but to Russia as a whole. A combination of ignorance, superstition, corruption, inefficiency, graft, and abuse of power produced an environment in Russia only for dead souls—not for the living. Gogol called the child by its name. Small wonder that when Pushkin first heard the book read he cried: "God, what a sad country Russia is!"

Dead Souls was the most mature and the most profound work that Gogol produced—the crown of his creative imagination. As in the case of *The Brothers Karamazov* by Dostoyevsky, Gogol's masterpiece remained unfinished. Although, technically speaking, *Dead Souls* is a novel without a plot, the character of Tchitchikov binds all its separate parts together. The various chapters are like distinct sections of one big department store.

Before Gogol only individual protests were voiced against existing corruption and the misery of the underprivileged classes. Gogol not only summed these up but diagnosed the disease. His successors suggested remedies—remedies which fell into two main categories—Westernization and Slavophilism.

Oblomov, the classical Russian novel produced by Ivan Alexandrovitch Gontcharov (1812-1891), was an elongation of, if not a sequel to, *Dead Souls.* In abridged form it might have served as an additional chapter in that plotless novel. Both Gogol and Gontcharov diagnosed the national distemper—one labeled it *dead souls,* the other *Oblomovism.* However, in spite of Gontcharov's emphasis upon the negative side of human nature, *Oblomov* is not so gloomy as *Dead Souls,* and the atmosphere is fresher. When his novel first appeared, it made a tremendous impression, for the Oblomovs were more familiar to the reading public than the Tchitchikovs, and many a Russian recognized himself in Oblomov as in a mirror. As Turgenev once said, "As long as there remains one Russian, Oblomov will be remembered."

At the same time *Oblomov* paved the way for practically all of Turgenev's novels. All Turgenev's negative masculine types found their prototype in Ilya Oblomov, while Olga, Gontcharov's heroine, became the pattern for all the active feminine characters of Turgenev. It occasioned no surprise to many Russians when Gontcharov hurled the accusation of plagiarism against the great novelist of the century—Ivan Turgenev. But instead of being condemned, Turgenev was completely exonerated from this literary heresy—and justly so. The similarity of their ideas was a mere coincidence, for both novelists belonged to the same class, were confronted with similar problems, and in the course of everyday life came into actual contact with the types whom they portrayed.

In the classical novel *Oblomov,* Gontcharov depicted the life of the idle-rich nobility of the middle of the nineteenth century from the cradle to the grave. No other author in Russian literature known to us has ever given such a vivid and faithful portrait of Russia's Oblomovs. Oblomov spent the better part of his life in dressing gown and slippers— the outward symbols of the mental and physical stagnation of the wearer —and it took Gontcharov an entire chapter to get him out of bed! It is very difficult to give in English the exact connotation of the Russian word *pokoy,* which implies *repose, seclusion,* and *unruffled peace.* Oblomov sacrificed everything to gain *pokoy.* This word supplies the key to Oblomov's character and to Oblomovism. *Pokoy* occupies the same prominent place in *Oblomov* as *smirenie* in the work of Dostoyevsky. *Smirenie* was a sublimation of *pokoy.* Both were distinctly Slavic traits, particularly characteristic of those directly or indirectly attached to the land. It was natural, therefore, that Oblomov and Oblomovism should become household words throughout Russia, just as Tartuffe in France, Pecksniff in England, and Babbitt in America. From this time on the idle-rich nobility became a legitimate target for attack, and many Russian authors were not slow to avail themselves of this opportunity.

In *Oblomov,* Gontcharov depicts the clash between tradition and innovation in nineteenth-century Russia—between the old patriarchal landowners and the new industrial bourgeoisie represented by the successful and enterprising businessman; between rural life and urbanization; between culture and civilization. In this respect Gontcharov may be considered a forerunner of Tchekhov, whose own version of Oblomovism is to be found in all his plays. Throughout Tchekhov's works— and this is particularly true of *The Cherry Orchard*—there runs like a scarlet thread the same clash between the old and the new in Russia. Ranevsky in *The Cherry Orchard* was Tchekhov's version of Oblomov, and Lopakhin his version of Stolz. Tchekhov skilfully wove the problem of ruralism versus urbanization into the texture of this play.

Oblomov at his best was, as we have seen, a true representative of a declining patriarchal society whose roots were fixed firmly in the past. It took many generations to achieve the society of which Oblomov was, perhaps, the last representative. Gontcharov's novel was therefore in a sense a monument to that past. Until the dawn of the "practical age" Oblomovism represented an ideal devoutly to be wished. When Gontcharov wrote, *pokoy,* the *summum bonum* of life to every Oblomov, was rapidly becoming a lost horizon. When the age of industry began to encroach upon patriarchal society, in protest against the hustle-bustle of the practical businessman, the Oblomovs turned their backs upon it all and defied the world in dressing gown and slippers. They clung till the last ditch to what they believed to be the Russian heritage.

Gontcharov, himself a *barin* (nobleman), dealt with Oblomov sympathetically. He did not condemn everything in Oblomovism, and upon Oblomov himself he bestowed more positive than negative traits. It was not even Gontcharov's purpose to deprive the Oblomovs entirely of *pokoy,* for he was never an enemy of the existing order—but rather to place a price upon it. He wanted to purge Oblomovism of its less desirable attributes, laziness and neglect, and to add to it a new meaning. *Pokoy* as the reward of labor and the exercise of practical ability was his ideal.

In Stolz, Gontcharov attempted to portray the practical and enterprising businessman—the antithesis of Oblomov—whom he prophetically recognized as the leader of the new age. Gontcharov seems to have realized that it would take many Stolzes under Russian names to change the inherent characteristics of the Oblomovs. He would like to have seen Oblomov co-operate with Stolz. But Oblomov could not bring himself to adopt a mode of life which necessitated work and action, as well as everyday contact with the seamy side of life from which he held himself aloof, and he turned a deaf ear to Stolz's dreams of the approaching age of industrialism. There remained, therefore, only a choice between Oblomovism and Stolzism, and, as we have seen, Gontcharov predicted the triumph of the latter. He could only hope that victory would not come at the expense of the strong points of Oblomov's generation. In these two characters, Oblomov and Stolz, we find the forerunners of the nation-wide controversy between the Slavophiles and the Westernizers. Oblomov's better traits were the source of Slavophilism. Stolz's ideas were echoed again and again by the Westernizers.

In the person of Olga, Gontcharov has drawn a portrait of the new woman in Russia who began to wrestle with Oblomovism. Herself a member of the St. Petersburg nobility, she was, nevertheless, ahead of her contemporaries. She was active and persistent, with a fine mind, yet deep and tender feelings. She was also honest, decent, and sincere. As yet she had not acquired an established outlook on life or settled convictions but she was in search of them. Because of her love for Oblomov, she tried to expose his weak traits, to arouse him from his inertia, and to induce him to assume his responsibilities. She did not dwell at length upon his positive features, but it was because of these that she loved him. Like Gontcharov, she believed that if Oblomov could be cured of these negative qualities, he could continue to play a leading role in Russian society without resigning his place to the Stolzes. Unfortunately Olga failed. Turgenev's heroines met the same fate of frustration when they sought to eradicate the Oblomovism of their time in their lovers. Next to Pushkin's Tatyana, Olga represented the best in Russian womanhood until the appearance of Turgenev's Liza.

In the person of Zahar, Gontcharov represented the eternal serf, loyal as a dog to his master, yet dishonest in trifles, inefficient, and incurably lazy. Although he does not contribute a great deal to the novel, he was an indispensable fixture in the structure of the society of his time.

All in all we may say that *Oblomov* from an historical standpoint, and more especially as a sociological study of Russia in the middle of the nineteenth century, is almost indispensable. Without *Oblomov* one cannot understand Turgenev and Tchekhov.

Of considerable historical interest even today is Gontcharov's account of his world tour (1852-1854), as recorded in *Frigate Pallada* (1855-1857). The volume on *The Russians in Japan at the Beginning of 1853 and the End of 1854* (1855) throws considerable light on Admiral Y. V. Putyatin's efforts to open Japan, which parallel those of the United States through Commodore Perry.

SLAVOPHILES AND WESTERNIZERS

Russian writers of the mid-nineteenth century became engulfed in a bitter controversy over Slavophilism and Westernism. Slavophilism was not a political movement but a natural outgrowth of the Russian temperament. It stood for no striking reforms but rather for a reassertion of the inherent good qualities in the Russian character. Its orientation was strictly national. Westernism, on the other hand, was an imported product which found many sponsors in Russia. In fact, the greatest liberals were almost automatically classified as Westernizers, although there were actually as many in the opposite camp. The Westernizers stood for a Western orientation, that is, they wanted their institutions, political, economic, and social, modeled upon those of Western Europe, particularly upon those of France and England.

The leading exponents of Slavophilism were A. S. Khomyakov (1804-1860), Ivan Aksakov (1823-1886), and Ivan Kireyevsky (1806-1856). According to Khomyakov, the principal factor in the historical process was not the state (West) but the people (Russia). It was the people who created the autocracy, which differed from Western absolutism, thereby achieving spiritual emancipation from politics. The autocracy in other words, was an expression of the political asceticism and the anarchistic spirit of the Russian people, who sought to free themselves from all the obligations of government. Khomyakov believed that the Russian people delegated not only their political power but also their authority in ecclesiastical affairs to the tsar. Such a people, Khomyakov concluded, was messianic in character—a chosen people —whose mission was to establish not an empire but a Holy Russia.

Aksakov was one of the outstanding advocates of Pan-Slavism. The unification of the Slavic world he regarded as vital to Europe and the world at large. It was his belief that Russia and the Slavic world were about to assume a world-wide historical role.

Kireyevsky, the most progressive thinker among the Slavophiles, was especially concerned with Russia's mission in Europe. While he acknowledged the West European contribution to Russian enlightenment, he believed that Europe had passed the zenith of its achievement and was already on the decline. There were only two states, he foresaw, that were capable of assuming leadership in the future—the United States and Russia. Since the United States was so remote, he believed that European leadership must inevitably revert to Russia.

In brief, the fundamental principles of Slavophilism were Autocracy, Orthodoxy, and Nationality. Its representatives agreed, on the whole, that the West was the legitimate successor to the First Rome and to its religious incarnation, Catholicism; that, on the other hand, the East, as embodied in Orthodoxy, was the Second Rome; and that the East, in its turn, transmitted its heritage to Russia, the Third Rome, which was destined, under the autocracy and the Orthodox faith, to perform a historic mission for the regeneration of Europe and the world.

The most outstanding Westernizers were T. N. Granovsky (1813-1855), Alexander I. Herzen (1812-1870), and Michael A. Bakunin (1814-1876). Granovsky's main contribution, as a well-known professor at Moscow University, was that he expounded and interpreted Westernism to the rising Russian intelligentsia. Herzen, exiled from Russia by Nicholas I in 1851 because of his criticism of the autocratic system, continued his propaganda for Westernism in London through the medium of the periodical *The Bell,* of which he was the editor. He attacked the Slavophile views in regard to the mission of Russia and belittled the Russian contribution to the development of civilization. Above all, he attacked Pan-Slavism. Like other Westernizers, Herzen looked upon the national life of Russia prior to the reign of Peter the Great as "ugly, poor, and barbarous." Among the most extreme Westernizers was Bakunin, the revolutionary anarchist. In brief, all West-ernizers believed that Russia should follow the path of European development, should overthrow the autocracy, abolish serfdom, and establish civil rights and law in line with Western models.

Whereas the foregoing writers were the philosophical and ideological exponents of Westernism and Slavophilism, the foremost literary exponents of these two movements were Turgenev and Dostoyevsky. Ivan Sergeyevitch Turgenev (1818-1883) was the most articulate mouthpiece of the Westernizers and around him this whole movement centered. Dostoyevsky filled a similar role for the Slavophiles. Only in this light can we understand the novels of these two leaders. Each of Turgenev's novels has its counterpart in a work by Dostoyevsky— the one expressing the point of view of the Westernizers, the other of the Slavophiles.

The Memoirs of a Sportsman affords what may be termed a preview of Turgenev's novels. Outwardly speaking a series of harmless sketches, the *Memoirs* were, if indirectly, at least partially responsible for the abolition of serfdom in Russia, as Alexander II himself admitted on one occasion. These sketches, more than any other work in Russian litera-ture, elicited sympathy for the plight of four-fifths of Russian humanity. While in *Dead Souls,* Gogol dealt indirectly with the institution of serf-dom, describing for the most part its physical status, in *The Memoirs of a Sportsman,* Turgenev most artistically depicted, for the first time, the life of the serf at its best. In this work he revealed the soul of the serf— a soul which was not so different from his master's, at times even supe-rior. The sketches displayed so much objectivity that they immediately won universal approbation and established Turgenev's reputation as an author.

Inasmuch as Turgenev read *Uncle Tom's Cabin* by Harriet Beecher Stowe, an allusion to which is found in his novel *Smoke,* some compari-son between the American classic and *The Memoirs of a Sportsman* may be of interest.

The institution of slavery began in America in 1619 when the first slave ship landed at Jamestown, Virginia, with slaves for the pioneer planters. Russian serfdom dates to 1581, in the reign of Ivan the Ter-rible, when the serfs were "affixed" to the soil for a period of years, and later for life. By the time of Catherine the Great (1762-1796) they had for all practical purposes become the personal property of Russian landed proprietors or of the Russian state. Thus in the nineteenth cen-tury America and Russia alike were faced with the problem of a subject people—in America a black people, but in Russia a people of the same race and religion as their masters. By the year 1852 slavery in America threatened to divide the Union, serfdom in Russia to upset the monarchy. In this year the two books mentioned above, both destined to play an important role in the abolitionist movement in their respective countries, were published.

These books were an "open sesame" to literary fame for both Turgenev and Mrs. Stowe. Turgenev was lifted from obscurity to the very first rank of Russian writers. For a time he had the distinction of being the only Russian novelist of international reputation. Through him Russian literature was introduced to France and the Western world.

The *Memoirs* revealed Turgenev's skill and delicacy in character analysis both of men and dogs. He depicted the peasants more sympathetically than the upper classes. His squires were invariably vulgar, cruel, or ineffective, whereas he took pains to emphasize the humanity, imaginativeness, intelligence, and dignity, as well as the poetic and artistic gifts of the peasants. Yet his characters were not overdrawn. Turgenev did not dwell on atrocities which were the exception rather than the rule, nor did he try to idealize his serfs. By painting life-portraits of sensible, reasoning, and affectionate human beings bowed down by the yoke of serfdom, side by side with life-portraits of their mean and shallow masters, the landed proprietors, he, in a wholly unobtrusive manner, awakened in his readers a consciousness of the injustice and ineptitude of serfdom.

Turgenev's novels may be regarded as sketches on a larger scale than those which composed *The Memoirs of a Sportsman,* and they dealt with different problems. The novels span a period of twenty years, from 1856 to 1876, a period which practically coincided with the reign of Alexander II. The era was one of relative freedom in Russia, during which serfdom was abolished, zemstvos were established, trial by jury introduced, the term of military service reduced, and many unpopular laws repealed or mitigated.

The reign of Alexander II may be called Russia's Victorian Age— an age in which liberalism kept pace with industrialism and in which the rights of the individual were respected and guaranteed. It was, moreover, the zenith of the golden age of Russian literature and art. To offset England's rostrum of famous writers, her Tennyson and Browning, Carlyle, Dickens, and Thackeray, the Alexandrian age produced Turgenev, Dostoyevsky, Tolstoy, and many other poets and thinkers of the first rank. But behind superficial resemblances there is a profound difference between the relative positions of Russia and Great Britain. In the England of Tennyson freedom had broadened slowly from precedent to precedent. Culture was the mellow fruit of a literary heritage based upon Chaucerian, Elizabethan, and eighteenth-century traditions. Russia bridged the gap from barbarism to culture within the brief span of a few decades. In England's golden age the loyalty of the masses to the throne reached its climax. In Russia the relaxation of the censorship let loose forces directed toward the destruction of the Romanov dynasty, among them Nihilism, which later amalgamated with the more positive but equally destructive Marxism.

Turgenev was chiefly responsible for making the novel of the Alexandrian age the vehicle for the expression of opinions on and criticism of the foremost political, social, and economic issues of the day. Each of his novels had its thesis, relevant to one or more of the specific problems which faced his contemporaries. When Turgenev became a convinced Westernizer he realized that simply to diagnose Russia's ills in the manner of Gogol or Gontcharov would never provide an adequate solution of her problems. He must go beyond constructive criticism and suggest a remedy. The remedy which he believed would solve all Russia's problems for generations to come was the substitution of constitutional for autocratic government. In his novels beginning with *Rudin* and ending with *Virgin Soil,* Turgenev carried on his search for a leader capable of achieving that aim. Only in this light can we understand the trend of thought revealed in these works. They form the best background for the history of the Russian Revolution, for, in his search for a leader, Turgenev parades before us in review his various candidates for the task, most of whom are failures. It took him twenty years to locate his leader, who emerged from his last novel, *Virgin Soil,* not in the role of the leading character, Nezhdanov, but in the person of Solomin, a representative of the middle class. Turgenev's remedy for Russian political, economic, and social problems was a strong middle class.

It was not until 1906 that the Russian Government began to take cognizance of this class and to sponsor it. Under the premiership of Stolypin (1906-1911), several million peasants were given the opportunity to form the nucleus of a middle class in Russia. Although Turgenev intended this class to champion reform—to aid in the creation of a liberal constitutional government in Russia—the Tsarist Government used it to strengthen the position of the monarchy. As a result the majority of this group was dispossessed by the Soviet Government during the first years of the Five-Year Plan.

When Turgenev looked about for a leader he naturally turned first in *Rudin* (originally *A Natural Genius*), to the student body. Many of his contemporaries thought that in the person of Dmitri Rudin, he described his friend and classmate at Berlin University, Michael Bakunin, the political anarchist. Others held that Rudin was a projection of Turgenev himself during his student days. But Rudin did not measure up to Turgenev's expectations. By nature he was more of an Oblomov than a man of action. When he finally decided to act he met death in a foreign cause, somewhere in France, and even for that he received no credit, for those who located his dead body believed him to be a Pole. In brief, in the person of Rudin, Turgenev has given us a most faithful and vivid portrait of the "superfluous" or "undesirable" man, who "speaks like a giant" but "acts like a pigmy."

Turgenev, after this denouement, was advised to abandon his search for a leader among the student youth and to seek him instead among the nobility proper. This he did in *A House of Gentlefolk* (also *A Nobleman's Nest*), which established his reputation as a novelist. Although the heroine, Liza Kalitin, stole the show in this novel, Turgenev's interest centered in Fyodor Lavretsky, a character who combined traits favorable both to the Westernizers and the Slavophiles, and who, therefore, had no enemies in Russia. But Lavretsky in practice symbolized the decadence of the landed aristocracy, as, with a sigh of resignation, he abandoned his task and passed the torch to the new generation in which he had great faith.

After this second frustration, Turgenev either lost faith in Russian characters or, more likely, he wished to delegate ideas, which would not have been popular with the authorities if uttered by a Russian, to a Bulgarian. For this purpose he chose the Bulgarian Insarov, who became the hero of his third novel *On the Eve*. Turgenev acknowledged that he owed the theme of this novel to V. Karatayev, a friend who was killed in the Crimean War. In *On the Eve* it was Turgenev's purpose to encourage all Russian liberals to emulate Insarov. Although Insarov's cause was, on the surface, national, in that he dreamed of the liberation of Bulgaria from the Turkish yoke, Turgenev's contemporaries were expected to read between the lines and, by substituting liberalism or constitutionalism for nationalism, to discover the real cause—the liberation of Russia from autocracy.

Turgenev's ruse calls to mind a similar expedient of the author of the Book of Job, who, when he wished to voice a protest against the world order of Jehovah and the plight of the people of Israel, selected a non-Jewish spokesman in the person of Job and permitted him to express statements which, from a Jew, would never have been tolerated. Turgenev's purpose was essentially the same, only the setting was different. Very few understood that purpose, and because Insarov was the only positive male character among Turgenev's heroes, Turgenev himself was condemned by many critics for conferring such an honor upon a foreigner whom he had dragged from the Bulgarian marshes.

When Insarov was rejected, Turgenev set out to prove that a Russian character was even more capable of assuming leadership than a Bulgarian. Bazarov, the hero of *Fathers and Children,* was supposed to be Turgenev's ideal type, stronger even than Insarov. Strange as it may seem, however, no sooner did he select a Russian character than that character proved a weakling whose every project met with frustration. Bazarov came to be known as a Nihilist. By setting forth the tenets of Nihilism, Turgenev, like Gogol and Gontcharov, assumed the role of diagnostician instead of supplying the remedy. Nihilism joined "dead souls" and "Oblomovism" in the list of Russian household words.

Strictly speaking, if we are to judge by the spirit of the work, Turgenev did not preach Nihilism in this novel. Nor did he create Bazarov —he discovered him. It was Turgenev's purpose to direct the attention of the authorities to this new movement which was rapidly taking root in Russian soil. Far from preaching violence or Nihilism through Bazarov, Turgenev sounded a warning against this dangerous newcomer, as if he would say—"Your type of government gave birth to this type of man. Mend your ways by introducing more and better reforms before it is too late. Do you not hear the threats of Bazarov?" Instead of heeding the warning, however, most of the authorities and conservative society, in general, were displeased with Bazarov and condemned Turgenev accordingly. Many members of higher Russian society chose to regard his novel as a serious attempt to negate the "culture of the nobility." On the other hand, the liberals, particularly the Westernizers, thought that, in Bazarov, Turgenev defeated his own purpose. *Fathers and Children* became, therefore, the most controversial and the most widely discussed novel in Russia and has remained so. The impression was given that Turgenev became frightened of his own creation: that he gave Bazarov a chance to expound his ideas, but when he reached the point where he was ready to translate those ideas into action, Turgenev, the *deus ex machina,* fearing that his hero might become a Frankenstein or a Golem, stepped into the arena in person and brought Bazarov's life to a premature end.

This novel likewise reflects the clash between the sciences and the humanities during the period in question. Very few are aware of the fact that Russian Nihilism, strictly speaking, was not so much a product of industrialism as of German science which invaded Russia in the form of an "ism" in the middle of the nineteenth century. The brothers Kirsanov represent the old traditional generation brought up on the humanities. Bazarov, the leading character in this classic novel is the forerunner of the new scientific age. The Nihilism of Bazarov was the result of science minus the humanities. Everything that savored of art and culture in the traditional sense was taboo to Bazarov, that prototype of Nihilism in its various forms. The duel between Bazarov and Pavel Kirsanov, ostensibly over Fenitchka, actually symbolized the clash between the two ideologies.

One of the few to understand the message of *Fathers and Children* was Dostoyevsky, who wrote what may be called its sequel from the Slavophile point of view in his novel *The Possessed.* Dostoyevsky began where Turgenev left off, by depicting the Bazarovs in action, with startling results. After reading *The Possessed* we are less likely to condemn Turgenev for the annihilation of his own creature.

When the furore over *Fathers and Children* died down, Turgenev produced *Smoke.* This novel, strictly speaking, was a rebuttal to the criticisms of those authorities and conservatives who misconstrued his message in *Fathers and Children.* He held up many of their ideas to ridicule and indirectly implied that they were incapable of grasping this message or the liberal recommendations of the Westernizers because they wasted their time on trivialities or, as he said, in trying to hypnotize a turtle.

Smoke was followed by *Spring Freshets,* in which, although it does not deal with the background of current events in Russia proper, Turgenev produced another negative type in the person of Sanin, who met with frustration in both love and business. In 1880 Turgenev omitted *Spring Freshets* from a volume containing his other six novels because he considered that he had not been sufficiently objective in his treatment of Sanin and the other characters. To Turgenev, objectivity was one of the most indispensable elements in any novel, and, since this one did not measure up to his own standards, he classified it as a separate story. Nevertheless *Spring Freshets* is an important link in the chain of Turgenev's novels. In the first place, many critics regarded Sanin as a self-portrait of Turgenev. In the second place, the novel caused some international repercussions. The German press, in Germany as well as in Russia, began a campaign against Turgenev because of his portrayal of the German character, Kluber, and the German officers, Baron von Dongof and Von Richter. After the publication of *Fathers and Children* and *Smoke,* Turgenev lost many Russian friends and followers; *Spring Freshets* likewise deprived him of his German friends and sympathizers.

As has been indicated previously, it was not until his last novel,

Virgin Soil, the most mature of all, that Turgenev finally reached his goal. Moreover, it was not his leading character, Nezhdanov, who measured up to the author's requirements for leadership, but Solomin, the practical factory manager and highly respected representative of the new industrial age. It was during this period that industry began

I. S. TURGENEV

Courtesy Sovfoto

to develop rapidly in Russia, and the businessman began to assert himself as in any industrial country. The practical man who talked seldom but acted often and with decision came into vogue. Solomin was Turgenev's version of Stolz in *Oblomov.*

We must remember that Turgenev was seeking political change rather than social revolution. Solomin, too, hoped that the new era could be inaugurated by evolutionary means rather than by violent revolutions. Although, as we have seen heretofore, Turgenev was at times inclined to side even with the revolutionists to effect the downfall of autocracy, either his aristocratic lineage or his native sagacity finally led him to distrust the leadership of the Bazarovs. Solomin was a man of different caliber—one who appealed to the majority of constructive liberals in Russia.

Virgin Soil is based chiefly on the *"Narodniki"* Movement ("Go to the People"), which came into vogue among the radicals at this time. Instead of working longer in the dark among small groups of adherents, the young revolutionists determined to popularize their message by carrying it directly to the people at large. They wanted to get a first-hand knowledge of the people whose conditions they hoped to ameliorate. As a result they discovered that they had overestimated the "People's" intelligence and maturity, or "consciousness." The soil must be prepared for revolution. Turgenev diagnosed the situation by calling his novel *Virgin Soil,* and he recommended through his mouthpiece, Solomin, a slower but a surer and more practical method of reform, by painstaking education of the people and by gradual evolution, rather than by sudden and violent revolution. History proves that both his diagnosis and his remedy were correct.

The study of Turgenev's novels, therefore, clearly indicates how closely interwoven Russian literature is with current events. His novels faithfully reflected Russian life and the controversial issues of the day. If we had no history whatever of the period in question we could still reproduce it in part from Turgenev's novels.

Although Turgenev is better known for his sketches and novels, his contribution to drama should not be overlooked. His ten plays (1843-1852) were written almost concurrently with the *Memoirs of a Sportsman.* One of them, *A Month in the Country,* has become a permanent part of the repertoire of the Russian theatre. In spite of the fact that it belongs to the pre-emancipation era, with the exception of a cursory reference to the 320 serfs belonging to Bolshintsov, Vera's unwelcome suitor, it might readily be included in a collection of Tchekhov's plays. In its portrayal of the inertia and boredom of country life, it has much in common with *The Three Sisters, Uncle Vanya,* and even with *The Cherry Orchard.*

As already stated, each of Turgenev's novels has its counterpart in a work by Fyodor Mikhailovitch Dostoyevsky (1821-1881). To understand the difference between Turgenev and Dostoyevsky is to comprehend the sharp distinction between culture and civilization. By culture is meant something organic and inherent. By civilization is understood something mechanical and artificial. Culture depends upon a certain locality and is, therefore, the natural outgrowth of a particular soil or environment. Civilization, on the other hand, does not necessarily depend upon geographical phenomena. It may appear everywhere or anywhere. Culture implies birth and growth; civilization calls to mind inventions and material betterment. For instance, if a person wishes to fly, he invents an airplane. That represents civilization. But, if the same person could grow wings on his body, that would denote culture. Character is culture; manners, civilization. If a person lacks character, nobody can give it to him. A character cannot be acquired, but good manners can be taught to anyone, even to an animal. To illustrate further, music is culture, the science of music is civilization. Anyone can study music, but not everyone can be a musician. Emerson represents American culture; Edison and Ford—American civilization. Culture is static; civilization, dynamic. Culture is feeling or emotion; civilization, rationalism and analysis. Culture is lyric; civilization, epic. We can tame or civilize practically every living thing; but we can cultivate only certain of them. We cultivate plants, but we do not civilize them. Thus a person may be highly cultured and possess little civilization, or *vice versa*. The East stressed culture—the West emphasized civilization. Civilization is the more objective, while culture is subjective. Culture stresses the heart; civilization the mind. The ancient Hebrews, for instance, were primarily a cultured people—the Romans predominantly a civilized nation; whereas the Greeks were fortunate in possessing both culture and civilization.

The novels of Dostoyevsky faithfully represent Russian character at its best and at its worst. In the works of Turgenev civilization predominates. In other words, the Slavophiles, whose most outstanding literary exponent was Dostoyevsky, consciously or unconsciously voiced the sentiment of Russian culture; while the Westernizers, whose principal champion was Turgenev, represented civilization—more specifically Western civilization. Only in this light can we grasp the underlying motives of these two great novelists.

Although he refrained from calling the child by its real name, Dostoyevsky always vigorously opposed the importation of foreign culture at the expense of Russian culture. In his own words, "No nation on earth, no society with a certain measure of stability, has been developed to order, on the lines of a program imported from abroad." This does not mean that Dostoyevsky blindly opposed everything foreign merely because it was alien. He was against foreign ideas when they threatened to supplant native influences. He had no objection to the introduction of foreign technique, mechanical equipment, inventions, and so

LEO TOLSTOY ON THE PLOUGHFIELD (1887)

The painting by Ilya Repin shows the great writer practicing what he preached.

forth. In other words, he was not antagonistic to the importation of civilization because that is transferable and changeable and does not depend on local environment. What he valiantly and consistently condemned was the importation of foreign "isms," that is, foreign culture, for he believed that culture could only be transplanted at the expense of native characteristics. Culture must grow like a tree.

There is no doubt but that most of the Westernizers were as good Russian patriots as the staunchest of Slavophiles, the difference being that the Westernizers for the most part exposed the shortcomings of the Russian character and the backwardness of their country in contrast to the rapid material progress and advanced ideas of the West. They presented the negative side of the picture, while the Slavophiles expressed their patriotism, rightly or wrongly, by advancing the strong points of Russian character and Russian culture in general—the positive side of the picture.

Dostoyevsky's method of characterization was the exact opposite of Turgenev's. Where Turgenev discovered his characters, Dostoyevsky for the most part created them. Turgenev's artistry stopped when the individual was completely drawn; Dostoyevsky's artistry began when the individual, having been almost scientifically portrayed, began to act and, although beset by seemingly insuperable obstacles, moved sincerely and artistically through a lifetime of climax. This incidentally throws an interesting light on the fact that Dostoyevsky's short stories were never so successful as his novels; while Turgenev's short sketches were greater works of art than his novels.

Turgenev was not great enough to control the characters he portrayed and to follow them through to their logical end—hence, the frustrations. In this respect Dostoyevsky proved himself the greater genius. Turgenev's characters differ from Dostoyevsky's principally in the degree of their individuality and stature. Turgenev's characters formed the loom on which Dostoyevsky's were woven. The latter are potentially similar to the former, but Dostoyevsky begins where Turgenev left off. He intensifies what conflict there is already and adds so much more that the proportion of adversity to normality becomes contorted to a degree which is invariably responsible for the insanity of the character in question. At this point Dostoyevsky is ready to begin the significant portion of his novel.

A few of Turgenev's characters might have been used to advantage and even with great profit by Dostoyevsky. He could have incorporated Lavretsky into his novels, after intensification to the point of abnormality. Bazarov, before his death, would have been an interesting

figure for Dostoyevsky to begin with, and Bazarov's parents would
have fitted admirably into one of his novels. "For such people as they
are not to be found in your grand society even in the daytime with
a light." (Bazarov.) Of them all, perhaps Fenitchka, the mistress of
the elder Kirsanov, came closer than the rest to being a creation of
Dostoyevsky. Bazarov once said of her: "She'll go to destruction
probably. Well, she'll extricate herself somehow or other." This was
the nearest that Turgenev ever came to Dostoyevsky in the field of
characterization.

Turgenev considered foreigners superior to most Russians (Insarov), and his more or less positive Russian types spoke at least a
foreign tongue (Solomin). On the other hand, Dostoyevsky considered most Russians superior to most foreigners. Every one of his
admirable characters was of pure Russian descent. In fact, according
to Dostoyevsky, there were no bad Russians. They became so only
when they came into contact with alien "isms." Even Sonya, the
prostitute, he implies, was better than all the foreigners. In other
words, according to Dostoyevsky, Russians are essentially good, if
they remain Russians.

In brief, Dostoyevsky was a genius, while Turgenev was an artist.
Turgenev achieved his mark through restraint—Dostoyevsky through
the absence of restraint. Turgenev was vivid through expression,
Dostoyevsky through passion. Turgenev was a man of the world,
Dostoyevsky an innocent. Turgenev wrote like an innocent, and
Dostoyevsky like a man of the world.

In the light of the foregoing explanation, Dostoyevsky's major
novels may seem more intelligible to Western readers. Let us consider
briefly his first short novelette, *Poor People*. An outsider, on reading
this novel in letters, may well wonder why it created such a sensation
in the Russian literary world, even prior to its publication in 1846.
Why did leading critics predict the rise of a new Gogol? In the first
place, Dostoyevsky revealed in this novel a remarkable maturity of
thought for a young man barely twenty-four years of age. Moreover,
his literary style was both powerful and polished, not by any means
inferior to the work of the best writers of his generation. Finally,
and most important of all, without detracting from the originality of
Poor People, Dostoyevsky enlarged upon Gogol's *Cloak,* which had
already become a classic, and which had been extensively imitated.
The literary exponents of the Russian poor enjoyed great popularity,
and, in consequence, their books were best-sellers, although this was
not their purpose. The title of Dostoyevsky's small novel might be

applied to an entire library of works produced by his contemporaries on the plight of the Russian poor. Later critics discovered in *Poor People* the germs of a philosophy which permeated all Dostoyevsky's subsequent novels—just as *Sevastopol* supplied a preview to the rest of Tolstoy's works.

Although the most popular of Dostoyevsky's novels among foreigners in general has a gruesome plot, *Crime and Punishment* was never meant to be a glorified detective story. Russian literature was not written for the entertainment of its readers, and the plot of *Crime and Punishment* is of secondary importance. The main idea, which runs like a scarlet thread through this and through his three subsequent novels, is the clash between the Slavophiles and the Westernizers. With *Crime and Punishment,* the controversy between these two camps began in earnest. The novel served both as a rebuttal to Turgenev and as an exposition of the Slavophile point of view on political, economic, and social matters. The reader must be warned again not to approach Dostoyevsky's major novels with Western tools. If Dostoyevsky had written his novels in the West, he might never have secured a publisher.

Crime and Punishment marks the breach between Dostoyevsky and the radicals. Like Turgenev he was in search of a leader, and, like him, he turned first to the student body. Raskolnikov is a much more interesting person, however, than Turgenev's Rudin or even Bazarov. Even the choice of his name served a particular purpose. The etymological derivation of Raskolnikov is *raskol,* meaning schism, rift, break, or detachment. It is another name for *bezpotchvenik,* a word coined by the Russian critic Grigorovitch, and extensively employed by the Slavophiles when they referred to the Westernizers. In free translation a *bezpotchvenik* is one who is detached from the soil, in contrast to one who is rooted in the soil. The name of Raskolnikov thus supplies the key to the entire novel. Before he was captivated by the rationalism of the West, our hero was decent and led a useful life. From the time he became a "Raskolnikov," he entered upon the path which led to crime.

Raskolnikov may be regarded as Turgenev's Rudin or Nezhdanov in action, presented from the Slavophile standpoint. His crime was the result of rationalism and cold logic, no feelings being involved. Not that Raskolnikov had no heart or emotions. But, according to Dostoyevsky, the science of the West, which was based on facts and laws, obliterated all human feeling. In *Crime and Punishment,* as in his three subsequent novels, Dostoyevsky emphasizes the struggle for supremacy between the heart and the mind. When the mind takes the upper hand, the result is crime; but when the heart prevails resurrection follows. As long as Raskolnikov remained under the influence of Western intellectualism, his life was miserable, and he became a detriment to society. When his Russian heart (soul) reasserted itself, he became a new man.

In other words, it was Dostoyevsky's conviction that the mind without the heart was like a body without a soul. Greek culture included both; Plato stressed the mind, Aristotle the heart. Greek culture would have been less interesting if either had dominated to the exclusion of the other. This, too, was the genius of Christianity—that it appealed both to the heart and to the mind, although the former predominated.

What was true of Raskolnikov may be applied to Sonya. She was not as well educated as he, but, according to Dostoyevsky, her thinking reflected the rationalism of the West. She became a prostitute, not from preference, but to save her family from starvation. The result was that she saved neither her family nor herself. When her Russian heart reasserted itself, she experienced a resurrection, breathed new life into Raskolnikov, and became a source of comfort and consolation to others. By way of digression, Dostoyevsky was the first author in Russian literature to lift a prostitute from degradation and contempt and to place her on a par with the most virtuous heroines of world literature. She became the moral force in the tragedy, and she served as a warning against a social order which was the product of Western rationalism. Dostoyevsky gave Sonya a new deal.

It may be of interest to observe that Dostoyevsky dealt with his criminals as the prophet of the Old Testament dealt with the erring members of his flock. They passed through four stages: sin (crime), punishment (suffering), repentance (resurrection), and forgiveness (love). It may seem strange that Dostoyevsky, who was imbued with the teachings of the New Testament, where forgiveness is not necessarily dependent upon punishment, should subject his heroes to this purge. This becomes clear when the reader bears in mind that to Dostoyevsky, Love, the greatest thing in the world, evolved only from suffering. It would be erroneous to accept the dictum of many critics who maintain that he made a religion or a fetish of suffering. He did not advocate suffering for the sake of suffering, but rather as a price which the individual, society, or nation must pay in life for the *summum bonum*.

Although the main issue in *Crime and Punishment* is political, there exists also an ethical problem. Was it ethical for Raskolnikov to murder the wretched pawnbroker, whom he regarded as a social parasite, so that he might use the blood money to complete his education and thereby become a useful member of society? Furthermore, was it ethical for his sister, Dunya, to marry a man she despised in order to finance her brother's education and assure his future? Finally, was it ethical on the part of Sonya to subject herself to humiliation, suffering, disgrace, and danger in order to feed a drunken father and a starving family? In Western Europe at that time many writers condoned as well as commended such a sacrifice of self. The individual thinking of the age might be transferred to the class. Was it ethical for one class or group, by implication the Westernizers, to destroy another in order to produce what they thought would be a better world?

In brief, Dostoyevsky's main purpose in *Crime and Punishment* was to show that Raskolnikov and his followers, when they fell victims to the imported "isms" of the West, became criminals; but after going through certain processes which restored them to their own culture and soil, they reasserted themselves and became useful members of society. All Dostoyevsky's criminals needed was a new start in life, and for this he felt that they required no assistance or enlightenment from the West. All that was necessary was for them to rediscover the potentialities of Russian culture and to develop them accordingly.

Crime and Punishment not only reflects the controversy between the Slavophiles and the Westernizers, but it is closely connected with economic conditions current in Russia in 1865; for in that year there was a severe economic depression in Russia. Money was so scarce that even persons with good security found it difficult or impossible to borrow the funds they required. There were many foreclosures on mortgages. Even Dostoyevsky himself was threatened with foreclosure on June 6, 1865, if he did not pay the lawyer, Pavel Lyzhin, a debt of 450 rubles. Possibly Dostoyevsky had this lawyer in mind when he described Dunya's unethical fiancé, Luzhin, in this novel. It has been suggested that Dostoyevsky might have called this novel "1865" instead of *Crime and Punishment*.

It is likewise interesting to note that the plot of *Crime and Punishment* was undoubtedly suggested to Dostoyevsky by the notorious case of the merchant's son, Gerasim Tchistov, who in the spring of 1865 killed two women with an axe, after robbing them of 11,260 rubles. Russian newspapers of that day made the most of this sensational case.

Although Dostoyevsky did not kill Raskolnikov as Turgenev did Rudin, he was through with him, once his resurrection was assured. In his next novel, he sought a more ideal type—one far removed from the poverty-stricken student. Like Turgenev he went to his "house of gentlefolk" for Prince Myshkin, the hero of *The Idiot*.

Prince Myshkin, Dostoyevsky's new candidate for leadership, differed materially from Turgenev's Lavretsky. He had a magnetic personality which immediately commanded attention. People who agreed or disagreed with him, whether wise or flippant, adults or children, of whatever rank or station, listened to what the prince had to say. No one hated him. It seemed as if he were about to assume leadership and settle all their problems by Peace. However, like Christ, whom Myshkin in certain scenes distinctly resembles, he was crucified by the mob who termed him an idiot. The action of the mob abruptly terminated Myshkin's career, although it was apparent that he was much wiser than they. At times it almost seems that the idiot is a projection of the author himself, for it is a well-established fact that the Westernizers not infrequently hurled the epithet of idiot or that of epileptic at Dostoyevsky. In this novel he takes pains to prove that the idiot is wiser and saner than all of them, that, in fact, they themselves are the idiots, and it is he who suffers for their transgressions.

Psychopathologists and criminologists have paid homage to the remarkable contribution of Dostoyevsky in *The Idiot,* in which he anticipated with a great degree of accuracy many modern scientific developments in these fields. Far from being distressed by his epileptic condition, Prince Myshkin, voicing the sentiment of Dostoyevsky, regarded this disease as an asset rather than a liability. In fact, he implied that his talent or genius was directly attributable to his infirmity. It is interesting to note that a number of historical figures have been victims of epilepsy. Theologians or scholars, as the case may be, have advanced the theory that the prophet Ezekiel, St. Paul, Mohammed, Caesar, Constantine the Great, Catherine the Great, Alexander I of Russia, Napoleon, and Dostoyevsky all suffered from this disease.

While the controversy still raged over Turgenev's *Fathers and Children,* Dostoyevsky, instead of continuing his hitherto fruitless search for a leader, wrote a sequel to Turgenev's novel, which he called *The Possessed (The Devils).* Strictly speaking, in *The Possessed* Dostoyevsky portrayed the Bazarovs in action. When the novel appeared in 1873 it shook Russian society profoundly, particularly the Western camp. Many of Dostoyevsky's adversaries branded him again as an idiot and an epileptic who exaggerated and defamed the liberal and socialist movements. Even as late as 1913 Maxim Gorky published a protest against the production of *The Possessed* by the Moscow Art Theatre. In spite of the anger of the Westernizers, this novel crowned

Dostoyevsky as the prophet of Russia. Within a few years of its completion the violence of the anarchists afforded convincing proof of the validity of his contentions. Although it may be true that *The Possessed* did not reflect the actual conditions of the time in which it was written, Dostoyevsky's keen psychological insight into the minds of the extreme radicals of his day enabled him to visualize the logical outcome of their thinking and activities.

The Possessed and *Fathers and Children* represent the best and perhaps the first primary literary sources on the Age of Nihilism in Europe. *Fathers and Children,* as already indicated, was the first to break new ground in this field by introducing the term *Nihilism* in its modern connotation. In Turgenev's main character, Bazarov, we have the prototype of the typical Russian Nihilist. On the other hand, *The Possessed,* published a decade later, not only reflects Russian Nihilism but is even more representative of German Nazism. Alfred Rosenberg, the Russianborn philosopher of National Socialism and father of Neo-Paganism in Germany, drew heavily upon *The Possessed* for his new mythology, although his interpretation betrays the immaturity and superficiality of his analysis. Although Dostoyevsky was obviously not in any position to foresee the actual circumstances of the rise of Nazism, the Nazis were undoubtedly influenced by Dostoyevsky's exponents of a "new order" as characterized in *The Possessed.*

Dostoyevsky's analysis of the theories of Shigalev, one of the characters of *The Possessed* (see especially Part II, Chapter VIII), provides the best possible background for the ideology expounded in Hitler's *Mein Kampf* and Rosenberg's *The Myth of the Twentieth Century.* Shigalovism, in brief, is an attempt to establish a perfect social order. It starts with the principle of absolute freedom and reaches the paradoxical conclusion of absolute slavery for nine-tenths of the human race. The remaining one-tenth constitute the directors with absolute power who demand absolute submission from the rest. In this new order, where everything must be reduced to a common denominator, and where the masses must be on the same level (Shigalev's interpretation of equality), there is no room for great minds, for genius, and for culture. Cicero would have his tongue cut out, Copernicus would be blinded, and Shakespeare stoned. All must work, however, and render obedience to the extent of submerging their individuality completely in the group. They must have no desires of their own.

To maintain rigid discipline and thereby preserve the new order for one thousand years, Shigalev invented a system of spying in which it became the duty of the slaves to spy upon one another. He even advocated the use of lies, legends (rumors), slander, incendiarism, murder, and "incredible corruption" to maintain the regime. To eliminate "boredom" and to hold the masses in terror, he worked out the idea of the purge (letting of fresh blood) as a regularly recurring shock. This, in Shigalev's opinion, would maintain a state of mental vacuum and prevent the organization of any subversive movements which were the product of a latent benevolence. Much of the theory and technique of Nazism can be found in Shigalevism.

Dostoyevsky implies that the characters of *The Possessed,* even the notorious Pyotr Verkhovensky, were essentially good, but for the fact that their energies had been directed into improper channels. Using Shatov as his mouthpiece, he maintained that they could only be redeemed by driving out the devils and making room for the healing properties of the Orthodox faith. By Orthodoxy, Dostoyevsky meant the ideal Church, the Church as conceived by Solovyov, Berdyaev, and Bulgakov—a Church of freedom of the spirit and high religious devotion. No matter what "ism" people professed, no matter what cause they espoused even to the extent of self-sacrifice, without religious faith Dostoyevsky believed that they built their foundation upon the sand. In other words, the foundation of all foundations, the philosophy of all philosophies, the cause of all causes, was religion—the Orthodox faith, without which people became "possessed."

Arriving at this conclusion, Dostoyevsky ventured another prophecy that Russia would eventually become the savior of Christian civilization. Since the Russian Church was dogmatically nearer to the Protestant Church and ritualistically closer to the Roman Catholic, he believed that it was destined to become the bridge which would eventually unite the three. In his opinion the Russian Orthodox Church was the only one which had retained its purity, since, in the West, science had practically eclipsed Protestantism, and the merits of Roman Catholicism were obscured by too much organization and temporal power. Although at times Dostoyevsky virulently attacked the Roman Catholic Church, especially in the chapter of *The Brothers Karamazov* entitled "The Grand Inquisitor," on the other hand, he paid great homage to certain virtues which are distinctly characteristic of Roman Catholicism. For this reason many Catholic critics have found him inconsistent and consider that he defeated his own purpose.

Since he believed Russia would be saved by a spiritual leader rather than by a statesman or revolutionist, Dostoyevsky sought the fulfilment of his dream in the person of Alyosha, one of the Brothers Karamazov. Unfortunately this, his final novel, remained unfinished, and his ideal hero, Alyosha, undeveloped. Whether or not Dostoyevsky planned to write four or five volumes on *The Brothers Karamazov* cannot be established with certainty in spite of certain allusions to the contrary. Whether, on the spur of the moment, he was tempted to change the nature of Alyosha and to transform him into a villain remains equally obscure. Following the spirit of the novel, it would seem that Dostoyevsky wished to make of Alyosha a Redeemer and a Russian leader. At times it appears that he lost faith even in Alyosha, believing that only a miracle could save Russia. Alyosha, coming as he did from the family of the Karamazovs, might well be considered a miracle.

The story of *The Brothers Karamazov* is, in many respects, an epic of Russian life. Each member of the family represented a slice of Russian society. Dimitri was an uncultured and unconscious Slavophile, whereas Ivan, the brain of the trio, directly or indirectly represented the Westernizers. Smerdyakov, the illegitimate son, stood for the imitative mob which follows the leader and becomes a tool in the hands of the theoreticians. His father, Fyodor Karamazov, belonged to the sensuous, indifferent, reactionary group of the old generation. Alyosha was destined to reconcile the classes represented by Dimitri and Ivan. If, as some critics maintain, Dostoyevsky possessed in turn the traits of each of the Karamazovs, this would merely tend to substantiate the fact that he more than any other Russian author truthfully reflected the Russian people at their best and at their worst.

It seems clear from the very outset that Dostoyevsky felt more sympathy for Dimitri than for Ivan. Dimitri, in spite of his shortcomings, was essentially good at heart. Purged by suffering for a crime which he did not commit, he might have been redeemed, might have become a normal being—an eventuality which was hardly possible in the case of Ivan. With his desire to dominate, it was very difficult for Ivan to bow even to circumstances. When he was forced to do so, he became mentally unbalanced. Although the actual murder of Fyodor Karamazov must be laid at Smerdyakov's door, it was Ivan's brain that engineered the crime. Dostoyevsky clearly suggests that Smerdyakov had Ivan's sanction to murder his father. Since Dostoyevsky's philosophy of life was almost identical with that of the Near East, where the motive of the sinner or criminal as a rule receives greater consideration than the actual deed, he therefore blamed Ivan for the crime and labeled Smerdyakov his blind tool.

In this novel, even more than in *The Possessed,* Dostoyevsky asserted the necessity of religion and faith in the Christ. In spite of his conviction that the Christian Church would eventually save Russia and make of it a model nation, whose light would radiate to the four corners of the earth, in this work he did not shut his eyes to the abuses and superstitions within the Church. Through Churchmen of the caliber of Father Zosima and Alyosha he hoped to remedy its faults.

In *The Brothers Karamazov,* Dostoyevsky made the most earnest attempt ever made in Russian literature to iron out the various controversial issues which confronted his countrymen. For this reason it is surprising to find that in this first volume he devoted more space to the arguments of his opponents than to his own rebuttal. No Westernizer ever presented his case more convincingly than Ivan in *The Brothers Karamazov.* No Westernizer has provided an equally clear analysis of the fundamental principles of Slavophilism. In fact, the Westernizers seem tacitly to have agreed to maintain a sort of censorship against Slavophilism in their writings, whereas Dostoyevsky, whom they termed a dogmatic Slavophile, was broad-minded enough to open his columns to his adversaries and to present the case of the Westernizers on the social order and on religion in a most articulate manner. No wonder Pobyedonostsev and his fellow-reactionaries were both frightened and shocked by the religious discussions between Ivan and Alyosha! They were only pacified when Dostoyevsky assured them of a rebuttal in the second volume. Death intervened before he could fulfill that promise, and Dostoyevsky died like a true Christian, turning the other cheek. Perhaps, for this reason, his message was all the more powerful.

To sum up, Dostoyevsky's novels are the noblest expression of nineteenth-century Slavophilism. Placing the heart above the intellect, he opposed all manifestations of foreign "isms" whose purpose was to supplant or eclipse Russian virtues, which were the product of many centuries of Russian joy and sorrow. In the field of "enlightenment" he felt that the West had nothing to offer Russia, since Russia possessed all the elements necessary for her own redemption—in particular, the Russian Orthodox Church. While he was against the encroachment of Western "isms," he readily acknowledged Western accomplishments in the field of invention and technique which benefited humanity as a whole, opposing only the importation and adaptation of things intrinsically cultural.

Dostoyevsky had still another reason for urging the Russian people to turn their backs on Western Europe. It was his belief, as expressed in his *Diary of a Writer* in 1881, that Europe must inevitably fall a prey to "degrading Communism," whereas Asia offered the greatest potentialities for Russia's future development and for the release of Russian energy. ". . . By turning to Asia, with our new concept of her, our country may experience something akin to what happened in Europe when America was discovered. For, in truth, Asia to us is like the then undiscovered America. With Asia as our aim, our spirit and forces will be regenerated. . . . In Europe we were hangers-on and slaves, but we shall go to Asia as masters. To the Europeans, we were Tartars, whereas in Asia, we, too, are Europeans. Our civilizing mission in Asia will serve as a bribe to our spirit and will lure us thither." According to Dostoyevsky, this orientation toward Asia "is necessary, because Russia is not only in Europe but also in Asia; because the Russian is not only a European but also an Asiatic." Dostoyevsky's conception of Russia's Asiatic mission dates back to his exile in Siberia, when in 1854 during the Crimean War he composed a little-known poem, "On European Events," in which he already insisted it was God's will that Russia should go to Asia under the banner of the White Tsar and the Orthodox Church to create a renaissance among the Asiatic peoples. Within a century Soviet leaders were going to Asia, as Dostoyevsky demanded, but in the name of a Red Tsar, Communism, and atheism.

During World War II Soviet literary critics ostensibly became enamored of Dostoyevsky, and the impression was given that he had been entirely redeemed and retrieved. In recent years, however, they have rediscovered in him a formidable, potential foe of the Soviet regime and system. With the defeat of Nazi Germany, the radical element that Dostoyevsky portrays so unfavorably, now inevitably becomes to the discerning Soviet reader, not German but Russian, and he is likely to find its counterpart in the Soviet Government. Whereas the Soviet Union proclaims itself the first and foremost socialist state, Dostoyevsky denounces socialism (Marxian socialism), based on materialism, in no uncertain terms as a danger to the world. According to Dostoyevsky, the salvation of Russia will come through a rejuvenated Orthodox Church. Although the present Soviet Government may not be averse to using the Orthodox Church as a tool or weapon to further its own interests, needless to say it has no intention of setting it up as a rival or successor. Finally, the Soviet Government, anxious to exalt the contemporary Soviet man, finds in Dostoyevsky only characters that are abnormal misfits who provide no worthy example for the emulation of the "contemporary man."

In the final analysis, Dostoyevsky's gallery of characters was composed of lunatics, perverts, epileptics, prostitutes, drunkards, and swindlers—the scum of society, afflicted with all manner of mental diseases. Most of them lived in the city slums or in the provincial metropolis,

Dostoyevsky assembled them all, demonstrated their plight, expressed their thought, aroused sympathy in their behalf, subjected them to a spiritual bath, and started them out all over again. To a certain extent he played for them the role of the Salvation Army, emphasizing their spiritual welfare rather than their physical necessity.

The same controversy, which is reflected in the works of Dostoyevsky and Turgenev, has been rehearsed in Russia today under a somewhat different nomenclature. The existing clash of opinions between the Right and the Left in the Soviet Union, between those who demanded a nationalist orientation ("Nationalist in form, socialist in content."—Stalin), and those who advocated an international platform, constituted a revival of the struggle between the Slavophiles and the Westernizers. At present—in partial fulfilment of Dostoyevsky's prophecy—the former seem to be gaining ground.[1]

The current vogue of existentialism is tempting many writers to draw comparisons between Dostoyevsky and Soeren Kierkegaard or Jean-Paul Sartre, two of the leading exponents of that philosophy. Of the two, there appears to be much more in common between Dostoyevsky and the nineteenth-century Danish philosopher, Kierkegaard, for whom the "arrogance" of rationalism spelled destruction to European civilization and Jesus Christ afforded proof of the existence of God. But if Dostoyevsky is to be ranked as a religious existentialist, Leo Tolstoy, in our opinion, merits even greater consideration.

Whereas Dostoyevsky introduced the slums and the middle-class into Russian literature, Lyev Nikolayevitch Tolstoy (1828-1910) confined himself to green pastures, to the nobility, and the peasantry. The one deified the Russian people, the other lauded to the skies the virtues of the Russian peasant. In this respect Tolstoy has more in common with Turgenev, for he began where Turgenev left off in his *Memoirs of a Sportsman*. But Tolstoy treated the peasants subjectively, whereas Turgenev viewed their most vital problem, that of serfdom, with remarkable objectivity.

Tolstoy's characters are simple, like the country folk he admired so greatly; Dostoyevsky's are complex. Tolstoy wrote, for the most part, of the sane, the healthy, and the normal individual; Dostoyevsky, of the criminal, the diseased, the insane, and the abnormal. In spite of his dynamic power, Dostoyevsky wrote like a humble man; Tolstoy with authority. "I say unto you" is the predominant tone of Tolstoy's work,

---

[1] For the Soviet attitude towards Dostoyevsky following World War II, see Yermilov, V., "F. M. Dostoyevsky and Our Critics," *Soviet Press Translations,* Vol. III, No. 5, March 1, 1948, pp. 155-160.

particularly in later years. Dostoyevsky underestimated his own greatness. Tolstoy was not only aware of his creative genius but, by implication, boldly announced to the world his opinion of himself. His ego defied even his own earnest attempts at humility, led him to project his personality into most of his works, many portions of which are auto-

Courtesy Sovfoto

MIKHAIL GLINKA (1804-1857), noted Russian composer.

biographical. Dostoyevsky rarely resorted to autobiography, an exception being his *Memoirs from a Dead House,* although he revealed his own Slavophile views in the person of Shatov and his own epileptic condition in the experiences of Prince Myshkin.

Tolstoy regarded himself as the foremost prophet and teacher of his generation, whereas Dostoyevsky in reality was both. The former raised disciples; the latter, imitators. Tolstoy was both a great teacher and

PETER ILYITCH
TCHAIKOVSKY

The music of this best-known Russian composer reflects his love for the Russian landscape, the Russian past, and Russian customs.

MODEST MUSSORGSKY

An exponent of realism in Russian music, Mussorgsky put into his operas and songs the spirit of the Narodniki Movement.

NIKOLAY RIMSKY-KORSAKOV

The last of the leaders of the nationalist school, Rimsky-Korsakov drew upon the themes of the literature of his day.

philosopher; Dostoyevsky, a disciple of Christ and a psychologist. Tolstoy emerged unscathed from his "mission," whereas Dostoyevsky was "crucified" as an idiot and an epileptic. Even posthumously Tolstoy has fared better than his great contemporary. His works were the first of the Russian classics to stage a comeback after the Revolution, while Dostoyevsky's works still await recognition. This is in spite of the fact that the New Russia reflects, under a new nomenclature, more of Dostoyevsky's philosophy than of Tolstoy's.

Whereas Turgenev was a Westernizer and Dostoyevsky a Slavophile, Tolstoy for a time combined the ideologies of both, until at length he established a teaching of his own known as Tolstoyism. In methodology, he was nearer Turgenev, but dogmatically and ideologically he was closer to Dostoyevsky. Like the latter, he repudiated Western civilization and, in particular, Western materialism. The philosophy of each was Oriental, the difference being that Dostoyevsky's was more of an elongation of the Near East plus Russia, whereas Tolstoy's was Russian plus the Taoism of the Far East. Tolstoy wrote extensively of Reason in his later years, often identifying Reason with God and with Knowledge, but the Reason he described emanated from the heart rather than from the head; for Tolstoy finds that Reason is inherent in every man, although often obscured or eclipsed by other factors. In order to reassert that Reason, it was only necessary, in his opinion, to listen to and obey the inner voice of conscience—which is again closer to the heart than to the mind. In brief, Tolstoy's Reason must not be identified with the Practical Reason of Kant. His is Russian Reason, grafted upon Oriental philosophy. In other words, it represents a combination of heart and mind, at times almost constituting an answer to Dostoyevsky's dream.

A significant factor in Dostoyevsky's Slavophilism was the Russian Orthodox Church. To Tolstoy, the Church—and by the Church he meant the Orthodox or Catholic Churches—distorted, institutionalized, particularized, obscured, and debased the Gospel of Christ, and he predicted its downfall. Dostoyevsky, although he admitted certain abuses and shortcomings (*The Idiot, The Brothers Karamazov,* and *Raw Youth*), believed that a rejuvenated Orthodox Church constituted the only hope for the salvation of Russia and of the world, and he predicted its ultimate triumph. Tolstoy was nearer the Protestant Church; Dostoyevsky, in spite of his attacks on Roman Catholicism, was nearer to it than he realized. Dostoyevsky dreamed of the universal application of Russian Christianity; Tolstoy of a universal religion, which would become the creed of Russia—a Christianity minus Churchianity. Tolstoy put to the test most of the world's leading religions. Like Nietzsche, he did not discard Christianity but became jealous of the Christ and established a creed of his own—Tolstoyism.

Tolstoyism belongs to the later years of Tolstoy's life, from 1879 to 1910, that is, from the time of his conversion until his death. These years are sometimes known as the period of "preaching" or the age of Tolstoy the Apostle. The essence of Tolstoyism is to be found in *Confession* and in his subsequent work, most of which is summed up in *Resurrection*. In fact, all the later works of Tolstoy, even his dramas, may be termed "confessions"—either confessions about himself, about the Russian nobility, authorities and institutions, or in particular about the Russian Church from which he was excommunicated in 1901.

Tolstoyism teaches that there is no God, other than the moral law inside man. Instead of being motivated by outward inducement, that moral law moves in obedience to an inward spontaneity. The inner life underlies the universe. The end or the goal of inner action is inner peace (happiness). By peace, Tolstoy does not imply Epicureanism but the doctrine of imperturbability or *quietism,* the essence of which is Taoism. In Tolstoyism, as well as in Taoism, there are elements of defeatism and anarchism, and also of domination. The *withdrawal* of the senses to a point where one no longer sees the things perceived implies all this. The idea that "To a mind that is still the whole universe *surrenders"* suggests domination—subjugation, rather than resignation. Thus, in spite of Tolstoy's later ethical teachings, in which "Resist no evil" occupies the most prominent place, he himself barely practiced it. In fact, Tolstoy recognized no authority above himself, for he was neither a disciple nor a follower. He was the founder of Tolstoyism—another creed.

Tolstoy is always more the moralist than the philosopher. He demands that everyone else see the light in the Tolstoyan way. Looking toward the Christian ideal of world brotherhood, he addresses his doctrine to every man. He has a positive energy which cannot be found in the quietly aloof spirit of the Taoist, who, after all, writes only for the few.

Taoism goes beyond Tolstoyism, historically and otherwise. Its truths, if truths they be, are more fundamental, for Tao is the Natural Way. Tolstoy loses sight of Tao when he sets up a code of morality, for morality comes into existence only when Tao is lost. Because the Tolstoyan's reason tells him to, he pursues his ideal, his way. About the Taoist philosophy there is something more elemental, more pliable, more "limpid" as Waley terms it. It is quite intangible; one can't see it;

and yet, if he once hits upon it there is an inexhaustible source of power, which also is indescribable, but even more potent because of its formlessness, its lack of definition. The Tolstoyan ideal is something one consciously attempts to reach, and there are definite rules for getting there. But the Taoist ideal of nothingness and complete harmony and mergence with the universe is something upon which one just falls.

The essential ideals are the same—the results are the same. Whether one reaches Tao or the Heavenly Kingdom is immaterial. Both are merely symbols of an inner, spiritual peace. Tolstoy has only modernized the route, putting up appropriate signposts along the way. Even with his better than average understanding of the philosophical ideals of the East, however, he is unable to make use of them in unadulterated form; hence with them he combines the Western ideals; not wholly Western either, because Christianity, too, is an Eastern philosophy. It is Tolstoy's plan to give us the basic truths of Christianity which find their complement and likeness in the great truths of the Far East. And in such a combined form, he gives the Eastern beliefs, meant in the first place only for a select few, a universality which makes them accessible to the whole of mankind.

In brief, Taoism is esoteric in nature, its fundamental premise being that the *summum bonum* in life is to lose oneself in the world through non-action. On the other hand, Tolstoyism has a wide, popular appeal, teaching, as it does, that the *summum bonum* in life is to find oneself in a world in which non-action is only a prelude to action.

The most representative work Tolstoy produced during the first period of his literary career, 1852 to 1862, was *The Cossacks.* Although this novel was published in January, 1863, he first projected it in 1852, wrote it in 1860, and added the finishing touches to it in 1862, prior to his marriage. Tolstoy had no intention of publishing this work for some time. It would, perhaps, have shared the fate of *Hadji Murad,* which appeared posthumously in 1911, had Tolstoy not used it to settle a gambling debt at a time when he was otherwise short of funds.

The Cossacks ranks next in importance to Gogol's *Taras Bulba.* Gogol's narrative was historical, but Tolstoy wrote of the Cossacks of his own day whom he knew in person. Gogol's work was a tale of adventure; Tolstoy's was philosophical in tone. *Taras Bulba* has its vivid climax, leaving the reader a glorious picture of triumphant fierceness of exaltation in the face of actual death. *The Cossacks* closes with an anticlimax, when Olenin returns to his former empty life, without Maryanna, and without having found the "inner peace" he sought in the Caucasus.

Gogol's work was epic in tone, whereas Tolstoy's is lyric. Olenin also proved to be a new version of Petchorin in *The Hero of Our Times*.

Tolstoy's greatest contribution in *The Cossacks* was that he revealed the everyday life of the Caucasians, presenting their strong, rather than their weak points, against a magnificent scenic background. His was a sympathetic account and an appreciative understanding of customs which were strange to the Russian people as a whole. Maryanna, Lukashka, and Yeroshka were soon as familiar to Russians as Turgenev's characters in his *Memoirs of a Sportsman*. Tales of the Caucasus have always held a certain fascination for the Russian people. The greatest Russian poets and a few outstanding writers received their literary baptism amid the scenic grandeur and the picturesque customs of the Caucasus. As we shall see, F. A. Korsh, the founder of the first private theatre in Moscow, was a native of the Caucasus; and V. I. Nemirovitch-Dantchenko, who established the Moscow Art Theatre, came from the same region.

In *The Cossacks* we can detect the symptoms of Tolstoy's later philosophy, particularly his preference for the simple life close to nature. In the person of Olenin we find that same restlessness which pursued Tolstoy all his days. For in this autobiographical novel he was just beginning his search for an answer to the riddle of life.

Tolstoy's three sketches, entitled *Sevastopol* (December, 1854, May, 1855, and August, 1855), also belong to the first period of his literary career. Written while he was on active service at Sevastopol during the Crimean War, these sketches marked Tolstoy's first attack on war in general, particularly upon war between Christians. His descriptions of the horrors of war and his discrimination between real and false heroes were only excelled in his later masterpiece, *War and Peace*. In *Sevastopol,* Tolstoy did for the common soldier what Turgenev in his *Memoirs* did for the serf. He directed attention to the services rendered by the ordinary soldier, who, more often than not, received no recognition of his sacrifice, since all the glory and honor went to false heroes. In Tolstoy's estimation, the common soldier was more patriotic than his superiors who spent most of their time talking about promotion. The army never forgave Tolstoy for this exposure, regarding him as a renegade from his own class.

The bulky novel *War and Peace,* together with *Anna Karenina,* may be termed the product of the "honeymoon period." After his marriage in 1862, Tolstoy conceived plans for writing works of an historical nature. Had it not been for the Countess, however, he would never have been able to give to the world these two masterpieces. In her own handwriting she painstakingly copied and recopied the manuscripts of both novels many times.

Originally Tolstoy intended to write a history or a novel of the Decembrist Movement of 1825, which shook Russia profoundly. This first revolutionary attempt to secure a constitutional government involved the flower of the Russian nobility. Many paid for this revolt with their lives; others were exiled to Siberia, where they laid a foundation for culture in that remote region. The stories and legends about them which circulated throughout Russia, especially among the nobility, provided ideal subject matter for a novel. Tolstoy had only published three chapters of *The Decembrists,* however, when he became absorbed in the reign of Alexander I. His interest gradually focused on the Napoleonic campaigns, and he abandoned the Decembrists for *War and Peace,* a novel which was five years in the making. Tolstoy intended this novel as an introduction and background to the Decembrist Movement—a purpose which it fulfills to the letter, since *War and Peace* ends where the Decembrist Movement begins. It appeared first as a serial, and later in book form in 1869.

War and Peace is justly called the national novel of Russia. It is a colossal prose epic, reflecting the whole range of Russian life at the beginning of the nineteenth century. Once again Tolstoy paid homage to the simplicity and strength of the common people in contrast to the artificiality of the upper classes. Being an officer himself, it was natural that he should devote more space to descriptions of battles than to other phases of Russian life. Nevertheless, one finds here a true reflection of the life of the various classes in Russia—of their life during peace and war, as well as during the aftermath of war; of the various superstitions and beliefs which were the product of war, as well as of the positive benefits arising from a just struggle.

In this novel, even more than in the Sevastopol sketches, Tolstoy denounced war as an instrument for the settlement of disputes between nations. He tried his level best to minimize the sagacity of the strategists and the heroic exploits of the superior officers. Some critics have seen in this approach the recurrence of an old fatalism in a new guise. But this was not fatalism. Tolstoy merely sought to minimize the achievements of the war lords and the glory of war. Perhaps here, too, he had already acquired a habit, which became more pronounced in after years, of consciously or unconsciously minimizing the achievements of others in his own field—in this case, the army.

Although Tolstoy's main purpose was to strip war, particularly imperialistic war, of its vain glory and to discourage men from seeking a military career, some critics feel that he accomplished just the reverse. Unintentionally, *War and Peace* became the text for patriotism in Russia, and the battles so vividly described and so artistically delineated, served rather as an inducement for men to enter the army than as a deterrent to military service. In spite of his antiwar message, Tolstoy, in this book, said practically nothing in opposition to defensive wars. It was not until later, after his conversion, that he advocated a literal application of the Christian doctrine, "Resist no evil." In this novel, Tolstoy was more objective than in his previous or in his subsequent works. Absorbed in others, he, for the first time, with a few exceptions, left himself entirely out of the picture. In *War and Peace* there are several heroes of equal importance, none of whom is Tolstoy, although Prince Andrey and Pierre Bezukhov no doubt reveal Tolstoy's outlook at that time.

There is a feeling of spaciousness in this novel. It leaves the reader with the impression of being part of a vast audience, watching a performance of the epic of a nation, in which Russians from one end of the country to the other flit across the stage before his eyes.

Although *Anna Karenina* was based upon an actual incident which took place not far from Tolstoy's estate, its central idea was a natural outgrowth of *War and Peace*. While Vronsky and Anna, so far as the plot goes, are the main characters, Levin was the soul of the novel so far as Tolstoy was concerned. In fact, Levin was Tolstoy himself—the transitional Tolstoy of the period between *War and Peace* and *Confession*. Levin's ideas on labor and the social order incurred all the hostility from members of the nobility that Tolstoy himself experienced from his own people—even from his own wife, the Countess. Levin, in a rather artificial fashion, put into practice some of his ideas, which Tolstoy himself never succeeded in doing. In studying the personality of Tolstoy and his philosophy, especially after 1879, much attention should be paid to the character of Levin and even to Kitty, his wife. One almost infers that, at times, Tolstoy would have preferred a wife like Kitty to the Countess.

Although Levin is the personification of Tolstoy, there is much of Tolstoy in Vronsky too. Before he met Anna, Vronsky was just a man in a uniform, *"un homme comme il faut"*; from the bureaucratic standpoint, a man with a chequered past, not unlike Tolstoy prior to his marriage. This was the first time that Vronsky had actually fallen in love. Although an illicit love, it was nevertheless the real thing. Tolstoy shows that even an illicit love might prove a resurrection for a Vronsky, while it meant death for Anna. From the time Vronsky met Anna, his star began to rise, hers to decline. He was resurrected because of her love, and when she had done everything for him within her power, she gave him the last she had to offer—her life. There are indications that Vronsky's love for Anna began to grow cold—not so Anna's. Having given up everything in the world for him, she made Vronsky the center of her universe, and her love became a jealous passion. When she realized that her attitude would only bring him unhappiness, she took her own life.

In this novel, as in *War and Peace,* Tolstoy swung his lash at the military class with its unbalanced code of morals. He did for Anna what Dostoyevsky did for Sonya, although they belonged to different classes. One thing they had in common—adultery. Whereas Dostoyevsky gave Sonya a new start in life, Anna Karenina, because of her position, character, and culture, and the conventional attitude of her class, could not begin life anew. Although Tolstoy himself disapproved of Anna's action, he portrayed her in such a fashion that her sin was almost obscured and eclipsed by her charm and courage. He presented her fall from grace in a most natural manner, as something which might happen to anyone, irrespective of background, rank, or station. As a warning to those who might presume to pass judgment upon one who paid a heavy price for her sin, he prefaced his book with the Biblical injunction, "Vengeance is Mine. I will repay!"

Subsequent to the publication of a few other works, a drastic change took place in Tolstoy's life. In 1879 he began his *Confession,* in which, for the first time, he preached his new creed of Tolstoyism. This is a theological treatise, in which Tolstoy openly voiced his opinion of the Orthodox Church, and his personal recollections of the inconsistency of his own upbringing with the actual teachings of Christ, although those who reared him posed as Christians. He asserted, here as elsewhere, that the influence of the Church upon true Christianity was detrimental, implying that the Church did for Christianity what Buddhism did for Taoism. Just as Taoism degenerated into superstition and mysticism until it consisted of a debased ritual which bore no resemblance to the original teaching of Lao-Tzu, so the ritualistic and other functions of the Christian Church, in his opinion, distorted and degraded the ethical teachings of Christ. In other words, it was in this book that Tolstoy for the first time openly advocated a Christianity minus Churchianity.

After another interval, during which additional publications appeared, Tolstoy produced *The Kreutzer Sonata* in 1889, followed by his explanatory *Afterword* to it in 1890. This short novel caused a sensation, not only in Russia, but throughout Europe. For a time it was even banned in the United States. Without going into details, it may be mentioned that this was the first sex novel in Russian literature. Tolstoy wrote two novels on sex. The other was *The Devil*, published posthumously in 1911. Strangely enough, in this novel, as in *War and Peace*, his achievement was in direct opposition to his intentions. *War and Peace* was intended to discourage the glorification of army life, but it served rather as an inducement to that very thing. The same was true of *The Kreutzer Sonata*. It was a didactic work, a moral novel, against "conventional" marriages. It opened the door to a stream of sex literature in Russia. It seems strange that Tolstoy, the moralist, should pave the way for writers like Artzibashev (*Sanine*), in whom this crude, licentious, abusive approach to the sex problem reached its culmination. *Sanine* was, in more ways than one, "a Russian tragedy." When *The Kreutzer Sonata* was first published, it was regarded as an attack on all marriage—which was not true. Tolstoy's attack was directed at light marriages, which he termed legal prostitution.

Tolstoy's last great novel, *Resurrection,* was written in 1899, and sold to the highest bidder to defray in part the expenses of the migration of the persecuted Dukhobors (Christian communists) to Canada. It was the most loosely constructed novel that Tolstoy has written. He himself acknowledged that he obtained the idea for this work from the resurrection of Raskolnikov, recorded in the epilogue of Dostoyevsky's *Crime and Punishment.* Tolstoy's *Resurrection* is a working out of the regeneration Raskolnikov achieved through Sonya's great love, but with an entirely new character, a different crime, and much the same setting.

Dostoyevsky's *Crime and Punishment* was a psychological study of the criminal mind. *Resurrection* is a sociological study of prisons and prisoners. Tolstoy began where Dostoyevsky left off. A consecutive reading of *Crime and Punishment* and *Resurrection* leaves one with two very moving, but quite distinct, experiences—the first a glimpse into the mind of a man; the second, into his heart. Both novels were concerned with criminals. Fundamentally the idea of both novelists was the same—that persons who commit crimes are normal people not unlike ourselves, but who, because of the injustice and inequalities of their social environment and certain ideologies, run counter to the law and to the legal machinery set up to ensnare them. *Resurrection* tells us much about the prison system and so-called criminal justice, but nothing of the mental and spiritual anguish to which the individual is subjected before his punishment is meted out to him. *Crime and Punishment,* on the other hand, tells what goes on in the mind of one man before and after

he commits his crime, but next to nothing about his life in prison. Dostoyevsky brought out the "inner good" in Raskolnikov; Tolstoy
related Nekhludov's search for "inner peace." In *Crime and Punishment,* the individual is the center of attention; in *Resurrection,* society
predominates. Both novelists revealed some understanding of Russian
society: Dostoyevsky, of the lower stratum; Tolstoy, of both the upper
and the lower classes.

Resurrection summed up Tolstoy's "confessions." In this final novel,
he not only advocated a theory, but through Nekhludov he put his own
theories into practice. Tolstoy accepted as gospel truth the old Oriental
adage that "The greatest hero is he who can overcome himself," and he
believed that the only prerequisite to the practical application of his
theories was courage.

In spite of the fact that Nekhludov is Tolstoy himself, he does not
hesitate to reveal the limitations of Nekhludov even after his resurrection. It is strongly suggested that all Nekhludov's sacrifices were made
from an egotistical motive—in order to achieve inner peace. His trip
to Siberia with the convicts and his proposed marriage with Katusha
Maslova were the price he expected to pay for this inner peace. There
was nothing altruistic about it.

Katusha Maslova was infinitely superior to Nekhludov. Although
of peasant origin, she had greater moral and spiritual stamina than the
prince. His resurrection was the product of remorse—hers, of love.
In not one of the many criticisms of Katusha has justice been done to
her. Her love was a Russian love, a kind which is difficult for the West-
erner to grasp—just as it is difficult for him to understand Anna's final
sacrifice for Vronsky. When Katusha rejected Nekhludov's proposal
of marriage, she did it because she loved him, because she knew he did
not love her, and because of the social gulf that separated them. Hers
was an unselfish renunciation. He, knowing that she loved him, was
obviously relieved at her decision, which he accepted with alacrity at
its face value. Nekhludov found "inner peace" at Katusha's expense.

THE NOBILITY AND THE PEASANTRY IN TOLSTOY'S NOVELS

A member of the higher nobility himself, Leo Tolstoy was perhaps
the most famous and the most popular portrayer of aristocratic life in
Russia. Reared in a cultured environment and accustomed to consort
with the elite, he was thoroughly acquainted with the best as well as
with the worst traits of his class. In describing the life of the nobility,
he confined himself to three groups: the first consisted of statesmen and

prominent officeholders—men like Karenin, Oblonsky, and Shtcher-batsky; the second included military officers, such as Vronsky and Nekh-ludov; and the third was composed of rich landowners, represented by Nekhludov and Levin.

To the casual observer the Russian nobility was a gay, witty peo-ple, whose time was spent in search of pleasure. Tolstoy gives us a vivid picture of a class, which in Russia no longer exists, and of which there remain only a few last representatives in exile. In the painting of such scenes he had no superior in Russia.

Tolstoy depicted this class at work and at play. He described their formal balls, as in *Anna Karenina,* where, against a background of beau-tiful gowns, smart uniforms, gay music, and graceful dances, the love between Anna and Vronsky was born before the very eyes of the dis-tressed Kitty. Time and again he described their intimate informal par-ties, where at dinners, at homes, and musical evenings, groups of close friends gathered to discuss the latest scandals, political and war news, philosophical questions, literature, music, art, in fact, almost every con-ceivable subject which was not of an ultra-serious nature. Where gos-sip and light conversation became a fine art, the accomplished hostess dreaded a moment's awkward silence for fear it might ruin the entire evening. Tolstoy's novels covered the entire range of the normal activi-ties of his class—not only the balls, but the skating party, where Levin renewed his acquaintance with Kitty; the horse races frequented espe-cially by the officers; the hunting expeditions, which were an integral part of the curriculum of every nobleman; and even the new vogue for tennis.

In Tolstoy's novels we can follow the noble from youth to old age, for he described the education of both men and women of his class. Like himself, the majority of the men attended university for a time even if they did not graduate. They tasted the discipline of army life and observed its rigid code of honor. Their women were educated for mar-riage, learning, in addition, music, dancing, drawing, French literature, and languages. It was imperative for the Russian woman of aristocratic origin to marry as soon as possible, with the question of love a minor problem to be settled as satisfactorily as possible after the wedding. Before marriage they met men in society under strained, artificial con-ditions that did not lead to a real knowledge of character. As Tolstoy indicates in the case of Kitty, it was the height of humiliation and social disgrace for a woman to be dropped by a young man who had paid her any noticeable attention. Both men and women were proficient linguists, and they all spoke French, the smart language of society, although

German and English were popular. It was the custom at the evening salons Tolstoy described so well for both men and women to intersperse foreign words and phrases in their ordinary conversation.

In *Anna Karenina,* perhaps better than elsewhere, Tolstoy revealed the double moral standard for Russian men and women of the aristocracy. The typical nobleman, like Vronsky, was permitted, even expected, to have as many affairs as possible. The more women who fell in love with him, the more popular he became. The typical officer, like Vronsky, or like Olenin in *The Cossacks,* drank too much, gambled for high stakes, conquered as many women's hearts as possible, and in general lived a reckless and extravagant life.

The married aristocrat had to be more discreet about his affairs, when he chose to leave the straight and narrow path, especially if the object of his devotion was a woman of a lower class. In *Anna Karenina,* when Stiva had an affair with the former governess of his children, his wife, Dolly, could not forgive him, not because he had an affair, but because he had one with a woman of an inferior class.

A woman's affairs, even if she were married, were not particularly condemned as long as they did not become a topic for common gossip, and as long as her husband's professional reputation was not injured. When Karenin found out that Anna was unfaithful, he thought not of the immorality of the situation but only of his own reputation, fearing that this might cost him his career in politics. Anna's friends continued to accept her, even though they suspected her guilt, until she and Vronsky openly admitted their relationship to the world by going off and living together. Then they refused to associate with her any longer. Her women friends were more harsh in their uncompromising condemnation than the men, who might have forgiven her. Vronsky, however, was in a better position than Anna. He lost no respect and no friends and, had he given her up and returned to the army, he could have started again just where he had left off, with as good a chance for advancement as before.

In brief, Tolstoy, on the one hand, showed the life of the nobility at its best—its glamor, excitement, luxury, culture, and brilliant social life. The *raison d'être* of the nobility depicted in his major novels was ably summed up by Oblonsky in *Anna Karenina*: "The aim of civilization is enjoyment." But Tolstoy was among the first of the outstanding Russian authors to have the temerity to point out the corrupt and degenerate mode of living tacitly accepted by its members—a constructive criticism. He revealed its shallowness, its incongruous moral code, its extravagance, its unbalanced sense of values, the amount of valuable time wasted on ridiculous pastimes. In his novels he showed that the artificiality, restlessness, and boredom of the average noble demanded a far heavier price than he lavished on his own entertainment. Levin and Nekhludov bore witness to the serious problem of land management which faced the rural nobility; Karenin and Oblonsky, to the political wire-pulling necessary in order that the city official might not only retain his position but secure a better one.

Finally, Tolstoy exposed to the light of day the unhappy condition of any country where a small percentage of the population did none of the labor, yet lived in the lap of luxury, while the vast majority who did all the work lived in miserable poverty, with no educational opportunities and barely enough to eat. Of the three representative groups of the nobility with whom he dealt—the prominent officeholders, the military officers, and the rich landowners—Tolstoy pinned his hopes on the third, believing that they might be instrumental in bringing a new era to the Russian peasantry.

Although Tolstoy painted a vivid portrait of the nobility of his day and generation, the peasants were dearer to his heart, at least in his later years, than any members of his own class. Tolstoy approached the peasants from a different angle than Gogol, Turgenev, or even Pisemsky. He not only regarded them as human beings, but he was not satisfied until he had placed them on a pedestal, until, in fact, he had almost deified them. Not only did he describe sympathetically their physical conditions but also their philosophy of life, their ideas, emotions, and opinions, in such a way that he left no doubt that he was their personal champion. Tolstoy, in other words, approached the peasants subjectively, with the result that one finds a better appreciation of them in his works than in those of any other Russian writer.

In the chapters about Levin and the management of his estate (*Anna Karenina*), Tolstoy revealed the peasant as an intelligent human being with a quick mind and a fine character. Simple living and hard manual labor had made of him a noble superior creature of lofty thoughts and strong character. Tolstoy believed that luxurious, artificial, idle living weakened a man's character and destroyed his peace of soul: that the most admirable type of existence was one of simplicity and hard work coupled with brotherly love and the practice of the Golden Rule. He thought the peasants came much nearer this ideal of perfection than the aristocracy. Therefore, he wanted to follow Christ's injunction to the rich young ruler, that is, to give up all that he had and become a peasant himself. He believed that since the peasants had more of the inner peace which comes from the attainment of these ideals than the aristocracy, they found greater favor in the eyes of God.

Levin, in *Anna Karenina,* who is really Tolstoy himself, voices his philosophy and thoughts. He has the distinction of being the most ideal landowner in Russian fiction. In his attempt to find some meaning in life, he associated with the peasants at harvest time, working side by side with them on an equal footing. During the dinner hour, he ate with an old man, and they became good friends. Tolstoy says that Levin "felt much nearer to the old man than to his own brother, and could not help smiling at the affection he felt for him." That night, after a hard day's work, Levin felt more at peace with himself than he had for a long time, and he reached the decision that it was more important to be a competent farmer than a rich but idle nobleman. In this passage, Tolstoy's account of the peasants swinging their scythes is typical of his fine descriptive powers.

Levin did not join the peasants at harvest in any spirit of condescension. The reader feels that he regarded them with an envy and admiration which were entirely new in Russian literature. Because he believed that the life of the peasant was an ideal life—not one to be pitied—he wanted them to be free to acquire land of their own, provided they themselves did not have serfs. Levin, or in reality Tolstoy, was a complete democrat in this respect. Serfdom was already abolished when he wrote *Anna Karenina;* it only remained for the aristocratic landowner to share his spoil with the peasants on an equal footing.

In *Resurrection,* Nekhludov attained this aim, by parceling out his land among his peasants. Unfortunately, Nekhludov's peasants had been subjugated and cheated so often by their landlords that they simply failed to understand that he was actually giving them the land, and they regarded his scheme as merely another ruse to extract money from them. It was almost impossible for them to realize that he was doing something for them at no profit to himself, and at first they bluntly refused to accept his offer. Such were the peasants with whom Tolstoy himself had to deal, and whose conditions he sought to alleviate.

Tolstoy's idealization of and preoccupation with the peasants and peasant life go far to explain his attitude toward Shakespeare's work, which he never liked. To Tolstoy, any writer or artist who failed to appreciate the fundamental importance of the agricultural worker, or who depicted him as a clown for the sole purpose of entertaining an audience, failed to merit the laurels which the world had bestowed upon him. In fact, even writers who overlooked, while they did not disparage

the peasants, lost caste with Tolstoy. This may well explain his negative attitude toward Leonid Andreyev.

To sum up, Tolstoy's literary career is one of the most absorbing in
the history of Russian literature. His life was practically coincident
with the Golden Age. His literary activity spanned a period of some
fifty-eight years, from 1852 to 1910. In versatility, he was unexcelled
by any writer of his time. He was not only a novelist, but a short-story
writer, an essayist, a dramatist, a theologian, a philosopher, an artist, a
preacher, and the founder of a creed of his own. No writer surpassed
him in describing the life of the nobility in pre-Revolutionary Russia,
or in appreciation of the Russian peasantry. His works reflected all the
ideas and ideals that prevailed in the Russia of his day and generation.
He was the only author in Russian literature who could speak with
authority even to his rulers, who could prophesy their downfall, and
yet emerge unscathed. In Tolstoy one visualizes the patriarch of old,
who raised his powerful voice in protest against the injustice and corruption of his time. In short, Tolstoy was an institution by himself in
the Golden Age of Russian literature.

Although in the study of Russian literature the novel occupies the
most prominent place, an understanding of Russian life as revealed
through that literature would scarcely be complete without some consideration of Alexander Nikolayevitch Ostrovsky (1823-1886), the
dramatist. While, in the novel, Turgenev and Tolstoy were depicting
the life of the Russian nobility or peasantry, and only incidentally refer-
ring to other slices of Russian society, a new class was making a niche
for itself in the drama—namely, the Russian merchant (*kupetchestvo*).
Whereas, in the literature we have already discussed, the underlying
motives were political, social, philosophical, and idealistic, in the plays
of Ostrovsky the economic factor predominates.

If Russian drama may be defined as "life relived," as a genuine trans-
migration of the souls of characters portrayed, then Ostrovsky is the
most representative Russian dramatist. He placed the drama on a par
with the novel. What Turgenev did for the serf, and Tolstoy for the
nobility and peasantry, Ostrovsky did for the merchant. For almost
half a century he dominated the Russian stage. He produced more than
fifty plays, forty-seven of which he wrote himself, five in collaboration
with others, while twelve were translations and adaptations for the
Russian stage.

In spite of his popularity in Russia, Ostrovsky's plays are the most
difficult to stage abroad. One reason for this is that his language was
the vernacular, both regional and local, of the merchant class, and as

such it often defies translation. As a result much of the content of his plays has been misconstrued or has failed to be appreciated in the West. In recent years a few of his plays have been translated, but the translator has sometimes departed so far from the original text that his final product contains little or nothing of Ostrovsky. Some translators have felt constrained to transform Ostrovsky's Russian merchants into American Rockefellers, American Babbits, or American workers.

Three-quarters of Ostrovsky's plays deal with the everyday life of the merchant class, with their strong as well as with their weak points. Ostrovsky's approach was clearly revealed in one of his letters:

> Let the Russian be gay rather than sad when he sees himself reproduced on the stage. Let others assume the role of reformers if they wish. In order to claim the right to correct the shortcomings of a person without insulting him, it is essential to prove that you are also aware of his strong points. That is exactly what I am trying to do in my comedies.

This approach is particularly well illustrated in his two plays, *The Sleigh* and *Poverty Is No Crime*. Because he adopted this methodology even in his comedies, stressing not only the incongruities but also the positive qualities of the Russian merchant class, many Westernizers accused Ostrovsky of Slavophilism. Such was the fate of any writer who attempted to portray the better qualities of Russian individuals or classes. On the other hand, when Ostrovsky had the temerity to champion the cause of the liberal merchant in his struggle with the hidebound traditionalists, many Slavophiles branded him as a Westernizer. As a matter of fact, Ostrovsky belonged to neither political camp. His purpose was to describe the life of the class of which he himself was a product, as it actually was—realistically and naturally. Inasmuch as any group has its merits and defects, it was therefore natural that the rival political camps alternately suspected him of partiality to one or the other.

Ostrovsky's merchant class, from the Russian standpoint, was neither a middle nor an upper class, but comprised the representatives of many classes. Within its ranks were to be found destitute members of the nobility, who, as a last resort, sought to retrieve their fortunes in the business world rather than by the management of their estates. It included the *nouveau riche,* the merchant capitalist, whose success only served to convince him of the power of the Almighty Ruble. Here, too, were to be found many ex-peasants, who had transferred their activities from the seasonal occupation of the farm to the more lucrative world of business, not to mention innumerable clerks and office employees who were the hangers-on of commerce and business. To the nobility described by Turgenev and Tolstoy, the running of an estate or the management of a business was usually a last resort, only to be undertaken in the face of desperate financial reverses, or when life held nothing but bitterness, disillusionment, and defeat. Ostrovsky's merchant class, on the other hand, devoted their lives to business management, and, far from regarding it as a disgrace, they elevated it to an art.

This class had its Russian Rockefellers as well as its Russian Babbitts. When Ostrovsky wrote, the merchant class was mainly responsible for the support of various social and cultural institutions, including art galleries. Its members not only subsidized talented writers, artists, dancers, and musicians, but produced them within their own ranks—as in the case of Ostrovsky himself. They helped to raise the standard of living not only for their own class but for others. In fact, their contribution to Russian culture and civilization has never received due recognition. On the other hand, they were also responsible for much bribery and corruption, prostitution, and vice, and for making a god of the Almighty Ruble.

In general, Ostrovsky voiced the sentiment of the liberal merchant. The plays which reflect this best are *The Storm* and *The Poor Bride*. *The Storm,* by general consensus, is considered one of the best, if not the best, of his many works. Here, as nowhere else, he presented the clash between the older generation of traditionalist merchants, the *samodurs* (domestic tyrants or bullies) like Madame Kabanova and Dikoy, whose roots were fixed in the feudal society of the past, and the younger and more liberal group (Katerina, Boris, Kuligin, Varvara), who strove for freedom of expression, liberty of action, and a more equitable division of authority. Balked by the *samodurs* from finding any legitimate outlet for their feelings, they sometimes, as in the case of Katerina and Boris, mistook license for liberty and indulged in serious lapses from the conventions. Even Tikhon, once he was beyond the reach of his mother's caustic tongue, cast everything else to the winds, in order to crowd as much pleasure as possible into a fortnight of freedom.

In *The Storm* it was the domestic tyranny of Martha Kabanova and Dikoy which bred license—a tyranny which demanded blind, unreasoning obedience from the younger members of the family. This tyranny produced both mental and physical suffering. Not only did Katerina have to submit to the constant nagging of her shrewish mother-in-law, but she had to endure a beating at the hands of her husband in accordance with her mother-in-law's orders—a beating which was supposed to make her a better wife. She was forced to kneel before her husband on the eve of his departure on a business trip and promise not to look at other men during his absence—just as he had to kneel before his domineering mother and pay heed to her countless instructions.

The chief object of Ostrovsky's dramas, particularly of this one, was the destruction of the *samodur,* and the triumph of honesty, moderation, and genuine goodness. Unlike Tolstoy, who practically sought to transform the nobility into a peasantry, or Tchekhov, who sought to supplant the nobility by a middle class, Ostrovsky was not seeking the destruction of the merchant class. He merely wished to rid it of its more undesirable elements, to eliminate the *samodurs*—in fact, to ethicize the business profession.

In *The Poor Bride* the power of the ruble is ably illustrated. In the first place a bride without a dowry was a frozen asset in a merchant's family, especially if she lacked beauty. If she were good looking, she could still hope to be sold to the highest bidder—to some rough, uncouth, and none too respectable merchant like Benevolensky. Anna Petrovna Nezabudkina was a product of the older traditionalist generation, for whom wealth covered up a multitude of sins, and who could unhesitatingly sacrifice her daughter to a man like Benevolensky in order to improve her financial position. Marya, representing the younger generation, accepts her mother's choice reluctantly, but unselfishly, in a fine spirit. On the one hand, Ostrovsky shows greed, selfishness, and disregard for human values; on the other, love and self-sacrifice.

To sum up, Ostrovsky gave a faithful description of the practical, materialistic merchant class, which was about to supplant the idealistic nobility. The final triumph of this class is reflected in Tchekhov's plays, particularly in *The Cherry Orchard.*

Although Anton Pavlovitch Tchekhov (1860-1904) was a prolific writer of short stories, novels, and plays, practically all his ideas are summed up in his last drama, *The Cherry Orchard,* A Comedy in Four Acts, published in 1904. Technically speaking, and from a universal standpoint, *The Three Sisters* (1900) is perhaps his masterpiece; but from an historical point of view *The Cherry Orchard* is much more significant. For that reason we have confined our discussion to this play.

In general, *The Cherry Orchard* was more popular and more widely discussed than any of Tchekhov's previous writings. The main reason for its phenomenal success was that it voiced the prevailing political, economic, and social sentiment of the Russian people. This play appeared during the Russo-Japanese War, and almost on the eve of the Revolution of 1905, when the common platform of all political parties was the urbanization (industrialization) of Russia. By general consensus there were far too many villages and "cherry orchards" in Russia, when what the country actually needed was cities, factories, railroads, machinery, and a vast program of industrial development.

It should be pointed out that the Russian village of the period in question was not like a European village or an American farming community. Many of them were several hundred miles from a railroad station, and the roads leading to them were unpaved and often impassable. There were no libraries, no clubs, no daily newspapers, and very little connection with the outside world. In such an atmosphere people vegetated in boredom. A stranger from town, more particularly from Moscow, was sure to become an absorbing center of interest for the entire community. Most of the enterprising people marooned in these villages, like the "Three Sisters," spent their time planning how to get out, how to get to Moscow, the land of dreams. Some left of their own free will—others, because of the mismanagement of their estates, were forced out by the Lopakhins. To understand Tchekhov better, one should read Turgenev's *A Month in the Country,* where the theme, the negative side of country life, is the same, minus the Lopakhins, who have not yet appeared on the scene.

Tolstoy idealized the peasant and the simple naturalness of village life. In Tchekhov we see that too much village life retards the material progress of Russia. His plays mark a distinct reaction against the idealism of Tolstoy—a reaction which expressed the general sentiment of the people. In *The Cherry Orchard,* more than in any other contemporaneous work, this clash between ruralism and urbanization, between the impractical, traditionalist, and often impoverished members of the nobility, and the impatient, ruthless businessman, is faithfully depicted. Tchekhov makes it quite apparent that a new era is beginning, and that the architect of the industrial age is the merchant capitalist.

In this play Madame Ranevskaya and her brother Gayev represent the unbusinesslike, impractical, decadent members of the "House of Gentlefolk," who have retained only the shadow of the former glamor which surrounded the nobility of *Anna Karenina,* and who contribute to the vegetation and stagnation of other classes by supporting "superfluous people" in idleness. On the other hand, Lopakhin, who seems to have stepped out of the pages of Ostrovsky, stands for the new, prosperous merchant class, not far removed from serfdom, which inherits the family estates of the Ranevskys, destroys the cherry orchards, together with all that they stood for symbolically and otherwise, and replaces them with suburban villas, the symbol of the new age.

In *The Cherry Orchard* the star of the Lopakhins is in the ascendancy—that of the Ranevskys is setting. The reader is confronted with a clash between sentimentalism on the one hand, and dollars and cents on the other; between static life and dynamic life; between culture and civilization; between that which was old and familiar and that which is new and unknown. The new way had a stronger appeal because the old way had been tried and found wanting. The new way promised concrete returns in the shape of higher wages, shorter hours, better living conditions, popular education, and so on, at the expense of the Oblomovs, dilapidated manors, and run-down cherry orchards. The dissatisfied elements, therefore, pinned their hopes on industrialization or, as they called it, urbanization, which promised all this in return for the sacrifice of a group which was numerically insignificant.

Although it seems apparent that Tchekhov's sympathies lay with the Lopakhins, of which class he himself was a product, nevertheless, he was fair enough and objective enough to lay bare the strong and the weak points of both sides in the struggle. The crude methods of Lopakhin reveal the destructive element latent in him. At times his coarseness assumes such proportions that one wonders which the merchant capitalist wanted more—a new world of his own making or revenge for the injustice and inequalities of the past—perhaps both. On the other hand, the sentimental Ranevskys, who cherished every stick and stone of the ancient and decrepit manor house, thoughtlessly abandoned the eighty-seven-year-old footman, Firs, who had served the family for forty years. When Firs discovered his predicament, his first thought was not for himself but for his master and whether he had remembered to wear his fur coat. Like Turgenev, Tchekhov, perhaps consciously, points out that the serf may reveal a nobler spirit than his master.

In *The Cherry Orchard,* the clash between the old and the new ends with the defeat of the old and the triumph of the new. The merchant capitalist, whose victory was foreseen by Gontcharov, whose leadership was sought by Turgenev and whose representatives take precedence in the works of Ostrovsky, finally in *The Cherry Orchard* displaces the old nobility. The triumph of Lopakhin is also the triumph of the Stolzes and the Solomins, whereas the defeat of the Ranevskys is likewise the defeat of the Oblomovs and the Lavretskys.

The merchant capitalist dealt his death-blow with the axe that cut down the cherry orchard—a blow that was heard throughout Russia— and which proved to be the first signal of the approaching revolution. For the Revolution of 1905 was not, in the final analysis, a social revolution. It put the merchant capitalist in the saddle, where he remained until 1917. Strangely enough, it was his children who provided the leaders for the 1917 revolution; and it was this very class, which, by its contributions to the revolutionary money chests, blindly dug its own grave. The merchant capitalists were ousted, not by the axe, but by firing squads and "liquidation."

Abroad, and particularly in England, Tchekhov became the most popular of the Russian dramatists—even upon occasion a rival of Shakespeare. There are several reasons for this. In the first place, Tchekhov, with his humorous short story, broke new ground in Russian literature from the standpoint of the foreigner. By showing that the Russian could laugh as well as sigh, he was for them like a ray of light in "the monotonous gloom" of Russian literature. In Europe, moreover, the short story enjoyed an immense popularity, and in Russia, where it had reached its nadir, Tchekhov elevated it to an art. Furthermore, his dramas, although less amusing, expressed a reaction against sentimentality which coincided with English taste at the beginning of the twentieth century. The attention of the English public may have been attracted to the denouement of his plays, particularly in the case of *The Three Sisters* and *Uncle Vanya,* which are somewhat reminiscent of Goldsmith's *Deserted Village.* To be sure, in Goldsmith, the depopulation of the countryside was bemoaned as a tragedy, whereas in Tchekhov it is welcomed, but the milieu is the same. Finally, the merchant capitalist, depicted by Tchekhov, was an even more familiar figure in the industrial centers of Western Europe than in Russia itself. To the Englishman, as well as to Tchekhov, he was a practical man who stood for material progress.

Although *The Cherry Orchard* is for Americans undoubtedly the best-known Russian play, it may in the future, because of the popularity of Margaret Mitchell's *Gone With the Wind,* be even better understood and appreciated. For both works deal with the passing of a traditional way of life, based upon a landowning aristocracy and the institution of serfdom or slavery.

Tara meant to Scarlett what the cherry orchard meant to Madame Ranevskaya. Both women faced the loss of their property to men who, from their standpoint, were upstarts or white trash. Lopakhin, a product of the new industrial capitalism, insisted on buying the cherry orchard, where his father had been a serf. Jonas Wilkerson, the typical carpetbagger of the post-Civil War era, sought to buy Tara, where he had once served as an overseer, prior to his discharge on moral grounds.

Both women refused to capitulate to the new social and economic order. But Madame Ranevskaya, who was more of a sentimentalist, expected a miracle to save her. Scarlett, in whom the materialist prevailed, was ready to go to any length, even to sell herself to a man she did not love, in order to save Tara, that she might never be hungry again. Although Madame Ranevskaya lost her cherry orchard, she remained an aristocrat. Scarlett kept Tara, but in doing so she stooped to the level of the white trash she so utterly despised.

A parallel reading of *The Cherry Orchard* and *Gone With the Wind* suggests further comparisons between Gayev and Ashley Wilkes, neither of whom was fitted to cope with the new way of life.

In brief, Tchekhov's works, especially *The Cherry Orchard,* mark the transition between the downfall of the "House of Gentlefolk" and the advent of the proletariat—sometimes called Russia's "Twilight Period."

Maxim Gorky (1868-1936), like Tchekhov, believed that the future of Russia lay in further industrialization rather than in agricultural development. Both writers resented Tolstoy's idealization of the peasantry and traced much of the wretchedness and misery in Russia to peasant influence. Tchekhov, however, hitched his chariot to the merchant capitalist, as his agent for urbanization, whereas Gorky lined himself up with the urban workers—the proletariat. Moreover, Gorky, unlike his contemporaries, demanded a change through revolution rather than by education and evolution. In literature he did for the urban "serf" what Turgenev did for the rural serf.

Although Gorky is better known as the classic interpreter of Russian proletarian culture, he evinced his real talent in the portrayal of the Russian underworld. In his idealization of the underworld Gorky undoubtedly sounded a new note in Russian literature. He was the uncrowned king of the Russian *bosyak* (tramp or hobo) before he became the writer-laureate of the proletariat. Not all of his works— and he was a prolific writer—reflect Gorky. The Gorky who found a niche for himself among the writers of the classical age was the Gorky who championed the underworld and interpreted the prewar Russian proletariat. Although this Gorky belongs essentially to the Golden Age, he was not a genius of the same caliber as Turgenev, Dostoyevsky, and Tolstoy. He was a man of great talent.

No other author, prior to Gorky, has given us such a characteristic and sympathetic description of the Russian *bosyak.* Gorky's tramps differ sharply from the members of the American underworld, or from those of any other country, except perhaps Germany and Italy. This partly explains the popularity of his works in these two countries. The Russian underworld described in *The Lower Depths* was not made up of racketeers, gunmen, and bootleggers, driving high-powered automobiles and wearing tuxedos and dress shirts. It was composed rather of "creatures that once were men." For the most part these human derelicts were victims of the social order rather than violators of the law. Their chief weapon was their fists—or, as a last resort, a knife. They were invariably penniless. Money, when they had it, burned holes in their pockets. Except for thieves and robbers, this underworld constituted an army of unemployed and unskilled laborers, who wandered from place to place in search of work. So true to life was Gorky's portrayal of this slice of Russian society that his name became a byword in the mouth of every tramp, and he was recognized as the patron of the underworld. To upbraid a hobo for his laziness might well bring the retort: "You never can tell—I might become a Gorky!"

By assembling the various types of the Russian underworld in a basement night lodging, Gorky, in his play *The Lower Depths,* was able to sum up his ideas concerning them. Although of diverse antecedents, barons, Tartar princes, thieves, prostitutes, or card-sharpers, they have this in common—that they are the victims of the social order, and they meet here on a plane of equality. Such a play, for the majority of people, broke new ground in Russian drama.

Originally this play was entitled *Na Dnye Zhizni* (The Lower Depths of Life); but, at the suggestion of V. I. Nemirovitch-Dantchenko, Gorky dropped the last Russian word. The play was first produced at the Moscow Art Theatre on December 31, 1902, and its thirty-fifth jubilee was held at the close of 1937. Germany, especially, went wild over the play. From 1903 to 1904 it enjoyed an uninterrupted run of 500 nights in Berlin alone. English translations have appeared under various titles: *In the Depths, A Night Shelter, Submerged, Down and Out,* as well as *The Lower Depths.*

Whereas in Tchekhov's plays, the idle-rich nobility and other "superfluous" people vegetate in boredom in the Russian village, Gorky's hoboes vegetate in idleness and trivialities, sometimes reluctantly, in the dark damp basements where they seek a temporary lodging. In spite of their sordid surroundings, Gorky's heroes still have faith in a better future. They do not spend their time cursing the system or lamenting their misfortunes. The pinnacle of their discussion, as led by Luka, the vagabond pilgrim, and his interpreter, Satin, the card-sharper, is "the better man." Far from being crushed in spirit, some of them regard their wretched conditions as the price of their freedom. To Tchekhov's idle-rich, life spelled boredom; although physically better off than Gorky's tramps, they were spiritually crushed. The human failures of Gorky's underworld, in spite of their environment, are spiritually the stronger of the two. They still have hope; they take life as it comes, sometimes in happy-go-lucky fashion; they sing, and they keep their faith in humanity. Man to them is the norm. Whether he turns out to be a carpenter, a card-sharper, a Napoleon, or a Mohammed, he is still a man, free and deserving of respect. Strangely enough they would prefer "a better man," even a better underworld. Gorky's philosophy of "the better man," expressed by Luka and Satin, almost approaches Tolstoy's "inner peace."

In other words, Gorky discovered a world in the underworld. His implication is clear enough—that tramps or hoboes with such beautiful souls should not be lost to humanity because they are the victims of an unjust social order. In this field Gorky had no predecessor, and herein lies his chief contribution to Russian literature.

Less artistic, but of greater political significance, was his proletarian novel, *Mother*. This was the first novel subsequent to the 1905 revolution to portray the life of the urban worker in the factory, at home, at political meetings, on parade, and so forth. Although it truly reflects the life of the proletariat during the period in question, there were few mothers like Pelagueya Vlasova. It seems quite evident that Gorky wished other mothers to emulate her, but he has given us a portrait of the ideal, rather than of the real, proletarian mother.

If we did not know that Gorky's novel was produced in Russia in 1906, we could never guess that it ran the gauntlet of the world's most rigid censorship. This novel was an open challenge to the government—an appeal to the worker to emulate the Vlasovs and, by force or revolution, to bring about the new social order. Gorky did not mince words in the appeals of his agitators. In a country where freedom of speech exists, speeches like those of Pavel would be regarded as soapbox oratory or casually dismissed as Red propaganda. But in Russia, during the period in question, the activities of the Vlasovs and their supporters constituted a serious menace to the old regime. Yet this book could be found in every library, accessible to anyone capable of reading it. This was chiefly due to the efforts of the Russian intelligentsia, in welcoming into Russian literature a real proletarian novel, without altogether subscribing to the ideas expressed in it.

Gorky's *Mother* is by no means a work of art. It is rather a political document of the tumultuous years 1905 and 1906. As we have already intimated, Gorky is really at home only in the underworld. In the world he is less of an artist and more of a propagandist. *The Lower Depths* is a sociological study—*Mother,* a political tract.

For a better appreciation of Gorky, American readers should turn to John Steinbeck. Of all American writers, Steinbeck is the one who most nearly approaches Gorky. There is a great deal of the Gorky philosophy in the works of Eugene O'Neill and in Erskine Caldwell's *Tobacco Road,* not to mention others, but Steinbeck is the American version of Gorky.

Both Gorky and Steinbeck succeeded in awakening the general public and the authorities to the existence of a class of people living under conditions almost beyond their comprehension. Both writers championed the cause of these lower depths and presented their characters in such a light that the public realized they were, after all, human beings, albeit tramps or migrants.

Gorky in *Lower Depths* and Steinbeck in *Grapes of Wrath* not only succeeded in gaining recognition of the plight of the Satins, the Lukas, and the Joads, but they made the public lament such a great waste of valuable human material. People not only wondered what could be done for these lower depths, but what they, in a better environment, could do for their countries. In other words, what could the Satins and Lukas do for Russia? What could the Joads do for America?

Any comparison of Gorky and Steinbeck should not overlook the fact that, although both were out-and-out realists, Gorky, always the artist, attained the same effects without the crudeness and profanity found in Steinbeck. In this respect, Steinbeck has more in common with the contemporary Soviet writer, Mikhail Sholokhov, than with Gorky.

In short, Gorky did for the tramp and for the proletarian what Tolstoy did for the peasant, Andreyev for the Jew, and Turgenev for the serf. He idealized him. The impression derived from a study of his works is that he stands at the head of a great mass of humanity, seeking recognition and a new life. With Gorky began the era of the domination of the proletariat.

This summary of Russian literature would not be complete without reference to the Symbolist movement, which began in the 1890's and came especially to the fore in Russia after 1905. Its most outstanding representatives were Leonid Andreyev (1871-1919), Vyatcheslav Ivanov (1866-1949), Andrei Bely (1880-1934), and Alexander Blok (1880-1921). The Symbolist movement projected itself into what was a virtual vacuum in the Russian literary world, when after the 1880's no outstanding novels were being produced. It matured and became more articulate after 1905, as a result of widespread disillusionment over the achievements of the revolution in that year. At first the Symbolists attributed the chaotic state in the political and social life of Russia to what they alleged were wrong emphases in nineteenth century Russian literature, especially to over-emphasis on social problems. In the process of their revaluation and reinterpretation of that literature, however, most of them became enamored of it and emerged as its staunch supporters. In particular, the Symbolists were responsible for the rediscovery of Dostoyevsky, whose works they made extremely popular. Indeed they found in Dostoyevsky, as in no other novelist, substantiation of their own distrust of and reaction against industrialism, materialism, and atheism. The Symbolists provided an important link between the Golden Age and Soviet literature. Their ideas and their experiments in technique influenced many Soviet writers, especially in the 1920's.

LITERARY CRITICISM

It is very difficult to provide non-Russians with a concise and yet comprehensive definition of a Russian critic or of Russian literary criticism. Ostensibly the critics interpreted Russian literature. Actually, because of the very nature of that literature, the scope of their work was much greater. Because the great writers of the Golden Age championed the cause of political freedom and social reform, the Russian critics devoted their articles mainly to an analysis of the great questions at issue in their time and to the remedies advanced. Their greatness lies in the fact that they did it boldly and at the risk not only of their careers but of their very lives. The history of Russian literary criticism is a record of martyrdom.

Although by the outside world most of these critics were regarded as atheists because of their attack upon organized religion, they actually took many of their ideas of social justice from Christianity. In other words, like the French philosophers of the eighteenth century, they attacked churchianity, not Christianity, as Belinsky's *Letter to Gogol* so clearly demonstrates. Many of these critics were the children or grandchildren of priests and had themselves attended a theological seminary. It was because of this background that they became conscious of the gulf between Christian principles and the practice of the official

Courtesy Sovfoto

VISSARION GRIGORYEVITCH BELINSKY (1811-1848)
Russian literary critic.

Church, which in Russia had become a tool of the state, thereby constituting a reactionary force which impeded progress. In their denunciation of corruption in the Orthodox Church, the Russian critics performed much the same role from without that the Reformers achieved from within the Catholic Church during the era of the Reformation in Western Europe. For in nineteenth-century Russia the Church as an institution never did champion the cause of the serfs or take a stand for the betterment of their position. That Christian task, strange as it may seem, had to be taken up through secular channels by writers and critics—the so-called atheistic intelligentsia.

It stands to reason, therefore, that the Russian critics had to do far more than analyze books from the standpoint of art and technique. Their outlook had to be broad, their understanding deep, and their courage unflinching. As political and social reformers they had to face the antagonism of both Church and state. The Russian critic had to assume in turn the role of a Protestant Reformer, a French Encyclopedist, an American Revolutionist of the 1776 variety, and a contemporary columnist.

It is not surprising that the Russian critics have been very popular with the leaders of the new regime in Russia. By and large, both critics and revolutionary leaders shared the same fate of imprisonment and exile on behalf of their ideals. N. K. Krupskaya, the wife of Lenin, for example, testified to her husband's great affection for Tchernyshevsky and to the frequent references he made to the great critic in his writings. The most important contribution of the Soviet regime in this respect is that it has republished the works of the critics and has made them popular. Especially since the adoption of the new constitution in 1936 and the Pushkin Centennial in 1937, several works about the critics have appeared. To date, strictly speaking however, only a beginning has been made. The study of Russian literary criticism is still a virgin field.

Although there were many Russian literary critics during the Golden Age, three of the greatest among them will suffice here to represent their role in Russian literature and their chief contributions. These are Belinsky, Tchernyshevsky, and Dobrolyubov.

Vissarion Grigoryevitch Belinsky (1811-1848) was the founder of literary criticism in Russia. In fact he elevated it to an art and a science. He was practically the first who dared to criticize established writers in various fields. Before his time, writers were held in high esteem, and there was such respect for the printed word that hardly anyone had the temerity to criticize prominent authors. In his "Literary Reflections" Belinsky appealed to Russians to follow the example of West European critics and to point out the weak as well as the strong points of a writer's work, irrespective of his position. The impression is that he, himself, wished to set an example for others in this respect, for in this same work, while presenting a survey of Russian writers from Lomonosov to Pushkin, he went so far as to assert that there was still no such thing as Russian literature.

The importance of Belinsky's stand in favor of literary criticism should not be overlooked. It did have the salutary effect of inducing many writers to be more careful about what they wrote. Especially during the life of Belinsky, Russian writers became critic-conscious, fully aware that what they wrote could never escape his watchful eye. Belinsky left his imprint on Russian readers as well as upon Russian writers; the limited but select circle of Russian readers was a highly intelligent group who often paid as much attention to the critic as to the author. The reader of Belinsky's works inevitably gains the impression that he wrote with authority. Only one Russian writer excelled him in this respect and he was Leo Tolstoy. Belinsky's bid for criticism, however, did in practice open the door to the mediocre critic and encouraged a tendency on the part of Russian critics in general to expose the weak points rather than to commend the strong points of the work whose value they assessed.

Belinsky's indictment of Russian literature emanated from his failure to discover a single genius in that field. Although he found many great talents, he did not believe that any of them, with the exception of Pushkin, revealed even a spark of genius. A talented person—Belinsky implied in his essay—is at best only an artisan, whereas a genius is an artist. An artisan merely recreates, whereas an artist actually creates. It seems that the main purpose of Belinsky in writing his "Literary Reflections" was to reconnoiter the field in order to discover a genius. But Pushkin was the only man of great promise he found. His main reasons for elevating Pushkin above the rest were, first, that Pushkin's work reflected the national qualities of the Russian people and, second, that his poetry was free from any motivation.

With regard to Pushkin's place in world literature, Belinsky in his "Survey of Russian Literature in 1841" said that Pushkin stood in the same relation to the great European poets as Russia did to Europe, and vice versa.

Belinsky attributed the absence of any genius in the field of Russian literature to the lack of a national (*narodnaya*) literature. Too many Russian writers, he complained, had merely imitated the works of foreign writers. Belinsky's article in reality constituted an appeal for such a national literature, for he conceived the cosmos as a unit, comprised of national entities, each of which was destined to make its own distinctive contribution.

The real prerequisite to the understanding of Belinsky and the other leading Russian critics is not only a knowledge of the political and social system extant in Russia during the period in question, including the ritual and dogma of the Orthodox Church, as well as a comprehensive background of Russian and comparative literature, but also some familiarity with the ideas of the leading German philosophers of the eighteenth and nineteenth centuries.

Writers on Belinsky have ordinarily divided his literary career into several well-marked stages, according to the influence upon him of Schelling, Fichte, and Hegel. The consensus is that the Schelling period was ushered in by the appearance of the "Literary Reflections" in *Molva* in 1834. Judging by this work, Belinsky understood Schelling to mean that the universe is permeated with one eternal idea; that in the course of history this idea manifests itself in the life of peoples, each of which must express one aspect of the universal idea; and that this manifestation is the only justification of a people's existence. In art Belinsky found the best expression of the unique qualities of a people. At the time he wrote, Belinsky felt that Russian literature did not yet express the national qualities of the Russian people.

Following the Fichte period, which lasted for only a brief interlude (1836-1837), came the Hegelian period (1837-1840). As in Europe, so in Russia, Hegelian philosophy was subject to many interpretations by Conservatives (Rightists) and Liberals (Leftists). To Russians in these years it was summed up in a nutshell by the assumption that whatever was real was rational and should be accepted. The Slavophiles in Russia interpreted this to mean acceptance of Orthodoxy and Autocracy as they existed, but the Westernizers contended that, since life was dynamic, change must be accepted as reality. Belinsky, although fundamentally a Westernizer, came very near at times to voicing the interpretation of the Slavophiles as regards Orthodoxy, Autocracy, and Nationality.

As a result, Belinsky at times enjoyed the plaudits of both Westernizers and Slavophiles. His influence upon Dostoyevsky, the foremost literary exponent of Slavophilism, was particularly great. From the "Literary Reflections," Dostoyevsky undoubtedly derived his concept of the mission of the Russian people.

Belinsky also took cognizance of the comparative dearth of juvenile literature in Russia during his lifetime. In his article on "Two Books for Children" in 1840, he made a strong appeal for greater effort in this field. Too many Russians, he felt, looked upon children's books with contempt and bought them mainly for their colorful illustrations. Belinsky was aware of the importance of good literature for children. Far from believing that anyone could write books for children, he pointed out that only a genius could fill this gap. Turgenev was the first among Russia's great writers to take this admonition seriously with the publication of *Byezhin Prairie* (*Memoirs of a Sportsman*, 1852). He was the first in Russia to produce what may be termed standard juvenile literature.

As early as 1843 Belinsky was already in a position to announce the existence of a Russian literature. This was a far cry from his first survey in 1834, when he denied that there was such a thing as Russian literature. The progress of a decade led him to conclude that Russian literature was no longer confined to Pushkin but included a whole roster of outstanding writers. By 1847 ("Russian Literature in 1847") he admitted that even Russian literary criticism had been established on a sound basis.

In his survey of Russian literature in 1846, however, Belinsky warned his readers that they should not approach the field with the same gauge they used to approach other literatures. Just as the history of Russia did not follow the same pattern as the history of other countries, he pointed out that Russian literature, too, was unique. Unless this were borne in mind, he insisted that Russian literature would remain a riddle and a mystery.

To sum up, it may be said that Belinsky was largely instrumental in producing a national Russian literature and in laying the foundations of Russian literary criticism. He likewise made another outstanding contribution by interpreting standard European literature to the Russians, both through European and Russian glasses. In this respect, he therefore paved the way for comparative literary criticism in Russia, which flourished in the nineteenth century. Furthermore, in the interpretation of Belinsky's role in Russian literature, greater stress should be laid in the future on two aspects of his achievement. First, it is important to note the extent to which, in spite of his reputation as a Westernizer, Belinsky reflected the age of Nicholas I, with its growing emphasis on nationalization and Russification. This is particularly evident in his annual surveys of Russian literature from 1834 to 1847. Not only was Belinsky at his best in these surveys, but they provide a first-hand history of Russian national literature during its most formative years. Second, the influence of Belinsky on Dostoyevsky should no longer be overlooked.

Nikolai Gavrilovitch Tchernyshevsky (1828-1889) has done for Gogol what Belinsky did for Pushkin. He correctly interpreted the historical significance of the Gogol period of the 1830's and 1840's in Russian literature. Although like Belinsky, Tchernyshevsky also recognized the genius of Pushkin, he found in Gogol's satirical sketches, which were themselves replete with criticism and analysis of the existing social system, the spark which produced modern Russian literary criticism. The implication is that both Tchernyshevsky and Belinsky, in laying the foundations of Russian literary criticism, derived much inspiration from Gogol.

Tchernyshevsky was not only a critic of Russian writers; he was also a critic of Russian critics, especially of Belinsky. This was done at a time when the mere mention of Belinsky in print was forbidden. In his

Essays on Russian Literature in the Days of Gogol, Tchernyshevsky returned Russian criticism to the tradition of Belinsky.

With Tchernyshevsky began the attack on the Russian intelligentsia as weaklings. Although the repudiation of the intelligentsia really emerged first in Turgenev's novels, where the characters he portrayed as leaders for the founding of the new social order turned out to be weaklings and failures, it was Tchernyshevsky who was responsible for classifying all such progressives as typical representatives of the Russian intelligentsia, and who made them the butt of criticism and ridicule for their inability to achieve positive results. The attack on the Russian intelligentsia continued practically without respite until the 1930's.

A study of Tchernyshevsky's works reveals that in general he advocated reform by a gradual evolutionary process rather than by revolution. For he believed that any fundamental improvement in the Russian social system depended upon increased enlightenment and education for the illiterate, inarticulate, and unorganized masses (*narod*), who comprised four-fifths of the nation, as well as upon the ability of the intelligentsia to convince the rulers of Russia that reforms were necessary and should come voluntarily from above rather than by force from below.

Just as Belinsky was influenced by Hegel, Tchernyshevsky came under the spell of the German philosopher, Ludwig Feuerbach (1804-1872). This in itself marks a change in outlook on the part of the intelligentsia from idealism and mysticism to materialism, as well as from the philosophy of reconciliation to a realization that concrete action must be taken to bring about a change in existing conditions. Just as Feuerbach put man at the center of the universe and insisted that everything should be done for man and through man, so Tchernyshevsky put the people (*narod*) first and claimed that everything should be done by the people and through the people.

As a careful perusal of his works indicates, Tchernyshevsky began as a philosopher, then turned to history, and finally to political economy. It is clear, however, that for him materialism was a means to an end rather than an end in itself. He reached the conclusion, however reluctantly, that materialism more than idealism would assist the revolutionary forces.

This transition from idealism to materialism is reflected in Tchernyshevskys' preference for Gogol, the realist, to Pushkin, the idealist. Whereas Belinsky had predicted that Pushkin would remain the model for Russian writers who sought to give expression to Russian genius, Tchernyshevsky, in his *Essays on Russian Literature in the Days of*

Gogol, claimed that Gogol rather than Pushkin was the real founder of the school of national Russian writers. For Gogol, unlike Pushkin, was free from foreign influence. His works were devoted exclusively to a realistic portrayal of Russian life. Although his books were works of art, he was not motivated by art for art's sake, but rather by art for life's sake or for the sake of the *narod.* Since the *narod* was the center of his thinking, Tchernyshevsky placed the poet Nekrasov above Pushkin. In his judgment, Nekrasov was a product of the people, worked all his life for the people, and accomplished everything through the people.

Another reason why Gogol appealed particularly to Tchernyshevsky was that, unlike many other writers who blamed only individuals or specific groups or classes for the state of affairs in Russia, both men agreed in placing the blame upon the entire social structure. There were no redeeming characters belonging to any social stratum in either *The Revizor* or *Dead Souls.*

Tchernyshevsky subordinated writers like Griboyedov, Pushkin, Lermontov, and Koltsov to Gogol because none of them established a school of writers as Gogol did. It seems likely that Tchernyshevsky's elevation of Gogol contributed greatly to the advancement of Russian prose at the expense of poetry and made the novel, which was a more realistic medium than the poem, the true vehicle of the Golden Age of Russian literature.

Among his own contemporaries, Tchernyshevsky preferred Tolstoy, for whom he predicted a great future, Nekrasov, and Dobrolyubov.

In spite of his premature death, the influence of Nikolai Alexandrovitch Dobrolyubov (1836-1861) was such that by 1885 four editions of his works had been published. In Soviet Russia today, Dobrolyubov enjoys the same popularity as the other leading Russian critics.

The most striking feature of Dobrolyubov's political ideology is that, unlike most of his fellow-Westernizers, he advocated the American political system, in preference to any European model, to replace the existing autocratic regime in Russia. He favored the American system for many reasons, as outlined in an article written in 1859,[1] but mainly because he believed that it did more to advance the welfare of the people as a whole than any other system. Since Dobrolyubov worked for the good of the *narod,* it was natural that he should approve of America as the country which best served the interests of the people in contrast to most of Europe where the people were expected to serve the state.

---

[1] A critical review by Dobrolyubov of *Travels in North America, Canada and the Island of Cuba* by Alexander Lakier (2 Vols., St. Petersburg, 1859).

In fact, Dobrolyubov in 1859 grasped the spirit of America as it was reflected some years later in Lincoln's Gettysburg Address. "Government of the people, by the people, for the people" was exactly what Dobrolyubov and his fellow critics were crusading for at the risk of their lives in Russia. America had already achieved it.

The Puritanic principle, derived from the *Old Testament* (*Leviticus* 25:23), that all the land belonged to God and that any man was entitled to the amount he could till, likewise appealed greatly to Dobrolyubov, who felt that it was carried into practice in America. In the process of westward expansion there was always land available for those Americans who were willing and able to till and exploit it. To the sponsors of the *narod* in Russia, confronted for the most part by a landless peasantry, in a country which was in 1859 still on the eve of the abolition of serfdom, the American example suggested a near approach to paradise on earth.

To most Europeans, because of the unusual absence of government interference, this freedom of the individual to go and take the land spelled anarchy. But Americans have termed it "rugged individualism." Strictly speaking, rugged individualism is the real essence of Russian idealistic anarchism, which has been so generally misinterpreted by Western scholars. If a critic like Dobrolyubov had lived in the United States in 1859 he would have qualified as a good American patriot and as a rugged individualist. In Russia he was denounced as a radical, undesirable citizen, and even as a venomous snake! Had he not, like Belinsky, died young, Dobrolyubov would undoubtedly have been exiled to Siberia, as were Tchernyshevsky and many others who displayed an active interest in the welfare of the people.

Dobrolyubov was a combination of Belinsky and Tchernyshevsky, but he surpassed them both in his impatience for immediate action to reform the Russian political and social system. In fact, he called as loudly for action as did his contemporary, Alexander Herzen (1812-1870), although Herzen, who left Russia in 1847, wrote from the safe vantage point of London, whereas Dobrolyubov dared to ring his bell inside Russia. Because he was downright conscience-stricken over the plight of his countrymen, Dobrolyubov, more than his fellow critics, belabored the intelligentsia, of which he himself was a member, for standing idly by and doing nothing. Dobrolyubov who, like Tchernyshevsky, was a strong believer in the strength and efficacy of public opinion, felt that, where no other recourse was possible, the intelligentsia should at least take a stand, even though it meant assuming the cross of martyrdom. This protest against inaction explains Dobrolyubov's interest in Gontcharov's novel, *Oblomov*, published in 1859.

What Belinsky did for Pushkin and Tchernyshevsky for Gogol, Dobrolyubov did for Gontcharov, with special emphasis on Oblomovism. To the average American the listless and parasitic Oblomov seems like an exaggerated version of the superfluous man. Dobrolyubov, on the contrary, felt that among the intelligentsia Oblomovism, to a greater or less degree, was unfortunately the rule rather than the exception. He compared the Russian intelligentsia, who were supposed to furnish leadership for the *narod,* to the Oblomovs who made flowery speeches full of promises, but who had neither the energy nor the courage to carry their promises into effect.

Next to Gontcharov, Dobrolyubov acclaimed Ostrovsky, in particular his play, *The Storm,* with its revelation of the status of women and its portrayal of Katerina's struggle for freedom and self-expression. Of Turgenev's novels, he preferred *On the Eve* (1860), upon which he based his article, "When Will the Real Day Come?" It was natural that the energy and purposefulness of Insarov, the only dynamic character among Turgenev's men, should appeal to a lover of action like Dobrolyubov, although he was by no means satisfied with the way the novel ended—hence his query about when the real day would come. To a limited extent, it did come with the abolition of serfdom on March 3, 1861. Dobrolyubov died a few months later.

Belinsky, Tchernyshevsky, and Dobrolyubov, this foremost trinity among the Russian literary critics of the Golden Age, were true representatives of the Russian intelligentsia of the nineteenth century. Intelligentsia is a term of Russian origin which is often translated into English as "the intellectuals," "the elite," or "the educated," sometimes even those with a modicum of education in contrast to the *narod,* who were mainly illiterate. Actually, it is as difficult to translate the Russian term *intelligentsia* into English as it is to translate the English word *gentleman,* with all its denotions and connotations into the Slavic and other continental European languages. Although many books and articles have been written about the Russian intelligentsia, it is doubtful if anyone has yet given a concise scientific definition of the term which would be universally accepted.

Irrespective of the definition that may eventually be coined, it is clear that the Russian intelligentsia did not consist only of Westernizers, as is sometimes implied, but also included Slavophiles and even Monarchists. It was no regimented group with but a single idea or a single solution for the betterment of existing conditions in Russia. Some of its members were purely doctrinaire in their approach to the burning issues of the day. Others preferred to present these problems to the public through the medium of fiction or drama. Still others were impatient with delay and hoped for the coming of a new political and social regime in the twinkling of an eye. In other words, some leaned heavily in the direction of evolutionary means to attain the ends in view, while others insisted on conducting a revolutionary crusade. But regardless of differences in outlook, the Russian intelligentsia were the leaders who molded and shaped Russian thinking in the nineteenth century. Inasmuch as their thoughts were focused upon ways and means for the betterment of the lot of Russians in general, they actually represented the conscience of the Russian people.

It is regrettable that the world outside Russia has derived a distorted impression of the Russian intelligentsia, especially of the Russian critics. Literary men abroad naturally preferred the restraint, the polished phrases, and the artistry of a novelist like Turgenev to what they called the sermonizing and the shrill, scolding tone of the critics. They have helped to perpetuate the impression that the Russian intelligentsia consisted of a group of hot-headed radicals of plebeian origin, mainly atheists and impractical idealists, who talked much and accomplished little. Englishmen and Americans who lived in countries where most of the reforms the Russian critics crusaded for had already been achieved often failed to observe the unselfishness of the motives of men like Belinsky, Tchernyshevsky, and Dobrolyubov and their influence on the leading writers of the day. Writers abroad, unless they could read Russian, must have depended largely upon hearsay rather than upon a first-hand knowledge of the works of the critics, few of which have ever been translated. For the false impression that the intelligentsia were impotent and ineffectual the Russian critics, themselves members of the intelligentsia, were largely responsible. Conscience-stricken because of the condition of the *narod* and exasperated at their inability to achieve results as fast as they wished, they often scolded one another and voluntarily shouldered the blame for the limited progress that was made.

After a careful study of the life and works of leading critics like Belinsky, Tchernyshevsky, and Dobrolyubov, one has to conclude, in view of the unselfishness of their motives and the Christian character of their objectives, that if they had been able to carry on their crusade for the *narod* inside the Church, using theological terminology instead of scientific nomenclatures, the Church would have revered them as martyrs and would undoubtedly have canonized them as saints.

MUSIC

Russian music, like Russian literature, received a decided impetus from the growth of national consciousness that followed the Napoleonic invasion. Foreign influences, especially Italian, were predominant in the field of Russian music at the dawn of the nineteenth century, but they were soon challenged and supplanted by the new national orientation. One of the chief sources of inspiration for Russian composers, as for Russian writers, was the wealth of folklore and legends, which enjoyed great popularity as a result of the strong upsurge in nationalism and the reawakened interest in the Russian past.

As in the case of the writers, most Russian composers of the nineteenth century belonged to the ranks of the nobility and were *dilettantes* in the field of music. In other words, the founders of Russian music were not ordinarily professionals, who depended on music for their livelihood. They more often served in the armed forces, the bureaucracy, or in some other profession, in addition to their musical activity—a situation which partially accounted for the limited output of some of them. While they were, in most cases, therefore, under no compulsion to cater to public taste, they did, like the writers, have to cope with the Russian censorship.

The pronounced Oriental, especially Caucasian and Middle Eastern, influences that permeated Russian music in the nineteenth century were undoubtedly the product of a combination of factors, including the imprint of the Mongol invasions and the expansion of Russia into the Caucasus, Central Asia, and the Balkans.

The founder of national Russian music was Mikhail Glinka (1804-1857). He stands in the same relation to Russian music as Pushkin to Russian literature. In fact Glinka was a contemporary and friend of Pushkin and Gogol. His *Capriccio on Russian Themes* (1833), composed in Berlin, was one of the first fruits of his effort to write music in the Russian style. It was followed in 1836 by a Russian opera, *A Life for the Tsar* (originally entitled *Ivan Susanin*), which reflected the new nationalism by its glorification of the Romanov dynasty and won the composer the favor of Nicholas I. Strictly speaking, this opera, which dealt with the founder of the Romanov dynasty, began where Pushkin with his *Boris Godunov* (published 1831) left off. With the appearance of *A Life for the Tsar* Glinka gained recognition as the foremost composer in Russia. In his *Ruslan and Lyudmila* (1842), Glinka resorted to a Pushkin subject based on a popular fairy tale. The Oriental effect achieved by the inclusion of Tartar melodies in this opera exercised considerable influence over later Russian composers. *Kamarinskaya,* the symphonic dance which Glinka produced in 1848, became the model for Russian composers in the orchestration of Russian folk melodies. Tchaikovsky later wrote: "The present Russian symphonic school is all in *Kamarinskaya,* just as the whole oak is in the acorn." In other words, *Kamarinskaya* played much the same role for Russian music as Gogol's *The Overcoat* for Russian literature. Since his death in 1857 Glinka has remained a national hero, revered alike by Slavophiles and Westernizers. Under the Soviet regime, *The Great Glinka,* a film based on his life, has been produced.

Although Glinka is regarded as the founder of national Russian music, it was Mily Balakirev (1837-1910) who became the head of the national Russian school of music. More important for his guidance of others than for his own compositions, Balakirev was the leader of the group known as "the mighty handful" or "the Big Five," which included César Cui, Borodin, Mussorgsky, and Rimsky-Korsakov. Balakirev prepared a collection of Russian folk songs, which appeared in 1866, and likewise collected Oriental themes in the Caucasus. He displayed a similar interest in the folk music of the other Slavic countries. In his emphasis upon folk music and Eastern themes he carried still further the development of the Russian-Oriental musical idiom which had begun to take form in the music of Glinka. Balakirev also played an important part in the establishment and activities of the Free School of Music (founded 1862) in St. Petersburg, which became a center for the national school.

The first Russian composer to achieve an international reputation was Alexander Borodin (1833-1887), a physician and scientist as well as a composer. He is best known for his opera, *Prince Igor,* based on a Russian epic which is as important to Russians as the Arthurian legends to the English. "The Polovetsky Dances" from Act II of this opera were based on authentic melodies collected among the tribes of Central Asia. These wild Eastern dances, with their intoxicating rhythms, and the Choral Finale of the opera have attained world-wide popularity. Borodin likewise broke new ground with his *Second Symphony* (1877), which has been called a panorama of Russian epical chronicles. In 1880 appeared his orchestral tone-picture, *In the Steppes of Central Asia,* which likewise bore the imprint of the Russian Orient and achieved success abroad. Although Borodin died before the completion of *Prince Igor,* this work was put into final form by Alexander Glazunov (1865-1936) and Rimsky-Korsakov. It is of interest that the Soviet Government has honored Borodin for his medical services to the Russian people.

The Russian composer who has emerged, with the passage of time, as the most outstanding representative of Balakirev's "Big Five," is Modest Mussorgsky (1839-1881). A true successor of Alexander Dargomyzhsky (1813-1869) rather than of Glinka, Mussorgsky was an exponent of realism in Russian music. His close observation of old women and peasants, of the *muzhiks,* and the life they led, has made his operas and songs a reflection of the spirit of his time—especially of the Alexandrian Age. The liberation of the serfs had drawn the attention of the aristocracy and the intelligentsia to the common people. By going to the people in the field of music, Mussorgsky put into practice the precepts of the Narodniki Movement.

Mussorgsky's *magnum opus* was his *Boris Godunov,* based on the Puskin drama of that name. His first version of this opera, finished in 1870, in which he exalted the role of the people in several scenes, proved unacceptable to the authorities, and he was compelled to make a number of changes in it. Until recently this opera has been known to the public largely through the more polished version prepared by Rimsky-Korsakov, a version which sacrificed much of the flavor and "truth" of the original. In 1928, however, the Soviet Government published the score of the original Mussorgsky version, which now appears to be gaining favor both in the Soviet Union and in the United States.

Khovanshchina (begun 1873), another of Mussorgsky's national operas which he left unfinished, was based on the story of the Old Believers of the seventeenth century. The Prelude, which describes daybreak over Moscow, is strongly national in tone. In *The Fair of Sorotchintsi* (begun 1874), a comic opera based on Gogol's story, Mussorgsky made use of Ukrainian folk songs. Another of Mussorgsky's works, the short opera, *Marriage* (1868), was drawn from one of Gogol's plays. It is not remarkable that Gogol, the realist, was Mussorgsky's favorite author. Both men, one in literature, the other in music, had a deep understanding of the psychology of the Russian people. Both were Slavophiles. Mussorgsky's colorful *Pictures at an Exhibition* (1874), noted for its variety of characterization and humor, was based on an actual exhibit of the sketches, water-colors, and stage designs of Victor Hartmann, noted Russian architect and friend of the composer. Mussorgsky's *Nursery Cycle* and his numerous songs in themselves constituted a unique contribution to Russian music.

The fame of Nicholas Rimsky-Korsakov (1844-1908), the last of the leaders of the nationalist school, rests on his numerous operas. His early works, including *Maid of Pskov* (1868) and *Sadko* (1894), show the influence of Glinka and the Balakirev circle. *Sadko* recalls

Prince Igor, and *Maid of Pskov,* which tells of the efforts of Ivan the Terrible to humble the proud cities of Pskov and Novgorod, has been termed a lesser counterpart of *Boris Godunov.* Like other Russian composers, Rimsky-Korsakov often found his themes in the literary work of his day. *May Night* (1878), a comic opera, was based on one of Gogol's tales. Two of his operas, *Tsar Saltan* (1899-1900) and his final work, *The Golden Cockerel* (1907), were drawn from Pushkin's fairy tales. Rimsky-Korsakov revelled in Russian folklore and legends, which provided the inspiration for much of his music. This was true, not only of *Sadko,* and *The Tsar's Bride* (1893), but of *The Snow Maiden* (1882), a truly national opera based on Ostrovsky's epic of the Slavonic legend of spring. Among his other well-known works are *Scheherazade* (1881) and the religious opera, *The Invisible City of Kitezh* (1907).

Rimsky-Korsakov became a national martyr among Russian liberals when in 1905 he resigned his honorary membership in the Russian Musical Society in protest against the closing of the Conservatory by the authorities in their efforts to suppress student revolutionary activities. It was at this time that he orchestrated *Dubinushka,* one of the popular revolutionary songs of the day. A temporary ban on the performance of all Rimsky-Korsakov's compositions served only to increase their popularity. *The Golden Cockerel,* his final opera, which was in reality a satire on the stupidity of autocracy, came under the ban of the censor and was not produced during the composer's lifetime.

As professor at the St. Petersburg Conservatory of Music from 1871 to 1905, Rimsky-Korsakov helped to train a distinguished group of Russian musicians, including Alexander Glazunov, who carried on the traditions of the national school, Liadov, Arensky, Ippolitov-Ivanov, and Igor Stravinsky. Few Americans are likely to recall that it was in his capacity as a *gardemarine* on the Russian clipper *Almaz,* rather than as a musician, that Rimsky-Korsakov visited America with the Russian naval squadron which remained in American waters from October 1863 to April 1864, during the critical days of the Civil War.

Peter Ilitch Tchaikovsky (1840-1893) is undoubtedly the best-known Russian composer, and his works have enjoyed world-wide popularity. A prolific and highly versatile composer, Tchaikovsky has given the world ten operas, six symphonies, three ballets, four concertos, four suites, and twelve overtures, not to mention more than one hundred romances, an equal number of piano pieces, four string quartets, a piano trio, a string sextet, and several additional chamber works. Almost two-thirds of his music is still unknown in the United States.

A. S. PUSHKIN

A portrait of "the Shakespeare of Russia" by Orest Kiprensky

Although he was not a member of the "Big Five," or the so-called national school, Tchaikovsky's music reflects the composer's love for the Russian landscape, the Russian past, and Russian customs, whereas some of his works, including his symphonies, especially the *Second Symphony* (Little Russian, 1872) and the popular *1812 Overture* (1880) have deep national roots. The Soviet composer, Dmitri Shostakovitch, calls him the founder of the great school of Russian music. In contrast to the "Big Five," however, his music was intensely subjective and introspective, reflecting man's struggle to overcome the blind elemental forces. Like the Greek tragedians, he was concerned primarily with the element of conflict, with a sense of the tragedy of life. Soviet musical critics, who refuse to consider him a pessimist, regard him as a great realist philosopher in the field of music.

In 1877 there began the unusual relationship between Tchaikovsky and the wealthy widow, Nadejda von Meck, whose generosity provided financial independence for the composer for some fourteen years and left him free to devote his entire time to musical composition.

Tchaikovsky is perhaps best known in the United States for his six symphonies, the last three of which are a standard part of the American concert repertory of all major American symphony orchestras. All his symphonies include song and dance themes and are marked by that lyrical quality so characteristic of Tchaikovsky and Glinka. His *Fourth, Fifth,* and *Sixth Symphonies* convey the same message, the tragic struggle of man against an inexorable fate. Among Tchaikovsky's programme works, his finest symphonic poems, the *Romeo and Juliet* Fantasia—Overture (1869) and *Francesca da Rimini* (1876) are respectively among the most powerful interpretations of Shakespeare and Dante in music.

Tchaikovsky's three best-known operas are *Eugene Onegin* (1878), *Mazeppa* (1884), and *The Queen of Spades* (1890), all based on Pushkin themes. In all his operas, Tchaikovsky was concerned primarily with the inner world of his heroes. This lyrico-psychological approach constituted his main contribution to world opera. In Russia, *Eugene Onegin* has become a permanent feature of the repertory of the famous Moscow Bolshoi Theatre, which in 1938 gave its 800th performance of this opera.

In addition to his symphonies and operas, which reveal his predilection for dance melodies, Tchaikovsky contributed greatly to the revival and regeneration of ballet music in Russia. His three ballets, *The Swan Lake* (1876), the most popular ballet in the USSR, *The Sleeping Beauty* (1889) and *The Nutcracker* (1892), all concerned with the world of fantasy, have exerted a profound influence on the subsequent ballets of Glazunov, Stravinsky, Prokofiev, and Khatchaturian, among others.

Tchaikovsky did much to popularize chamber music, including the chamber ensemble, in Russia. His *First Quartet,* Opus 11, in D-Major (1871) contains the famous *Andante Cantabile,* with its stirring folk *motif,* which moved Leo Tolstoy, Tchaikovsky's favorite author, to tears when he first heard it. His *Trio for Piano, Violin, and Violoncello in A-Minor,* Opus 50 (1862), was dedicated to the memory of Nikolai Rubinstein of the Moscow Conservatory. His chamber music is extensively performed in the USSR.

The music of Tchaikovsky dominated the last quarter of the nineteenth century. Since that time it has exerted a vast influence on world music. On his American tour in 1889 the composer himself discovered that he was "ten times more famous in America than in Europe." Tchaikovsky exerted a marked influence over the early works of the noted Bohemian composer, Gustav Mahler (1860-1911), whose works have recently experienced a revival in the United States. Inside Russia Tchaikovsky has become as vital a part of the national consciousness in music as Pushkin in literature. Other Russian composers, including Arensky, Glazunov, Ippolitov-Ivanov, and especially Sergei Rachmaninov (1873-1946) owe much to the Tchaikovsky traditions of melody and harmony, while the Russian modernist, Scriabin, was influenced by Tchaikovsky in his treatment of philosophical and psychological problems. Under the Soviet regime, Tchaikovsky's reputation has waxed rather than waned. All the outstanding Soviet composers, including Shostakovitch, Myaskovsky, Khatchaturian, and Dzerzhinsky, have acknowledged their indebtedness to Peter Ilitch Tchaikovsky. Throughout the years, little or no adverse criticism of Tchaikovsky has come out of Russia.

The so-called modern school of Russian music (as distinguished from the Soviet) is best represented by Alexander Scriabin (1872-1915) and Igor Stravinsky (1882-   ). Scriabin's best-known works are *The Divine Poem* (1903), *The Poem of Ecstasy* (1907-1908), and *The Poem of Fire* (*Prometheus,* 1909-1910). His technical innovations, which include the six-note or "mystic" chord and esoteric harmonies, are characteristic of modern music and they influenced later Russian composers. From 1900 on Scriabin, strongly influenced by the Russian mystic philosopher, Prince S. N. Trubetskoy, and by the philosophy of Nietzsche, began his efforts to fuse music with philosophy. Scriabin's experience in America in 1906, like that of Gorky, proved unfortunate, and he was forced to leave because of popular indignation concerning his private life.

Igor Stravinsky (1882-   ), onetime student of Rimsky-Korsakov, and the recognized leader of Western modernism, has spent much of his life abroad, having left Russia for France before World War I, and France for the United States in 1939. His well-known ballets, *The Fire-Bird* (1910) and *Petrushka* (1911), both based on Russian folklore, were commissioned by Sergei Diaghelev for his *Ballet Russe* in Paris. Stravinsky's most revolutionary score, which best illustrates his disregard for conventional form and harmony, was *The Rites of Spring* (1913), based on the pagan rituals of Russia. His choral symphony, *Symphonie des psaumes* (1930) was commissioned by the Boston Symphony Orchestra and first performed in 1931. Even while abroad, Stravinsky has carried on the tradition of Russian national music.

Any study of Russian culture in the century between the Napoleonic wars and the Russian Revolution clearly reveals how intimately the literature and music were related to current events and to one another, and how all three reflected the underlying national current of that era.

III

The Soviet Union 1917-1960

IO

The Two Revolutions

THE MARCH REVOLUTION: THE PROVISIONAL GOVERNMENT

(March 12, 1917, to November 7, 1917)

S PREVIOUSLY indicated [1] the Fourth Duma defied the emperor's *ukaz* of March 11, 1917, which prescribed its dissolution, thus precipitating the revolution in Petrograd. While the revolution was in progress in the capital, the people in outlying districts knew very little of what was in progress. It took three days for the news of the startling events to seep through to the cities of the provinces. When the overthrow of the monarchy became known, the nation went wild with excitement. The new Provisional Government, with Lvov and Kerensky at its head, enlisted the ardent support of the populace, who now foresaw a new era for Russia in the government's promise of free press, free speech, and the release of political prisoners. The end of the war seemed at hand. In the streets complete strangers embraced and kissed in their exuberance of joy.

On March 22, 1917, the United States took the lead in granting recognition to the Provisional Government. Shortly afterward, Great Britain, France, and Italy also recognized the new government. In the following month the United States entered the world war. This step was of tremendous moral influence in Russia, as well as in all of Europe.

From the very first the Provisional Government encountered opposition from the Soviet of Workers' and Soldiers' Deputies. The latter organization assumed so much authority that to all intents and purposes two governments were trying to function in Russia. The first, the Provisional Government, which had been recognized by the Allies, was responsible for the political revolution and had in mind social reforms

---

[1] See p. 186.

273

in the future. The second, the Workers' and Soldiers' Soviets, represented a social revolution and looked forward to great political reforms. On March 14, 1917, each government issued a decree. The decree of the Provisional Government established freedom of speech, freedom of the press, universal suffrage, and announced that a constituent assembly would be summoned. The police force was to be replaced by a civil militia. Revolutionary troops stationed in the capital were not to be sent to the front. Soldiers, when not in service, were to be granted civilian rights. Workers were to be allowed the privilege of forming unions and engaging in strikes. A general emancipation of all national minorities was to be effected. A general amnesty was declared for all political, religious, and military prisoners, which amnesty resulted in the freeing of many dangerous criminals. The decree of the Soviets was the famous "Army Order Number I" by which the Russian army was undermined and destroyed. All power was concentrated in the "Soldiers' Committees," which even had the control and disposal of all weapons. In the event that orders of the military commission of the Provisional Government conflicted with Soviet orders, the former were not to be obeyed. On May 22, Kerensky issued the "Declaration of Soldiers' Rights," addressed to the army and navy. His order confirmed practically all the demands of "Order Number I" and even exceeded its provisions. "Order Number I" was a death blow to army existence. Certain officers, who refused to agree to it in its entirety, met death at the hands of the soldiers, and soon the entire army became completely demoralized. Within two months there were from one to two million deserters. According to Lenin, the army "voted for peace with its legs."

Internal difficulties were further complicated by the burning question of the continuance of the war. Had the Central Powers been alive to their own interests they might have followed a course of procedure which would have resulted in advantages to themselves as well as to Russia. For instance, if Germany had announced her unwillingness to carry on war with the new government and had withdrawn her troops in proof thereof, it would have created a powerful sentiment in her favor among all classes in Russia. As a result there would have been no further Russian attacks against the Central Powers, whose position at the end of the war would have been appreciably better in consequence. The new Russian government might also have taken a step, which would have materially altered the course of the war. As usual the Allies were importuning Russia to "deflect German forces" from the Western Front. This would have been the time for the Provisional Government to say bluntly that Russia would no longer engage in any active fighting but would only keep her soldiers under arms until the end of the war. Such a stand would have been quite justified in view of the services which Russia had already rendered to the Allies and the small returns she had received from them. However the government did not choose to take this position, and on March 18, in a meeting of the Allied representatives at Petrograd, Milyukov, minister of foreign affairs, pledged the active participation of Russia in the war until its conclusion. He also made known that as a reward for this, she expected to come into possession of the city of Constantinople. (See Milyukov's note on war aims, May 1, 1917, published in the daily newspaper, *Ryetch,* May 3, 1917.)

To the people at large, it seemed that the war was starting over again, and a storm of protest arose on all sides especially from the Soviets. Soldiers asked of what use the Revolution had been if it could not put an end to the war. Crowds of excited citizens staged street parades which were joined even by loyal regiments. These crowds sent up the cry, "Down with Imperialism! Down with Milyukov! We want peace without annexation or indemnities!"

Addressing the Congress of the Cadet (K.D.) Party on May 22, 1917, Milyukov made the following statement:

I admit quite frankly and stand firmly by it, that the main thread of my policy was to get the Straits for Russia. I fought, unfortunately, in vain, against those who favored the new formula (no annexation, and no indemnity, and the right of self-determination), and that Russia should free the Allies from their obligation to help her secure sovereign rights over the Straits. I would say, and say it proudly, and regard it as a distinct service to the country, that until the last moment that I was in office, I did nothing which gave the Allies the right to say that Russia has renounced the Straits.[1]

The decision of the government to remain in the war and Milyukov's declaration paved the way beautifully for the Bolsheviks, who were not slow to take advantage of their opportunity. Already in March 1918 the Party had changed its name to the Russian Communist Party (Bolshevik). Two prominent leaders, Lenin and Trotsky, both of whom had been living abroad,[2] returned to Russia promptly, the former arriving in Petrograd April 16, and the latter on May 15. Others who joined

---

[1] See Golder, F. A., *Documents of Russian History 1914-1917,* Century Co., 1927, p. 334.

[2] The German government, seeing an opportunity to use Lenin to destroy Russian military power, transported him in a sealed railroad car from Switzerland to Russia. Trotsky returned to Russia from the United States via England. He did not join the Bolshevik Party until July 1917.

them included Nikolai Bukharin from New York, Maxim Gorky from Capri, Vyatcheslav Molotov and Joseph Stalin (Joseph Vissarionovitch Djugashvili, 1879-1953) from Siberia, and many others who, now that the ban was lifted, streamed back to Petrograd and dedicated themselves heart and soul to the achievement of the Bolshevik Revolution. Lenin, who received a somewhat mixed reception from the Soviet upon his arrival, nevertheless threw himself fearlessly into the task of encouraging fraternization among the soldiers at the front and seizure by the peasants of estates throughout the country. He placed no confidence in the Provisional Government or its leaders, whom he regarded as compromisers. In opposition to them he stood for the end of the war, social revolution, a government of Soviets, and a world-wide proletarian uprising. Already on May 3, the first Bolshevik demonstration against Milyukov had taken place, including a demand for the transfer of all power to the Soviets. Although there was a patriotic counter-demonstration on May 4, the Provisional Government considered it expedient to take steps to abate the hostility of the Soviets. Milyukov and the minister of war, Gutchkov, were induced to resign, and a new cabinet, from which they were omitted, was organized on May 17. Although Prince Lvov was still premier, the real head was Kerensky. On the following day this new cabinet acceded to the Soviet demand that the country seek a peace "without annexation or indemnities on the basis of self-determination by the people."

It is difficult to estimate accurately Kerensky's place in the Revolution and the value of his services. For a time he was the most popular leader in Russia. The masses worshipped him and accepted his word as gospel. The conservatives always hated him, regarded him as a most dangerous person, and held him responsible for the coming of the Bolshevik regime. We may safely state that he had the interests of his country at heart. Unfortunately, however, he did not really understand the Russian people. Both the military and the civilian population had become accustomed to severe army discipline and had grown to expect it. What the country needed at this time, in addition to a popular leader, was a strict disciplinarian, and this Kerensky most emphatically was not. Moreover, while he was gifted with a magnetic personality and persuasive powers, he was himself susceptible to the influence and persuasion of others. Thus he was unable to resist the pressure brought to bear upon him by the Allies and yielded to their insistence that a new offensive be launched against the Central Powers.

The Western Allies might perhaps have saved the situation, had they been better informed as to Russian conditions, had they been able to break the stalemate on the Western Front, and had they organized the dispatch of military supplies to Russia with greater expedition. In June the United States did set aside credits amounting to $325,000,000 for the purchase of munitions and supplies for the Provisional Government. But the supplies from the United States and England proved to be too little and came too late. Instead of easing the pressure on the Eastern front by a stepped-up offensive in the West, the Allies called for a new Russian offensive. Under the circumstances, this offensive had not the slightest chance of success. The soldiers were utterly disgusted with war, and they and their families were eager for their return from the front so that they might get their share of the land which had been appropriated by the peasants. Incited by the Bolsheviks, the peasants had refused to await the election of a Constituent Assembly and a legal partition of the land, but had taken possession of the estates of the *pomiestchiki* and others, which they were now dividing among themselves. Moreover a most undesirable element had been introduced into the army by a large number of former members of the police force who had been drafted to replace disabled veterans and civilian recruits. The chief fighting experience of this group had been acquired through pogrom making, and they knew nothing else. Responding to their instincts and training, they made pogroms on the Jews and Ukrainians of the invaded territory, with the result that army discipline and morale were badly shaken. A German counterattack resulted in the complete collapse of the Russian offensive.

From July 16 to 18, the Provisional Government was called upon to put down a Bolshevik uprising in Petrograd. Realizing that they had lost for the time being, the chief Bolshevik leaders, Lenin and Zinoviev, fled from Russia, thus escaping Kerensky's order for their arrest, which was issued on July 19. Trotsky and a few others were seized but were not held long. Immediately all members of the Bolsheviks resumed their former secret tactics, which were directed by Lenin from his refuge in Finland. Kerensky, who now replaced Lvov, failed to heed the lesson of the "July Days," or to take the necessary measures to strengthen the position of the government in preparation for the next test of power with the Bolsheviks.

General Brusilov, who was commander-in-chief of the army, disagreed with Kerensky's general policy toward the army and toward the Bolshevik leaders. Therefore Kerensky dismissed him and on July 30 appointed General Kornilov in his place. The folly of this appointment speedily became evident, for Kornilov began to move against Petrograd with the avowed intention of seizing power. All but a few reactionaries were in deadly terror of Kornilov's Cossacks, especially his "wild division," which was commanded by General Krimov. People recalled how the Revolution of 1905 had been crushed by the army upon its return from the war with Japan and feared a repetition of such procedure. However the Provisional Government with the aid of the Soviets was able to cope with the situation. General Kornilov was arrested and court-martialed.[1] Previous to this General Krimov had committed suicide. The loss of prestige resulting from the Kornilov affair contributed greatly to the decline and fall of the Provisional Government.

Despite the fact that it had been able to avert a counter-revolution, the Provisional Government had lost the support of many of its former adherents. There was a growing sentiment in favor of the politically astute and well-organized Bolsheviks, who were slyly disseminating their propaganda in all quarters, particularly in the army and navy. Their constant demand for peace caused many soldiers to desert and won for them the attention of people who would otherwise have repudiated their principles. For many, the term "Bolshevism" came to be synonymous with peace, hence their movement received the enthusiastic approval of the unlettered classes, or, in other words, the vast majority of the Russian people. They also received support from some aristocrats who hoped to regain their lost power by the overthrow of the Kerensky government. The Kornilov affair was a most opportune occurrence for the Bolsheviks. On September 18, just six days after his advance had failed, they gained control of the Petrograd Soviet. In October they elected Trotsky President of the Soviet.

On October 23, a German squadron entered the Gulf of Riga and attacked the weak remnant of the Baltic fleet, thus threatening Petrograd. The attempt of the Provisional Government to leave the city was bitterly criticized and opposed. The Soviets raised the cry of "treason," and even conservatives denounced the government. The situation was deteriorating rapidly, when on October 30 Kerensky prophetically told the American journalist John Reed: "The Russian people are suffering from economic fatigue—and from disillusionment with the Allies! The world thinks that the Russian Revolution is at an end. Do not be mistaken. The Russian Revolution is just beginning. . . ."[2] Everything now depended upon the election of the Constituent Assembly, scheduled for November 25. To forestall the government and a possible counter-

---

[1] When the Bolsheviks overthrew the Kerensky government, Kornilov managed to escape. He later joined the White army and was killed April 18, 1918. The Kornilov affair is still a matter of controversy. For Kerensky's version, see Kerensky, A. F., *The Prelude to Bolshevism*, New York, 1919.

[2] Reed, John, *Ten Days That Shook the World*, Modern Library, p. 39.

revolution, the Bolsheviks took advantage of the extensive support which they had gained and called an All Russian Congress of Soviets for November 7, in Petrograd. That night, Bolshevik troops took possession of the chief government buildings, and the inhabitants awoke the next morning to find the city placarded with announcements of the establishment of the Soviet regime.

The election of the Constituent Assembly was still in the future, and moreover the results thereof were doubtful. The Bolsheviks, on the other hand, promised the immediate consummation of popular hopes and desires, including peace, land, and bread. Therefore, the army and the people failed to support the Provisional Government. Kerensky fled, his government collapsed like a house of cards, and the Bolsheviks imposed their regime upon the country.

THE BOLSHEVIK REVOLUTION: MILITANT COMMUNISM 1917-1921

Whereas the March Revolution of 1917, carried out by the Fourth Duma without the active participation of the revolutionary parties, voiced the sentiment of the majority of the Russian people, the November Revolution of the same year, perpetrated by the Bolsheviks, was, strictly speaking, a counter revolution, imposed by a demagogical minority. In other words, the spontaneous revolt of the Fourth Duma against Romanov tyranny in a sense represented Russia's "finest hour," in that it cleared the way for the establishment of a Russian democracy. The Bolshevik usurpers, however, who seized the reins of power, reversed the trend of the Revolution and substituted a Party tyranny beside which the tyranny of the dynasty paled into insignificance.

On November 7, 1917, Bolshevik forces in revolt against the Provisional Kerensky Government (March 12—November 7, 1917) took possession of the chief government buildings in Petrograd (Leningrad). The following day (November 8) the Second Congress of Soviets met and officially approved the Bolshevik program. A Council of People's Commissars was formed with Nikolai Lenin as President. The other members of this Cabinet were Leon Trotsky, commissar of foreign affairs, Alexei Rykov, commissar of the interior, Joseph Stalin, commissar of nationalities, and Anatole Lunatcharsky, commissar of education. Thus was the Soviet Government established.

Inasmuch as there existed both passive and active resistance to the newly formed Soviet Government, one of Lenin's first acts as President of the Council of Commissars was to issue an order on December 20, 1917, for the creation of a Special Commission for the Suppression of Counter-Revolution, Sabotage, and Profiteering, better known as the Tcheka (Cheka). Felix Dzerzhinsky, a Polish Bolshevik sometimes called "the Saint-Just of the Russian Revolution," was named the head

Courtesy Underwood & Underwood

ALEXANDER KERENSKY, pre-Bolshevist premier in 1917.

of this agency. In 1922, when the Tcheka became very unpopular, the name was changed to OGPU, in 1934 to Narkomvnudel (NKVD), and in 1946 to MVD.

When Soviet forces seized the reins of control from the Provisional Government, the initial reaction of the Russian people was neither overwhelmingly in favor nor violently opposed to the new set-up. The other major political parties, such as the Mensheviks, Social Revolutionaries,

THE BOLSHEVIK ATTACK ON THE WINTER PALACE

Soviet artist V. Kuznetsov shows the Bolsheviks storming the headquarters of the Provisional Government on November 7, 1917.

Kadets, Bund (Jewish Labor Organization), for the most part ignored the new regime or engaged in sabotage on a small scale. Outside the political parties, which in the main were committed to the continuation of the war on the side of the Allies, the majority of the people, without approving the Bolshevik program, were willing to accept the Soviet regime temporarily, simply because it promised peace. Facing the fourth winter of the war, with serious shortages of food and equipment, heavy casualty lists and low morale, the war-weary masses wanted nothing so much as "Peace and Bread," which constituted plank number one on the Bolshevik program. In this connection, it should be stated that no inconsiderable number of wealthy business magnates, who were implacably opposed to the Kerensky regime, financed the Bolsheviks with the idea of using them as tools to rid the country of the Provisional Government, after which they planned to establish a constitutional government, or, in the case of the reactionaries, to restore the old regime.

The Soviet Government, confident of securing the support of the vast majority of the people because they advocated an immediate peace, at first not only tolerated the existence of other political parties but actually permitted the election of the Constituent Assembly projected by the Kerensky regime. When this assembly met in Petrograd on January 18, 1918, and it became apparent that the majority of the delegates consisted of Social Revolutionaries, not Bolsheviks (the former polled 16,500,000 votes to 9,000,000 for the Bolsheviks), the Soviet Government promptly arrested all delegates who belonged to parties other than their own. On January 20, the Constituent Assembly was officially dissolved. By June 14 the estrangement between the Bolsheviks on the one hand and the Mensheviks and Social Revolutionaries on the other was such that the Soviet Central Executive Committee, after accusing them of counter-revolutionary intrigue, expelled them from membership and established the one-party state which is still characteristic of the Soviet regime. By the time the first Soviet Constitution was adopted in July 1918, the Social Revolutionaries, Mensheviks, and Kadets were at war with the Communists.

It was not until after the attempted assassination of Lenin by a Social Revolutionary on August 30, 1918, however, that the Council of People's Commissars in retaliation issued a decree (September 10) instituting the Red Terror. The Tcheka, as the instrument of the Terror, ruthlessly suppressed every evidence of opposition to the Soviet regime. It is difficult to establish with certainty how many people were "liquidated" in this purge, but the consensus is that the numbers ran into the tens of thousands. So effective was the purge that it was some time

NIKOLAY LENIN

before the opposition forces could organize to wage civil war against the Soviet regime.

Although by the terms of the Inter-Allied agreement of September 5, 1914, the Tsarist Government had bound itself not to make a separate peace, Soviet leaders, as soon as they were in the saddle, prepared to redeem their pledge to the Russian people to negotiate an immediate peace with the Central Powers. Under the circumstances, this was the only logical step for them to take to justify to the masses their overthrow of the Provisional Government, which had pledged itself to carry on the war. Inasmuch as the people in general had no idea of the kind of peace the Germans had in store for them, this gesture on the part of the Soviets was received with widespread approval.

Before entering into direct negotiations with the Central Powers, Leon Trotsky, commissar for foreign affairs, proposed to the Allied ambassadors in Petrograd on November 22, 1917, that an armistice be declared on all fronts, preparatory to a general peace based upon principles of self-determination for all subject peoples, without annexations or indemnities. Since a general cessation of hostilities at that time would have redounded to the advantage of the Central Powers, it was natural that Trotsky's proposal should evoke a bitter protest from the Allies. On the other hand, the Allied leaders who, by exerting pressure, had hitherto succeeded in prevailing upon the Russians to remain on the offensive and to open new fronts in time of Allied need, obviously had no real conception of the opposition of the Russian army and people to the continuation of the war, of the paucity of Russian military equipment, and of the general disorganization and disunity within the country. The Russians had been fighting for thirty-nine months, during which time approximately 15,000,000 men had been mobilized. Of these, some 5,500,000 had been killed or wounded and 2,417,000 captured. By the early autumn of 1917 not more than 3,000,000 remained in the field to defend a front more than 2000 miles in length. The Kerensky offensive during the summer of 1917, which cost the Russians around 170,000 killed and wounded, as well as 213,000 prisoners, was largely responsible for the downfall of the Provisional Government. Even before the overthrow of the Provisional Government, the Russian High Command estimated that about 1,500,000 soldiers had simply taken "French leave" from the army and gone home. Only Sir George Buchanan, the British Ambassador to Russia, seems to have realized that, under the circumstances, Allied pressure against the conclusion of a separate peace by the Bolsheviks was ill-advised and likely to contribute in the final analysis to the advantage of Germany, but his sober warning of November 27 was ignored.[1]

The Soviet Government therefore terminated hostilities against the Central Powers on November 29, 1917, and shortly thereafter entered into peace negotiations with the representatives of the German government. These negotiations, after some interruption and delay, culminated in the Peace of Brest-Litovsk, March 3, 1918. One of the best accounts of this treaty is to be found in *The Forgotten Peace, Brest-Litovsk, March, 1918,* by John W. Wheeler-Bennett.

During the negotiations for the Peace of Brest-Litovsk, there was a fundamental difference of opinion between Lenin and Trotsky over accepting the terms. Trotsky revolted against the humiliating peace and favored procrastination, by one means or another, until there should be a revolution in Germany. Lenin, on the other hand, was anxious to accept any terms which would provide the necessary breathing spell to permit reorganization and consolidation of the new regime. Trotsky, who had lived in America, had imbibed some of the technique of Anglo-Saxon politicians, who are inclined to support a waiting policy in the hope that circumstances may change. Lenin, who had lived in a German environment, knew this would be of no avail as long as the Russians were confronted by a powerful and undefeated German army. Both Lenin and Trotsky anticipated a revolution in Germany. Trotsky expected it to come from within—a mass uprising of the German people behind the lines. Lenin realized that unlike Russia, where the Revolution brought about the collapse of the Russian army, in Germany only military defeat and the collapse of the German armed forces could produce the revolution. Events proved Trotsky wrong and Lenin right.

The deadlock at Brest-Litovsk led Trotsky to break off negotiations, after refusing either to sign a treaty or to resume the war. But the "neither peace, nor war" proposition broke down when the Germans denounced the armistice, resumed the offensive, and soon threatened the capital. Although preliminary steps had been taken toward the end of January 1918 for the voluntary recruitment of a Red army, very little had been accomplished. Lenin's proclamation on February 21 that the "Socialist Fatherland was in danger" rallied enough Soviet detachments to halt the German forces temporarily. But the situation remained untenable. In spite of the fact that the Germans now submitted even more drastic conditions for peace than those Trotsky had rejected, Lenin saw no possibility of continuing the war without an army. By

---

[1] Buchanan, Sir George, *My Mission to Russia,* Boston, Vol. II, pp. 225 ff.

concluding peace he hoped to create at least a breathing spell for Russia, while the "imperialist" forces, as he understood them, continued to devour one another. His insistence on peace at any price, however, very nearly split the Party.

By the Treaty of Brest-Litovsk, Russia was forced to recognize the independence of the Ukraine, Poland, Finland, Esthonia, Latvia and Lithuania, as well as to surrender the Provinces of Kars and Ardahan in Transcaucasia to Turkey. All in all, the Russians lost some 522,676 square miles of territory, including a population of about 66,000,000 people. More specifically, this peace deprived Russia of 34 percent of her population, 32 percent of her agricultural land, 85 percent of her sugar beet land, 54 percent of her industrial undertakings and 89 percent of her coal mines. In August 1918, a codicil to the treaty provided for the demilitarization of the Russian army and fleet, the payment of an indemnity of 6,000,000 marks and additional German commercial rights in Russia.

In short, the Treaty of Brest-Litovsk—" a peace by violence," as Lenin's representatives called it—not only dismembered and disarmed Russia but transformed that country into a kind of colonial hinterland for German exploitation. G. J. Sokolnikov, head of the Soviet peace delegation, summed up Soviet reaction to the peace terms on March 3 as follows: "We openly declare before the workers, peasants and soldiers of Germany, before the workers and the exploited classes of the entire world, that we are forced to accept an ultimatum, dictated to us by the party which is stronger at this moment. We sign this ultimatum without discussing it." According to John Wheeler-Bennett the Treaty of Versailles, as compared with that of Brest-Litovsk, was almost a model of justice and liberty.

It is of interest to note that President Wilson was by no means averse to a treaty based on the principle of no annexations, no indemnities and self-determination, and that his famous Fourteen Points, set forth on January 8, 1918, constituted a direct response to the Russian peace program. Indeed, Point Number 6 called for the establishment of a Russian peace on the following basis:

The evacuation of all Russian territory and such a settlement of all questions affecting Russia as will secure the best and freest co-operation of the other nations of the world in obtaining for her an unhampered and unembarrassed opportunity for the independent determination of her own political development and national policy and assure her of a sincere welcome into the society of free nations under institutions of her own choosing;

and, more than a welcome, assistance also of every kind that she may need and may herself desire. The treatment accorded to Russia by her sister nations in the months to come will be the acid test of their good will, of their comprehension of her needs as distinguished from their own interests, and of their intelligent and unselfish sympathy.

Since neither the Allies nor the United States took steps to implement this doctrine, the Treaty of Brest-Litovsk was ratified by the Congress of Soviets on March 16, 1918, by a final vote of 784 to 261.[1] Five days later Ludendorff launched the great spring offensive on the Western Front, which very nearly ended in catastrophe for the Allies.

By signing the Peace of Brest-Litovsk, Soviet leaders, at the risk of a serious breach in the Party, redeemed their pledge to the Russian people to end the war. They still had to fulfill their promise to provide the population with bread. This task was rendered more difficult, since the peace had deprived the Soviet regime of the Ukraine, the Baltic states and other productive areas. Subsequent food shortages naturally aggravated dissatisfaction with the new government; although the peo- had wanted peace, they did not expect dismemberment and the loss of their best food-producing regions.

In this predicament, the Soviet Government dealt with the urban centers first, because the cities included the most articulate elements of the population. Here were the most ardent supporters of the regime and likewise its most bitter opponents. Since there was a shortage of almost all the necessities of life, all large-scale industry was nationalized (June 28, 1918) and available food supplies were requisitioned. In November private trade was outlawed, plans having been made to substitute state and co-operative stores. Private banks were likewise nationalized, although no steps were taken as yet to stem the tide of inflation. The authorities instituted a system of rationing, with a twofold purpose in view: to supply food for all, and to ensure support for the government, since any opposition involved the confiscation of ration cards and consequent starvation under prevailing conditions. In order that ration cards might be distributed in accordance with the best interests of the Soviet

---

[1] As late as March 5 Trotsky sounded out Colonel Raymond Robins, head of the American Red Cross in Russia, as to the possible American reaction in the event of Soviet refusal to ratify the treaty, but there was no response. See Hard, William, *Raymond Robins' Own Story*, N. Y., 1920, pp. 151 ff., and Harper, Samuel N., *The Russia I Believe In*, Chicago, 1945, pp. 112-113. The position of the American ambassador, David R. Francis, was very anti-Bolshevik. See Francis, D. R., *Russia from the American Embassy*, N. Y., 1921. The role of America at this time is fully discussed in Schuman, Frederick L., *American Policy Toward Russia Since 1917*, N. Y., 1928, pp. 70-91.

regime, the population of the cities was classified according to three categories: Communists, government employees, craftsmen, and unemployed. The "declassed" or "unproductive element," comprised mainly of members of the former nobility, bourgeoisie, and intelligentsia, received no ration cards. The plight of the "declassed" in this period beggars description.

A ration card entitled its possessor to purchase about half a pound of bread daily. This fact merits additional comment. In Russia, bread is literally the staff of life and not a mere accessory to an otherwise well-filled dinner plate. In the words of the Russian proverb, "Dinner is not dinner without bread and salt." The average Russian consumes a minimum of one pound of bread daily, no matter how plentiful other foods may be. In the army, this amount was sometimes doubled or even trebled. At a time when meat, herring, and vegetables had either disappeared or become extremely scarce, it is therefore easy to understand the predicament of Russians whose ration cards limited them to a mere half pound of bread per day. The shortage of bread, which was enough to make any government unpopular in Russia, together with the excessive zeal of certain local commissars, particularly in provincial towns, who followed their own judgment in confiscating surplus shirts, chairs, and household articles, increased the agitation against the new regime in the urban areas.

Having established a modicum of order in the cities but finding themselves still confronted with food shortages, it was natural that Soviet authorities should turn their attention to the rural population, which comprised nearly four-fifths of the peoples of the Soviet Union. For some time the rural population had remained undisturbed by the distress and disorder in the cities. Following the advice of the Bolshevik leaders who opposed the Kerensky regime, millions of peasants had appropriated the property of large landowners and the Crown lands, while others took advantage of the general confusion to increase their meager allotments. By the spring of 1918, having satisfied their land hunger, the peasants became very independent in their dealings with city dwellers. Since the latter had little but worthless paper money to offer in exchange for farm produce, the peasants refused to do business with them.

Confronted with this situation, the Soviet Government was forced to send "Food Battalions" to the villages to requisition farm products. In anticipation of such a procedure, entire villages organized to resist the Soviet agents and even went forth to battle. This was possible because, when the army disintegrated, many soldiers returned home with their weapons and some villages secured artillery pieces. In some instances, the peasants liquidated the "Food Battalions," whereupon in retaliation the Soviets destroyed the villages.

To combat the unified opposition to Soviet policy in many villages where the traditional communal spirit prevailed, the Soviet Government divided and classified the rural population in accordance with the policy pursued in the cities. It divided them into *kulaki,* or rich peasants, whose income exceeded $88 per year; *seredniaki,* or middle peasants, who had an income of around $46 per year; and *bedniaki,* or poor peasants, who earned $39 per annum or less. In addition, there were the *batraki,* or hired farm laborers. Control in the villages was exercised mainly by the *bedniaki,* who were organized into Committees of the Poor and given authority to seize surplus grain and cattle. Private trade in grain was replaced by a state monopoly, and, in spite of the bitter class war in the villages, the Communists managed to establish a few state and collective farms. By the middle of 1918 the Soviet Government had established its control firmly in the rural districts as well as in the cities.

It was but natural that the foregoing drastic regulation of urban and rural life should have created widespread discontent among the various groups and nationalities inside Russia. The Soviet regime likewise faced a hostile world outside Russia. This situation was largely due to three factors: Soviet repudiation of foreign debts, Soviet propaganda for world revolution, and Soviet persecution of the Church, accompanied by hostility toward all religions.

So far as the outside world was concerned, Soviet repudiation of foreign debts on February 8, 1918, was the first great blunder of the new regime. It made the USSR unpopular everywhere, particularly in France, where large numbers of Frenchmen held Russian bonds for debts incurred by the Tsarist Government. By supporting any and every effort to overthrow the Revolutionary regime, outside investors hoped to retrieve their losses. Soviet leaders blundered because they did not realize the significance attached by the Western capitalist democracies to the matter of honoring debts. Even Trotsky, who had lived in America, was not familiar with the outlook of the typical businessman. Today there are many who know nothing about Finland beyond the fact that the Finns have paid their debts. Had Soviet leaders made a token payment, or even asked for a moratorium, it is doubtful whether the business interests of creditor countries would have backed any intervention by their respective governments. Unfortunately, however, the Soviet Government persisted in denouncing all debts incurred by the tsarist and Kerensky regimes, as obligations for which the masses of the people could not be held responsible. This was one of the principal factors contributing to foreign intervention.

Soviet propaganda for world revolution was another factor which aggravated relations between the USSR and the Western democracies. Not every strike abroad was due to agitation from Moscow, since in every country the war and its aftermath had resulted in much dislocation in commerce and industry. Nevertheless, Soviet propaganda in favor of strikes, sabotage, and world revolution resulted in the Soviet regime being branded as the chief instigator of labor and political unrest everywhere, especially through its agency, the Comintern, established in March 1919, in Moscow.

The third reason for Soviet unpopularity abroad was the persecution of the Church, in particular the Orthodox Church, and Soviet efforts to indoctrinate the masses with atheistic propaganda. In approaching the whole problem of religious persecution and atheism in the USSR, it is important to recall that before 1917 the official Russian Church was a tool of the Tsarist Government. Within the ranks of the Russian clergy there did exist a small minority that would have welcomed the separation of Church and state in order to free the Church from its political bondage to the state. The fact is that immediately following the Revolution of 1905 sixty-one out of sixty-three Russian bishops, asked by the Holy Synod to express their views on Church reform, declared in favor of disestablishment.[1] In contrast to America, this was done in Russia at the risk of liberty, position, and security. In this particular instance, the intrepid Russian clergy were condemned by both Church and state.

In tsarist times, the official Russian Church never protested against government persecution of religious minorities. As a body, it never championed the cause of the persecuted and downtrodden. For the most part, it preached resignation and acceptance of the *status quo.* In fact, in Russia, Churchianity became synonymous with reaction, especially after 1905, when the Church as an institution actively aided the government in liquidating the constitutional reforms wrung by the people from the tsarist regime on October 30, 1905. In this light, it is possible to understand the attitude of Soviet leaders toward the Church as an institution. Care must be taken, however, not to confuse Orthodoxy with the Church. Had Orthodox Christianity been practiced in Russia, the Church would have had far greater support from the people during and following the Revolution.

---

[1] See Zernov, Nicolas, *Moscow the Third Rome* (London, 1937), p. 88.

Another matter about which the outside world has been ill informed is that under the old regime in Russia there existed no racial hatred. Persecution was motivated chiefly by religious and political animosity. In the United States, on the other hand, Americans have enjoyed religious tolerance, but until recently in some areas there has existed racial discrimination. Since many Soviet leaders attributed most of the discrimination characteristic of the old regime to religious hatred, they therefore concluded that, if the Church were uprooted, its influence in government and education eliminated, there would be an end to dissension and persecution.

Irrespective of the motives of the Soviet Government in repudiating foreign debts, disseminating propaganda for world revolution and divesting the Church of its power and wealth, nevertheless, its actions were greatly instrumental in bringing about foreign intervention and civil war in Russia.

CIVIL WAR

AND

FOREIGN INTERVENTION

The Soviet regime faced opposition from yet another source. Prior to the Revolution, substantial numbers of Czech prisoners, who had served in the Austrian army, cast their lot with the Russians and took part in the 1917 offensive against the Central Powers. When the Soviet regime withdrew from the war these Czech troops, about 40,000 in all, asked to be sent to the Western Front to continue their fight against the Germans. The Czechs were being evacuated by way of Siberia, but, when the first contingent reached Vladivostok in May 1918, Trotsky, supposedly as a result of pressure from the Germans, first ordered that they be disarmed and then that they be interned as prisoners of war. The enraged Czechs promptly revolted and seized the chief cities along the Trans-Siberian railroad from Samara (Kuibyshev) to Vladivostok, taking possession of the latter city on June 29, 1918. Forthwith rebellion against the Bolsheviks became general throughout Siberia and eastern Russia.

The spring of 1918 also brought foreign intervention along the Russian periphery in both Europe and Asia. Immediately following the Treaty of Brest-Litovsk in March 1918, Russia's former ally, Great

Britain, on the pretext of preventing Allied supplies from falling into the hands of the Germans in Finland, landed troops at Murmansk. French and American marines soon joined the British. Early in April the Japanese, taking advantage of the general confusion and ignoring American protests, landed at Vladivostok. Following the decision of the Supreme War Council of the Allies on July 2, 1918, in favor of military intervention in Russia, approximately 15,000 additional Allied troops occupied Archangel early in August, while British forces seized Baku and the rich oil fields in the Caucasus. In July, units of the United States Asiatic Fleet under Admiral Austin Knight reached Vladivostok, followed in August by an American expeditionary force of 7000 men under the command of General William S. Graves. President Wilson with the greatest reluctance had countenanced American intervention, admitting to his confidant, Colonel House, in July 1918 that "he had been sweating blood over the question what is right and feasible to do in Russia." However, Japanese action in pouring 73,400 troops into Eastern Siberia aroused American fears as to the possibility of a permanent Japanese occupation, to which the United States was opposed. Within a few weeks it became only too clear that Allied objectives in Russia were altogether at variance with those of the United States. Americans took no very active part in the fighting in Siberia beyond what was necessary to guard the railways. Two American efforts to effect a reconciliation between the opposing Russian factions failed to succeed. Finally, after the German military collapse in November 1918, which led to the withdrawal of the German army from the Ukraine, French forces occupied the Black Sea port of Odessa.

The Russians who revolted against the newly established Soviet regime organized what are ordinarily known as the "White" armies. Foreigners frequently misunderstand the use of the term "White" in this connection. Many have been under the impression that these anti-Bolshevik armies came from the region known as White Russia. In reality, however, the White armies, which fought the Red army from 1918 to 1920, included men from every part of Russia. They were called "White" merely to distinguish them from the "Reds." The White armies were armed and equipped almost entirely by foreign powers—Russia's former allies. Later they received substantial support from the armies of the intervening powers, particularly from the Big Four, Britain, France, Japan, and the United States.

The White forces in South Russia were led by General Anton Denikin, who organized the "Volunteer Army." Those in the Baltic region were led by General Nicholas Yudenitch, while those in the North and in Siberia came under the direction of Admiral Alexander Koltchak. Because Koltchak was better known abroad than Denikin, the Supreme War Council of the Allies in Paris communicated with him early in 1919, promising him every aid in overthrowing the Soviet regime. In the White armies this was understood to mean that the Allies favored Koltchak as commander-in-chief and as temporary head of the Russian government. For the sake of unity, Denikin forthwith acknowledged Koltchak as his superior in command. As compared with the Red Army, the White armies, together with the troops supplied by their foreign allies, constituted a very formidable force.

Although Trotsky was not the first to conceive the idea of a Red army, his name is nevertheless associated with its organization and early achievements. The decree establishing the Red army was issued on February 23, 1918, by the Sovnarkom (Council of People's Commissars). Although the Red forces enjoyed the great strategic advantage of inner lines of communication, in contrast to the White armies they were ill clad, often underfed, poorly equipped, short of officers, and frequently undisciplined. They inherited most of their weapons and ammunition from the tsarist army. Many of their officers were veterans of the imperial army and therefore suspect to the Soviets, who in the summer of 1918 appointed political commissars to keep them under constant surveillance. Prominent among the Red officers of this period were Semyon Budenny, Klementy Voroshilov, and Joseph Stalin. Stalin and Voroshilov achieved fame for their spirited defense of Tsaritsyn (Stalingrad) in the fall of 1918, when the city was called the "Red Verdun." Although conscription was introduced in 1918 it is estimated that the Red army never had more than 600,000 troops available for action at any one time. Both the Red and the White armies had to contend with deserters during this critical period.

In view of the conditions described above, it is not surprising that the Allies expected the White armies to annihilate the Soviet forces in *Blitzkrieg* fashion and that they confidently anticipated the early establishment in Russia of a constitutional regime on which they could depend to re-establish the Eastern front against Germany. In spite of the tremendous odds faced by the Red army and the initial gains made by the Whites and their allies on all fronts, it was the Soviet forces which, by fighting what was in a sense "the first total war of the 20th century,"[1] emerged triumphant. In order to do so, they were forced to mobilize industry, agriculture and man power and to resort to psychological warfare.

---

[1] Schuman, F. L., *Soviet Politics at Home and Abroad*, N. Y., 1946, p. 160.

In retrospect, it is not difficult to account for the Soviet victory. In the first place, although Denikin's slogan, "Russia, One and Indivisible," served well enough as a rallying cry for tsarist nationalists, it aroused fear and dismay among the nationalistic Poles, Finns, Ukrainians, the Baltic peoples, Georgians, Armenians, and even some of the Cossacks. Although most of these national minorities were vehemently opposed to the Soviet regime, they had no desire to fight to restore the one and indivisible tsarist monarchy and thereby sacrifice their own aspirations for independence.

Second, the atrocities committed by the White armies were more instrumental than anything else in bringing about the ultimate downfall of the anti-Soviet forces. In many regions, the White Terror surpassed the Red Terror in cruelty. In South Russia, the greatest sufferers were the Ukrainian peasants and the Jews, the majority of whom were in favor of private property and free enterprise.

The initial successes of the White armies, particularly in the Ukraine, were chiefly due to large-scale plundering permitted by commanding officers. Although the army included many bona fide, patriotic and intelligent Russians, the bulk of these forces, which were otherwise practically unpaid, was attracted by the unlimited opportunities for license, loot, and booty. The leaders responsible for these excesses made every effort to behave in exemplary fashion in places where foreign consuls were located, such as in the Crimea, Odessa, and Kharkov, but the news of atrocities committed by the Whites nevertheless reached foreign countries and protests were forthcoming. Inside Russia, it was difficult for the victims of the White Terror to understand why these Whites were supported by foreign countries which claimed to be fighting to make the world safe for democracy. When, because of unfavorable reaction at home and abroad, orders were given to desist from robbery and assault, the offensive came to an end and the retreat of the Whites began.

The White atrocities in Siberia under the Koltchak regime were even more disastrous to the anti-Soviet cause than were those perpetrated in South Russia by Denikin's "Volunteer Army." Notorious bandits like Kalmykov, Semyonov, Annenkov and Rozanov, in their efforts to save Siberia from Bolshevism, did Koltchak irreparable harm by their thirst for blood and booty, as did the fanatical Baron von Ungern-Sternberg in Outer Mongolia in 1921. According to an American eye-witness, General William S. Graves, "The deeds of the two White chieftains, Atamans Semyonov and Kalmykov, would have done credit to Genghis Khan." Graves incurred the displeasure of the leaders of the English, French, and Japanese forces for his condemnation of the excesses of the White armies, but his circumspect attitude later redounded greatly to the credit of the United States. Further authentic information on these atrocities and on the downfall of Koltchak may be found in *The White Armies of Russia* by George Stewart and in *The Testimony of Koltchak and Other Siberian Materials,* edited by Harold H. Fisher and Elena Varneck.

The third great mistake of the White leaders was the fatal decision of Denikin's successor, Baron Peter Wrangel, after everything else failed, in favor of calling for Polish assistance to overthrow the Soviet regime. On April 20, 1920, the Poles invaded the Ukraine and under the leadership of Joseph Pilsudski **they** occupied Kiev on May 6. This move on the part of Poland in reality operated to the advantage of the Soviet forces. Profiting by the outraged national feeling which the Polish invasion aroused, the Red army attracted to its ranks many who had heretofore been bitterly opposed to the Revolution. Even General Brusilov, who had been living in Moscow since his dismissal by Kerensky, was induced to issue a statement urging all Russians to rally to the support of the Soviet Government in expelling and punishing the Poles.

Under the stimulus of popular enthusiasm and support, the Red army advanced against Kiev and drove the Poles out on June 6. Far from content with this, however, it pursued the Poles all the way to Warsaw, which by July 10 was in danger of falling to the Russians. With their capital threatened, the Poles promptly appealed to the Allies for aid. The French, who were the first to respond, sent a military mission to Warsaw under the command of General Maxime Weygand. On August 11, the British prime minister, David Lloyd George, issued an ultimatum to the Soviet Government to suspend the drive on Warsaw or the British fleet would bombard Leningrad. Meanwhile the Red army, which had overreached itself and which was hard-pressed by the Poles under the direction of Weygand, began to retreat, August 14-17. It was driven back in disorder almost to Minsk. On September 12 the Soviets signed an armistice with Poland and a month later (October 12) a preliminary peace was made. The final peace between Poland and the Soviet Union was signed at Riga on March 18, 1921. Its provisions remained in effect until September, 1939.

It was during the crisis occasioned by the Soviet threat to Poland that Secretary of State Bainbridge Colby of the United States found an opportunity in his note of August 10, 1920, to the Italian ambassador to clarify the American position with regard to Russia. Although he minced no words as to American opposition to the Soviet regime and American determination not to grant it official recognition, he expressed himself just as vigorously in opposition to the dismemberment of the country. It was on this ground that he explained the American refusal to recognize the Baltic States, although he condoned the separation of Poland, Finland, and Armenia.

The United States feels that friendship and honor require that Russia's interests must be generously protected, and that, as far as possible, all decisions of vital importance to it, and especially those concerning its sovereignty over the territory of the former Russian Empire, be held in abeyance. By this feeling of friendship and honorable obligation to the great nation whose brave and heroic self-sacrifice contributed so much to the successful termination of the war the Government of the United States was guided in its reply to the Lithuanian National Council, on October 15, 1919, and in its persistent refusal to recognize the Baltic States as separate nations independent of Russia. The same spirit was manifested in the note of this Government of March 24, 1920, in which it was stated, with reference to certain proposed settlements in the Near East, that no final decision should or can be made without the consent of Russia.

Not until July 27, 1922, under the Harding Administration, did the United States, while still reaffirming its opposition to "the alienation of Russian territory," grant recognition to Esthonia, Latvia, and Lithuania.

Another reason for the defeat of the White armies was the establishment of the Comintern or Third International, which was organized under the auspices of the Soviet Government in Moscow, March 2-6, 1919, under the presidency of Gregory Zinoviev. While the First International (1864) [1] and the Second International (1889) were primarily

---

[1] The First (Socialist) International, known as The International Workingmen's Association, was organized in London in 1864 and dissolved in New York in 1876. Its primary purpose was economic, the object being to improve the lot of the workers. The Second International, or The World's Labor and Socialist Parties, was more political in nature than its predecessor. Moreover, it was admittedly pacifist and advocated that workers, in the event of war, should strike and refuse to fight. The Second International collapsed when it failed to avert the War of 1914-18. The Third (Communist) International, 1919-43, was a casualty of World War II, at which time it became clear that the workers of Germany and her satellites not only participated in the invasion of the USSR but committed atrocities there such as no capitalist nation had ever perpetrated. What is usually termed a Fourth International was formed by the followers of Trotsky abroad who became bitter enemies of the Stalin program in the Soviet Union. In October 1947, after relations between the Soviet Union and her allies in World War II had seriously deteriorated, Moscow proclaimed the existence of the Cominform, comprised of nine states within the Soviet orbit, most of them Slavic.

defensive in nature and included Socialists and workers of various shades of ideology, the Comintern or Third International was composed exclusively of Communists whose aims were alternately aggressive and defensive.

In retrospect, it may be said that the Third International was first and foremost an act of desperation growing out of the Civil War and foreign intervention. Soviet leaders, confronted by a shortage of weapons and ammunition, acted on the principle that the best defense was the offensive. They resorted to the establishment of the Comintern as a kind of secret weapon, designed to spread demoralization among the armed forces of their enemies as well as to hamper them on the home front. In other words, the founders of the Third International hoped by means of Comintern activities abroad to keep capitalist countries so busy with their own affairs that they would have no time or opportunity to intervene in the USSR. That this became the underlying motive of Soviet leaders is substantiated by a statement of Maxim Litvinov to the Associated Press in Stockholm as early as January 21, 1919, when he explained that Russian propaganda "was an act of self-defense" to which any nation invaded by foreign troops would have resorted.[1]

Soviet resort to political and psychological warfare, although it operated against the establishment of better relations with foreign governments, nevertheless increased the chances of the Soviet regime for survival. Soviet propaganda among Allied troops led in March 1919 to a minor mutiny among American forces in the White Sea area, after which the United States army promised to withdraw all American soldiers from there by June 1919. This Archangel expedition cost 200 lives and some $3,000,000. In April, French sailors at Odessa raised the Red flag, with the result that French naval forces had to be withdrawn. Desertions among Russians conscripted by the armies of the intervention steadily increased in number.

Although Soviet propaganda proved an effective weapon of defense against foreign intervention, it achieved only transitory success as a weapon of aggression abroad. Bela Kun succeeded in establishing a Soviet regime in Hungary on March 21, 1919, but the counter-revolutionary forces of Admiral Nicholas Horthy and Rumanian invaders crushed the new regime by the end of July. An uprising of Sparticists in defeated Germany had already led to the murder of the revolutionary leaders, Karl Liebknecht and Rosa Luxemburg, in January 1919. A Bavarian Soviet established in Munich on April 7 was suppressed by the Reichswehr before the end of the month. While fighting for their

---

[1] Quoted in A. U. Pope, *Maxim Litvinov*, p. 153.

existence at home, Soviet leaders were unable to send aid to revolutionaries abroad.

On April 6, 1920, five days after the last American forces evacuated Vladivostok, the Far Eastern Republic of Siberia was, in accordance with the advice of Lenin, established at Verkhne-Udinsk under the presidency of Krasnoshchekov, a former Chicago lawyer in sympathy with the Soviet cause. The capital of the new republic, which extended east from Lake Baikal to the Japanese-occupied Maritime Province, was later transferred to Chita.

In the belief that a Communist state would only serve to promote further Japanese aggression, the Far Eastern Republic recognized private property, proclaimed freedom of the press, a universal franchise, and other attributes of a democratic regime. In reality, it served as a buffer state between the Soviet Union and the Japanese-occupied Maritime Province on the Pacific Coast, with the tacit consent of both the Soviets and the Japanese. The Soviet Government granted recognition to the Far Eastern Republic on May 16. By the close of 1920 the Japanese puppet government at Vladivostok had followed suit. Although it failed to secure recognition from the major Allied powers, the Far Eastern Republic sent a trade delegation to the Washington Conference (1921-22)—a conference at which the Soviet Union was otherwise not represented.

After the withdrawal of the last Japanese troops from Vladivostok, the Far Eastern Republic was no longer needed. On November 13, 1922, this Soviet puppet state voluntarily surrendered its sovereignty in order to rejoin the Russian Socialist Federation of Soviet Republics (RSFSR). With the dissolution of the Far Eastern Republic the unity of the Soviet Union was established. Japanese troops remained in Northern Sakhalin, however, until January 1925.

Thus revolutionary Russia, in the very process of forming a new state, was beset on all sides by foreign powers, German and Turkish, as well as Allied. True, these powers were not united, were in some instances even more suspicious of their fellow interventionists than of the Bolsheviks, and never at any time succeeded in making an all-out, concerted effort to suppress the Soviet regime. Nevertheless the active intervention of so many of the major European, Asiatic, and American powers left an indelible impression on the Russians in general, and on the Soviet government in particular, which has continued to affect that country's relations with foreign powers to the present day. Moreover the intervention left its stamp on every aspect of the domestic organization of the Soviet Union, which was molded and shaped under conditions of civil war and in a life-and-death struggle against foreign arm- ies. Not only did foreign intervention fail to achieve its goal of estab- lishing a second front against Germany or suppressing Bolshevism, but from the standpoint of practical politics it proved to be a blunder of the first magnitude. In retrospect it is clear that the United States was right in questioning "the wisdom of intervention" and in assuming that it would only arouse "a hot resentment" in Russia, without accomplish- ing any of the desired objectives.[1] The foreign intervention may be said to have contributed more than anything else to putting the Soviet regime in the saddle.

A note of caution should be sounded here on the use of Soviet primary sources for the history of the Civil War and foreign inter- vention. Since the rise of Stalin, and especially during the Cold War that followed World War II, there has been wilful and wholesale falsifi- cation and distortion of the history of this period in the Soviet press, in Soviet historical publications, and even in Soviet fiction.

---

[1] See the United States note to the Japanese and Allied Governments, dated March 5, 1918, quoted in Bunyan, James, *Intervention, Civil War, and Communism in Russia, April-December 1918,* Baltimore, 1936, pp. 65-66.

II

The Constructive Period
1921-1941

THE NEW ECONOMIC POLICY (NEP)
1921-1928

BY 1921 it was clear that the Soviet regime was in the saddle. Victory against opposition at home and abroad had been achieved, however, at a tremendous price. After seven years of war, civil strife, and foreign intervention, the Russian people were exhausted, hungry, and ill clad. To add to their misery a severe drought in the Volga Region brought famine in its wake. In other parts of the country the peasants, in retaliation for the forced requisition of farm products, stopped producing more than they required for their personal use. Not more than half of the prewar farming area remained under cultivation. Industrial production, moreover, had declined to 15 percent of the 1914 level and the country was faced with economic debacle. Transportation facilities were inadequate to permit proper distribution of food on hand. Among those who suffered most were the "declassed"—members of the former bourgeoisie, aristocracy, and clergy, who had not cast their lot with the Soviets and who were denied ration cards. Several million of them died of starvation in 1920 and 1921.

The mortality would have been higher if the American Relief Administration (ARA) under the direction of Herbert Hoover had not rendered timely assistance. This organization, assisted by the American Red Cross and other agencies for relief in the United States, rendered invaluable service to the destitute in Russia during these critical years. The American Relief Administration and the Red Cross spent approximately $62,000,000 and cared for fully 4,173,339 children and 6,316,958 adults. Various Jewish organizations, such as the Joint Distribution Committee and People's Relief, aided by relatives of the destitute Russians, contributed over $40,000,000 for Russian relief. Thus the entire sum furnished by the United States was in the neighborhood of $100,000,000.

Meanwhile the sporadic revolts and strikes which occurred in 1920 and 1921 were ruthlessly suppressed by the Soviet regime. One of these revolts, however, while no more successful than the others, made the government pause and consider. Red sailors at Kronstadt, whose assistance had formerly turned the tide in favor of the Soviets, staged an uprising on March 2, 1921, calling for "Free Soviets." Among other things, they demanded the restoration of freedom of trade, freedom of the press, a secret ballot, and the calling of a Constituent Assembly. Since the Red sailors could in no wise be regarded as counter-revolutionaries, Soviet leaders were sufficiently startled to realize that the time had come to take stock of the situation. The Soviet government began to grope its way toward the building of a new economy on the ruins of the old.

While the sailors' revolt was in progress, the Tenth Congress of the Communist Party met in Moscow, March 8-16, 1921. The most vital problem before it was the matter of increased production, and this was the keynote of Lenin's speech before the session. Without circumlocution he confessed, "We are in a condition of such poverty, ruin and exhaustion of productive powers of the workers and peasants, that everything must be set aside to increase production." The Lenin who uttered these words was not the same man who assumed the presidency in 1917. In the years from 1919 to 1921 he had been learning from bitter experience. Although to him Communism was a religion, he was a realist. "For me," he said, "theory is only a hypothesis, not the Holy Scripture; it is a tool in our daily work." Beginning in 1919, he permitted the introduction of different economic systems in various provinces of the Union. Whereas one province was placed on a strictly Communistic basis, another became semi-communistic and a third remained semi-capitalistic. A close check was kept on the manner in which each system operated and the results were tabulated. Thus, for the first time in history, a socialistic experiment was conducted along scientific lines. It goes without saying that this experimentation was attended by much suffering and privation on the part of the human guinea-pigs who were involuntarily subjected to it. However the value to humanity as a whole of the services rendered by Lenin's experiment cannot be overestimated, for it afforded conclusive proof that Communism had failed to work.

It was Lenin's dream to transform backward, agrarian Russia into an industrial nation, thereby establishing "a new technical base" for

Communism. With this in mind, as early as 1920 he called for the drafting by the State Planning Commission (Gosplan) of a ten-year economic program, an important phase of which was his own pet scheme for the electrification of Russia. This was the design for the future, but it provided no solution for the existing predicament of the Russian people. Lenin was an honest, as well as a highly intelligent man, and when he appeared before the Tenth Congress, equipped with hard facts rather than far-fetched and idealistic theories, he courageously made his confession. It was this—that his investigations had convinced him that a strictly Communistic system, the realization of which had been his life dream, was unworkable, at least for the time being. No one but Lenin would have dared to make such a pronouncement, and no one but he had the power to institute a change of policy which, if carried to its logical conclusion, would have banished militant Communism from the USSR.

From Lenin's confession was born the New Economic Policy, better known as the NEP. Lenin himself described it as "a strategic retreat," undertaken to permit the country to recuperate before the resumption of the Socialist offensive. Although the NEP was not intended to do more than provide a breathing spell, many Russians believed that if his life had been prolonged, Lenin would have made of the USSR a semi-capitalistic state and brought the country back to "normalcy." As it was, his appearance before the Tenth Congress may be said to close his career as a great political leader. Shortly thereafter his health began to fail. On May 22, 1922, he was seized with a paralytic stroke from which he never fully recovered. He died on January 21, 1924, at Gorky following a second stroke.

One of the first changes to follow the introduction of the NEP was the establishment of free trade inside the Soviet Union. Although the land and the "commanding heights" of heavy industry remained nationalized, and the state retained its complete monopoly of foreign trade, there was a tendency to leave small-scale production in the hands of private individuals. The Socialist form of production was replaced by what might be termed state capitalism. A system of "trusts" on the German or American model replaced the single management of industry. Simon Liberman, for example, set a precedent by establishing and heading the trust for the timber industry, which enlisted the services of a number of Russia's former capitalists, well known abroad, and proceeded to restore the export trade in timber so as to create a gold

RED SQUARE AND THE LENIN MAUSOLEUM

From Lenin's tomb (lower right), Soviet officials review parades passing through the Square. In the center is the cathedral of St. Basil, begun by Ivan Grozny to commemorate the conquest of Kazan (1552), and now a museum. On the right is part of the historic Kremlin Wall.

reserve.[1] Forced labor was abolished, and concessions were granted to foreign capital. Peasants, after paying a heavy tax in kind, were allowed to dispose of their surplus. As a result of these concessions to industry and agriculture a new Soviet *bourgeoisie* began to make its appearance.

Toward the end of 1921 a State Bank was established which accomplished the stabilization of Soviet currency by June 1924. The "chervonetz," with a value equal to ten gold rubles or a little more than five dollars, became the standard, and metal coins began to replace the stamp money and other worthless paper in circulation. Briefly stated, the introduction of the NEP was followed by an immediate revival of industry and agriculture. By 1926-1927 industrial production on the whole had returned to the 1913 level, although some industries, such as iron, were lagging rather far behind. During the years of NEP operation, 1921 to 1928, there was sufficient food, business in general was active, and the people enjoyed relative health and contentment. The Soviet Union prospered under a system which was neither socialistic nor capitalistic; it was the NEP system.

With the NEP the wall of Soviet isolation was breached and a beginning was made toward the re-establishment of economic relations with other countries. As early as January 16, 1920, the Allies had lifted the blockade they had imposed against the Bolsheviks. Although the world was not yet ready to recognize the Soviet Government, there were soon indications that, however reluctantly, they were prepared to trade with it. France, in particular, needed Russian timber for reconstruction, as England required it for railroad construction. For Russian gold, Sweden was willing to sell railroad equipment, especially locomotives, and even sawmill equipment to the Soviets. Lloyd George was favorably disposed toward the development of Anglo-Soviet trade. "After all," he said, "we deal with cannibals too." Thus in March 1921 the Soviet Government made its first trade agreement with England. Shortly thereafter Russia secured credits up to £1,000,000 from Lloyd's Bank.

In order to promote the rehabilitation of Russia Lenin was even prepared to invite foreign capital to participate in the development of the country. Wherever foreign capital was granted concessions, however, the Soviet Government closely supervised its activities. That Soviet leaders proceeded with all due caution is clear from the fact that, whereas in the years from 1921 to 1928 some 2400 applications were

---

[1] See Liberman, Simon, *Building Lenin's Russia,* Chicago, 1945, pp. 96-100.

received for foreign concessions, the state signed only 178 contracts, and by October 1928 only 68 of these concessionary enterprises were still functioning, representing a capital of 61,000,000 rubles and a personnel of 20,000.[1] Among the more outstanding concessions under the NEP was the American manganese concession at Chiaturi in the Transcaucasus, headed by W. Averill Harriman, the prominent industrialist who later became ambassador to Moscow. A British company had an important concession for a time in the Lena goldfields of Siberia, and the Japanese secured concessions in Kamtchatka. Lenin often found it difficult to convince his colleagues that Russia could profit from this resort to foreign capital.

Lenin was right in assuming that the resumption of trade relations, even on a limited scale, would pave the way for the official recognition of the Soviet regime. In 1924 Britain, Italy, Norway, Austria, Greece, Sweden, China, Denmark, Mexico, and France recognized the Soviet Government, followed by Japan in January 1925. The United States therefore remained the only great power that refused to establish normal diplomatic relations with the new regime, although from the standpoint of the world at large it was becoming "respectable." American engineers, however, did contribute to the reconstruction of the country, and trade relations were re-established through the Russian-American Trading Corporation organized by Sidney Hillman.

The success of the NEP did not meet with universal approval. Since in practice it amounted to "restricted capitalism," it was natural that uncompromising Communists in the Soviet Union should regard it almost as a betrayal of the Revolution. As early as the Eleventh Congress of the Communist Party in March 1922, the cry had been raised that the "retreat on the economic front" must be checked. Dissension among the leaders of the Communist Party, already apparent before the death of Lenin, crystallized in the spring of 1925 when, upon the recommendation of Stalin, the Fourteenth Party Conference made additional concessions to the middle-class peasants, or kulaks, which allowed them to lease land and hire labor.

Left-wing opposition to this extension of the NEP was led by Trotsky, a former Menshevik, who had joined forces with Lenin after the March Revolution of 1917, and who had already voiced his objections to the NEP in his *Lessons of October,* published in 1924. When Trotsky failed to return from South Russia for Lenin's funeral, Party control was vested in a Triumvirate comprised of Kamenev, Vice-Chairman of the Council of People's Commissars, Zinoviev, head of the

---

[1] See Liberman, *op. cit.,* p. 143.

Comintern, and Stalin, Secretary of the Party. It was this triumvirate which carried through the policy of concessions to the peasants, with the support of a Right-wing faction of the Party, which included Bukharin, the editor of *Izvestia*, and Rykov, premier of the Soviet Union, who favored still greater concessions. Trotsky and his followers attacked the "bourgeois" tendencies of the Party, accused the Party Central Committee of being autocratic, and demanded the application of the principles of Communism to agriculture as well as to industry.

The fundamental difference between Trotsky and Stalin, however, concerned the issue of world revolution. Trotsky, the internationalist, "the slashing sword of the Revolution," believed that socialism could never succeed in the USSR alone—that it must be established by revolution throughout the world. To achieve this end, he was willing to devote the entire resources of the Soviet Union to foment revolution. Stalin, on the other hand, espoused the belief that socialism, irrespective of the fate of the Revolution abroad, could succeed in the USSR. The Soviet Union, in his estimation, differed from other countries by being almost a continent and a virtual league of nations in itself. He was therefore ready to abandon the principle of world revolution in favor of the more nationalistic ambition of achieving socialism in one country—the USSR.

The course of events abroad from 1921 to 1927 only served to strengthen Stalin's convictions in this respect. World revolution as fomented by Moscow had not only failed to achieve more than transitory results in Europe, but in practice it led to reaction and Fascism. Fascism under Mussolini had already superseded the Communist movement in Italy. In May 1926, the Polish Republic was overthrown by a military *coup d'état* led by Pilsudski. Following the failure of the general strike in England in the same year, the Baldwin Government severed diplomatic relations with the Soviet Union in 1927. The climax came when in April 1927 Chiang Kai-shek and the Kuomintang Party broke with the Chinese Communists and expelled Soviet advisers from China. These successive reverses convinced Stalin that Soviet resources could be put to much more constructive use in the building of a Socialist state at home.

The decline and fall of Trotsky were accomplished in the five-year period following Lenin's death. In April 1925, he was removed from the influential post of War Commissar and, after a term of "sick leave," was transferred to lesser administrative jobs, including that of Commissar of National Economy. When the Fourteenth Party Congress of December 1925 upheld Stalin against Kamenev and Zinoviev on the

JOSEPH V. STALIN, JULY 1948

issue of building Socialism in the Soviet Union in preference to foment-ing world revolution, these two members of the Triumvirate joined the opposition under Trotsky. Zinoviev was shortly thereafter re-moved from the headship of the Comintern. Since Trotsky repeatedly conspired to return to power, he was dismissed from the Politburo in July 1927, expelled from the Party at the Fifteenth Congress in December 1927, and exiled to Alma Ata in Turkestan in January 1928. Even in distant Turkestan, however, Trotsky refused to abandon his efforts to build up an effective underground movement, with the result that he was exiled from the USSR in January 1929. Trotsky thereupon took refuge in succession in Turkey, France, Norway, and finally in Mexico, where he continued to direct Trotskyite opposition to the Stalin regime and where he was finally assassinated in August 1940 (died August 21).

The clash between Stalin and Trotsky has underlined the contro-versy over the interpretation of the NEP. Some writers have regarded "the strategic retreat" as proof of the failure of socialism or Marxism under the Soviet regime, and as an indication of a drift toward state capitalism. Others have persisted in regarding it as a temporary "respite" in the march toward socialism. It was natural that since it combined some of the features of capitalism and socialism it did not appeal to uncompromising supporters of either system. One thing, however, seems clear. The compromise saved the Soviet regime from almost certain collapse. Moreover the NEP whetted the appetites of Communists and non-Commnunists alike for constructive work, which was soon to find its expression in the Five-Year Plans.

THE FIVE-YEAR PLANS
1928-1941

No sooner was Trotsky ousted from power than Stalin began to pur-sue the task of building socialism at home, using some of the very meth-ods advocated by the Trotskyite opposition. At the Fifteenth Party Congress of December 1927, which expelled Trotsky, Stalin secured the adoption of an accelerated program of industrialization and collec-tivization, commonly known as the First Five-Year Plan. This Plan, which was expected to cost over three and one-half billion dollars, out-lined a course of procedure for the five-year period, beginning with the Soviet fiscal year, October 1, 1928, and continuing until October 1, 1933. Every phase of life in the USSR was subject to its control, including agriculture, education, transportation, the mining, fishing and

THE DNIEPER DAM AT ZAPOROZHYE IN THE UKRAINE

The postwar Stalin Five-Year Plan has provided for the reconstruction of the dam, destroyed in 1941.

forestry industries, public health, recreation, and others, the idea being that by the end of the stipulated period there would be a well-established socialistic and industrial state in the Soviet Union. The Plan was expected to provide Soviet citizens with an abundance of all the necessities and even the luxuries of life, while leaving a considerable surplus for export. In short, the First Five-Year Plan promised the coming of a socialist millenium.

Although the original blueprint of the First Five-Year Plan was roughly divided into three parts—heavy industry, light industry, and surplus commodities or consumer items—circumstances largely beyond the control of Soviet leaders caused them to revise the program drastically in the direction of heavy industry. Soviet leaders soon realized that the transformation of the USSR was a task of such magnitude that it could not possibly be achieved in five years. More important still, the Japanese occupation of Manchuria in 1931 forced the Soviets, in the interests of defense, to place more emphasis upon heavy industry, with the result that the other phases of the program lagged far behind schedule. Before the end of the First Five-Year Plan the Soviet Government began to prepare public opinion for a Second Five-Year Plan (1933-1938) to stress light industry, and for the prospect of a series of such programs to follow. The First Five-Year Plan was declared to have achieved its goal a full nine months ahead of schedule, and the new program was inaugurated early in 1933. By January 1933, however, Hitler was in the saddle in Germany and strategic considerations required a redoubling of Soviet efforts in the direction of security. The Third Five-Year Plan (1938), which afforded some prospect of supplying Soviet citizens with the long-awaited consumer goods, was interrupted when Hitler precipitated Germany and Europe into World War II. Following the end of the conflict Stalin announced the beginning of a Fourth Five-Year Plan in February 1946.

In brief, in spite of all obstacles, the Five-Year Plans laid the foundations of a powerful iron and steel industry in the Soviet Union, including the establishment of new centers of heavy industry in Siberia. In complete contrast with efforts under the tsarist regime to "Westernize" Russia, the new industrial offensive was conducted without recourse to foreign loans, and without returning to the policy of foreign concessions, characteristic of the NEP, although quantities of industrial equipment were obtained on credit terms ranging from six months to several years. Foreign technical assistance played an important and indispensable role in these undertakings. For instance, an American engineer, Hugh L. Cooper, designed and supervised the construction of

KARL MARX COLLECTIVE FARM IN KABARDINO BALKARIA

Article 7 of the USSR Constitution permits some measure of individual ownership on collective farms. In this picture there can be seen the neatly cultivated plots allocated to individual farmers for their personal use.

the great Dnieprostroy dam, begun in 1927 and formally opened in the summer of 1932. Another American engineer, Alexander Vasilievitch Winter, designed the power plants, the capacity of which was 625,000 kilowatt hours.[1] Other Americans have left interesting records of their experiences in the USSR during these years, as did John Scott, who, in his *Behind the Urals* (1942), tells the fantastic story of the building of the huge steel center of Magnitogorsk, where he worked for some five years; and John D. Littlepage, an American mining engineer, who from 1928-1937 held a key position in the Gold Trust, opened up new mines in various parts of Siberia.

Other major items of construction included the giant tractor factories at Stalingrad, Kharkov, and Tchelyabinsk, designed to facilitate the mechanization of agriculture; the Molotov motor works at Nizhni-Novgorod (Gorky); also the great steel plants at Magnitogorsk in the Southern Urals and at Kuznetz in Siberia, which served as the arsenal of the Soviet Union in World War II.

Similar strides were made in the field of transportation. Not only did the Soviets undertake to double-track the Trans-Siberian Railroad, but in certain strategic areas, five or six parallel stretches of track were laid. The Turkestan-Siberian (Turk-Sib) Railway, linking Tashkent with Alma Ata and Novosibirsk, was completed in 1930. Great locomotive works were established at Voroshilovgrad. Soviet airlines increased from 1300 kilometers in 1928 to 89,500 kilometers in 1936. The commercial and strategic potentialities of Soviet inland waterways were greatly extended by a series of important canals, which linked the Moscow River with the Volga, the Volga with Lake Onega, and Lake Onega with the Baltic and White Seas. Another canal, intended to join the Volga and the Don Rivers, was unfinished when Germany invaded the Soviet Union. The completion of this project which was ultimately accomplished in 1952, was intended to make water transport possible from the Black and Azov Seas to the Caspian, Baltic, and White Seas. Moscow was to become a port of five seas and one of the world's largest river ports. Beginning in 1932, when the Soviet icebreaker, *Sibiryakov,* made its first successful voyage from Archangel to Vladivostok in a single season, the Northern Sea Route Administration directed every effort toward opening the Arctic as a normal artery of shipping during the summer months. During the Third Five-Year Plan special emphasis was placed on the development of this Northern Passage in order to secure regular communications with the Far East.

---

[1] Littlepage, J. D., and Bess, Demaree, *In Search of Soviet Gold,* N. Y., 1937.

It was during the Second Five-Year Plan that the famous Moscow subway was constructed under the direction of Lazar Kaganovitch.

The growth of Soviet cities was one of the most striking features of the program of industrialization. From 1926 to 1939 the urban population more than doubled. In the same period, the population of Moscow increased from 2,000,000 to 4,000,000; that of Leningrad, from 1,500,-000 to 3,000,000. The following cities doubled, or very nearly doubled, their population: Kharkov, Baku, Tashkent, Dnepropetrovsk, Kazan, Kuibyshev, Minsk, and Vladivostok. Others like Voronezh, Novosibirsk, Sverdlovsk, Stalingrad, and Gorky tripled their numbers, while Archangel and Tchelyabinsk quadrupled their population. New cities, especially those founded in Siberia, like Magnitogorsk, Sverdlovsk, and Komsomolsk, mushroomed in size. All told, more than ninety large industrial centers were established during the First Five-Year Plan. Although World War II brought devastation to many of the Soviet Union's European cities, it very considerably increased those in Siberia.

The crusade for collectivization of peasant holdings likewise revolutionized Soviet agriculture. The Revolution of 1917 had led to the confiscation of the great landed estates of the Russian aristocracy and their division among the peasantry. The number of private plots was thereby increased from some 16,000,000 to approximately 25,000,000. In order to effect the restoration of agriculture, Soviet leaders had made important concessions to these peasants during the NEP and many kulaks had waxed prosperous. The Five-Year Plan now reversed the trend by calling for the consolidation of private family plots into collective farms (*kolkhozi*). The war cry went forth for the liquidation of the kulaks and those who resisted the program of collectivization by hiding or burning their grain, refusing to plant their crops, slaughtering their cattle, and other forms of sabotage. Hundreds of thousands of the recalcitrants were transported to Siberia to work in the forest or mines, or on roads or canals. Others starved during the famine which swept the Ukraine in the early 1930's, particularly in 1932. This return to "class war in the villages" gave rise to a first-class agricultural crisis. Even as early as March 1930, Stalin had to condemn collectivization "by military force" and to decry those who thought they could begin a collective "by pulling down church bells" and other extreme measures.

By these drastic means, Soviet agriculture was revolutionized. Whereas in 1928 there were only 1600 collective farms, by 1930 the number had risen to 85,900, embracing some 6,000,000 households. By January 1946, according to official figures, there were 217,000 collective farms in the Soviet Union, comprising 85 percent of the peasant

OIL WELLS AT BAKU ON THE CASPIAN SEA

households of the country. The Soviet Union by 1937 had become the world's foremost producer of agricultural machinery, including combine harvesters. On the eve of the German invasion of the Soviet Union in June 1941, some half million tractors were making large-scale agriculture possible. Since 1913 agricultural production had doubled. Before World War II entirely new agricultural areas were opened up in the Urals, Siberia, the Soviet Far East, and Kazakhstan. The irrigation of arid regions, as in Central Asia, contributed greatly to the increase in production. The area of irrigated land almost doubled between 1913 and 1940, at which time it amounted to 17,291,000 acres.

Throughout the era of the prewar Five-Year Plans, the Communist Party and the Komsomol, or League of Communist Youth, exerted the greatest possible pressure upon the peoples of the Soviet Union to increase production. According to the late Samuel Harper of the University of Chicago, a frequent visitor to Russia during these years, the new slogan might well have been: "Build until it hurts." Such unemployment as existed on the eve of the First Five-Year Plan disappeared. The haste with which revolutionary changes in industry and agriculture were achieved involved untold hardship for the masses and resulted in numerous mistakes due to ignorance or sabotage. On the one hand there were miracles of courage and achievement, and on the other appalling waste and sacrifices. In the process of effecting a complete transformation of the country at a war tempo, Russians had to cope with appalling shortages of food, clothing, and other necessities of life, with rationing (until 1934-1935), overcrowding, and endless red tape. For them these were years of "blood, sweat, and tears," during which there were inevitably many casualties. In a prophetic warning issued in 1931, Stalin explained to the Russian people the necessity for maintaining the high "Bolshevik tempo" of production:

We are fifty to a hundred years behind the advanced countries. We must cover this distance in ten years. Either we do this or they will crush us.

Ten years later, on June 22, 1941, the Soviet Union was invaded by Nazi Germany. Meanwhile, it became the objective of the Soviet people to overtake and surpass America in ten years. Some slight idea of the task they confronted in the training of competent personnel alone can be derived from the account of one American engineer:

None of the workmen had had any experience with mechanized mining, and even the older engineers had never seen any of the new milling equipment except as pictures in catalogues. I saw that it would be necessary to teach each individual workman drilling, timbering, blasting, operation of the milling machinery, and, especially, care of equipment. I put on some digging clothes and went to work with the men, and I followed that practice during all my years in Russia.[1]

Since, as in the early days of the NEP, everything was subordinated to the battle for production, it was logical that the Soviet Government should provide every possible incentive and reward to citizens who devised ways and means of speeding up the program. In June 1931, on the eve of the Japanese occupation of Manchuria, piece work was introduced and wage scales were readjusted to make remuneration commensurate with the type of labor performed. In other words, the more a worker was able to produce, the greater his income. Some Communists opposed this marked deviation from the Marxist principle of compensating each worker "according to his *need.*" That the change proved effective as an incentive to production is clearly indicated by its ultimate incorporation in the Soviet Constitution of 1936, which expressly stipulated (Chapter I, Article 12) that "He who does not work shall not eat." Socialism in the USSR, according to the same Article, was being realized by application of the principle, "From each according to his ability, to each according to his *work.*"

The compulsory aspects of the Five-Year Plans were tempered still further by the rewards, especially in the form of bonuses, and the publicity showered upon workers who exceeded their quotas and raised the standards of workmanship. One of the most outstanding instances of such recognition, which fired the imagination of the Russian workers, was the case of Alexei Stakhanov, a Donetz coal miner. In 1935 Stakhanov, by a combination of team work plus piece work, so increased his quota at the mine that he was depicted throughout the USSR as a national hero whom other workers should emulate. Stakhanovism, by and large, amounted to nothing more nor less than the setting of new production records by means of a division of labor. The Stakhanov movement swept the country, contributing greatly to the speed-up of production. It is a well-known fact that it lent a tremendous impetus to the Second Five-Year Plan.

To increase agricultural production and to compensate in some measure for the dizzy pace of collectivization, similar concessions were made to collective farmers. In 1933, for example, collective farmers were guaranteed the perpetual use of their land, together with the right to private ownership of three cows, as well as an indefinite number of pigs, sheep, and poultry. Their earnings, over and above what was due to the

---

[1] Littlepage and Bess, *op. cit.*, p. 40.

state, were likewise recognized as private property and could be invested in interest-bearing bonds. With the unhappy fate of the kulaks in mind, collective farmers did not rest until these and similar concessions were incorporated in the 1936 Constitution (Chapter I, Articles 7-10). This Constitution not only recognized the right of Soviet citizens to personal ownership of their income from work and savings, of their homes and household goods, but also their right to inherit private property (Article 10). These concessions to private initiative supplemented but did not replace the basic principles of collectivism in the USSR.

To make Asiatic Russia, especially Eastern Siberia, self-sufficient from the standpoint of food supply, every incentive was offered following the Japanese entry into Manchuria to encourage farmers to settle there. Special concessions, including free transportation, credits and tax exemptions were offered to entice pioneers to establish themselves in regions strategically exposed to enemy attack. In 1928 a Jewish homeland was founded in Birobijan west of Khabarovsk on the borders of Manchuria, where Jewish settlers established collective farms and their own industries. Between 1928 and 1936 the Jews increased the area under production in this frontier region two and a half times. In 1934 Birobijan became the Jewish National Autonomous Region.

When the Germans invaded the Soviet Union on June 22, 1941, the USSR was still far from achieving its goal of "overtaking and surpassing America" as an industrial power. It had nevertheless succeeded in laying the foundations of heavy industry, which without doubt enabled the country to survive invasion. To appreciate the significance of the Five-Year Plans, it should be understood that the underlying motives were as much strategic as economic. From the economic standpoint American economists and engineers may claim with some justification that this Soviet industrial revolution was achieved at too great a price, due to the enormous waste, the serious blunders, and the extent of human misery involved in putting through a program of such magnitude in such haste and with such a dearth of trained technicians. Nevertheless World War II amply demonstrated the urgency, in fact the indispensability of industrialization, and its success from the strategic point of view. By 1941 the Soviet people were, in large measure, economically independent of the Western world.

In addition to the significance of the Five-Year Plans from the standpoint of national defense, it is important to take cognizance of their psychological effects. The thirteen years prior to the Nazi invasion were years of constructive achievement. In spite of the manifest opposition of the population to certain phases of the program, the people of the USSR as a whole, especially the youth, were eager for constructive work. Against the somber background of this battle against time, it should not be overlooked that a new generation of Soviet citizens not only learned to read and write, but to handle the tools of modern industry and agriculture, which was for many a thrilling experience that paved the way to a brighter future. In retrospect, it seems apparent that the Five-Year Plans lent wings to the imagination of the Soviet people—that they provided a new horizon. High-sounding revolutionary theories no longer sufficed to maintain the enthusiasm of the average Soviet worker or peasant. The fact that during the Five-Year Plans they could actually come down to earth and participate in a practical manner in the building of socialism in their own country, and that they could see, as time progressed, positive results—all this acted like a tonic to the people. Through constructive activity, the nation found its salvation.

In proportion as the program took shape and results became apparent, it produced a marked sobering effect upon the Soviet people which was reflected in their theories regarding the family, law, the Church, education, etc. The new outlook is well illustrated by the Soviet writer, Boris Pilnyak, in his novel on the Five-Year Plan entitled *The Volga Falls to the Caspian Sea* (1930), in which the engineer Poltorak explains to his colleague:

> . . . And it turns out that morality may be squandered, just like boots and grain; the revolution has squandered it. Morality will have to be restored like boots and sown areas, because morality is a simple and an actual economic unit, no less necessary than coats or potatoes. . . .

The Soviet people, in the process of building a new world, also made peace with the past, began to revaluate past achievements and to revive and cherish national traditions. They likewise displayed a wholesome tendency to make peace with the outside world in order that they might continue their constructive program without let or hindrance. "This policy of international peace," declared the Communist Party at its Fifteenth Congress, "is at the same time a fundamental condition for the development of socialism within the USSR." The Soviet Union proceeded to adhere to the Kellogg-Briand Peace Pact of 1928 and to enter into nonaggression pacts with its neighbors. Those Russians whose vision was still confined to the destructive phases of militant Communism were purged or liquidated without compunction when they sought to obstruct or sabotage the new program of construction.

A careful analysis of the Five-Year Plans indicates that the measure of success achieved was due largely to Soviet resort to capitalistic methods and guidance rather than to socialism. Such expedients as the introduction of piece work, bonuses for higher production, concessions to collective farmers, recognition of a modicum of private ownership, etc., stimulated competition and increased production. American brains and American know-how provided the blueprints for many Soviet projects, whereas imported American equipment made

MOSCOW SUBWAY

Courtesy Sovfoto

possible their early completion. The best recognition of this situation is to be found in the popular Soviet play *Tempo* (1929) by Nikolai Pogodin, in which the prescribed model for all Soviet workers to emulate is the American engineer Carter. The term "American" became synonymous with "efficiency." While Americans were thus rendering invaluable constructive service to the program for the industrialization of the Soviet Union, the Comintern during the so-called Red Decade helped American subversive elements to foment strikes and to infiltrate government agencies with the intent of achieving the ultimate overthrow of the American system of government. It would be difficult to find a more striking instance of base ingratitude for American aid.

Needless to say, the "great retreat" of the 1930's gave rise to opposition on the part of Communists who decried any deviation from the fundamentals of Marxism with as much vehemence as in the days of the NEP. In particular, they feared the growth of a middle class of collective farmers and piece workers, which would mark the end of the "classless society" proclaimed by the Revolution. Moreover, many irreconcilables still hankered for world revolution as distinct from "Socialism in One Country." The forces of the opposition also included tsarist engineers and "specialists," whose services were enlisted during the Five-Year Plans, but who did not want any Soviet program to succeed. Last, but not least, some foreign countries, especially Germany, having observed Soviet technical progress with growing dismay, were anxious to block the rise of a powerful Soviet state by conspiring to overthrow the Stalin regime. To achieve this, they required the collaboration of Soviet generals, some of whom appear to have fallen into the trap.

Irrespective of the causes, which were complex, the leading Soviet victims of the purges, 1936-1938, would have been included on any Communist Roll of Honor during the 1920's. At the first trial conducted by the Supreme Military Tribunal of the USSR in August 1936, Kamenev and Zinoviev, previously implicated in the assassination of Stalin's close friend and associate, Sergei Kirov, in December 1934, were now found guilty of a plot to murder Stalin and were executed. At the second trial, which took place in January 1937, well-known Communists like Pyatakov, former Commissar of Heavy Industry, Muralov, who led the Red troops in triumph into Moscow in 1917, Yagoda, the head of the OGPU, Radek, a brilliant Soviet journalist, and Sokolnikov, commissar of finance under the NEP, were denounced as Trotskyites, who conspired with the aid of foreign powers to overthrow the Stalin regime. In June 1937, there followed the famous secret trial of Marshal Tukhatchevsky, assistant commissar for defense, and seven high Soviet generals, namely, General Putna, a former Soviet military attaché in London, General Yakir, General Ulorevitch, General Feldman, chief of personnel for the Red army, General Kork, head of the Soviet Military Academy at Frunze, General Primakov, and General Eideman, president of *Osoaviakhim* (the Society for Chemical and Aviation Experiment), who were condemned for treason and shot. They were accused of planning a military *coup d'état* with foreign aid, in return for which they were prepared to sacrifice the Ukraine. The fourth and last of the famous purge trials occurred in March 1938, when two famous Right-wing Communists, Nikolai Bukharin, a close friend of Lenin and editor of *Izvestia,* as well as Alexei Rykov, former premier of the USSR, 1924-30, were accused of collusion with the Trotskyites to effect the overthrow of Stalin.

Altogether sixty well-known Communists were tried, convicted and, with a few exceptions like that of Radek, were promptly liquidated. They included representatives of the Council of Commissars, the Central Committee of the Communist Party, leaders in the Red army and navy, as well as members of the Soviet diplomatic corps. They all admitted their complicity in plots to overthrow the Stalin regime. Subsequent revelations by Czech government leaders have substantiated accusations against the Red army generals of treasonable contacts with the Germans.

Along with the Communist leaders, thousands of citizens of lesser rank throughout the Union became victims of the purges. Undoubtedly the innocent suffered along with the guilty. Some engineers accused of "wrecking" were in all probability victims of their own inexperience and ignorance rather than "enemies of the people." Shortly thereafter, in 1937, the Soviet Government raised the standards of education in order to provide better specialists for the future. Because of the excess zeal displayed by many local Soviet officials in conducting the purges and the demoralizing effects of this conduct upon the people at large, the Soviet Government in 1938 called a halt to further arrests.

Although the purges gave rise to widespread confusion, fear, and dismay among Soviet officials at home and abroad, the masses of the people were not greatly disturbed by them. In fact, they were often satisfied to find that officials who themselves had been guilty of much bloodshed and untold misery were now reaping what they formerly sowed. Many Russians felt that, as a result of the ruthless liquidation of the opposition, the Soviet regime emerged stronger and more unified than ever before. The outbreak of war, with its subsequent revelation of powerful fifth columns in many European countries, helped to confirm this opinion.

Beyond the borders of the USSR, however, the purges confused and shocked public opinion. Many supporters of the Soviet regime were antagonized by this "reign of terror," attacked Soviet "barbarism," and declared that Stalin had betrayed the Revolution. Friends and acquaintances of the victims, former Leftist journalists, and many Communists abroad "confessed" the error of their ways in books, articles, and public lectures in a campaign of unrelenting hostility against the USSR. As a result of the purges, the Soviet Union lost much prestige abroad. The liquidation of the top generals of the Red Army General Staff convinced military experts in Britain and the United States of the "weakness" of the Soviet Union, which was frequently described as a "Colossus with feet of clay." Lord Halifax, British foreign secretary under Neville Chamberlain, was so convinced of the weakness of the Red army that he believed Poland would prove to be a stronger and more effective ally of Great Britain than the USSR. In spite of the havoc played by the Stalin regime with the top Red Army leadership, World War II produced a galaxy of brilliant military strategists, including Timoshenko, Zhukov, Konev, Malinovsky, Rokossovsky, Govorov, Bagramian, Tchernyakhovsky, Voronov, Vasilevsky, and others, to replace Marshal Tukhachevsky and his associates who were purged.

CONSTITUTION OF 1936

It is a long, long trail from the adoption of the constitution of the Russian Socialist Federated Soviet Republic (RSFSR) by the Fifth All-Russian Soviet Congress on July 10, 1918, to the adoption of the New Constitution of the Union of Soviet Socialist Republics (USSR), better known as the Stalin Constitution, on December 5, 1936. The constitution of the RSFSR was the first of the Soviet constitutions, a product of the era of militant Communism, which reflected the spirit of Karl Marx's Communist Manifesto of 1848. It declared Russia to be "a Republic of Soviets of Workers', Soldiers', and Peasants' Deputies." Supreme power was vested in an All-Russian Congress of Soviets, chosen by a process of indirect election, in which greater preponderance was accorded to the urban as against the rural Soviets, while bourgeois and clerical elements of the population were disfranchised. The above-mentioned Congress elected a Central Executive Committee, which in its turn appointed as its executive organ a Council of Commissars (Sovnarkom). This constitution made no specific reference whatsoever to the Communist Party. While the Constitution of 1918 was limited to the RSFSR, as soon as counter-revolution was suppressed and Soviet Republics were established in Byelorussia, the Ukraine, and the Transcaucasus, a Union of Soviet Socialist Republics (USSR) was established by treaty in December 1922. The first constitution of the USSR, modeled after but more cumbersome than that of the RSFSR, was adopted by the Central Executive Committee of the Union on July 6, 1923, and ratified by the Second All-Union Congress of Soviets on January 31, 1924.

With the rapid and revolutionary changes that took place in the USSR during the course of the Five-Year Plans, it soon became apparent that the constitution adopted during the period of the NEP needed overhauling. In 1935, therefore, the Seventh All-Union Congress of Soviets called for a Constitutional Commission to revise the USSR Constitution of 1924 in the light of the rapid growth of socialist industry and the collectivization of agriculture, so as to dispense with unequal suffrage, indirect elections, the open ballot, and so on. On June 12, 1936, this Commission, of which Stalin was president, published the New Projected Constitution of the USSR. Throughout the length and breadth of the Union this draft was discussed by Soviet citizens, who proceeded to recommend some 43,000 changes, mostly of a minor nature. During the six months prior to its final adoption on December 5, 1936, the draft was overhauled, with the result that forty-three amendments were introduced, including Soviet recognition of the right to inherit private property. The final draft of the Stalin Constitution was believed to embody the gains already achieved by the Soviet people in their march toward Communism, namely the end of class conflict, socialist ownership of the instruments of production, and the dictatorship of the working class. Although the words "democracy" and "democratic" do not appear in the new constitution, Stalin, in addressing the Extraordinary Eighth Congress of Soviets on November 25, 1936, claimed that it was "the only democratic constitution in the world."

Even the foregoing brief summary bears witness to the dynamic nature of Soviet constitutional development since the Revolution. During these years constitutional changes have paralleled changes in the economic structure of Soviet society. It may even be said that they have trailed after rather than set the pace for changes in the Soviet economy. In view of what has already happened, it may be assumed that the Stalin Constitution does not represent the last word in Soviet constitutional development, but that additional changes will be instituted as circumstances and the evolution of Soviet society render them feasible or necessary. "Naturally, of course," said Stalin in his report to the Eighteenth Congress of the Communist Party, "the forms of our state will again change in conformity with the change in the situation at home and abroad." Indeed, since 1936 many important amendments have been introduced.[1]

In Chapter I of the Stalin Constitution the USSR is defined as "a socialist state of workers and peasants." Here likewise are defined the limits of public and private ownership. Although the socialist system is specified as the predominant form of economy in the USSR, provision is

---

[1] For the official text of the Constitution of the USSR as published in English in 1959, see Appendix, p. 463.

Norwegian Sea

White Sea

March 1940

SWEDEN   FINLAND

NORWAY

from   Finland

L. Onega

G. of Bothnia

March, 1940

Oslo

Vänern

Stockholm

Helsinki

L. Ladoga

Vättern

Hangö (by Lease)

G. of Finland

Tallinn

ESTONIA

Baltic States
June, 1940

Riga
LATVIA

Moscow°

Baltic Sea

LITHUANIA

Kaunas

U. S. S. R.

Wilno
to Lithuania
Sept., 1939

Berlin

from Poland
Sept., 1940

Warsaw

GERMANY

Government
General
of Poland

SLOVAKIA

from Rumania
June, 1940

Russian Accretions:
1939 ~ 1940

HUNGARY

BUCOVINA

BESSARABIA

International Boundaries:

The Territorial Gains Are
Identified on the Map by Date.

R.E.Falconer

Black

Miles: 0   100   200   300

RUMANIA

Sea

nevertheless made for private economy on a small scale, as long as this does not involve exploitation of the labor of others. According to Article 10 individuals are entitled to personal ownership of their income from work and savings, their homes, and household articles, and they have the right to inherit such personal property. As an indication of the pressure upon all Soviet citizens for greater and greater production, Article 12 specified that workers would be compensated "in accordance with their work," rather than as heretofore in accordance with their need.

Chapter II, which lists the Republics of the Union (eleven in 1936; sixteen by 1941), also defines the limits of the jurisdiction of the federal government and the authority retained by the individual republics. As in the Constitution of the United States, certain "enumerated" powers are vested in the federal government, the residuary powers remaining with the republics. The nature and extent of Soviet federalism, however, constitute a subject which has given rise to much divergence of opinion among historians and political scientists outside the USSR. On paper, Article 17 provides that each Union Republic has the right "freely to secede" from the USSR. The Constitution was amended in 1944 to permit each republic to conduct its own relations with foreign states (Article 18a), as well as to maintain its own military formations (Article 18b). Nevertheless the binding force of the Communist Party, which transcends republican boundaries and is strongly centralized in Moscow, acts as a brake upon the exercise of autonomy by the republics. It is scarcely conceivable, in spite of Article 17, that one of them would be permitted peacefully to secede from the Union. Moreover the Constitution provides that in the event of a discrepancy between a law of the Union and a law of a republic, the Union law prevails. In contrast to the United States, where the constitutionality of a state law is a matter for judicial determination, in the USSR the Presidium of the Supreme Soviet can annul any decision or order of a Union Republic (Article 49).

Chapter III provides an outline of the structure of the government of the USSR. The highest organ of government in the Soviet Union is the Supreme Soviet, which consists of two Chambers, of equal authority—the Soviet of the Union and the Soviet of Nationalities—each being elected for a four-year term. In joint session, the Soviet of the Union and the Soviet of Nationalities elect a Presidium, consisting of a Chairman, sixteen Vice-Chairmen representing each of the constituent republics, a Secretary and twenty-four members. The Supreme Soviet also appoints the Government of the USSR, that is, the Council of

Ministers (known as the Council of Commissars until March 15, 1946). Thus, in commonplace English, the Supreme Soviet and the Presidium constitute the legislative branch, whereas the Council of Ministers is the executive branch of the government of the USSR. From the standpoint of structure, the Stalin Constitution was a marked improvement upon the Constitution of 1924, with its cumbersome Congress of Soviets and bicameral Central Executive Committee. The student of Soviet politics must always bear in mind, however, that it is the Communist Party that exercises real authority over all branches of the Soviet Government. Yet the Communist Party receives only somewhat casual mention in the 1936 Constitution (Articles 126 and 141).

Chapter IV outlines the structure of the government of the Union Republics, which is largely modeled upon that of the federal or All-Union Government. Chapter V defines the authority and functions of the Council of Ministers of the USSR; Chapter VI does virtually the same for the Union Republics. Chapters VII and VIII deal respectively with the structure of government of the Autonomous Soviet Socialist Republics and with the local organs of state authority. Chapter IX deals with the judicial branch of the Soviet Government, including the Office of Procurator.

Chapter X, on paper one of the most important in the Constitution, may be termed the Soviet "Bill of Rights." Unlike its American counterpart, however, it includes not only the rights of Soviet citizens but also their obligations to the government (Articles 130-133). These rights include the right to work, to rest and leisure, to maintenance in old age or sickness, to education, equal rights for women, race equality, freedom of religious worship as well as of anti-religious propaganda, the guarantee of freedom of speech, of the press, of assembly, of street processions and demonstrations, the right to unite in public organizations, such as trade unions, co-operative associations, youth organizations, sport and defense organizations, cultural, technical and scientific societies, inviolability of the person and home, and finally the right of asylum to foreign citizens. The duties of Soviet citizens include their obligation to abide by the Constitution and obey the laws, to safeguard public, socialist property, to perform military service, and to defend the fatherland.

From the standpoint of internal conditions, it is worth noting that the new Constitution guaranteed to the peoples of the Soviet Union four freedoms: freedom of speech, freedom of the press, freedom of assembly, including the holding of mass meetings, and freedom of street processions and demonstrations (Article 125). The last paragraph of this

Article, however, virtually cancels these four freedoms, since the facilities essential to their exercise are entirely at the disposal of the Soviet Government. Citizens of the Soviet Union have no access to printing presses, stocks of paper, public buildings, and communications facilities, without the express permission of the government which controls them. Unless these qualifications are removed, the four freedoms of Article 125 amount to no more than window dressing. Certainly these freedoms, as they are understood by the Western democracies, do not exist in the USSR, where there is no "free trade in ideas" and where, although there is a surprising amount of "self-criticism" in regard to the shortcomings of some particular bureaucratic office or official, there is no independent criticism of governmental policy or of the higher officials of the government. The government and the Party as such are regarded as infallible. It is possible to criticize the inferior quality of matches produced by some factory, or the failure of a particular industry to fulfill the requirements of the Five-Year Plan, but not to launch an attack on the foreign policy of the Soviet Union. Soviet leaders have consistently opposed toleration of dissentient opinons, hostile to the Soviet Union, as a symptom of weakness, contrary to the interests of "Soviet democracy."

As in the case of the four freedoms, the right of Soviet citizens to unite in public organizations of any description, guaranteed by Article 126, is virtually negated by a similar qualifying clause to the effect that Communist Party members must provide "the leading core" of all such organizations. The Communist Party, as Stalin explained in his well-known work, *Problems of Leninism,* "must stand at the head of the working class; it must see farther than the working class; it must lead the proletariat, and not follow in the tail of the spontaneous movement." He virtually conceived the dictatorship of the proletariat to be *"in essence* the 'dictatorship' of its vanguard, the 'dictatorship' of its Party."

One of the highlights of the Soviet Bill of Rights was its guarantee of racial equality (Article 123), which was included in the Constitution precisely at the time when the Nazis were making a fetish of racism and were discriminating against those they termed "subject" or "inferior" peoples, including the Jews. In 1948-49, however, it was widely rumored among the Western democracies that a revival of anti-Semitism had begun in Russia. Although there were undoubtedly some incidents in the Ukraine following the end of the German occupation, the Soviet press appeared to concentrate its attack, not on Jews as such, but on Zionism, and on either Jews or Gentiles who advocated a Western orientation—political or cultural. In January, 1953, however, a TASS dispatch in the Soviet press alleged that a terrorist group of doctors, most of whom were affiliated with the international Jewish organization JOINT, had conspired to bring about the death of Soviet leaders Andrei Zhdanov and A. S. Shcherbakov. This was followed by a temporary break in diplomatic relations with Israel (February 11-July 20, 1953), on the ground that the Israeli government had conspired in the explosion of a bomb on the premises of the Soviet legation in Tel Aviv. Although in April the charges against the doctors were repudiated, the tone of the accusations clearly indicated that anti-Semitism was by no means dead in the USSR.

The Constitution also marked the beginning of a new deal for the Church in the USSR (Article 124). Persecution of the Church, especially the Orthodox Church, inaugurated by the Soviet Government in the era of militant Communism, gave way to a modicum of religious freedom. While the new Constitution enfranchised the clergy and recognized freedom of religious worship, it still guaranteed freedom of anti-religious propaganda.

Chapter XI deals with the electoral system of the USSR. In contrast to the previous Soviet constitutions, provision was made for "universal, equal, and direct suffrage by secret ballot" (Article 134). For the first time, all citizens eighteen years of age and over, irrespective of "race or nationality, sex, religion, education, domicile, social origin, property status or past activities" were granted the right to vote (Article 135). Those formerly disfranchised on the basis of their social origin, their bourgeois or clerical activities, have thus been reinstated as full-fledged Soviet citizens. It is clear that in the eyes of Soviet leaders they no longer constituted a danger to the Soviet Union.

Unlike the United States, the Soviet Union conducts no primary elections. The sifting of candidates is accomplished at the nomination meetings of "Communist Party organizations, trade unions, cooperatives, youth organizations and cultural societies," where, after the usual debates for and against the candidates, the list is reduced to a single slate, instead of two or more as in the United States. Any Soviet citizen who is still dissatisfied with the results can register his protest on election day by means of a blank ballot. It should be noted here that the Soviet Constitution recognizes only one political party, the Communist Party, although candidates for election are not necessarily limited to Party members. Of the 1143 deputies elected to the Supreme Soviet in 1937, in the first election under the Stalin Constitution, 855 were Party members and 288 non-Party members.

To those Americans who wonder why such a totalitarian regime bothers to hold elections at all, Merle Fainsod (*How Russia is Ruled,* 1953, p. 323) provides an effective reply: "Soviet elections serve as a form of national mobilization. Like the plebiscites under Napoleon and Hitler, they are intended to demonstrate both to the world outside and the enemy within, that the people of the Soviet Union are solidly aligned with the regime."

Chapter XII of the Soviet Constitution deals with miscellaneous items, such as insignia and the capital of the USSR, which is designated as Moscow. The final Chapter XIII outlines the procedure for the amendment of the Constitution. According to Article 146, amendment is accomplished by means of a two-thirds vote in each of the two Chambers of the Supreme Soviet. In this respect, the Soviet Constitution is less "rigid" than the American Constitution which, in addition to a two-thirds majority in both Houses, also requires the approval of three-fourths of the states.

For the outside world, the purges obscured the significance of the Constitution which was adopted on December 5, 1936.[1] Although many of the high-sounding promises of the new Constitution have been observed neither in spirit nor in letter, it is highly significant that its guarantees are printed in black and white, that they are read and reread by the peoples of the USSR. The time may come when these Soviet citizens under the impact of Western democracy will demand the implementation of the guarantees which exist as yet only on paper.

Although the Stalin Constitution provided the framework of political democracy, it did not establish democracy any more than it established communism. As the Russians themselves acknowledge, it recognized the existence of a socialist state still subject to the dictatorship of the Communist Party. By American standards the Soviet Union, politically, has all the earmarks of a police state. Economically, it represents not communism or socialism but state capitalism, in which the workers are the chief victims of exploitation by the government.

---

[1] For representative interpretations of the Soviet Constitution see Schuman, F. L., *Soviet Politics at Home and Abroad,* Chapter VII, pp. 287-344; Timasheff, N. S., *The Great Retreat,* Chapter V, pp. 72-104; Harper, Samuel N., and Thompson, Ronald, *The Government of the Soviet Union,* 2nd edition, 1949; Maynard, *op. cit.,* Chapter XXVI, pp. 496-514; Laserson, Max M., *Russia and the Western World,* Chapters II and III, pp. 58-114; Towster, Julian, *Political Power in the USSR,* especially Chapter XIV, pp. 375-411; Fainsod, Merle, *How Russia Is Ruled,* 1953. See also Kirichenko, M., "The First Soviet Constitution," *Izvestia,* July 10, 1958.

12

Soviet Foreign Policy from 1917 to 1941

EUROPE

THE KEY to an understanding of Soviet foreign policy from the Peace of Brest-Litovsk to the outbreak of World War II is that the Soviet Government acted through weakness rather than through strength and was primarily concerned with the defense of the USSR against foreign invasion. The real turning point in this respect came in August 1920, when the Soviet hordes were stopped at the gates of Warsaw. The Soviet Union emerged from the Civil War and foreign intervention weak and dismembered, badly in need of a long breathing spell to enable the new regime to establish order and to proceed with the industrialization and collectivization of the country. The main object of Soviet foreign policy was, therefore, the avoidance of war. Throughout the entire period Soviet leaders displayed an almost pathological fear and distrust of the outside world. Until the rise of Hitler, the chief objects of their distrust were France and Britain in Europe, and Japan in the Far East. After 1932 their uneasiness was focussed mainly upon Germany and Japan. At no time during the interlude between 1917 and 1939 were Soviet leaders in a position to carry out, nor did they contemplate, aggressive military action against the outside world. Their aggressive moves were confined to propaganda. The transition from a defensive to an aggressive and imperialistic Soviet foreign policy came with the Nazi-Soviet Pact of August 23, 1939. This pact not only unleashed the forces of Hitlerite aggression against the West, but by scrapping the status quo in Eastern Europe, it paved the way for continued Soviet expansion, which was soon to constitute a major threat to world security.

Since 1917 Soviet foreign policy has passed through many phases. During the first period, from 1917 to 1928, the USSR stood for world

Courtesy Sovfoto

SESSION OF THE SUPREME SOVIET OF THE USSR

Joint meeting of the Soviet of the Union and the Soviet of Nationalities in the Large Kremlin Palace on June 13, 1950.

revolution, using the Third International as its agent. The persistent refusal of the Soviet leaders to recognize debts incurred by the tsarist and Kerensky regimes, unless they secured compensation for the damage done by foreign interventionists, was a further cause for the continued estrangement between Russia and the West. The United States, in particular, according to President Coolidge, did not propose to enter into relations with a regime "which refuses to recognize the sanctity of international obligations." Excluded from the League of Nations, it was logical that the two international outcasts, Germany and the Soviet Union, should reach an understanding to their mutual advantage at the Rapallo Conference in 1922. This understanding provides the key to Soviet foreign policy for almost a decade until the rise of Hitler. As an outgrowth of it Germany was able, to a limited extent, to obviate the disarmament provisions of the Treaty of Versailles, and the Russians secured German technical aid in industrial and military organization. The substance of the Rapallo Treaty was reaffirmed in the Soviet-German nonaggression and neutrality pact of April 24, 1926. Between 1920 and 1925, in spite of world-wide opposition to the spread of revolutionary doctrines by the Comintern, the Soviet Union secured recognition from most of its neighbors and from all the major powers with the exception of the United States.[1]

---

[1] Recognition was secured as follows: In 1920, from Esthonia, Lithuania, Latvia and Finland; in 1921, from Poland, Iran, Afghanistan, Turkey and Outer Mongolia; in 1922, from Germany; in 1923, from Italy; in 1924, from England, Norway, Austria, Greece, Sweden, China, Denmark, Albania, Mexico, Hungary, and France; in 1925, from Japan.

During the second period, from 1928 to 1934, there was a marked shift in Soviet foreign policy from its former emphasis on world revolution to a nationalist orientation. The reasons for this change are fairly obvious. Trotsky, the chief exponent of internationalism and world revolution, was expelled from the Union in 1927 and replaced by Stalin, the nationalist. With the inauguration of the First Five-Year Plan (1928-1932), Stalin focused his efforts upon a program of building socialism in one country—the USSR. To do this successfully, the Soviet Union needed peace and security. One of the cardinal features of Soviet foreign policy during this period was, therefore, the conclusion of a series of nonaggression and neutrality pacts with neighboring states. While these bilateral agreements met Soviet needs for the time being, they were equally advantageous to Russia's weak and insecure neighbors.

Such pacts had already been arranged with Turkey in December 1925, with Germany, Lithuania, and Afghanistan in 1926, and with Iran in 1927. In 1932 similar treaties were signed with Finland, Latvia, Esthonia, Poland, and France. In December 1931, and again in November 1932, the USSR offered to conclude a nonaggression pact with Japan, but these proposals were rejected. Even as late as 1933, the Soviet-German Pact of 1926 was renewed, and Italy joined the impressive list of states which had reached nonaggression agreements with the USSR. The USSR was likewise the first power to ratify the Kellogg-Briand Pact of 1928, thereby renouncing war as an instrument of national policy and agreeing to settle all disputes by peaceful means. It seemed apparent that the Russians had reached a *modus vivendi* with the capitalist world.

During this second period, the USSR also sought and obtained recognition from the United States, with the object not only to secure moral support but also more machinery and technical assistance for the successful completion of the Soviet program of heavy industry. Franklin D. Roosevelt, prior to his election as president in 1932, had intimated a willingness to abandon the policy of nonrecognition. The effects of the depression on United States foreign trade and the Japanese occupation of Manchuria in 1931 were largely responsible for the change in American policy. That our recognition of the Soviet Union on November 16, 1933, was of mutual advantage to both countries concerned is suggested by the fact that it sufficed to postpone Japanese preparations for aggression against Asiatic Russia, at a time when the USSR was ill prepared to resist and when the United States was highly desirous of "containing" further Japanese expansion. Joseph C. Grew, American ambassa-

dor in Japan, appraised the results of United States recognition of the
USSR as follows:

> . . . American recognition of Soviet Russia has injected an important
> psychological element into the situation and gives pause to those in authority
> in Japan, for regardless of the pacific policy of the United States, American
> action in the event of a Japanese-Soviet conflict would be to the Japanese
> an unknown and disturbing factor, necessarily to be taken into considera-
> tion. Military plans may be regarded as infallible; but the attitude and
> possible action of the United States constitute the element of uncertainty
> and therefore an unknown hazard. American recognition has increased
> self-confidence in Moscow, but no one believes that the Soviet Union will
> commence hostilities. I therefore believe that our recognition of the Soviet
> Union has injected into the situation a restraining influence, probably of
> greater effect than any other single integral.[1]

Although recognition, in the words of Roosevelt, "strengthened
the structure of peace" in the Far East, it failed to establish mutual confidence between the United States and the USSR. William C. Bullitt,
the first American ambassador to the Soviet Union, failed to secure the
expected agreement on the troublesome debt issue, because the Russians
made any such settlement conditional upon the receipt of loans for the
purchase of United States supplies. American businessmen, who hoped
that recognition would result in Soviet purchase of tens or even hundreds of millions of dollars worth of American goods, were soon disillusioned. The Johnson Act, which forbade loans to foreign governments that had defaulted on previous obligations, was interpreted to
apply to the Kerensky debts, with the result that the necessary loans to
promote large-scale commercial intercourse between the two countries
were not forthcoming and a deadlock resulted. A trade treaty was
signed, however, in July 1935, by which the USSR agreed to make pur-
chases amounting to $30,000,000 within the course of the next twelve
months. The convening of the Seventh, and incidentally the last, Congress of the Third International in Moscow in the summer of the same
year nevertheless aroused much antagonism in the United States, where
it was interpreted as a breach of the terms of recognition. The purges
contributed still further to the estrangement of American sentiment
toward Russia.

During the third period, from 1934 to 1938, Soviet foreign policy
was based upon collective security within the framework of the League
of Nations. During these years, the USSR was threatened by the rise

---

[1] Grew, Joseph C., *Ten Years in Japan*, N. Y., 1944, pp. 119-120.

of Hitler to power in the West and by Japanese expansion in the Far East. Largely because of the efforts of France, the USSR joined the League of Nations on September 18, 1934, having received a permanent seat on the League Council. Soviet entry into the League, which followed the withdrawal of Germany, indicated a fundamental change in attitude toward that organization, which Soviet leaders originally regarded with suspicion as an "imperialist instrument of capitalist states," likely to resort to collective action against the USSR. As the Soviet Union resumed normal diplomatic relations with other countries and the Comintern receded more and more into the background as an agent of Soviet foreign policy, the USSR had taken part in sundry League activities of an economic and humanitarian nature, as well as in the Preparatory Commission on Disarmament. Having finally, in the quest for security, agreed to enter the League, the Soviet Union became one of the staunchest supporters of Articles X and XVI of the Covenant. In spite of the vote in the League Assembly of thirty-eight to three in favor of Soviet entry, the general attitude of the powers toward the USSR was clearly demonstrated when Maxim Litvinov, the Soviet representative on the League Council, was appointed chairman of the unimportant Committee on Seaweeds.[1] Litvinov's subsequent speeches before the League, in which he criticized the ineffectiveness of that organization in achieving disarmament and preventing aggression, proved highly disconcerting to some of his Geneva colleagues. Membership in the League, in other words, did not result in effective collaboration between the USSR and the West.

Soviet membership in the League proved to be the prelude to a defensive alliance between the USSR and France, ratified on May 2, 1935, and a pact with Czechoslovakia (May 16, 1935), which guaranteed Soviet military aid to the Czechs if and when France fulfilled her pledge to come to the assistance of Czechoslovakia. For the second time in less than fifty years the threat of German aggression in Europe had led to the establishment of a Franco-Soviet alliance, this time reinforced by alliances with Czechoslovakia, in order to forestall German expansion at their expense. The preservation of this alliance, as events were soon to prove, was the principal basis for an effective bulwark against Nazi aggression. But just as all efforts in the direction of collective security foundered on the shoals of Munich, so the Soviet-French alliance and the Czech Pact were likewise virtually to be annulled by the same Munich pact of 1938.

---

[1] See Pope, Arthur Upham, *Maxim Litvinoff*, p. 349.

From 1935 to 1938 Hitler and his associates worked incessantly to break the Franco-Russian-Czech alliance, which barred the way to German expansion. Unable to effect this alone, the Germans achieved their objective with the apparently tacit support of the Chamberlain Government of Great Britain. During the Munich crisis of September 1938, which resulted in the partition of Czechoslovakia, the Soviet Union, despite its alliances with both France and the Czechs, was deliberately excluded from all participation in the conferences. "Events," according to Winston Churchill, "took their course as if Soviet Russia did not exist." [1] Former President Beneš of Czechoslovakia later affirmed that the Russians not only announced their readiness to live up to the terms of their alliance but even offered to support the Czechs in the event of German invasion, regardless of the action taken by France. But Soviet protestations were of no avail. The exclusion of the USSR from the Munich discussions constituted a complete negation of the Franco-Soviet alliance and therefore the attainment of Hitler's long-sought objective. In brief, the Czechoslovak crisis of 1938 was in the nature of a colorful façade which obscured the real issue—the scrapping of the Franco-Russian-Czechoslovak system of alliances as the only serious obstacle to German expansion.

From September 1938, to August 23, 1939, the Soviet Union made a final bid for collective security against Nazi Germany. Immediately following the German occupation of Prague in March 1939, Litvinov called for an international conference of all nations opposed to aggression, but the proposal was rejected as "premature." In April, however, mainly at French insistence, Anglo-French representatives went to Moscow, ostensibly to negotiate an agreement to stop Hitler. Unfortunately the Chamberlain Government rejected the offer of Anthony Eden to represent England in the Moscow negotiations and selected in his stead William Strang, a Foreign Office official of no special standing, thereby seriously offending the Russians. The replacement of Litvinov by Vyatcheslav Molotov as foreign commissar on May 3, 1939, provided fair warning to the Western powers of a forthcoming change in Soviet policy, since Litvinov had been closely associated with all Soviet efforts toward collaboration with the West, whereas Molotov was at that time by no means a specialist in matters of foreign policy. The Germans were not slow to take advantage of the situation. Following a hint from Molo-

---

[1] See Churchill, Winston, *The Second World War*, Vol. I, *The Gathering Storm*, p. 305, as well as Chapters 16 and 17, with reference to the British role at this time, and his own efforts to secure the collaboration of England, France, *and Russia* against Hitler.

tov on May 20, the German Foreign Office decided within the next ten days "to undertake definite negotiations" with the Soviet Union.[1] Thus the USSR proceeded, at one and the same time, to carry on negotiations with Germany, on the one hand, and with France and England on the other.

Soviet leaders, with the Munich background in mind, doubted the sincerity of the Anglo-French governments in their dealings with the USSR. The undue procrastination and hesitation of the two Western democracies, together with the revelation in London in both Parliament and press of an English scheme to advance a loan of £1,000,000,000 to Nazi Germany,[2] induced the Russians to take direct action in the interests of their own immediate security. In August 1942, Stalin explained the Soviet position to Churchill, during the latter's visit to the Kremlin, as follows:

We formed the impression that the British and French Governments were not resolved to go to war if Poland were attacked, but that they hoped the diplomatic line-up of Britain, France and Russia would deter Hitler. We were sure it would not.

The Russians had learned that in the event of war with Germany the French were prepared to put approximately one hundred divisions on the Western Front, the English only two at the outset and two later, whereas the Red army, according to Stalin, would have to provide more than three hundred divisions for the Eastern Front.[3]

The forthright tactics of the Germans during these critical weeks, their manifest willingness to recognize Russian interests in the region from the Baltic to the Black Sea, and their readiness to send German Foreign Minister Ribbentrop to Moscow to conclude negotiations, made a profound impression on Soviet leaders, especially as compared with the half-hearted efforts of England and France regarding either a political or a military understanding. A Soviet-German trade agreement was concluded on August 19, by which the Russians obtained substantial credits for the purchase of German goods in return for the allocation of certain raw materials to Germany. This commercial agreement proved to be the prelude to a political understanding.

---

[1] Sontag, R. J., and Beddie, J. S. (Editors), *Nazi-Soviet Relations, 1939-1941*, N. Y., 1948, pp. 6, 15.

[2] See especially *The New York Times*, July 21-25, 1939; Dallin, David J., *Soviet Russia's Foreign Policy, 1939-1942* (Yale University Press, 1942), pp. 47-48; Schuman, Frederick L., *Night Over Europe* (Knopf, 1941), p. 204.

[3] Churchill, Winston, *op. cit.*, Vol. I, p. 525.

Laurence Steinhardt, American ambassador in Moscow, who ever since July had foreseen a possible change in Soviet foreign policy, repeatedly warned Washington of an impending Soviet-German agreement.

Following the previous example of England (September 30, 1938) and France (December 6, 1938), the USSR, to the consternation and dismay of the Western democracies, entered into a nonaggression pact with Nazi Germany on August 23, 1939. Contrary to popular opinion, this was not an alliance but a nonaggression pact, basically similar in scope to those already concluded by Britain and France with Germany, which were hailed as "bringing peace in our time."

Documents uncovered in the German Foreign Office and released by the State Department of the United States include a "Secret Protocol" to the above-mentioned nonaggression pact,[1] which defined the respective spheres of influence of Germany and the Soviet Union in the event of any territorial and political readjustment in Eastern Europe. In such an event, the Protocol specified that Lithuania would fall within the German orbit, and the other Baltic States within the Soviet sphere. The Protocol included no specific arrangement with respect to the future of Poland, since that could only be "definitely determined in the course of further political developments," but the Soviet and German spheres were said to be "bounded approximately by the line of the rivers Narew, Vistula, and San." In Southeastern Europe Germany recognized Soviet interest in Bessarabia. Such a definition of spheres of influence did not differ materially from the arrangement reached by the Anglo-Russian *Entente* of 1907 with respect to the Middle East.

By their appeasement of Hitler at Munich, so the Soviets seem to have reasoned, the British and French governments had hoped to deflect Hitlerite aggression, if they could not prevent it entirely, to the East against the USSR and thereby save themselves. The Soviet-German nonaggression pact was regarded as forestalling any such program. When, following the conclusion of this pact, Hitler promptly invaded Poland (September 1, 1939), thereby forcing England and France reluctantly into war, the Western democracies accused the USSR of double-crossing them by giving the Nazis "the green light" in the West. There seems to be no definite proof, however, that either Hitler or Stalin expected England and France to rush to the aid of Poland any more than they had gone to the rescue of Czechoslovakia. From the standpoint of Soviet strategy, it gave the Russians a breathing spell

---

[1] Sontag, R. J., and Beddie, J. S., *op. cit.*, p. 78.

of almost two years in which to prepare for the coming conflict, and it prevented any immediate Nazi invasion of the USSR, under conditions which would have permitted England and France to remain passive onlookers.

Irrespective of the motives of the Stalin Government, whether they were designed to forestall an Anglo-French deal with Nazi Germany

Courtesy Sovfoto

SIGNING OF SOVIET-GERMAN AGREEMENT
(August 23, 1939)

Molotov, Soviet Commissar for Foreign Affairs and Chairman of the Council of People's Commissars, signing the non-agression pact between the Soviet Union and Germany.

In the group (l. to r.) are J. Von Ribbentrop, under-secretary of State Gauss, Josef Stalin, Legation attaché Hilger, Molotov, and Count Von der Schulenberg, German ambassador to the USSR

which would have given Hitler a green light in the East, or whether they were the product of a diabolical intent to release the forces of Nazism against the West while the USSR stood aloof, waiting for an opportunity to profit from the holocaust—the fact remains that the Nazi-Soviet Pact scrapped the containment policy that held Nazi

Germany within bounds and thereby provided the immediate cause for the outbreak of World War II. It likewise launched the Soviet Union on a policy of aggressive imperialism that was to affect the destinies, first of Eastern Europe and later of Eastern Asia for years to come.

From the invasion of Poland on September 1, 1939, to the Nazi invasion of the USSR on June 22, 1941, Soviet foreign policy pursued an independent course. Allegations to the effect that with the signing of the Soviet-German nonaggression pact Stalin became the tool of Hitler are not substantiated by events. Hitler's tool could never have occupied Bessarabia and Northern Bukovina, half of Poland and the Baltic states of Esthonia, Latvia, and Lithuania, not to mention advanced bases in Finland—all at Hitler's expense. With the conclusion of the Soviet-German agreement of August 23, 1939, and the outbreak of war thereafter, Hitler was, for the time being, at least, helpless to prevent the Soviet advance. The Germans, in view of the Allied blockade, became more dependent on Russian imports. There were repeated wrangles over the new German-Soviet boundary, and the Soviet Union made importunate demands upon the Germans for machine tools for the manufacture of munitions.

Under the telling blows of the Nazi *Blitzkreig* the Polish state was virtually destroyed and her government was obliged to flee the country, all within about two weeks' time and without any immediate assistance, beyond a formal declaration of war, from Poland's Western Allies. Then on September 17, after repeated prodding from Ribbentrop,[1] the Soviet army itself crossed the Polish borders and occupied Eastern and Southern Poland. On September 29, in Moscow, the Soviet and Nazi governments reached a tentative border agreement,[2] based mainly on the Curzon Line,[3] although this was modified later in favor of the Germans. Their prolonged delay in reaching such an agreement seems to afford further evidence that no explicit prior arrangement for a common Soviet-German boundary in Poland had been reached when the Stalin-Hitler nonaggression pact was signed in August. On November 1, following elections on the Soviet pattern, the Ukrainian and

---

[1] *Ibid.*, pp. 86-96. Ribbentrop began to call for the movement of Soviet troops into Poland as early as September 3.

[2] *Ibid.*, pp. 105-107. At this time Lithuania was transferred from the German to the Soviet sphere, in return for the Polish Province of Lublin and parts of the Province of Warsaw, which fell to the Germans.

[3] Ethnographical boundary line dividing Poles from Russians (and roughly following the Bug river) drawn up by the Allied Supreme Council, December 8, 1919, and formally recommended to the Poles by Lord Curzon, British Foreign Secretary.

Byelorussian areas of Soviet-occupied Poland were incorporated into the Ukrainian and Byelorussian Republics.

The Soviet occupation of Eastern Poland effectively blocked German access to the Rumanian border, to the Soviet Ukraine, and in general to the Near East, at a time when Franco-British defenses in the last-mentioned area were practically nonexistent. As a result of Soviet action, it was a full year before German troops were in a position to reach Rumania via another route—that of Hungary. Although the USSR was bitterly attacked abroad for its occupation of Eastern Poland, both Lloyd George and Winston Churchill of Great Britain acknowledged the strategic necessity of the Soviet move from the standpoint of Soviet defense against the Nazi menace.

Immediately after the collapse of Poland, the USSR took steps to improve its strategic position against Germany by expansion in the Baltic region. The Baltic states of Esthonia, Latvia, and Lithuania, which had fallen under German influence after the rise of Hitler, were now forced to become Soviet protectorates. The USSR signed mutual assistance pacts with Esthonia (September 28), Latvia (October 5), and Lithuania (October 10), whereby Soviet military control was extended to the Baltic, and the Soviet right to maintain strategic bases there was recognized. In August 1940, the three Baltic states were incorporated into the USSR as Union Republics. Although recognition of their independence was refused by the United States from 1917 to 1922, on the ground that these Baltic States rightfully belonged to Russia, neither the United States nor Great Britain recognized their incorporation into the Soviet Union in 1940.

Soviet pressure on Finland to improve the strategic position of the USSR in the Gulf of Finland on the Leningrad front, which was within artillery range of the Finnish border, and along the Baltic-White Sea Canal, did not produce similar results. Although Soviet security undoubtedly required some modification of the Finnish border, especially in view of previous collaboration between the Germans and the Finns in 1918, the blunders of Soviet diplomats and the stubborn refusal of the Finnish government to compromise in time led to a short but bitter conflict which began on November 30, 1939, and lasted until March 12, 1940. The Soviet-Finnish War greatly increased the antagonism of the Western powers, especially Britain, France, and the United States, against the USSR, led to the abrupt expulsion of the Soviet Union from the League of Nations (December 14, 1939) and from the International Labor Organization (February 5, 1940). It very nearly precipitated another war between Britain and France on the one hand and the USSR on the other.[1] France undertook military preparations aimed at an invasion of the Soviet Union via Turkey and the Caucasus—a move designed in part to halt the export of Soviet oil to Germany. In England plans were laid for the dispatch of an expeditionary force of six divisions via Sweden to Finland. Had Sweden not refused the right of transit and the Finnish War not been abruptly concluded in March 1940, there might even have been an Anglo-French attack on the USSR, which would in all probability have resulted in an outright Soviet-German alliance against the West.

Initial Soviet reverses in the war against Finland, due largely to the failure of the Soviet Government to anticipate Finnish resistance, blinded the Western powers to the actual military strength of the Soviet Union and led them to overlook the significance of the sudden collapse of the supposedly impregnable Mannerheim Line under the Red army offensive of February-March 1940. The terms imposed upon Finland in March 1940 were more severe than those offered by the Soviet Union prior to hostilities. The USSR acquired the Karelian Isthmus, including Viborg and the adjacent islands in the Gulf of Finland, a lease of the strategic Hango Peninsula, the northern and western shores of Lake Ladoga, a strip of territory in the Arctic along the watershed of the Kemi River to provide greater security for the Murmansk Railroad, and a part of the Petsamo Peninsula, although the port of Petsamo was returned to the Finns. The Karelo-Finnish Republic of the USSR was established in July 1940.

On the very eve of the Nazi absorption of Rumania, following hard upon the heels of the collapse of France in June 1940, the Soviet Union demanded from Rumania the return of Bessarabia and the cession of Northern Bukovina, with its Ukrainian population. In spite of manifest German displeasure at this "surprise" move, Soviet occupation of these areas began on June 28, just prior to the harvest of the sugar-beet crop and was rapidly completed. In August 1940 Northern Bukovina and Southern Bessarabia were incorporated into the Ukrainian Republic, while the rest of Bessarabia became the thirteenth, or Moldavian, Republic of the USSR.

Thus, from August 1939 to June 1941, while Germany was deeply involved in Poland and in Western Europe, the Soviet Union materially improved its strategic position by the reincorporation of territory, almost all of which had previously belonged to tsarist Russia. The

---

[1]See Dallin, *op. cit.*, pp. 167-168; Schuman, *op. cit.*, p. 389; Coates, W. P., and Zelda, K., *A History of Anglo-Soviet Relations*, pp. 628-636.

number of Union Republics was thereby increased from eleven to sixteen. The USSR likewise increased its population to approximately 193,000,000.

It seems apparent that for a time German-Soviet collaboration redounded to the advantage of both powers. Russian supplies were regarded by the German government as "a very substantial prop to the German war economy." A German Foreign Office Memorandum of September 28, 1940,[1] indicates that since the new commercial arrangements had gone into effect Russia had supplied Germany with "over 300 million Reichsmarks worth of raw materials, roughly 100 million Reichsmarks of which was grain." Such commercial contacts as Germany was able to maintain with Iran, Afghanistan, Manchukuo, Japan, and even South America depended on the route across the Soviet Union. The Russians, on their part, were able to readjust their strategic frontiers on the Baltic and Black Seas, and to obtain important machine tools and equipment from Germany, although the disproportion between German and Russian deliveries by September 28, 1940, is apparent from the German admission that only 150,000,000 Reichsmarks worth of German goods had been sent to the USSR. The war made it increasingly difficult for Germany to furnish the type of equipment the Russians demanded.

Soviet-German relations began to deteriorate when the spectacular German victory in the West, especially the collapse of France in June 1940, made the Germans more arrogant. Friction between the two countries arose out of the reinterpretation by each of the delimitation of their respective spheres in Eastern Europe. With the Soviet absorption of the Baltic states and Bessarabia, Germany had lost important sources of raw materials. There was friction over the establishment of the German-Lithuanian boundary. Russian suspicions were aroused by unilateral German intervention in the Balkans, especially in regard to the Rumanian cession of Transylvania to Hungary and Germany's guarantee of the rest of Rumania. During his visit to Berlin in November 1940, Molotov made an issue of the passage of German troops through Finland to Norway, since Finland was within the Soviet sphere. Although ostensibly Molotov's visit to Berlin was intended to broaden Soviet-German collaboration and link Moscow more effectively with the Rome-Berlin-Tokyo Axis, Soviet insistence on the withdrawal of German troops from Finland, on a Soviet guarantee of Bulgaria, and upon the need for a Soviet base at the Dardanelles proved an insuper-

---

[1] Sontag, R. J., and Beddie, J. S., *op. cit.,* pp. 199-201.

WAR IN WINTER

Red Army men, garbed in white and supported by Soviet artillery, attack German fortifications. March 1942.

able obstacle to another deal. Relations had so deteriorated by December 1940 that the German *Wehrmacht* received instructions to "be prepared *to crush Soviet Russia in a quick campaign* even before the conclusion of the war against England." [1] Ribbentrop informed Japanese Foreign Minister Matsuoka during his visit to Berlin in March 1941 that relations between Germany and the USSR, while correct, were "not very friendly." He complained that for some time the Russians "had demonstrated their unfriendliness to Germany whenever they could," asserting that since the appointment of Sir Stafford Cripps as English ambassador to Moscow "ties between Russia and England were being cultivated in secret and, at times, relatively openly." Matsuoka was given to understand that "a conflict with Russia was always within the realm of possibility." The Yugoslav crisis in April 1941, immediately following the conclusion of a treaty of friendship and nonaggression between the USSR and Yugoslavia, contributed still further to the worsening of relations between the Soviet Union and Germany. As hostilities became imminent, both countries proceeded to concentrate troops along the common frontier.

In summing up Soviet foreign policy in Europe, we may safely conclude that during the years following the Revolution of 1917 Soviet leaders, still smarting from the Intervention (1918-1922), assumed that the USSR stood alone against the world, and that all foreign agreements were directed against her. Their reaction to the Washington Conference (1921-1922), to which the Soviets were not invited, was the Rapallo Agreement of 1922 with Germany and the Treaty of Friendship and Recognition with Japan in 1925. In response to the Locarno Agreement of 1925, the Russians made a series of nonaggression pacts with their neighbors. To offset the Anglo-French nonaggression pacts with Germany after Munich, the Russians entered into a similar arrangement of their own with the Nazis, followed by a five-year neutrality pact with Japan in the Pacific (1941). In other words, when the great powers isolated or ignored the Soviet Union, Soviet leaders took parallel action in the interests of Soviet security.

In retrospect, it can be said that whether it sought the collaboration of Britain and France, recognition by the United States, or signed nonaggression or neutrality agreements with Germany and Japan respectively, the Soviet Government was concerned first and always with the problem of making the USSR strategically strong and secure. As

[1] *Ibid.,* Directive No. 21 (Operation Barbarossa), pp. 260-264. Preparations were to be completed by May 15, 1941.

Stalin himself stated so clearly and vigorously on the eve of the Soviet reforms of 1935:

We never had any orientation toward Germany, nor have we any orientation toward Poland and France. Our orientation in the past and our orientation in the present is toward the USSR and toward the USSR alone.

ASIA

1. Far East

In the Far East, Soviet foreign policy followed the tsarist tradition to this extent—when Russia was threatened from both the East and the West, Russian interests in the East were subordinated to those in the West. Thus the Soviet Union subordinated its Far Eastern policy to the European and even made important concessions to the Japanese in the belief that the threat from the West (Hitler) was of greater consequence. After the Japanese entry into Manchuria in 1931, however, the Soviet Government made provision for the rapid colonization and industrialization of Siberia. This served the twofold purpose of deterring the Japanese from their designs against Siberia, and of providing an arsenal and training ground for the USSR in the conflict with Germany.

Since the Western powers, partly for ideological considerations, pursued the same policy in the Far East as in Europe of isolating and ignoring the Soviet Union, even on occasion encouraging China to do the same (1927), it was but natural that the Russians should find it expedient to take parallel action in the interests of Soviet security by coming to terms with Japan in Asia as they did with Germany in Europe. Japan, having emerged from World War I the strongest power in Eastern Asia, only to be thwarted in her designs of further aggrandizement by the Western powers, particularly by the United States, likewise found it advantageous to come to an understanding with the USSR. It is significant, however, that the initiative in the direction of better Soviet-Japanese relations ordinarily came from the Japanese rather than from the Russians.

After the Russo-Japanese War the Tsarist Government, as substantiated by the Russo-Japanese Treaties of 1907 and 1916, saw eye to eye with Japan regarding the partition of China. The Soviet regime, on the other hand, wanted a strong and friendly China and an alliance with America in the Pacific at the expense of Japan. Beginning with Lenin (Seventh Congress of Bolsheviks, 1918), Soviet leaders regarded Japan as the greatest Far Eastern threat not only to the USSR but to the world at large. In this connection, it is significant that one of the early Soviet writers, Karl Radek, as early as September 28, 1922, in an article in *Pravda,* argued in favor of an outright Soviet-American alliance in the Pacific. He also tried to convince Americans that it was to their interest to support the new nationalist movement in China, with the objective of creating a strong China to offset Japan.

By sending Michael Borodin and other Soviet experts to China in September 1924, Soviet leaders apparently did not intend to, nor did they believe that they could, execute there a revolution of the 1917 vintage. They did hope to achieve a revolution like that of 1905 in Russia. They therefore appealed to Chinese national pride in China's rich and ancient cultural heritage, and to the need for Chinese national unity and independence—a procedure which the Comintern did not adopt in any other country, not even in Soviet Russia at that time, for the Soviets ordinarily emphasized social and economic exploitation on a class basis to the exclusion of other factors.

The Soviet justification for interference in China was Soviet interest in creating a strong and friendly China to offset Japan in the Pacific, in the belief that, if the Russians did not establish their influence there, the Japanese would. In this respect, Soviet leaders were correct. In the Pacific, as in Europe, the Soviets were motivated by strategy rather than by economics.

Soviet-Chinese relations, however, were overshadowed by the rise of an aggressive Japan, particularly after 1931. Yet the Russians, even after the conflict between China and Japan began in 1937, supplied the Chinese with more than 60 percent of the aid they received from abroad, at a time when England and the United States, as if in doubt as to whether the creation of a strong China were to their own interest, sent scrap iron and oil to Japan. In view of the hostility and suspicion of the Western democracies toward the Soviet Union both in Europe and in Asia, Soviet spokesmen were quick to assume that the democracies sent aid to Japan because the USSR was helping China.

To understand Soviet-Japanese relations, it is necessary, by way of recapitulation, to turn back to the Russo-Japanese Treaty of 1907, which was supplemented by the two additional treaties of 1910 and 1912. These treaties were the first step in the direction of a Russo-Japanese alliance aimed at the Western powers, in particular against America. They indicated the reorientation of Russo-Japanese policy following the Russo-Japanese War, 1904-1905.

In spite of their recent triumph over Russia the Japanese, dissatisfied with the attitude of the Western powers toward the emergence of a strong Japan, took the initiative in an effort to appease the tsarist regime. The Russian government, in spite of Theodore Roosevelt's efforts at Portsmouth to ameliorate the peace terms demanded by Japan, resented Western sympathy for the Japanese and what they regarded as Western efforts to foment revolution inside the tsarist realm during the conflict. The Russians believed that they lost the war chiefly because of internal revolution rather than because of Japanese military and naval superiority. After 1905 Japan and Russia therefore were brought together by their distrust of the Western democracies.

The next step was taken in 1916 when Japan, in bitter resentment over American protests against the Twenty-one Demands on China (1915), took the initiative to secure from tsarist Russia a secret treaty aimed against any "third power" which might seek to establish a protectorate over China. The "third power" was America. It is now obvious that Japan, far from content with the prospect of securing the former German colonies in the Pacific, was making elaborate preparations for further expansion in Asia with the tacit consent of the tsarist regime, which expected to share the spoils. The Revolution of 1917, however, thwarted Japanese designs and forced them to postpone their program indefinitely, although they did not yield without a struggle.

When the Japanese occupied Eastern Siberia (1918-1922) during the Allied Intervention in Russia, they were able to convince many Russians that their purpose was to restore the tsarist regime and to revive the Treaty of 1916. As late as 1919 Vladimir Purishkevitch, a former monarchist deputy of the Duma and one of the chief propagandists of the Koltchak-Denikin regime, openly advocated the establishment of a kind of *"Dreikaiserbund,"* including Germany, Russia, and Japan, as the best guarantee for the maintenance of world peace, and as a bulwark against democracy and communism.

When the Washington Conference (1921-1922), from which Soviet Russia was excluded, also aroused the bitter resentment of Japan by denying her naval equality with Britain and the United States and forcing her to withdraw from Siberia, the way was paved for a Soviet-Japanese *rapprochement*. The Treaty of Friendship and Recognition between the USSR and Japan in 1925 was reminiscent, in some respects, of the treaty between tsarist Russia and Japan in 1916. This agreement not only guaranteed the "neutrality" of the USSR in the event of a conflict between Japan and a third power but also promised delivery of oil to the Japanese fleet during such a conflict. The Soviet Union again was taking parallel action.

Three years later, in 1928, after the Nanking Government had broken off diplomatic relations with the USSR (1927), ostensibly because of Comintern activity but undoubtedly with Anglo-American support, the Russians proceeded to renew their 1907 Fisheries' Agreement with Japan. The fisheries agreement, which expired in 1936, was renewed annually thereafter, with progressive modifications in favor of the Soviet Union. On March 30, 1944, when the agreement was renewed for a period of five years, the Japanese, in addition to the surrender of twenty-four fishing lanes of strategic importance to the USSR, likewise agreed to the termination of Japanese coal and oil concessions in Northern Sakhalin, which had been granted to Japan in 1925 for a forty-five year term and which still had twenty-six years to run.

In May 1933 the Soviet Union agreed to sell the Chinese Eastern Railway, long a bone of contention between Tokyo and Moscow, to Japan. Ever since the Japanese occupation of Manchuria the Russians had met with obstacle after obstacle in their operation of the railroad, culminating in a complete impasse in 1933. After almost two years of negotiations an agreement was finally signed on March 23, 1935, whereby the Japanese were to pay the USSR 140,000,000 yen, plus approximately another 30,000,000 yen in pensions to Soviet railroad personnel. There seems little doubt that the Soviet Government, in disposing of the Chinese Eastern Railroad, which had been operated jointly by the USSR and China since 1924, was intent upon removing one more threat to peace with Japan in the Far East, the better to cope with the growing menace of the European situation. It was on March 16, 1935, that Hitler denounced the military clauses of the Versailles Treaty. This was followed in May of the same year by the conclusion of the Franco-Soviet alliance.

The designs of Japanese nationalists and militarists on Siberia, so nearly realized in the period of foreign intervention, were never laid to rest. Soviet leaders believed that Japan's incursion into Manchuria was directed as much against the USSR as against China. Their assumption has been corroborated by evidence produced at the War Crimes Tribunal in Tokyo.[1] As Japanese Ambassador Oshima informed Ribbentrop on April 18, 1943:

One thing that is incontestable is that for twenty years all the plans of the General Staff have been developed with a view to an offensive against Russia. . . .

---

[1] See "The Tokyo Trial of the Chief Japanese War Criminals," *Soviet Press Translations,* Vol. III, No. 7, April 1, 1948, pp. 195-202. Far Eastern Institute, University of Washington.

Manchuria was to be the Japanese base of operations for the invasion of Siberia. The Japanese constructed strategic rail and motor roads in Manchukuo—most of which led to the borders of the USSR. By 1941 they had 287 airfields and landing strips in Manchukuo and 53 in Korea. Disclosures at the War Crimes Trial indicate that a secret agreement attached to the Anti-Comintern Pact, signed by Germany and Japan in 1936, and by Italy in 1937, envisaged joint measures against the USSR. The Three-Power Pact of September 27, 1940, according to the *Memoirs* of Prince Konoye, the Japanese prime minister, transformed the tripartite agreement of 1936 into a military alliance directed against the Soviet Union. In reality, however, it encouraged the Japanese to pursue an expansionist policy in the South and, as events were soon to indicate, it by no means impelled them to join the other signatories in a conflict against the USSR.

The USSR, as already indicated, took appropriate action to counteract Japanese designs on the Soviet Far East by speeding up the industrialization, colonization, and defense of Siberia, and by furnishing aid to China. In March 1936 the Soviet Union and its puppet, the Mongol People's Republic, concluded a mutual aid agreement. This was followed by a treaty of nonaggression between the USSR and the Republic of China in August 1937. By the time the Japanese, emboldened by their initial successes in China, attacked the Red army in force at Changkufeng (Khasan) at the juncture of the borders of the USSR and Korea in 1938, with a view to the possible encirclement of Vladivostok, and again at Nomanhan on the Mongolian frontier, the back door to the USSR, from May to September 1939, the Soviet forces were ready for them and inflicted a decisive defeat upon the Japanese in each engagement. Having incurred 42,000 casualties, including some 20,000 killed at Nomanhan, the Japanese abandoned any intentions they may have had of immediate aggression against the Soviet Union. Moreover, the exposed position of the Dutch East Indies following German occupation of the Netherlands, and the fall of France in June 1940, deflected Japanese ambitions clearly and unmistakably to Southeast Asia.

The Soviet-German pact of August 23, 1939, profoundly shocked the Japanese. They soon made an opportunity, however, in conjunction with Foreign Minister Matsuoka's trip to Berlin, to follow the German example and concluded a five-year neutrality pact with Soviet Russia on April 13, 1941. There is some evidence to the effect that during the existence of the Soviet-German nonaggression pact Germany, in her own interest, encouraged Japan to normalize her relations with the USSR and to expand southward in the direction of Singapore, thereby bringing England to her knees. Ribbentrop was still pursuing this objective during Foreign Minister Matsuoka's visit to Berlin in March 1941. Even in the event of a Soviet-German conflict Ribbentrop advised Matsuoka that "Japan would best help the common cause if she did not allow herself to be diverted by anything from the attack on Singapore." [1] Unlike the Western democracies, the Japanese did not anticipate a successful Nazi *Blitzkrieg* against the USSR, following the German invasion of Soviet Russia on June 22, 1941. Japan had already discovered the strength of the Red Army in the Far East.

Just as the Soviet-German nonaggression pact deflected temporarily Nazi aggression from the USSR toward the Western democracies, so the Soviet-Japanese neutrality pact of 1941 served to deflect Japanese aggression from the direction of Siberia to the possessions of the Western democracies in the South Pacific. However, just as Hitler did not dare to move against the Soviet Union until he had subdued the rest of the continent of Europe, Japan did not risk moving south until the Nazis had invaded the Soviet Union and the fall of Moscow seemed imminent.

Actually, so far as the USSR and Japan were concerned, each was relieved to find the other involved in a life-and-death conflict. Neither country showed any disposition to break the neutrality pact of 1941 until the USSR, in compliance with the Yalta and Potsdam agreements, invaded Manchuria in 1945.

2. Near and Middle East

Realizing that they did not have the wholehearted support of the Russian population, especially of the Slavic element, nor tangible backing from the European proletariat, the Bolsheviks turned to the East, in particular to the Muslim East inside and outside the Russian borders. Although ostensibly anticipating a revolution in the West, they turned their heavy propaganda artillery toward the East, where they expected more tangible results. In spite of the fact that many European workers sympathized with the Bolshevik Revolution, they were not ready to submit themselves to Russian leadership. In the Orient, however, especially in the Middle East, the Bolsheviks sensed their opportunity to assume command. It was logical enough for them to appeal to the largest of the Russian minorities, the Muslims, who constituted about 10 or 12 per cent of the population, and through them

---

[1] Sontag, R. J., and Beddie, J. S., *op. cit.*, p. 309.

to the Muslims of the world. Within a month of their seizure of power, on December 5 (November 22 O.S.), 1917, the Council of People's Commissars of the Bolshevik regime issued an "Appeal to the Muslims of Russia and the East" [1] to rally to the support of the Revolution and to cast off the yolk of imperialism.

A careful analysis of the "Appeal to the Muslims," and of other literature pertaining to the period, suggests that the Soviet Government believed the success of the Bolshevik Revolution to be contingent upon its alliance with the Muslim Orient. In other words, the success of the October Revolution and the liberation of the Muslim World were regarded as inseparable and interdependent. This position was substantiated by a resolution of the Seventh All-Russian Congress of Soviets on December 5, 1919:

> In greeting the representatives of Soviet Turkestan and Soviet Bashkiria, the Seventh All-Russian Congress of Soviets of workers, peasants, Red Army soldiers and Cossack deputies regards their presence not only as proof that a feeling of solidarity with the toiling masses of the USSR has penetrated the Muslim toiling masses, but that the conviction has penetrated the Muslim East that the RSFSR, located as it is between capitalist Europe and the peoples of Asia enslaved by imperialism, is their stronghold in their struggle for liberation from national oppression.

The "Appeal" of the Council of People's Commissars likewise marked a turning point in the attitude of Muslims toward Russia. Bolshevik denunciation of Tsarist imperialism and renunciation of Tsarist claims on Constantinople and the Straits, as well as of all treaties that infringed on the sovereign rights of adjacent Muslim states, including Iran and Afghanistan, mitigated Muslim hatred of Russia, at least temporarily. In the minds of many Muslims, England superseded Russia as the symbol of oppression. Prior to World War I, England held sway over the largest area of Muslims. At the conclusion of that conflict, she extended appreciably her Muslim possessions, which stretched from Egypt to India. England, therefore, became the main target of Soviet propaganda. This propaganda took deep root among Muslims and other Asians.

In identifying the Bolshevik Revolution with Muslim liberation, Soviet leaders revised the traditional concept of the Eastern Question. To the average person under the Tsarist regime the Eastern Question

---

[1] For an English translation of this "Appeal," see Spector, Ivar, *The Soviet Union and the Muslim World, 1917-1958,* University of Washington Press, Seattle, 1959, pp. 33-35.

was synonymous with the partition of the Ottoman Empire, including the Russian threat to Constantinople, the Dardanelles, and the Bosphorus. The "Appeal to the Muslims" appeared to remove the threat of Russian expansion at the expense of Turkey and the Muslim World. Not only did the Soviet Government publicly renounce the secret agreements by which the Tsarist regime paved the way for further annexations, but it redefined the Eastern Question as one which involved Soviet aid for the liberation of enslaved peoples from the domination of "England, France, the United States, and other capitalist countries." Moscow was to become "the Mecca and Medina of all enslaved peoples." The Soviets, moreover, extended the scope of the Eastern Question to include the problems of oppressed colonial peoples in Africa and South America, as well as in Asia. According to Mikhail Pavlovitch, Soviet editor of *Novyi Vostok* (*The New Orient*), "a war against any of these countries of the Orient is a war against the USSR, just as a war against the USSR is a war against the Orient." In the Soviet interpretation of the significance of the October Revolution one can easily detect the signs of a new Soviet imperialism on a global scale, which was soon to constitute a threat, not only to the West but to the Orient itself.

Subsequent events prevented the Bolsheviks from taking effective measures to implement their "Appeal to the Muslims of Russia and the East" to join the revolutionary bandwagon. The German-dictated Treaty of Brest-Litovsk (March 3, 1918), which recognized the independence of the Ukraine, Poland, Finland, Esthonia, Latvia, Lithuania, and Georgia, and surrendered to Turkey the Transcaucasian provinces of Kars and Ardahan, including Batum, virtually dismembered Russia in Europe. Immediately thereafter, the Bolsheviks were placed strictly on the defensive by the intervention of Great Britain, France, and the United States, Ottoman Turkey, and Japan to stem the tide of revolution and to support the White Russian Armies engaged in Civil War with the Communists. The counterrevolutionary forces of Denikin and Kolchak, as well as those of the British and French invaders, made regular communication with the Muslim East for some time impossible.

By July 1920, the time seemed ripe for another attempt to rally the Muslims to the cause of the Revolution. Already the Soviet regime was confident of victory over the White Armies and foreign interventionists, and reasonably sure that the war-weary Russians were in no position to offer a serious challenge to Soviet authority. In Turkey, the "revolutionary core" of the East, the Nationalist forces of Kemal

Pasha were challenging the Entente powers. In neighboring Iran, a Soviet republic had been established in Gilan, and there was an uprising in Khorassan. Georgia, although its independence was recognized by a treaty signed with the Soviets on May 7, 1920, was still regarded as the "kept mistress of the Entente," and the Bolsheviks feared that the theatre of Entente military operations had been removed from Russia proper only to be re-established in Transcaucasia.

It was the Second Congress of the Third International, rather than the Soviet Government (Council of People's Commissars, RSFSR), which seized the initiative in July 1920, by summoning the First Congress of the Peoples of the East at Baku on September 1. The Comintern determined, first, to instigate strikes, riots, and subversion in Europe and America, especially in those countries that led the foreign intervention, in order to discourage any repetition of the invasion of Russia. Second, it planned to attack the colonial periphery, "the Achilles' heel of imperialism," to deprive the Entente of its sources of raw materials and fuel. The summons to Baku, therefore, was a summons to the Muslim World to organize a counterattack against the foreign invaders of Russia, in order to expel them from the lands adjacent to the Soviet republics, including Turkey, Iran, Armenia, and Mesopotamia. The Comintern's invitation was more aggressive in tone than the "Appeal" by the Council of People's Commissars in 1917. Its main purpose was to create the machinery needed to implement the Sovietization of the Muslim World. It summoned the "faithful" Muslim proletariat (workers and peasants), in order to bring about a Jihad, or Holy War, against the colonial powers, especially England.[1]

It was no accident that Baku was chosen as the site for the First Congress of the Peoples of the East. For years the Baku oilfields had served as a magnet to Persian, Turkish, and Tatar migrant workers. With its motley proletariat, the city was a focal point for the dissemination of socialist revolutionary propaganda directed against Tsarist Russia. It was geographically accessible to the Muslim peoples of Soviet Russia, as well as to the Persians, Turks, and Arabs to the south. A conference at this strategic location could serve to consolidate Soviet power among the Soviet Muslim minorities, much of whose territory had been occupied without considerable difficulty by the English, French, and Turks during the period of foreign intervention. Wide-

---

[1] For a complete English translation of the Comintern's invitation to the peoples of the East to come to the Baku Congress, published in *Izvestia*, July 3, 1920, see Spector, Ivar, *The Soviet Union and the Muslim World, 1917-1958*, pp. 48-52.

spread disaffection among anti-Soviet forces in the area still constituted a threat. In the city of Baku itself, Communist power had been re-established as recently as April 1920. Even while the Congress was in session, a serious revolt erupted in Daghestan.

According to the Bolshevik record, 1891 delegates answered the summons of the Comintern. Of these, 1273 were said to be Communists, 266 non-Party, 100 failed to indicate their affiliation, and 55 were women. All the Muslim peoples of Soviet Russia, and those linked by treaty relations with it, were represented. In addition to the Turks (235 delegates), Persians (192), and Armenians (157), specifically summoned by the Third International, there were Chinese (8), Kurds (8), and Arabs (3), as well as Georgians (100).

The high watermark of unity among the delegates was reached during the keynote address by Gregory Zinoviev, president of the Comintern, who issued a fiery summons of the Muslims to a Jihad, primarily against English imperialism. A Holy War against English imperialism was something that Arabs, Turks, Persians, and other Muslims could understand and which they could wholeheartedly endorse. The record indicates that the Zinoviev address was punctuated by "stormy applause" and "prolonged hurrahs." The aroused Muslims, convinced that they were participating in one of the most important events in history, in a frenzy of excitement rose from their seats and brandishing their swords, daggers, and revolvers, swore to undertake the fight against imperialism.

Although Lenin, Stalin, and others had warned the delegates of the Comintern to exercise caution in their approach to the Muslims, especially in regard to religious issues, Zinoviev and his cohorts evinced their ignorance of the Muslim Orient by attacking Islam, its leaders, and institutions. In brief, the Baku Congress urged the Faithful to substitute the red flag of revolution for the green banner of the Prophet, the Third International for Islam, Lenin for Mohammed. The price of liberation from England was the repudiation of religion —of Islam. The Muslim delegates, as a whole, were alienated by the Comintern's antireligious propaganda.

Zinoviev's second blunder was an attack on Turkey, which the Soviet Government intended to use as its key agent to win over the rest of the Muslim World, especially the Near and Middle East. Thus the Baku Congress revived Muslim suspicions of Russians, which the Soviet Government had been taking such pains to eradicate. It served as an eye-opener to the most "progressive" Muslims of the kind of "liberation" the Third International had in store for them.

The lone delegate to sound an Anti-American note at Baku was the American, John Reed of Oregon, best known as the author of *Ten Days that Shook the World*. In his attack on United States policy in the Philippines, Central America, and the Caribbean Islands, he undertook to warn the assembled delegates that "the peoples of the East, the peoples of Asia, have not yet experienced the power of America."

The sudden collapse of Germany in 1918 caught Turkey unprepared, leaving its people face to face with disaster. By the Anglo-Turkish truce signed at Mudros on October 30, 1918, Allied forces occupied the Turkish forts at the Straits and their warships gained access to the Black Sea. The uncompromising terms exacted by England included the surrender of Turkish garrisons in Arabic countries (Iraq, Syria, Hejaz, and Yemen), the evacuation of Turkish forces from Iran and Transcaucasia, the immediate demobilization of the Turkish Army, Allied control over Turkish communications, and the right of the Allies to occupy Batum, Baku, or any part of Turkey deemed essential to Allied security. Although the Sultan and his government remained in Constantinople, the spontaneous resistance of the Turks to the Allied occupation soon assumed the proportions of a political and national revolution in Anatolia, of which the national hero, Kemal Pasha, became the leader in 1919.

When news of the Turkish Revolution reached Soviet Russia, the Soviet Government and the official Soviet press regarded it as a counterpart and an elongation of the October (Bolshevik) Revolution. It was hailed by the editor of *Izvestia* "as the first Soviet Revolution in Asia" (April 23, 1919). Of immediate importance to the hard-pressed Soviet Government, then confronted by civil war and foreign intervention, was the strategic position of Turkey. Revolutionary Turkey was expected to protect the exposed Russian flank in the Caucasus and to serve as a bulwark for revolutionary Hungary. Even more important, however, was the fact that Soviet leaders appear to have sensed an opportunity to make use of revolutionary Turkey, not only as an ally against the Entente powers, but as the vanguard of Bolshevik Revolution in the Muslim World, especially in the Near and Middle East. In the words of Stalin at the Tenth Congress of the Russian Communist Party, in March 1921, "Turkey, the most politically developed country among the Muslim peoples, raised the banner of revolt and rallied around itself the peoples of the East against imperialism."

In its "Appeal to the Muslims of Russia and the East," on December 5, 1917, the Soviet Government completely renounced all Russian claims to Turkish territory:

> We declare that the secret treaties of the dethroned tsar regarding the seizure of Constantinople, which were confirmed by the deposed Kerensky, now are null and void. The Russian Republic and its government, the Council of People's Commissars, are against the seizure of foreign territories. Constantinople must remain in the hands of the Muslims.

Although Soviet leaders continued to boast of this renunciation, at least until 1947, there is reason to believe that the Turkish Revolution of 1918-1922 produced a sudden "about-face" in their policy. Of special interest, in this connection, is an article by Yu. Steklov, published in the official government newspaper, *Izvestia,* on April 23, 1919:

> The famous question of the Dardanelles now assumes a somewhat different color. Russian imperialism of the tsarist and bourgeois period continually dreamed about these Dardanelles. German imperialism intended to seize these Dardanelles. But, actually, it was Anglo-French imperialism that took possession of them. And recently we learned that American imperialism is stretching out its greedy hand for them. Now the Turkish Revolution is returning the Dardanelles to the Turkish masses and through them to the world proletariat, which includes the Russian. Thus, what Russian imperialism failed to realize by virtue of centuries of intrigue, now as a ripe plum will fall to the Russian working class.

In other words, the Soviet Government expected to fall heir to Constantinople and the Straits, not as a result of the secret agreements of 1915-1916, but by means of a "Soviet" revolution in Turkey.

In spite of the efforts of the Sultan, the Germans, and later of Allied censorship, news of the revolutionary upheaval in Russia had spread quickly throughout Turkey. Turkish prisoners of war returning from Russia following the Bolshevik seizure of power were already indoctrinated with the Communist virus, while those returning from Germany were influenced by Spartacist ideology. They helped to organize trade unions in Istanbul. A leading Turkish Socialist, Mustapha Subhi, interned in Russia during World War I, played a prominent role in the indoctrination of "thousands" of Turkish prisoners. He edited a Turkish propaganda organ, *Yeni Dünya (The New World),* first in Moscow and then in Baku, and took an active part in the Baku Congress before returning to Turkey in November 1920 to organize Communist groups. These groups, together with some formed earlier (1918-1919) in Anatolia and in Istanbul, led to the creation of the Turkish Communist Party in 1920. Weak as it undoubtedly was, even by Soviet admission, it was instrumental in distributing quantities of Communist literature in the Turkish language, thereby promoting dissension at a critical period in the country's history.

Confronted by foreign occupation and the prospect of the dismemberment of their country by the Entente victors, Kemal Pasha appeared to regard Communist infiltration as the lesser evil, to be dealt with under more favorable circumstances. Having severed all connections with the Ottoman Government in Constantinople, he called for the election of a Turkish Grand National Assembly, which held its opening session in Ankara, on April 23, 1920. Its first decision, according to Kemal Pasha, was to send a mission to Moscow. This initial effort to establish Soviet-Turkish diplomatic relations and to secure Soviet military aid for the beleaguered Turkish nationalists soon bogged down in disagreement over frontiers.

It was Turkish reaction to the Treaty of Sèvres (August 10, 1920), that induced the Kemalist regime to turn once again to Soviet Russia. This treaty provided for the dismemberment of the Ottoman Empire. In this respect, it was comparable to the Treaty of Brest-Litovsk (March 3, 1918), imposed on Russia by the Central Powers. Ironically enough, the Allies sought to accomplish in regard to Turkey what the Central Powers did to Russia, and what Tsarist Russia had long dreamed of accomplishing in Turkey. Under such circumstances, Kemal Pasha in desperation was ready to secure help from any source, even from Communists.

On March 16, 1921, after several months of frustrating negotiations, Turkey and the RSFSR finally signed a "treaty of friendship and fraternity." This treaty established a boundary settlement, by which Kars, Ardahan, and Artvin were ceded to the Turks and Batum was restored to the Russians (Georgian SSR). The troublesome Straits question was to be settled by a conference of the Black Sea powers, with the proviso that there should be no infringement of Turkish sovereignty and that Constantinople should remain in Turkish hands. In brief, the Moscow Treaty normalized relations between Turkey and Soviet Russia. It was followed by subsidiary treaty arrangements with the Transcaucasian Soviet Republics (Armenia, Azerbaijan, and Georgia) in October 1921, and with the Ukrainian SSR early in 1922.

In spite of their criticism of the Kemalist Government, Soviet leaders recognized that this treaty strengthened the international position of the Soviet Government. From the Soviet point of view, this treaty, together with similar treaties concluded with Persia and Afghanistan in the same year, was instrumental in strengthening the cause of peace, served to encourage the national liberation movement in the Near and Middle East (Article IV), "paralyzed" the Allied intervention in Transcaucasia, and in general weakened the position of the Entente camp.

During the Turkish Revolution, and for some time thereafter, the character of Turkish relations with the Soviet Government was contingent upon the policy of the Entente toward Turkey. In other words, whenever the Turks were hard pressed by the Entente and threatened with the dismemberment of their country, they turned inevitably, even though reluctantly, to Soviet Russia for support. In proportion as the Entente powers eased their pressure and displayed a willingness to compromise, the Soviet-Turkish rapprochement cooled off appreciably.

Kemal Pasha's victorious campaign against the Greeks in 1922 led the Entente powers, especially England, to retreat from their now untenable position based upon the Treaty of Sèvres, and to come to terms with the Turkish Nationalists while Kemal Pasha could still serve as a bulwark against Communism in the Near and Middle East. Turkey emerged from the Lausanne Conference of 1923 independent of both the Soviets and the Allies. The Treaty of Lausanne was greatly instrumental in stemming the tide of militant communism of the pre-NEP vintage in Iran, Afghanistan, and the Arab countries. The loss of Turkey as the key Soviet agent for the spread of revolution in the East signified the loss of Soviet leadership in the Muslim World.

Since the outcome was most unfavorable to the Soviets, the Soviet press tried to divert attention from this situation by claiming that the Turks owed their victory to the very existence of the Soviet Republic and to Soviet support. "Why," asked Soviet Foreign Commissar Chicherin, "did the world powers make the greatest concessions to little Turkey? Because they were afraid of Soviet Russia." The Soviet Government refused to ratify the Straits Convention, which internationalized the strategic passage between the Aegean and Black Seas.

In 1925 the Mosul dispute and the Locarno Pact contributed to the revival of the Soviet-Turkish rapprochement. After Lausanne, the English and the Turks were at loggerheads over the disposition of the oil-rich Mosul area, on which no settlement had been reached. The problem was aggravated in February 1925 by a revolt of the Kurdish tribes in southeastern Anatolia under the leadership of Sheikh Said of Palu, who protested the establishment of the Turkish Republic (April 1924), demanded the restoration of the Shariat, and land reforms. Although the revolt was suppressed, the Mosul dispute was settled by the League of Nations on December 16, 1925, in favor of Iraq, with the proviso that the British mandate over that country should continue for twenty-five years. The following day the Turkish foreign minister rushed to Paris to conclude a deal with the Soviet Union.

The USSR was apprehensive over the signing in October 1925 of the Locarno Pact, which, from the Soviet standpoint, constituted the formation of an anti-Soviet bloc and a possible prelude to the renewal of foreign intervention in Russia. Since both Turkey and the Soviet Union remained outside the League of Nations, once again they chose to make common cause in time of emergency. On December 17, 1925, they concluded a treaty of friendship and nonaggression, which was tantamount to an alliance. By this treaty, Turkey and the USSR agreed to remain neutral in the event that either was attacked by a third power, or by a combination of powers (Article 1). Each contracting party undertook to enter into no alliance and to make no political agreement directed against the other (Article 2). This treaty, concluded for ten years, was extended and supplemented on several occasions until it was denounced by the Soviet Union on March 19, 1945, as an outgrowth of World War II. Its basic value to the Soviet Union consisted in the assurance it provided against aggression from the Straits in the event of war between Russia and the Western powers. It provided the basis for Turkish neutrality until the closing months of the Soviet-German conflict in World War II. The Turks, for their part, derived immediate profit from the alliance, which facilitated the settlement of their Mosul dispute with England in 1926.

Soviet relations with Iran subsequent to the Bolshevik Revolution in some respects paralleled those with Turkey. On January 14, 1918, Trotsky officially reassured the Iranian Government of Soviet renunciation of the Anglo-Russian Convention of 1907, and of all other conventions infringing upon the independence of Iran. With the completion of the evacuation of Tsarist forces from Iran in the summer of 1918, English troops pushed north to fill the "vacuum," ostensibly to forestall the Turks in Transcaucasia. The subsequent Anglo-Iranian Treaty of August 9, 1919, virtually transformed Iran into a British protectorate. It was a triumph for the diplomacy of

Lord Curzon, who had long regarded Russian encroachment on Persia as a major threat to British possession of India.

In spite of English pressure, this Iranian version of the Treaty of Sèvres was never ratified by the Mejlis, due to widespread opposition from Iranian nationalists and effective Soviet propaganda. In protest, the Iranians, like the Turks after the Treaty of Sèvres, turned to Soviet Russia for support against English "imperialism."

In the spring of 1920, a Soviet-Iranian rapprochement became possible. After the restoration of Soviet authority in Baku at the end of April, Iranian merchants began to insist on the resumption of trade and diplomatic relations with Soviet Russia. In May, the withdrawal of the English from Enzeli and Resht in advance of Soviet troops weakened British prestige and rendered even less likely the ratification of the Anglo-Iranian Treaty of 1919. On May 5, 1920, Vossuq-ed-Dowleh asked the Soviet Government to establish normal diplomatic and trade relations and to conclude an "equal" treaty based upon earlier Moscow proposals. He was even ready to recognize the Soviet Republic of Azerbaijan. The advance of Soviet Azerbaijanian forces into Gilan and the subsequent proclamation of the Soviet Republic of Gilan on May 20, 1920, not only aroused profound apprehension in Iranian Government circles, but it demonstrated the need for an understanding, especially in view of the fact that protests to Moscow and the League of Nations produced no results.

In spite of strenuous English opposition, a Soviet-Iranian treaty was concluded in Moscow on February 26, 1921, as the first official act of the new Government of Seyyid Zia ed-Din and Colonel Reza Khan, who had seized power by army *coup d'état* five days earlier. The second official act of the new regime was the repudiation of the treaty with England, on the pretext that the Mejlis had failed to ratify it.

The main purpose of Reza Khan, an Iranian counterpart of Kemal Pasha, was to free Iran from both English and Soviet interference, and to introduce drastic reforms in the country, which in the Muslim World is tantamount to secularization. Just as Kemal Pasha used the Russians to offset English and French encroachment, Reza Khan first used the English to help him consolidate his power. The Treaty of Friendship between Iran and the RSFSR enabled him in turn to force a British withdrawal from Iran and to abandon the Anglo-Iranian Treaty of 1919. The subsequent failure of Kuchuk Khan, with the support of Soviet advisers and reinforcements from Soviet Azerbaijan, to conduct a successful march on Teheran, precipitated the withdrawal of Soviet forces from Iran by September

1921. This insured the speedy collapse of the Soviet Republic of Gilan.

The Soviet-Iranian Treaty of 1921, with minor adjustments on both sides, restored the Russo-Iranian boundary of 1881. It likewise confirmed the restoration to Iran of numerous concessions and properties of the Tsarist Government, including roads, railroads, telegraph and telephone lines, Church properties, etc., and canceled Tsarist loans. Each contracting party agreed to refrain from intervention in the internal affairs of the other and to prohibit hostile organizations and groups from operating on the territory of the other. The Iranians secured the right to free navigation on the Caspian Sea.

The full significance of Articles VI and XIII, which did infringe upon the territorial sovereignty of Iran, and constituted a serious potential threat to Iranian independence, was not apparent until World War II. Article VI provided as follows:

If a third party should attempt to carry out a policy of usurpation by means of armed intervention in Persia, or if such Power should desire to use Persian territory as a base of operations against Russia, or if a foreign Power should threaten the frontiers of Federal Russia or those of its allies, and if the Persian Government should not be able to put a stop to such menace after having been once called upon to do so by Russia, Russia shall have the right to advance her troops into the Persian interior for the purpose of carrying out the military operations necessary for its defence. Russia undertakes, however, to withdraw her troops from Persian territory as soon as the danger has been removed.

Article XIII further provided:

The Persian Government, for its part, promises not to cede to a third Power, or to its subjects, the concessions and property restored to Persia by virtue of the present Treaty, and to maintain those rights for the Persian nation.

When the Iranian Government in November 1921, in apparent violation of Article XIII, granted an oil concession formerly held by a Georgian of Russian nationality to the Standard Oil Company of New Jersey in the five northern provinces of Iran, vehement protests from the Soviet Government led to the annulment of the concession. The same fate befell the Sinclair Oil Company in a similar venture in 1923.

Article VI did serve as a basis for Soviet intervention in Iran on August 25, 1941, to forestall German occupation in World War II. Both articles nevertheless proved of direct service to Iran, Article

VI by facilitating British withdrawal, and Article XIII by preventing the concessions and properties restored by Russia from reverting to any other foreign power.

One reason the Soviet Government was prepared to make major concessions to Iran in 1921 was that the prevalence of famine in Soviet Russia made peace abroad a virtual necessity. These concessions came on the eve of the introduction of the New Economic Policy, which stemmed the tide of militant Communism at home and abroad. With the conclusion of the Soviet Iranian Treaty, the Soviet Government appeared to abandon any immediate prospects for the establishment of a Soviet regime in Iran. This treaty formed the basis for all later agreements between the USSR and Iran. It helped to restore peace and order in the midst of chaotic conditions on both sides of the border.

From 1927 to 1941 there was no major Soviet action directed against the Muslim countries of the Near and Middle East. The Soviets drafted their blueprint for Communism in this area, represented by the *Communist Programs for Turkey and the Arab Countries.*[1] They provided instructions and guidance to local Communist groups, which were weak and inarticulate, and which, in most cases, had been driven underground.

---

[1] For a complete English translation of these Communist Programs, see Spector, Ivar, *The Soviet Union and the Muslim World, 1917-1958.*

13

The USSR in World War II
1941-1945

ON JUNE 22, 1941, breaking a ten-year nonaggression pact
with the Soviet Union signed on August 23, 1939, Germany invaded the USSR without a prior declaration of
war. The Germans were joined by Italy, Slovakia, and
Rumania on the same day, by Finland on June 25, and by Hungary on
June 27. Although the Churchill Government had warned Soviet leaders of the approaching invasion, Stalin and his associates apparently
did not believe that Germany would risk a war with the Soviet Union
at that time. They may not have realized the extent to which Soviet
military prestige had suffered abroad, even in Germany, as a result of
the Finnish War. Moreover, the Russians, who feared an attack via
Finland and the north more than one through the Ukraine, felt that the
Finns had been so weakened by the Soviet-Finnish War of the winter
of 1939-1940 that they would not permit the Germans to use their
country as a stepping stone from which to attack Leningrad. In this
respect they were mistaken. It has since been revealed that the Finns
were collaborating with the Germans for some time prior to the actual
invasion. At least by December 18, 1940, when "Operation Barbarossa" was drafted, the Germans were certain that they could "count
on the active participation of Rumania and Finland in the war against
Soviet Russia," and their special roles in the coming conflict were
defined.

To understand why the Germans, who refused to risk an invasion
of the USSR in 1939, when they might have attempted it with the tacit
support of the Western democracies, were nevertheless confident in
1941 of a victory over the Soviet Union in approximately six weeks,
it is important to remember, first, that the Germans had practically all
Europe in their grasp from Norway and Finland to the Balkans. Second, until they could dispose of the Red army at their backs, which had

been actively encroaching upon the German sphere in Eastern Europe, the Germans did not dare to undertake the subjugation of Britain. As Hitler informed Mussolini on the very eve of the German invasion of the USSR, he would not hesitate to use his entire air force against England "if, aside from all other conditions, I at least possess the one certainty that I will not then suddenly be attacked or even threatened from the East." He expressed the fear that if he did resort to an all-out air attack on England "Russia will then begin its strategy of extortion in the South and North, to which I would have to yield in silence from a feeling of air inferiority." In other words, Germany failed to invade England not only because of the heroic resistance of the Royal Air Force but also because of the danger from the East.[1] Hitler believed it essential to put an end to the Russian menace first. Because of a serious miscalculation, moreover, the Nazis seem to have believed that England would make peace once the German armies turned to the East. Third, the Germans in 1941 could count on the Murmansk-Leningrad front, opened by the Finns, to immobilize nearly a million Red army troops, while the Rumanian divisions actively engaged a large Soviet army in the South. Fourth, Hitler was also in a position to secure Italian, Hungarian and Spanish divisions, not to mention divisions of "Volunteers" from various parts of conquered Europe. Finally, he could count on the slave labor of 130,000,000 conquered people to run the factories and to produce the food necessary to sustain the fighting forces of Germany and her satellites. In 1941, it was by no means a case of 70,000,000 Germans waging a war against 193,000,000 Russians. With all Europe under Germany hegemony, with England stunned by Dunkerque, and the United States still neutral, Germany was able virtually to denude her Western front in order to begin the campaign in the East with tremendous odds in her favor.

Actually, the reaction abroad to Hitler's invasion of the USSR did not meet German expectations. Winston Churchill, prime minister of Great Britain, promptly welcomed the Russians as allies. As early as July 12, 1941, the British and Soviet governments concluded an agreement for mutual aid, with the following provisions:

1. The two governments mutually undertake to render each other assistance and support of all kinds in the present war against Hitlerite Germany.

[1] Sontag, R. J., and Beddie, J. S., *op. cit.*, p. 350; see also Shirer, William L., *The End of a Berlin Diary*, p. 275, where General Jodl corroborates this view; see likewise Churchill, Winston, *The Second World War*, Vol. II, *Their Finest Hour*, p. 577, where Churchill states that "Like Napoleon in 1804, he [Hitler] recoiled from the assault of the island until at least the Eastern danger was no more."

2. They further undertake that during this war they will neither negotiate nor conclude an armistice or treaty of peace except by mutual agreement.

The British people heaved a sigh of relief, recognizing the invasion of the USSR as the salvation of Britain. Even in the United States, in spite of the aftermath of the Finnish War, there was a noticeable improvement in public sentiment toward the USSR. By August 1941, the Roosevelt Administration had agreed to afford "all economic assistance practicable" to the Soviet Union, including unlimited export licenses and priorities equal to those enjoyed by Great Britain. In neither Britain nor America, however, were there any great expectations that the USSR would be able to withstand the Nazi onslaught for more than a few weeks, or at the most, a few months. General Marshall, then American Chief of Staff, is reported to have warned press correspondents confidentially that a Russian collapse was to be expected in a matter of a few weeks.[1] According to Gallup public-opinion polls taken shortly after the German invasion began, 70 percent of the American people expected the early collapse of the Red army. At the Atlantic Charter Conference in August 1941 Winston Churchill, in a bid for the lion's share of lend-lease, spoke with certainty of the ultimate fall of Moscow and the end of Russian resistance.[2] Not all Americans shared the prevailing pessimism with regard to the Russian campaign. Joseph E. Davies, former American ambassador to Moscow, predicted in an interview with the United Press that the Red army would amaze and surprise the world. Harry Hopkins, who was dispatched on a special mission to Moscow in July 1941 to ascertain Soviet needs for the conduct of the war, returned in time for the Atlantic Charter Conference convinced that lend-lease aid to the USSR was justified, and he was able to convince Roosevelt that the Russians would hold out.

Hitler launched his great *Blitzkrieg* against the USSR with an armed force of 170 divisions, his immediate objective being to strike directly at Moscow and Leningrad, to encircle and destroy the Red army, and to force the Soviet Union to capitulate within a period of approximately six weeks. During the first great German offensive, from June 22, 1941, until the German tide was stemmed before Moscow on December 6, the Red army had to depend almost entirely on Soviet military resources, without help from abroad. According to official

[1] Shirer, *op. cit.*, p. 263.
[2] Roosevelt, Elliott, *As He Saw It*, p. 30.

Soviet figures, the USSR lost 490,000 killed, 1,112,000 wounded and 520,000 missing—a total of 2,100,000 in the course of this campaign.

In spite of such heavy casualties, the Red army emerged from the initial onslaught of the Germans with two important achievements to its credit. First, it had demonstrated to the world that the German *Blitzkrieg* could be stopped and thereby refuted the many "military experts" in the Western democracies who had contended otherwise. Although the Germans had been in the USSR for nearly six months instead of the anticipated six weeks, they were no nearer their objective of destroying the Red army than before. Second, the Red army, in spite of extensive territorial losses in the West, had saved Moscow. From the beginning of the invasion, Red army strategy, focused on the defense of Moscow, had led to the concentration of the best-equipped Soviet ground and air forces in the Moscow area. The significance of Moscow, often overlooked by the Western democracies, was such that its capitulation might well have had psychological as well as military repercussions that would have enabled Hitler to achieve his objectives in the USSR. General Halder, Chief of the German General Staff at the beginning of the conflict with the USSR, blames Hitler's decision to take Kiev for the failure of the German army to break through Timoshenko's defenses on the Central Front and take Moscow in 1941.[1]

The achievements of the Red army during the first phase of the war forced a revaluation on the part of military authorities throughout the world of certain prior assumptions concerning the nature of modern war. It had been generally assumed that mechanized warfare, as waged by the German *Panzer* divisions, eliminated the need for large military reserves of man power. "Give us the tools," said Churchill to Americans, at the same time disclaiming the need for American troops, "and we will finish the job." The invasion of the USSR demonstrated, on the contrary, that without its vast reserves of man power, the Red army could never have sustained such losses as those incurred during the first six months and still have survived. The Red army stand also forced military strategists to recognize the important role of the infantry, and even of cavalry, which sometimes had been considered "dead," in any modern mechanized war conducted on a scale as vast as that of the Eastern front. The weakness of German infantry and artillery, which could not keep pace with the *Panzer* units, has been regarded as one of the serious mistakes of the German High Command in its invasion of the USSR—a mistake which caused the German offensive to bog down around Smolensk on the road to Moscow.

---

[1] Shirer, *op. cit.*, pp. 265-268.

To the utter amazement of the outside world, the Red Army not only stopped the Nazi *Blitzkrieg* before Moscow, but it launched a major Soviet offensive on the eve of the Japanese attack on Pearl Harbor, at the very moment when the German offensive had spent itself. The Red army offensive, launched by General (later Marshal) Zhukov on December 6, 1941, continued until March 8, 1942. Red army strategy concentrated on driving back the 50 German divisions on the Moscow front. During the first month of this campaign the Red army admittedly lost another 434,000 men killed and wounded. Without a second front and still without lend-lease aid from abroad, Soviet forces drove the Germans 100 miles west from Tikhvin and 240 miles west from Moscow to Kholm.

The Red army offensive demonstrated to the Soviet people and to the anti-Hitlerite forces abroad which, since December 7, 1941, had included the United States, that the Germans could not only be stopped, but that their best legions could be forced to retreat. Had the Germans been compelled to fight on another front at this time, so the Soviets claimed, the Nazi retreat might even have become a rout and the War might have been measurably shortened. Hitler's legions were surprised by the offensive and they were not prepared for military action in midwinter, at which time they expected to be comfortably housed in Moscow and Leningrad. They were likewise confronted by mutiny among the Italian troops, thousands of whom were freezing to death. The absence of substantial combat aid from Britain during this spectacular Red army offensive gave rise to the bitter controversy over a second front, which continued until the landing of the Allied expeditionary forces in France in June 1944. For all practical purposes, Hitler was able to conduct a one-front war in the East from June 22, 1941, until the invasion of North Africa in November 1942.

When it became apparent that the USSR would survive the initial Nazi onslaught, the British government dispatched Anthony Eden to Moscow in December 1941 to discuss Anglo-Soviet relations during and following the war. These conversations paved the way for the Twenty-Year Alliance between Britain and the Soviet Union, which was signed by Foreign Commissar Vyatcheslav Molotov in London on May 26, 1942. By the terms of this alliance the British and the Soviets pledged themselves "to afford one another military and other assistance and support of all kinds in the war against Germany and all those states which are associated with her in acts of aggression in Europe," and they agreed not to conclude a separate peace. Article VII provided that neither Britain nor the Soviet Union would conclude any alliance

A STREET IN STALINGRAD DESTROYED BY GERMAN BOMBARDMENT

The battle of Stalingrad marked the turning point of World War II on the Eastern Front

or take part in any coalition directed against the other high contracting party.

Immediately following the conclusion of the Anglo-Soviet alliance Molotov flew to Washington, where an agreement was concluded on American lend-lease aid for the Soviet Union. As a result of these discussions a rather ambiguous joint communiqué was issued to the effect that "full understanding was reached with regard to the urgent tasks of creating a second front in Europe in 1942.[1] Although there now seems to be little doubt that the United States and the USSR at the time saw eye to eye in interpreting the foregoing statement to mean that a second front would actually be opened in Europe in 1942, the British government later maintained that it was only agreed to recognize the urgency of the task of opening such a front—not that the Western Allies were obligated to do it. When the Soviet Government showed signs of being disturbed over this denouement, Churchill flew to Moscow in August 1942 to convince Stalin of the impossibility of opening a second front in Europe and to announce the compromise solution of an Anglo-American landing in North Africa in November.

That this compromise failed to satisfy the Soviet Government and that Churchill's visit was unable to accomplish its objective of removing Soviet suspicions of Anglo-American policy were clearly revealed in Stalin's reply to the inquiries of Harry Cassidy, an American correspondent in Moscow, on October 3, 1942:

As compared with the aid which the Soviet Union is giving to the Allies by drawing upon itself the main forces of the German fascist armies, the aid of the Allies to the Soviet Union has so far been little effective. In order to amplify and improve this aid, only one thing is required: that the Allies fulfill their obligations fully and on time.

On November 6, 1942, on the eve of the twenty-fifth anniversary of the Revolution and of the Allied landings in North Africa, Stalin announced that Britain was immobilizing only 4 German and 11 Italian divisions in Egypt and Libya, with the result that the Germans were still able to concentrate 240 divisions on the Eastern Front.

It has now been revealed that President Roosevelt, General Marshall, and General Eisenhower argued in favor of a second front in

---

[1] Molotov drafted this statement. See Sherwood, Robert E., *Roosevelt and Hopkins,* p. 557. For political as well as military reasons Molotov wanted a second front capable of drawing 40 German divisions from the Russian front in 1942.

Europe in 1942 in preference to the landing in North Africa.[1] They seem to have regarded it as the most effective method of rendering assistance to the Russians, thereby keeping them in the war, and the quickest means of defeating the Germans with the smallest loss in American lives. Although the American High Command believed a European front to be more important strategically and also less hazardous than the North African venture, the British remained unalterably opposed to such a move. Churchill favored an attack on the "soft underbelly of Europe," preferably through the Balkans, to a landing in the West. A cross-channel invasion was approved "in principle" at the Quebec Conference in August 1943, but Churchill was still trying to substitute a Balkan campaign at the Cairo Conference in November of the same year. In brief, Churchill reluctantly agreed to the program of a second front in 1944, although he would have preferred a further postponement until 1945. It seems likely that the second front issue will go down in history as one of the most controversial issues of World War II. In this connection, it should be pointed out that Russian wrath was directed not so much against the United States as against Great Britain, with which country the USSR had a twenty-year alliance that called for "military and other assistance and support of all kinds" in the war against Germany and her allies. The absence of any second front in Western Europe from 1941 to June 1944 seems also to have surprised the Germans. In November 1943 in a lecture on "The Strategic Position in the Beginning of the Fifth Year of the War," General Jodl commented that "according to our ideas it is totally incomprehensible that the Anglo-Americans should have avoided forming the second front in the west that their Russian allies have been demanding for over 2 years. . . ."[2]

The Germans launched their second summer offensive against the Red army on June 13, 1942. By November 10, when this offensive was brought to a halt at Stalingrad, the Germans had advanced from Kursk to Voronezh on the Central Front and from Taganrog on the Azov Sea to the vicinity of Grozny in the Caucasus. The main objective of the German High Command was to cut off Moscow by encirclement

---

[1] See the diary of Capt. Harry C. Butcher, USNR, *My Three Years with Eisenhower*, which was first serialized in *The Saturday Evening Post*, beginning December 15, 1945, and appeared in book form in 1946. See also Roosevelt, Elliott, *op. cit.*, pp. 108-109, 128, 144, 147-148, and 183-184, on the second front controversy; Sherwood, Robert E., *op. cit.*, Chapter XXIII, pp. 518 ff; and Eisenhower, Dwight D., *Crusade in Europe*, pp. 45-48, 52-54, and especially 66-71, where Eisenhower states that "later developments" convinced him that the landing in North Africa was preferable to a "small" second front in France in 1942.

[2] Quoted in Shirer, W., *op. cit.*, p. 285.

THE BIG THREE AT TEHERAN

from the south via Stalingrad and the Volga. The city of Stalingrad was subjected to a five-month siege, beginning on August 22. That Soviet retention of this city was likely to determine not only the fate of Moscow but also the success of the German advance to the Near East was fully appreciated in Great Britain, as evidenced by Churchill's flight to Moscow in August and by the British presentation of the Stalingrad sword to Marshal Stalin at the Teheran Conference in December 1943. In this campaign, the German army extended its occupation of Soviet territory to a maximum of 580,000 square miles.

In October 1942 during the siege of Stalingrad the United States army took over from Great Britain the main responsibility for the Iranian supply route.[1] Since the close of 1941 the British had been shipping limited quantities of rubber, jute, tin, lead, and other products from India and the Far East to the USSR via Iran. By May 1943, the American army was moving 100,000 tons of military and other supplies a month by the Iranian route. Whereas in 1941 the United States dispatched only 150 airplanes and 8500 trucks, tanks, and other mechanized equipment to the Soviet Union, in 1942 it was in a position to send 2500 airplanes and 82,000 trucks and military vehicles.[2] By 1943, the number of airplanes reached 5150, and that of trucks and other vehicles, 144,000. In 1942, however, twelve ships out of every hundred which sailed for the Soviet Union were sunk. The Murmansk route was the more dangerous because of the establishment of Nazi air and submarine bases in Norway and Northern Finland. By 1943 only one ship out of one hundred was lost en route to the USSR. Among American lend-lease supplies shipped to Russia were jeeps, Tommy guns, barbed wire, field telephones and wire, machine tools, rails and locomotives, oil refineries, a tire factory, steel, aluminum, copper, boots, food, and seeds. However, since none of these supplies reached the USSR in really mass quantity until the late spring of 1943, the Red army had to rely almost entirely upon Soviet resources on a front nearly 2000 miles in length.

The second Soviet winter offensive was launched on November 19, 1942, and lasted until March 31, 1943. In this historic campaign, which marked a turning point in the tide of warfare on the Eastern Front, the Red army retrieved 184,000 square miles of German-occupied Soviet territory, advancing as much as 400 miles in some sectors on a front

---

[1] See Stettinius, Edward R., Jr., *Lend Lease: Weapon for Victory*, N. Y., 1944, pp. 203-229.

[2] See Wesson, Major-General Charles M., "Administering Lend-Lease for the Soviets," *The American Review on the Soviet Union*, Vol. VI, No. 1, November 1944, pp. 3-10.

that reached from Leningrad to the Caucasus. The foremost achievement in this campaign was the encirclement and capture of the 22 German divisions (330,000 men) of General von Paulus before Stalingrad, together with vast quantities of usable German equipment. Shortly thereafter, on January 18, 1943, the Red army lifted the sixteen-month siege of Leningrad. Other Soviet victories included the capture of Voronezh (January 25), of Krasnodar in the North Caucasus (February 13), as well as Rostov on the Don and Voroshilovgrad (February 15). Although Kharkov was temporarily liberated (February 18), the Germans, by the transfer of 30 new divisions from Western Europe, were able to recapture this city on March 14 and to recover large areas in the Donbas. Stalin, in his Order of the Day for February 23, 1943, on the twenty-fifth anniversary of the Red army, claimed that: "In view of the absence of a second front in Europe the Red army alone is bearing the whole weight of the war." On May 19, 1943, Winston Churchill announced that "Russia has already inflicted injuries upon the German military organism which will, I believe, prove ultimately fatal." According to official Soviet figures, the USSR lost 4,200,000 men killed and missing during the first two years following the Nazi invasion.

The third and last summer offensive of the German armies in the USSR, launched on July 5, 1943, consisted of an all-out effort by 38 German divisions to secure a break-through on the Kursk-Belgorod salient of the Central Front. The most destructive tank and artillery battle of the war took place on this narrow front from July 5 to July 23, in the course of which almost 3000 tanks, 1400 airplanes, over 1000 guns and 70,000 troops were lost by the Germans. The Western Allies of the Soviet Union, who had come to assume that the Red army was capable of conducting only a winter offensive, followed with growing amazement the gigantic summer offensive launched by the Soviets on July 12, which reached the Dnieper by the end of September and accomplished the liberation of 115,000 square miles of territory within two months. The retreat of the Germans was so rapid that in the United States speculation was rife about "a deal" between the Soviets and the Nazis. The scale of the fighting on the Eastern Front, which involved some 500 German and Soviet divisions, was difficult to comprehend. In spite of Anglo-American expectations that the Germans would stop the Red army at the Dnieper River, Ukrainian troops crossed it in October, recovered Dnepropetrovsk on October 25, and the historic city of Kiev on November 6.

Soviet-American relations had improved considerably during the course of the war, although much mutual distrust still existed. The problem created by the United States refusing to recognize Soviet incorporation of the Baltic states and Eastern Poland was temporarily shelved. American public opinion viewed with satisfaction Soviet adherence to the Atlantic Charter in 1941, and the signing by Litvinov, as Soviet ambassador to Washington, of the Declaration of the United Nations on January 1, 1942. Soviet dissolution of the Comintern, or Third International, on May 22, 1943, aroused more confidence in the United States with regard to the possibility of future collaboration between the two countries. Nevertheless the second front issue still bred ill will and suspicion in Moscow, as General Deane at once discovered upon his arrival there as head of the American Military Mission in October 1943.

Closer collaboration between the Soviet Union, on the one hand, and England and the United States, on the other, was achieved at the first wartime conference of the foreign ministers of the three powers in Moscow, October 19-30, 1943. In a joint declaration, to which China also subscribed, the four powers pledged themselves to continue their collaboration after the war and recognized the necessity of establishing a general international organization for the maintenance of peace and security. The three powers then issued declarations denouncing fascism in Italy, pledging the independence of Austria, and the punishment of war criminals. At Moscow, by promising to set the date for the second front, Secretary of State Cordell Hull secured Soviet consent to a "Big Three" conference of Roosevelt, Stalin, and Churchill, to be held at Teheran in late November.

The Teheran Conference, November 28-December 1, 1943, marked the first real effort at co-ordinated planning of the conduct of the war. Plans for a cross-channel invasion in late May or early June 1944 were discussed, as well as for a Soviet offensive in the East, timed to coincide with the opening of the second front in the West. It was at Teheran that Stalin first hinted that Soviet help would be forthcoming in the Pacific once the war in Europe was over. According to General Deane, who was present at Teheran, at that time and "almost until the final collapse of Japan the President and the Chiefs of Staff attached the greatest importance to Soviet participation in the Pacific war."[1] A

---

[1] Deane, John R., *The Strange Alliance*, N. Y., 1947, p. 41. It has since been revealed that at Teheran rather than at Yalta Roosevelt intimated to Stalin that the USSR might have access to the port of Dairen in Manchuria. See Sherwood, *op. cit.*, p. 792.

RUSSIAN TROOPS ENTER BERLIN

Soviet tanks pass by a building that bears an inscription: "Berlin shall always remain German."

three-power declaration issued at Teheran expressed the desire of England, the USSR, and the United States to maintain the independence, sovereignty, and territorial integrity of Iran. One of the most immediate results of the Teheran Conference was the conclusion in Moscow by President Beneš on December 12 of a twenty-year alliance between the Soviet Union and Czechoslovakia—an alliance which was earlier opposed by London and Washington, since it would bring Czechoslovakia within the Soviet orbit.

During the spring of 1944, while United States-British bombing raids devastated German cities like Cologne, Hamburg, and Berlin, the Red army liberated Odessa (April 10) on the Black Sea and invaded Rumania. The Crimean campaign was brought to a successful conclusion in May with the capture of the remains of Sevastopol. By D-Day on June 6, 1944, when the landing in Normandy of the Allied Expeditionary Force under General Dwight D. Eisenhower made the long-awaited second front a reality, the Red army had liberated practically all Soviet territory except the Baltic fringe, Eastern Poland, and Bessarabia.

In the summer of 1944 the Soviet Union redeemed its pledge to support the Allied campaign in the West by means of a Soviet offensive in the East. In July the Red army liberated Vilna, reached the Vistula, and captured Brest-Litovsk. Winston Churchill (August 2) promptly credited the Red army with having done "the main work of tearing the guts out of the German Army." Late in August, as the Americans entered Paris (August 24), Soviet forces swept rapidly across Rumania and entered Bucharest (August 31). Rumania then joined the Red army as a co-belligerent in the invasion of Hungary. Early in September Soviet troops entered Yugoslavia and East Prussia, while on another front the Red army reached the borders of Czechoslovakia. On September 14, hostilities between Finland and the USSR were terminated, and the Finns joined Soviet forces in the expulsion of Nazi troops from their country. Eleven days after the Soviet Union declared war on Bulgaria (September 5), the Soviet army entered Sofia (September 16), whereupon the Bulgarians joined the ranks of the Soviet co-belligerents to drive the Germans from the Balkans. In October the important Baltic port of Riga, Latvia, was captured, and Czechoslovakia and Northern Norway were penetrated. With the aid of Yugoslav partisans under Marshal Tito, Belgrade was liberated. As late as November 1944, however, the Red army still faced 204 German and Hungarian divisions, 180 of which were German.

On the eve of the twenty-seventh anniversary of the Revolution (November 6) Stalin paid tribute to the effectiveness of Allied assistance in the West, following the establishment of the second front:

There can be no doubt that without the organization of the second front in Europe, which pinned down 75 divisions of the Germans, our troops would not have been able in so short a time to break down the resistance of the German troops and drive them from the confines of the Soviet Union. Thus it is equally without doubt that without the mighty operations of the Red army in the summer of this year, which pinned down some 200 German divisions, the troops of our allies would not have been able so quickly to deal with the German troops, and thrown them out of the area of middle Italy, France and Belgium.

By this time, with the exception of a German pocket holding out in Western Latvia, the Soviet frontiers from the Barents to the Black Sea had been cleared of enemy forces. Before the end of the year the Red army completed the encirclement of Budapest.

On January 12, 1945, Soviet forces launched their final winter offensive in South-Central Poland. Ruined Warsaw was taken on January 17, and the German border in Silesia was reached two days later. On January 21, after the capture of Tannenberg in East Prussia, the Red forces invaded Germany proper. After a fifty-day siege, Budapest fell to the Russians on February 13. As a result of corresponding advances on the Western Front, troops of the United States First Army crossed the Rhine at Remagen on March 8.

As the war in Europe approached a victorious climax, the "Big Three" held a second and highly significant conference at Yalta in the Crimea, February 4-11, 1945, at which the immediate problems of the war and those of the postwar world were discussed. This was the conference which, according to Secretary of State James F. Byrnes, marked the "high tide of Big Three Unity." [1] It was the first major conference after the opening of the second front in June 1944, and already the Allies were preparing to launch an offensive across the Rhine, while the Russians had commenced their drive on Germany's eastern frontier. One of the main issues of this conference, therefore, concerned what was to be done with Germany. Serious consideration was given to the idea of partitioning Germany into several small states, the respective zones of occupation of England, the United States, the USSR, and France were defined, and a central control commission was

---

[1] Byrnes, James F., *Speaking Frankly*, N. Y., 1947, Chapter II, pp. 21-45.

decided upon. According to Secretary Byrnes, the main interest of Russia in the German question at Yalta concerned reparations. Stalin held fast to his contention that those countries which carried the main burden of the war should have priority as regards reparations. In order to obviate a deadlock on this vital issue, President Roosevelt finally agreed that the Reparations Commission should take as "a basis for discussion" the Soviet suggestion of reparations payments totaling $20,000,000,000, of which 50 percent was to go to the Soviet Union. The phrasing of the reparations clause was to cause an infinite amount of trouble at a later date.

Another major issue which confronted the powers at Yalta, one in which they were all interested, was that of Poland. England had an alliance with Poland, undertaken by Chamberlain on the eve of World War II, in spite of the fact that he was then in no position to render the Poles any effective assistance. The United States, with its sizable and articulate Polish minority, was also concerned about the future of Poland. The Soviet Union, mindful of how Poland had been used after World War I as a Western bulwark against the USSR, and aware of the claims advanced by White Russian and Ukrainian minorities now incorporated in the Union, was prepared to be satisfied with nothing less than the Curzon Line and the provision that Poland should be given compensation at the expense of Germany. The insistence of the Russians on a "friendly" Poland led, after much argument, to a decision in favor of reorganizing the existing Provisional (Lublin) Government of Poland on "a broader democratic basis," so as to include representatives from the Polish government in exile in London, which had shown itself to be, by and large, hostile to the Soviet Union. Actually, since the Red army already occupied Poland, this was regarded by the Russians as a major concession to Allied unity. The acrimonious disputes later precipitated by this decision seriously affected, according to General Deane, all preparations for Allied co-operation in the Pacific war.

The United States, looking ahead to the postwar world, was fundamentally interested at Yalta in advancing the cause of international organization, on the basis of decisions reached at the Dumbarton Oaks Conference in the fall of 1944. The major issue decided at Yalta concerned the voting procedure in the Security Council, in regard to which the American delegation itself proposed the now famous "veto right" of the five major powers, which was accepted by the USSR and later adopted by the San Francisco Conference in April 1945. It was likewise agreed at Yalta that the Ukraine and the

Byelorussian Soviet Republic should have separate representation in the United Nations Organization.

At the closing session of the Yalta Conference, which at the time won almost universal applause, Stalin made a statement prophetic in nature:

It is not so difficult to keep unity in time of war since there is a joint aim to defeat the common enemy, which is clear to everyone. The difficult task will come after the war when diverse interests tend to divide the Allies. It is our duty to see that our relations in peacetime are as strong as they have been in war.[1]

During the final weeks of the victorious 1945 campaign, the Germans were permitted no respite. The Red army entered Austria on March 30 and completed its occupation of Vienna on April 13 after seven days of street fighting. On April 21 Soviet troops under Marshals Zhukov and Konev entered Berlin and soon accomplished the encirclement of that city. Four days later, on April 25, American troops of the United States First Army under General Courtney H. Hodges joined forces with Marshal Konev's First Ukrainian Army near Torgau on the River Elbe, thereby splitting Germany in two. After Berlin fell to the Russians on May 2, the end came fast. British forces under Field Marshal Sir Bernard L. Montgomery contacted Marshal Konstantin Rokossovsky's Second White Russian Army south of the Baltic in Mecklenburg Province on May 3. Finally, on May 7 at Rheims the German armed forces agreed to surrender unconditionally to the Allies. The final capitulation was signed in Berlin the following day, and the war in Europe was over.

Although no Soviet territory had been retrieved by Allied military forces, part of the credit for the remarkable Soviet record during the war must be attributed to the increased supplies of lend-lease equipment reaching the Soviet Union. Major-General Charles M. Wesson, Director, Division for Soviet Supply, Foreign Economic Administration, has stated that by the end of June 1944 the United States had sent supplies valued at $5,931,944,000 to the USSR. By the time the second front was established in France, Americans had provided the Russians with 10,800 airplanes, 318,500 trucks and other mechanized equipment, in addition to substantial quantities of tools, raw materials, and food.

Two years later, President Truman reported to Congress (June 14, 1946) that from March 11, 1941, to December 31, 1945, the United

---

[1] Quoted in Byrnes, *op. cit.*, p. 44.

States supplied its allies with lend-lease totaling $49,096,000,000. Of this total, the USSR received slightly less than 23 percent, or $11,141,470,000, whereas the British Empire got more than 60 percent, or $30,753,304,000. Major-General John R. Deane, head of the wartime American Military Mission in Moscow,[1] states further that from October 1, 1941, to May 31, 1945, there were 2660 ships sent to the USSR which carried a total of 16,529,791 tons of supplies. Since 52 of these ships were diverted to the United Kingdom and 77 were lost en route, some 15,234,791 long tons of supplies reached the USSR. Among these supplies he lists 427,284 trucks, 13,303 combat vehicles, 35,170 motorcycles, and 2328 ordnance service vehicles; 2,670,371 tons of petroleum products; 4,478,116 tons of canned meats, sugar, flour, salt, etc.; 1900 steam locomotives, 66 Diesel locomotives, 120 tank cars, 35 heavy machinery cars, 9920 flat cars, and 1000 dump cars. Over $1,000,-000,000 worth of machinery and industrial equipment were sent, millions of dollars worth of medical supplies, and vast quantities of Quartermaster items, such as cloth, underwear, shoes, and bedding. More than half of these lend-lease shipments reached their destination via the Pacific and the Trans-Siberian Railroad. For purposes of comparison, it is interesting to note that, according to former Secretary of the Treasury Henry J. Morgenthau, Jr., it cost the United States roughly $6,000,000,000 to fight its way from Naples to Rome. It stands to reason that, because of the tremendous scale of warfare on the Eastern Front, the real arsenal of the Soviet Union still consisted of those Soviet factories which were not overrun by Nazi Germany. American aid and mechanized equipment nevertheless made the difference between an early and victorious conclusion of the conflict in Europe and further protraction of the war.

In March 1947, Soviet Foreign Minister Molotov informed the Council of Foreign Ministers that the war against Germany and Japan cost the Soviet Union $357,000,000,000, in addition to the destruction wrought by the German invasion and occupation which amounted to $128,000,000,000, making a total cost of $485,000,000,000. Some idea of the destruction wrought by the Axis powers in the Soviet Union is indicated by Molotov's announcement that 1710 towns, 70,000 villages and hamlets, and 6,000,000 buildings were destroyed, making some 25,000,000 people homeless. In addition, 35,000 plants and factories and 40,000 hospitals were lost.

With the approach of victory in Europe, there was growing concern in the United States over the Soviet interpretation of the Yalta Agreements, especially in regard to Rumania and Poland. It soon became

----

[1] Deane, *op. cit.,* pp. 88-95.

apparent that the United States and the USSR entertained entirely different concepts of what constituted governments "broadly representative of all democratic elements." Wisely or unwisely, since the Red army occupied all of Eastern Europe, England and the United States made an issue of the installation of the pro-Soviet Groza Government in Rumania and of the inclusion of the London Poles in the reorganized government of Poland. Each side accused the other of breaking the Yalta Pact. The death of President Roosevelt on April 12, 1945, on the very eve of the San Francisco Conference (April 25-June 26, 1945), did not improve prospects for the early settlement of delicate and controversial political issues that had already superseded military problems in importance. Although Stalin, as a gesture toward Allied unity, sent Molotov to San Francisco, disagreement between the Anglo-American delegations and the Soviet delegation was manifested on almost every issue before the conference. While the San Francisco Conference was preparing the final draft of the Charter of the United Nations Organization, President Truman sent Harry Hopkins once again to Moscow to iron out differences that had arisen over the United States' insistence on the admission of Argentina to the United Nations, the composition of the Polish government, and other problems contributing to the deterioration of Soviet-American relations. To his credit, Hopkins was able to reach a *modus vivendi* with reference to Poland, whereby a new government including Stanislaw Mikolajczyk was formed, Poland was admitted to the United Nations Organization as a charter member, and recognition for her was obtained from the United States. Hopkins also helped to solve the San Francisco deadlock over the "veto right" by prevailing upon Stalin to agree that the veto should not apply to procedural questions.

The Potsdam Conference (July 17-August 2, 1945), held three months after the victory in Europe, afforded still further evidence of the difficulties to be encountered before an equitable European settlement could be reached. Of the "Big Three" who negotiated at Teheran and Yalta, only Stalin remained. President Truman now took the place of Roosevelt, and before the Conference came to a close Winston Churchill and Anthony Eden, as a result of the sweeping Labour victory in England, were replaced by Clement Attlee and Ernest Bevin. The discussions at Potsdam were fraught with disputes over such issues as the role of France and China in the drafting of the European peace treaties, the interpretation of the Yalta Pact, the situation in Greece and Yugoslavia, the question of trusteeship over the Italian colonies, the Straits question, the Polish-German frontier, and the vital reparations issue.

Agreement was nevertheless reached on the establishment of a Council of Ministers, which was to undertake first the drafting of peace treaties with Italy and the Balkan states. Although the Anglo-American delegates were greatly perturbed over the Soviet procedure of transferring to Poland the administrative control of German territory as far west as the Neisse River, they bluntly refused to recognize the *fait accompli* as a permanent settlement of Poland's western frontier and postponed the issue until the peace conference. England and the United States did, however, agree to support the transfer of the East Prussian capital of Königsberg to the USSR. After much debate the conference determined that reparations should not be handled by cash payments, as after World War I, but rather by payments "in kind." It was decided that the reparations requirements of each of the powers should be satisfied out of its own zone, with the Russians securing another 15 percent of the industrial equipment of the Western zones. For additional equipment from the Western zones the Russians agreed to pay the equivalent value in food, coal, timber, and raw materials from the Eastern zone. The American delegation remained adamant in its opposition to the payment of reparations out of current production, until such time as German exports were sufficient to cover the cost of German imports, thereby making American loans unnecessary. Although by this settlement the conference avoided an open rupture on the subject of reparations, events were soon to prove that it by no means put an end to the controversy. An agreement was also reached as to the equal division of the German fleet and merchant marine among the three powers. In the words of Secretary of State Byrnes, the Potsdam Conference showed that "agreements reached in conference must be hammered out on the hard anvil of experience."

The American public had never ceased to speculate on whether or not the USSR would join the war in the Pacific against Japan once hostilities ceased in Europe. There were clear indications that the Japanese government was ready to offer major concessions to the Soviet Union in order to preserve Soviet neutrality. It has since been revealed (August 10, 1945) by the former American ambassador to the USSR, Admiral William H. Standley, that as early as 1943 Stalin informed Secretary of State Cordell Hull of the Soviet decision to enter the war against Japan when Germany surrendered. On February 11, 1946, Secretary of State James F. Byrnes made public a top secret military agreement on the Kurile Islands, signed at the Yalta Confer-·

ence on February 11, 1945, by Roosevelt, Stalin, and Churchill, which provided for Soviet entry into the Pacific War within three months after the surrender of Germany.

According to this agreement the Big Three recognized the *status quo* in Outer Mongolia, agreed to restore the former rights of Russia violated by Japan in the Russo-Japanese War of 1904-05, such as the return of Southern Sakhalin to the Soviet Union, the restoration of the lease of Port Arthur as a naval base, and "the preeminent interests" of the Soviet Union in the internationalized port of Dairen. The agreement likewise provided for joint operation of the Chinese Eastern Railway and the South Manchurian Railroad by the USSR and China, on the understanding that "the preeminent interests" of the Soviet Union should be safeguarded and that Chinese sovereignty over Manchuria should be maintained. It was also agreed that the Kurile Islands would be handed over to the USSR. Since the United States, Great Britain, and China, at the Cairo Conference in November 1943, agreed to the principle of restoration of former colonies and possessions in the Far East, it was therefore logical that the USSR should expect the same treatment accorded other powers. Because the Yalta agreement was reached without consulting the Chinese government, it was necessary at the time of the Potsdam Conference for Britain and the United States to take steps to secure a Sino-Soviet accord confirming the foregoing decisions. Such a treaty was finally signed at Moscow by Chinese representatives on August 12, 1945.

In accordance with its commitments in the Yalta Pact, the Soviet Union declared war on Japan on August 8 (effective August 9), just three months after the surrender of Germany and two days after the first atom bomb was dropped on Hiroshima. Judging by material extant, it is safe to say that the Soviet Union would have entered the war against Japan, with or without the concessions made by the Allies at Yalta. The Japanese, who had already tried to transmit peace overtures through the Russians to the Potsdam Conference, accepted the Potsdam ultimatum to surrender, providing assurances were forthcoming that the emperor's sovereignty would be maintained. Meanwhile, the Red army invaded Manchuria, Korea, and Southern Sakhalin. Although Japan announced her surrender on August 14, General Alexei Antonov, the Red Army Chief of Staff, declared that Soviet forces would continue the war in East Asia until the Japanese laid down their arms. On August 17 the Japanese Kwantung army, the pride of Japan, surrendered unconditionally to Marshal Vasilevsky. Three days later the Red army entered Mukden, Harbin, and Changchun, virtually completing the conquest of Manchuria. On August 22 Soviet airborne troops landed at Dairen, Port Arthur, and at Shimushu in the Kuriles. General Derevyanko represented the Soviet Union when General Douglas MacArthur accepted the Japanese surrender on board the battleship *Missouri* in Tokyo Bay on September 2.

It has been officially disclosed that during the month-long Soviet campaign and mopping-up operations in the Far East Red army casualties numbered 8219 killed and 22,264 wounded. The Soviets claimed that 80,000 Japanese were killed, 20,000 wounded and 594,000 captured, including 148 generals. There can be little doubt that whereas the Red army bore the main brunt of the fighting against Germany in Europe, the Americans, together with the Chinese, bore the brunt of the fighting against Japan in the Far East. Whether the dropping of atomic bombs on Hiroshima and Nagasaki or the Soviet declaration of war was more effective in precipitating the final surrender of Japan is a matter upon which opinions will continue to differ. Japanese peace overtures had begun before either of these steps was taken. It must be acknowledged, however, that the winning of the war in the Pacific would have taken longer and would have proved far more costly had the Red Army not immobilized the best military forces of Japan in Manchuria ever since Pearl Harbor.

Whereas Russia emerged from World War I dismembered, disorganized, in the throes of civil war and foreign intervention, the Soviet Union emerged from World War II the strongest land power in Europe and Asia. At the end of World War I the Western powers feared Russian weakness and turmoil and proceeded to ignore her at the Peace Conference at Versailles. At the end of World War II the Soviet Union was a strong, united state, which had not only reincorporated most of the territories lost in 1918, but included some new acquisitions and seemed disposed toward further expansion. Thus in 1945 the other powers feared Soviet strength and the possibility of unilateral action on the part of the USSR in Europe. Since only two first-rate powers emerged from World War II—the United States and the Soviet Union—the other powers proceeded to group themselves around one of the two, with the result that Europe soon faced a division into a Western and an Eastern bloc. In 1945 it was no longer possible to ignore the Soviet Union, but it had become increasingly difficult for the other powers to reach an agreement with her in the conclusion of a satisfactory postwar world settlement.

14

Soviet Culture

SOVIET LITERATURE, 1917-1960[1]

I N ANY consideration of contemporary Soviet literature the novel
ranks first, as in the past. Next in importance comes the drama.
At the dawn of the Revolutionary era, when Alexander Blok,
Sergei Yesenin, Boris Pasternak, and Vladimir Mayakovsky were
at the height of their fame, it seemed as if poetry would supersede both
the novel and the drama. With the lapse of time, however, it has
become apparent that the national genius is again expressing itself
best in prose, thus following the tradition of the past. The novel in
particular has reasserted itself.

Soviet literature has been, on the whole, propagandist in nature. In
this respect, however, the best of it does not differ as much from the
Russian literature of the past as the uninitiated may sometimes suspect.
The bulk of the pre-Revolutionary literature was likewise propagandistic
—and the term is not used here in any derogatory sense—because
writers like Gogol, Turgenev, Dostoyevsky, and Leo Tolstoy invariably
championed a cause and sought through the medium of so-called fiction
or drama to win converts for the abolition of serfdom, educational
reforms, improvements in local or provincial government, and so on.
The main difference between the propaganda of the old and that of the
new regime is that in pre-Revolutionary times propaganda was ordinarily directed against the existing government, whereas under the
present regime it supports the new order and is leveled against those

---

[1] In this chapter the author has drawn heavily upon his article on "Contemporary
Russian Literature: Katayev, Tolstoy, Sholokhov," published in *The English Journal*,
Vol. XXXII, No. 6, June 1943, 295-302.

who fail to conform to its tenets. In other words, writers under the old regime achieved fame because the government was in passive or active opposition to them. Writers under the Soviet regime, on the contrary, owe their early recognition and widespread popularity to government support. They have been expected to serve as the teachers and educators of the vast masses of the people in the struggle for collectivism, industrialization, greater production, and the war effort.

Soviet literature owes a great deal to the patronage and guidance of Maxim Gorky, who died in 1936. Since his later books are essentially an elongation of his pre-Revolutionary work, discussed elswhere in this book, and since so much has already been written about him in English, it seems advisable to omit further reference to him here in order to devote more space to other leading Soviet authors. In 1934, however, toward the close of his career, Gorky was responsible for launching a new style in Soviet literature and the arts—that of socialist realism, which in its implementation since his death has led to outright dictatorship over creative art in the USSR.

Soviet literature has been closely interwoven with current events, and consequently its writers, consciously or unconsciously, have reflected the evolution in the USSR from militant Communism to a Socialist (collectivist) and nationalist orientation. For a study of the Soviet Union, therefore, the literature is a necessary, often an indispensable collateral, and at times serves as an important primary source.

For example, the poet and dramatist, Vladimir Mayakovsky (1893-1930), truthfully reflected the era of militant Communism and the policy of world revolution, as his play *Mystery-Bouffe* ("The Permanent Revolution") clearly indicates. Pantaleimon Romanov (1884-1936), especially in his novel, *Three Pairs of Silk Stockings*, reflected Soviet outlook and problems during the NEP (1921-1928). The aftermath of the Civil War and the problems of reconstruction were effectively presented in Feodor Gladkov's novel, *Cement* (1926). Valentin Katayev (1897-   ), in his well-known play, *Squaring the Circle* (1928), portrayed the changing attitudes of Soviet youth on the eve of the First Five-Year Plan. Another Soviet writer, Boris Pilnyak (1894-1937), in his novel, *The Volga Falls to the Caspian Sea* (1930), dealt with the many problems involved in the construction of a great canal project under the Five-Year Plan. This novel likewise marked an attempt toward the revaluation of moral issues, which later culminated in the re-establishment of the sanctity of the family in the USSR. Even the casual reader of Pilnyak's novel could not fail to note the change in the Soviet outlook, not only regarding the family but on other moral problems. For his realistic approach, the unfortunate Pilnyak paid the penalty exacted of so many Soviet writers and artists. He disappeared from view in 1937 and his works have since been ignored in the Soviet Union. The works of writers like Alexei Tolstoy (1882-1945) and Mikhail Sholokhov (1905-   ) reflected the revival of the historical novel as a highly important literary medium in the USSR. The significance of the historical novel in the achievement of racial and national unity, especially in the recent war years, and its bearing on postwar problems, have not yet been fully evaluated.

Among the host of Soviet writers, three of the most outstanding have been Katayev, A. Tolstoy, and Sholokhov.

Although Katayev began to write before 1917, his best works belong to the post-Revolutionary period. In general they are characterized by humor and satire. Among others he has written *The Embezzlers* (1926); *Squaring the Circle* (1928); *Time, Forward!* (1933); *Peace Is Where the Tempests Blow* (1936); *For the Soviet Power* (1949), and short stories like *The Golden Pen, The Father,* etc.

Katayev's best work to date, from the literary as well as from the historical standpoint, is his play, *Squaring the Circle,* which has been successfully produced in America. This comedy occupies, in contemporary Russian literature, a similar place to that held by Gogol's *The Revizor* in the nineteenth century. Although both plays reflect a certain period, now outmoded, they will continue to make people laugh in the future as they did in the past. *Squaring the Circle* has proved to be one of the most popular plays on the Soviet stage.

Contemporary Russian drama, like that of the nineteenth century, has found its best expression in the comedy, probably because the comedy has always served as the best medium for constructive criticism of the seamy side of the existing order and its institutions. When *Squaring the Circle* was first published and staged here in America, many at first refused to believe that it was the work of a Soviet writer living in Russia, and that it had actually been produced inside the USSR. It held up to ridicule the whole Komsomol organization, its principles and ideas, as no other writer has dared to do before or since. The fact that such a play was published and staged in the Soviet Union at that time is a clear indication that someone in power was as interested as Nicholas I, with regard to the publication and staging of *The Revizor,* in constructive criticism and in letting the people know that their leaders were aware of the shortcomings of petty officials—in this case of the Komsomol. Katayev's work may be said to have ushered in the period of "self-criticism."

In brief, just as his novel, *The Embezzlers,* a clever satire about two rascally Soviet officials who abscond with some 12,000 rubles of the state funds, is a new version of Gogol's *Dead Souls,* so *Squaring the Circle* is a contemporary counterpart of Gogol's *The Revizor.* Katayev was influenced by Gogol more than by any other Russian writer. In this respect, he does not differ from his predecessors of the pre-Revolutionary era, who found inspiration in the same source.

On the death of Gorky in 1936, A. N. Tolstoy (1882-1945) became the recognized dean of contemporary Russian writers. An extremely versatile person, he obtained recognition as a poet, journalist, playwright, historian, and novelist, although he is best known for his outstanding historical novels, *Peter the First* (1929-1934) and *The Road to Calvary* (1921-1942).

Perhaps the main reason for the popularity of *Peter I* was the striking parallel it afforded between the Russia of Peter the Great (1689-1725) and the Russia of the Five-Year Plans. The Peter presented by Tolstoy is one who attempted to revolutionize the traditional mode of Russian life and to Westernize Russia in a single generation, regardless of obstacles and in spite of the opposition of privileged landowners, hostile clergy, and an apathetic and indifferent public. The picture inevitably calls to mind the efforts of Stalin to bring about the collectivization of agriculture and the industrialization of Russia by means of the Five-Year Plans.

It should be understood that *Peter I* has been chiefly responsible for a revaluation and reinterpretation of the Russian past on the part of contemporary Soviet writers. From the Russian standpoint, it is an epoch-making work, since it has restored the link between the present Russia and the past, which was broken by the Revolution of 1917. When Part I of this novel was filmed in 1937 Alexei Tolstoy became the most widely known writer in the USSR, with the possible exception of Sholokhov.

To be sure, historical novels were being produced in the USSR before *Peter I.* But they were for the most part based on the Revolution and the Civil War which followed, with only an occasional excursion into the more remote past to portray, as Tchapygin did in his *Stenka Razin* (1927), a revolutionary hero of another age. Meanwhile, outstanding Russians of the pre-Revolutionary era had been ignored or were taboo because of their bourgeois or noble origin. With the appearance of *Peter I* it became increasingly clear that there were far-sighted and capable monarchs, military leaders, statesmen and writers before the Revolution, and that it was no longer possible to tar them all with the same brush. It was therefore no accident that heroes of the past like Alexander Nevsky, General Suvorov, and even Ivan Grozny were resurrected and are now being presented from the standpoint of Soviet realism, which no longer ignores the parallels between their day and ours.

The renaissance of the historical novel and drama in the USSR, ushered in by *Peter I,* effected two purposes so far as the masses of the Russian people were concerned. It showed them how Russians had met and overcome the attacks of hostile invaders and other obstacles in the past. It likewise indicated that in the old days, as in the present, the Russian people had to endure restrictions and privations in order to attain a better life. In other words, Peter sacrificed thousands of Russian serfs to construct St. Petersburg; in parallel, many Russians were uprooted from their traditional mode of life or died of starvation in the process of collectivization and industrialization in Soviet Russia. The nomenclature was different, but the parallels were clearly drawn.

Another of Alexei Tolstoy's historical novels, *The Road to Calvary,* was awarded the Stalin prize for *belles lettres* in 1942. Here Tolstoy provides a picture of Russian society throughout World War I, the Revolution, and the Civil War period. In Soviet Russia this novel helped to create a better appreciation and understanding of the role of the Russian intelligentsia, which was an object of attack for many years following the Revolution. Just as his *Peter I* showed that some tsars were better than others, *The Road to Calvary* indicated clearly enough that a corresponding distinction must be made between intellectuals. Although *Peter I* reveals much careful scrutiny of the original sources, Tolstoy has the advantage of having been a participant himself in the events covered by his later novel.

The Soviet writer who, at least for the time being, has eclipsed his contemporaries, and whose works are today the most widely read and quoted in the USSR, is Mikhail Sholokhov.[1] He is likewise better known outside the Soviet Union than either Katayev or A. Tolstoy by his literary masterpiece, *The Silent Don* (1926-1940), and the opera by Ivan Dzerzhinsky, based upon the novel.

Sholokhov is a Don Cossack. Among his best works are *Lazorevaya Steppe,* a collection of short stories about the Don River region pub-

---

[1] For a recent Soviet interpretation of Sholokhov, see Khmelnitskaya, Tamara, "The Realism of Sholokhov," *Soviet Press Translations,* Vol. IV, No. 10, May 15, 1949, pp. 301-314. Far Eastern and Russian Institute, University of Washington.

lished in 1925; *Virgin Soil Upturned* (1932), which described Soviet efforts to promote collectivization among the Cossacks during the Five-Year Plans; and a series of short stories, including *The Family Man, The Worm-Hole,* and *The Foal.* His main contribution to contemporary Russian literature is *The Silent Don,* begun in 1926 and completed in 1940. During World War II he began work on another epic novel, *They Fought for the Motherland.*

The *Silent Don* is a contribution not only to Soviet literature but to Russian literature as a whole. It reveals, for the first time, the various aspects of Don Cossack life from the cradle to the grave. In this epic, Sholokov interprets the family life and institutions, religious beliefs, and occupations of the Don Cossacks, their role in World War I and in the Civil War as no writer has dealt with them before. Although Lermontov, Gogol, and Leo Tolstoy have enriched Russian literature with their vivid tales of Cossack life, at best they dealt with certain phases or episodes, and their stories often remind us of the adventures of our own American cowboys and Indians. On the other hand, Sholokhov's work is an all-embracing, all-inclusive epic of the most colorful Cossacks in the history of Russia—the Don Cossacks—presented from the standpoint of realism rather than romanticism.

The *Silent Don* likewise breaks new ground by creating an understanding and appreciation of the Cossacks throughout Russia. Russians who read Gogol's *Taras Bulba,* Lermontov's poems of the Cossacks of the Caucasus, and Leo Tolstoy's *The Cossacks* and *Hadji Murad* could not help but admire the dashing heroism of the Cossacks, but they were often repelled and horrified by their actions. In Old Russia, the Cossacks were feared, partly because they were used by the tsars to crush revolts and strikes. Sholokhov, describing rich Cossacks and poor, good and bad, Red and White, has eliminated this element of fear by showing that the Cossacks are ordinary human beings, with joys and sorrows like those of any other people.

In the past, Russian writers have championed the cause of other oppressed minorities and groups. It remained for Sholokhov to elicit a long-delayed recognition of the contributions of the Don Cossacks. In this respect, *The Silent Don* carries on the tradition of classical Russian literature and is perhaps more representative of it than any other Soviet work. It serves, therefore, as the best link between pre-Revolutionary and contemporary Russian literature.

Like A. Tolstoy's *Peter I* and Leo Tolstoy's *War and Peace,* masterpieces with which the Sholokhov epic is often compared, *The Silent Don* is a historical novel. But whereas both Tolstoys wrote of the distant past which they knew only from books and records, Sholokhov deals with contemporary history which he himself helped to make, in a region where he knew both the people and the countryside as intimately as he knew himself. *The Silent Don* is therefore more than a historical novel. It is a historical record of first-class importance. In this respect it has much in common with Alexei Tolstoy's *The Road to Calvary*.

Any person unaware of the time and place of writing of *The Silent Don* would never for a moment suspect that it was published in a country where freedom of speech was circumscribed by the necessity of depicting the new regime in a favorable light, especially from the ideological standpoint. Katayev, it is true, exposed some of the limitations of Komsomol ideology; but, accidentally or otherwise, he took care to point out that the deviations from the established practice, which he portrayed so sympathetically, would not hurt the Revolution. Even then, he did not entirely escape the consequences of his temerity.

Sholokhov, on the other hand, writes as a free Cossack, making no concessions whatever, even when dealing with his hero, Grigory Melekhov; it is Dzerzhinsky's opera, and not Sholokhov's novel, which makes of Grigory a real Soviet hero. In the novel, Grigory believes he would have been wiser to remain with the Reds, instead of drifting from side to side in the Civil War, but in reality he returns home, disillusioned with the excesses of both factions. Whether it was because Sholokhov for the first time depicted the class struggle among the Cossacks, whether it was due to his reputation as a proletarian writer and member of the Communist Party, or for some other reason, his *Silent Don* is one of the rarest examples of freedom of speech in contemporary Russian literature.

In view of the rapid and dramatic transformation of Asiatic Russia under the Soviets, and especially of Siberia, it is already apparent that contemporary Russian writers are falling under the spell of the Russian East and of the Russian Arctic frontier. This trend will bear close watching in the future. The literature of Russia in the nineteenth century began in the North. However, Russian writers derived much of their inspiration from the South, particularly from the Ukraine and the Caucasus, which then corresponded to the American "Wild West." Because of the scenic grandeur of the Caucasian Mountains, and the colorful and variegated life of the peoples of South Russia, including the Cossacks, this region is likely to continue to inspire the best literary talent Soviet Russia produces. Nevertheless, it may be assumed that, in the future, Siberia—where a wealth of folklore has been compiled in recent years, where a center of culture is being established, and where many writers are already living—will provide the setting and the milieu for a larger output of literary work. *The Every Day Arctic* by Boris Gorbatov has led numerous writers to seek literary inspiration in the Soviet North. For some time it has been the fashion for Soviet writers to accompany exploratory and scientific expeditions to the Arctic frontier. Whether Siberian literature will prove to be a distinctive *genre*, whether it will be an elongation of the Far East as Caucasian literature was of the Near East, or whether it will merge with the main stream of Soviet literature remains to be seen.

Some mention should be made here of the literature which has been produced under the Soviet regime by representatives of the national minorities. This contribution is a direct result of the recognition and encouragement of the native languages of minority groups by the Soviet Government. It is impossible as yet to estimate how much of this will prove to be of permanent value. Much has already been translated into Russian. Since Russian is now studied and spoken throughout the USSR, it stands to reason that the best of the works emanating from the minorities will find a niche among the Russian classics, and that they may well make Russian literature one of the most colorful and most representative in the world.

In World War II there emerged a whole flock of new Soviet writers, whose work was largely journalistic in nature. Among the most prominent is Konstantin Simonov (1915-   ), author of the nostalgic poem, *Wait for Me,* of the patriotic play, *The Russian People* (1942), produced in this country by the New York Theatre Guild, of the first novel on the epic siege of Stalingrad, *Days and Nights* (1945), and of the widely discussed play, *The Russian Question* (1947), which aroused indignation in the United States because of its criticism of the American press. Wanda Wasilevskaya (1905-   ), Polish-born wife of the playwright, Alexander Korneytchuk, wrote a graphic account of life in a Russian village under the Nazi occupation in her novel, *The Rainbow,* which was awarded the Stalin Prize in 1943. The significance of this work and of the film based upon it, in connection with the Soviet war effort, has not yet been fully evaluated outside of Russia. Other wartime writers whose works have revealed distinct literary merit are Leonid Sobolev, noted especially for numerous sea stories based upon his experiences with the Red Navy, some of which have appeared in *The Soul of the Sea,* and Vasily Grossman, a Ukrainian, whose *Stalingrad Sketches* and *No Beautiful Nights (The People Immortal)* reflect the bitter struggle of the years of retreat. A. Stepanov's mammoth historical novel on *Port Arthur* (1944) foreshadowed the return of the Russians to that highly strategic Far Eastern port.

Since the war a new trend has appeared in Soviet literature, which marks a reaction from the idealization of the past encouraged during the war years. The vogue for historical fiction has been severely criticized. Soviet writers have been urged to tear their eyes from the past and to fix them on the present, so that they may "hail the creative labor of the Soviet man." Literature, like the other arts, was harnessed to the Stalin Five-Year Plan and the great task of reconstruction. In keeping with political and international events, Soviet postwar literature reveals a distinctly anti-Western trend, which at times assumes the guise of a kind of neo-Slavophilism. Emphasis is still placed on folk literature, as indicated by the praise accorded Pavel Bazhov's *The Malachite Box* and other fairy tales of the Ural region, best known to Western readers from the Soviet technicolor film, *The Stone Flower*. Fundamentally, however, the real demand today is for literature about the contemporary Soviet man.

No sooner did Soviet writers concentrate on the delineation of the "contemporary Soviet man" than they were told that this Soviet man must be a positive, not a negative type. The champions of the positive Soviet type discovered that existing Soviet literature provided them with a foundation on which to build and with examples for them to emulate. They traced the positive type back to Gorky, especially to his novel *Mother;* to A. Serafimovitch's *The Iron Stream* (1924); to D. Furmanov's *Tchapayev* (1923), where the power behind Tchapayev is Klytchkov, the Commissar; to A. Fadeyev's *The Rout (The Nineteen)*, which is recommended even more than his recent novel, *The Young Guard;* to Sholokhov's *Virgin Soil Upturned;* to P. Pavlenko's *Happiness;* to S. Babayevsky's *The Cavalier of the Gold Star;* and to Mikhail Bubennov's recent work, *The White Birch,* where the Commissar, Yakhno, although not the main character, plays the same role as Klytchkov in *Tchapayev.*

Two novels which, because of their wide popularity, became the focal point of much of the discussion about positive and negative types, were Alexander Fadeyev's *The Young Guard* (1945) and Boris Polevoy's *A Story of a Real Man* (1947).

The Young Guard stressed the superiority of the existing Soviet system from a military, political, economic, and especially from an educational standpoint. By 1947, however, the author was accused of "deviation," because of his failure to portray the leading Bolshevik characters as positive and active types. In compliance with the new trend Fadeyev in 1951 brought out a revised version of his novel, in which the leader of the underground youth organization, Lyutikov, and his associates stand out as positive characters, worthy of emulation.

A Story of a Real Man (1947), by Boris Polevoy, appeared as if in answer to the prayers of Soviet propagandists for some means of stemming the tide of discontent over domestic conditions in the USSR after the close of World War II. It became virtually an integral part of the Soviet program for the readjustment and rehabilitation of millions of Soviet veterans and displaced persons who had returned to their homes following that cataclysm. Although ostensibly a war novel the indomitable hero, Meresyev, served as an example for all maimed or destitute Soviet citizens to emulate. The "real man" was soon identified with the "contemporary man" or the "Soviet man," as distinct from the "historical man" who rose to unprecedented popularity in the war years.

Some Soviet writers and critics like Vera Panova, best known as the author of *The Train* (*Companions,* 1946), resisted the growing pressure for a ban on negative characters. They argued that if all leading characters were to be positive and unmarred by negative traits they would cease to be typical and Soviet literature could no longer claim to be realistic.

This literary debate over the delineation of positive and negative characters continued until G. M. Malenkov, in his report to the Nineteenth Party Congress on October 5, 1952, handed down from above a new definition of the term "typical," which at once set the tone for Soviet writers throughout the length and breadth of the land:

". . . In creating artistic images," said Malenkov, "our artists and writers must always bear in mind that the typical is not only what is most often encountered. The typical is that which most fully and vividly expresses the essence of a given social force. In the Marxist-Leninist concept, the typical does not necessarily mean a specific statistical average. Typicalness corresponds to the essence of a given social-historical phenomenon and is not simply what is most widespread, most often repeated, most common. A deliberately magnified image, brought out in salient relief, does not exclude typicalness, but more fully reveals and emphasizes it. Typicalness is the main sphere of the manifestation of partisanship in realistic art. The problem of typicalness is always the problem of politicality."

If we are to read between the lines of the comments of Soviet writers and critics following the Malenkov pronouncement, it is clear that the leading characters in Soviet drama and fiction must be Communists and *ipso facto* they must be positive types, since no Communist can be delineated as a weakling. If negative characters must be introduced, they should be so depicted as to make it clear that they are foreign to the Soviet environment. Such a line of argument represents an attempt to implement in literature Article 126 of the Constitution of the USSR.

In brief, Soviet critics want their writers to become contemporary Gogols, using the technique of Gogol to create, not negative but typical positive characters who will have as great a grip on the popular imagination as did Tchitchikov. They want Soviet writers to depict the Soviet man as he ought to be rather than as he is, in the hope that the people may emulate his example.

If the current trend in Soviet literature should continue for the next few years, it can produce only a distorted and idealistic rather than a realistic portrait of the Soviet man. The characters will be neither positive nor negative, neither realistic nor typical. They can be typical only of the State apparatus—of the Party. This distortion of realism can produce only "lives of Soviet saints." The only redeeming feature connected with this Soviet hero worship is that it may result in an unlooked for and unwanted revival of individualism, which could eventually prove detrimental to communistic ideas and to statism.

The publication in 1956 of V. Dudintsev's novel, *Not By Bread Alone* (*Novyi Mir,* Nos. 8, 9, 10), which clearly revealed the struggle of the positive individual against collectivism, left those responsible for the molding and shaping of Soviet literature profoundly shaken. Although his hero proved to be right and the collective power wrong, obviously it was not the purpose of Dudintsev to undermine the Soviet system of collectivism. His emphasis on the frustrating experiences of the inventor, Lopatkin, who designed a centrifugal pipe-casting machine of considerable value only to have it rejected by the Soviet bureaucracy, nevertheless produced that result. Because of the disturbance created by this novel, Soviet critics who continued to advocate the delineation of the positive character emphasized early in 1957 that this must not be done at the expense of collectivism and Communist discipline: "Creative activity in the field of literature and art must be imbued with the spirit of the struggle for Communism, must instill in the heart courage and firmness of conviction, must develop socialist consciousness and comradely discipline."

As was the case with many of his predecessors, Dudintsev succumbed to pressure and "revised" his novel. Its very title nevertheless challenged forty years of Soviet materialistic indoctrination, serving as a reminder to the peoples of the USSR that "man does not live by bread alone. . . ."

A year later, in 1957, there appeared another novel, which evoked even stronger repercussions, both inside and outside the Soviet Union. This was *Doctor Zhivago,* by one of Russia's foremost poets, Boris Pasternak (1890-1960). Rejected for publication in the USSR, it appeared first in Italy and was immediately thereafter translated into many other languages. Although Pasternak was awarded the Nobel Prize in Literature in October 1958, the furore aroused in the USSR by the almost fabulous success of his novel abroad ultimately forced him to refuse the honor.

Like Dudintsev, Pasternak championed the cause of the individual. But he did more than that. He wrote a novel about the Russian Revolution, which was highly critical of Communism, Marxism, and collectivism. In brief, *Dr. Zhivago* was an indictment of the men, methods, and results of the Communist upheaval. In contrast to the "idealists" who led the Russian Revolution of 1905, Pasternak portrayed those of the October Revolution as professional revolutionists —fanatics, with one-track minds. The social betterment they preached, he claimed, was far from being practised. After twenty-five years of silence on the part of the poet, it was heartening to find that Pasternak's novel revealed a thirst for religion, highly reminiscent of Dostoyevsky.

SOVIET MUSIC, 1917-1960

In the early years of the Soviet regime there was, in music as in literature, a good deal of experimentation and a drift toward extreme modernism. By and large, however, Soviet music has followed the traditions of the great Russian composers of the nineteenth century. Whenever it has betrayed a disposition to abandon them in favor of the satirical, exaggerated effects characteristic of Western modernism, Soviet criticism has stemmed the tide.

Among the more outstanding composers of the USSR are several who have likewise achieved fame and popularity in the United States, including Nikolai Myaskovsky (1881-1950), Sergei S. Prokofiev (1891-1953), Dmitri Shostakovitch (1906-   ), and Aram Khatchaturian (1904-   ).

Myaskovsky, who until his death in 1950 ranked as the dean of Soviet composers, began his musical career under the old regime. From 1921, as Professor at the Moscow Conservatory, he helped to train and influence the younger generation of Soviet composers, including

Khatchaturian, Shebalin, Muradeli, and Kabalevsky. His own work— he has twenty-four symphonies to his credit—shows the influence of Mussorgsky and Borodin, and carries on the traditions of Russian classical symphonic music.

Prokofiev, a student of Rimsky-Korsakov and Liadov, spent some years abroad in Germany, France, and the United States after the Revolution but returned to the USSR in 1933, where he was recognized as one of the leading Soviet composers. Some of his early works, *The Buffoon, The Scythian Suite,* and *The Love for Three Oranges,* the last-mentioned produced in Chicago, show the same tendency toward sarcasm and caricature found in Mussorgsky's musical works and the literary masterpieces of Gogol. After his return to the USSR, however, Prokofiev's works increasingly reverted to patriotic themes. He wrote the music for several Soviet films, including *Lieutenant Kije, Alexander Nevsky,* and *Ivan the Terrible.* His *Alexander Nevsky Cantata* (1939), based upon the music for the Sergei Eisenstein film, is a powerful work on the Russian defense of Novgorod against the Teutonic Knights in 1242. Prokofiev's operas, *Semyon Kotka,* based on one of Katayev's works dealing with the Civil War period, and his more recent *War and Peace,* composed during World War II, have been criticized for their lack of a broad melodic treatment and for the excessive use of recitative as a substitute for melody. Among the works of Prokofiev that have won considerable acclaim abroad are his early *Classical Symphony* (1917) and the *Second Concerto for Violin and Orchestra in G Minor* (1935), which Jascha Heifetz has classed among the great violin concertos. His unique *Peter and the Wolf* (1936) appears to have won a place for itself in the repertoire of music for children.

Dmitri Shostakovitch, who achieved world-wide fame during World War II, is regarded by many as the most gifted composer produced yet by the Soviet regime. He has written nine symphonies; the *First* (1926) still ranks among his best works, although the *Seventh* or *Leningrad Symphony* (1942), which served as a "patriotic call to arms," was widely heralded during the war years. The Shostakovitch ballet, *The Golden Age* (1929-1930), representing a clash between Soviet and Fascist visitors to a capitalistic industrial exhibition, was written in a satirical vein. His opera, *Lady Macbeth of Mtsensk* (1932), based on Nikolai Leskov's novel, *Katherine Ismailova,* aroused a storm of criticism in the Soviet Union on account of its "jarring, irritating, and affected intonations." A *Piano Quintet*

(1940) was received more favorably and, like the *Leningrad Symphony,* won the Stalin Prize.

Since 1942 the Soviet Armenian composer, Aram Khatchaturian, has attracted increasing attention abroad. Like Shostakovitch he is a product of the new era, although his music is steeped in the folklore of his native Armenia, the Caucasus, and the Transcaucasus. Khatchaturian's best-known works include a *Concerto for Piano and Orchestra* (1936), a *Concerto for Violin and Orchestra* (1940), a *Second Symphony* (1941-1942), and his highly colorful and rhythmic *Gayne Ballet* (1942), a recording from which became a best-seller in the United States.

Other Soviet composers whose works have attracted attention are Dmitri Kabalevsky (1904-   ), known also as a music critic, Vissarion Shebalin (1902-   ), who follows the Tchaikovsky tradition of melody, Ivan Dzerzhinsky (1909-   ), already mentioned in connection with his "model opera," *The Silent Don,* and Ivan Muradeli (1908-   ), Georgian-born composer whose opera, *The Great Friendship,* was in 1948 condemned for its formalism, thereby sharing a fate comparable to that of *Lady Macbeth of Mtsensk.*

According to Juri Jelagin, in *Taming of the Arts,* the autobiographical record of his experiences in the Soviet theatrical and musical worlds, Soviet composers and musicians enjoyed an additional ten years of relative freedom after the Soviet theatre was reduced in 1936 to the common denominator of socialist realism. During this decade, 1937-1947, Russian composers produced an outstanding and remarkably varied body of works, including many of those listed above.

Since the end of the war there has been in music, as in literature a reaction against Western influences. Whereas the Soviet writer has been called upon to portray the Soviet man and forget the past, the Soviet composer has been urged to abandon affectations, eccentricity, and formalism and return to "the noble traditions of Russian music." Emphasis is placed on melody and folk themes rather than on "cacophonous roar and rumble"—on music that the Soviet masses can understand and appreciate. In pursuit of this aim the first All-Union Congress of Soviet Composers was convened in Moscow in April 1948.

Ilya Ehrenburg, writing in *Znamya* (October 1953), and Aram Khatchaturian in *Sovietskaya Musika* (November 1953) protested against rigorous bureaucratic controls in literature and music respectively and demanded greater freedom for creative artists in the USSR. Whether this marks a turning point or just another temporary breathing spell for the long-suffering Soviet writers and musicians was not yet clear by 1960.

15

The USSR After World War II

DOMESTIC AFFAIRS

SINCE 1945 there has been an almost unprecedented upsurge of nationalism in the Soviet Union. Although for some years prior to World War II there were indications of a revival of Russian nationalism, the war itself, with the invasion of Russian territory and the ultimate victory, greatly intensified this trend, as wartime literature, and especially the historical novel, clearly revealed. Ever since the end of the war—in proportion as the rift between the East and West has widened—Soviet nationalism has taken deeper root, until by 1948 it far exceeded the national Slavophilism of the nineteenth century and might well be termed *neo-Slavophilism,* albeit under socialistic nomenclature. It seems that there is being enacted in the Soviet Union today a controversy comparable in some respects to that between the Slavophiles and Westernizers of the nineteenth century, which contributed so much to the golden age of Russian literature. Whereas at that time, however, in spite of the autocracy and censorship, both the Slavophiles and the Westernizers had a platform from which to express their ideas, in the current controversy between the neo-Slavophiles and neo-Westernizers only the former have a chance to express themselves, while the views of the neo-Westernizers are derided and, at least for the time being, silenced. There is not today the same balance of opposing views as in the nineteenth century litera-ture and press.

The Soviet postwar trend toward nationalism has not been con-fined to politics, the international arena, or even to the revival of pan-Slavism in Eastern Europe. It has invaded every phase of Soviet life and thought, including education, music, literature, and the arts, as well as science. The Soviet Government, under the aegis of the

Communist Party, has launched a campaign in each of these spheres to rid the country of alien Western "isms," and to exalt Russian and Soviet leaders and achievements over and above those of the West. Whereas the Soviet regime, which came into power after World War I, for some years pursued a policy of militant communism, it has emerged from World War II with a policy of militant nationalism.

In what might well be termed a "USSR First" program, the Soviet Union has been exalting the role of Russian scientists, in some instances giving them credit for discoveries or inventions ordinarily attributed to Western scholars. Alexander S. Popov, for example, instead of Marconi, is hailed as the real discoverer of radio. Dmitri Mendeleyev is acclaimed as the world's greatest chemist, who discovered the Periodic Law and thereby paved the way for the disclosure of the secrets of atomic energy. Zhukovsky is given credit for laying the theoretical foundations of aerodynamics and aviation, while A. P. Karpinsky, "the father of Russian geology," is said to have been far ahead of the Western geologists of his time.

From the standpoint of science, however, the breach between the East and the West was most clearly revealed at a session of the V. I. Lenin Academy of Agricultural Sciences (July 31 to August 7, 1948), at which the I. V. Mitchurin school of biological science under the leadership of Academician T. D. Lysenko emerged triumphant over those Soviet scientists (I. I. Schmalhausen, B. M. Zavodovsky, A. R. Zhebrak, and N. P. Dubinin) who represented Western concepts on genetics as developed by J. G. Mendel the Czech, August Weismann the German, and Thomas H. Morgan the American biologist. The Mitchurinites, in line with the basic tenets of dialectical materialism, contend that a change in the environment of an organism leads to changes in its heredity, thereby discarding the thesis of most Western biologists who maintain that the properties of heredity are completely independent of the living conditions of plants and animals. The Presidium of the Academy of Medical Sciences has likewise officially adopted the Mitchurin thesis. Some outstanding Western scientists, including H. V. Muller, President of the Genetics Society of America, and Henry Dale, President of the Royal Society of Great Britain, who deplored the dogmatic stand of their Soviet colleagues and believed it to be entirely unsubstantiated, resigned their membership in the Academy of Sciences of the USSR in 1948. The whole controversy, which as indicated has had its repercussions far beyond the boundaries of the Soviet Union, has shown that in the USSR today there is no such thing as "science for science's sake," any more than there is a recognition of the principle of "art for art's sake." Only those scientific efforts are encouraged which in the opinion of Soviet Party leaders contribute in practice to the material betterment of the USSR. There is no such thing as a science divorced from politics, according to the Presidium of the Academy of Sciences of the USSR in its reply to H. V. Muller (*Pravda,* December 14, 1948). In order to disseminate the officially accepted theories on heredity to the effect that acquired traits can be inherited, the Soviet Ministry of Cinematography on January 2, 1949, released the widely advertised technicolor film *Mitchurin* and urged all Soviet citizens to attend the showings.

The same admixture of extreme nationalism and Party dogmatism has characterized of late the official approach to education, linguistics, and historical research. Numerous Soviet textbooks for the higher schools have been denounced for subservience to the West and for underrating or ignoring Russian achievements. Even the outstanding linguistic scholar, V. V. Vinogradov, author of *The Russian Language* (1947), was castigated for " the absence of a militant, patriotic spirit, and an exaggeration of the contribution of foreign linguistics. . . ." The climax of the postwar linguistic controversy was reached when, after a series of articles, pro and con, in *Pravda* (May 9-August 2, 1950),[1] Joseph Stalin himself stepped in to dethrone the uncrowned king of Soviet linguistics, the late Academician N. Ya. Marr. Even a cursory reading of these articles raises the question as to whether the Lysenko theory of genetics is not in some respects out of line with Marxism-Leninism as applied to the new Stalin version of linguistics. Linguistic scholars were criticized for paying undue attention to the study of ancient languages and taking no interest in the contemporary language in the process of formation. The same criticism was directed against historians who buried themselves intellectually in the remote past and neglected the study of the Soviet Union.

Among scholars in various fields, there has been waged since the war a campaign for a return to Marxist-Leninist doctrines and for their active propagation in the schools. There have been complaints about courses in which the teachings of Marx and Lenin have been completely ignored, or in which they are perfunctorily presented to the students as "a series of formulae which bear an extremely remote relation to contemporary social life." [2] Soviet educators are being told to make clear the advantages of the socialist economic system over the

---

[1] See *The Soviet Linguistic Controversy,* edited by Ernest J. Simmons, New York, 1951.
[2] *Pravda,* March 10, 1947.

capitalist, and "to expose" contemporary "bourgeois" economic concepts for what they are. In brief, the Soviet Government since 1945 has
been engaged in an all-out effort to uproot everything it regards as
un-Soviet in the ideological and political training of Soviet youth and

Courtesy Sovfoto

MOSCOW STATE UNIVERSITY

Soviet citizens. For the time being, at least, there is no tolerance of
opposing viewpoints.[1]

Another factor which has contributed greatly to Soviet nationalism
and neo-Slavophilism in the postwar years is the isolationism, sometimes referred to as the "iron curtain," which has been in part a volun-

---

[1] See Spector, Ivar, "The Russians Conquer Marx," *The Saturday Review,*
January 31, 1953.

tary Soviet withdrawal from the West and in part a result of the concerted opposition of the West toward the Soviet Union. In the past, when Russia has gone isolationist, autocracy and reaction have dominated the domestic scene. Russians were discouraged from studying or traveling abroad, especially in Western Europe, and foreigners were unwelcome in Russia. The best examples are the reign of Nicholas I (1825-1855) and that of Alexander III (1881-1894). A somewhat parallel situation prevails today in the USSR. Since 1945, when the isolationist spirit reasserted itself, the Soviet Government has been ruthlessly uprooting the evidences of Western thought and culture which penetrated Russia during the years of collaboration with the West.

In the domestic field, the high tide of Soviet nationalism in the post-war years has been directed first toward the reconstruction of the devastated regions of the motherland. After World War I the process of reconstruction was retarded by miltant communism, civil war, and the expectation of an imminent world revolution. In World War II, however, reconstruction followed directly upon liberation, even in some instances before hostilities ceased and often with the involuntary aid of prisoners of war.

Soviet leaders in the beginning anticipated that the road to reconstruction would be eased and accelerated by the payment of at least $10,000,000,000 in German reparations and by foreign, principally American, loans to replace lend-lease, which was terminated at the end of the war. When reparations payments failed to meet their expectations and no American loans were forthcoming, the Soviet Government increased its demands on Soviet-occupied Europe and came to rely perforce more and more on its own resources, as well as on the extensive use of slave labor. Under worse circumstances, the Soviet regime had survived and built up the country after 1918. Soviet leaders were confident that, although the process of rehabilitation would of necessity be slower, they could meet the new challenge alone if necessary. It seems apparent that Soviet nationalism was thereby accentuated.

Other factors notwithstanding, the Soviet people attributed their victory in World War II basically to their Soviet social and state system, and to the three Five-Year Plans (1928-1941), which constituted a preparedness program. It was this planned economy which in their opinion had laid the foundations of heavy industry, collectivized agriculture, and modern military techniques which enabled the Soviet Union to continue resistance even after the Germans and their satellites had occupied Soviet territory to a depth of some 800 miles.

The Fourth or Stalin postwar Five-Year Plan, adopted by the Supreme Soviet on March 18, 1946, was designed primarily to repair the ravages of war and to carry on new construction in the part of the Soviet Union untouched by the conflict. After World War I and the Civil War it took the USSR about six years to restore industrial production to the 1913 level. The new Stalin Five-Year Plan had as its goal the restoration of the prewar level in industry and agriculture by 1948, and a substantial increase in that level thereafter. By 1950 industry was expected to exceed the 1940 level by almost 1.5 times, agriculture by more than 25 percent, and transport by more than 33 1/3 percent.[1]

Of the total volume of major works outlined by the Plan, almost half was directed, at least in the beginning, toward the rehabilitation of the devastated areas of European Russia.[2] The scope of this task can be realized perhaps if we remember that, according to Soviet figures, some 1710 cities and towns were partially or wholly destroyed, that 70,000 villages were demolished, more than 40,000 miles of railway track destroyed, including 13,000 bridges, not to mention the mines, factories, power stations, equipment, livestock, homes, and last, but not least, the loss of human life. Indeed, General Eisenhower has stated [3] that on his flight to the USSR in 1945 he did not see a house standing from the time he passed the Soviet frontier until he reached the environs of Moscow. He was told that so many Russians had been killed that the Soviet Government would never be able to obtain an exact estimate of the total. During the war, more than 1300 enterprises had been evacuated to the East in advance of the German invaders. Soviet leaders estimated that in the years from 1946 to 1950 they must restore or build some 5900 enterprises in the USSR.

The basic reconstruction program involved the restoration of such projects as the Dnieper Dam, the Zaporozhe Steel Plant, the naval base at Sevastopol, the mines of the Donbas, the rebuilding on more modern lines of cities like Stalingrad and Minsk, and the repair of major damage done to Leningrad, Odessa, Kiev, Kharkov, Pskov, and other cities in European Russia. Among railroads requiring reconstruction were the Moscow-Leningrad, the Moscow-Minsk-Brest, and the Moscow-Kiev-Odessa trunk lines. The Stalin White Sea-Baltic Canal was likewise slated for rebuilding.

Although the major emphasis of the Stalin Five-Year Plan was upon heavy industry (iron and steel, fuel, and machine tools, etc.) and

---

[1] *Pravda*, October 26, 1946.
[2] *Ibid.*
[3] *Crusade in Europe*, p. 469.

railway transport, provision was also made for greatly increased agricultural and livestock production by means of mechanization, electrification, and, where necessary, irrigation. According to the program, the increased production of food and consumer products would make possible the early discontinuance of rationing and price reductions. Emphasis was likewise placed on the improvement of living conditions by construction of more schools, hospitals, rest homes, cinemas, and housing facilities. Indicative of the fact that Soviet security was still a matter of primary concern, the Plan called for the strengthening of the defensive power of the USSR and the equipment of the armed forces with up-to-date weapons, as well as "the building of a strong and powerful Navy." In his speech of February 9, 1946, Stalin summed up ultimate Soviet objectives as follows:

We must achieve a situation where our industry can produce annually up to 50,000,000 tons of pig iron, up to 60,000,000 tons of steel, up to 500,000,000 tons of coal and up to 60,000,000 tons of oil. Only under such conditions can we consider that our motherland will be guaranteed against all possible eventualities. That will take three more Five-Year Plans, I should think, if not more. But it can be done and we must do it.

In brief, the avowed object of the Soviet Government was to complete the building of a socialist society and continue the gradual transition from socialism to communism. From the figures cited, however, it is clear that, even when the Stalin objective is achieved, the Soviet Union will still lag far behind the industrial production of the United States.

In drafting the postwar Five-Year Plan, the State Planning Commission provided for the distribution of industrial projects throughout the Union, rather than for their concentration in a few already highly developed areas. For example, their blueprint for the all-round development of the iron and steel industry envisaged not only the restoration of prewar enterprises in the Donbas, the expansion of facilities already developed in the Urals, Siberia, and the Far East, but new iron and steel mills in Georgia and Kazakhstan, as well as in the Leningrad area. A pipe-rolling mill was located in Azerbaijan. Novo-Troitzk in the Urals, which in 1942 comprised some sixteen cottages, by 1946 had become the center of a new steel combine and boasted a population of 20,000 inhabitants. At Sverdlovsk in Siberia an entirely new industrial district was developed for the production of heavy chemical machinery. At Magadan, an industrial center with auto-repair shops and ship-repair yards on the Sea of Okhotsk, the first steel in the Soviet Far East was smelted in 1948.

As the East-West tension increased after 1945, special emphasis was placed on construction in Asiatic Russia, even, it seems, at the expense of reconstruction in European Russia. At Molotov in the Urals the Soviet press claimed that there was not a factory where existing shops were not enlarged and new ones constructed. Meanwhile, the reconversion of plants from a wartime to a peacetime basis went on apace. The Stalin Tank Building Plant in the Urals changed over to the construction of railroad cars, and the Urals Heavy Machine Building Plant at Sverdlovsk instead of tanks began to produce blast furnaces, rolling mills, drills, and so on.

The experience of World War II having demonstrated that industrial cities like Stalingrad, Leningrad, and Moscow were more vital points of resistance to an invading army than rural areas, the Soviet Government has since the war undertaken the construction of new industrial centers on the periphery, especially in the Far East. In the Maritime Province of Siberia a number of such centers, including Komsomolsk, Magadan, Raitchikhinsk, Birobijan, Sovietskaya Gavan, Artem, and Okha have grown up in the past twenty years, and many others are not yet on the map. Vladivostok has become the largest port in the Soviet Union. In 1947 and 1948 Dalstroi, the Far Eastern Construction Trust, advertised for all types of engineers, technicians, doctors, teachers, office workers, and other specialists for Kolyma and Tchukotka, an indication of unprecedented activity in the northeastern periphery of the USSR directly across from Alaska. An electric power station has been built at Usmun on the Indigirka river, in the vicinity of the world's cold pole, and mining operations are under way.

Nor has Southern Sakhalin, recently recovered from the Japanese, been neglected. To this Far Eastern outpost, where the sun rises seven hours earlier than in Moscow, settlers have come from all parts of the Soviet Union to develop the fishing, mining, and timber industries, and incidentally to increase the defensive potentialities of that highly strategic area which provides the USSR with free access to the Pacific and with important bases against any future threat of aggression from Japan. Demobilized soldiers have been encouraged to remain in Sakhalin. As an additional incentive to settlement, *Trud,* the labor newspaper, reported (September 26, 1948) that the newcomers have been provided with thousands of head of cattle, sheep, and pigs for their individual use.

The extensive redistribution of population required by the development of new industries in widely scattered parts of the Soviet Union has been achieved in part by inducement and in part by coercion. All sorts of incentives have been offered by the Soviet Government to induce settlers to "Go East." In Southern Sakhalin these include ten years' exemption from taxation. In many instances, they involve opportunities for better wages, bigger wage bonuses, more comfortable housing, free transportation, loans to private persons for housing construction, the purchase of cows, and household goods, etc. In Omsk, for instance, in 1946 comfortable private dwellings were constructed and wages raised as an incentive to settlement and increased productivity.

The Soviet Government has been making every effort to develop cultural, scientific, artistic, and educational institutions in Siberia. The new Opera House of Novosibirsk rivals, if it does not excel, those of Moscow and Leningrad. Tomsk University is conducting extensive research directed toward the further development of Siberian resources. It is somewhat reminiscent of an old American pioneer custom that school raising bees have been held by settlers in the *taiga* and in the Sverdlovsk Region. Moreover, the government is beginning to bring electricity and paved roads to the *taiga*. To meet the needs of the increasing flow of new settlers, prefabricated houses are already being constructed in Kamtchatka, and a new plant was scheduled to begin production in Yakutia early in 1949. The press reported as early as 1946 that more young people were arriving every month to swell the population of Komsomolsk on the Amur.

Where labor requirements cannot be met by this voluntary trek of prospective settlers to the East, the Soviet Government now as in the past can rely upon the forced labor of political prisoners and convicted criminals. The abolition of capital punishment on May 27, 1947 (reestablished on January 13, 1950, for treason, espionage, and sabotage), reflects a practice long prevalent even in tsarist Russia of commuting the death penalty to labor in Siberia. No official statistics are available as to the number of prisoners so employed. GULAG, the Soviet Slave Labor Trust and a division of the MVD, maintains scores of penal labor camps throughout the Soviet Union, and estimates as to the number of its prisoners have ranged from five to twenty millions. German and Japanese prisoners of war have likewise been used to ease the widespread labor shortage of the postwar years, as well as large numbers of Poles, Esthonians, Latvians, Lithuanians, and Finns, deported from their homelands.

With the improvement of transportation facilities, it has become apparent that the Soviet Far East is no longer to remain a remote and isolated hinterland. In April 1948 a regular air transport completed the round trip between Moscow and Khabarovsk in three days instead of the usual seven. Parts of the Trans-Siberian Railroad are being electrified (e.g. from Omsk to Tatarskaya), and a new harbor with extensive shipyards has been developed at Sovietskaya Gavan, north of Vladivostok.

Courtesy Sovfoto
Moscow today. The tall building near Krasnye Vorota.

It seems apparent that the marked emphasis in the postwar years on increased housing construction (including private homes), the production of more automobiles, radios, bicycles, musical instruments, and all types of consumers' goods—the signs of a higher standard of living—is designed to prove to Soviet citizens that they have within their grasp at home many of the advantages hitherto provided only in the West, and especially in America. Of special interest in this respect was the decree issued by the Presidium of the Supreme Soviet on August 29, 1948, permitting Soviet citizens to buy or build private houses of not more than five rooms in size or two stories in height, and granting them perpetual use, but not ownership, of the building sites. This decree followed widespread criticism in the Soviet press of inadequate housing accommodations, especially in coal mining and other industrial areas in both the East and the West. The extent of the current vogue for home ownership was inadvertently admitted by Soviet authorities (*Trud,* February 18, 1953) when the press revealed that in the city of Kiev alone workers and employees have used government loans to construct more than 6,000 private homes since World War II. It is worth noting that in a period of emergency the Soviet Union is inclined to make concessions to private initiative, as during the NEP following World War I and again in order to speed the process of reconstruction after World War II. On the other hand, capitalist countries, when confronted by emergency, have frequently resorted to socialist expedients, such as public works programs, etc.

On December 16, 1947, the Soviet Government likewise put an end to rationing and simultaneously introduced monetary reform. This was done, according to *Pravda* (December 17, 1947) in order "to liquidate the aftermath of World War II as it affected the circulation of money, to restore the full value of the Soviet ruble, and to facilitate the transition to trade at uniform prices without rationing." As explained by Soviet Party leaders, the enormous military expenditures of the war years had required that huge quantities of money should be put into circulation. Much of this which could not be exchanged for goods flowed into the hands of speculators who took advantage of the gap between controlled state prices and those on the unorganized *kolkhoz* market. Following the German occupation there were likewise quantities of counterfeit money in circulation. The abolition of rationing without monetary reform would, according to the Soviet press, have played into the hands of speculators and led to increased inflation. The Government therefore took the bold and determined step of monetary reform simultaneously with the abolition of rationing in the belief that a sound currency was essential to the successful fulfillment of the postwar Five-Year Plan.

As interpreted by Moscow this reform—which involved the exchange of privately accumulated money on the basis of one new ruble for

ten of the old, which retained the wage rates in effect, and simultaneously reduced price levels on many commodities—represented a real
gain for the overwhelming number of workers, particularly because
the bank savings of the great majority, those amounting to no more
than 3000 rubles, retained their former value. For many, of course,
especially for speculators or for peasants who had hoarded their savings
in their own private "strongboxes," the reform was tantamount to
confiscation. Irrespective of the motives of the Soviet government in
the devaluation of the ruble, one thing is clear: the ruthless methods by
which it was accomplished could only have been adopted by a totalitarian state.[1] Rumors of another devaluation of the ruble following the
death of Stalin in 1953 resulted in so much panic buying of durable
goods in Moscow that the Soviet Government was forced to deny that
further monetary "reform" was contemplated.

Immediately following the abolition of rationing there was a campaign against the production of shoddy goods and inefficient trade practices. It was widely acknowledged in the Soviet press that many Soviet
enterprises had been fulfilling or exceeding their quotas by sacrificing
quality to quantity. Soviet leaders warned that goods produced must
be such as would please the consumer or he would not buy. The consumer, it was stated, would no longer "accept poor or useless goods in
exchange for the full-value Soviet ruble." [2] He demanded merchandise
of higher quality and better service from trade co-operatives and state
enterprises.

As international tension has mounted in the postwar years, the
tempo of the Soviet campaign for greater production, for higher quality
goods, and for reduced costs of operation has increased. In February
1947 the Soviet Constitution was amended to provide for a basic eight-
hour, instead of the prewar seven-hour, working day (Article 119).
Enterprises of all kinds have been urged to exceed the norms set by
the Plan, and to complete their annual quotas ahead of time. Those
that do so have received a great deal of favorable publicity in the Soviet
press. There has been an equivalent amount of ruthless "self-criticism"
of those who lag behind and of those *kolkhozi* and machine tractor stations that fail to keep their farm equipment in repair or fail to deliver
their quotas of grain to the state on time. In 1948 the slogan went forth
that the Stalin Five-Year Plan should be completed in four years, that
is, in 1949.

[1] For a more detailed analysis, see Schwartz, Harry, *Russia's Soviet Economy*,
New York, 1950, pp. 405-407.

[2] *Pravda*, December 26, 1947.

In fact, in 1948, just one hundred years after the publication of Karl Marx's *Communist Manifesto,* there was conducted throughout the Soviet Union a high-pressure campaign for profits. It was no longer enough that socialist enterprise should produce more and better items all the way from machines to consumer goods—they were expected to do it more efficiently and more economically so that the profits thereby secured might be used for new projects. Party organs in 1948 began to insist on the introduction of intraplant cost accounting in Soviet enterprises, with the object of effecting additional savings in excess of the plan. Moscow enterprises took the lead in a Union-wide competition for "profits."

Courtesy Sovfoto

The Vladivostok railroad station, terminus of the trans-siberian railway, showing the city in the background

Thus by 1948 the Soviet Government, in its efforts to compete with the capitalist West, talked as never before in terms of business efficiency, reduced production costs, the need for meeting consumer demands, the necessity for a sound currency, and, above all, of bigger and better profits. These are terms that the capitalist world understands. Indeed, the economic trend in the Soviet Union appeared to be, at least for the time being, in the direction of state capitalism rather than toward communism, with the state or state trusts running business enterprise instead of private concerns. The Soviet Government was at once confronted with the fact that it needed trained economists, state planners, and accountants, of whom there was a serious shortage, and it called upon its educational institutions to provide better training in these respects.

Meanwhile production was pushed ahead at a feverish pace. It was in the all-out effort to complete this program in 1949 that Soviet writers, actors, musicians, artists, scientists, and the press were drafted willingly or unwillingly to do their part. By the close of 1948 Soviet economy appeared to have made substantial strides toward the completion of the postwar Five-Year Plan, especially as regards heavy industry and the fuel economy. Progress was admittedly less spectacular in agriculture and livestock production, while housing construction still lagged considerably behind the Plan. Although in 1948 there was a marked increase in production of consumers' goods, the average urban worker's standard of living had not yet attained the prewar level. Western economists are inclined to believe that such Soviet figures on production as are available tend to exaggerate the results actually achieved. The substantial gains that have been made are attributed in part to the early restoration of numerous industrial enterprises in European Russia.

In a series of important decisions from 1947 to 1950, the Soviet Government drafted the main outlines of what is now called the Stalin Plan for Remaking Nature. This program includes the multiple hydro-electric, irrigation, afforestation, transport and development projects now under way along the Volga, Don, Dnieper, and Amu-Darya river systems in European and Central Asiatic Russia.

On July 11, 1952, the Soviet Government announced the completion of the V.I. Lenin Volga-Don Navigation Canal, which was officially opened on July 27. At the same time, another unit in the project, the Tsimlyanskaya Hydro-electric Plant on the Lower Don was put into operation. The projects under construction include the Stalingrad and Kuibyshev Hydro-electric Stations, those at Gorky on the Volga and Molotov on the Kama, as well as the Turkmenian Irrigation Canal, stretching from the Caspian to the Aral Sea. On July 3, 1953, *Izvestia* reported the completion of the Ust-Kamenogorsk Hydro-electric Station on the Irtysh River in Siberia. A similar power project was started in 1952 on the Angara River near Irkutsk in Central Siberia. The Nineteenth Congress of the Communist Party on October 12, 1952, announced the addition to the new Five-Year Plan of still another great hydro-electric plant on the River Ob at Novosibirsk.

Courtesy Sovfoto

VOLGA DON CANAL

Although ostensibly this vast network of construction projects is designed to improve economic conditions and "to banish drought and famine forever" from large areas of the USSR, it seems obvious that Soviet leaders are undertaking them also because of their great strategic value. In contrast to countries where free enterprise prevails, in the Soviet Union these public works projects are accomplished at terrific cost in human life, with the use of vast numbers of forced and slave laborers. In fact, many of the concentration camps are located in the areas where such developments are in progress.

Eighteen months after the announcement of the completion of the Fourth Five-Year Plan, the Nineteenth Congress of the Communist Party on August 20, 1952, outlined its directives for a Fifth Five-Year Plan (1951-1955), calling for a marked increase in the output of most major items of industrial production, such as pig iron, steel, rolled metal, coal, oil, electric power, steam turbines, hydro-turbines, oil equipment, etc. Following the death of Stalin in 1953 the Soviet Government sought to allay public discontent by promising the long-suffering peoples of the USSR that it would take immediate steps to remedy the continued embarrassing shortages of consumer goods and housing facilities. Even if the USSR should fulfill all the quotas set for 1955, its industrial output will remain far below that of the country it aims to surpass, namely, the United States.

FOREIGN POLICY

The Soviet Union emerged from World War II with two main objectives: 1. To prevent Germany ever again from constituting a threat to the Soviet Union and its Slavic satellites. 2. To block the revival of Japanese militarism, which would constitute a threat to Asiatic Russia. These objectives might have elicited some measure of support from the Western allies had the Soviet Government not undertaken to implement its policy by ruthless suppression of all independent action on the part of countries within the Soviet orbit in Eastern and Central Europe and by Communist domination of China. Because of Soviet aggression in Europe and the Orient, the Western allies had no sooner defeated the Axis powers than they were forced to support the rehabilitation and militarization of Germany and Japan against a vastly greater Soviet threat to world security.

As previously indicated, relations among the Allies, and especially between the United States and Great Britain on the one hand, and the

USSR on the other, began to deteriorate some months before the end of the war. The difficulties which cropped up at San Francisco in the spring of 1945 became even more apparent at Potsdam in July and August. It is often claimed that one of the chief factors in the growing estrangement was the change in leadership in 1945 in both the United States and Great Britain, where Roosevelt and Churchill were replaced by President Truman and Prime Minister Attlee, neither of whom had carried on negotiations with Stalin during the difficult war years. While in the ranks of the opposition Churchill has been most outspoken in his attacks on the Soviet Union, the Churchill who bore the responsibility of office was, as experience has demonstrated, both able and willing to reach a *modus vivendi* with the USSR.

The termination of World War II in August 1945 was another factor which contributed to the East-West rift in matters of international diplomacy. It is by no means unique that wartime allies should find it increasingly difficult to pursue a common policy once military operations have ceased and the fear of a common enemy no longer exists. After the Napoleonic Wars, it will be recalled, there was a comparable breach between England and Russia. After World War I, French preoccupation with security as defined by Georges Clemenceau estranged both England and the United States, and France was long regarded as the problem child of Europe.

Indeed, it was in their efforts to win not the war but the peace that the United States and Great Britain parted ways with the Soviet Union. Even as early as the signing of the Atlantic Charter in 1941, before the United States was an active participant in the conflict, Americans began to create the peace in their own image. Inevitably they conceived of it as an Anglo-American peace, founded on the very real community of interest between the two great English-speaking peoples, which, it was assumed, the rest of the world would approve and accept. Unfortunately, that did not prove to be the case. Two powers emerged from the war—not England and America, but the United States and the Soviet Union. The Russians, too, wanted a peace in their image—one that would meet their concept of security, their need for reparations, postwar loans, and industrial equipment. On account of their terrific sacrifices in men and the devastation of their land, they expected that America would accept their version of the peace. They, too, proved wrong and soon became as bitter and as disillusioned as their erstwhile Allies.

There is every indication that, although the Russians may have anticipated American expansion in the Pacific at the expense of Japan, they expected that, in line with United States policy after World War I,

the Americans would soon withdraw from Europe and the Mediterranean. They were not prepared for America's rise to world leadership,
especially in so far as it involved an active and vigorous participation in
European affairs, in particular those of Central and Eastern Europe.

To a very considerable degree, American policy in postwar Europe
has been the result of English initiative. As early as the spring of 1945
official English policy showed signs of change. Having exerted every
effort during the war to achieve a closer understanding between the
USA and the USSR, England, as the end of the war approached, was
confronted by the unpleasant prospect that continued Soviet-American
collaboration would provide little or no opportunity for her to influence
peacetime policies. In the early years of the war England had expected
the USSR either to succumb before German armed might or to emerge
from the conflict so weak as to carry little weight in mapping the postwar
world. Instead, the end of the war found the Soviet Army in occupation of Eastern and much of Central Europe, with a frontier that temporarily at least reached out to the Elbe and the Adriatic.

For a time England might have hoped, as revealed by Field Marshal
Jan Christian Smuts, to play off the new and unwelcome colossus of
the East against the United States, the colossus of the West, to the ultimate advantage of England and the British Empire. When it became
apparent that England had not emerged from World War II in a strong
enough position to assume such a decisive role, the English Labor Government, in line with traditional English policy of maintaining the balance of power, urged the United States to assume the role of "leadership" in Europe, in order to forestall a further westward expansion of
the USSR. It fell to Winston Churchill to give clear expression to
British policy, when, in his now famous address at Fulton, Missouri,
on March 5, 1946, in the presence of President Truman, he called for
what amounted to an Anglo-American alliance directed against the
Soviet Union. Whether because of this British effort, or for other reasons, the fact remains that the United States, for better or for worse,
and often without adequate preparation, was soon inextricably involved
in European affairs, from the Baltic to the Mediterranean, and from
the Atlantic to the Dardanelles. In giving priority to Europe in the
moulding of the peace, as in the waging of the war, the United States
of necessity was distracted from the highly explosive situation in Asia,
in the previous handling of which Americans had achieved considerable
success and greater prestige than the other Western powers.

The USSR emerged from World War II with very definite ideas as
to what constituted Soviet security—as definite as those of the French

after World War I. Having recovered prior to the Nazi invasion most of the territory along her western border that had belonged to tsarist Russia and which the Bolshevik regime had surrendered by the peace of Brest-Litovsk (including a slice, but not all of Finland, the Baltic states of Estonia, Latvia, and Lithuania, eastern Poland, comprised mainly of Byelorussians and Ukrainians, and Bessarabia, together with Northern Bukovina, which had never belonged to tsarist Russia), the USSR showed no disposition whatsoever to relinquish this territory. Only in the United States does there appear to have been much anticipation that the USSR would voluntarily, or even under pressure, abandon the 1939-1940 acquisitions, which once again provided direct access to the Baltic and the mouth of the Danube. From the Soviet standpoint the revised frontier constituted, not expansion, but the restitution of a strategic boundary.

As a result of the war, Soviet leaders contemplated a further adjustment of this frontier, at the expense of Finland in the Petsamo region, together with a Soviet naval base in the southwest in the Porkkala-Udd area, by the acquisition of Koenigsberg in East Prussia, the annexation by agreement with Czechoslovakia of the Carpathian Ukraine to do away with a possible center of Ukrainian irredentist propaganda abroad, the establishment of a base at the Dardanelles to secure the Soviet exit to the Mediterranean, and possibly a trusteeship over one of the Italian colonies in North Africa. The Yalta Agreement had already recognized Soviet right to the Kurile Islands and Southern Sakhalin, as well as to the return of Port Arthur and certain former tsarist interests in Manchuria.

The United States, unlike the Soviet Union, sought no territorial acquisitions on the continents of Europe and Asia. The American Government nevertheless deemed the acquisition of the former Japanese mandated islands in the Pacific, the retention of wartime bases in the Caribbean and North Atlantic, and the establishment of a Mediterranean base essential to the preservation of American security.

The opposition of the Western powers was aroused not so much by the strengthening of the Soviet frontier as by Soviet determination to maintain a series of "friendly governments" in countries bordering on the USSR in Europe. Following the Bolshevik Revolution England and France had taken the lead in encouraging the establishment of a series of bulwarks against Communism along the Soviet border from the Baltic to the Black Sea. Without exception, the governments of Finland, the Baltic states, Poland, Czechoslovakia, and Rumania had remained basically hostile to the Soviet Union, and in the interval between World Wars I and II pursued a pro-British, pro-French, and at times a pro-German policy. Convinced that this situation contributed to the outbreak of World War II and remained a threat to Soviet security, the Soviet Government was determined that it should not be restored in 1945. The Soviet Government therefore intervened actively in these border states where the Red army was in occupation to see that "friendly governments" were established and maintained. The Western powers, especially England and America, protested time and again that the Russians were violating the Yalta Agreement for the holding of "free and unfettered" elections and the establishment of democratic regimes in these states, especially in Poland, Rumania, and Bulgaria— later in Hungary, and in 1948 in Czechoslovakia.

One of the major issues which revealed the growing rift between the East and the West in the postwar years was the negotiation of the peace treaties with Italy, the Balkan states, and Finland. Not long before his death, President Roosevelt had hinted that it might not be necessary to hold a peace conference following World War II. Some Americans, including Secretary of State Byrnes, felt that instead of another Versailles Peace Treaty concluded when passions were still hot it might be better to have "a cooling-off period" before major decisions likely to affect the peace of the world for years to come were reached. Partly on this ground, no doubt, and because the opposing views of the East and West made peace without appeasement seem unattainable, there was no haste in effecting a general European peace settlement.

The Potsdam Conference had provided for the setting up of a Council of Foreign Ministers to draft the terms of the peace. Since the United States delegation at Potsdam received the impression that the USSR was not anxious to come to grips with the German treaty immediately, it was deemed best to begin with the Italian and Balkan treaties and thereby acquire the experience with which to approach the major European and Far Eastern issues. Americans would have preferred an arrangement by which the small powers played a more important role in the drafting of these treaties. According to the Potsdam decision, however, the treaty with each enemy state must be drafted by those powers that signed the armistice with it, the exception being that France was to help draft the Italian peace treaty.

The Potsdam Conference had already indicated some of the basic differences of opinion between the Western powers and the Soviet Union as regards the peace settlement. The London Conference of Foreign Ministers in September 1945 resulted in a complete deadlock over the Italian boundaries, disposition of the Italian colonies, the sum total of

Italian reparations, the character of the Balkan governments, and the role of China and France in the preparation of the Balkan treaties. The American delegation was greatly concerned over Soviet demands on Turkey for the return of the Provinces of Kars and Ardahan (lost by the Treaty of Brest-Litovsk), and for a base at the Dardanelles. The English delegation was still more alarmed at Soviet insistence on a trusteeship over one of the Italian colonies in North Africa, preferably Tripolitania, which constituted a threat to British predominance in the Mediterranean. Convinced that Soviet expansionism was going too far, the Western powers stood "firm" in their opposition to Soviet demands, and no agreement was reached.

The deadlock at London was broken at the second session of the Council of Foreign Ministers in Moscow in December 1945, at which time the Russians agreed to the calling of a twenty-one nation peace conference to discuss the treaties with the Balkan nations, Finland, and Italy. A compromise was reached in connection with the troublesome Balkan issue, whereby after further "broadening of the Rumanian and Bulgarian governments," and the holding of "democratic elections," the United States and Great Britain would extend diplomatic recognition to those states. A wide area of agreement was reached as regards the establishment of an Atomic Energy Commission in the UNO, the joint Soviet-American supervision of Korea, creation of an Allied Control Council in Japan, and continued support for a unified China. Although Secretary of State Byrnes was unable to reach an agreement with the Soviet Union on Iran, he felt that considerable progress had been made on other issues. The American press, however, was beginning to suspect any agreement with Russia as evidence of "appeasement."

In spite of the success of the Moscow Conference, more than six months were to pass before the Big Four could reach an agreement on the summoning of the peace conference of twenty-one nations at Paris on July 20, 1946, to discuss the five treaties. From July 20 to October 15 some three hundred amendments to the treaties were considered—a victory for American insistence on "full and free" discussion, as against the Soviet position that the Conference should but confirm the agreements already reached by the Council of Foreign Ministers. The real issues at Paris were three—the fate of Trieste, the fixing of reparations totals, and the control of the Danube. After bitter debate and mutual recriminations about an Eastern and a Western bloc, the Conference rejected Yugoslav claims to Trieste and provided for its international control. The reparations payable by Finland, Bulgaria, and Rumania were set at $300,000,000 each, with Bulgaria pledged to pay $125,000, 000 to Greece. The USSR, Yugoslavia, and Greece were each awarded reparations amounting to $100,000,000 from Italy, while Ethiopia received $25,000,000, and Albania's claim was rejected. On the Danubian question, the Russians argued for control by the riparian states alone, and the Western powers demanded the restoration of the international system of control which had been in effect since 1856, and which had provided for the representation of non-Danubian states such as France and England. Since both sides remained "firm," the powers had to be satisfied with a recognition of the principle of the free navigation of the Danube and the scheduling of a further conference of the Big Four and the riparian states six months after the ratification of the peace treaties. The United States was unable to secure Soviet approval, either at Paris or at the subsequent session of the Council of Foreign Ministers in New York (November 4-December 11, 1946), to the discussion of a peace treaty with Austria. When the treaties were finally signed in Paris on February 10, 1947, after American negotiators had almost abandoned hope of securing an agreement, Secretary of State Byrnes remarked that they were "as good as we could hope to get by general agreement for a long time to come." [1] Following Soviet ratification of the treaties in August 1947, *Pravda* expressed somewhat similar views in notifying the Soviet people that the treaties "are the best that could be worked out in view of the multilateral negotiations." [2]

In spite of admitted shortcomings, the treaties did represent an important step in the restoration of stability in Europe. They likewise paved the way for the ultimate withdrawal of Allied forces from Italy, Bulgaria, and Finland, although the Soviet Union continued to maintain reduced forces in Rumania and Hungary to protect its supply lines to Austria. The treaties had demonstrated at least that, with patience and perseverance, agreement between the East and the West could be achieved, and that not just one but both sides would make concessions to achieve that end. Events seemed to indicate that even an imperfect peace was preferable to no peace at all.

Not only in the drafting of the peace treaties with the five enemy states but in the operation of the United Nations Organization, established with such high hopes at San Francisco in the spring of 1945, was the growing rift between the East and the West revealed. In the absence of a basic understanding between the two great powers—the USA and the USSR—the United Nations Organization was unable to function

---

[1] *Speaking Frankly*, p. 154.
[2] *Pravda*, August 30, 1947.

smoothly and efficiently but served rather as a platform for the waging of power politics. Among the many controversies which beset the UNO were the Iranian question, the "veto" problem, and the control of atomic energy.

Hardly was the United Nations Organization set in motion than in January 1946 the Soviet Union was haled before the Security Council by Iran for allegedly instigating rebellion in the northern province of Azerbaijan adjacent to the Soviet oil fields on the shores of the Caspian Sea. In the belief that England was behind this Iranian move the USSR, as in the years prior to World War II, promptly resorted to counter-action by calling for an investigation of the continued presence of British troops in Greece and Indonesia. When Iran undertook direct negotiations with the Soviet Union on January 26, the charges made by both sides were permitted to lapse, only to be renewed when it became clear that Soviet troops would not be withdrawn from Iran by March 2, 1946, as previously agreed. Once again, however, as a result of direct negotiations between Iran and the USSR, an agreement was reached involving the withdrawal of Soviet troops by May 6 and the establishment of the Russian Iranian Petroleum Company for the exploitation of the oil resources of northern Iran. Although the arrangement as to oil was ultimately rejected by the Iranian Parliament in October 1947, Soviet influence remained strong in northern Iran, just as British influence predominated in the south. In view of its prompt and vigorous action in the Iranian dispute, the Western powers credited the United Nations Organization with a victory in halting Soviet aggression. The Russians continued to regard the action of the Security Council as unwarranted, since the Soviet-Iranian treaty of February 26, 1921, and the wartime Soviet-British-Iranian treaty of 1942 permitted the presence of Soviet troops on Iranian soil for the purpose of maintaining order.

Although the United States was originally responsible for the inclusion in the United Nations Charter of the veto right of the five permanent members of the Security Council, it has been the Soviet Union which to date has made the most effective use of that power. Soviet exercise of the veto power to block action against the Balkan states for their alleged interference in the Greek Civil War, against Albania in her dispute with England over the placing of mines in the Corfu Channel, against the admission to the UNO of such new members as Eire, Transjordan, and Portugal, against any appeasement of Franco Spain, and so on, led to demands on the part of other powers for the restriction or abolition of the veto, even for the rewriting of the UN Charter.

The Russians themselves referred to the veto right as the "unanimity rule." As explained by Molotov, the then Soviet Foreign Minister, this unanimity rule "prevents two or three or even four powers from reaching an agreement among themselves and taking action against one or the other of the five major powers. The veto spurs the great powers to work together and makes it difficult for them to intrigue one against the other, which is undoubtedly in the interest of all the United Nations and in the interests of world peace." [1] In other words, the Russians believed that unless the major powers could act unanimously, they should not act at all. The Soviet approach, which many Westerners regarded as unwarranted "obstructionism," in reality had its roots deep in the Russian past—in the Russian *mir* and State Council, where a unanimous vote was likewise the rule, and where, especially in the *mir,* one who failed to conform was labeled a *raskolnik,* or dissenter. In the Soviet Union today, although there may be much discussion of a measure pro and con, the final vote of the Supreme Soviet is ordinarily unanimous.

In the United Nations Organization, however, especially in view of the growing rift between the East and the West, it became increasingly difficult to secure unanimity among the great powers on most controversial issues. Although it seems hardly likely that the United States, any more than the Soviet Union, would consent to surrender its veto power, Americans have felt that the frequent use of the veto by the Soviet Union resulted in deadlock rather than in unanimity and has paralyzed the efforts of the Security Council.

One issue on which agreement has yet to be reached is the international control of atomic energy. Provision was made at Moscow in December 1945 for the setting up of a UN Atomic Energy Commission to include all countries on the Security Council and Canada. The Canadian spy revelations early in 1946, involving the leakage of atomic secrets to the USSR, aroused much opposition to the release of further information on atomic weapons until adequate arrangements had been made for international inspection. A proposal by Bernard Baruch, senior American presidential adviser, in June 1946 made full inspection of the atom bomb stockpiles of the United States dependent on the surrender by the Big Five of the veto power on atomic matters. Andrei Gromyko, Soviet representative on the Security Council, in reply called for the immediate destruction of existing stocks of atomic bombs, the outlawing of such weapons, and the retention of the veto. The crux of

[1] *Pravda,* September 15, 1947.

the matter has been whether existing stocks of atom bombs should be destroyed prior to institution of a system of international inspection or after inspection. The Soviet Union contended that evidence of the development of atomic energy for civilian use might serve as an excuse for the United States to retain its stockpiles. Since neither side showed a disposition to yield, the Atomic Energy Commission in December 1946 undertook to proceed with its own plan without the Soviet Union. Although the USSR has somewhat modified its position on the use of the veto in regard to the control of atomic energy, it has so far refused to surrender it in matters involving the punishment of violators and has continued to insist on the prior outlawing of the bomb. On November 6, 1947, on the eve of the thirtieth anniversary of the Bolshevik Revolution, Molotov announced that there was no longer any secret about the atom bomb, thereby causing much speculation as to how far Soviet research in this field had progressed. Although the USSR has continued to call for world disarmament and the outlawing of atomic weapons, agreement as to ways and means of accomplishing this end has not yet been reached.

The Western powers tried to overcome the stalemate in the United Nations Security Council by the transfer of controversial issues to the General Assembly where no veto right prevailed. Because of the long intervals between the sessions of the General Assembly, however, in October 1947, over the objections of the Soviet Union, a United Nations Interim Committee, better known as the Little Assembly, was set up. The troublesome veto question was transferred to the Little Assembly, which likewise attempted to solve the deadlock on Korea and on the admission of new members. Since the Soviet Union refused to recognize or participate in the Little Assembly, it has so far not proved to be an effective substitute for an East-West *modus vivendi* in the settlement of world problems.

Outside the United Nations, the Big Four met with no greater success in the solution of Europe's number one problem—Germany. The basic issues involved were the future political structure of Germany, the settlement of reparations, control of the important Ruhr industrial area, denazification and disarmament of the country, and the joint administration of Berlin. To the Russians, Western advocacy of dismemberment, or at best of a loosely federated Germany, meant the consolidation of Western control over the vital Ruhr area. Soviet championship of a united Germany was in Western eyes but a veiled attempt to pave the way for a Communist Germany.

The war was barely over when in October 1945 American economists began to doubt the possibility of implementing the Yalta and
Potsdam formulae on reparations. Time and again the Russians re-
iterated their claim for $10,000,000,000 in reparations from current
production, industrial equipment, and foreign assets, to be distributed
over a period of eighteen years. Such payments, from the standpoint of
the United States, would prevent the economic rehabilitation of Germany, and that country would remain a millstone about the neck of the
American taxpayer. When, on December 2, 1946, Great Britain and
the United States reached an agreement for the economic fusion of
their occupation zones in Germany into what came to be known as
Bizonia, the Russians regarded this move as a step towards the transformation of the Ruhr into a base for the supremacy of American capital
in Europe at the expense of those countries that had been the victims
of Hitlerite aggression. Molotov's demand for four-power control of
the Ruhr was ignored.

Convinced by the spring of 1947 that a satisfactory agreement with
the USSR was not to be found in Europe or in Asia, inside or outside
the United Nations Organization, the United States determined, with
the collaboration of such other powers as were prepared to accept American leadership, to proceed with world rehabilitation and a world settlement without the Soviet Union. Announcement by Great Britain of
her intention to withdraw support from Greece at the end of March precipitated American action. In his memorable speech before Congress on
March 12, 1947, now better known as the Truman Doctrine, the President, by-passing the UNO, called for the expenditure of $400,000,000
to save Greece and Turkey from totalitarian aggression. Drafted under
the guidance of Secretary of State Marshall, this doctrine was based
on military strategy rather than on diplomacy as one phase of an
over-all program for the "containment" of Communism. It may be said
to mark the transition from a "firm" to a "tough" policy, that is, to
the so-called "cold war." This projection of American power into the
Balkan arena and the Straits question was regarded by the Russians as
a direct threat to their security. The Soviet press straightway became
more inimical toward America than ever before in history.

In response to a Communist coup in Hungary, the United States
took its next important step in the direction of "containment" of the
USSR on June 5, 1947, when Secretary of State Marshall at the
Harvard University commencement exercises presented the vague out-
lines of a European aid program, better known today as the Marshall
Plan. "Our policy," said Marshall, "is directed not against any country

World War II

or doctrine, but against hunger, poverty, desperation, and chaos. Its purpose should be the revival of a working economy in the world. . . ." He thereupon promised aid to all countries ready and willing to promote the task of recovery and threatened to withhold such assistance from those that obstructed this program.

A conference of sixteen European nations hastily summoned at Paris discussed measures of "self-help" which were to be the prerequisite to American aid. Although the Soviet Union at first somewhat dubiously agreed to participate in the Paris Conference, the Soviet press attacked the American plan as an extension of the Truman Doctrine for the further interference of the United States in European affairs. When it became clear that the lion's share of American aid would go to England, and the Russians suspected that the program might involve political as well as economic commitments, Molotov and his sixty-nine Soviet economic experts on July 2 withdrew from the conference, charging that the plan would split Europe, that it by-passed the UNO, and that it was geared to the reconstruction of Germany. The Western powers appeared not to regret the Russian withdrawal.

With the withdrawal of the Soviet Union and the nonparticipation of states in the Soviet sphere, the Marshall Plan assumed more and more the character of an exclusive Western bloc. The United States, England, and France proceeded without the USSR to draft a program for the economic rehabilitation of Western Germany and the co-ordination of its three zones. Economic aid was provided for England, France, Italy, and the Benelux countries, with the avowed purpose of creating a bulwark in Western Europe against Communism. In the Far East, American policy veered likewise in the direction of the economic rehabilitation of Japan, as the nucleus of a future Eastern bloc against Communism.

Charging that three- instead of four-power decisions on the future of Germany constituted a violation of the Potsdam Agreement, the Soviet Union proceeded at once to consolidate Soviet economic and political power in Eastern Europe under what Americans sometimes call the Molotov Plan. Czechoslovakia, under Moscow pressure, withdrew from the Marshall program and cast its lot with the Eastern bloc. A series of trade agreements was concluded between the USSR and the so-called satellite states, and Moscow tightened its grip on industry and transport in the Danube area. "Joint companies," in which there was fifty-fifty ownership by the USSR and the local government, multiplied. What the Soviet Union had failed to obtain in the form of reparations from Germany, it tried to exact by other means in Soviet-occupied Europe.

The threat of German revival proved to be a powerful incentive toward the consolidation, at least temporarily, of the Slavic states of Eastern Europe in opposition to the Marshall Plan. On October 5, 1947, the organization of the Cominform (Communist Information Bureau) with headquarters in Belgrade, representing the Communist parties of Eastern Europe, France, Italy, and the USSR, was announced. More regional in scope than the Third International which was disbanded during the war years of Allied collaboration, the Cominform was nevertheless, like its predecessor, both defensive and offensive in character. It was designed to resist further expansion of Western influence at the expense of the Eastern bloc, and at the same time to obstruct, and if possible wreck, the operation of the Marshall Plan in Western Europe. Shortly thereafter in February 1948 the Communists took over Czechoslovakia, and Communist propaganda noticeably increased in the Far East. The moving spirit of the Cominform until his death in 1948 was Andrei Zhdanov, a member of the Politburo, whose efforts to revive a militant Communist program abroad were accompanied by an all-out pressure campaign for increased production at home, in which ideology was subordinated to profits. The subsequent defection of Marshal Tito of Yugoslavia in 1948 indicated that complete harmony did not reign in the Eastern any more than in the Western bloc, where France eyed the restoration of Germany with dismay.

The cold war reached a new high in 1948 with the application by the Soviet Union of the Berlin blockade in retaliation for unilateral Western action on German monetary reform and its extension to Berlin. Instead of forcing the withdrawal of the Western powers from Berlin, the blockade produced the American-organized "air lift" which, costly as this temporary expedient proved to be, amazed both the East and the West when it was maintained through the winter months of 1948-1949. The blockade was lifted by the Soviets on May 12, 1949, in return for the summoning of a Big Four conference in Paris on May 23 to consider the German question.

As the cold war progressed, anti-Soviet sentiment in the United States reached a new peak. One factor promoting this was undoubtedly the presence in the United States of substantial and articulate minorities representative of countries absorbed into the Soviet sphere. The American press, however, displayed an almost unprecedented unanimity in placing the blame for the existing crisis in international affairs squarely on the Soviet Union. Some of those who took a leading role in the anti-Soviet campaign were at one time leading exponents of Soviet theories in the United States, who now attacked the USSR with as much fanaticism as they displayed in favor of it during the so-called "Red decade." The internal repercussions of the cold war in America included Congressional and state investigations of Communists and fellow-travelers, and the listing by the Attorney General's Office of what were termed "subversive, un-American organizations."

In the Soviet Union likewise the anti-Western campaign reached a new peak. Soviet writers and scientists whose works betrayed the influence of Western scholarship were accused of un-Soviet activities. Even failure to attack the West rendered them suspect. The atmosphere was such in both countries that sober minds became alarmed over the prospects for world peace.

Although the Marshall Plan as originally conceived was designed to furnish economic rather than military aid to Western Europe, it became increasingly difficult to draw a hard-and-fast line between the two or to stop with economic aid. In the fall of 1948 the initial steps were taken in the direction of a North Atlantic military alliance, backed by American aid for the rearmament of states adhering thereto and American commitments in the event of aggression. The tension eased somewhat following the American elections in November. Trade agreements were signed between England and Poland, Italy and the USSR, and Yugoslavia entered into similar negotiations with England and the United States. Preparations were made for the resumption in February 1949 of peace negotiations with Austria, postponed by the cold war, and the Soviet Union agreed to negotiate the settlement of its Lend-Lease obligations to the United States. Nevertheless President Truman's inaugural address of January 20, 1949, the substance of which recalls his previous enunciation of the Truman Doctrine on March 12, 1947, clearly indicated America's intention of continuing and extending the European economic aid program to combat Communism, and of providing military aid and guarantees to such countries as were willing to collaborate in the attainment of this objective. In line with this policy, the Foreign Ministers of twelve Western nations (Belgium, Canada, Denmark, France, Iceland, Luxembourg, The Netherlands, Norway, Portugal, the United Kingdom and the United States) on April 4, 1949, signed the North Atlantic Treaty in Washington, in the presence of President Truman, who termed it "a shield against aggression and the fear of aggression."

Although by 1949 the United States had made substantial gains in its program for the economic rehabilitation of Western Europe, the Soviet Union, which in the East-West duel of the turbulent postwar years held a trump card in its championship of agrarian reform, had likewise made considerable headway in Eastern Europe and the Orient. After World War I the Russian experiment appealed basically to labor groups in Western capitalist countries. This challenge was met, generally speaking, by the efforts of government and industry to improve the living standards of the masses and to steal the Soviet thunder by extending the program of social reform. After World War II, the Soviet Union met with a greater measure of success when it advanced into basically agrarian areas in Europe and Asia—areas where industrially-minded Westerners were initially at a disadvantage. This Soviet expansion was accompanied by widely-touted measures of agrarian reform. The large estates of the Junkers in East Prussia, of the landed aristocracy of Poland, Hungary, and the Balkan states, and in some instances of the Church, were sequestrated and divided among small farmers and landless peasants. Although the dispossessed who succeeded in escaping to the West were loud in their protests, they were of necessity few in number, whereas the peasants whose land hunger was thus appeased acquired a vested interest in the new regime. The rift between the Tito regime in Yugoslavia and the Soviet Union was due largely to the Yugoslav leader's resistance to collectivization. Since the spring of 1949 there has been a rising tide of opposition to a Soviet-inspired policy for the collectivization of agriculture in the satellite countries of Eastern Europe, which by 1953 resulted in sporadic uprisings behind the Iron Curtain. Reports of widespread hunger in parts of Soviet-occupied Europe in the summer of 1953 prompted a United States offer of food to alleviate the unhappy lot of these subject peoples.

The idea of agrarian reform has likewise caught the imagination of masses of people in the Far East, including China, Korea, and the colonial areas of southeast Asia. There, as in Europe, the Western powers in their world-wide anti-Communist front have frequently found themselves in the position of supporting the *status quo,* sometimes represented by corrupt, reactionary regimes, against the crying need for widespread social and economic reform. In the United States, which has long prided itself on the pursuit of progressive, anti-imperialistic policies in the Orient, many Americans have deplored the new line-up and drawn attention to the dangers inherent in it for America in the event that the old regimes were overthrown. There were signs, as the spring of 1949 approached and the leadership of Mao Tse-tung replaced that of Chiang Kai-shek in North China, that the USSR was preparing to follow up its initial advantage by supplying agricultural machinery, even at the expense of domestic needs, from stock-piles in Siberia to the peasant masses of China. The United States, with its superior industrial techniques, did not overlook the opportunities provided by deep-seated agrarian unrest in various parts of the globe. No doubt President Truman had this in mind when in the aforementioned inaugural address he announced that the United States would promote the industrial and scientific development of backward areas throughout the world. Today this plan is better known as the Point Four Program.

Although the United States continued to direct its main efforts toward the rehabilitation and preservation of Western Europe as a bulwark against Communism, the foreign policy of the Soviet Union, at least until the close of the Stalin regime, consistently subordinated Europe to Asia and successfully expanded the Soviet orbit in the Far East. In 1949 the Chinese Communists under Mao Tse-tung drove the legitimate Nationalist Government of Chiang Kai-shek from the Asiatic mainland to Formosa. The subsequent Sino-Soviet alliance of February 14, 1950, constituted the greatest potential threat to the Western World since the rise of Nazism. Under the tutelage of Moscow, the Chinese Communist regime proceeded to occupy Tibet, actively aided and abetted the Communist Vietminh forces of Indo-China (Vietnam), and in November 1951 entered the Korean conflict to save the remnants of the North Korean Communist Army from imminent defeat at the hands of the United Nations troops under General Douglas MacArthur. Soviet propagandists boasted, in poetry and in prose, that the Soviet orbit was 800,000,000 strong, extending from Hungary and Czechoslovakia in the West to China and Tibet in the Orient.

The invasion of South Korea by the North Koreans on June 25, 1950, came as surprise to Americans. In the Soviet press, however, there was never any secret about the ultimate intention of the North Korean Soviet satellite to absorb American-sponsored South Korea. The speedy intervention of the United States, supported by the United Nations, halted the North Korean *Blitzkrieg* and upset the time-table of Communist aggression, not only in Korea but elsewhere in Asia. Frustrated Soviet leaders undertook a world-wide propaganda drive designed to pin Korean war guilt on the United States. Although this propaganda campaign had little or no impact on the Western

Courtesy Sovfoto

A. Y. VYSHINSKY SIGNING THE TREATY BETWEEN THE USSR AND THE CHINESE PEOPLE'S REPUBLIC February 14, 1950

Left to right: A. A. Gromyko, N. A. Bulganin, N. V. Roshchin, Chou En-lai, A. I. Mikoyan, N. S. Khrushchev, K. Voroshilov, V. Molotov, J. V. Stalin, Mao Tse-tung, B. V. Podtserop, N. T. Federenko, Wang Chia Hsiang, G. M. Malenkov, Chen Po-ta, L. P. Beria, Mr. Azizov, and L. M. Kaganovich

World, some Asians appeared ready to accept the Soviet-Chinese war-guilt thesis and even the fantastic Communist charges of American perpetration of "germ warfare" in Korea. The USSR overlooked no opportunity to arouse Asiatic pride with the argument that Asian armies (Red Chinese and North Korean) had withstood the most highly mechanized land and air forces that the United Nations were able to assemble on the Korean front. By late 1952 Americans, who were bearing the main brunt of the Korean conflict, were impatiently calling upon President-elect Eisenhower for more effective action to end the Korean stalemate.

Although, technically speaking, the USSR did not enter the Korean conflict and continued to pose as the foremost "champion of peace," Soviet foreign policy was directed toward the prolongation of the war. Truce negotiations begun at Kaesong in July 1951 and continued at Panmunjon reached a deadlock over Communist opposition to the voluntary exchange of prisoners. It was not until July 26, 1953, that a truce was finally signed.

American diplomacy achieved greater success in forestalling, at least temporarily, Soviet designs against Japan. Although the USSR refused to participate, the United States succeeded in negotiating a separate peace treaty with Japan, which was signed by forty-nine countries at the San Francisco Conference, September 5, 1951.

Although in the Orient the United States suffered its most serious setback in the fall of China to the Soviet orbit, in Western Europe American policy met with a considerable measure of success. This was true in regard to the economic rehabilitation of war-devastated countries and the consequent decline of Communist political power. The United States even prevailed upon the vacillating members of the North Atlantic Treaty Organization (NATO) to make more concerted efforts for military preparedness to offset the threat of further Soviet expansion in Europe. When in 1952 American efforts to create an effective European Army by means of West German participation appeared likely to succeed. Soviet leaders at once betrayed their concern. In his last major public speech before the Nineteenth Congress of the Communist Party of the USSR on October 14, 1952, Stalin gave the Party a green light for more aggressive Communist action in the Western European democracies. There were signs that the USSR would attempt to disrupt the NATO program, especially insofar as it rested on the revival of German military power. Whether this indicated a major shift in emphasis of Soviet foreign policy from Asia back to Europe was obscured by the death of Stalin on March 5, 1953.

16

The Post-Stalin Era

The death of Stalin, following years of adulation that virtually amounted to deification, raised the problem of the Soviet succession—a problem that has plagued many dictatorships in the past. Since none of the eligible successors—Malenkov, Beria, and Molotov—had attained Stalin's stature, there was temporarily, at least, a division of power among them, with Georgi M. Malenkov assuming the Premiership but surrendering the strategic post of Secretary of the Central Committee of the Communist Party to Nikita S. Khrushchev;[1] with Lavrenti P. Beria serving as Deputy Premier and Minister of Internal Affairs; and Vyacheslav M. Molotov, likewise a Deputy Premier, returning to his old post as Minister of Foreign Affairs. The inevitable struggle for supremacy among the Soviet Big Three culminated in the announcement on July 10, 1953, of the overthrow of Beria, the head of the dread Soviet secret police (MVD).

The triumvirate lost no time in playing down the "cult of personality" that had elevated Stalin to the skies and established his reputation for infallibility. In the months that followed his death Stalin's name was rarely mentioned in the Soviet press and then largely in conjunction with the historical figures of Marx, Engels, and Lenin. It seemed as if the triumvirate thus paved the way for a departure from Stalin's policies.

In addition to the contest over the succession, there were at least two factors following the death of Stalin that threatened the continued dominance of the Communist Party in the Soviet Union, namely, the rise of strong upper and middle classes and the reassertion of the power of the Soviet Army. Both the upper and middle classes and the military caste were opposed to the domination of the Party. It was logical, therefore, that the new regime, to preserve the authority of the Party, should make concessions to these two elements, by a further

---

[1] On September 12, 1953, the plenary session of the Central Committee of the Communist Party of the Soviet Union (CPSU) elected Khrushchev as first secretary of the Central Committee of the CPSU, thus formalizing his position.

432

NIKITA S. KHRUSHCHEV

reduction of prices and promises to raise the living standards, by the inclusion of popular Army leaders in key positions, and by curbing the power of the secret police through the removal of Beria. The Supreme Soviet was convened on August 5, 1953, in part, at least, to reassert the badly shaken authority of the Communist Party.

To allay popular discontent over the chronic shortages of consumer goods Anastas I. Mikoyan, Minister of Trade, in his report to the All-Union Conference of Trade Workers on October 17 (*Izvestia-Pravda,* October 25, 1953), promised the long-suffering Soviet citizen more of everything from meat and butter to vacuum cleaners, refrigerators, kitchen gadgets, television and radio sets, bicycles, and automobiles.

In the fall of 1953, with no general peace settlement in sight and alarmed at the speed with which the United States in self-defense was establishing a string of bases encircling the USSR, the Soviet Government abruptly shifted its emphasis from foreign to domestic affairs. The importance attached by Soviet leaders to the re-establishment of unity on the domestic front was emphasized by a decree ordering a 72 per cent increase in domestic consumer goods' distribution by the end of 1954. To insure the success of this program the Soviet Government shelved the Five-Year Plan for one year and provided for the expenditure of one billion dollars in gold to import food and consumer goods from abroad. The intent of the new regime in thus subordinating foreign to domestic affairs appeared to be twofold: to satisfy the Soviet people and to accumulate stores of food in the event of war. Soviet policy at the Berlin Conference (January-February 1954), which stubbornly upheld the *status quo* and blocked a European settlement, offered further substantiation of the priority accorded at that time to domestic issues.

The next step in the contest for power among Soviet leaders occurred on February 8, 1955, when Malenkov resigned as premier, allegedly due to inexperience and to the unsatisfactory state of Soviet agriculture. He was succeeded by Marshal Nikolai A. Bulganin. The power of the Red Army was emphasized by the appointment of Marshal Grigory D. Zhukov as Minister of Defense. For a time, it appeared that the Army might dominate the Government, at the expense of the Communist Party.

The rise of Nikita S. Khrushchev to power dated from his spectacular indictment of Stalin, February 24-25, 1956, before the Twentieth Congress of the Communist Party. Khrushchev met the challenge, first of the Stalinist faction which disapproved his economic policy of decentralization of agriculture and industry, and second, of the Army. On July 3, 1957, Malenkov, Molotov, Kaganovitch, and Shepilov, all accused of anti-Party activity, were ousted not only from the Party Presidium and Central Committee, but from their Government posts. Instead of liquidating his fallen opponents, as Stalin would have done, the victorious Khrushchev placed Malenkov in charge of a hydroelectric station at Ust-Kamenogorsk in eastern Kazakhstan, made Molotov ambassador to Outer Mongolia, Kaganovitch director of a cement plant in the Urals, and Shepilov a school teacher, first in Central Asia, and later at the Institute of Economics in Moscow.

Having thus strengthened his grip on the Communist Party, Khrushchev proceeded to reassert the power of the Party over the military. On October 26, 1957, Marshal Zhukov was relieved of his post as Minister of Defense and was replaced by Marshal Rodion Y. Malinovsky. Accused of promoting his own "cult of personality" and of resisting Party control of the Red Army, the popular Zhukov was expelled from the Party's Presidium and Central Committee in November. With the threat of the man on horseback removed, on March 27, 1958, the Supreme Soviet re-elected the aging Voroshilov as chairman of its Presidium. Behind this "front" emerged Nikita Khrushchev as chairman of the Council of Ministers (premier) of the Soviet Union, replacing Bulganin. Thus, by the spring of 1958, Khrushchev combined in his own person, as did Stalin before him, leadership of the Party and the Government. In the struggle for supremacy, the Party had reasserted its authority over the Red Army.

As Khrushchev gained control of the Party's Central Committee, he was able to carry out drastic reforms in Soviet agricultural policy. On June 18, 1958, the Government terminated compulsory deliveries of agricultural products, or what amounted to payment in kind of grain and other products for work done by machine-and-tractor stations (MTS). This action removed a long-standing grievance of Soviet farmers, who for years had delivered farm produce to the Government for almost nothing. Collective farmers anticipated a higher income in the future, although their purchase of machinery formerly rented from the MTS temporarily increased their expenses.

Khrushchev likewise proceeded, in 1957 and 1958, to carry out a radical decentralization of Soviet industry and to effect some improvement in working conditions. In April 1957, the working day was reduced to six hours in the mines, and to seven hours in heavy industry. In October 1958, the details of a new Seven-Year Plan were disclosed—designed to achieve by 1965 the goals originally set for

1972. The new program was said to be required by economic decentralization, new mineral discoveries, and new developments in power, plastics, and synthetic fibers. Khrushchev boasted that its purpose was to enable the USSR to surpass the United States in production.

Ostensibly the Khrushchev program for agriculture and industry was intended to accelerate the transition from Socialism to Communism. A careful analysis of his policies, however, seemed to indicate that once again the Soviet Government was resorting to capitalist "tools." In other words, when the Soviet goal was to surpass the United States, the USSR of necessity had to adopt American methods.

Stalin's successors continued to pursue his policy of emphasizing the industrial and technological development of the Soviet Union. If the growth of the urban population is a valid indication of technological development and if Soviet figures are accurate, some substantial progress was made. *Izvestia* reported (September 11, 1953) that the Soviet urban population had reached 80,000,000, as compared to 26,-000,000 in 1926. By 1956, 44 per cent of the Soviet population of approximately 200,000,000 lived in the cities.

To make the twentieth century the era of Soviet technological development, the Soviet Government accorded priority to the sciences over the humanities in education. The decree of the Council of Ministers of the USSR on the occasion of the opening on September 1, 1953, of the new buildings of the Moscow State University called after N. V. Lomonosov specifically directed the university administration to begin instruction and research at once in physics, chemistry, mechanical-mathematics, geology, and geography. In 1954, there were 54,000 graduates from Soviet engineering schools. By 1956, Soviet institutions of higher learning were said to be graduating almost twice as many scientists and engineers as were the institutions in the United States.

The urgency behind the Soviet priority for science and technology was revealed in memorable fashion in 1957. In August, the Soviet Government announced its possession of an intercontinental ballistic missile (ICBM), with a range of 5,000 miles, at 13,000 miles per hour. This was used in the autumn of the same year to place Sputniks I and II into orbit. On October 4, the free world was shocked to learn that the USSR had successfully launched a 184-pound earth satellite which, at 18,000 miles per hour, reached a maximum altitude of 560 miles. On November 3, a 1,129-pound rocket cone, which carried the dog Laika, began circling the earth at a maximum height of 1,056 miles. The Sputnik Age had dawned.

The Soviet Government likewise proceeded to exploit atomic energy for nonmilitary purposes. In September 1958, at a conference in Geneva on the peaceful uses of atomic energy, Soviet delegates revealed that the USSR had constructed in Siberia what they claimed was the world's largest atomic power station, with a capacity of 1,000,-000 kilowatts.

When Vice-President Richard Nixon visited Siberia in July 1959, he inspected one of the newest manifestations of the Soviet concentration on science. Near the great new hydroelectric dam at Novosibirsk, a "science city" was under construction on the banks of the Ob River. Here the Soviet Government plans to build a scientific center that will rival the centers at Leningrad and Moscow. The project includes a science university to accommodate from 1,500 to 3,000 carefully selected students, with a faculty twice the size of the student body. The purpose of this development is to exploit the undeveloped resources of Siberia for the industrial and technological progress of the USSR.

FOREIGN POLICY

The death of Stalin precipitated what appeared to be an about-face in Soviet foreign policy. Perhaps as a result of internal instability, the Soviet Government appreciably stepped up its peace offensive abroad, not only on the diplomatic but on the economic front. It extended the olive branch to East Germany, and especially to Turkey, by officially abandoning on May 30, 1953, all Soviet territorial claims against the latter. It held out prospects of increased trade with the USSR, China, and the Soviet satellites to Western nations that were anxiously scanning the international horizon in search of new economic outlets. Although, in view of past experience, Soviet overtures were received with outright skepticism, the bait was sufficiently tempting to constitute a threat to the unity of the free world.

The fear on the part of the West that Soviet leaders were staging no more than a temporary retreat on the international front was enhanced by Malenkov's announcement on August 8, 1953, before the Supreme Soviet that "the United States has no monopoly in the production of the hydrogen bomb. . . ." Even from the ranks of steadfast allies of the United States this announcement produced a call for a return to diplomacy and renewed efforts in the direction of international control of atomic weapons.

In the post-Stalin era, Soviet foreign policy continued to be oriented toward Asia. Although the preservation of the Sino-Soviet alliance continued to have first priority, renewed and more intensive emphasis was placed on the Near and Middle East. As in the early postwar years, Soviet expansionist aims encountered the opposition of the United States.

To offset the Sino-Soviet alliance of 1950 the United States sponsored closer ties between Turkey and Pakistan in the Middle East. The Turkish-Pakistani Mutual Aid Agreement of April 2, 1954, constituted a major diplomatic and strategic victory for United States foreign policy. To put more teeth into that pact the United States and Pakistan signed an agreement on May 19 providing American military aid and technical assistance to Pakistan. The Turkish-Pakistani Pact united the two strongest Muslim states, comprising about 100,000,000 people, or one-fourth of the Muslim World, located on the southern periphery of the USSR. Following the unanimous ratification of the agreement by the Turkish Grand National Assembly on June 11, 1954, Turkey and Pakistan announced that they would henceforth shift from a passive to an active policy in seeking to induce other Muslim countries of the Near and Middle East, especially those in the north, to join forces with them to establish an effective system of collective security.

Because the Soviet people are still impressed by manpower, at times even more than by technology, the impact on the USSR of the Turkish-Pakistani Agreement was instantaneous. It resulted in large-scale, strategic countermeasures involving the status of the 30,000,000 Muslims inside the borders of the Soviet Union. Soviet Central Asia, where the bulk of these Muslims resided, was the bulwark for the defense of the Ural region, the backbone of Soviet industrial development.

Under the guise of a campaign to increase Soviet food production, the Soviet Government in the spring of 1954 instituted a program for the reclamation of virgin and idle lands and the opening up of new agricultural areas in Kazakhstan, West Siberia, the Ural and Volga regions, and the North Caucasus. These are highly strategic areas with reference to the Near and Middle East. One of the principal areas selected for cultivation and reclamation was Soviet Central Asia, known before the Revolution as Russian Turkestan, but which now comprises the Soviet republics of Kazakhstan, Kirghizia, Tadjikistan, Turkmenistan, and Uzbekistan.

The Soviet drive to cultivate virgin and idle lands in Central Asia was designed to populate the rural areas with non-Muslim peoples. The ultimate purpose of the Soviet Government was that both the urban and rural areas of Soviet Central Asia in time should be absorbed largely by the Slavs, in which event the fate of the native peoples in all probability would be that of the Crimean Tatars and Kalmyks. This drastic genocidal program was launched under the impact of the alliance between Turkey and Pakistan, two Muslim countries strategically located on the Soviet periphery.

The extent of Soviet concern over the Turkish-Pakistani rapprochement can be gauged by the character and quality of the colonists dispatched to the Central Asian Republics. The Malenkov regime sent, not slave laborers or even common laborers, but members of the Komsomol (Young Communist League), who constituted the cream of the crop of Soviet youth, each one a trained agitator, picked for qualities of leadership and unquestioned loyalty to the Soviet regime. Judging by the Soviet press campaign from April to June 1956 for the extension of this program, and by Khrushchev's appeal for another half million from the reservoir of 18,500,000 Komsomol members for Kazakhstan, Siberia, and the Far East, the Soviet Government was seeking to establish not only a Slavic, but a Komsomol Belt along this strategic frontier of the USSR. The inclusion of the Far East in this drive to populate Soviet Asia suggested that precautions were being taken against any future expansionist aims on the part of Red China. In addition to the Komsomol colonists, the Soviet Government in 1955 dispatched entire regiments of demobilized soldiers, together with their commanders, to the Central Asian Republics. These Soviet veterans served at least three purposes: they reclaimed fallow land and thereby increased the food and cotton crops; they augmented the Slavic element in the population; and they were available for mobilization at a moment's notice for purposes of defense or offense. From the Soviet standpoint, the strategic advantages surpassed even the economic benefits.

In the field of foreign affairs, the Soviet Government betrayed manifest alarm over the impact of the Istanbul-Karachi agreement on the 350,000,000 Muslims beyond Soviet borders, stretching from Chinese Turkestan and Southeast Asia to Morocco and West Africa. Even without waiting for the formal conclusion of the pact, the Soviet Government in an official note of protest to Turkey (*Pravda-Izvestia,* March 20, 1954) predicted that this agreement would "aggravate the situation in the Near and Middle East, and also in Southeast Asia, and would have a direct bearing on the security of the Soviet Union." It accused the United States of planning to use "the human resources" of this area to carry out American policy, and of "forging a bloc by instalments."

Far from intimidating Turkey and Pakistan, Soviet pressure facilitated and accelerated the extension of their alliance by means of the series of agreements which comprised the Baghdad Pact of 1955. In November 1955, the premiers of Iraq, Iran, Pakistan, and Turkey met with the British Foreign Secretary, Harold Macmillan, to establish a permanent political, military, and economic organization, with headquarters in Baghdad. The United States, which originated the idea of the pact but was not a signatory, was represented by political and military observers. On November 22, the five powers comprising the Middle Eastern Treaty Organization (METO) announced the establishment of the "Council of the Baghdad Pact," the purpose of which was defense against "aggression or subversion."

By the Baghdad Pact the Middle East was linked with the North Atlantic Treaty Organization (NATO) through Turkey and Great Britain, and with the Southeast Asian Treaty Organization (SEATO) through Pakistan. It marked the conclusion, at least on paper, of a United States-sponsored chain of alliances stretching from Norway to the Philippines, the object of which was to prevent further expansion on the part of the Sino-Soviet axis. In the Middle East, although the Baghdad Pact established a 3,000-mile ideological and military *cordon sanitaire* against further Soviet penetration, it still required implementation. The signatories, realizing that the effectiveness of the pact depended upon the United States, looked forward to ultimate American membership and to the inclusion of other Arab states. The Iraq Government hastened to announce that its adherence to the pact in no wise conflicted with its membership in the Arab League. The implication was that the pact might be used to aid any Arab state which became the object of aggression. Nevertheless, the Baghdad Pact split the Arab World, at least temporarily, thereby creating a situation which the USSR quickly exploited to its own advantage.

The abstention of Afghanistan left another gap in the Baghdad Pact. Spurred into action by the Turkish-Pakistani Agreement of 1954 and by the United States-Pakistan Arms Pact, the Soviet Government had already taken steps to strengthen its ties with Afghanistan, regarded as the one truly "neutral" Muslim state lying athwart the USSR and Pakistan. Soviet action had taken the form of economic aid—the construction of an oil pipeline from Uzbekistan to the Afghan city of Mazar-i-Sharif, and of two huge wheat silos in Kabul and Pul-i-Khumr—and of support for Afghan nationalist demands for a plebiscite among the Pathan tribes of Pakistan's northwest frontier province. A Soviet-Afghan agreement in the fall of 1955 for the reciprocal free transit of goods relieved Afghanistan of dependence on Pakistan. With extensive atomic research reported in Soviet Kirghizia, northeast of Afghanistan, the USSR could not afford to let its Afghan neighbors go by default into the American-sponsored Muslim alliance in the Middle East. Following the adherence of Iraq and Iran to the Baghdad Pact, and as a climax to the trek of Bulganin and Khrushchev to Kabul, the Soviet Government announced on December 18, 1955, a loan of $100,000,000 to Afghanistan and a ten-year extension of the 1931 Soviet-Afghan Treaty of Neutrality and Mutual Nonaggression.

Although Afghanistan remained officially "neutral" between the Soviet and Western blocs, the Soviet-Afghan rapprochement appeared to give the USSR a foothold there, which served a twofold purpose: In the first place, it enabled the Soviet Union to maintain the gap in the METO chain of defense along the southern Soviet frontier, thereby compensating in part for the loss of Iran. Second, it afforded an opportunity for the USSR to outflank both Pakistan and Iran.

Soviet strategy in the Middle East became clear, when the USSR thereafter tried to acquire a foothold in Egypt by providing that country with arms from Czechoslovakia and by seeking a contract for the construction of the Aswan Dam. Once successful in Egypt, the Soviet Union would outflank METO in the west as it did via Afghanistan in the east. It would thus hold the Middle East in a pincer grip that would constitute a direct threat to Western defense of that area. By intimidation and economic pressure directed against Iran, Turkey, and Pakistan, the Soviet Government made valiant efforts to accomplish the defection of one or more of these states from the Baghdad Pact, and thus to block or delay the implementation of the United States program for an effective alliance of the Muslim states against Communism. A Turkish Foreign Ministry official voiced his Government's continued suspicion of Soviet tactics, as follows: "Turkey feels that this activity on the part of the Soviet Union proves beyond a doubt the value of the Baghdad Pact and that the Pact is doing just what it was supposed to accomplish."

Another important factor in Soviet-Muslim relations in the post-war period was the resurgence of the Muslim population of Red China. The creation of new Muslim states in the Middle East, such as Pakistan, had its impact on the Muslim minority in China, which sought greater autonomy for its own members. The Soviet and Red Chinese Governments proceeded to organize the Muslim elements under their jurisdiction, in order to make use of them in other parts of the Muslim World, especially in the Near and Middle East. Soviet-Chinese efforts in this direction found expression in a speech by Burhan, chairman of the preparatory committee of the China Islamic Association, delivered before Muslim delegates from various countries at the Peace Conference of the Asian and Pacific Regions, on October 18, 1952. This Muslim Conference was held concurrently with the Nineteenth Congress of the Communist Party in Moscow, at which Stalin made his last major speech on foreign policy.

Early in 1956 it became clear that Red China and the USSR were taking parallel action in the Near East and Africa, possibly as a result of the Asian-African Conference in Bandung. The most conspicuous parallels were to be seen in their diplomatic and trade overtures to Lebanon, Syria, Egypt, the Sudan, and Liberia. The trek to Cairo in June of the new Soviet Foreign Minister, Dmitri Shepilov, to celebrate the end of three-quarters of a century of English occupation of the Suez Canal Zone was followed in July by the visit of Chou En-lai to commemorate the third anniversary of the Egyptian revolution of 1953. Thus, no sooner had the Western powers reconciled themselves, albeit reluctantly, to the necessity for recognizing the USSR as a factor in eastern Mediterranean affairs, than they were confronted by the sudden and unwelcome impact of Red China in that area.

Post-Stalin Soviet policy in Asia raised another new problem for the West. Prior to 1953 the USSR presented a challenge to the West as an ideological and as a military force. It has since emerged also as an economic competitor. Having observed the effectiveness of the Marshall Plan in Europe, of United States aid to Turkey and other underdeveloped areas, the Soviet Government adopted these tactics as its own, not only in Eastern Europe, but in large parts of Asia and Africa.

Although the USSR had made a few sporadic efforts to provide economic and technical aid to such Middle East countries as Turkey and Yemen prior to World War II, it was not until the death of Stalin that the Soviet Government made a concerted effort to meet the challenge of the United States by implementing its own program of economic assistance to the developing countries of Asia outside the Communist orbit. This program included the dispatch of Soviet technicians to at least fourteen countries and the training of hundreds of Asian specialists in Soviet institutions. In its bilateral agreements the USSR, in contrast to the United States, preferred long-term, low interest rate loans and barter deals to outright grants, frequently accepted as payment such raw materials as Egyptian cotton, Burmese rice, and Indian jute, when these products were a glut on the world market, and supplied limited quantities of machine tools and industrial equipment to accelerate the industrialization of Asian countries. The object was to render the recipients of Soviet aid, such as Egypt, Afghanistan, Yemen, and Syria, economically dependent on the Sino-Soviet orbit and to cut their ties with the West.

One of the more spectacular examples of Soviet technical assistance, which created an impression in many countries of the Middle East, was the Soviet-Indian agreement of February 2, 1955, by which the Soviet Union undertook to provide India with a steel plant and equipment at Bhilai, as well as to furnish Soviet technicians to supervise its construction. In November 1956, the USSR extended a new $126,000,000 credit to India, primarily for the purchase of heavy machinery. In spite of Indian occupation of the Communist state of Kerala, the Soviet and Indian Governments late in 1959 negotiated another loan for approximately $378,000,000 to support the Third Indian Five-Year Plan.

The Soviet Government achieved only limited success in its efforts to extend economic aid to the countries of the Baghdad Pact. Under a 1956 trade pact, the Batala Engineering Company of Pakistan, for instance, arranged for the purchase of 14,000 tons of pig iron and steel billets. Turkey, confronted in 1957 by a critical lack of foreign exchange and credits with the countries of the Western bloc, was persuaded to turn experimentally to the Soviet foreign aid program. It was significant that Nikita S. Rijov, then USSR Ambassador in Ankara, was the Soviet engineer who had supervised the construction of the Kayseri textile mill for the Turks in 1934. In any event, a Turkish delegation representing the Ish Bank returned from a 40-day sojourn in Moscow with a contract for the construction in Turkey of a sheet glass factory and a caustic soda plant, designed to free the Turkish Republic from its dependence on foreign glass imports. In August 1957, Himmet Olomen, a Turkish Democratic deputy in Parliament, explained that if the United States could not fulfill Turkish needs for industrialization, Turkey would have to look elsewhere. As in the case of the Pakistani and the Turks, the Iranians were wary of Soviet trade propositions. The Soviet regime was content for a time to provide planes, pilots, and specialists to assist Iran in combatting the annual locust invasion, which destroyed crops on both sides of the Soviet-Iranian border. In April 1957, however, a

Soviet mission headed by First Deputy Foreign Minister Kuznetsov succeeded in settling not only long-standing border problems but in making a three-year trade agreement by which the USSR would exchange machinery, cars, and sugar for Iranian minerals, agricultural products, and rugs. Another major concession won by Iran was the right of free transit through the USSR for all commodities, irrespective of origin.

The stepped-up Soviet trade offensive in Asia included all the countries of the Soviet orbit. According to United States estimates, Red China accounted for 20 per cent of the total Sino-Soviet bloc trade. Although the Chinese drive was directed mainly toward the countries of Southeast Asia and India, Red Chinese trade delegations did not overlook the Middle East, especially Jordan, Egypt, and Syria. Since 1957, the Arab countries have strengthened their economic ties with the Soviet European satellites and with Yugoslavia. By 1958 the United Arab Republic of Egypt and Syria had reached trade and payments agreements with practically all of the Soviet European satellites, as well as with People's China

After several years of concerted effort the Soviet bloc's economic offensive was still limited in scope. It had nevertheless made significant gains in the Middle East, so much so, in fact, that the Vice-President of the United States in October 1957 termed it a greater cause for concern than the Soviet launching of the first earth satellite (sputnik). In periods of crisis, it presented the countries of the Middle East with alternatives. If the West refused to build hydroelectric plants, dams, steel plants, roads, and oil refineries, the Soviet Union was ready to exploit the opportunity to its own advantage. The Soviet expert, D. Byeloshapkin, writing in *International Affairs* (Moscow), in July 1958, nevertheless admitted that the USSR "cannot as yet fill all the needs of strengthening the economic independence of the Arab states."

As of February 1, 1958, Soviet bloc aid in the Near East was focused upon three Arab states—Egypt ($485,000,000), Syria ($294,-000,000), and Yemen ($19,000,000).[1] The total United States aid to all Arab lands in this area was approximately one-fifth of the $798,-000,000 extended by the Soviet bloc to the United Arab Republic and Yemen, now known as the United Arab States. The Soviet Union, according to some Arabs, has been much more prompt than the United States in implementing the aid it has promised, not to mention the fact

---

[1] *The Sino-Soviet Economic Offensive in the Less Developed Countries,* Department of State Publication 6632, May, 1958.

that its political position was "correct" during the Suez dispute and certain other crises in the Near and Middle East (*New York Times,* February 8, 1958). As compared to the limited amount of aid advanced to Arab countries, the United States over the same period advanced $283,382,000 in aid to Israel and $437,210,000 to Turkey. In 1958 the extension of foreign aid appeared to have a direct bearing on the allegiance of the states of the Near East to the Soviet and Western blocs. The announcement by Khrushchev, on October 23, that the Soviet Union would lend the United Arab Republic as much as 400 million rubles ($100,000,000) for the construction of the Aswan High Dam clearly indicated that United States foreign policy must be geared to confront the Soviet challenge in the Near and Middle East. No sooner was ground broken in January 1960 for the construction of the first stage of the Aswan High Dam than the USSR agreed to advance $400,000,000 to finance the second stage of this "Great Pyramid of the twentieth century."

The USSR continued to accelerate its economic aid program to Asian and African countries in 1959. Soviet extension of $100,000,-000 in credits to Ethiopia in July—a spectacular move—appeared to herald a major offensive to penetrate Africa, both economically and politically. Nor was Southeast Asia neglected. The Indonesian Republic on Asia's Muslim fringe, in addition to $100,000,000 previously advanced, received a Soviet loan of $17,500,000. It was significant that Soviet agreements with both Ethiopia and Indonesia provided for the development of technical training of students. In August, another Soviet loan for Ceylon financed a $21,000,000 iron and steel project, including smelting furnaces and a rolling mill. Soviet contracts and commitments for the past year alone, according to C. Douglas Dillon, undersecretary of state for economic affairs in Washington, amounted altogether to $1,000,000,000. In order to "tool up" to provide "a global approach" to Soviet economic and diplomatic activity in various parts of the world, the State Department, in August 1959, transferred the handling of Soviet issues from the Office of Eastern European Affairs to a newly created office of Soviet Union Affairs.

The prospects for further Soviet encroachment in the Near East, especially in the Arab East, were enhanced by the withdrawal, July 19-20, 1956, of Anglo-American offers to help Egypt finance the building of the Aswan High Dam on the Nile. By this action, according to Senator J. William Fulbright (August 14, 1957), "we handed communism a key to the Middle East." In retaliation, President Gamal Abdel Nasser on July 26 decreed the nationalization of the Suez Canal

Company twelve years prior to the end of its concession, with the avowed object of securing revenue to finance the Aswan Dam. This action was approved without delay by the Soviet press. Without full assurance of Soviet support, it seems unlikely that Egypt would have recklessly defied the Western Powers on so crucial an issue.

Since Tsarist Russia was a signatory of the Contantinople Convention of 1888, the Soviet Government clearly indicated its intention to participate in any revision of that settlement and demanded the inclusion of the Arab succession states of the Ottoman Empire. Although unwilling in 1947 that Turkey should have exclusive control of the Dardanelles and Bosphorus, the USSR now posed as the principal champion of Egyptian sovereignty over the Canal, rejecting Anglo-French plans for its internationalization. After September 12, 1956, Soviet pilots came to Nasser's rescue to keep the Canal open. On September 16, in a major pronouncement, the Soviet Government warned that "any disturbance of peace in the Middle East cannot but affect the security and interests of the Soviet state," and demanded a peaceful settlement through the United Nations.

No sooner had the Israeli invasion of Egypt begun (October 19, 1956), closely followed by Anglo-French intervention, than Bulganin appealed to India and to Indonesia for a special session of the Asian-African bloc that comprised the Bandung Conference. On November 3, Voroshilov promised Soviet aid to visiting President Shukri al-Kuwatly of Syria. Two days later the USSR warned England, France, and Israel of Soviet readiness to use force "to crush the aggressors." Bulganin's call for joint United States-Soviet action to end the Egyptian War was promptly labeled "unthinkable" by the Eisenhower administration.

Sino-Soviet intervention in the Suez crisis strengthened the position of President Nasser and the Arab states. Temporarily, at least, the prospect of Soviet "volunteers" in the Near East, augmented by Red China's offer of another 250,000, gave rise to near panic on the part of Egypt's invaders. Without the threat of imminent Soviet military intervention, it is doubtful whether the United Nations emergency Assembly would have ordered and achieved a cease-fire in Egypt so quickly, that it would have proceeded so rapidly to authorize and to move into Egypt the new United Nations police force, and that England, France, and Israel would have agreed to withdraw from Egyptian territory in favor of U.N. occupation forces. Among the Arabs, however, the prestige of the United States, which had vigorously opposed the Anglo-French-Israeli invasion of Egypt, easily matched that of the

USSR. The Arabs have since contended that this was "America's finest hour."

The invasion of Egypt, unfortunately, coincided with the Hungarian revolt against Communist tyranny in Europe. Aggression, whatever its motives and justification, is still aggression. The resort to force by England, France, and Israel muted the protest against Soviet aggression in Hungary. Under other circumstances, it might have been possible to mobilize world sentiment in the United Nations to bring irresistible pressure to bear against the ruthless suppression of the Hungarian uprising by the Red Army.

To prevent any repetition in the future of the possible use of Soviet "volunteers" in the Arab World, on January 5, 1957, President Eisenhower called upon Congress to authorize the use of United States armed forces against Communist or Communist-dominated aggression in the Middle East. An amended version of the so-called Eisenhower Doctrine (Middle East Doctrine), after prolonged debate in Congress, became law on March 9.

Following a series of articles in the Soviet press denouncing the proposed Eisenhower Doctrine, the Soviet and Red Chinese Governments on January 18 signed in Moscow a joint declaration condemning it and announcing their readiness to support the peoples of the Near and Middle East in order to prevent "aggression" and interference in their internal affairs. This "Sino-Soviet Doctrine," as reported in the Soviet press, met with an immediate and favorable response in some parts of the Arab World, especially in Cairo and Damascus.

It was perhaps unfortunate that the Eisenhower Doctrine was directed solely against the threat of "armed aggression from any country controlled by international communism." At a time when United States prestige had soared to new heights in the Muslim World, American leadership overlooked an opportunity to propose an ironclad guarantee of protection of the Middle East against aggression from any source, communist or noncommunist. As it was, the Eisenhower Doctrine appeared to offer no protection against a repetition of the Anglo-French-Israeli invasion of Egypt which, in the minds of Arab leaders, constituted the real threat to peace and security in the Arab World. Not only did the Eisenhower Doctrine fail to win the unanimous support of the Muslim World, but temporarily, at least, it split the Arab states, thereby providing the USSR with still another opportunity to use the breach to secure a Soviet foothold there.

There was widely divergent reaction in the Middle East to the implementation of the Eisenhower Doctrine in the summer of 1958.

Following hard upon the heels of disturbances in Lebanon and revolution in Iraq, United States troops landed at Beirut, in July, at the request of the Lebanese Government, to forestall further internal unrest. Whereas the Turks regarded United States action as "sublime," Lebanese opinion was sharply divided, and in Cairo the official press and radio voiced unqualified opposition. The revolutionary government of Major General Abdul Karim Kassim of Iraq, undoubtedly under pressure from the Soviet Union which provided the new regime with substantial military aid, virtually abandoned the Baghdad Alliance months before its formal withdrawal on March 24, 1959. This breach in the so-called Northern Tier, which for time threatened the very existence of the Baghdad Pact, amounted to a victory for the Soviet Union. To offset further defection, the United States, which had joined the Pact's Military Committee following the Suez crisis of 1956, now agreed to participate in its antisubversive activities. Instead of formally joining the alliance, the Eisenhower Government signed separate defense agreements with Turkey, Iran, and Pakistan, providing guarantees against aggression.

Since World War II, the relations of the Soviet Union and the United States, with few exceptions, have been based on strategy rather than on diplomacy. A series of international crises during the postwar years has clearly demonstrated that the continuation of strategic moves by the United States and the USSR in Europe and Asia could lead to armed conflict. By 1957 there appeared to be no place for either adversary to move with safety on this planet, although the launching of the first sputnik pointed the way to future competition in other spheres. This deadlock left but one alternative short of war—a return to diplomacy. The obstacles strewing the path of the United States Government in making diplomatic overtures to the USSR were manifold, as indicated by efforts to achieve a summit conference in 1959, but the issues at stake seemed to make another attempt imperative.

Premier Nikita Khrushchev's visit to the United States in September 1959 proved to be a step in the direction of improved Soviet-American relations. Following in the footsteps of Peter the Great, Khrushchev appeared to be opening a new "window to the West." His subsequent action indicated that he was strongly impressed by the might and wealth of the United States. No sooner did he return to the USSR than he introduced the "Made in America" program of credit buying on the installment plan, which was widely acclaimed by the Soviet population. This was followed by the introduction of a new system of bonuses for Soviet factory and other managers based on a reduction of costs (or inversely on an increase in profits) rather than on quantitative output. In other words, profit has become indispensable to production in a manner highly reminiscent of Western capitalism.

The return to diplomacy has been facilitated since 1958 by vastly increased contacts between the leaders and peoples of the Soviet Union and those of the Western democracies. Indicative of the new trend was the Soviet-American Cultural Agreement of January 27, 1958, for the exchange of films, broadcasts, and reciprocal visits of artists, scientists, students, teachers, athletes, and journalists. Historically, whenever Russia has opened its doors to the ideas and peoples of the West the impact of these contacts has led the Russian Government (Tsarist or Soviet) to ameliorate conditions for the Russian peoples at home. Contrary to general belief, the Soviet leaders are highly sensitive to criticism from abroad. The American impact on the Soviet Union ultimately may serve to enlarge the horizons of freedom and to improve living conditions both for the peoples of the USSR and for those of the Soviet satellites.

Nikita Khrushchev for some time had contended that the easing of world tension and the promotion of international understanding required a summit conference of the great powers. Although Western diplomats did not subscribe unqualifiedly to this point of view, a summit meeting was scheduled to be held in Paris on May 16, 1960. On May 1, however, an American U-2 plane on an intelligence flight from Pakistan to Norway was shot down over the Siberian city of Sverdlovsk. To the dismay of people throughout the world and of diplomats already assembled in Paris, Khrushchev on May 16 unequivocally refused to participate in summit talks without a public apology from President Eisenhower for the incident, assurance that there would be no repetition of it, and the punishment of those responsible for the flight. The summit conference, on the success of which so much depended, promptly collapsed. When the storm of accusations died down, it became apparent that both parties to the dispute were seeking to keep the door open for the renewal of summit negotiations at some future date.

Bibliography

GEOGRAPHY AND POPULATION

Balzak, S. S. *et al.*, *Economic Geography of the USSR*, New York, 1949.
Berg, L. S., *Natural Regions of the USSR*, New York,
Crankshaw, Edward, *Russia and the Russians*, London, 1947.
Cressey, George B., *The Basis of Soviet Strength*, New York, 1945.
Goodall, G., *Soviet Russia in Maps*, London, 1942.
Jorré, Georges, *The Soviet Union: The Land and Its People*, New York, 1950.
Lamont, Corliss, *The Peoples of the Soviet Union*, New York, 1946.
Lorimer, Frank, *The Population of the Soviet Union: History and Prospects*, Columbia University Press, 1946.
Mikhailov, N., *Land of the Soviets*, New York, 1939; *Soviet Russia: The Land and Its People*, New York, 1948.
Mirov, N. T., *Geography of Russia*, New York, 1951.
Shabad, T., *Geography of the U.S.S.R.*, Columbia University Press, 1951.
Shimkin, D. B., *Minerals: A Key to Soviet Power*, Harvard University Press, 1953.

RUSSIAN HISTORY—GENERAL

Baring, Maurice, *The Mainsprings of Russia*, London, 1914.
Beazley, R., Forbes, N., and Birkett, G. A., *Russia from the Varangians to the Bolsheviki*, Oxford, 1928.
Chadwick, N. K., *The Beginnings of Russian History: An Enquiry into Sources*, Cambridge University Press, 1946.
Cross, Samuel H. (Translator), *The Russian Primary Chronicle*, Cambridge, Mass., 1930; *Slavic Civilization Through the Ages*, Harvard University Press, 1948; *Mediaeval Russian Churches*, Cambridge, Mass., 1949.
Florinsky, M. T., *The End of the Russian Empire*, Yale University Press, 1931; *Russia: A History and Interpretation* (2 vols.), New York, 1953.
Graham, Stephen, *Boris Godunov*, Yale University Press, 1933; *Ivan the Terrible*, Yale University Press, 1933; *Peter the Great*, London, 1929; *Tsar of Freedom: Alexander II*, Yale University Press, 1935.
Grekov, B. D., *The Culture of Kiev Rūs*, Moscow, 1947.
Grégoire, Henri and others (Editors and Translators), *La Geste Du Prince Igor*, New York, 1948.
Karpovich, M., *Imperial Russia, 1801-1917* (Berkshire Studies), New York, 1932.
Kerner, R. J., *The Urge to the Sea: The Course of Russian History*, University of California Press, 1942.

Kliuchevsky, V. O., *A History of Russia,* New York, 1911-28.
Kohler, Phyllis P. (ed. & tr.), *Journey for Our Time: The Journals of the Marquis de Custine,* New York, 1951.
Kohn, Hans, *Pan-Slavism: Its History and Ideology,* University of Notre Dame Press, 1953.
Kornilov, A., *Modern Russian History,* New York, 1952.
Laserson, M. M., *The American Impact on Russia: Diplomatic and Ideological, 1784-1917,* New York, 1950.
Leroy-Beaulieu, A., *The Empire of the Tsars and the Russians* (3 vols.), New York, 1902-1903.
Levin, A., *The Second Duma,* Yale University Press, 1940.
Lobanov-Rostovsky, A., *Russia and Europe, 1789-1825,* Duke University Press, 1947.
Martin, John Stuart (ed.), *A Picture History of Russia,* New York, 1945.
Masaryk, Thomas G., *The Spirit of Russia,* London, 1919.
Mavor, James, *An Economic History of Russia,* 2nd ed., London, 1925.
Maynard, Sir John, *The Russian Peasant and Other Studies,* London, 1942.
Mazour, Anatole G., *The First Russian Revolution, 1825,* University of California, 1937.
Michell, R. and Forbes, R. (eds. & trs.), *Chronicle of Novgorod, 1016-1471,* London, 1914.
Mirsky, D. S., *Russia: A Social History,* London, 1927.
Mohrenschildt, Dimitri S. von, *Russia in the Intellectual Life of Eighteenth Century France,* New York, 1936.
Paléologue, G. M., *The Enigmatic Czar: the Life of Alexander I of of Russia,* London, 1938.
Pares, Bernard, *A History of Russia,* New York, 1947; *The Fall of the Russian Monarchy,* New York, 1939.
Platonov, S. F., *A History of Russia,* New York, 1929.
Pobedonostsev, C., *Reflections of a Russian Statesman,* London, 1898.
Putnam, Peter (ed.), *Seven Britons in Imperial Russia, 1698-1812,* Princeton University Press, 1952.
Rambaud, Alfred, *The History of Russia,* Boston, 1879.
Robinson, Geroid T., *Rural Russia under the Old Regime,* New York, 1949.
Seton-Watson, Hugh, *The Decline of Imperial Russia, 1855-1914,* New York, 1952.
Soloveytchik, G., *Potemkin,* New York, 1947.
Sorokin, Pitirim, *Russia and the United States,* New York, 1944.
Strakhovsky, L. I., *Alexander I of Russia,* New York, 1947.
Strakhovsky, L. I., (Editor), *A Handbook of Slavic Studies,* Harvard University Press, 1949.
Sumner, B. H., *A Short History of Russia,* New York, 1943; *Peter the Great and the Emergence of Russia,* London, 1950; *Peter the Great and the Ottoman Empire,* New York, 1950.

Tarle, Eugene, *Napoleon's Invasion of Russia—1812,* New York, 1942.

Thomson, G. S., *Catherine the Great and the Expansion of Russia,* New York, 1950.

Tiesenhausen, V. (Compiler and Editor), *Collection of Materials Relating to the History of the Golden Horde* (In Russian), Volume II, Moscow, 1941.

Tompkins, S. R., *Russia Through the Ages; from the Scythians to the Soviets,* 1940.

Treviranus, G. R., *Revolutions in Russia: Their Lessons for the Western World,* New York, 1944.

Vernadsky, George, *Ancient Russia,* Yale University Press, 1943; *A History of Russia,* New York, 1944; *Medieval Russian Laws,* Columbia University Press, New York, 1947; *Kievan Russia,* Yale University Press, 1948; *The Mongols and Russia,* Yale University Press, 1953.

Walsh, Warren B., *Readings in Russian History,* Syracuse University Press, 1948.

Wipper, R., *Ivan Grozny,* Moscow, 1947.

SOVIET RUSSIA

Alexander, Grand Duke of Russia, *Once a Grand Duke,* New York, 1932.

Barghoorn, F. P., *The Soviet Image of America. A Study in Distortion,* New York, 1950.

Bauer, R. A., *The New Man in Soviet Psychology,* Harvard University Press, 1952.

Baykov, Alexander, *The Development of the Soviet Economic System,* New York, 1948.

Beck, F. and Goden, W., *Russian Purge and the Extraction of Confessions,* New York, 1951.

Berdyaev, Nicholas, *The Origin of Russian Communism,* New York, 1937.

Bunyan, James, *Intervention, Civil War, and Communism in Russia (April to December, 1918),* Baltimore, 1936.

Caldwell, Erskine, *All Out on the Road to Smolensk,* New York, 1942.

Carr, E. H., *The Soviet Impact on the Western World,* New York, 1947; *The Bolshevik Revolution, 1917-1923* (3 vols.), New York, 1950-1953.

Chamberlin, Wm. H., *Russia's Iron Age,* Boston, 1934; *The Russian Enigma,* New York, 1943; *The Russian Revolution, 1917-1921* (2 vols.)

Chernov, Victor, *The Great Russian Revolution,* Yale University Press, 1936.

Dallin, David J., *The Real Soviet Russia,* Yale University Press, 1944.

Dallin, D. J. and Nicolaevsky, B. S., *Forced Labor in Soviet Russia,* Yale University Press, 1947.

Davies, Joseph, *Mission to Moscow,* New York, 1941.

Deutscher, I., *Stalin,* New York, 1949.

Duranty, Walter, *I Write as I Please,* New York, 1935.

Essad-Bay, M., *Stalin,* New York, 1932; *Blood and Oil in the Orient,* New York; *OGPU,* New York, 1933.

Fainsod, Merle, *How Russia is Ruled,* Harvard University Press, 1953.

Fischer, George, *Soviet Opposition to Stalin,* Harvard University Press, 1952.

Fischer, Louis, *Men and Politics: An Autobiography,* New York, 1941.

Fisher, H. H., *The Famine in Soviet Russia, 1919-1923,* Stanford, 1935.

Francis, David R., *Russia from the American Embassy,* New York, 1921.

Gankin, O. H., and Fisher, H. H., *The Bolsheviks and the World War: the Origins of the Third International,* Stanford University Press, 1940 (2 Vols.).

Graves, William S., *America's Siberian Adventure,* 1918-20, New York, 1931.

Gsovski, Vladimir, *Soviet Civil Law: Private Rights and Their Background Under the Soviet Regime* (2 Volumes), Ann Arbor, 1948.

Guillaume, General Augustin, *Soviet Arms and Soviet Power,* Washington, 1949.

Gurian, W. (ed.), *The Soviet Union: Background, Ideology, Reality,* University of Notre Dame Press, 1951; *Bolshevism, An Introduction to Soviet Communism,* University of Notre Dame Press, 1952; (ed.), *Soviet Imperialism: Its Origins and Tactics,* University of Notre Dame Press, 1953.

Harper, Samuel, *The Russia I Believe In,* University of Chicago Press, 1945.

Harper, Samuel N., and Thompson, Ronald, *Government of the Soviet Union,* 2nd ed., New York, 1949.

Hazard, John N., *The Soviet Housing Law,* New Haven, 1940.

Hindus, Maurice, *The Great Offensive,* New York, 1933; *Mother Russia,* New York, 1943; *Crisis in the Kremlin,* New York, 1953.

Inkeles, A., *Public Opinion in Soviet Russia,* Harvard University Press, 1950.

Jasny, N., *The Socialized Agriculture of the U.S.S.R.,* Stanford University Press, 1949.

Johnson, The Very Reverend Hewlett, *The Soviet Power,* New York, 1940.

Koestler, Arthur, *Darkness at Noon,* New York, 1941.

Kournakoff, Sergei N., *Russia's Fighting Forces,* New York, 1942.

Krivitsky, W. G., *In Stalin's Secret Service,* New York, 1939.

Laserson, Max M., *Russia and the Western World,* New York, 1945.

Liberman, Simon, *Building Lenin's Russia,* Chicago, 1945.

Lyashchenko, P. I., *History of the National Economy of Russia to the 1917 Revolution,* New York, 1949.

Lyons, Eugene, *Assignment in Utopia,* New York, 1939; *The Red Decade,* 1941.

Magidoff, Robert, *The Kremlin Versus the People,* New York, 1953.

Maynard, Sir John, *Russia in Flux,* New York, 1948.

Mirsky, D. S., *Lenin,* Boston, 1931.

Mosely, Philip E. (ed.), "The Soviet Union Since World War II," *The Annals of the American Academy of Political and Social Science,* May, 1949.

Pares, Sir Bernard, *Moscow Admits a Critic,* London, 1936; *Russia* (A Mentor Book, 1949); *A Wandering Student,* Syracuse University Press, 1948.

Pope, Arthur Upham, *Maxim Litvinoff,* New York, 1943.

Readings in Leninism, 5 Vols., International Publishers, 1937.

Reed, John, *Ten Days that Shook the World,* Modern Library, 1935.

Report of Court Proceedings in the Case of the Anti-Soviet Trotskyite Centre, USSR, 1937.

Reshetar, John S., *A Concise History of the Communist Party of the Soviet Union,* New York, 1960.

Rosenberg, Arthur, *A History of Bolshevism,* Oxford University Press, New York, 1934.

Schueller, George K., *The Politburo,* Stanford University Press, 1951.

Schwartz, Harry, *Russia's Soviet Economy,* New York, 1950.

Scott, John, *Behind the Urals,* Boston, 1942.

Seton-Watson, Hugh, *Eastern Europe Between the Wars, 1918-1941,* New York, 1946; *From Lenin to Malenkov,* New York, 1953.

Shapiro, Leonard, *The Origin of the Communist Autocracy, 1917-1922,* Harvard University Press, 1955.

Shirer, Wm. L., *End of a Berlin Diary,* New York, 1947.

Shub, David, *Lenin: A Biography,* New York, 1948.

Simmons, E. J. (ed.), *USSR,* Cornell University Press, 1947.

Snow, Edgar, *People on Our Side,* New York, 1944; *The Pattern of Soviet Power,* New York, 1945.

Souvarine, Boris, *Stalin,* New York, 1939.

Sukhanov, N. N., *The Russian Revolution 1917,* Oxford University Press, New York, 1955.

Strakhovsky, L. I., *Intervention at Archangel,* Princeton, 1944.

Tchernavin, Tatiana, *Escape from the Soviets,* New York, 1933.

Timasheff, Nicholas S., *The Great Retreat,* New York, 1946.

Tolstoy, A., *I Worked for the Soviets,* Yale University Press, 1935.

Towster, Julian, *Political Power in the U.S.S.R., 1917-1947,* New York, 1948.

Treadgold, Donald, *Twentieth Century Russia,* Chicago, 1959.

Trotsky, L., *The History of the Russian Revolution,* New York, 1936; *Stalin,* New York, 1946.

Voznesensky, N. A., *The Economy of the U.S.S.R. During World War II,* Washington, 1948.

Vyshinsky, Andrei, *The Law of the Soviet State* (Translated by Hugh W. Babb), New York, 1948.

Walsh, E. A., *The Fall of the Russian Empire,* New York, 1928.

Webb, Sidney and Beatrice, *Soviet Communism: A New Civilization,* New York, 1936.

Werner, Max, *Military Strength of the Powers*, New York, 1938; *Battle for the World*, New York, 1941; *The Great Offensive*, New York, 1942.
Werth, Alexander, *Moscow War Diary*, New York, 1942; *Year of Stalingrad*, Hamilton, 1946.
White, D. Fedotoff, *The Growth of the Red Army*, Princeton, 1944.
Wolfe, Bertram, *Three Who Made a Revolution*, New York, 1948.

ASIATIC RUSSIA

Baddeley, John F., *Russia, Mongolia, China*, London, 1919; *The Russian Conquest of the Caucasus*, New York, 1908.
Baidukov, George, *Over the North Pole*.
Collins, Percy McDonough, *A Voyage Down the Amour*, 1860.
Cressey, George, *The Basis of Soviet Strength*, New York, 1945.
Davies, R. A., and Steiger, A. J., *Soviet Asia, Democracy's First Line of Defense*, New York, 1942.
Fisher, Raymond H., *The Russian Fur Trade, 1550-1700*, University of California Press, 1943.
Gennin, G. W. de, *A Description of Ural and Siberian Industries in 1735* (in Russian).
Gerrare, Wird, *Greater Russia*, New York, 1903.
Golder, F. A., *Russian Expansion on the Pacific, 1641-1850*, Cleveland, 1914.
Gruber, Ruth, *I Went to the Soviet Arctic*, New York, 1939.
Kennan, George, *Siberia and the Exile System* (2 vols.), New York, 1891.
Kerner, R. J., *The Urge to the Sea, the Course of Russian History*, University of California Press, 1942.
Krist, Gustav, *Alone Through the Forbidden Land. Journeys in Disguise through Soviet Central Asia*, London, 1938.
Kunitz, Joshua, *Down Over Samarkand: The Rebirth of Central Asia*, New York, 1935.
Lantzeff, George V., *Siberia in the Seventeenth Century: A Study of the Colonial Administration*, University of California Press, 1943.
Littlepage, J. D., and Bess, Demaree, *In Search of Soviet Gold*, New York, 1937.
Lobanov-Rostovsky, Prince A., *Russia and Asia*, Ann Arbor, 1951.
Mandel, William, *The Soviet Far East*, New York, 1944.
Miller, G. F., *A History of Siberia* (in Russian), Leningrad, 1937.
Norins, Martin R., *Gateway to Asia: Sinkiang*, New York, 1944.
Norton, H. K., *Far Eastern Republic of Siberia*, London, 1923.
Ravenstein, E. G., *The Russians on the Amur; Its Discovery, Conquest, and Colonization*, London, 1861.
Scott, John, *Behind the Urals*, New York, 1942.

Semyonov, Yuri, *The Conquest of Siberia,* London, 1944.

Shoemaker, Michael Myers, *The Great Siberian Railway from St. Petersburg to Pekin,* New York, 1904.

Stewart, George, *The White Armies of Russia,* New York, 1933.

Strakhovsky, L. I., *The Origins of American Intervention in North Russia, 1918,* Princeton University Press, 1937.

Taracouzio, T. A., *Soviets in the Arctic,* New York, 1938.

The Siberian Encyclopedia (in Russian).

Varneck, E., and Fisher, H. H., (eds.), *The Testimony of Kolchak and Other Siberian Materials,* Stanford University Press, 1935.

Wright, G. F., *Asiatic Russia.*

Yarmolinsky, A. (Trans. and ed.), *The Memoirs of Count Witte,* Garden City, 1921.

FOREIGN POLICY

Bailey, T. A., *America Faces Russia: Russian-American Relations from Early Times to Our Day,* Cornell University Press, 1950.

Beloff, Max, *The Foreign Policy of Soviet Russia,* Vol. I, Oxford University Press, 1947; Vol. II, New York, 1949; *Soviet Policy in the Far East, 1944-1951,* Oxford University Press, 1953.

Browder, Robert P., *The Origins of Soviet-American Diplomacy,* Princeton University Press, 1953.

Butcher, Harry C., *My Three Years with Eisenhower,* New York, 1946.

Byrnes, James F., *Speaking Frankly,* New York, 1947.

Cahen, Gaston, *Histoire des Relations de la Russie avec la Chine, sous Pierre Le Grand* (1689-1730), Anastic Edition, 1941.

Churchill, Winston S., *The Second World War,* New York, 1948-53. Vol. I, *The Gathering Storm;* Vol. II, *Their Finest Hour;* Vol. VI, *Triumph and Tragedy.*

Coates, W. P., and Zelda K., *A History of Anglo-Soviet Relations,* London, 1943.

Dallin, David J., *Soviet Russia's Foreign Policy, 1939-42,* New Haven, 1942; *Soviet Russia and the Far East,* Yale University Press, 1948; *The Rise of Russia in Asia,* New Haven, 1949.

Dean, Vera M., *The United States and Russia,* Harvard University Press, 1947.

Deane, John R., *The Strange Alliance,* New York, 1947.

Degras, J. (ed.), *Soviet Documents on Foreign Policy* (2 vols.), New York, 1951-1952.

Dennett, Tyler, *Roosevelt and the Russo-Japanese War,* Garden City, 1925.

Dennett, Raymond and Johnson, J. E. (eds.), *Negotiating with the Russians,* Boston, 1951.

Dulles, Foster Rhea, *The Road to Teheran,* Princeton, 1944.

Eisenhower, Dwight D., *Crusade in Europe,* New York, 1948.

Fischer, Louis, *The Soviets in World Affairs,* New York, 1951.

Gantenbein, James W. (Editor), *Documentary Background of World War II,* New York, 1948.

Gleason, J. H., *The Genesis of Russophobia in Great Britain,* Harvard University Press, 1950.

Helmerich, Ernest C., *The Diplomacy of the Balkan War, 1912-1913.*

Hendel, Samuel (ed.), *The Soviet Crucible,* D. Van Nostrand Co., Inc., Princeton, N. J., 1959.

Hilger, G. and Meyer, A. G., *The Incompatible Allies: A Memoir-History of German-Soviet Relations, 1918-1941,* New York, 1953.

Jelavich, Charles, *Tsarist Russia and Balkan Nationalism,* University of California Press, Berkeley, 1958.

Konovalov, S. (ed.), *Russo-Polish Relations: An Historical Survey,* Princeton University Press, 1945.

Korff, S. A., *Russian Foreign Relations During the Last Half Century,* New York, 1922.

Marriott, J. A. R., *Anglo-Russian Relations, 1689-1943,* London, 1944.

Moore, Harriet L., *Soviet Far Eastern Policy, 1931-1945,* Princeton University Press, 1945.

Morse, H. B., and McNair, H. F., *Far Eastern International Relations,* Boston, 1931.

Mosely, Philip E., *Russian Diplomacy and the Opening of the Eastern Question in 1838-1839,* Harvard University Press, 1934.

Price, E. B., *The Russo-Japanese Treaties of 1907-1916 Concerning Manchuria and Mongolia,* Baltimore, 1933.

Rubinstein, Alvin Z., *The Foreign Policy of the Soviet Union,* New York, 1960.

Schuman, Frederick L., *American Policy Toward Russia Since 1918,* New York, 1928; *Soviet Politics at Home and Abroad,* New York, 1946.

Seton-Watson, Hugh, *The Eastern European Revolution,* New York, 1951.

Shapiro, L. (ed.), *Soviet Treaty Series,* Georgetown University Press, 1951, Vol. I, 1917-1928.

Sherwood, Robert, *Roosevelt and Hopkins: An Intimate Study,* New York, 1948.

Smith, Walter Bedell, *My Three Years in Moscow,* New York, 1950.

Sontag, R. J., and Beddie, J. S. (Editors), *Nazi-Soviet Relations, 1939-1941,* New York, 1948.

Stettinius, Edward R., Jr., *Roosevelt and the Russians,* New York, 1949.

Sumner, B. H., *Russia and the Balkans, Oxford,* 1937.

Taracouzio, T. A., *War and Peace in Soviet Diplomacy,* New York, 1940.

Tompkins, P., *American-Russian Relations in the Far East,* New York, 1949.

Vandenberg, A. H., Jr., and Morris, J. A. (eds.), *The Private Papers Senator Vandenberg,* Boston, 1952.

Vernadsky, George, *Political and Diplomatic History of Russia,* Boston, 1936.

Weigh, Ken Shen, *Russo-Chinese Diplomacy,* Shanghai, 1928.

Wheeler-Bennett, John W., *The Forgotten Peace, Brest-Litovsk, March, 1918,* New York, 1938; *Munich: Prologue to Tragedy,* New York, 1948; *The Nemesis of Power: The German Army in Politics, 1918-1945,* New York, 1953.

Williams, Wm. A., *American-Russian Relations: 1781-1947,* New York, 1952.

White, J. A., *The Siberian Intervention,* Princeton University Press, 1950.

Wuorinen, John H., *Finland and World War II 1939-1944,* New York, 1948.

Yakhontov, Victor, *USSR Foreign Policy in the Far East,* New York, 1945.

Young, G. W., *The International Relations of Manchuria,* Chicago, 1929.

Zabriskie, Edward H., *American-Russian Rivalry in the Far East: A Study in Diplomacy and Power Politics, 1895-1914,* University of Pennsylvania, 1946.

NEAR AND MIDDLE EAST

Berliner, Joseph S., *Soviet Economic Aid to Underdeveloped Countries,* New York, 1958.

Goitein, S. D., *Jews and Arabs—Their Contacts Through the Ages,* New York, 1955.

Hitti, Philip K., *History of the Arabs,* 5th ed., London, 1953.

Hurewitz, J. C., *Diplomacy in the Near and Middle East,* 2 Vols., D. Van Nostrand Co., Inc., Princeton, N. J., 1956.

Kirk, George, *A Short History of the Middle East,* New York, 1955.

Laqueur, Walter Z., *The Soviet Union and the Middle East,* New York, 1959.

——— (ed.), *The Middle East in Transition,* London-New York, 1958.

Lenczowski, George, *The Middle East in World Affairs,* Ithaca, N.Y. 1956.

Nasser, Gamal Abdel, *Egypt's Liberation,* Washington, D.C., 1955.

Sand, William (ed.), *Tensions in the Middle East,* Washington, D.C., 1956.

Sayegh, Fayez A., *Arab Unity: Hope and Fulfillment,* New York, 1958.

Spector, Ivar, *The Soviet Union and the Muslim World, 1917-1958,* University of Washington Press, 1959.

The Development of United States Policy in the Near East, 1945-1951, Washington, D.C., 1952.

Zeine, Zeine N., *Arab-Turkish Relations and the Emergence of Arab Nationalism,* Beirut, 1958.

Zenkovsky, Serge A., *Pan-Turkism and Islam in Russia,* Harvard University Press, 1960.

MINORITIES

Allen, W. E. D., *The Ukraine: A History,* Cambridge University Press, 1940.
Anders, W., *An Army in Exile. The Story of the Second Polish Corps,* London, 1949.
Bilmanis, Alfred, *A History of Latvia,* Princeton University Press, 1951.
Buell, Raymond L., *Poland—Key to Europe,* New York, 1939.
Chamberlin, W. H., *The Ukraine: A Submerged Nation,* New York, 1944.
Dubnov, S. M., *History of the Jews in Russia and Poland,* Philadelphia, 1918.
Greenberg, Louis, *The Jews in Russia* (2 vols.), Yale University Press, 1944.
Halecki, Oscar, *A History of Poland,* New York, 1943.
Hindus, Maurice, *The Cossacks,* New York, 1945.
Hrushevsky, Michael, *A History of the Ukraine,* Yale University Press, 1941.
Karski, S., *Poland: Past and Present,* New York, 1933.
Konovalov, S. (ed.), *Russo-Polish Relations,* Princeton, 1945.
Kunitz, Joshua, *Russian Literature and the Jew,* Columbia University Press, 1929.
Meiksins, Gregory, *The Baltic Riddle,* New York, 1943.
Reshetar, J., *The Ukrainian Revolution* (1917-1920), Princeton University Press, 1952.
Schmitt, Bernadotte (ed.), *Poland,* University of California Press, 1945.
Schwarz, Solomon M., *The Jews in the Soviet Union,* Syracuse University Press, 1951.
Shotwell, J. T., and Laserson, M. M., *Poland and Russia,* New York, 1945.
Vernadsky, George, *Bohdan, Hetman of the Ukraine.*

LITERATURE AND CULTURE

Abraham, Gerald, *Eight Soviet Composers,* New York, 1943.
Barghoorn, Frederick, *The Soviet Cultural Offensive,* Princeton University Press, 1960.
Berdyaev, Nicolas, *The Russian Idea,* New York, 1948.
Borland, H., *Soviet Literary Theory and Practice during the First Five-Year Plan, 1928-1932,* New York, 1950.
Bunt, Cyril G. E., *A History of Russian Art,* London and New York, 1946.
Cournos, John (ed.), *Short Stories Out of Soviet Russia,* New York, 1929; *Treasury of Russian Life and Humor,* New York, 1943.
Counts, George S. and Lodge, Nucia, *The Country of the Blind,* Boston, 1949.
Deutsch, Babette and Yarmolinsky, A. (translators and editors), *Russian Poetry: An Anthology,* New York, 1927.

Fitzsimmons, Thomas, *et al., USSR Its People Its Society Its Culture* (Survey of World Cultures), New Haven, 1960.

Gudzy, N. K., *History of Early Russian Literature* (Translated by Susan W. Jones), New York, 1949.

Guerney, Bernard G. (ed.), *Treasury of Russian Literature,* New York, 1943.

Guterman, Norbert (translator), *Russian Fairy Tales,* New York, 1945.

Hare, Richard, *Pioneers of Russian Social Thought,* New York, 1951.

Hecht, David, *Russian Radicals Look to America, 1825-1894,* Harvard University Press, 1947.

Jarintzov, N., *Russian Poets and Poems,* New York, 1917.

Jelagin, Juri, *Taming of the Arts,* New York, 1951.

Johnson, Wm. H. E., *Russia's Educational Heritage,* Pittsburgh, 1950.

Kaun, Alexander, *Soviet Poets and Poetry,* University of California Press, 1943.

Kelly, Marie Noele, *Mirror to Russia,* London, 1952.

Kunitz, Joshua (Editor), *Russian Literature Since the Revolution,* New York, 1948.

Lavrin, Janko, *An Introduction to the Russian Novel,* London, 1942.

London, Kurt, *The Seven Soviet Arts,* New Haven, 1938.

Lossky, N. O., *History of Russian Philosophy,* New York, 1951.

Maslenikov, Oleg, *The Frenzied Poets: Andrey Biely and the Russian Symbolists,* University of California Press, 1952.

Menshutkin, B. N., *Russia's Lomonosov, Chemist, Courtier, Physicist, Poet,* Princeton University Press, 1952.

Miliukov, Paul, *Outlines of Russian Culture,* Philadelphia, 1942.

Mirsky, D. S., *A History of Russian Literature,* New York, 1949.

Noyes, Rapall (ed.), *Masterpieces of the Russian Drama,* New York, 1933.

Poggioli, Renato, *The Poets of Russia 1890-1930,* Harvard University Press, 1960.

Reavey, George, *Soviet Literature Today,* Yale University Press, 1947.

Riasanovsky, N. V., *Russia and the West in the Teaching of the Slavophiles,* Harvard University Press, 1952.

Rice, T. T., *Russian Art* (Penguin Books), London, 1949.

Rubissow, Helen, *The Art of Russia,* New York, 1946.

Schlesinger, Rudolf, *Soviet Legal Theory: Its Social Background and Development,* New York, 1945.

Seroff, Victor, *The Mighty Five,* New York, 1948.

Seton, Marie, *Sergei M. Eisenstein,* New York (n.d.).

Simmons, E. J., *English Literature and Culture in Russia, 1553-1840,* Harvard University Press, 1935.

Simmons, E. J., (ed.), *Through the Glass of Soviet Literature,* New York, 1953.

Slonim, Marc, *The Epic of Russian Literature: From Its Origins Through Tolstoy,* New York, 1950; *Modern Russian Literature: From Chekhov to the Present,* New York, 1953.
Sokolov, Y. M., *Russian Folklore,* New York, 1950.
Somerville, John, *Soviet Philosophy,* New York, 1946.
Seltzer, Thomas (ed.), *Best Russian Short Stories,* New York, 1925.
Seven Soviet Plays, with Introduction by H. W. L. Dana, New York, 1946.
Spector, Ivar, *The Golden Age of Russian Literature,* Caxton Printers, Revised and Enlarged Edition, 1952.
Struve, Gleb, *Soviet Russian Literature, 1917-1950,* University of Oklahoma Press, 1951.
Tompkins, Stuart R., *The Russian Mind: From Peter the Great Through the Enlightenment,* University of Oklahoma Press, 1953.
Varneke, B. V., *History of the Russian Theatre,* New York, 1951.
Voyce, Arthur, *Russian Architecture: Trends in Nationalism and Modernism,* New York, 1948.
Wiener, Leo, *Contemporary Drama of Russia,* Boston, 1924.
Yarmolinsky, Avrahm, *Treasury of Great Russian Short Stories,* New York, 1944; *A Treasury of Russian Verse,* New York, 1949.
Zenkovsky, V. V., *A History of Russian Philosophy* (2 vols.), Columbia University Press, 1953.

RELIGION

Anderson, Paul B., *People, Church and State in Modern Russia,* New York, 1944.
Bulgakov, Sergius, *The Orthodox Church,* New York, 1935.
Casey, Robert P., *Religion in Russia,* New York, 1946.
Curtiss, J. S., *The Russian Church and the Soviet State,* Boston, 1953.
Feodotov, R. P., *Religion in Russia,* New York, 1946; *A Treasury of Russian Spirituality,* New York, 1948.
Timasheff, Nicholas S., *Religion in Soviet Russia,* New York, 1942.
Zernov, Nicholas, *Moscow the Third Rome,* London, 1937.

ALASKA

Andrews, C. L., *The Story of Alaska,* Idaho, 1938.
Chevigny, Hector, *Lost Empire: The Life and Adventures of Rezanov,* New York, 1937.
Chinard, Gilbert, *Le Voyage de Laperouse sur les Cotes de l'Alaska et de la Californie* (1786).
Denison, B. W. and Associates, *Alaska Today,* Caldwell, Idaho, 1952.
Farrar, Victor J., *The Annexation of Russian America to the United States,* Washington, D. C., 1937.

Golder, F. A., *Russian Expansion on the Pacific, 1641-1850,* Cleveland, 1914.

James, James Alton, *The First Scientific Exploration of Russian America and the Purchase of Alaska.*

Okum, S. B., *The Russian-American Company,* Harvard University Press, 1951.

BIBLIOGRAPHICAL GUIDES

Grierson, Philip, *Books on Soviet Russia, 1917-1942,* London, 1943.

Kerner, Robert J., *Slavic Europe: a Bibliography,* Harvard University Press, 1918.

Mazour, Anatole G., *Modern Russian Historiography,* 2d ed., D. Van Nostrand Co., Inc., Princeton, N. J., 1958.

Walsh, Warren B., *Russia Under Tsars and Commissars: A Readers' Guide,* Syracuse, 1946.

Yakobson, Sergius, *Five Hundred Russian Works for College Libraries,* Washington, 1948.

PERIODICALS

The American Review on the Soviet Union.

The American Slavic and East European Review.

The Slavonic and East European Review (London).

The Russian Review.

Current Digest of the Soviet Press, 1949—

Soviet Press Translations, Far Eastern and Russian Institute, University of Washington, 1946-1953.

Soviet Survey (London).

Appendix

CONSTITUTION

(Fundamental Law)

of the

UNION OF SOVIET
SOCIALIST REPUBLICS [1]

As Added to and Amended up to the Ninth Session
of the USSR Supreme Soviet, Fourth Convocation

CHAPTER I

THE SOCIAL STRUCTURE

ARTICLE 1

The Union of Soviet Socialist Republics is a socialist state of workers
and peasants.

ARTICLE 2

The political foundation of the USSR is the Soviets of Working People's Deputies, which grew and became strong as a result of the overthrow
of the power of the landlords and capitalists and the conquest of the dictatorship of the proletariat.

ARTICLE 3

All power in the USSR belongs to the working people of town and
country as represented by the Soviets of Working People's Deputies.

ARTICLE 4

The economic foundation of the USSR is the socialist system of economy and the socialist ownership of the instruments and means of production, firmly established as a result of the liquidation of the capitalist system
of economy, the abolition of private ownership of the instruments and
means of production, and the elimination of the exploitation of man by man.

---

[1] Published by USSR, No. 12 (27), Washington, D. C., 1959.

ARTICLE 5

Socialist property in the USSR exists either in the form of state property (belonging to the whole people) or in the form of cooperative and collective farm property (property of collective farms, property of cooperative societies).

ARTICLE 6

The land, its mineral wealth, waters, forests, mills, factories, mines, rail, water and air transport, banks, communications, large state-organized agricultural enterprises (state farms, machine and tractor stations and the like). as well as municipal enterprises and the bulk of the dwelling houses in the cities and industrial localities, are state property, that is, belong to the whole people.

ARTICLE 7

The common enterprises of collective farms and cooperative organizations, with their livestock and implements, the products of the collective farms and cooperative organizations, as well as their common buildings, constitute the common, socialist property of the collective farms and cooperative organizations.

Every household in a collective farm, in addition to its basic income from the common collective farm enterprise, has for its personal use a small plot of household land and, as its personal property, a subsidiary husbandry on the plot, a dwelling house, livestock, poultry and minor agricultural implements—in accordance with the rules of the agricultural artel.

ARTICLE 8

The land occupied by collective farms is secured to them for their use free of charge and for an unlimited time, that is, in perpetuity.

ARTICLE 9

Alongside the socialist system of economy, which is the predominant form of economy in the USSR, the law permits the small private economy of individual peasants and handicraftsmen based on their own labor and precluding the exploitation of the labor of others.

ARTICLE 10

The personal property right of citizens in their incomes and savings from work, in their dwelling houses and subsidiary home enterprises, in articles of domestic economy and use and articles of personal use and convenience, as well as the right of citizens to inherit personal property, is protected by law.

ARTICLE 11

The economic life of the USSR is determined and directed by the state national economic plan, with the aim of increasing the public wealth, of steadily raising the material and cultural standards of the working people, of consolidating the independence of the USSR and strengthening its defensive capacity.

ARTICLE 12

Work in the USSR is a duty and a matter of honor for every able-bodied citizen, in accordance with the principle: "He who does not work, neither shall he eat."

The principle applied in the USSR is that of socialism: "From each according to his ability, to each according to his work."

CHAPTER II

THE STATE STRUCTURE

ARTICLE 13

The Union of Soviet Socialist Republics is a federal state, formed on the basis of a voluntary union of equal Soviet Socialist Republics, namely:

The Russian Soviet Federative Socialist Republic
The Ukrainian Soviet Socialist Republic
The Byelorussian Soviet Socialist Republic
The Uzbek Soviet Socialist Republic
The Kazakh Soviet Socialist Republic
The Georgian Soviet Socialist Republic
The Azerbaijan Soviet Socialist Republic
The Lithuanian Soviet Socialist Republic
The Moldavian Soviet Socialist Republic
The Latvian Soviet Socialist Republic
The Kirghiz Soviet Socialist Republic
The Tajik Soviet Socialist Republic
The Armenian Soviet Socialist Republic
The Turkmen Soviet Socialist Republic
The Estonian Soviet Socialist Republic

ARTICLE 14

The jurisdiction of the Union of Soviet Socialist Republics, as represented by its higher organs of state power and organs of state administration, embraces:

(a) Representation of the USSR in international relations, conclusion, ratification and denunciation of treaties of the USSR with other states, establishment of general procedure governing the relations of Union Republics with foreign states;

(b) Questions of war and peace;

(c) Admission of new republics into the USSR;

(d) Control over the observance of the Constitution of the USSR, and ensuring conformity of the Constitutions of the Union Republics with the Constitution of the USSR;

(e) Confirmation of alterations of boundaries between Union Republics;

(f) Confirmation of the formation of new Territories and Regions and also of new Autonomous Republics and Autonomous Regions within Union Republics;

(g) Organization of the defense of the USSR, direction of all the Armed Forces of the USSR, determination of directing principles governing the organization of the military formations of the Union Republics;

(h) Foreign trade on the basis of state monopoly;

(i) Safeguarding the security of the state;

(j) Determination of the national economic plans of the USSR;

(k) Approval of the consolidated state budget of the USSR and of the report on its fulfillment; determination of the taxes and revenues which go to the Union, the Republican and the local budgets;

(l) Administration of the banks, industrial and agricultural institutions and enterprises and trading enterprises of all-Union jurisdiction; general guidance of industry and construction under Union-Republican jurisdiction;

(m) Administration of transport and communications;

(n) Direction of the monetary and credit system of all-Union importance;

(o) Organization of state insurance;

(p) Contracting and granting of loans;

(q) Determination of the basic principles of land tenure and of the use of mineral wealth, forests and waters;

(r) Determination of the basic principles in the spheres of education and public health;

(s) Organization of a uniform system of national economic statistics;

(t) Determination of the principles of labor legislation;

(u) Determination of the principles of legislation concerning the judicial system and judicial procedure and of the principles of criminal and civil codes;

(v) Legislation concerning Union citizenship; legislation concerning rights of foreigners;

(w) Determination of the principles of legislation concerning marriage and the family;

(x) Issuing of all-Union acts of amnesty.

ARTICLE 15

The sovereignty of the Union Republics is limited only in the spheres defined in Article 14 of the Constitution of the USSR. Outside of these spheres, each Union Republic exercises state authority independently. The USSR protects the sovereign rights of the Union Republics.

ARTICLE 16

Each Union Republic has its own Constitution, which takes account of the specific features of the Republic and is drawn up in full conformity with the Constitution of the USSR.

ARTICLE 17

The right freely to secede from the USSR is reserved to every Union Republic.

ARTICLE 18

The territory of a Union Republic may not be altered without its consent.

ARTICLE 18A

Each Union Republic has the right to enter into direct relations with foreign states and to conclude agreements and exchange diplomatic and consular representatives with them.

ARTICLE 18B

Each Union Republic has its own Republican military formations.

ARTICLE 19

The laws of the USSR have the same force within the territory of every Union Republic.

ARTICLE 20

In the event of divergence between a law of a Union Republic and a law of the Union, the Union law prevails.

ARTICLE 21

Uniform Union citizenship is established for citizens of the USSR. Every citizen of a Union Republic is a citizen of the USSR.

ARTICLE 22

The Russian Soviet Federative Socialist Republic includes the Bashkirian, Buryat-Mongolian, Daghestan, Kabardinian-Balkar, Karelian, Komi, Mari, Mordovian, North Ossetian, Tatar, Udmurt, Checheno-Ingush, Chuvash and Yakut Autonomous Soviet Socialist Republics; and the Adygei, Gorny Altai, Jewish, Kalmyk, Karachayevo-Cherkess, Tuva and Khakass Autonomous Regions.

ARTICLE 23

REPEALED.

ARTICLE 24

The Azerbaijan Soviet Socialist Republic includes the Nakhichevan Autonomous Soviet Socialist Republic and the Nagorno-Karabakh Autonomous Region.

ARTICLE 25

The Georgian Soviet Socialist Republic includes the Abkhazian and Ajarian Autonomous Soviet Socialist Republics and the South Ossetian Autonomous Region.

ARTICLE 26

The Uzbek Soviet Socialist Republic includes the Kara-Kalpak Autonomous Soviet Socialist Republic.

ARTICLE 27

The Tajik Soviet Socialist Republic includes the Gorno-Badakhshan Autonomous Region.

ARTICLE 28

The solution of problems pertaining to the administrative-territorial structure of the regions and territories of the Union Republics comes within the jurisdiction of the Union Republics.

ARTICLE 29

REPEALED.

CHAPTER III

THE HIGHER ORGANS OF STATE POWER IN
THE UNION OF SOVIET SOCIALIST REPUBLICS

ARTICLE 30

The Highest organ of state power in the USSR is the Supreme Soviet
of the USSR.

ARTICLE 31

The Supreme Soviet of the USSR exercises all rights vested in the
Union of Soviet Socialist Republics in accordance with Article 14 of the
Constitution, in so far as they do not, by virtue of the Constitution, come
within the jurisdiction of organs of the USSR that are accountable to the
Supreme Soviet of the USSR, that is, the Presidium of the Supreme
Soviet of the USSR, the Council of Ministers of the USSR, and the Min-
istries of the USSR.

ARTICLE 32

The legislative power of the USSR is exercised exclusively by the
Supreme Soviet of the USSR.

ARTICLE 33

The Supreme Soviet of the USSR consists of two Chambers: the Soviet
of the Union and the Soviet of Nationalities.

ARTICLE 34

The Soviet of the Union is elected by the citizens of the USSR voting
by election districts on the basis of one deputy for every 300,000 of the
population.

ARTICLE 35

The Soviet of Nationalities is elected by the citizens of the USSR voting
by Union Republics, Autonomous Republics, Autonomous Regions, and
National Areas on the basis of twenty-five deputies from each Union Republic, eleven deputies from each Autonomous Republic, five deputies from
each Autonomous Region and one deputy from each National Area.

ARTICLE 36

The Supreme Soviet of the USSR is elected for a term of four years.

ARTICLE 37

The two Chambers of the Supreme Soviet of the USSR, the Soviet of the Union and the Soviet of Nationalities, have equal rights.

ARTICLE 38

The Soviet of the Union and the Soviet of Nationalities have equal powers to initiate legislation.

ARTICLE 39

A law is considered adopted if passed by both Chambers of the Supreme Soviet of the USSR by a simple majority vote in each.

ARTICLE 40

Laws passed by the Supreme Soviet of the USSR are published in the languages of the Union Republics over the signatures of the President and Secretary of the Presidium of the Supreme Soviet of the USSR.

ARTICLE 41

Sessions of the Soviet of the Union and of the Soviet of Nationalities begin and terminate simultaneously.

ARTICLE 42

The Soviet of the Union elects a Chairman of the Soviet of the Union and two Vice-Chairmen.

ARTICLE 43

The Soviet of Nationalities elects a Chairman of the Soviet of Nationalities and four Vice-Chairmen.

ARTICLE 44

The Chairmen of the Soviet of the Union and the Soviet of Nationalities preside at the meetings of the respective Chambers and have charge of the conduct of their business and proceedings.

ARTICLE 45

Joint meetings of the two Chambers of the Supreme Soviet of the US-SR are presided over alternately by the Chairman of the Soviet of the Union and the Chairman of the Soviet of Nationalities.

ARTICLE 46

Sessions of the Supreme Soviet of the USSR are convened by the Presidium of the Supreme Soviet of the USSR twice a year.

Extraordinary sessions are convened by the Presidium of the Supreme Soviet of the USSR at its discretion or on the demand of one of the Union Republics.

ARTICLE 47

In the event of disagreement between the Soviet of the Union and the Soviet of Nationalities, the question is referred for settlement to a conciliation commission formed by the Chambers on a parity basis. If the conciliation commission fails to arrive at an agreement, or if its decision fails to satisfy one of the Chambers, the question is considered for a second time by the Chambers. Failing agreement between the two Chambers, the Presidium of the Supreme Soviet of the USSR dissolves the Supreme Soviet of the USSR and orders new elections.

ARTICLE 48

The Supreme Soviet of the USSR at a joint sitting of the two Chambers elects the Presidium of the Supreme Soviet of the USSR, consisting of a President of the Presidium of the Supreme Soviet of the USSR, sixteen Vice-Presidents, a Secretary of the Presidium and fifteen members of the Presidium of the Supreme Soviet of the USSR.

The Presidium of the Supreme Soviet of the USSR is accountable to the Supreme Soviet of the USSR for all its activities.

ARTICLE 49

The Presidium of the Supreme Soviet of the USSR:

(a) Convenes the sessions of the Supreme Soviet of the USSR;

(b) Issues decrees;

(c) Gives interpretations of the laws of the USSR in operation;

(d) Dissolves the Supreme Soviet of the USSR in conformity with Article 47 of the Constitution of the USSR and orders new elections;

(e) Conducts nation-wide polls (referendums) on its own initiative or on the demand of one of the Union Republics;

(f) Annuls decisions and orders of the Council of Ministers of the

USSR and of the Councils of Ministers of the Union Republics if they do not conform to law;

(g) In the intervals between sessions of the Supreme Soviet of the USSR, releases and appoints Ministers of the USSR on the recommendation of the Chairman of the Council of Ministers of the USSR, subject to subsequent confirmation by the Supreme Soviet of the USSR;

(h) Institutes decorations (orders and medals) and titles of honor of the USSR;

(i) Awards orders and medals and confers titles of honor of the USSR;

(j) Exercises the right of pardon;

(k) Institutes military titles, diplomatic ranks and other special titles;

(l) Appoints and removes the high command of the Armed Forces of the USSR;

(m) In the intervals between sessions of the Supreme Soviet of the USSR, proclaims a state of war in the event of military attack on the USSR, or when necessary to fulfill international treaty obligations concerning mutual defense against aggression;

(n) Orders general or partial mobilization;

(o) Ratifies and denounces international treaties of the USSR;

(p) Appoints and recalls plenipotentiary representatives of the USSR to foreign states;

(q) Receives the letters of credence and recall of diplomatic representatives accredited to it by foreign states;

(r) Proclaims martial law in separate localities or throughout the USSR in the interests of the defense of the USSR or of the maintenance of public order and the security of the state.

ARTICLE 50

The Soviet of the Union and the Soviet of Nationalities elect Credentials Committees to verify the credentials of the members of the respective Chambers.

On the report of the Credentials Committees, the Chambers decide whether to recognize the credentials of deputies or to annul their election.

ARTICLE 51

The Supreme Soviet of the USSR, when it deems necessary, appoints commissions of investigation and audit on any matter.

It is the duty of all institutions and officials to comply with the demands of such commissions and to submit to them all necessary materials and documents.

ARTICLE 52

A member of the Supreme Soviet of the USSR may not be prosecuted or arrested without the consent of the Supreme Soviet of the USSR, or, when the Supreme Soviet of the USSR is not in session, without the consent of the Presidium of the Supreme Soviet of the USSR.

ARTICLE 53

On the expiration of the term of office of the Supreme Soviet of the USSR, or on its dissolution prior to the expiration of its term of office, the Presidium of the Supreme Soviet of the USSR retains its powers until the newly-elected Supreme Soviet of the USSR shall have formed a new Presidium of the Supreme Soviet of the USSR.

ARTICLE 54

On the expiration of the term of office of the Supreme Soviet of the USSR, or in the event of its dissolution prior to the expiration of its term of office, the Presidium of the Supreme Soviet of the USSR orders new elections to be held within a period not exceeding two months from the date of expiration of the term of office or dissolution of the Supreme Soviet of the USSR.

ARTICLE 55

The newly-elected Supreme Soviet of the USSR is convened by the outgoing Presidium of the Supreme Soviet of the USSR not later than three months after the elections.

ARTICLE 56

The Supreme Soviet of the USSR, at a joint sitting of the two Chambers, appoints the Government of the USSR, namely, the Council of Ministers of the USSR.

CHAPTER IV

THE HIGHER ORGANS OF STATE
POWER IN THE UNION REPUBLICS

ARTICLE 57

The highest organ of state power in a Union Republic is the Supreme Soviet of the Union Republic.

ARTICLE 58

The Supreme Soviet of a Union Republic is elected by the citizens of the Republic for a term of four years.

The basis of representation is established by the Constitution of the Union Republic.

ARTICLE 59

The Supreme Soviet of a Union Republic is the sole legislative organ of the Republic.

ARTICLE 60

The Supreme Soviet of a Union Republic:

(a) Adopts the Constitution of the Republic and amends it in conformity with Article 16 of the Constitution of the USSR;

(b) Confirms the Constitutions of the Autonomous Republics forming part of it and defines the boundaries of their territories;

(c) Approves the national economic plan and the budget of the Republic and forms economic administration areas;

(d) Exercises the right of amnesty and pardon of citizens sentenced by the judicial organs of the Union Republic;

(e) Decides questions of representation of the Union Republic in its international relations;

(f) Determines the manner of organizing the Republic's military formations.

ARTICLE 61

The Supreme Soviet of a Union Republic elects the Presidium of the Supreme Soviet of the Union Republic, consisting of a President of the Presidium of the Supreme Soviet of the Union Republic, Vice-Presidents, a Secretary of the Presidium and members of the Presidium of the Supreme Soviet of the Union Republic.

The powers of the Presidium of the Supreme Soviet of a Union Republic are defined by the Constitution of the Union Republic.

ARTICLE 62

The Supreme Soviet of a Union Republic elects a Chairman and Vice-Chairman to conduct its sittings.

ARTICLE 63

The Supreme Soviet of a Union Republic appoints the Government of the Union Republic, namely, the Council of Ministers of the Union Republic.

Chapter V

THE ORGANS OF STATE ADMINISTRATION OF
THE UNION OF SOVIET SOCIALIST REPUBLICS

ARTICLE 64

The highest executive and administrative organ of the state power of the Union of Soviet Socialist Republics is the Council of Ministers of the USSR.

ARTICLE 65

The Council of Ministers of the USSR is responsible and accountable to the Supreme Soviet of the USSR, or, in the intervals between sessions of the Supreme Soviet, to the Presidium of the Supreme Soviet of the USSR.

ARTICLE 66

The Council of Ministers of the USSR issues decisions and orders on the basis and in pursuance of the laws in operation, and verifies their execution.

ARTICLE 67

Decisions and orders of the Council of Ministers of the USSR are binding throughout the territory of the USSR.

ARTICLE 68

The Council of Ministers of the USSR:
(a) Coordinates and directs the work of the all-Union and Union-Republican Ministries of the USSR and of other institutions under its jurisdiction, exercises guidance of the Economic Councils of the economic administration areas through the Councils of Ministers of the Union Republics;
(b) Adopts measures to carry out the national economic plan and the state budget, and to strengthen the credit and monetary system;
(c) Adopts measures for the maintenance of public order, for the protection of the interests of the state, and for the safeguarding of the rights of citizens;
(d) Exercises general guidance in the sphere of relations with foreign states;
(e) Fixes the annual contingent of citizens to be called up for military service and directs the general organization of the Armed Forces of the country;
(f) Sets up, whenever necessary, special committees and central ad-

ministrations under the Council of Ministers of the USSR for economic and cultural affairs and defense.

<h3 style="text-align:center">ARTICLE 69</h3>

The Council of Ministers of the USSR has the right, in respect of those branches of administration and economy which come within the jurisdiction of the USSR, to suspend decisions and orders of the Councils of Ministers of the Union Republics and of the Economic Councils of the economic administration areas and to annul orders and instructions of Ministers of the USSR.

<h3 style="text-align:center">ARTICLE 70</h3>

The Council of Ministers of the USSR is appointed by the Supreme Soviet of the USSR and consists of:

The Chairman of the Council of Ministers of the USSR;

The First Vice-Chairmen of the Council of Ministers of the USSR;

The Vice-Chairmen of the Council of Ministers of the USSR;

The Ministers of the USSR;

The Chairman of the State Committee of the Council of Ministers of the USSR on Planning;

The Chairman of the Commission of the Council of Ministers of the USSR on Soviet Control;

The Chairman of the State Committee of the Council of Ministers of the USSR on Labor and Wages;

The Chairman of the State Committee of the Council of Ministers of the USSR on Science and Technology;

The Chairman of the State Committee of the Council of Ministers of the USSR on Aircraft Technology;

The Chairman of the State Committee of the Council of Ministers of the USSR on Defence Technology:

The Chairman of the State Committee of the Council of Ministers of the USSR on Radioelectronics;

The Chairman of the State Committee of the Council of Ministers of the USSR on Shipbuilding;

The Chairman of the State Committee of the Council of Ministers of the USSR on Construction;

The Chairman of the State Committee of the Council of Ministers of the USSR on Foreign Economic Relations;

The Chairman of the Committee on the Security of the State under the Council of Ministers of the USSR;

The Chairman of the Administrative Board of the State Bank of the USSR;

The Chief of the Central Statistical Board under the Council of Ministers of the USSR.

The Council of Ministers of the USSR includes the Chairmen of the Councils of Ministers of the Union Republics by virtue of their office.

ARTICLE 71

The Government of the USSR or a Minister of the USSR to whom a question of a member of the Supreme Soviet of the USSR is addressed must give a verbal or written reply in the respective Chamber within a period not exceeding three days.

ARTICLE 72

The Ministers of the USSR direct the branches of state administration which come within the jurisdiction of the USSR.

ARTICLE 73

The Ministers of the USSR, within the limits of the jurisdiction of their respective Ministries, issue orders and instructions on the basis and in pursuance of the laws in operation, and also of decisions and orders of the Council of Ministers of the USSR, and verify their execution.

ARTICLE 74

The Ministries of the USSR are either all-Union or Union-Republican Ministries.

ARTICLE 75

Each all-Union Ministry directs the branch of state administration entrusted to it throughout the territory of the USSR either directly or through bodies appointed by it.

ARTICLE 76

The Union-Republican Ministries, as a rule, direct the branches of state administration entrusted to them through corresponding Ministries of the Union Republics; they administer directly only a definite and limited number of enterprises according to a list confirmed by the Presidium of the Supreme Soviet of the USSR.

ARTICLE 77

The following Ministries are all-Union Ministries:
    The Ministry of Foreign Trade;
    The Ministry of Merchant Marine;

The Ministry of Railways;
The Ministry of the Medium Machine-Building Industry;
The Ministry of Transport Construction;
The Ministry of the Chemical Industry;
The Ministry of Electric Power Stations.

ARTICLE 78

The following Ministries are Union-Republican Ministries:
The Ministry of Internal Affairs;
The Ministry of Higher Education;
The Ministry of Geological Survey and Conservation of Mineral
    Resources;
The Ministry of Public Health;
The Ministry of Foreign Affairs;
The Ministry of Culture;
The Ministry of Defence;
The Ministry of Communications;
The Ministry of Agriculture;
The Ministry of Trade;
The Ministry of Finance;
The Ministry of Grain Stocks.

CHAPTER VI

THE ORGANS OF STATE ADMINISTRATION
OF THE UNION REPUBLICS

ARTICLE 79

The highest executive and administrative organ of the state power of
a Union Republic is the Council of Ministers of the Union Republic.

ARTICLE 80

The Council of Ministers of a Union Republic is responsible and accountable to the Supreme Soviet of the Union Republic, or, in the intervals
between sessions of the Supreme Soviet of the Union Republic, to the Presidium of the Supreme Soviet of the Union Republic.

ARTICLE 81

The Council of Ministers of a Union Republic issues decisions and
orders on the basis and in pursuance of the laws in operation of the USSR

and of the Union Republic, and of the decisions and orders of the Council of Ministers of the USSR, and verifies their execution.

ARTICLE 82

The Council of Ministers of a Union Republic has the right to suspend decisions and orders of the Councils of Ministers of its Autonomous Republics, and to annul decisions and orders of the Executive Committees of the Soviets of Working People's Deputies of its Territories, Regions and Autonomous Regions, as well as decisions and orders of the Economic Councils of the economic administration areas.

ARTICLE 83

The Council of Ministers of a Union Republic is appointed by the Supreme Soviet of the Union Republic and consists of:
The Chairman of the Council of Ministers of the Union Republic;
The Vice-Chairmen of the Council of Ministers;
The Ministers;
The Chairman of the State Commission on Planning;
The Chairman of the State Committee of the Council of Ministers of the Union Republic on Construction and Architecture;
The Chairman of the Committee on the Security of the State under the Council of Ministers of the Union Republic.

ARTICLE 84

The Ministers of a Union Republic direct the branches of state administration which come within the jurisdiction of the Union Republic.

ARTICLE 85

The Ministers of a Union Republic, within the limits of the jurisdiction of their respective Ministries, issue orders and instructions on the basis and in pursuance of the laws of the USSR and of the Union Republic, of the decisions and orders of the Council of Ministers of the USSR and the Council of Ministers of the Union Republic, and of the orders and instructions of the Union-Republican Ministries of the USSR.

ARTICLE 86

The Ministries of a Union Republic are either Union-Republican or Republican Ministries.

ARTICLE 87

Each Union-Republican Ministry directs the branch of state administration entrusted to it, and is subordinate both to the Council of Ministers of the Union Republic and to the corresponding Union-Republican Ministry of the USSR.

ARTICLE 88

Each Republican Ministry directs the branch of state administration entrusted to it and is directly subordinate to the Council of Ministers of the Union Republic.

ARTICLE 88A

The Economic Councils of the economic administration areas direct the branches of economic activity entrusted to them, and are directly subordinate to the Council of Ministers of the Union Republic.

The Economic Councils of the economic administration areas issue within their jurisdiction decisions and orders on the basis and in pursuance of the laws of the USSR and the Union Republic and decisions and orders of the Council of Ministers of the Union Republic.

CHAPTER VII

THE HIGHER ORGANS OF STATE POWER IN THE AUTONOMOUS SOVIET SOCIALIST REPUBLICS

ARTICLE 89

The highest organ of state power in an Autonomous Soviet Socialist Republic is the Supreme Soviet of the Autonomous Republic.

ARTICLE 90

The Supreme Soviet of an Autonomous Republic is elected by the citizens of the Republic for a term of four years on a basis of representation established by the Constitution of the Autonomous Republic.

ARTICLE 91

The Supreme Soviet of an Autonomous Republic is the sole legislative organ of the Autonomous Republic.

ARTICLE 92

Each Autonomous Republic has its own Constitution, which takes account of the specific features of the Autonomous Republic and is drawn up in full conformity with the Constitution of the Union Republic.

ARTICLE 93

The Supreme Soviet of an Autonomous Republic elects the Presidium of the Supreme Soviet of the Autonomous Republic and appoints the Council of Ministers of the Autonomous Republic, in accordance with its Constitution.

CHAPTER VIII

THE LOCAL ORGANS OF STATE POWER

ARTICLE 94

The organs of state power in territories, regions, autonomous regions, areas, districts, cities and rural localities (stanitsas, villages, hamlets, kishlaks, auls) are the Soviets of Working People's Deputies.

ARTICLE 95

The Soviets of Working People's Deputies of territories, regions, autonomous regions, areas, districts, cities and rural localities (stanitsas, villages, hamlets, kishlaks, auls) are elected by the working people of the respective territories, regions, autonomous regions, areas, districts, cities or rural localities for a term of two years.

ARTICLE 96

The basis of representation for Soviets of Working People's Deputies is determined by the Constitutions of the Union Republics.

ARTICLE 97

The Soviets of Working People's Deputies direct the work of the organs of administration subordinate to them, ensure the maintenance of public order, the observance of the laws and the protection of the rights of citizens, direct local economic and cultural affairs and draw up the local budgets.

ARTICLE 98

The Soviets of Working People's Deputies adopt decisions and issue orders within the limits of the powers vested in them by the laws of the USSR and of the Union Republic.

ARTICLE 99

The executive and administrative organ of the Soviet of Working People's Deputies of a territory, region, autonomous region, area, district, city or rural locality is the Executive Committee elected by it, consisting of a Chairman, Vice-Chairmen, a Secretary and members.

ARTICLE 100

The executive and administrative organ of the Soviet of Working People's Deputies in a small locality, in accordance with the Constitution of the Union Republic, is the Chairman, the Vice-Chairman and the Secretary elected by the Soviet Working People's Deputies.

ARTICLE 101

The executive organs of the Soviets of Working People's Deputies are directly accountable both to the Soviets of Working People's Deputies which elected them and to the executive organ of the superior Soviet of Working People's Deputies.

CHAPTER IX

THE COURTS AND THE PROCURATOR'S OFFICE

ARTICLE 102

In the USSR justice is administered by the Supreme Court of the USSR, the Supreme Courts of the Union Republics, the Courts of the Territories, Regions, Autonomous Republics, Autonomous Regions and Areas, the Special Courts of the USSR established by decision of the Supreme Soviet of the USSR, and the People's Courts.

ARTICLE 103

In all Courts cases are tried with the participation of people's assessors, except in cases specially provided for by law.

ARTICLE 104

The Supreme Court of the USSR is the highest judicial organ. The Supreme Court of the USSR is charged with the supervision of the judicial activities of all the judicial organs of the USSR and of the Union Republics within the limits established by law.

ARTICLE 105

The Supreme Court of the USSR is elected by the Supreme Soviet of the USSR for a term of five years.

The Supreme Court of the USSR includes the Chairmen of the Supreme Courts of the Union Republics by virtue of their office.

ARTICLE 106

The Supreme Courts of the Union Republics are elected by the Supreme Soviets of the Union Republics for a term of five years.

ARTICLE 107

The Supreme Courts of the Autonomous Republics are elected by the Supreme Soviets of the Autonomous Republics for a term of five years.

ARTICLE 108

The Courts of Territories, Regions, Autonomous Regions and Areas are elected by the Soviets of Working People's Deputies of the respective Territories, Regions, Autonomous Regions or Areas for a term of five years.

ARTICLE 109

People's Courts are elected by the citizens of the districts on the basis of universal, direct and equal suffrage by secret ballot for a term of three years.

ARTICLE 110

Judicial proceedings are conducted in the language of the Union Republic, Autonomous Republic or Autonomous Region, persons not knowing this language being guaranteed the opportunity of fully acquainting themselves with the material of the case through an interpreter and likewise the right to use their own language in court.

ARTICLE 111

In all Courts of the USSR cases are heard in public, unless otherwise provided for by law, and the accused is guaranteed the right to defense.

ARTICLE 112

Judges are independent and subject only to the law.

ARTICLE 113

Supreme supervisory power to ensure the strict observance of the law by all Ministries and institutions subordinated to them, as well as by officials and citizens of the USSR generally, is vested in the Procurator-General of the USSR.

ARTICLE 114

The Procurator-General of the USSR is appointed by the Supreme Soviet of the USSR for a term of seven years.

ARTICLE 115

Procurators of Republics, Territories, Regions, Autonomous Republics and Autonomous Regions are appointed by the Procurator-General of the USSR for a term of five years.

ARTICLE 116

Area, district and city procurators are appointed by the Procurators of the Union Republics, subject to the approval of the Procurator-General of the USSR, for a term of five years.

ARTICLE 117

The organs of the Procurator's Office perform their functions independently of any local organs whatsoever, being subordinate solely to the Procurator-General of the USSR.

CHAPTER X

FUNDAMENTAL RIGHTS AND DUTIES OF CITIZENS

ARTICLE 118

Citizens of the USSR have the right to work, that is, the right to guaranteed employment and payment for their work in accordance with its quantity and quality.

The right to work is ensured by the socialist organization of the national economy, the steady growth of the productive forces of Soviet society, the elimination of the possibility of economic crises, and the abolition of unemployment.

ARTICLE 119

Citizens of the USSR have the right to rest and leisure.

The right to rest and leisure is ensured by the establishment of an eight-hour day for industrial, office, and professional workers, the reduction of the working day to seven or six hours for arduous trades and to four hours in shops where conditions of work are particularly arduous, by the institution of annual vacations with full pay for industrial, office, and professional workers, and by the provision of a wide network of sanatoria, holiday homes and clubs for the accommodation of the working people.

ARTICLE 120

Citizens of the USSR have the right to maintenance in old age and also in case of sickness or disability.

This right is ensured by the extensive development of social insurance of industrial, office, and professional workers at state expense, free medical service for the working people, and the provision of a wide network of health resorts for the use of the working people.

ARTICLE 121

Citizens of the USSR have the right to education.

This right is ensured by universal compulsory seven-year education; by extensive development of secondary education; by free education in all schools, higher as well as secondary; by a system of state grants for students of schools of higher education who excel in their studies; by instruction in schools being conducted in the native language; and by the organization in the factories, state farms, machine and tractor stations and collective farms of free vocational, technical and agronomic training for the working people.

ARTICLE 122

Women in the USSR are accorded equal rights with men in all spheres of economic, government, cultural, political and other public activity.

The possibility of exercising these rights is ensured by women being accorded an equal right with men to work, payment for work, rest and leisure, social insurance and education, and by state protection of the interests of mother and child, state aid to mothers of large families and unmarried mothers, maternity leave with full pay, and the provision of a wide network of maternity homes, nurseries and kindergartens.

ARTICLE 123

Equality of rights of citizens of the USSR, irrespective of their nationality or race, in all spheres of economic, government, cultural, political and other public activity, is an indefeasible law.

Any direct or indirect restriction of the rights of, or, conversely, the establishment of any direct or indirect privileges for, citizens on account of their race or nationality, as well as any advocacy of racial or national exclusiveness or hatred and contempt, is punishable by law.

ARTICLE 124

In order to ensure to citizens freedom of conscience, the church in the USSR is separated from the state, and the school from the church. Freedom of religious worship and freedom of anti-religious propaganda is recognized for all citizens.

ARTICLE 125

In conformity with the interests of the working people, and in order to strengthen the socialist system, the citizens of the USSR are guaranteed by law:

(a) Freedom of speech;
(b) Freedom of the press;
(c) Freedom of assembly, including the holding of mass meetings;
(d) Freedom of street processions and demonstrations.

These civil rights are ensured by placing at the disposal of the working people and their organizations printing presses, stocks of paper, public buildings, the streets, communications facilities and other material requisites for the exercise of these rights.

ARTICLE 126

In conformity with the interests of the working people, and in order to develop the organizational initiative and political activity of the masses of the people, citizens of the USSR are guaranteed the right to unite in public organizations: trade unions, cooperative societies, youth organizations, sport and defense organizations, cultural, technical and scientific societies; and the most active and politically-conscious citizens in the ranks of the working class, working peasants and working intelligentsia voluntarily unite in the Communist Party of the Soviet Union, which is the vanguard of the working people in their struggle to build a communist society and is the leading core of all organizations of the working people, both public and state.

ARTICLE 127

Citizens of the USSR are guaranteed inviolability of the person. No person may be placed under arrest except by decision of a court or with the sanction of a procurator.

ARTICLE 128

The inviolability of the homes of citizens and privacy of correspondence are protected by law.

ARTICLE 129

The USSR affords the right of asylum to foreign citizens persecuted for defending the interests of the working people, or for scientific activities, or for struggling for national liberation.

ARTICLE 130

It is the duty of every citizen of the USSR to abide by the Constitution of the Union of Soviet Socialist Republics, to observe the laws, to maintain labor discipline, honestly to perform public duties, and to respect the rules of socialist intercourse.

ARTICLE 131

It is the duty of every citizen of the USSR to safeguard and fortify public, socialist property as the sacred and inviolable foundation of the Soviet system, as the source of the wealth and might of the country, as the source of the prosperity and culture of all the working people.

Persons committing offenses against public, socialist property are enemies of the people.

ARTICLE 132

Universal military service is law.

Military service in the Armed Forces of the USSR is an honorable duty of the citizens of the USSR.

ARTICLE 133

To defend the country is the sacred duty of every citizen of the USSR. Treason to the motherland—violation of the oath of allegiance, desertion to the enemy, impairing the military power of the state, espionage—is punishable with all the severity of the law as the most heinous of crimes.

CHAPTER XI

THE ELECTORAL SYSTEM

ARTICLE 134

Members of all Soviets of Working People's Deputies—of the Supreme Soviet of the USSR, the Supreme Soviets of the Union Republics, the Soviets of Working People's Deputies of the Territories and Regions, the Supreme Soviets of the Autonomous Republics, the Soviets of Working People's Deputies of the Autonomous Regions, and the area, district, city and rural (stanitsa, village, hamlet, kishlak, aul) Soviets of Working People's Deputies—are chosen by the electors on the basis of universal, equal and direct suffrage by secret ballot.

ARTICLE 135

Elections of deputies are universal: all citizens of the USSR who have reached the age of eighteen, irrespective of race or nationality, sex, religion, education, domicile, social origin, property status or past activities, have the right to vote in the election of deputies, with the exception of insane persons and persons who have been convicted by a court of law and whose sentences include deprivation of electoral rights.

Every citizen of the USSR who has reached the age of twenty-three is eligible for election to the Supreme Soviet of the USSR, irrespective of race or nationality, sex, religion, education, domicile, social origin, property status or past activities.

ARTICLE 136

Elections of deputies are equal: each citizen has one vote; all citizens participate in elections on an equal footing.

ARTICLE 137

Women have the right to elect and be elected on equal terms with men.

ARTICLE 138

Citizens serving in the Armed Forces of the USSR have the right to elect and be elected on equal terms with all other citizens.

ARTICLE 139

Elections of deputies are direct: all Soviets of Working People's Depu-

ties, from rural and city Soviets of Working People's Deputies to the Supreme Soviet of the USSR, are elected by the citizens by direct vote.

ARTICLE 140

Voting at elections of deputies is secret.

ARTICLE 141

Candidates are nominated by election district.

The right to nominate candidates is secured to public organizations and
societies of the working people: Communist Party organizations, trade
unions, cooperatives, youth organizations and cultural societies.

ARTICLE 142

It is the duty of every deputy to report to his electors on his work
and on the work of his Soviet of Working People's Deputies, and he may
be recalled at any time upon decision of a majority of the electors in the
manner established by law.

CHAPTER XII

ARMS, FLAG, CAPITAL

ARTICLE 143

The arms of the Union of Soviet Socialist Republics are a sickle and
hammer against a globe depicted in the rays of the sun and surrounded by
ears of grain, with the inscription "Workers of All Countries, Unite!" in
the languages of the Union Republics. At the top of the arms is a five-
pointed star.

ARTICLE 144

The state flag of the Union of Soviet Socialist Republics is of red cloth
with the sickle and hammer depicted in gold in the upper corner near the
staff and above them a five-pointed red star bordered in gold. The ratio of
the width to the length is 1 :2.

ARTICLE 145

The capital of the Union of Soviet Socialist Republics is the City of
Moscow.

Chapter XIII

Procedure for Amending the Constitution

article 146

The Constitution of the USSR may be amended only by decision of the Supreme Soviet of the USSR adopted by a majority of not less than two thirds of the votes in each of its Chambers.

Index

491

INDEX

DATE DUE

1: 2188954			
1/30/87			